Journey to
the Heart Centre

Copyright

Copyright © John J. Rieger / Shenreed (2015)
Self-Published by: Shenreed Publishing

Paperback edition ISBN # 978-0-9810900-6-1

Source: Canadian ISBN Service System (CISS) Library and Archives Canada

All rights reserved.
The following **(*)** fair use exception and conditions are hereby granted

* Share: You are free to copy and distribute portions of this work without prior permission from the author/publisher, provided that full credit is attributed to the author and a working link is provided to the author's website – http://shenreed.com/index.html

* Attribution: You must attribute the work in the manner that neither suggests, or implies, that the author endorses you, or your use of the work. The author maintains all moral rights.

Note: This fair use exception is granted with the specific understanding that any and all shared material is:

* Non-commercial: You may NOT copy and use this work or any remixed, adapted, altered or transformed versions of this work for any commercial purposes whatsoever, including any and all third party or silent partner agreements. Any distribution of this work, (other than as previously specified) be it in a digital, print, audio, video, radio, TV, screenplay or film format, including any publicity, translations and foreign distribution, must have specific approval, in writing, from the author, John J. Rieger and publisher, Shenreed Publishing. Contact can be made via email at one of the following addresses: info@shenreed.com, shenreed@gmail.com, or through other contact information found at shenreed.com

Public Domain: Whereas this work and any of its elements are in the public domain, that status, nor anything in this license, impairs or restricts the author's rights.

Journey to the Heart Centre

Healing begins in the Heart

John J Rieger / Shenreed

Dedicated to Heart

Epigraph

Zen Philosophy

It is the simplest of words and phrases with the deepest of knowing and feeling, that until it has been experienced the words may be words, may intrigue, may confuse but when felt is the YES of enlightenment. These words have the deepest of meaning and continue to grow as awareness moves through them, that you are not trapped in the words but the words grow out from the experience and share the experience.

Now these are some of the words.
You know much and pretend to know little.
You feel much and pretend to feel nothing.
You fear little but experience it much.
You live as one but fight to remain separate.
You give much but allow little.
You dream always but awaken slowly.
You need self but ignore truth.
You are Divine but need no one.
You long for love from behind a locked door.
You reach for truth with one eye open.
You walk ahead with one leg.
You stand tall while on your knees.
You are a friend to all and a friend to no one.
You fear what you love.
You help give freedom to others while remaining in a cage.
You are all of these and none of these.
Feel your way through and share the words on this page.

© Channeled by Jen Goodwin, 1997 Sept. 3

Ignorance

You fear what you do not know.
You protect what needs no protection.
You love what you fear,
yet fear what you love,
and do not know the difference.
Some say ignorance is bliss.
Some say ignorance is Hell.
Soo Long :)

Channeled by John Rieger / Shenreed 2002 Jan. 8

Preface

We think that just because we are aware of ourselves and our physical surroundings, that we are fully conscious of our reality. Unfortunately, that belief is far from the truth. As an analogy, while we know how to operate and can relate to the activity on a computer, that doesn't mean we know all the behind the scenes technology and programming that is involved in creating what we see and do. In the same way, we go through our lives thinking that we are having a real, meaningful and productive life, yet we are unaware that we are living an illusion based on our old imprints, programs and beliefs that we blindly accept as truth. We are unaware of all the background and underlying conditions that create it, including our ignorance of the unseen role that denial and avoidance play in creating our reality. We are living our life according to the imprints, programs and beliefs we have, and like a computer and its programs, we respond in the same way, garbage in, garbage out.

We go through our lives striving to be happy, accepted and successful, and even if we are fortunate enough to achieve our goals, we still feel empty. We always want something bigger, better or faster, and we are never satisfied or fulfilled with what we have. If on the other hand, we believe that our hopes, dreams and desires are out of reach, we accept our pain and suffering as our lot in life, and hope for a better life after death. It's a never ending battle as whatever we do, it's never enough or good enough. We then come to the realization that we're chasing an illusion and that our life is also a part of that illusion. We then begin to ponder and question the meaning of life as well as ask other age-old questions like; who are we? Why are we here? Why do some of us have to struggle and suffer while others just seem to have a good time? Why is there evil in this world? What is love?

People search for love and hope to find their true soul mate in an attempt to add meaning and purpose to their life, and bring them the joy and happiness they desire. Yet when in a relationship it is either one or the other, or both, that are not happy or satisfied. We then struggle to keep our dream and image of a perfect relationship and life alive by trying to be kind, caring, considerate, sharing, understanding, compromising, co-operative, self-sacrificing, and any other noble virtues we feel we need to have in order to maintain the illusion. But, no matter what we do or say, it's never enough, said or done in the right way, or at the right time to make them or us happy. We have been led to believe that in order to be loved and accepted, that we need to give love and accept what others give us. That we need to put the needs and feelings of others, our husband, wife, boyfriend, girlfriend, family, children, friends, peers, etc. ahead of ours. We're taught that self-sacrifice and thinking of others is loving and unselfish, but when we really begin to look

Preface

deeper we see that the reason we're really doing all these things is to get some form of acceptance and feeling of self-worth and purpose.

We look to another person, place or thing to make us happy, to make us feel loved and accepted and so the cycle continues, unaware that we are looking for love that is outside ourselves to fill the emptiness we feel inside. We are oblivious to the fact that what we're searching for is what is within us. This concept is nothing new as many people throughout history have alluded to this fact. While it has been said, what hasn't been said is how do we do that, how do we find self-love, besides doing what we have always been doing in the past except in a different form, and that we know doesn't work. People know the truth, that love lies within our very Being and that we need to love ourselves in order to be happy, but when attempting to live the truth, we still get caught up in trying to get love from the outside, unaware of the underlying imprints, programs, beliefs, denial and guilt that are at play. We also believe that we can love others unconditionally, but that is also false as we can't give what we don't possess. We can't give an apple if we don't possess an apple. It's an illusion, a mental word game meant to trick the Mind into unquestionably believing and accepting guilt and self sacrifice as unconditional love.

We search for truth and unconditional love and we've all been taught "the truth" and how to "be loving," (notice they are not one and the same) but in all the thousands of years of teaching it has never been successful. Why? Is it because we are ignorant or because the present teachings are flawed, or both? People search for the truth yet are afraid to speak or hear the truth, so how can we ever find the truth if it's always denied? Emotions and feelings are a part of who we are or we wouldn't have them, and to deny them is to deny a part of who we are, and to deny a part of who we are is to deny ourselves unconditional love. By denying a part of our Being, we give ourselves conditional love which always feels incomplete and controlling, and it's this same conditional love that we then share with others, even though we don't like to call it that. It's only when our lives begin to fall apart that we begin to question if this life is real and what our purpose in all this is. Religions, science, and social customs and traditions all have differing points-of-view, but none can give us the answers that we can use in the here and now that will change our life in a meaningful way, and one that is not based in denial and avoidance.

It's when we have a crisis in our life that we are faced with having to make a difficult choice, of either accepting the illusion that we call life and try to make the best of a bad situation, or to keep digging for the truth to find out what is really going on. We reach a point in our lives when we realize that our hopes, dreams and desires are not possible, or at least not possible in the way and manner we have been trying to achieve them. That there has to be an alternative solution, one that will not only work, but also feels right and is not just more emptiness, heartbreak, terror and rage that we are presently experiencing. So the questions we then ask ourselves are; how can we experience what we desire, and how can we uncover the truth about how we can do that without the present limitations or conditions?

We also have the belief that if we just had the power to be in control of the people, places and things in our lives, that we would be able to make the necessary outer changes that would then bring us the happiness we desire. Of course, we can overpower and control others to get what we want, but that doesn't make us or them happy, and there will always be someone waiting in the shadows to overpower us, and that is the same game that we have been playing for thousands upon thousands of years, and we know it doesn't work. So now if we know that the present system doesn't work and has never worked, we need to uncover the reason why and what the alternative is. We then realize that the alternative to changing others and the world is to do the opposite, and that means that instead of trying to change others, we change ourselves. But, there is always the proverbial but, as people generally assume that when faced with an issue, they think that if they do the opposite of what they were doing that they will have solved their issue or problem. People think that if they are in an abusive relationship that the solution is to leave the relationship. That if they are alcoholics, they need to stop drinking, if they are smokers, they need to give up cigarettes, and if they are over-eaters, they need to go on a diet, and the list goes on and on.

What people fail to realize is that while they are on the right track in their thinking in that they need to do the opposite of what they have been doing, they missed the mark as that thought is only a part-truth and is NOT the solution. They have to go deeper and not just look at and address the symptoms, but to find and address the cause. Using the smoker as an example, doing the opposite is not about quitting smoking, it's about ending denials and looking for the cause, the reason why they began to smoke in the first place and are now addicted to smoking, and that is the opposite to what they have been doing. When they look at the reason they started, they will uncover what they have been trying to cover up by smoking. They will begin to remember experiences and the feelings and emotions that they don't want to feel. If they were to simply stop smoking without addressing the underlying cause, they would just find another habit or way to deny and avoid their feelings.

To know what life is, we need to know what life is not, and we can only do that by experience and by how we feel about what we experience. To know what truth is, we need to know what is not the truth. When we strip away all that is false, the truth becomes evident. To know what love is, we need to know what love is not. When we strip away all that we feel is not love, we are left with Unconditional love, which is what we have been searching for, that fills us from the inside out, and not vice versa. While the

Preface

questions are many and complicated, the answers are simple and obvious. When we strip away what doesn't work, we find what does work. We know that denial and avoidance doesn't work, so therefore, what will work is the opposite, ending our denial and avoidance.

Once we begin to dig beneath the surface by removing all that is false, we uncover the truth, the real issues, and it is then that we can begin the process of healing and empowering ourselves. In ending our denials and empowering ourselves, it's not important what other people do or don't do, but what we do or don't do. There is no quick fix or magic pill that will solve our problems and issues that are preventing us from creating and enjoying the reality we desire. If we have bent intent and all we do is talk our talk, and not walk our talk, then nothing really changes except the form of our experiences and we will just keep going in circles, remaining unaware, disempowered and unenlightened.

Enlightenment is about self-empowerment and bringing light and love to heal those aspects of ourselves that we have denied and are in the dark. It's about finding our balance and the freedom to create and experience the life we have always dreamed of here on Earth. Self-empowerment also means that we need to take responsibility for all of our well-being. We have to do it for ourselves, but we don't have to do it alone. It doesn't matter whether we begin with the repressed and denied emotions, the mental blocks holding them down, or the imbalances held in the physical body. When we can truly accept all of our selves in the moment, with love in our Heart, then we are in balance and in harmony with our Spiritual Essence.

In this moment, I believe that:

- We are a Spiritual Being clothed in a physical body and that everything including our thoughts, emotions and physical body are a form of energy and that everything is connected.
- We need to take responsibility for our well-being, to empower ourselves, and to no longer accept the bandage approach of treating the symptom and not healing the cause.
- True healing can take place when we are in balance, when we can accept and express all our emotions, thoughts and desires without fear, denial, judgment, guilt or shame.
- True freedom and self-empowerment can be realized when we are able to live in the present moment, no longer controlled by beliefs, imprints and programs that limit our experience or the expression of who we really are.
- To be able to express the love, joy and the magic in our Hearts is who we really are, and to share our unique expression and our humanity is what true life is all about.

Acknowledgements

I would first like to express my gratitude to my Divine Mother and Father for the opportunity to be a part of the transformation that is taking place, not only within us, or on Earth, but one that is affecting the entire Universe.

I'd also like to express a heartfelt thank you to my family, my father, mother, brothers and sisters, my ex-wife, son and daughter, and to my extended family, for giving me the opportunity to experience what I needed to, that would enable me to heal the lost parts of my Being.

A big thank you also goes out to all the others that have been a part of my life experiences; partners, friends, acquaintances, neighbors, co-workers and society in general. Everyone that I've met in person, on the phone, through correspondence, or over the internet has been a part of my journey and without them there would be no experience and no journey. While I've mentioned those I've met, those that I haven't met are also part of my experience, in fact, all life on Earth is a part of my journey, if not directly, then indirectly as we are all connected.

I'd also like to say a special thank you to Ceanne DeRohan, author of "The Right Use of Will" (RUOW) series of books, for her courage to not only channel, but to also make this material public that enabled me to begin to heal and transform my life.

And lastly, I'd like to specifically acknowledge and thank three exceptional women that came into my life to help me on my journey of healing and self-discovery; they are, in order of appearance:

- Rita Miotto, who helped me explore and develop many of the tools I use on my healing journey and which I share in my book, "Journeys from the Heart Centre."
- Jen Goodwin, who helped me not only expand the tools, but also with developing the application of the tools and with whom I did most of my emotional work that enabled me to find what I was missing in my life, self love, my Heart centre.
- Irene Robitaille, who not only gave me a physical home when I was homeless, but also helped me on my healing journey and encouraged me to write.

Thank you all.

John

"Healing begins in the Heart"

Note to reader: While this book will explore, discuss and make reference to material from the Right Use Of Will (RUOW) series (books 1-8), I'd like to note that Ceanne DeRohan, the author of the RUOW series, is not involved with, nor does she endorse this book, or any comments made. On the other hand, I strongly recommend that you use the RUOW books as a companion to this and my other books.

Table of Contents

Table of Contents	xii
Introduction	1
Chapter 1 - Some Personal Background	12
My Early Years	12
Leaving Home	20
Marriage and Family	23
Being My Own Boss	26
My World Falls Apart	30
Chapter 2 - 1990 - My Journey Begins	35
Fulfilling a Dream	37
My Inner Journey begins	40
Chapter 3 - 1997 - The Winds of Change	46
What is Your Desire?	47
Clearing the Astral Plane	47
An Introduction to Healing	49
Receiving Love	52
Message from the Pharnoos	55
Awareness, Lifting the Veils	57
Full Circle	58
Vocabulary	59
Awakening Others	59
Animals	60
Awareness and Awakening	63
Need to Know	66
Shalom	68
Word Judgments	69
Chapter 4 - Emotions Begin to Surface	71
The Truth Shall Set You Free	75
Fountain of Youth	81
Speak Your Truth	82
Awareness of Your Denials	84
Loving Intent	85
Relationships and Limitations	88
Moving Blocks	89
Relationships and Balance	90
Chapter 5 - My Lost Child	91
Growth and Balance	91
Moving Anger and Rage	101
Healing and Your Path	102
Releasing Your Anger	103
Judgments and Beliefs	103

Table of Contents

    Consciousness 104
Chapter 6 - Releasing the Old 106
    The Journey Begins 106
    Experiences and Growth 112
    Limitations and Expectations 117
    Surrendering the Ego 119
    Turmoil and Struggle 119
    What is Your Intent? 120
Chapter 7 - 1998 - Transitions 122
    The Coming Changes 122
    Vows and Curses 126
    A New Chapter Begins 128
    Forthrightness and Silence 130
    Being in the Now 132
    Power and Essence 134
    Transformation and the Butterfly 136
    Read Your Messages 137
    Indeed, INDEED, IN-DEED 138
    Fear of the Unknown 140
    Free Will and Denial 140
    Trust Foundation 142
    Unlovingness and Shadow Feelings 143
    Freeing Yourself 146
    Ambivalence 148
    Flight of Love 148
    Clarify Your Intent 150
Chapter 8 - Faltering Steps 151
    Levels and Changes 151
    Dare to Dream and Be 152
    Self-Empowerment 154
    Relationships and Self 154
    Letting Go of the Past 156
    Beauty and Sexuality 158
    Becoming Balanced – Ending Denials 158
    Responsibility and Empowerment 161
    New Beginnings 161
    Intent and Action 163
    Manifesting What You Want 164
    Self-love and Self-acceptance 166
    A Shift in Consciousness 171
    Earth Changes and Inner Changes 172
    Breaking Free of the Quicksand 174
    Denial Spirit and Spirit in Denial 179

- The trickster 183
- Your Brothers and Sisters 185
- The Golden Age 185
- Levels and Layers 191
- Right Place and Asking 192
- Sexuality 193
- Opportunities for Change 194
- Sexuality and Denial 195
- Right Place and Right Time 197
- First Step of a Journey 198

Chapter 9 - A New Beginning 200
- Healing Heart and False Feelings 201
- Balance and the Heart Centre 202
- The Spiritual Warrior 206
- Faith and Trust 207
- Repairing and Healing 208
- Fellowship and Actors 209
- Healing and Understanding 210
- Movement and Momentum 211
- Vulnerable and Strength 213
- Paths and Being Who You Are 215

Chapter 10 - Owning My Feelings 217
- Duality and Polarity 217
- Surrender and Acceptance 219
- The Healing Power of Love 226
- Anger and Self-hatred 227
- Coyote Medicine 229
- Fear of Asking and Trust 230
- Duality of Light and Dark 230
- Inner Battle of Spirit and Will 232
- Message for Jen 234
- Fear is your Ally 236
- Stop Trying to Be Real 237
- Feeling of Aloneness 237
- Hope, Faith and Preference 237

Chapter 11 - The Power of Denial 241
- True Understanding and Knowing 241
- New Beginnings and Changes 244

Chapter 12 - 1999 - Going Deeper 246
- Healing Intent 247
- Denial and Pressure 247
- Movement and Acceptance 251

Chapter 13 – My First Level of Healing 263

Table of Contents

- Re-claiming Your Power 267
- Healing and Transformation 271
- Abundance 274
- Gratitude and Self-acceptance 275
- Be the Change 276
- Higher-Self 285
- Lost Greatness 286
- Intent and Fear 286
- Heart Reborn and Heartlessness 289

Chapter 14 - My Terror and Heartbreak 290
- The Power of Love 292
- Hopelessness 293
- Acceptance 300
- The Heart Centre Purpose 301
- Recovering Lost Will 310
- Judgments on Doing 318
- Inner Battle and Choice 320
- Denials, Judgments and Reality 320
- Purpose and Trust 323
- Self Forgiveness 324
- Time and Space 324
- Accepting Your Gifts 326
- Judgments and False Feelings 326
- Letting Go, Ending the struggle 327
- Ending Limitation 328
- Unconditional Love 333

Chapter 15 - Survival and Circling 335
- Doing Verses Being 341
- Power 345
- Talents and Gifts 346
- Uniqueness 350

Chapter 16 - 2000 - The New Millennium 355
- On Being Human 356
- Power of Love and the Word 356
- Remembering 359
- Raw Emotions and Beliefs 362
- False Will 366
- Secrets and Purpose 367
- Remaining Issues 369
- Memory, Denial and Fear 370
- The Five Tornadoes 371
- Primal Expression 373
- Time and in the Moment 376

Journey to the Heart Centre

- Words 377
- Differentiation and Fragmentation 380
- Being at One 386

Chapter 17 - Lost and Alone 388
- Reawakening Your Powers 389
- Activating Emotions by Touch 390
- Letting Go and Opening to Love 392
- Raising Your Vibration 394
- Forgiveness of Self 394
- Crystals and Helping Others 395
- Trust and Betrayal 398

Chapter 18 – My Second level of Healing 401
- Boundaries and the New World 408

Insights and Conclusion 420
Listing of Channeled Messages 435
About the Author 439

Introduction

To give you a basic idea of the work I'm sharing, this trilogy consists of the following books.

- **Journeys from the Heart Centre – Meditation as a tool for healing and Self-empowerment** – is a how-to manual and guide that uses non-denial based meditation/visualizations as a tool to not only expand your conscious awareness, but to also allow you to seek the underlying causes to the stress, fears, and issues in your life and begin to heal them. It also includes notes, insights, and understandings to assist you on your personal journey.
- **My Journey - Three Levels of Healing – Feeling, healing and understanding Emotions** – covers numerous topics and issues, and contains key insights and understandings into the nature of the human psyche that are vital in not only healing your Emotional Being, but also in unlocking the mystery of your Mind, how it works, and why it does what it does. Finally, I share three personal healing experiences that are directly related to the previous material.
- **Journey to the Heart Centre – Healing begins in the Heart** – While considered an autobiography, it also contains numerous channeled messages from my Spirit guides. I begin with a brief background of my significant life events, and while my journey began in 1990, the main focus is on four years, (1997 - 2000) and the trials and tribulations I went through that enabled me to experience my first two levels of healing.

This book was actually my original unpublished manuscript that included an appendix containing an abbreviated version of the meditation/visualization tools that I use on my journey. Years later, I decided to remove the appendix (no pun intended) and expand the meditation/visualization tools to create a new book. I added some basic insights and understandings that weren't in the original manuscript and this revised appendix then became my first book. After I published it, I felt that there were a lot more understandings and insights that I needed to share, based on the three major levels of healing I had now experienced. These insights and understandings, as well as my three healing experiences became my second book. I consider it to be a companion to the first book and another tool to help you on your healing journey.

Journey to the Heart Centre

This book now completes the trilogy, and while it's my autobiography, I also consider it co-written as it contains numerous channeled messages that I received from my guides in the Spirit realm. In this book, I share the trials and tribulations I went through that finally enabled me to experience my first two major levels of healing. It focuses on four years of my journey (1997 - 2000) and the struggles I went through in trying to put the esoteric concepts from the "Right Use Of Will" books that I was reading, and the messages I was receiving from my guides, into action, into physical reality. When I finally succeeded, it allowed me to experience what has eluded me in all my existence, that of actually manifesting unconditional love and to feel the power that one possesses when one is not in denial and is living in the "now" moment. If you happened to pick this book to read first, you will need to read the others so that you can put the pieces of the puzzle together, as the books are interconnected and very little material is repeated.

As previously mentioned, I began writing this book in 2000, and during the process of reading and transcribing the material from my journals to my computer, I would at times be activated by what I was reading, and I added those "now" thoughts and emotions to the book. Several years have now passed and as I was editing this book for publication, I was going to delete all those "now" moments, but instead, I decided to include them as they too were part and parcel of my healing process and journey. I also felt I needed to share the numerous channeled messages that I received that helped me on my journey. The dilemma I had in formatting this book was how to differentiate the channeled messages and my now moments, from the main body of the book. Originally, I used two different fonts, one for the main body of text, with the now moments in italics, and another for the channeled messages. I've now decided to use one font for the entire book and to use clipart images as symbolic markers to identify the channeled messages, my emotional moments, and my quotes.

The image of a dove will now serve as a marker to indicate the beginning of a channeled message. As an aside note, I've also included an alphabetical listing of all the channeled messages, with page numbers at the end of the book for quick reference.

The Heart image will now indicate my emotional "now" moments I had when compiling or editing my book, and a small ♥ symbol to signify the end.

Finally, the quotation mark image will identify my quotes that are inserted throughout the book. These quotes will also be shown in ***bold italics***.

Introduction

Note: The following "now" section is from my original introduction when I began writing my manuscript back in August of 2000. I kept it intact as I wanted to show you what I was feeling and going through at the time.

♡ In this moment, this book feels like an impossible task. Some of my issues in writing this book are in both the organizing and the writing of it as I've never written a book before. I feel that I'm no writer and there is so much to say with so many layers, twists and turns, that I feel I will only confuse those that are trying to gain some insights into their issues. I feel like the blind leading the blind and that I'm not any kind of authority on the subject of self-empowerment. I'm not a lettered man, nor do I have any diplomas, certificates or status (including New Age) that states who, or what I am, as I don't believe that defines who I am anyway. But here again, are those old programs, beliefs and judgments coming up that say that unless I have the approval of those in a position of power, and that I have met their qualifications and standards, that what I say isn't true and that I won't be taken seriously.

What I'm going to be sharing with you is from personal experience, which I feel is the best teacher. This is not to say that I haven't read and studied others works, but I feel that I've had to travel down those paths to find out for myself, for my own experience, if that was, or wasn't what I was looking for. While what I read offered some part truths, I always felt that something was missing. After reading numerous New Age, self-help, and scientific books, and examining various religions, I decided to expand my search and explore where there were no paths, to boldly go where no one had gone before, (sounds like "Star Trek") to find the truth.

This book is in part, an autobiography, a part of my life that I'm afraid to share, and another part that I feel will read like a new age fiction story, one that is not real and that I've made up. This book is about the ending of my old life and reality and the beginning of my new life in a new world reality. This is difficult for me as I don't know what I'm going to end up writing. I'll be sharing some of my personal experiences, feelings, trials and tribulations as well as my triumphs and joy. I'm going to be as honest as I can and present this book in a manner so that you'll know that I'm human and on a journey to discover, heal and empower myself. That I too am struggling with my personal issues and demons that would have me stop this journey and to just get on with it, and make the best of a bad situation.

I'm also wondering how I'm going to include my family, friends, and acquaintances in this book without infringing on their space, their privacy, and their life. At this time, I don't have the perfect answer, but I know and trust that I will get it when the time comes, so here goes a big leap of faith. I've also been wondering how I'm going to merge the messages and guidance I've received with my journal notes and make it all fit and flow. I began by

Journey to the Heart Centre

entering my messages and notes into the computer from seven years ago and I realized that my beliefs of what I thought was the truth have changed, and for that matter, are still changing. I had this preconceived notion that I was going to write a book with only what I believe to be the truth today, and that it had to be perfect and not change. So I needlessly toiled and lamented, postponed and became frustrated with myself at even the thought that I could write this book. I then laughingly realized that this is the perfect moment to begin to write my book, and all those moments that I'm now typing into my computer were perfect moments at that time and place, as I was not ready for anything else. I now realize that I needed to go through those experiences to gain the awareness so that I could move on to the next experience. Not that all the choices I made were the right ones, but that too was perfect to allow me to gain experience and hindsights, to see where I would now choose differently. It makes me smile to see how a little twist in thoughts and words can change the whole meaning, perception and feeling of an idea. How easily we can get caught up in "trying to be perfect" when in actuality, we are in the perfect time and place to be all that we are capable of being and are aware of in the moment.

I just realized that writing this book is going to be another level of healing for me, to look at all the things I don't like to see, that bother me, and to also look at all my judgments and issues that it will bring up that I need to heal. ♥

This book is part of my personal on-going journey of discovery, healing, and self-empowerment that began in 1990, when the bubble burst and my personal and small business world collapsed. Frustrated with my life and traditional social and religious dogma that gave me no meaningful answers, I began my journey, my search for truth and the meaning of life. During the next few years, I read over 250 books on almost every New Age self-help topic, as well as various other books on medicine, science, and religion, trying to find answers to my probing questions. My journey is an eclectic blend of science and spirituality, (not religion) as I explore the middle ground between what science can't see, hear, feel or prove and thereby states doesn't exist, and what religion doesn't want you to find out is real for yourself. What I was searching for in the books I read was the common thread that would link them all together, and while all books offered some part truths, something was always missing or didn't feel right. I challenged everything I read as I continued to ask who, what, where, when, why and how. As I ventured into the great unknown, I had no guide, no signposts, only my mind and my feelings, which I didn't trust, to help me find what was missing in my life. I was blinded by a fog, aware only that I was searching for something but not

Introduction

knowing what I was searching for, how to find it, where to look for it, or to even know if I had found it when I did, and then what to do with it when, and if I found it.

Not satisfied with the answers I was getting with my outer search, I decided to expand my search and explore where there were no paths. In 1994, I began my inner search when I was introduced to meditation. During the next three years, it expanded to include past life regression, meeting animal guides and totems, life guides and higher self, astral journeys, channeling, among other things. While all these "tools," as I came to call them, expanded my conscious awareness and opened new frontiers and experiences for me, I also felt that something was missing and didn't feel right.

I continued to simultaneously explore my outer and inner reality still looking for the common thread, and it wasn't until early 1997, when I obtained the book, "Right Use of Will" (RUOW) by Ceanne DeRohan, that things began to click and make sense for me that felt right, even though I didn't understand it in the moment. I also found the common thread that had eluded me in all the books I had read and the meditations/visualizations I had experienced. What I found that was common was not what was being said, but what was not being said, what was being denied, and that was the definitive turning point in my search. Reading the RUOW books continued to expand my awareness of the role that denial was playing in my life. It was at this time that besides writing about my experiences and the channeled messages I was receiving, I also began writing about my thoughts, feelings and emotions.

I also realized that the meditation/visualization tools I had been using were all based in denial, and that I now needed to combine the tools with the esoteric points-of-view and the emotional work that RUOW provided. I then modified the meditation/visualization tools, changing them from a denial-based format (denial and suppression of feelings and emotions) to a non-denial format, where I would allow my feelings and emotions an opportunity to be expressed. This change allowed me to expand the tools to include working on finding the cause of my issues, and to begin to heal my inner and outer child. As I worked with these new tools, I began to merge and apply the insights and understandings I was getting on my inner experiences, with those of my outer life experiences. As I ventured further into this new and unknown emotional territory, it took me through feeling almost every possible emotion as well as some experiences that are beyond belief. I continued to write about my experiences, thoughts, feelings, emotions, insights, understandings, and the channeled messages and guidance that I was receiving, knowing that I would be writing books, and that these entries would form the basis of those books.

As I continued my inner journey, I was always asking, who, what, where, when, why and how, and when I'd get an answer, I'd repeat the sequence again and again. I was filled with questions upon questions, but for every answer I'd receive, I'd also have another ten questions. Many times it seemed like an endless and impossible task, but I knew that I would never know the truth unless I tried, and kept trying and going deeper until I found the answer. I was awash in a sea of feelings and emotions and being dragged down by my imprints, programs and beliefs that were telling me that my feelings and emotions were wrong, and that healing was impossible. I knew from my past mini healing experiences I had when using the meditation/visualization tools, that healing was possible and that I was on the right track to also heal my big issues, but I just didn't know how to get to them, or what I needed to do when I did. It was a slow and gradual process as there were more issues, mini healings, hindsight's, insights and understandings that I needed to experience. I also realized that I needed to go through all those experiences in order to gain awareness so that I could move on to the next experience. Not that all the choices I made were the right ones, but that too was what I needed to enable me to gain experience and hindsight, to see what didn't work, and where I could choose differently the next time I was being activated.

What drove me on my quest was my heartfelt desire and intent to heal those lost and tortured parts of me that I had discovered during my meditation/visualization journeys. At that time, I didn't know how to heal them, I only knew that I would never know unless I tried and kept trying, peeling off layer by layer, level by level, going deeper until I found the real cause. Slowly, step by step, by trial and error, I had to find the answers to my probing questions myself. In order to find out what was really going on and to get to the truth and heal the lost parts of me, I found that I needed to constantly challenge all my old imprints, programs and beliefs, not defend them. I felt that if I searched long and hard enough, that eventually I'd find what I was looking for, as I had no desire to simply do the best I could. I wanted answers, but I not only wanted answers, I wanted answers that would allow me to heal and empower myself. Unwilling to give up, I returned again and again to the issues that were tormenting me for two reasons. One was that I wanted to become aware of the unseen role that denial played in these experiences, and secondly, that I was determined to find and heal the cause of my issues and recover the lost parts of me. It was, and still is, confusing and frustrating as I go through the gradual processes and the different stages and levels of healing. At times I feel that I'm just going in circles and that "I can't see the tree for the forest" as I'm still unaware that I'm locked in an unseen cycle of denial and self-hatred.

Love was one thing that I didn't expect to discover in my search for truth as I felt that I was already a "loving" person. To begin to know the truth of what love is, I had to know what love is not. While I had a healing experience in February of 1999, it wasn't until August of 2000, that I

Introduction

consciously experienced unconditional self-love for the first time in my life (in my existence) and I was awakened, so to speak, as what I experienced was a 180-degree shift, a complete reversal of what I had believed love was. It was a day before I experienced my second level of healing that I began to write about my journey, as I felt that I needed to share what I had already experienced with others that were also searching to heal and understand their feelings and emotions.

It took me eleven years to move from the first stirrings of awareness and the beginning of my search, through the process of finding the tools that I needed, learning how to use them, to finally entering the gap and reaching my awakening point, that of bringing conscious love and acceptance to the lost parts of me with unconditional self-love. It was then that I discovered how and why it was really me that was being unloving to myself, and that my present experiences were actually based on false thoughts, feelings and emotions that were also a reflection and a reaction to the unloving experiences I had as a child that were as yet, unresolved. Now, I'm on the journey to integrate this new awareness into the physical world, to heal all aspects of me, to "walk my talk" and to bring Heaven to Earth. I know that what I've found, many are also searching for and hope to find, and this is what I want to share. What I share is what I have lived and personally experienced, and what I've experienced, felt and know in my heart can't be studied in any present form, and thus the reason for this and future books.

I'm going to present this book in a chronological order so that you can see the interactions between my messages and my experiences, to give you a feel for the flow and the processes taking place. Some things also repeat themselves but this too is part of the process, the not so merry-go-round that I'm on, and that I can't seem to get off of. I feel that in order for you to understand what I'm sharing, that it's necessary to first give you a bit of my personal background so that you can get a feel of where I'm coming from, the issues I have, and what I have been dealing with all my life. Some of these details are hard for me to share because I still have some unresolved issues that I need to heal, but in writing about them, that will also mean that I will have to face them, and if I admit they happened, then I'm no longer avoiding and denying them. When I have acceptance for them, then I also have the opportunity to heal them.

During the course of writing this book, I searched my journals for key events, moments and experiences to include in my book. I noticed that in the beginning, I wrote mainly on what I was doing, how I was keeping busy, keeping my Mind occupied and focused on trying to find a mental solution to fix the problems I was experiencing. I've purposely omitted most of the details of my daily work based activity as it really doesn't serve the purpose of this book. What I was doing wasn't as important as what I wasn't doing, and as you will see, I was, for the most part, caught up in the doing, trying to be successful, make money, be happy, and not being me. By being me, I mean being real, being who I am in the moment. Being real isn't something that you can just do, as to be real you also need to know what not being real is. We think we are being real by doing and experiencing things that will make us, or others happy, or even when we are sharing the pain of our issues, but that is not the being real I'm talking about. While I thought that what I was doing was important, I gradually began to see that what I was feeling was also important if healing was my intent, and although I knew differently, I was still, for the most part, caught up in the doing and not being real and in denial of my feelings and emotions. As you follow my journey you will notice that at first I was controlling my feelings and emotions, and then slowly, I began to allow them to be expressed, yet unaware of the imprints, programs, beliefs, judgments, false feelings and emotions, as well as the role of guilt, shame, and the unseen role of denial that I was running on. I was too busy doing what I thought was me, my life, my purpose, not realizing that I couldn't be further from the truth in that I wasn't being real and in the moment. Until you have the awareness that something is there, you can't see it or know that it's there. You can be looking at a tree and not see the bird in it until it moves. In the same way, you can't see what you are denying, preventing from moving, until you allow it to move by ending your denials.

Ending denials and exposing secrets is the exact opposite of what everyone is doing and that is not only new, but also frightening as it's not considered normal, appropriate, or even safe. What is also not acceptable is expressing our true feelings and emotions when they are considered to be negative and are not what others want to hear. We can only heal our emotions by ending our denials of them, not by controlling and denying them as we have been doing. We can't fix something if we keep denying it's broken or keep pushing it away. When faced with our issues, we think that if we do the opposite of what we were doing that we will have solved and healed our issue or problem. As mentioned, ending an abusive relationship, quitting smoking, drinking, or drugs, is not solving and healing our issues, but is instead, going to the opposite end of the denial teeter-totter. What each of these issues have in common is the unseen role of denial, the unresolved and denied emotional issues, the feelings and emotions that we don't want to remember. We need to face our fears, not find ways and means of avoiding and denying them. To begin to heal, we need to convince our mind to change its point-of-view. By that I mean, we need to look at the problem in a different light, that instead of controlling and repressing our feelings and emotions, we now express all that has been denied and avoided. In other words, facing and accepting our fears instead of denying and avoiding them. It's a catch 22 situation. Although many will talk about being open minded, facing their fears, healing their emotions, and taking their power back, most do not "walk their talk," and

Introduction

when given the mental, emotional, and physical opportunity to do so, will either fight to justify their old beliefs, run, or just give up.

In writing this book, I didn't include all the mini healings I experienced, either personally or when I was working with Jen, nor did I share the countless activations I had when reading the RUOW books. Instead, I tried to focus on what I felt was important for you the reader, and that was my shift away from being in control of my feelings and emotions, to allowing myself to express them. Another thing I tried to do was to show how I was repeating the same feelings and emotions and how they related to the things I was experiencing in my outer reality. As I've previously mentioned, I included most of the channeled messages I received as I felt they were important and needed to be shared.

As you read this book, you will notice that any realizations, hindsights, and insights that I wrote about are the ones I had during that part of the journey, and that many are only part-truths as I really wasn't able to expand and understand them until I had more information. There was more that I needed to experience, feel, and heal, to understand more of my reality. What I share in this book is what I was going through at the time, without all the understandings and insights that I now have, and that I share in my other books. This was a work in progress, a slow, step-by-step journey where, through trial and error, I slowly and methodically began to put the pieces of the puzzle together.

As you progress into my story, you will notice that Jen becomes a major player in my healing experiences. While much of the mini-healing work can be done by yourself, you will find that you need others to reflect to you what you are unable to see for yourself. If you have a partner that is also on their healing journey, then you will heal your issues quicker. I feel I need to make a comment here in that I didn't write much about the good times and experiences I had with Jen. Not that we didn't have them, the long talks, the movies, the shopping, and the special moments we shared, not to mention all the journeys and healing work we did together. These touched me to my very Heart and Soul, and even though I didn't write about them, I'll always have them. Much of what I wrote in my journals is what I couldn't or didn't express verbally with Jen in the moment I was activated, so my only form of expression was to write. After I expressed myself in writing, I would share what I was going through and what I had written the next time I talked to her. It's these deep denied emotions and issues that are at the core of my healing and is what I feel others need to read and feel in order to touch these parts that they too have difficulty in expressing.

Although I was working with Jen, I was also on my own in that I had to work it out for myself to find out what was really going on, so that I could finally reach and heal the lost parts of me. Jen would activate me into my issues and denials and I would gap. Once I gapped there was nothing more that she could do to help me, but only activate me further into my denied issues and self-hatred. Then there were the times when the roles were reversed and I'd activate her into her issues of denied heartbreak, terror, anger, rage and self-hatred, and she would gap, but try as I might, I couldn't reach her either, as nothing I could say or do would help her anymore than she could help me when I was in denial and in the gap. These were the times that we had to go into our feelings and issues on our own until such time that we were able to end our denials and heal those denied parts of our Being, but until they were healed, the activations just kept coming back in one form or another. It seemed that the bigger and deeper the issue, the more it was denied, and the stronger it became at the next activation

Early in our relationship, actually, it was during our first phone call, we both mentioned we were searching to heal our emotions and to become whole. We then made an agreement, knowing that we were both going to go into places, issues, and pain that would activate us, and that no matter what happened, we would not abandon the other. That we would move through or into our pain, knowing that it wasn't the other person's intent to harm us and that they were only activating the other into their issues to help bring healing. Sometimes we would be triggered and just hate the other person, but when we touched and felt our real issues and emotions, we had only love and gratitude for the other person, that they stayed with us through our darkest moments when we were pushing them away. There were other times when one person would have a mini healing experience and we would both feel a love and a connection beyond words, but then within five minutes, we would be activated again, or it would be the other person that would be activated and going into their issues. If this were an ordinary relationship, we would have been long gone.

While much of what I write about in my experiences with Jen seems like I'm just plain stupid and desire to experience all the issues that are torturing me, that was not my intent. I returned because it was my desire to heal those tortured parts of me that I didn't know how to heal, but I would never know unless I tried and kept trying, until I found the real cause. It was the same for Jen. We knew from our past mini-healing experiences that this form of healing was working, so we felt that it would also work on the BIG issues that we hadn't healed yet, it was just that we didn't know how to get to them or do it. We had experienced many good times together and had many bad times turn to healing experiences, that to part company because we just couldn't seem to get through a particular issue wasn't how we worked. We also felt that we wouldn't have been brought together if it wasn't for our highest purpose and good, or that healing wasn't possible.

In the early stages of my journey, I worked more with Jen and her issues, as she was more open to expressing her feelings and emotions than I was. At the time, I also judged her needing more help than I did as she was

Introduction

struggling physically, emotionally and mentally. As you will notice, I write very little about what I am feeling in the early stages of my journey, it is only later, that I allow myself to open up. I also wrote notes and messages for Jen in my journals, but as they are of her personal experiences and issues, I feel that they are her story and not mine to share. Neither do I share her journey experiences or my experiences when I empathically picked up on her denied emotions and physical pain. While they were for my experience, they too are not a part of my journey and as such, were omitted for the most part with only the occasional reference made to enable you, the reader, to tie together what I was going through and how I was activated into my issues. I also did the same with notes and messages that I had for Irene. Likewise, there were other people that came into my life, and while they played a direct role in my experiences and personal issues, I didn't include any of their personal stories.

Part of the reason for writing the book the way I did was to show you the gradual and oft times frustrating and repetitive processes, and the different stages or levels that take place, and that true healing is not a "quick fix." As you read this book you will discover a map, so to speak, markers along the path that will relate to your personal experiences and issues. If you are able to feel and see what I went through and what I did and didn't do on my journey, then you can use that as a guide to see what is going on with the issues in your life. Even though we may have different experiences, deep down the feelings of terror, heartbreak, anger, rage, and all the other feelings and emotions are the same, and all are related to denial and a lack of self-acceptance and self-love. Using all three books will give you the tools and a greater understanding of not only the issues you are facing, but also how to heal them in a much shorter time than I did. It is only your intent and dedication to heal and find self-love, to empower yourself, that will determine your journey.

Chapter 1 - Some Personal Background

My Early Years

I was born on the prairies of Canada, in Melville, Saskatchewan in 1944, to parents of Polish/German descent and devout Roman Catholics. It was customary in those times for people with certain ethnic and cultural backgrounds to band together in small towns and communities. My grandparents had immigrated to Canada when they were children, and while both my grandparents and parents had gone to school and could read and write English, German was the only language that was spoken in the home. The fact that I couldn't speak English and was unable to communicate with my teachers and peers when I started school was to have a traumatic effect on my life.

One of the earliest childhood memories I have was when I was around four years old. It was late fall, early winter and we were moving from one farm to another. A team of horses was pulling the hay wagon loaded with our furniture and belongings, and I was sitting on top of them. As we made the trip I can remember the fight my parents had over my dad losing the farm because of his drinking and gambling. We then lived on the share crop farm until I was nine years old, when we moved into the village of Dubuc, where I had been going to school. The school had four classrooms and taught grades one to twelve, with three grades per room.

I was excited about going to school and meeting other children. I remember the first day of school and hearing a strange noise as I walked into the school with my dad. The foreign noise was the English language. Not only was I confused by the language, but being intuitive, I was also picking up on what the other children were thinking and feeling, especially any thoughts or feelings that were being directed at me. I asked my father to take me home, that I didn't want to be here. I remember my father telling me that I would be okay, and that all I had to do was to watch and listen, and learn to be like the other children. We lived on the farm at that time, and he told me that he would be back after school to pick me up, but I didn't know when that was. I didn't want him to leave me, but I had no choice. It's important to note that there wasn't a single person in the school that knew any German that could act as a translator for me. When my father left, I was totally alone in a foreign and hostile environment. I remember the teacher talking to me, asking me questions, and the children laughing and taunting me because I couldn't understand or speak English. Later that morning, I felt humiliated and

Chapter 1 – Some Personal Background

shamed because I couldn't tell the teacher that I needed to go to the bathroom and I peed my pants in class. To make matters worse, I had to sit in them all day. The verbal abuse and sneering laughter was not all that I got, as when recess and lunch time came, so did the bullies and the physical beatings. My father was late in picking me up after school, and so I suffered more verbal and physical abuse.

Being intuitive, I knew when, where and how they were going to attack me, but there was nothing I could do to prevent it. I hated school and didn't want to go back, but I had to tolerate the verbal abuse and beatings. The only help I got from my parents was the advice to grow a thicker skin. There was also no compassion from the teachers I had, and it wasn't until grade four when I got Mrs. Stokes as a teacher, that I started to pull out of my shell. She would ask me to clean the black boards or do errands for her if she felt that I might get beat up at recess. Although she tried to protect me, it also caused another problem as the kids now called me the teacher's pet and I'd get beat up for that. At lunchtime she would read a chapter from a book like the Hardy boys or Treasure Island, and I'd stay inside as I not only liked the stories but it also saved me from some verbal abuse and beatings.

The verbal and physical abuse carried on until I was in grade six when I felt I had had enough, and that it was time for a change. Although I was small for my age, I now felt I was strong enough to beat up the bullies, not all at once, but one at a time. After a beating, I followed the smallest bully and beat him up. The next day, they ganged up on me and beat me, but then later, I caught another and beat him up. I slowly made my way through the pack until I got to the last, the biggest one and beat him up. After that, things changed and I was no longer bullied.

We were a poor family and there were many hard times. I was the eldest of five children; I have two brothers and two sisters. I can remember when my dad was sick in bed for almost a year and couldn't work, and how the neighbors and relatives would drop off food and hand me down clothes to get us through. My dad recovered and took a job at a gas station in town but that was not enough to support a wife and five children. I remember helping my mother clean the local hall on Saturday mornings after the Friday night movie, and then setting up for the Saturday night dance. We would clean up again on Monday and set the chairs back up for the movie on Friday night. I would also get up early on Sunday morning, sometimes at 5 a.m., and go to the hall to pick up the beer bottles, which I would cash in for 1 cent a bottle. That enabled me to buy one or two comic books for 10 cents each and maybe a coke and some candy that I shared with my brothers and sisters who would get an allowance because they were younger than me and couldn't earn money like I did. I also collected the tickets from people going to the movie on Friday night. As payment, I was allowed to watch the movie for free.

Journey to the Heart Centre

Another experience that I remember was when I was in grade six. I was going to the general store to get my comic book and a coke, and I saw a pocketknife that I really wanted; I think it cost $1.00. I didn't have enough money to buy it and I never stole anything before, so I was very anxious and nervous. I watched to see if Mr. Steinberg, the storeowner, was looking and when he turned his back to me, I put it in my pocket. I went up to the counter, paid for my comic book and coke and left. I came back about a half hour later, as guilt and shame had been eating away at me for having stolen the pocketknife. I thought I was unnoticed as I put it back on the shelf. I turned to leave when Mr. Steinberg asked me if I was looking for a job and wanted to make some money. I eagerly stated that I was. He said that Mr. Clark, my one armed neighbor, a war veteran, was going to be building a garage for him and that if I would help him; he would pay me $10.00. I replied that I'd really like the job as I looked back at the knife on the shelf. Mr. Steinberg said, "Good, and I'll put that pocketknife aside for you as I know you want it."

♡ I'm emotional at this point and tears are streaming down my face as I haven't remembered that kindness and love for many years. I realized at that time, that he knew I stole the pocketknife when I left the store the first time but he said nothing and let me take it. After the garage was built, Mr. Clark said that I did a fabulous job helping him, and he later had me help him (with pay) anytime he needed a pair of small and willing hands. Both Mr. Steinberg and Mr. Clark were like a father to me in a way that my own father could never be. I have a pain in my heart at this moment and I have to stop typing to feel this. I felt the denied heartbreak that I had been holding since I was twelve or thirteen years old when we moved from Dubuc. I also remembered my teacher, Mrs. Stokes, who also showed me the same love and acceptance. After years of abuse, I was finally beginning to be accepted and loved, only to lose it when we moved away, and again, I had no choice or say.
♥

After I completed grade six, we moved to the city of Regina, where my dad got a job in the hospital. My mother wasn't working as my youngest brother and sister were not in school yet. We were enrolled in a Catholic school where I just completed grade seven, I say just, as it was mid May when we were excommunicated from the Catholic Church. The reason was that I was going to confession twice a week, on Sundays with my family in church, and then again on Monday at school. I was making up lies on Monday and then confessing my lies on Sunday. When I finally decided that I wasn't going to lie anymore, that was when the trouble started, resulting in our excommunication. This event deeply affected my life and I see I still have guilt and shame over what happened, as for years it alienated our family from our Catholic relations of some thirty-six aunts and uncles and over one

Chapter 1 – Some Personal Background

hundred and fifty cousins as well as our Catholic friends. We were still over a month from the end of the school year and final exams, but they didn't want us back so they gave me and my siblings passing grades and told us to take a hike. That also affected my schooling, especially math, as I was never able to catch up on what I had missed.

As far as religions go, after our excommunication from the Roman Catholic Church, I became an atheist, as I felt I had lost my religion and my faith. I believed that if there was a God, why did he do this to me? I did everything he said. I tried to be good. I listened to my parents as best I could, and did what I thought they wanted me to do. I said my prayers. How did I fail? Why did he let this happen? Why do bad things happen to good people? I didn't believe, or feel, that God was the loving and just God that he made himself out to be, so therefore for me there was no God, not a God of love anyway. There were too many unanswered questions that religion couldn't, or didn't want to answer to my satisfaction. This of course didn't sit well with my mother who bounced around from church to church, looking for the right religion. I now believed that science had the answer, that Darwin was right and that we all came from apes. But science didn't fill the bill to my satisfaction either as a lot of what they said was based on assumptions, puffed up to be fact. So then I moved to being a scientific agnostic, with the belief that there is a God, but he isn't to be found in any religion as such.

Other events that would also have an effect on me was the fact that from grade six to grade ten, we moved four times and I went to five different schools. I was a loner and an outsider as I was the new and unknown one. Trouble had no problem finding me, and I was always threatened, bullied or beaten. If that wasn't enough, during the grade seven summer holidays, I had an accident. I was playing tag and had jumped up onto a picket fence. To avoid being tagged, I jumped off to the other side, but in the excitement, I didn't realize that my shoelace had gotten caught on a board until it was too late. I landed head first on the edge of a wooden sidewalk, breaking seven of my upper teeth. They were broken at the roots and some were also chipped. The doctor and dentist recommended that I keep them until I was at least sixteen years old, and then I could get an upper denture. For the next three years I had a mouthful of rotting teeth. Biting my fingernails was a compulsive habit, and the only time I had fingernails was for the six months when I had no upper teeth, while I was waiting for my gums to heal. During my adolescence and into my early twenties, I also had a bad case of acme. I always active and had to be doing something, something that required physical movement.

Although I was always on the outside, I was always trying to prove myself to get accepted, but that never worked either. In grade seven I got a job as a "helper" on a newspaper route, and in grade eight, he moved away and I got his paper route of fewer than 30 newspapers, where the average route size was 50 plus papers. It was the lowest subscriber route for that drop area, although there were a quite a few homes that were scattered over a large area including a couple of farmhouses outside the city limits. The paper put on a contest to gain subscribers and our incentive was to win a trip to Chicago. I increased the route from 30 to over 150 papers, and I was one of the winners. The trip was exciting and confusing at the same time, as I had never been away from home alone. After the contest, other carriers wanted my route to be split up but the manager said that as I was the one who built it up, that it would be mine until I decided to quit the route. I didn't make any friends with that move except for the two helpers that got the route when I moved in grade nine.

I was also the fastest bike rider in our neighborhood and had the best balance and coordination with the bike games that we played. These skills encouraged me to enter the provincial bicycle rodeo and I made it to the finals. I had won it on my riding skills but lost points when it came to bicycle inspection. I did all my repairs and adjustments so the bike was as safe as I could make it, but one of the judges, who weighed about 250 pounds, came over to my bike, grabbed my handle bars and put his weight on them, moving them down a couple of inches. He then went to my bicycle seat and twisted that too. After he finished inspecting my bike, he went to my nearest competition. I could see that he only pretended to be pushing on his handlebars, as he looked at me with a smirk. That was enough for me to lose the championship and take second place. What was really heartbreaking was in later overhearing the two of them talking and laughing; they were related.

In grade eight I took woodworking for the first time since my days working with Mr. Clark. I made a small cedar jewelry box, a footstool with a hinged upholstered lid, and a plastic ring with a fake diamond insert. My woodworking teacher entered all my projects in the Saskatchewan grade eight woodworking exhibitions where I won two first prizes and a second. I was happy at being recognized for my achievements but again it brought me pain, as others were jealous and there was more fighting. It didn't pay to be too good.

In sports, I had similar experiences. In grade nine I took physical education and the coach asked me to try out for track and field. I was the fastest runner in my class and in the hop, skip and jump, I landed on the grass on the other side of the pit. I wasn't praised by my peers for these feats, but criticized for showing off. After school, or on weekends, I had similar experiences when playing pick-up baseball and football. I was not only a fast runner, but also a good catcher and an accurate and strong thrower. In baseball, I was also a consistent home run hitter. It got so bad that the team I was chosen to play on would have to give the other team a handicap, either in points or in extra players. Sometimes I would even have to bat one handed and not wear a glove when fielding, and then other times, I was just not

Chapter 1 – Some Personal Background

allowed to play. After a while, playing sports and games wasn't fun. I never tried out for any high school athletics as I figured what's the use. Also in grade eight, in order to feel like I belonged and was part of something, I joined the Air Cadets for a year. After that, I joined the militia for another year. While the lowest military ranks had to march to the same drummer, military life also has its "social" structure, and if you didn't fit in with your peers or the chain of command, you were given a hard time.

♡ As I'm typing this into the computer I can feel how I've stopped myself from doing what I love, or being the best, as that only brought more rejection and heartbreak. I can feel the heartbreak of always having to be less than others to be accepted by them, and then to be rejected because I'm not as good as the others. It was a no win situation. ♥

In grade ten, I had all my broken and rotten teeth pulled out, and I had to go to school for six months with no upper teeth or dentures, as my gums had to heal before I could get my dentures fitted. It was also the last time that we moved as a family, as my parents bought a small two-bedroom house. I also got my first car in grade ten, a 1950 Plymouth. Now I had the freedom to not only get away from home, but to also get a part time job at the other end of the city and earn some money so that I could be more independent.

I didn't know what I wanted after high school, but I kept my options open for university until grade twelve, when I dropped my university credits to focus on shop and automotive subjects. After I graduated and had the summer to think about it, I went back for a second year in grade twelve to get the university credits that I dropped the year before. I was now re-considering university but I still wasn't sure of my direction, as psychiatry, psychology, archaeology, architecture, and electronic engineering were all appealing to me.

The following summer I took a job at Kentucky Fried Chicken for a few months, and then decided to take a better paying job with the Department of Highways as a lab tech, so that I could save up for university. During the summer and fall, I worked 10–12 hours a day, 6 or 7 days a week, in a small 6' x 8' trailer. I'd collect asphalt road samples, wash them with carbon tetrachloride to remove the asphalt, then heat the remaining gravel to remove all the moisture content so that the samples could be sieved for analysis. I can remember times when my head would be spinning and I'd have to get out of the trailer to clear my head. Years later, I discovered that carbon-tetrachloride is super toxic. After a year, I quit to go to work with my cousin cleaning up new and used cars. It was during this time that I enrolled in a home study course in electronics through DeVry Tech.

I never had a girl friend; I had "girl" friends, or rather girls that I knew from school or work, that I would sometimes drive home, but I never had a girl friend. Joan was my first real girlfriend when I was 21 years old. This is difficult for me as no one in my family out west knows about this, or I don't think they do, but Joan and I had been dating a few months and it was one of those nights that we were making out in my car. She had just finished her period a few days before so we never used any protection. It was my first sexual experience and also my last for a few years. Joan became pregnant. We talked about getting married and I even bought her a wedding ring. She didn't want to get married and refused to talk about it as her parents were sending her away to have the baby and then put it up for adoption. I was cut out of any discussions or decisions, and she was forbidden to ever talk or see me again. I was devastated and heartbroken, and also filled with guilt and shame. I felt that I couldn't turn to my parents for help, and neither could I turn to my friends, as I never really had any real friends. I felt utterly lost and alone. At that time, a popular song that resonated with me was the Beatles, "Yesterday."

I would now like to share with you the only three poems that I have left from my late teens and early twenties. I feel that as you read them, you will get the gist of the inner struggles that I was going through at that time.

NOT ME
Not me I say,
It wouldn't happen to me.
To others yes,
But not to me.

Will of steel,
Heart of stone.
Conscience and wisdom,
Overthrown.

It didn't happen!
No, it couldn't be.
Nothing like that,
would happen to me.

Temp-Anger
Anger in silence.
Anger inside.
Anger in calmness.
Anger and hide.

Hurt in silence.
Hurt inside.

Chapter 1 – Some Personal Background

Hurt with calmness.
Hurt and hide.

Hot………Cold.
Quick…….Still.
Fight……...Run.
Shout…….Unheard.

Heal in silence.
Heal inside.
Heal with calmness.
Heal and hide.

Forgive in silence.
Forgive inside.
Forgive with calmness.
Forgive and forget.

GOD
They say there's a God,
And know not why.
There must be a God,
Or who am I?

They believe there's a God,
And know not why.
There is a God,
Or who am I?

They know there's a God,
And know not why.
The eternal God,
Or who am I?

Too weak to reason,
Afraid to think.
Custom and tradition,
Narrow the mind.

Is there a God?
I want to know why?
The cause of all things,
Who am I?

Journey to the Heart Centre

Leaving Home

There was nothing holding me in Saskatchewan any longer. I had enjoyed the home study course in electronics, so in the spring of 1966, I packed two suitcases and boarded the train heading east to Toronto, to take up electronic engineering. My first experience in Toronto was a real eye-opener. When I got off the train, I hailed a cab to take me to the school to register and to get the name of a place where I could get room and board. I remember asking the cab driver why it was taking so long, and why we passed, what I later found out to be Casa Loma, three times. Amazingly, ten minutes after my comment, he dropped me off at the school.

♡ I have denied rage coming up as I'm transcribing this, as I'd like to hurt him for taking advantage of someone's innocence and confusion to make a buck. I hope you choked on it. ♥

During the first year I stayed at two different boarding houses, and then moved into a basement apartment with three fellow students. I moved out of the first boarding house after only a couple months. I complained that I had been finding cat hair in my sandwiches, as did a couple of other roommates. I was persuaded to bring the subject up after supper, but the others never supported me as they said they would. The next school day, she made sure that there was hair in my sandwich. I opened my cheese sandwich and it was literally covered in hair, as if it had been dropped on the cat a few times. I showed it to my roommates who were having lunch with me. They quickly checked their sandwiches, but they were fine. When I went home, I showed it to her, but she denied she made it that way, and again, my roommates kept quiet.

Within a week, I moved to my second rooming house, also full of DeVry students, and after a few weeks, I was beginning to settle into my new home. I also had a couple of part-time jobs in the evening and on weekends, and I saved some money and bought myself a 1958 Zephyr with leather interior for $75.00. One Friday afternoon, shortly after I got the car, the landlord telephoned his son and asked him to ask me if I would give his car a boost as his battery was dead, and he was stuck at the shopping centre with the groceries. I drove over and helped him start his car, and then drove home to finish my homework before supper so that I could go to work. When supper was ready, he called to us from the bottom of the stairs, to come and get it. As I came down the stairs, he extended his hand and thanked me for helping him. I looked into his eyes and as I shook his hand, I felt that in his heart, he was saying good-bye. I felt uneasy about it, and after supper a couple of the other students asked me what that was all about as he had never done that before. I told them what I felt and they just laughed. The next morning

Chapter 1 – Some Personal Background

the landlord went to work and died of a heart attack. I was devastated, both by his death and by my roommates who shunned me as if I had caused him to have a heart attack. The place no longer felt like a family and I moved out a short time later. I then took up sharing a basement apartment with three other students.

Being intuitive, I've been keenly interested in psychic and extraordinary powers since I was a child. I remember in grade four or five, telling my mother that my aunt was coming over to visit and what she was going to say and do. When she arrived and said and did everything I said she would, my mother flipped out and said that it was the work of the devil, and that I'd go to hell if I did or said anything like that again. Throughout my life I've always felt energies, knew things about people, or knew things were going to happen but I wouldn't give them acceptance or expression, and in most cases I dismissed them as soon as the knowing and feelings came up. If I did express them to others and when they came true, like with my mother and landlord, I felt that I was looked upon as something evil and that they thought I had caused whatever happened to happen. I thought it best to just keep quiet and to act only when it directly affected me, and it has saved my life and the lives of others a few times, mainly while driving or working. I would deny that I had any precognition or guidance, and just pass it off as just being lucky.

Speaking of the extraordinary, I've also been interested in UFO's and aliens since I was young, and in March of 1967, I saw my first UFO. It was late evening and I was out with a girl friend. We were parked overlooking a small park near Bathurst St. and Shepherd Ave. in Toronto. There were four 20-story apartments to the right, and a tree-filled valley in front of us. I had recently traded in my Zephyr for a 1960 Pontiac convertible, and as it was a warm evening, I had the top down. We were facing East, looking at the stars, when we spotted a bright light in the evening sky. At first, I thought it was the landing light of an airplane, as Downsview Air Force Base was nearby, but it was coming in too fast. As the light came nearer, I could see that it was a sphere. Within seconds it was upon us and suddenly exploded into a churning ball of fire, but without making a sound. At the time the sphere exploded, I estimated that it was about 10 feet in diameter, and about 100 feet above the ground and about 200 - 250 feet from us. It exploded near the tenth floor of the nearest apartment building.

I reached for the Kodak instamatic film camera in the glove box, and managed to snap two pictures of the fireball and the piece of smoking material that was spiraling down to the trees in the valley. The ensuing white smoke from the explosion rose effortlessly into the night sky. When I followed the smoke upward, I saw the UFO hovering just above the top of the apartment building. It looked like two soup plates with the smaller one inverted and on top of the bottom upright one. The top portion had five round portal type windows and the whole ship looked like polished aluminum, but it also seemed to shine from within, as if the aluminum was transparent. I took three more pictures as it hovered, floating on air, like a boat floats on water after it has shut down it engines and just rises and falls in its own waves. My girl friend was screaming and hysterical, but I just kept taking picture after picture. It hovered briefly over the apartment building before slowly making its way towards and over us, where it again paused momentarily. I knew it was about to take off as it slowly began to shift position. It then accelerated like nothing I had ever seen and within three seconds, it was out of sight in the western sky. During all of this, there was no sound of any kind from either the explosion or the UFO, only the traffic noise of the street behind us. The whole experience lasted for a minute or so.

We went to the apartment and told my roommates what we saw, and we decided to return to see it we could find what had drifted to earth. When we came to the intersection, there were two police cars at the corner gas station. I was in the left turn lane at the lights and I made an illegal right turn to see the police. I told them what I saw and they said that they had gotten a couple of strange calls from the apartment building and were sent to investigate. But having said that, they then began making me out as a weirdo and asking me what I was smoking and other ignorant rubbish. One officer did talk to me privately and said that there were a lot of reported UFO sightings that night. I was asked to follow them to the apartment building where there were two more police cars in the parking lot. A man in the back seat of one of them was giving them a statement. He briefly talked to me and told me that he had seen a fireball outside his window on the tenth floor. I guess the police where giving him the same routine they gave me, as when I told him that I saw the fireball too, he told the officers, "See I'm not crazy." But when I continued to tell him about the UFO I saw, he smiled and asked, "What you been smokin man, no way." I thought to myself, right, what's the use? Just keep your mouth shut. Later when I thought about it, I realized that he couldn't have seen it as it was above his building.

The police gave me the trumped up story that the EMO (Emergency Measures Organization) was conducting tests in the valley. The next day I drove into the valley and talked to the woman who owned the property, she told me that no one had been doing any kind of tests on her property which occupied most of the valley in question. There were numerous reports of UFO sightings that night and the following week in the newspaper. I always believed that we were not alone, and this sighting strengthened that belief.

I left DeVry after my first year and settled for "Electronic Technologist," as algebra and calculus were not my strong points that I needed to continue in the engineering program. It was in the spring of 1967 that I began my illustrious career in the new communications industry of Cable TV. I started with Metro Cable as an installer/serviceman. This first job

Chapter 1 – Some Personal Background

lasted about a year before I was asked to either quit or be fired, as I was making waves and asking too many questions that management felt I had no business asking. Most were related to the companies disregard to employee safety. Again, I stuck my head out for others that said they would back me, but when the time came, I was on my own. Of course things changed after I left, but that was of little consolation.

Marriage and Family

In the spring of 1968, I started my second Cable TV job working at York Cablevision, where I met Marian, who also worked there. We began dating and in the fall we set our wedding for March of '69. I had moved a couple more times and by 1969, I was living in a tenth floor apartment with three other guys; one was to be my best man. Three days before the wedding, I came home to find that the superintendent had changed the locks to the apartment, along with a bailiff note posted on the door relating to back rent. Marian and I had recently rented an apartment which we started furnishing, but all my stuff was still in this apartment. I jimmied the lock (Cable TV savvy) and got my stuff out. While I could open the door to my old apartment, I couldn't lock it again after I left. I moved all my stuff to the new apartment and slept on the floor for the next couple of days. I found out later that someone had taken the sign off the door, and when my best man came back to the apartment that evening, he was unaware that the superintendent had changed the lock, or that I had picked it. The superintendent happened to check the apartment and found him in it. He was arrested for breaking and entering, and spent the next two days in jail, unbeknownst to anyone. I was in a panic, besides being my best man; he also had the wedding rings. The night before the wedding, he reappeared, dirty, unshaven, in blue jeans and a soiled shirt. He told us that he was sorry, that he had taken the rent money and spent it on marijuana. This wasn't the first time he had been late with the rent, but this was one time too many, and hence the changing of the lock. With all of this happening, I also had reservations about getting married, but I was told that it was just "the jitters." We were married in the spring of 1969, and for appearance sake, we pretended that we were Christians and got married in a church to appease the families.

Our relationship changed on the first evening of our honeymoon when I told her how happy I was that now, not only did I have a friend and a lover, but also a wife and the future mother of our children. She coolly replied, "I'm not your friend or lover, I'm your wife and you're my husband." Suddenly she had all these programs come up as to what a wife and a husband was or had to be, and there was no more closeness and friendship in our relationship. I tried to talk to her about it but it was futile. I was confused and thought my feelings were wrong, and that if I was patient I would learn what was expected of me and how to be the husband she thought I should be, after all, she seemed to know what it meant to be a wife. We began a new life together, buying new furniture and decorating our first apartment that was also in a new building.

A few months after we were married, I walked out/was fired from York Cablevision, but Marian still continued to work for the manager that I had the argument with and who had fired me. She was feeling unsettled and depressed and said that if we had a child, that she could quit work and that a child would make her feel better. She got her wish and our son Bryan was born in December of 1970.

We then moved into a two-bedroom apartment in an older building where we stayed for a year until we bought our first house in 1972. It was a three-bedroom bungalow in the little community of River Drive Park, about 45 minutes north of the city of Toronto. I felt excited and overwhelmed at the same time. Now we had a home, but we also had a $20,000.00 first mortgage and a $2,500.00 second, and that meant I needed to keep my job in Toronto.

♡ At this point in writing this book, I searched my mind for hours, trying to piece together my marriage and family years, but could find very little, only small fragmented memories here and there. Reluctantly, I called Marian late one evening to ask her some questions. She was busy but said she wasn't, and hesitantly gave me some details. As I began to remember pieces of this lost puzzle, I was deluged with more questions. She was surprised that I didn't remember, and laughed, saying that old age was setting in. She then asked me why I wanted to know all this now. When I told her it was for my book, she said that she wanted to see it before I published it, or that she'd sue me. That statement brought up more fears but before I could really express myself, she ended our telephone conversation. I didn't write anything that evening as I was perplexed at the thought that I had lost those memories. I later realized that I must have really been in denial for them to be buried so deeply. ♥

Now back to my story. During the next few years I bounced from cable company to cable company. Having a child didn't make Marian feel better as she had been progressively feeling more depressed after Bryan was born. Our son wasn't a year old when she thought that going back to work would make her happy and so she decided to go to work at RCA, where she worked for the next few years, while her mother, who lived in Toronto, looked after our son. We only had one car at that time and I would drop Marian off at her work, then drop Bryan off on my way to work, and in the evening, I would do the reverse procedure. When she reminded me of this, I

Chapter 1 – Some Personal Background

thought to myself, how in the hell did I manage to do all that, and everything that I did around the house after I got home?

After working for a couple of years, Marian was still feeling depressed and was now eager to quit work and have another child. Janice was born in November of 1975; she was six weeks premature, but healthy. Marian tried to cope as best she could, but was feeling even more depressed. I tended to Janice during the evening and late night, and then was up by 6:30 a.m., getting ready to commute an hour to work. Six months or so after Janice was born; I decided to have a vasectomy.

♡ I'm just remembering changing diapers on both Bryan and Janice and how I had to slip a clothespin (reversed) over my nose, or I would gag on the smell of a dirty diaper. I was in real trouble one evening when Bryan laughingly pulled the clothespin off my nose. ♥

After our daughter was born, Marian took a part time job at the bank, as she wanted to get out of the house and also add to our family income. She worked a schedule of Thursday and Friday nights and Saturdays for the next three years, leaving me to tend the family and house during that time. In 1978 Marian decided to take a full time job. Janice was put into a day-care while Bryan went to school and was dropped off at the day care after school. I'd usually pick them up after work. We sold our first house and bought a new one in 1978, in the town of Newmarket, as we felt that there were more things for the kids to do in Newmarket, and that we wouldn't have to be driving them to all their activities. I really don't remember too much of my marriage, family or even work. A lot of these details are from my conversations with Marian. I feel I was on autopilot, doing what I had to do to survive.

Ever since I started my first job in Cable TV, I was always trying to work my way up in position only to quit, be fired, or have the company I was working for, sold to a previous employer. Whenever that happened, I would either have to take a lower paying position, or leave. In 1980, I was again in such a position and I was now transferred to another division where I had a two hour (one-way) commute that was taking its toll on me, but I also knew that I was running out of companies to work for. It was then that I met a young woman, Nicky that worked in the main secretary pool and was assigned to the planning department that I was supervising. She was aware of what was going on, and encouraged me to start my own business. Starting my own business was a big step as I was unsure of myself even though I had worked my way up the ranks and could work at any position and with any equipment. As previously stated, I started out in installations, but then I also had experience in service, dispatch, maintenance, lab, head-end, planning, sales, accounting, and then with moving from company to company, I was also familiar with different equipment and techniques. As Cable TV was a growing industry, I also knew aerial and underground cable TV construction specifications and techniques, as well as those related to apartment construction. I spent many years in the planning department, so I not only applied all my cable TV know how and skills to planning and designing the various aspects of a cable TV system, but I also had contacts with Bell Canada, Ontario Hydro, local hydro companies, city planning departments and developers, etc. I also knew what and how things needed to be done. I was an expert, but with an attitude when it came to people bullshitting me.

♡ Note: 2010 Nov. – As I'm re-editing this book, I'm laughing at my last sentence as I'm realizing that nothing has changed. I had worked my way up and had experienced the various aspects of Cable TV, making me an expert in my field, and now I'm writing my books on what I have experienced and know, making me an expert in my own right. While the two areas of expertise are different, there is one thing that is the same and that is that people say I have a negative attitude when I call them on their ignorance or bullshit. The only difference is that now I don't care what people think of me, as I don't need to make them happy so that I can have a job, make money and buy a little happiness. ♥

Being My Own Boss

By the fall of 1980, I was again looking for a job. For a month, I tried to get a job but no one was hiring, or at least willing to hire me. After a few weeks with no money coming in, things were getting financially tight so I reluctantly applied for UI (Unemployment Insurance) benefit's, but the rules had changed and because I had quit work, I had to wait six weeks from the date I applied before the benefits would kick in. That was not good news. Frustrated that I wasn't getting a job, I decided to start my own Cable TV planning and design consulting company, called Systems 80. What was also frustrating and discouraging was that my wife, family and friends had no real support for me starting my own business, as they took my getting fired and quitting the different cable companies as a sign that I had a problem, and therefore didn't have the mindset to start or run a business. So while I was starting my own business, I was also trying to get a job in the cable industry as that was all I really knew.

Two weeks after I received my first UI (Unemployment Insurance) cheque, I had to go in to the UI office and report on my employment status. I told them that I hadn't found a job, but that I had started my own business. They asked me when I started it and I told them a month ago. They then told me that because I was self-employed, that I was no longer eligible to claim UI benefits and that I would have to pay back any monies I had received, as I

Chapter 1 – Some Personal Background

was self-employed when I received my first benefit. I argued that I was just starting up, I had no real work yet, and that all I earned so far was $45.00 not counting expenses. There was no talking to them. I was on my own, as now I was even cutoff from receiving any UI (Unemployment Insurance) claims. I felt heartbroken and angry at the same time. I was angry and determined that the government could go and politely fuck themselves and that I didn't need them.

I felt lost and alone, but not only that, I felt a tremendous pressure on me as I had a wife and two children to support. I felt I had no choice, no one would hire me, the government cut off my UI benefits, so the only option I had was to make my business a success. What little savings we had was quickly being used up and so to make ends meet and to have some working capital, I decided to visit my local bank manager to see what he could do for me. I presented my business plan and talked with him about them, and also of my situation with the government. I was pleasantly surprised when he offered me an initial line of credit of $5,000.00, and more if I needed it, and, he did it without using the house as collateral. I was ecstatic. Here was a stranger who had faith in me. I felt that the government and its bureaucrats could go and fuck themselves, that I didn't need them, and that I'd show them.

I devoted all my energy and attention on getting my business going and by early 1981, I began doing contract work for the companies that I had worked for in the past. I started working out of the house, from a spare room off the master bedroom that I used as an office and work area. My first employee was Randy, a student from the local high school, who worked with me part-time by helping me with the drafting. I would set him up on the only drafting table I had in the office, while I did my planning and design on a small sheet of plywood that I laid on the bed in the adjoining master bedroom. As the business grew, I completed a small office and washroom in the basement that was actually at ground level at the front of the house. It comfortably served our purpose with five employees.

Within a year, we moved out to a new office, taking the lower level of a building. My wife had worked a short time in the business as a secretary and bookkeeper, before she decided that it was too much for her and I hired a woman to replace her. That space served the twelve employees that worked with me until the business was sold. I had trained all my employees, and only a couple of them had any cable TV experience. I actually preferred it that way as it was much easier to train an open mind than to reprogram one that had bad habits. Also, with all the experience I had, it was easy for them to pick up what was important, as then they would be able to figure out the small stuff by themselves.

By the fall of 1983, the business had grown to twelve employees and was about to double in size, or be reduced by 50%, as my biggest customer was now pressuring me to sell my company to them, as they were looking at diversifying. They already had a construction and installation department and were in the process of establishing a service and maintenance department. Now, to be able to provide a full turnkey Cable TV service, they were looking at a planning department and if they didn't acquire my company, they said that they would start their own and also take away the work that they had been giving me. Reluctantly, in January of 1984, after talking it over with my wife and employees, I decided to sell the business and become part of this larger organization as it looked like a win-win situation for all concerned.

It took me two weeks to realize that that was a big mistake, but by then it was too late. I didn't know that the jerk that I had as a previous supervisor would be made the director of operations of this new company. Along with him was a retired Bell Telephone Company executive whose exceptional managerial skills shone brightly, when at the first management meeting he suggested that washing telephone booths would be a real asset for the new planning department. I and a couple of others blinked our eyes in disbelief when he was given the mandate to pursue Bell Canada for a contract. I continued to work there, only to honor my one year contract and to also get the rest of the money that was being held back as insurance that I would fulfill my contractual obligations.

When I sold Systems 80, I had signed a non-competition agreement, so if I quit or was fired, I couldn't get back into Cable TV for five years, and that was all I really knew. I did however have a good amount of money that I could invest, so I began looking for something else to get into. I even entertained a partnership with a woman who had a line of athletic, school and fitness clothing. We had a good talk, tossing around several ideas, and while she and I were interested in forming a partnership, she already had a tentative deal with another person that was waiting for a government grant to buy into the company. That also ticked her off, as she couldn't get any help from the bank or government, yet this guy could. Unfortunately she had signed a tentative contract and there was no way out unless he didn't get the money. She called me a week later, stating that the deal had gone through and that she was sorry that things didn't work out for us, as she felt we could have really expanded the company.

Still looking for a business to invest in or buy, I was leaning over the fence, talking to my next door neighbor, who was telling me that he was selling a part of his business. I knew a bit about the business as I had helped him with some of the manufacturing when I had free time on my hands in the early days of Systems 80, as it was also a way to make some extra money.

In March of 1984, while I was still working for the cable TV company, I bought the small business that manufactured scale model scenery which I then called, "Vista Scenics." I hired two of the employees who formerly worked in the business and a new full time employee and a part time

Chapter 1 – Some Personal Background

student. Within a year, I went from working mostly with my mind and doing fine detailed drafting and selling a "service," to now doing general labor, (except for the sales and management end of the business) and selling a "product." I would work at the new business at night and on weekends, while working for the Cable TV Company during the daytime. Having me working and making good money and having money in the bank from the sale of the business was making my wife depressed. This time it wasn't that she wanted a child or to go back to work, this time she wasn't happy with our house and was looking at something new, something better. Within a few months, we bought a new house and rented out our old one.

By the end of 1984, I had fulfilled my contract and had received all the money from the sale of the business, and as I had another business started, there was nothing holding me back from speaking my mind. Things hadn't changed and weren't going to change at the company I was working for. In January of 1985, I attended a board meeting and was asked what plans I saw and had for the company for the New Year. I stated that my New Year's resolution was that I was tired of being screwed, and that I wanted to be the "fucker" instead of the "fuckee." That brought a few shocked looks, groans, gasps and a couple of chuckles and smiles. I told them that I didn't see any future for the company if they didn't make some major management changes, and that they would be down the tubes within a year. A week later, I had a meeting with the President and Vice president of the parent company, who I actually got along with, but as they couldn't, or wouldn't change what needed to be changed, and as I wasn't willing to kowtow to the two management idiots, I received my termination notice. I was wrong with my prediction, as the company lasted fourteen months before it went into receivership. Most of my original employees found work in other cable companies, three as planning supervisors, and others as planners. A couple of others took the experience and skills they learned and applied it to other trades.

In 1985, I decided to form a business partnership with the couple that I had bought the business from. This new joint venture meant getting a space that was going to be big enough to house both business operations. Needing space and not finding what we needed at a reasonable price in Newmarket, we decided to move (lock stock and barrel) to Barrie, Ontario, where property was more affordable, as Newmarket was in a growing boom at the time.

I looked into buying a large shop with a house, on ten acres of land outside the city of Barrie, but when that deal fell through due to zoning regulations, we just rented some industrial business space in Barrie. It was a lot of work in coordinating all the various aspects of the move, both business and personal. There was the job of finding a new business space and setting it up, and in sub-letting the old spaces. There was the physical move that required organizing it so that the businesses were still operational with minimum down time. Then there was the job of notifying all our customers of the move, as well as getting new services installed and connected, and old ones disconnected.

As all of this business activity was going on, we also had to deal with selling our two houses and buying a new one in Barrie, and then coordinating our personal move. As if that wasn't enough work, we also bought another smaller, new house as an investment, which we in turn ended up renting out to our new business partners. Of course there is more. On May 31, 1985, a powerful tornado ripped through Barrie and surrounding area, killing 12 people and leaving 800 homeless. It damaged the building that we were going to be leasing, but not enough that it couldn't be repaired before it was time for us to move in. It missed our new house that was under construction by a couple of blocks, but debris was littered all over the street and yard. It was amazing to see highway guard rails wrapped like pieces of bacon around large poplar trees that looked like they had been stripped by some giant hand. The landscape in the tornados path looked surreal.

By the fall of 1985, we had completed the move and set up the business as well as having moved into our new home. It had been a hectic period, but we were also enthusiastic about our new beginnings.

My World Falls Apart

This business relationship turned out to be disastrous and it ended in 1987. It was to have been a merging of the assets of our two private limited companies into a third joint company. With the merger of the two companies my partner and I looked after sales and production, with him doing more of the sales work, and I heading up production. My wife looked after accounts payable while the wife of my business partner looked after accounts receivables, and both shared the other office duties and also helped in production as needed.

Although I wasn't doing the books, I was aware of the value of the sales being shipped, as well as the new inventory coming in and the production that was going on. I repeatedly questioned accounts receivables in the third company which did not match the value of sales I saw going out, but I was told by my business partners and my wife that I was wrong, confused, didn't trust anyone, accused people of not doing their job, of stealing, or of me being a know-it-all and Mr. Perfect. Money was going out faster than it was coming in and what was supposed to be coming in to the third company wasn't. What was bothering me was that when there was a shortfall in revenue, I'd be asked to dip into the extra money I still had from the sale of my business to cover expenses. I was always assured that it was just a temporary loan until the accounts receivables came in, but that never seemed

Chapter 1 – Some Personal Background

to materialize, as a couple of months later there was still another shortfall and I wasn't being repaid. My issues over the money and my wife siding with my business partners were also straining our personal relationship.

During all this, my partners were secretly negotiating the sale of their 49% of the business to a third party for a tidy sum. That secret was finally brought forward in a form of a guilt trip, when they said that because I didn't trust them, that maybe we should part company, and that they had found a buyer for their share, but that he wanted 51% of the company. I agreed to a meeting with the potential new partner to negotiate the sale of 2% of my company and to see what cards were not being shown. After the meeting, I said that I needed time to consider my options. A couple of days later, I called him with my decision. I told him that I decided not to sell the 2% of the company, but instead, would offer him my full 51%, and that way he could work with my partners as they were already friends. He was agreeable and asked me to give him a number, which I did, and he was responsive and basically agreed to this new arrangement.

The next day I called a meeting and told my partners what I had decided. Needless to say, they went through the roof and said that the whole deal was a "no go" as far as they were concerned, even though they had repeatedly said that they loved the business and hated to give it up, but were doing it only because they couldn't work with me. They must have gotten in touch with him later that night as he called the next day and said the deal was off for now.

After a couple of weeks of more bullshit, I couldn't be talked out of what I felt was going on any longer. On a Friday, after closing, I noticed that my business partner had left her accounting books that she normally took home for "safety" reasons, as she feared a break in. I quickly gathered them up along with the other accounting books, accounts receivables, accounts payables and bank statements, and took them home with me. By late Saturday afternoon, I had sufficient proof of what I had suspected all along. I called a locksmith to have the locks changed at the shop. On Monday, when they found themselves locked out, they were outraged. They were quick to get a lawyer to have me sued and to give me a list of demands. I also contacted my accountant who referred me to a lawyer that I found to be very helpful and thorough. Besides running the business, I had to burn the midnight oil to try to sort out the accounting mess so that I could give my accountant something to work with. That was the only time in my life that I had to take a sleeping pill to go to sleep. I ended up only needing half a pill, otherwise I would sleep for ten hours and wake up groggy.

It was a trying time for the business as they wasted no time in spreading the word to some of my customers that either made me look like the villain, or they told them that the business had gone bankrupt. There was a lot of customer damage control that had to be addressed, and it took a couple of years before things returned to normal and there was some sense of order. They also wasted no time in setting up an identical business with the man who had been negotiating buying into the business, but whom they didn't want to be partners with. Within a month, that relationship fell apart when he saw them for what they were. I also suspected they had something to do with the fact that I started getting calls and letters from the government and the Federal Sales Tax Department. I also had numerous visits from a government Consumer Protection Agency, accusing me of selling products that were under weight. With each "surprise" visit, and upon checking, they found that all products were either on, or over weight. After their third visit, I accused them of harassment, saying that if I saw them again, that I would seek legal reprisals. I never heard or saw her again.

  Before all this happened, there were six people working in the business, my ex-partner and his wife, my wife, two part time employees, and of course, me. After the "event," I had to do a major reorganization as now I was basically running it by myself. My wife was refusing to work in the business, still arguing that I was wrong, and also that she couldn't take the stress any longer. At first I kept the part-time employees, as some of the operations needed three people to run the machines. As time went on and I examined my sales and costs figures, I decided to discontinue the products that were labor intensive and that didn't have high enough sales figures to justify producing them. I decided to eliminate a couple of product lines that enabled me to basically run the business by myself with less than a 4% decrease in sales, made up by reduced labor costs and inventory. While I eliminated some products, I also expanded existing profitable lines that increased sales with minimal inventory costs. Eventually, I reduced staff to one part-timer, and then none, as I simply became more efficient and cost effective. I also sold what I could of my ex-partners assets and took the rest to the garbage dump. That enabled me to downsized the rental space by 50%, thereby saving and making more money.

  This was a rough period for me as there was all the pressure of the lawyers and accountants, and the whole thing of being sued and having to counter sue. To make matters even worse, I had also rented them the house that my wife and I had bought as an investment. Now that they were not taking any money out of the business, they also decided to not pay rent. So not only did I have to deal with them on the business issues, I also had to personally go about getting an eviction notice and then suing them for back rent. It took almost a year before I was able to get them out of the house, which I then had to sell to make up for lost revenue in sales and to cover lawyer and accountant expenses. I also had to sell for other reasons that I'll explain now.

  As all of this was going on, my marriage was also falling apart. I remember being caught up in work, while at the same time, trying to get and

Chapter 1 – Some Personal Background

do all the things a man with a family should have and do. It was during this time that I also found out that my wife was having an affair with a family friend. He was married and they had two children around the same age as ours and we had visited each other's homes on a regular basis. I tried to save our marriage, but she insisted she loved him and wanted to be with him. It turned out that while she wanted him, he didn't really want her. In a ironic twist, he even phoned me, asking me to get my wife to stop phoning and bugging him. I laughingly told him that he wanted her and now he has her, and that he made his bed so now he had to sleep in it. We separated and started divorce procedures, but because of the money situation with the business, I continued to live in the house until it was sold, sleeping in the spare bedroom. My world was falling apart and crashing down around me.

In the fall of 1989, the papers were signed and we were formally divorced. I got to keep the business and my wife got the car, furniture and most of the money. Any money that I got from my share of the sale of the houses was used to buy out her share of the business. Of course, being the nice guy, I ended up with the shitty end of the stick, as I gave her half the business based on the previous year's book value, not taking into consideration any monetary losses credited to my ex-business partners sticky fingers, legal or accounting expenses, or loss of business. Of course that meant that I would be absorbing the total cost of all that.

While the divorce was basically friendly, because she got what she wanted, there were other issues that were not as easy to solve. My son, Bryan, was already off in college, but my daughter, Janice, who wanted to live with me, was forced to live with my ex-wife. She was fourteen years old at the time of the divorce and it would have meant a custody battle and years of costly court proceedings. My lawyer suggested that it would be quicker and cheaper, if I talked to my daughter and let her know that when she turned sixteen, that she could then legally move out and live with me, and that there would be no custody issues. I talked with my daughter and it was agreed. When she turned sixteen, she came to live with me until she finished high school and then went off to college.

It was in the fall of 1989, in the midst of all this turmoil and disaster that a shining light came into my life, her name was Barb. I feel this relationship gave both of us a means of coping and surviving, to re-group ourselves, and what I thought back then was, to heal our wounds. It was a grace period for both of us as she too was going through a separation/divorce and a mutual business wind-up. She also had two children that were living with her at the time. Her son was off to college the following year, leaving her daughter still in high school. Her daughter and I never got on as such; we tolerated each other but that was about as good as it got. During the next four years, Barb and I became involved in a lot of social activities including the curling club, canoe club and the ballroom dance club.

Journey to the Heart Centre

All the changes I made in the business also gave me more personal free time with which to pursue my new found relationship, including all the social activities we enjoyed. It also offered me the opportunity to begin my quest as I now had free time to read and meditate. Because the business had no retail sales, it had very little public traffic, so when I wasn't busy, I'd go into my office to read, or if I wanted to meditate, I'd lock the front door, and turn on the answering machine.

As a side note, I was never able to recover any of the lost money that was swindled from the business, but I was able to collect the back rent for the house. Because part of her book keeping was also written in a code, I could never place an exact dollar value on the amount that was missing, but between what I could identify and the legal and accounting expenses, it was well over $100,000.00, not counting any lost sales revenue.

Chapter 2 - 1990 - My Journey Begins

In the spring of 1990, I stopped in at Holmes Book Store, in Barrie, Ontario, and picked up, "The Edgar Cayce Primer," by Hurbert Puryear. It was a little black paperback that I found in the used book section. When I leafed through the pages I just so happened to stop on the page discussing the Akashic Records. Reading that sent a shock wave through me that said, wow, been there done that; finally here is somebody that makes sense and that I can relate to. I bought the book, and for the next five years I collected every Edgar Cayce book I could get my hands on, and yet, there was always something missing. The books were a piece of the puzzle but I felt there was more to it, and I was determined to find out what that more was.

During the next five years I picked up over two hundred and fifty books, everything from UFO's, mysteries of the paranormal, ancient civilizations, crystals, sound, color, magnets, pyramids, massage, Therapeutic Touch, Reiki, Reflexology, Acupressure, Aromatherapy, body movement, herbs and plants, runes, tarot decks, pendulums, past lives, chakras, native teachings, channeled books, new age magazines and the list goes on. Of all the channeled books I was reading "Bashar," by Darryl Anka, and "Bringers of the Dawn" and "Earth," by Barbara Marciniak had the biggest influence on me at this point in my journey. I started to read the New Testament and looked into what Eckankar, the Rosicrucians, and Scientology had to offer, but they weren't what I was looking for. Eastern religions and philosophy also interested me. I started to study them but I wasn't really drawn to anything other than meditation, chakras, reincarnation and karma, as those topics also provoked more questions than answers. The rest of the material appeared to be a takeoff, or had a similar spin to other religious beliefs, or vice versa, all saying the same thing more or less, just in a different way that still "felt" off. All these added to my knowledge, but it still left me feeling like something was missing. I was looking for a common thread, something that would link them all together, and so far it was eluding me.

During this period, I also went to a few psychic fairs where at first I would just walked around and watch and talk to those that appealed to me. After a couple of years, I finally got up enough nerve and stopped in to get a tarot reading. At the next psychic fair in Toronto, in the fall of 1993, I happened to walk by a partially curtained off area where Karen Langstaff was channeling a message. I stopped and was intrigued by what she was saying, and later stopped at her booth where she did a channeled reading for me and I was hooked, I had to know more about this thing called channeling.

Journey to the Heart Centre

She also informed me that she was holding meetings every Monday evening in Toronto, where people that were interested in channeling would come and share their experiences, and of course channel. It was a one hour drive from Barrie into Toronto, and after attending three or four meetings as an observer I enrolled in her class to learn how to channel. Up to this point, I had never even meditated so I was both excited and afraid. What if I became possessed? What if I couldn't get out of the trance like state? At this time she was still using the Edgar Cayce deep trance method of channeling for her main work, but she was also starting to work with conscious channeling, which is what interested me, and was what this class was to be about.

On a Saturday afternoon, a group of eight had gathered at a house on the outskirts of a small town north of Toronto, and I had my first channeling experience. I can remember the feeling of peace that came over me followed by what I would describe as getting a mild electrical shock. My body shook, trembled and twitched like I was spastic, and the words that came out of me were faint and jerky, but they came. I didn't remember much of what I had said, but I do remember hearing myself say the words. My last channeling experience later that day went a little smoother, and I was more aware of what was being said.

Later I was still afraid to do it on my own as I felt I needed to learn more about meditation before I would try verbal, conscious channeling again. It was during this time that I was also experimenting with automatic writing as it was a form of conscious channeling, but I didn't have to speak. From what I had read, seen and experienced to that point, I believed that I had to put myself into a more or less self-induced light hypnotic trance, aided by a form of meditation and breathing. I also believed that I must get in touch with my right brain, so that meant writing with my left hand. Most of this work was done while I was at work and when I was alone. As stated, I was in manufacturing at that time with no direct public sales, so I rarely received any unannounced callers and most of the sales were done by fax. I would begin by turning the phone ringer off and the answering machine on, and locking the front door. I'd go to my office, get my pen and paper, kick up my feet on the desk and begin to relax my body and do some deep breathing exercises. After a few minutes, when I felt I was ready, I'd slowly take my feet off my desk and prop myself up in my chair so as not to awaken myself from my dream like trance, and when I would feel that a spiritual presence was near me, I would ask my questions that I had prepared beforehand. As soon as I asked, I would begin to write whatever came to mind, even if it didn't make sense to me in the moment. In the beginning, I even tried not to look at my paper as I was writing, but I would have to when I felt the pen slip off the writing pad. I'm smiling now, remembering how I felt like I was cheating if I opened my eyes. I remember squinting to see where I was on the paper and

Chapter 2 – 1990 My Journey Begins

then pretending that I wasn't opening my eyes, as if somebody was watching me to punish me if I did.

I was naturally right-handed but I could also write with my left hand which was something I learned in my fifth and sixth grade, but I hadn't really kept it up, so now it was rather rough. I would write my channeled messages using my left hand and then afterwards, I would re-write above the words that were hard to read which made a real mess of the paper. I laugh at the time in April 1994, when I began writing the message with my left hand and then the pen fell to the floor. I reached down and picked it up with my right hand and unknowingly began writing where I had left off, with my eyes open. The next line read, "Indeed we are pleased to note that you now realize we are able to communicate with you using your right hand, as this will save you time in re-writing your left-handed notes." That was a big change for me and it still makes me chuckle.

I mentioned earlier that Barb entered my life in the fall of 1989. During the five plus years we were together, there were still past issues that Barb and I had to deal with individually, as well as issues in our relationship. Like most couples, we had our differences and disagreements, but we would always seem to work it out and get back together. Even though we were going out as a couple for five years, we still lived separately. By 1994, I was getting antsy and unsettled and was feeling that I needed to make a change in my life, and part of it was the dream of having a piece of property in the country where I could have a shop for the business and a home as well. Barb talked about having a country place and horses some day. We never got together on our plans, and instead, she ended up buying a townhouse in the same complex where I was renting one. It was in the beginning of 1994 that Barb and I had another argument and this was the longest time we had been apart.

Fulfilling a Dream

It was during this time when Barb and I were apart, that I found the property that I felt was what I was looking for. I had gone through some financial hard times the past few years, but I felt things were on the upswing. I felt comfortable in handling the mortgage as I was presently paying out over $1200.00 a month plus utilities for the shop and another $750 a month plus utilities for the townhouse. I viewed the property several times and it felt good, and it was also in the price range that I felt I could easily afford. Although it was what I desired, I had my doubts. I wasn't sure of a lot of things in my life and I was afraid to make a move. I drove up to the vacant property several times to have another look, as the owners had moved to British Columbia.

The last time I drove up I saw another Realtor showing the property and my heart dropped. I called up the listing Realtor and she suggested that if

Journey to the Heart Centre

I was really interested, that I should put in an offer, conditional on getting mortgage approval and see where it went. I thought about it that evening and the following day I put an offer in and it was quickly signed back. I considered it was a fair price and I accepted it; we had a tentative deal. It was also difficult for me as Barb and I were still not talking and I couldn't include her in my decision. That was a big step for me, doing something like that on my own, taking a risk, and it was also all about me, doing what I wanted.

I called my bank manager and set up an appointment to see him about getting a mortgage. He told me outright that he couldn't give me one, and that was an unexpected big disappointment. He informed me that now that I was no longer married, I was considered a risk, and because I had been married and had owned a house, I no longer qualified for the 5% down payment, I now had to put down 10%. I could make the 10% down payment, but that would cut into my operating capital for the business, which I really didn't want to do, especially now as summer was coming and sales were low and expenses were increasing as I had to build up inventory for the Christmas season. It also wouldn't leave me much of a cushion for moving expenses, and to get the business up and running in a new shop. But even if I did put down the 10%, that still wasn't good enough to get the mortgage. Because I was self-employed, that meant I was required to produce financial statements for the past seven years. Since my bank manager also knew that I had gone through financial difficulty with my ex-partner, he said he knew I would be turned down even though sales and profits had gone up over the past four years. He said he knew that I could easily carry the mortgage, utilities and taxes, but that wasn't good enough to get a mortgage.

I felt totally heartbroken and shattered, and felt the deal was dead. I called the Realtor and explained the situation and she suggested that there were several independent mortgage companies around, and to look at the possibility of getting a private mortgage. She was also going to see what the vendor would do. I did some calls and went to two mortgage companies and the second one said that he would give me a mortgage at 1% over the bank rate for two years, plus the standard 2% listing fee, but that I would need to put 10% down. I told him that I would get back to him. I wanted the property, but at the same time, I didn't want to put myself in a financial bind with the added costs. Now what do I do?

That evening I was thinking of my options and I remembered Barbs father telling me that if I ever needed any money, a loan for the business, whatever, that I should give him a call. I had big time guilt calling her father, as Barb and I were still not talking, and I felt like I was going behind her back if I went to her Dad for money. I finally decided to call him and to let him make the decision. I telephoned him and then went to his house where we talked about the property and the problems I was having getting a mortgage and that I was coming to him for help, even though Barb and I were not

Chapter 2 – 1990 My Journey Begins

talking to each other. I felt relieved when he said he thought that Barb and I would work out our "lovers spat," as he called it, like we always did. He said that he would lend me $15,000.00 at 10% with yearly repayment terms. I didn't expect him to offer me that much, but I also felt that this would take all the pressure off me, and that I could easily repay it in no time. With tears in my eyes, I accepted the offer and he said that he'd have the cheque for me the next day. The next day I picked up the cheque and held onto it, still pondering my decision. The following day, I deposited the cheque and made final arrangements with the mortgage broker and the Realtor.

In the summer of 1994, I fulfilled a dream. I bought a one and a half acre property in the country that had a century old school house that was built in 1867. It had been converted several years ago into a three-bedroom home with an office and a laundry room. It had a huge 12' x 30' cedar deck off the kitchen, running the length of the house and then extending around to the front entrance with a smaller 6' wide deck. It also had a 1200 sq. ft. workshop that was only three years old; all this was near the hamlet of Moonstone. It offered me peace and quiet as well as a place from which I could run my business. The property was bordered with mature sugar maple trees. It had two huge beech trees, one near the centre of the property on which I would later hang a truck tire swing mounted in a horizontal position, so that I could lay on it. It also had mature Delicious and Macintosh apple trees near the house, two of which would later come to support my hammock. There were also forty-five acres of mature forest bordering the east and north side of the property, and my closest neighbor was about three hundred feet to the west, that also had a stand of young pine trees separating us. Along the front of the property was a paved county road, and on the opposite side of the road was and abandoned barn and a building as well as several hundred acres of abandoned over grown farmland, spring fed streams and ponds and more forested areas. The yard did need some TLC, but as I loved gardening, this was not a problem and I was looking forward to it.

After I got possession of the property, I started moving the contents of the house up first, and then the business. It was a big job and one that I would not do again in the same way, which was mostly by myself, as I would bring up load after load, day after day. It was also good in a way in that I didn't have to do everything at once, as it gave me time to take down and set up the business storage units and still be able to fill and ship orders, but it was exhausting. Barb and I did get back together for a while and then we were "off" and "on" again one more time before our relationship was finally over in the fall of 1994.

♡ In this moment, I find that I still have more guilt as once Barb talked to her father and learned of my purchase, we got back together and she helped me a lot, both with the move and with setting up and in settling in to my new space. ♥

My Inner Journey begins

In the fall of 1994, I started to regularly attend a Meditation/Healing Circle being held in Barrie by Don Cheff, who coincidentally, I had met when I was taking Karen's Langstaff's channeling workshop earlier. In March of '95, I enrolled in an eight-week basic Chakra class and then in a Light Body class that was being facilitated by Don. During this period, I also experienced various mini treatments such as Acupressure, Shiatsu, Cranial Color Therapy, Aroma Therapy, Therapeutic touch, Sacral Therapy, Reiki, etc. I also had an extensive ear candling session that bought up a lot of past lives issues.

1995 April 23 - I went on a weekend workshop facilitated by Don Cheff and Kathy Roseborough. It was late Saturday afternoon and some twenty people were gathered around several long tables placed end to end. We had just gone through a guided meditation and were sharing our experiences as we were waiting to be called for supper. I had a profound emotional experience during my meditation and before it came to my turn to share, we were called to supper. I could hardly eat anything, and before we returned to the room I talked to Don and briefly told him what I had experienced. When we were all re-seated, Don looked at me and asked me if I would come to the front and share my experience with the group before the next session began. I was numb and also wrought with emotions as I made my way to the head of the table and stood beside Don.

I spoke emotionally of my experience, that I was the Centurion that took Jesus off the cross. I expressed what I saw and did, and also the shame, guilt and the heartbreak that I felt. I openly wept and sobbed in front of this group of strangers, as I only knew five people in the whole group. It was hard for me to stand up before a group and express myself but when I did, I felt this love flow around me. It was a different kind of love; the love I felt was that I had acceptance for my emotions and by expressing my emotions, I was loving myself and for that I was being loved. It was not for anything that I did in the past life, or for the release of the guilt or shame, but that I was loved, as I loved myself. As I returned to my seat several people spoke to me. I felt that some felt and understood my emotions while others said they did, but I felt empty words, mimicking what they heard others say, or what they believed were the right words to say.

Later, during the next meditation I had another past life experience. This time I was a woman, one of five that was going to be beheaded for being

Chapter 2 – 1990 My Journey Begins

a witch. As I made my way up to the chopping block, I looked at the man with the axe. He had a black hood over his head, yet I felt I knew him. I couldn't speak or utter a sound. I felt a calmness come over me as I felt my life force leave my body as my head tumbled toward the ground.

After that session, we all went out to the lounge to have a coffee, share our experiences and relax for the rest of the evening before going to bed. I had told Don what I experienced when we were coming out of the meeting room and about a half an hour later, I overheard Dave, whom I knew, talking to Don about his unsettling experience in the last meditation. He was explaining that he had a past life experience where he was a man with a black hood over his head, and that he had chopped off the heads of five women who were accused of being witches. I looked wide-eyed at both of them, while Don, open mouthed, looked at me in amazement and Dave looked puzzled. Don told him what I had shared earlier and I filled in the details. I knew Dave from our meditation classes and we were also sharing a room that evening. I felt a little uneasy but we joked about it, that I'd be sharing a room with the guy that cut off my head in a past life. It was a toss and turn night and I didn't get much sleep. Nothing eventful happened with the rest of the workshop that ended late afternoon the next day.

I returned home still in awe of the whole experience. I had seen the light but now the question was what was the light trying to show me? It wasn't about the light that was important, but about what the light was shining on, and to see that, I would have to look in the opposite direction. I don't know why, but I was drawn to the bible and I casually opened it and read any passages that jumped out to me. I was moved again when I realized that I too, am the Son of God. I didn't know what all that meant, but that was the day I began my search in earnest; I came to call that experience and moment, day zero.

1995 April 26 - Now that the weather was nicer I began running 4 km in the morning. I had just returned from my run and was resting under the Beech tree in the middle of the backyard, when I heard a voice coming from above me saying, "How are you doing down there little one?" I looked up into the branches and then laughed as I realized that it was the tree talking to me. I had my first conversation with a tree that day.

1995 May 10 - I attended my first sweat lodge, one that I will never forget. It was a pleasant spring late afternoon as I drove up to cottage of Star Bear/Heart Man and his wife Night Owl. I had gotten their name from a friend of a friend, and I had called for information and was invited up to the sweat. I had never met them or any of the people there that night, and this was all a "first" for me.

Journey to the Heart Centre

The cottage was nestled in amongst the rocks and forest of the Canadian Shield and overlooked a lake. A hundred feet or so from the cottage, perched on a outcropping of granite, nestled beside some cedar and under some towering pine trees was a small sweat lodge covered in Moose hide. There was a steep, sparsely treed bank descending to the lake on the left, and a giant granite cliff as a backdrop on the back and right side. A few steps from the lodge, four women and Night Owl were silently tending the crackling fire that was now beginning to cast dancing figures of light and shadows against the granite cliff.

I remember looking at the sweat lodge and wondering how the twelve men including myself were all going to fit in it. Star Bear called us together and informed us that Night Owl was going to be leading the sweat, as he was not yet qualified to do so. As the men inside the cottage began to get totally undressed for the sweat, he also said we could take a towel to sit on if we wanted to. I looked out toward the lodge and could see that Night Owl, who had been talking to the four women, was now also getting undressed as she was preparing to individually greet us before we entered the lodge. I was having reservations about being totally naked in front of all these strangers including the women, but I felt I was here for a reason so I was determined to see it through, but I did wait to be the last in line.

The sun was just beginning to set and from our viewpoint we could see dark clouds on the tangerine horizon; rain was coming. As I made my way to the lodge I could hear the crackling of the fire heating up a pit full of grandfather stones that were beginning to glow red-hot. In the distance, the trilling sounds of a pair of loons filled the night air as they hauntingly called to each other. As we slowly filed pass the fire I was aware of a feeling of warmth on my right side of my naked body and contrasting damp coolness on the left side. At the time, I didn't realize that because I was last in line, I also got the position closest to the door, second closest to the rock pit and heat, and right next to Night Owl.

We all managed to squeeze in, huddled naked against each other in a tight circle, knees pinned to our chest; shoulders stooped, head bent forward following the inside contours of the cedar lodge. For each ceremony, we were in almost total darkness except for the glowing red-hot stones in the pit, which grew dimmer and dimmer as the ceremony went on.

Before we entered the sweat, we were told that we could come out for a few minutes, but only after each ceremony and that if we left before the ceremony was finished, we couldn't get back in. I didn't think I'd make it through the first round but I did. I, along with three others, managed to crawl out on our hands and knees and lay face down, naked on the cool damp grass. I felt myself being nurtured by the Earth; cleansed by a gentle rain that was now falling, warmed by the crackling fire, and soothed by an ever so gentle breeze.

Chapter 2 – 1990 My Journey Begins

♡ I just realized in this moment that it was the four elements, Earth, Air, Fire and Water. I'm becoming emotional at the significance of all that and I'm wondering why I never picked up on it before. ♥

I returned to the sweat and came out again after the second round. This time I didn't feel so bad. The rain was coming down a little heavier now and I surrendered myself to it, feeling it gently beat on me, using my body as a drum. I could feel the rain trickling off my back and legs, and also running through my hair and then down the side of my face. Earlier I had reservations about being naked, but as we went through the various rituals I began to feel more comfortable and at ease with myself and the whole experience.

I returned for the third round and this time it was during our give away ceremony that the storm broke above us, and the lodge shook as the thunder rolled across the skies. We couldn't see the lightening as it was pitch black inside the sweat lodge, but we could feel the Earth and lodge shake when it was thundering. I came out after the third round not because I was in any pain but for the joy I was feeling, and I looked forward to the final ceremony.

It was as if the whole experience, including the storm had been orchestrated for the sweat. When we came out after the fourth ceremony, we all climbed down the steep bank to the lake and went for a refreshing quick dip in the icy water. Afterwards, we went back up to the cottage where we got dressed, and then shared our experiences and had a feast. Like I said, it was an experience I will always remember. Megwetch Night Owl (brings the dream) and Star Bear/Heart Man).

After Barb and I split up, I met Michelle at the Meditation/Healing Circle classes that I mentioned before, who was nineteen years younger than me. After a few months of getting together after classes for coffee and donuts with others in the group, we began dating. In the fall of 1995, Michelle and her five-year-old son, Justin moved in with me. Michelle was also searching for her path and this relationship opened us up to new ideas and experiences and activated a lot of emotional issues for both of us. Although spirituality and meditation was what brought us together, after she moved in, we didn't do too much in the way of meditating as I was mainly focused on work and what we were doing as family. At the same time, this relationship was putting me back into a lot of my old programs and patterns that I had been trying to break free from, and that created conflict in our relationship. By mutual consensus, we agreed to end our relationship at the end of the school year in June of 1996. She moved back to Barrie, but we continued to keep in touch.

I feel that I've drifted a bit here, but I felt it was necessary to let you in on that part of the story. After Michelle left, I felt that Moonstone was my sanctuary and also a turning point in my life. It gave me the solitude and the time needed to prepare me for my real journey. I felt I had taken all the classes I needed as nothing else appealed to me, and while Meditation and Visualization tapes were blissful, peaceful and uplifting, I felt there was more that I needed to experience. In the numerous books I was reading, I'd find only small parts that felt right, and I had this niggling feeling inside me saying that something was still missing. I wanted to find it but at the same time it all seemed so confusing and overwhelming. I was also beginning to do more channeling and even bought a voice-activated tape recorder along with a microphone and stand so that I could verbally channel and record my messages. This method offered limited success as I found it annoying to continually pause, rewind and playback my messages when I was transcribing them to my computer. I eventually abandoned that idea and settled for writing in a journal or on loose-leaf paper that I later put into binders.

In the fall of 1996, I decided to attend another group meditation facilitated by Don Cheff, in which I had another past life experience. After the session, I talked to Don about my experience and he lent me the book, "Right Use of Will," by Ceanne DeRohan. I read the part that he suggested and was fascinated in that the past life experience I had was very similar to what was in the book. I gave the book back before finishing it as I had other things going, but I ordered it in the spring of 1997.

That pretty much takes you up to where I'm going to begin the story of my journey. I'm going to be sharing my experiences as well as many of the messages I received from my guides. The purpose of this book is to show, in part, my journey including my fears, pain and joy, along with the insights and understandings I obtained. It will also allow you to see the transformation taking place, and how my beliefs changed with my experiences. How what starts out as being one thing turns out to be another, and to simply allow you to see the events of my journey and how they affected me, and maybe in some small way to assist you on your journey.

As you read the rest of this book, you will see that my journey and life will be deeply affected and changed by three exceptional women who are now about to come into my life, Rita, Jen and Irene. That's not to say that all the people I've known and met haven't affected or contributed to my life, my experiences and journey in some form or another. I thank them too for their part, because without them, I wouldn't have experienced what I did and be where I am now.

♡ At this moment I'm being flooded with a list of topics that will be dealt with, but I still don't know where to start, but at the same time I have, it's just that I haven't really admitted it. It will be a book for women, men, children, all ages, nationalities and eventually worldwide, in many languages, and will also be used by your alien brothers and sisters. *S*S* What? I didn't

Chapter 2 – 1990 My Journey Begins

hit the bold button… or type the net chat smile symbol ***S*** There it happened again. What's going on? ♥

This ain't no small project and I don't know if I really want this, but then again I do. I'm also afraid that I'll get corrupted and fall back into the old programs, beliefs and values. It is my intent to heal myself, all of me, and to spiritualize this physical body and bring heaven to earth. To live a life in love, joy, balance, abundance and peace.

> The journey of your life is about to begin. Embrace these shaking and doubtful moments and remember them, to hold them dear to you. For life as you know it is about to change and you will look back with fondness at all your memories and experiences, not with attachment but rather a knowing, sentimental feeling of acceptance and joy. You chose this task and journey and you are coming out from behind the veil that has kept you from knowing your true self. Blessings upon you this evening my son.   Father and Mother.

> I was going to delete the last two paragraphs but again it happened for a purpose, as it will also show you how I am going to be writing, by also sharing what is happening in the moment. ♥

Chapter 3 - 1997 - The Winds of Change

By the fall of 1996 my journey and search had intensified, or rather became more focused. Having just ended my relationship with Michelle, I was left to be with my two cats, my business, and myself. As I previously mentioned, the property I bought had a century old school house, a shop and a shed. While the manufacturing end of the business was located in a shop, I had the office in my home. This arrangement provided me with ample opportunity to pursue my spiritual growth. If there were no orders to ship, or stock and inventory to get ready, I'd put the phone on the answering machine and do whatever I felt like doing, as most orders came in by fax. As far as the business was concerned, fall was the busiest season as stores were gearing up for Christmas sales. But even though it was busy, I'd still take days off and ship orders at the end of the week, or next week, if they came in Thursday or Friday and I wanted to do something else. I didn't have that spark or drive to succeed like I used to have, as I felt that there was more to life than just work. When I wasn't working, I'd spend as much time as I could reading, meditating, channeling, talking on the phone, or going into town to the New Age books stores, and either looking for new books or just chatting with the owners and other customers.

I also found and joined a small local group that was holding meditation and channeling sessions once a week. This is where I met Rita, and after attending a few meetings, we exchanged phone numbers. A few days later I called her and we talked for over two hours that first night. We then began to regularly share our personal experiences and delve into topics that interested us. We also worked with each other doing journeys, sometimes into the small hours of the morning. All of our discussions and journeys were over the phone as she lived in Barrie that was some twenty miles from me.

It was on January 09, 1997 that Jen came into my life. I was telephoning a woman named Jan, a member of the local meditation /channeling group to follow up to see how she was feeling, as she had become deeply emotional the previous evening when I channeled a message for her. I dialed her telephone number but I got one digit wrong, and that's how I connected with Jen. We talked for over half an hour during that first wrong number call, and I gave her my phone number. Within a couple of weeks we were spending a lot of time on the phone, sharing experiences and doing journeys. I was also the go between Rita and Jen, as I'd share the experiences I had with Rita with Jen, and vice versa. I think they only talked to each other once or twice. Thankfully for me, none of these calls were long distance.

Chapter 3 - 1997 The Winds of Change

1997 Jan 18 - I was talking on the phone with Rita and we decided that since there was resistance to the channeling that we were doing in the local group, that we were going to begin a group called "Visions," that would hold meditation, channeling and past life sessions in the city of Barrie. Things were now beginning to really open up for me. Guided visualizations were a daily routine and channeling was becoming an interregnal part of our experiences, like this one that was spontaneous during our telephone conversation.

What is Your Desire?

It doesn't matter how long you have been on your "spiritual" path or even if you know what it is. It now matters only that you want to advance, to heal, to grow, to learn and become all that you can be. It doesn't matter if you understand all the terms and language. It matters only that you desire to learn, heal and evolve.

If you have the true desire and the will to learn and be guided quickly, quickly is what you will experience. If you think, "I will take it slow," slow is what you will experience. If you take the plunge, you get the experience quickly, just like learning how to swim. You will only experience the joy, thrill, and freedom of swimming if you are willing to "let go" of that which you hang onto or stand upon. Release your fear and you will have fun and joy beyond your wildest expectation. Risk children, let go, trust and believe that you will be supported.

Rita, Jen and I began to share more and more, and to do what I call journeys, where we would facilitate each other through guided visualizations. Sometimes our journeys became simultaneous as we'd both be experiencing the same events. With channeling came the awareness of different energies and I was also beginning to become aware of uneasy energies around me, energies that were trying to get my attention. I also received information on astral attachments or "cling-ons, as Rita and I later came to call them.

1997 Jan 29 - I received the following message.

Clearing the Astral Plane

Indeed, the healing now is also of those in the Astral plane for they are part of the planetary consciousness that needs awakening, not only those in the physical. Awakening these will also aid those on the planet to which some of these souls are attached for whatever reason. Releasing them now, giving them the opportunity not to be Earth bound, held by remorse, regret, or guilt, for those in the physical. This is the next clearing and you will notice new energies arriving to allow this to be accelerated. This will be a phenomenon like the flu. Suddenly Humans will be realizing that there are those energies around them that don't belong there, and they will feel anxious and will want to disassociate themselves with this energy, for although it is of a higher vibration than the physical, your light bodies are beginning to vibrate higher than the astral plane and hence the perception and the discomfort.

This awareness will be noticed and it will take time to release all those in the Astral plane that will want to be released. For the energies coming to Earth now not only affect Humans in the physical, but this energy is more directed to the souls in the Astral, for their healing, for their acceleration, to increase their vibration. Understand that as you prepare to meet this challenge, trust your guidance, your messages and your truth for you are protected always. They will come to seek you out as you are a portal, a doorway, and an answer to their question, to their dilemma. Simply acknowledge their presence and you may, if so directed, initiate a dialogue or simply be a beacon that will automatically inform them of what they desire to know and to show them the path to the light for growth and development. Simply say "I am the light, the truth and the way" and they will be given what is required to move into the light.

Understand also there will be those who are not simply lost, but who have attachments in varying degrees. These will usually be associated with those in the physical and the physical Humans will be coming for counseling, guidance, understanding and release from these shadows. This will be where considerable work will be required and all within the group and some outside the immediate group will be preparing themselves for this task. Adornia, Blessing unto you child.

Another brief message I got later was that "the Astral plane is next to be cleared in the physical, and that is what you're doing, that is what is holding a lot of people back, for a cloud is over them."

Clearing our astral plane and our attachments was one of the many things we worked on with ourselves, each other and with others who we felt were open. Attachments can be to people, living or dead, places or things, entities and even thought forms. I can't remember what Rita's attachments were that we cleared but with Rita's help; my first experience was that of releasing my mother who is very much alive. During the journey, I could see and feel that her attachment to me was her need to be in control, that she knew what was good for me and wanted to save me from myself. My attachment to her was that of feeling that I was responsible for her, that she is my mother and that I can't hurt her feelings. When I released my attachment to her I felt like the weight of the world had been lifted off my shoulders. As we progressed and became more confident in our journeys, I also became aware of other peoples attachments and found ways to help them clear themselves too.

Chapter 3 - 1997 The Winds of Change

1997 February 7 - I received the following message.

An Introduction to Healing

Blessings, for healers you are, not that you actually heal but that you are a facilitator to allow the self to heal, much like this channel. He does not think or ponder the words he writes, he merely writes. He is a conduit, a means of transferring energy from one space and time to another. So in a sense, he is a healer, healing with words, for the word has tremendous power that you have not yet begun to fathom and understand. All are healers, healers mostly of themselves first and then those around them that they can assist during this time of transition. There are as many ways of healing as there are Humans, and each is unique and each has special gifts. Some will heal with touch, some by sight, colour or shape, some with sound, and some with aroma and taste, by herbs, that which is ingested in the human form to assist the cells to function as per original plan.

There is no one path one must take to become the healer you are. Understand that you need not take any so-called courses to become the HEALER you are, for you already ARE that healer. You just don't know it yet and you haven't opened yourself to accept and EXPERIENCE your GIFTS. As you open and allow these gifts will come forward and they will be similar in some ways to what is already being practiced, BUT unique unto you. You may find that you are using ten to twenty different disciplines in your method of healing, of assisting others in their PHYSICAL, MENTAL and EMOTIONAL well Being.

For healing is not simply that of the physical. It must encompass all the bodies, for all is one. As you heal one, you must also heal the appropriate CAUSE in the other. For unless you assist in healing all the bodies, all the malfunctions of the DIS-EASE, the disturbances, you are merely doing what your doctors are doing now, putting a bandage on an injury, the disease. It may APPEAR to cure, to heal, but it is, we assure you, only temporary, for you have not addressed the major issue, all the issues surrounding the manifestation of the disease in the dense physical body which is the last to offer no resistance, no cover up. Oh yes, it can be made to cover up and mask the disease temporarily, but sooner or later it must surface in its full manifestation to be dealt with.

A further understanding that is required is that not all disease is to be cured. Being in the physical, you are here to experience, and hence, you can also CHOOSE to experience pain or the manifestation of certain diseases that are appropriate to the experiences you desire. Hence, by exposing your healing abilities through ego on a body that in fact wishes and desires the disease, you are disallowing that person the experience of the disease and are in fact, encumbering its soul growth, and YOUR soul growth. For you are, by your ego, trying to heal, to SAVE someone from what that someone wishes to experience, based on your beliefs. Understand that what you call healing, the abilities you have are also a responsibility, a responsibility to the highest purpose of yourself and the highest purpose of those that you deem to be sick and in DIS-EASE

As you begin to understand and apply yourself as true channels of Divine Love and Light you will begin to know and honor your gifts and know and honor their use. If you are compelled by what you call sympathy, empathy or compassion to assist or save someone, you must also be aware of the cause of the illness/disease. You may be directed to DO NOTHING but to allow the person to experience the pain and suffering however hard it is, you must detach yourself from wanting to save, to heal, for although this is a noble thought, it is out of ego. Ego is clever is it not, not that ego is wrong, it is simply being and doing what it thinks is right, what it thinks you are, and what it has have programmed to be and do. So we are saying that now is the time to consider not only HOW you heal, but WHY, WHEN, WHERE, WHAT and WHO you heal. For you are now at the stage, the phase of becoming who you are, and this is the mergement of your higher self and the ego, but until this is fully accomplished you will be flipping back and forth between spirit and ego. The higher you get in your vibration, the subtler will be the differences between them, and you must truly practice discernment, especially when attempting to be a channel in healing others.

Indiscretions you commit upon yourself are not as large, as misapplied, we are searching for words here to describe your actions upon others are harder to correct than the actions upon yourself. "Do onto others as you would have others do onto you," would probably fit the feeling we are trying to convey. Understanding will come with experience, and with experience will come wisdom. We are not here to chastise you, only to make you aware of what gift you have, and in your rushing to use it to save and heal your fellow man, what injury you can cause if you do not fully comprehend and apply yourself according to your highest purpose. In love and light we now conclude this introduction on healing, more will be given soon. Blessings, Adornia

> *Understanding will come with experience, and with experience, will come wisdom. - Shenreed*

It was during this time that I talked to Rita about selling my business as my heart wasn't in it anymore and hadn't been for a while, and that maybe I would sell my home too. She mentioned that she and her husband were also thinking of selling their home. This was a big step for me. I knew I was in for a change but I didn't know what, where, when or why, just that it was coming. I talked to some wholesalers and put out feelers in the industry to see if anyone was interested in the business. I got a couple of calls but no one was

Chapter 3 - 1997 The Winds of Change

really interested at this time. I thought that maybe I was to just carry on as I had been until I knew for sure what I wanted to do. I also began doing little things around the house and yard that I had been putting off which would make the place look better when, and if I did put it on the market.

As mentioned, Rita and I had also started a meditation/channeling/healing circle group, which we called "Visions" that met once a week at a Motel meeting room in Barrie. These sessions were audio taped and Rita would type our channeled messages for distribution the following week. During this time, we were also beginning to do past life regressions with journeys back to Atlantis, Lemuria, Pan, as well as multi-dimensional journeys. All these experiences were new to us but we were open, naive and also excited about what we were experiencing. Rita was also going through some shape shifting and manifesting experiences that were surreal.

At this point, we were mostly mental; by mental I mean thinking verses feeling. When we did have feelings and emotions come up, we dealt with them in a mental, controlling fashion. I can remember Rita and I saying that we needed to understand what we are doing before we could feel it, while Jen was adamantly opposed, saying that you need to feel it before you can heal and understand it. In the past life regressions that we had been doing, very little emotion was really being expressed, not that we were void of emotions, but we felt that emotions were one thing and spirituality was another. I feel this was a necessary step to enable us to experience what I would later come to call "tools." It was a step-by-step process to first open to the possibilities of such an experience and then to develop the tools to enable us to explore it more fully. Once we learned the techniques, we were then guided into feelings and emotions, and their role in these experiences.

Actually, during this period I was wrought with emotions, of unfinished issues with my last relationship with Michelle, of a business that no longer interested me, of declining revenues, and confusion as to where I was going with my life. I was in for major changes, and emotions were to become a big part of this change but I didn't know it yet. I was also going through flu like symptoms that put me flat on my back, which was something else for me to experience as I was rarely ever that sick in my life. One time I was so sick that I could hardly get out of bed for three days but I didn't clue in until later that this was a form of emotional release, which was being triggered by all the work we had been doing on our journeys.

1997 February 11 - I just now realized that I can no longer help those that I care about, that I must let them experience life on their own efforts. As above, so below. My guides, angels, archangels and the family of love and light, God, All that is, cannot DO it for me either, it goes against the law of growth, of higher purpose, of unconditional love. They can give me signals and symbols that will give me clues but they cannot directly interfere with what I (EGO) want to experience, however distorted I see it, and for whatever beliefs or conditions I agree or submit to. Once I make the conscious decision to change and do so, then I begin to create my own reality and the universe can then allow me to experience that. For instance, if I was a taxi driver and I asked for help, claiming that I now wanted to be a pilot. As long as I'm thinking, doing and being a taxi driver, I can't be helped to be a pilot because I'm still hanging on to being a taxi driver and they can't make me let go of what I'm hanging on to. I have to let go first and then they'll be able to help me, help myself. I don't know if that fully explains what I felt, as it's hard to express a feeling, especially one that you've never felt before.

♡ I later realized that in the messages I was receiving, that I was being spoken to in the language that I could understand, and I don't mean English. I mean that the words used were such that enabled me to mentally comprehend what was being presented in a form that I could relate to. As an analogy, it's like going to school and learning basic addition and subtraction, where the teacher uses materials that one can identify and relate to so that one can begin to grasp and comprehend the concepts that are being presented. ♥

1997 Feb. 14, 5:45 am - I awoke from a lucid dream where I had found myself drifting through people, objects and walls in a mall. I just went through them as if they were wisps of smoke or fog. I didn't change them; I just passed through them. I also went back and forth in time in the same space. The people adjusted to where they were and again they were like smoke. In both cases I felt that I could make them and myself solid and then we could just carry on in what we now call this physical reality. There was also a stack of dishes that I was able to control, as one by one I would make them disappear and then re-appear, or I'd re-arranged them with my thoughts and also make them rise up and fly around the room.

During the next couple of weeks, I was going through another series of body releases from hot sweats, cold chills, nausea, swelling, pain, sore and stiff muscles, sneezing, running nose, stuffed nose, sore throat and difficulty in swallowing. I was alone in my agony, pain and suffering.

Receiving Love

1997 Mar. 15 - It is I, Jehovah that comes to you this morning to bring you the understanding that you need to contemplate and experience so that you can bring it into your Being. It is one of non-commitment and one in which you always have choice and free Will; this is the understanding of Love.

Me; I don't understand?

Chapter 3 - 1997 The Winds of Change

That is why I bring this to you for your understanding. Love is all encompassing, non-judgmental, unconditional, freely given and freely received. You have no problem in giving but you do in receiving, for you think yourself not worthy. This is not only you, this is appropriate for many and some are in reverse, they can and want only to receive, but cannot give.

However, getting back to your situation, allow others to freely give you that which you desire to give or do. Allow them to do for you out of love, accept this, and allow this to come into your life. It is not an obligation or commitment to that person, it is merely letting that person express his or her love for you and you have merely to accept. You do not have to DO anything in return, for it is not a favor or a loan, it is a gift and it is unconditional. Just as you give and do not expect anything in return, so it is with them.

This is an area that you need to work on to experience and allow it into your life, to balance, for it is not a one way street. As you give, so shall you receive. There is imbalance, for you give and give of yourself, of your time, of your space, of your energy, always giving, but rarely do you accept. It is time for acceptance, acceptance in all the areas that you have been giving. Merely intend and ask that you desire to experience the acceptance of love.

I stopped channeling and made the statement, "I desire to experience the acceptance of love" three times out loud.

Good, your intention is heard and the universe will respond much like the picture you draw in its own way. This is a hard thing for you to realize and recognize (and others too) for in your heart you are kind, generous, loving, thoughtful, considerate, affectionate, allowing and eager to assist and help those that call upon you. This is fine and this is desirable to a point, but as I have said, you need to balance, not by doing or being less, but by allowing others to do unto you as you do unto others, unconditionally. As you do, so your life will begin to turn around and you will begin to see more clearly, for you will have a change of perspective. It is like breathing, you can't only exhale, you need also to inhale and as you inhale the love that others give you, you will also find that you will be able to give more to others. Practice this receiving on a conscious level and become aware of allowing the acceptance of love to come into your life. Recognize it for what it is and accept it.

The other end of this polarity, the stick as you want to call it, is that some people might want to impose their love upon you. Acceptance is also for your understanding and discernment. If what they give you is truly from the heart and unconditional, then accept and allow it, for although you may not need it directly, it may be used to get something else in exchange, that is if it is a physical thing. Acceptance as you sense, and which is also true, can clutter up your life if it is of those things that are of no use to you, but this will not happen unless you want it to, for your acceptance is of the things that you also give. So it would not be that you would receive that which you do not give.

Me; Yes, I understand.

Good, so trust, allow, and experience this new aspect into your life and you will enjoy even more the giving, the teaching and the sharing that you do. Blessings, YHVH

> **Intent: I desire to experience the acceptance of love. - Shenreed**

It was during this time that we were doing telephone journeys and in one journey, I guided Rita into her past life as Joan of Arc. It had some similarities to the current history version, except that in her remembrance, she wasn't burned at the stake, it was another girl that looked like her that was burned in her place. She had been tortured and crippled by having her right knee cap broken, and was then sent off to another country where she was married and died giving birth to one of her present children.

I also guided her in journeys to the Pleiadians. In one experience, she had bare feet with four toes but no toenails, long arms and hands with four long fingers, and again with no nails. She also had large dark eyes with a small nose and no lips on her mouth. She had long pink hair in braids decorated with beads and was wearing a flimsy gossamer robe that she had made and decorated with beads. During this experience, I had no actual involvement, but I was there as a witness, confirming what she was seeing, feeling and doing.

I was also beginning to do past lives with Jen. One of her experiences was of a life in Ireland where her sister had poisoned her on her wedding day. The belief that was put into place with that life/death was, don't be too happy or have too much, as you won't live to enjoy it. The second life she experienced during that regression was as a beautiful young black girl that was sold as a slave and kept for sex. Both black and white people shunned her and she eventually hung herself. The belief that was put into place in that lifetime was, don't be too attractive, too beautiful, as it will only bring you pain and suffering.

We also did simultaneous journeys, as I mentioned before, and one such experience was riding winged horses, Pegasus. We also rode on the backs of butterflies when we went to meet the fairies and Leprechauns. I still remember the meeting with Shimmy, the leprechaun. He was talking with an Irish, Gaelic accent and when I repeated his name as Jimmy, he was very quick and adamant to correct me. He told (us) me straight, that if his name was Jimmy, he would have told us so, and that his name was Shimmy and that

Chapter 3 - 1997 The Winds of Change

is what he wanted to be called. Both Jen and I laughed ourselves into hysterics at that exchange.

Besides numerous past life journeys and visits to other star systems and dimensions, we even got into simultaneous channeling. Rita had been channeling Quazar on a regular basis, and one evening while on the phone, we both channeled him at the same time, saying the same words as if reading from a book. That was a different, exciting and a joyful experience in that we felt that it was a confirmation for us, for both of us having the same message at the same time, it was real, even if we didn't understand it, or know how or why it was happening.

Rita and I were also involved in another unusual experience and that was in the form of two way channeling. Earlier, I had received the message that during our next weekly Meditation/Channeling classes, that Rita and I were going to be doing a channeling exchange. We were to take part of our consciousness to the Pleiades, to channel messages through the Pleiadians for others in their group, and at the same time, the Pleiadians were going to come through Rita and I, and we would consciously channel their messages for our group. We were going to be teaching the Pleiadians about emotions as during our recent journeys to the Pleiadians, both Rita and I observed that while there was peace and tranquility present, there was very little emotion, passion, or expression, the peaks seemed to be missing. I can remember during the class that I was flipping back and forth in consciousness and totally amazed at being able to be in two places at the same time and doing different things and wondering if Rita was doing the same and also knowing that she was.

♡ As I'm typing, I'm remembering the experience and becoming emotional. ♥

Another experience that Rita and I had was with the Pharnoos. I had received the message earlier that day saying that they wanted to get together with us, as we had with the Pleadians, but that they wanted us to come to them. I received the following message.

Message from the Pharnoos

We are the consciousness of the Pharnoos. We have no physical form but are here to observe this glorious transformation that is occurring at this time and we are in awe at the progress you and your little group are making in leaps and bounds. Crossing all thresholds as you dare search for the truth of who you are, and to express and experience yourselves to the fullest. It is truly amazing to see you re-group yourselves, these Starseeds are indeed awesome, have a character and zest for life and service unmatched in the universe. There is no stopping you, for you will take as long as is needed to do the task and when you reach a foothold, an opening, you go at it with an all consuming energy, devouring anything that stands in your way. Once you release your fears you are truly fearless, and with that strength of conviction you are unstoppable.

We are most interested in this aspect of being human and experiencing the polarity aspect of creation and that is why we are here. We offer to you and your company, the invitation to join us, to exchange, to come to know each other and to learn. For we have much to teach you and you us, it is simply a matter of trust. We are of light, as are you, but we have chosen to maintain our conscious form rather than manifest in the physical. We have had many opportunities to do so at different times and in different forms, but at this time, being human is the most intriguing. The offer is open anytime, call upon us as you can now manifest that, or we to you if you desire. Visit us and explore our form, we are open to receive you. Blessings and we wait further contact.

Later I spoke to Rita on the phone and we decided sure, why not go. We each went into our little meditative state of consciousness as we journeyed there together through a yellow/orange cloud or mist. We both felt we were there, but it felt strange that there was no one there to greet us, but at the same time, we felt we were being scanned. We were then told our emotions were too high and we were asked to adjust ourselves. We didn't know what we were doing but we made the conscious intent to lower our emotional vibration and we were told that it was still too high. Then it felt like they were beginning to probe us as it felt physically uncomfortable and Rita was beginning to panic. I asked them what they were doing but there was no reply, only more probing. I stated that if all they wanted to do was to probe us without consent and not talk to us as they originally stated, that we were leaving. I began to guide Rita and myself back and that was when they began asking us to stay. I said, "No, you had your chance," and we left.

Later we got the message that in the future, we are to only open ourselves to love and light, and only if it was in our highest purpose and for our spiritual growth, and that if it wasn't, to say no. As above, so below, just as we have to discern on Earth, so too we also have to discern with the other realms of existence. It was an important experience and lesson for both of us to feel.

1997 March 18 – Today I bought the first book in a series called "Right use of Will," Healing and Evolving the Emotional Body, by Ceanne DeRohan. I had read part of it a few months earlier when I was loaned a copy after sharing an emotional vision I had during a meditation and was told to read the chapter on "the land of Pan." Reading the part about the Light Wizard turning himself into and amethyst crystal, then experiencing the terror of being stuck in it, and then finally crawling out as a lizard, struck a chord in me, as that was the vision I had and the emotions I felt. I knew that I needed to read it and study the rest of the books too.

1997 March 19 - Rita called me that evening telling me that she had been out with her son's school class on a maple syrup tour. She said she got to supervise a group of twelve children that her son was in and that five of the children had ADD. After the tour, and while waiting for the bus, she had them all hold hands and form a circle, and they began to play a game that she had just made up. After the game was finished she could see that the bus would still be a few minutes; she didn't know why but she asked them all to stay in the circle and to close their eyes for a few moments. She then spoke to them telepathically saying that they would become aware of their attachments, their cling-ons, and that they would know what to do. When she could hear the bus approaching, she told them to open their eyes and form a line to get on the bus. She told me that they were all very subdued and quiet as they got on the bus and were seated. It was then that the five children with ADD all turned to her with big smiles on their faces and said to her in unison, "We're aware." Rita was dumbfounded, as she didn't know why she said that to them in the first place, secondly that they heard her, thirdly that they would even understand what she meant, and lastly to have them all turn and speak in unison. It freaked her out.

Awareness, Lifting the Veils

1997 Mar. 19 - Bittersweet is the knowledge and understanding that comes from awareness, for as the veils of illusion are lifting, all that is false is revealed and it is difficult, if not impossible, to even be in the atmosphere or environment that does not vibrate at your level. It is like being human and swimming underwater, for you need air to breathe and maintain life in your natural state. You can immerse yourself in the water and become one with it, but only for a very few minutes at most, before it becomes uncomfortable and you need to return to the surface to what you feel comfortable and natural in. In the physical we are dealing with emotional vibrations and not the air in your lungs, and therefore you can remain physically in an emotional environment for however long you choose, but its vibration will affect your emotional and physical bodies to the awareness that something is wrong.

Now suddenly you are faced with the awareness and you have to make a choice of letting go of old beliefs and systems that no longer vibrate to your new awareness. The dilemma immediately created is that of separation and a sense of loss, of connection with that with which you are familiar. This is the ego panicking at its loss of control. Understand that this will pass, for once you move into your new vibration and maintain it, you will also come to the realization that it was the old patterns and beliefs that were causing you

discomfort and pain. Removing the illusions removes the conflicts. Continue breaking down the walls, the barriers that have been put up by mass consciousness and by your limiting beliefs, and accept only those that continue to serve you. It might be a lonesome journey for a while but I assure you it's only temporary, for things are moving swiftly now and you'll soon meet others with whom you will link and progress.
Blessings YHVH

> *Removing the illusions, removes the conflicts. – Shenreed*

1997 March 20, 5:14 am - I channeled the following poem

Full Circle

Just as I am doing, I am being.
Just as I am being, I am knowing.
Just as I am knowing, I am becoming.
A sacred circle, unto myself,
Ever expanding, ever exploring.

This is the gift I give to you,
This is the gift I give to all.
To experience, to be, to know,
To learn and to grow.
To become all that you can possibly be.

And when you come full circle,
And know how grand you are.
Then you will know the simple truth,
That I say unto you my child.
It is God you have become.

I was also doing past life regressions and journeys with other people and I found that I could not only take them back into their past lives or on a journey, but that I was also able to tune in to what was happening with them. Rita and I were also working with people in the group and sometimes after the class had finished, we'd work with one or more. Sometimes we'd take them on a past life journey and other times it was clearing attachments. Jen was also doing the past life regressions with one of her friends. There was a lot going on and a lot of experiences in a relatively short time. I also got the feeling that past lives are not linear and that we can be living three, four or more lives then or now, and in different ages and sex.

Chapter 3 - 1997 The Winds of Change

Vocabulary

1997 March 25 - Your words and your vocabulary is for you now to be considered as a toddler, very limited in expression and experiences. As you experience more you will also learn how to express it, but for you now to hear a scientist talk about nuclear physics would leave you confused. We try to explain it in simple terms but what that does is to distort the true picture and your perception, and since your words are based on your present experiences this also adds to the distortion. Open yourself to feel not only the words spoken but also the words not spoken. Patience, trust and allow the process to take place and intend to understand to the fullest as you progress as you are doing now. Ask. We are here to assist you. Blessings.

I find it interesting how people get to meet each other and how our experiences are interwoven. It was at our regular Visions meditation meetings that we had a few new faces join the group, one of these was Ron. During our customary sharing session he started talking about music, and that he had been to a Medicine Wheel Ceremony last Thursday. During his story he mentioned a woman named Liz. Later, I talked to him about his experience and told him that I remembered Jen telling me about a friend of hers, Liz, who also went to a Medicine Wheel Ceremony last Thursday, but that I didn't know where it was or if it was the same Liz. He asked me how I knew Liz? I replied that I didn't know her personally, just what I heard through her friend Jen. He remarked that he knew a Jen, or Jennifer as he called her, from the Spiritualist Church in Orillia. I told him that Jen had told me that she had gone there a while ago. He said that he was talking to her recently and asked me if I was the guy that lived in Moonstone that she had met on the phone? I smiled and said I was, and that I had not met her yet, but that we sure talked a lot on the phone. We just looked at each other and smiled. Coincidence?

1997 March 28 - I awoke to write the following message.

Awakening Others

You are to bring people to awareness and to heal. The first to awaken will be those that are the writers, to awaken by the word, to bring understanding and to trigger them to seek answers to the questions they have. The time is fast approaching and the light workers that are still asleep, slumbering, so to speak, will need a crash course, a how to manual to activate themselves to the final integration and to aid humans in the times ahead. It will be in the form of what you call a manual, using both written and electronic media to perform these tasks. As you are sensing, begin to collect that which you are guided to and what you EXPERIENCE, for this is the KEY to your work, so shall you be able to teach and aid others. It is wondrous to watch this unfoldment in you and in others as your journey begins. Blessings YHVH

♡ I was just thinking of the paragraph on how I met Ron, and the coincidence of that. And now as I'm writing my book, I'm just seeing the above message in a different light. It's one that I got years ago but never really paid attention or focused on it. Coincidence? hummmmm? ♥

This was becoming an intensive period, as all of us were getting messages on a variety of topics and issues. Subject material ranged from relationships, sex, and ego, to past lives and multi-dimensional journeys. I was also beginning to get insights for other people and I started to pick up on their energy and the energies around them. I was also picking up on their emotions and even the pain in their physical bodies. Although this was all new and exciting, it was also very confusing and it seemed that we were not only getting overloaded with information and ideas, but also with feelings and emotions. My world was beginning to change and I felt that there was no going back.

♡ Looking back at this material now seems rather simplistic and general in nature, but I don't think I could have experienced it or understood it if I had received it in a different form than what I did. ♥

1997 March 30 - I got a message about animals and what they can show and teach us. There was a lot more but I lost the first part getting my pen and paper, so it starts in progress.

Animals

How Mosquito wants you to hear and feel all of life.
How Fly is buzzing around all the time and then practicing patience by becoming still.
How Spider shows that artistry is also a way of making a living.
How Beetle can have a hard shell to deflect its enemies, but also knows when its enemies are too big, and it flies away.
On Snail, who teaches simplicity and takes his home with him and is all he needs.
On Earthworm, whose softness can pierce the hardest Earth with love and patience.
On Ant, who shows service and cooperation.
On Caterpillar, who shows that life, and the change and transformation that is possible when one shuns the external and turns inward, on self.

I asked, "What about birds?"

Chapter 3 - 1997 The Winds of Change

On Robin, who wears his heart on his chest and sings his song of love for all to hear. He has many things to teach. How to listen and be still when there is something you want to hear or that is important in your life. To learn just to listen and feel with your whole body, you have merely to become like the Robin, to stop, listen, feel, to hear as Robin hears.

You experience what it is like to become any animal, by opening yourself to the experience and with a little practice and patience you will discover what their message is as a totem. As you increase your awareness, then so you will also become aware of their spirit, their language, so to speak, and you will be able to communicate with them, and they and you will become one. The same applies to plants, earth, rocks, water, air and fire. With all you can communicate, and yes you can call upon their help in time of need just like you remember in the Tarzan books and movies, they will come to you when you call. This is part of the gifts of opening that you will receive for yourself. There are many more gifts that you will become aware of, and no you are not going to lose them. It is simply that you do not yet know how to experience their energies.

Blessings this day upon you for now you are aware of your connection to the Earth, to nature, and yes you will also see and talk to the gnomes, fairies and the elementals. They are continually around you but you are unaware. Try not to try, for they are somewhat shy and make themselves present and visible only when they feel safe and when they feel they won't be seen. Call to them softly, they are now aware of you and they will come.

1997 Apr. 6 - Today was when I met Jen in person. We had been talking on the phone since January, sometimes for hours on end, and today we were finally going to meet in person. She only lived twenty minutes away from me but until now, she had felt uncomfortable at our meeting in person. Before I left home, I drew a happy face on a six-inch circle of cardboard and then taped it to a drinking straw. As I knocked at her door, I held it up to my face as I thought it would help to break the ice. It did and we had a laugh about it as she invited me in. She was about five-foot-five, slim and very attractive with a beautiful smile, blue eyes, and long curly dark brunette hair that she just casually gathered up and tied loosely on the top of her head. She was very creative and did a lot of craft work that was incredible. During our four-hour visit we talked and shared in the same way we did when we talked on the phone and even did some past life journeys.

1997 April 11 - I don't know why I'm putting this in my book, but when I was driving back from the city of Orillia, I kept getting the message blind-sided, so I drove with extra caution. As I approached my home I noticed a woman off to the side of the road doing something under a tree. She spotted me turning into my driveway and followed me into the yard, asking me if I had a cat. I replied I have two cats, Merlin a Seal Point Siamese, and Misha a big fluffy black and white Maine Coon. She said that she had been on walk and had noticed Misha at the side of the road waiting for a car to pass. When the car passed her, she ran across the road toward the house but was hit by a van coming in the opposite direction. The woman said she was blind-sided, that she was dead, that she never suffered much, and that she had put her under the tree across the road. I thanked the woman and she continued on her walk, while I went and got Misha. I buried her beside the large rock in the stone fence where she used to spend a lot of time. The house felt empty without her giant gentleness.

♡ As I'm typing this I am being filled with emotions as I never really grieved for him. I've always referred to him as her, I don't know why. He was big and weighed around 25 pounds with huge paws. He had long white hair with black and tan markings. He was twice the size of Merlin, but Merlin was the dominant cat. I miss him; I guess that's why I had to write about Misha. ♥

The meditation classes we were having were not growing as expected although there were a couple of times when there were fifteen or more, it still wasn't enough to cover expenses for the room rental. Rita and I had been splitting the difference on the short fall since the beginning and we never once broke even. We even changed the format from a donation to five dollars for the three-hour evening, but that didn't work either as people just didn't show up. It seemed they didn't want to pay for something they felt should be free. Looking back on it now I can see how we were meeting our own reflection and beliefs here.

> *If you can't see it for yourself,*
> *you need someone to mirror it for you. - Shenreed*

1997 Apr. 17 - This evening only one person showed up for the Visions group and that was Doug. Rita and I decided that the three of us would do our usual meditation and messages. I was giving what I felt was the last message of the evening and as I was nearing the end of the message, I began making a series of toning sounds that the message said were for activating, healing and alignment. I toned these flute-like sounds for maybe thirty seconds but it was enough to bring laughter to Doug and especially Rita who couldn't contain herself. She said later that she had received the similar messages and sounds but that she didn't channel them, but that when I did, it blew her circuits, her solar plexus and heart. The laughter brought everyone out of the meditation and we laughed until our sides hurt and then we laughed some more. Rita just couldn't stop.

Chapter 3 - 1997 The Winds of Change

      I could still hear Rita laughing as I was pulling out of the parking lot and when I got home, which was a good half-hour later, I got a phone call from her. She was still laughing at anything and everything and we must have laughed for another hour on the phone. The next day she called me and said that she laughed and giggled in bed all night. In the morning she was still laughing and her cousin, who was staying at her home, asked her what was going on with all the laughing. When Rita played the channeling tape for her, she also got activated and then there were two women laughing hysterically in the same house. Every time Rita called me she would burst into laughter as even saying, "Hello" would crack her up. Her laughter was infectious. She carried on with this laughing fit, day and night, for a full week.

At this time I'd like to share a couple of the messages that we got that evening. This is how Rita transcribed them from tape to paper. The first one I channeled was on;

Awareness and Awakening

      Understand children that as you grow and apply that which you have learned in your living, the living will become easier for you. (Definite Voice change, deeper and higher at the same time) And the insights that you gained, the wisdom that you gained can be applied to every situation and every experience that you encounter, or that you wish to encounter. You have control, so to speak, for you have choices and in that wisdom you can choose to act out of love, and you can see how other people are acting, or reacting, either out of fear or love. In your wisdom and understanding you will know where they are coming from and you can either choose to assist them, if it is appropriate, and then you will be guided, higher self to higher self, for the highest purpose. If the answer is no, just let them talk, let them be, let them do what they are doing and simply choose to do something else and in that you have power. Learning gets easier afterwards but the experience has to be applied, and the more you apply it with LOVE the easier it gets. Apply it with fear or out of ego and you will experience difficulties, and you will be aware of how you are re-acting and then you may choose again, to change, but that is the experience. Walk the path and if you don't like it, choose again. Choose out of love and not fear but not to deny your fear either.

      (Definite Voice change again, deeper and higher at the same time) It is a wondrous journey when you have the understanding and the wisdom, and the commitment to apply yourselves. For by applying yourselves do you truly learn and evolve, for you become aware of others around you who are unaware, are like in a sleep or stupor, even though they are talking to you, you know in your being what they are saying does not apply to the truth. It applies to their truth, their ego, to their point-of-view, and so allow it, and if you can make them aware of a higher truth so be it, and if not, it is not their time to awaken, let it be.

This awareness you might consider as putting your heads above clouds so that you can see better. You realize sometimes a lonely feeling for there is no one that you can talk to, or few that you can talk to that understand what you understand, and know what you know. Soon, very soon, those that are in the stupor will be awakened, and they will be searching for a truth, the truth, something that has been withheld from them for what seems to them an eternity. When they awaken, that's when your true purpose will begin, and then you can use your wisdom and understanding and guide them steadfastly to their path, to their purpose. Continue as you are doing, in applying yourself, and apply love and light to every thought, word and deed and you will continue to grow and grow magnificently. Blessings onto you beloved, it is I, Jehovah that has been with you this evening, feel me in your hearts as I feel you in mine.

A few moments later Rita channeled her message. Message from the Pleiadians:

Greetings, we are Pleiadians, our energies are all here now. We are traveling back and forth to a different place in the same time. Many of the feelings that you are experiencing are due to the shift that is occurring at this time. Do not be alarmed, the discomforts are minor, go with the flow. Your disorientation and confusion is due to the fact that can best be described as that you are actually thinking at the time of the actual CHANGE OVER and at that time you have nothing to go on, or nothing to fall back on as it is being newly created. These are mere fractions in your days, be aware of these fractions, and recognize them for what they are. Don't panic; rest assured you are in the midst of it now. We wouldn't tell you it will get better and we wouldn't tell you it will get worse, all that we can tell you is that it will progress and remember that you will not get more than what you can handle. Whatever is happening to you now is happening to many. Soon you will notice an epidemic developing but it won't really be an epidemic. It is exactly what you are going through now but the masses will try to put a name to it, a type of disease that doesn't respond to current therapies and there are those that will seek any kind of cure. It won't last for more than two to three weeks for them like it has for yourselves. This is to call attention to the masses that there is a major shift happening within their bodies as well as within the Earth. Many will learn from this, many won't, that's irrelevant, the point is the ones that are learning are going to be seeking like minded individuals to talk to, and to have explained and walked through what is to come. We feel privileged to be part of this night, to be able to share in this coming age with you. Blessings.

Chapter 3 - 1997 The Winds of Change

During this period, I was having a lot of dreams, this is one of them. I saw a battleship that was sinking and sailors who were trying to make their way up and off the ship as it was going down. I saw myself trying to help them but I was just passing through them. I realized that they had died but that their astral body was still attached to the ship that went to the bottom of the ocean.

> *Experience as a child, observe as an adult. – Shenreed*

♥ I now realize the significance of that dream. That when someone experiences a traumatic death, that their astral energy might remain in that space and time, and that part of the healing we need to do now is to also bring back that lost essence. Another thing I'm feeling here is that when someone has a fear of water, sailing or storms, etc., without any present life experience, that they are actually getting in touch with the lost essence they have in a past life that needs to be retrieved and healed. ♥

Rita and I were also getting more information and confusion on Ego, as we both felt that the ego had a lot to do with what was going on, but we weren't sure how or why? Last night, I was reading some of the material that I had written on the work I was doing with Jen and I feel that her Ego was blocking her, stopping her from reaching out and trying to stop her from expressing herself. Later, when we were on the phone, I felt that her Ego, or something, was trying to even block our higher selves from getting together. I feel that when Ego doesn't want to pursue anything it doesn't like, it tries to find some way to avoid having to deal with the situation. I was also getting information in my dream state that I was to start verbalizing my feelings and to even express them physically. I remember that my Ego voice was saying a big NO to that. The message I then got was to get Ego to assist in this process of expression.

Rita was now in a computer programming class and was having revelations as to how the computer, with its hard drive memory and programs are a lot like us. She was especially getting insights into the programming sequences and the retrieval and storage of memory.

I'd like to share another interesting technique that I found useful with Rita in doing some types of regression work. I would ask her to get herself into an altered meditative state and then I'd have her visualize a computer screen. When I asked her what the issue was that she was feeling, she would see the words on the screen and then we would follow them back to the source. In some ways it was like surfing the net. It also worked in other areas where information was to be retrieved or fears identified. We were also trying to do work with Ego using this technique. This work was mostly a mental process; that is to say it would identify what the issues and emotions were, but we still weren't really feeling the emotions at this time, except feeling that we didn't want to feel them. When we were working with Higher Self, guides, journeys, and the Inner Child, we still had to use the blue mist technique. Rita was also going through a dilemma and issues at this time that she felt she couldn't talk to me about and neither did she feel comfortable talking to Jen as she never really got to know her. She felt she had to and could do it on her own, and I felt she was beginning to distance herself from me.

Normally I had no problem sleeping at night as my head would hit the pillow and I'd take two or three deep breaths, yawn once or twice and I'd be off, but with all this work going on, my sleep patterns were changing. The following is typical of how some of my evenings went and sometimes I was lucky to get two or three hours of sleep. Thank goodness I was in a position where I could get catnaps in the late morning or afternoon. During these sleepless nights I would write my basic thoughts or feelings, and then maybe move into writing a channeled message and then back again. This was one such evening.

11:30 pm, I'm tired and yawning and I've been trying to go to sleep for what seems like ages but all I keep thinking of is the events of the day and past week. Finally I said to myself, might as well right it down and so here I go, I feel there's a message coming.

Need to Know

By the month of May, you will have triggered each other to the maximum and it will be part and parcel of your development, not development only, but purpose, not the end but the beginning. It will be the beginning of this relationship in a new format.

I lay back from writing, thinking about what does all this mean? Sometime later I received another message.

All is appropriate; we will not spoil this experience for you by communicating to you more than you need to know for the present time.

I rolled over and slipped the journal under my pillow and pondered what is appropriate. After a while I got the following message.

NEED TO KNOW; that is the KEY to communicating with others in the future. Those who don't know, don't need to know. Those that know, need to know, need to be assisted in working to their potential. It's also part and parcel of the Divine plan, all is appropriate.

Chapter 3 - 1997 The Winds of Change

I lay back again thinking, they're using those words again. Of course words are a KEY to communicating! If you don't use the right words in the right context, connotation and circumstance, then the meaning and intent of the communication is lost. I then got the message.

🕊 It is very important to be simple and specific at the same time so that all will receive part and parcel of what is appropriate for their growth and development at the time you are communicating to one or many, to part and parcel. All will receive what is appropriate by what you choose as your words, tone, pause, loudness, vibration and intent of your voice and the physical being as well as the clothes and colours you wear, for these also communicate.

Again, I turned out the light and lay back, this time I heard a song in my head. It was an Irish folk song from a tape I've been listening to recently. The words that came to mind were "No nay never no more... will I play the wild Rover... no never no more." I'll have to listen to that song tomorrow as there's a message in it. After that song, more thoughts and questions were going endlessly around in my mind. Then I got the following message.

🕊 It's part and parcel, (hee hee, I'm laughing, here we go again) of what changes are going on in your lives. For you don't have to say the obvious to communicate the obvious, there can be other subtle ways to get your message out however it is sent, so long as it is received. That is what is appropriate.

I lay there wondering how long this is going to be going on as I'm getting tired and this has been a long night as it's now 4:34 am

1997 Apr. 27 - Today I received a phone call from Liz, one of Jens friends. As time went on she too would become a part of my journey.

1997 May 7 - I received the following definitions.
- Knowing: that which comes from within, when one is connected to all that is.
- Doing: following that which creates excitement and applying that which you have knowing and understanding and now desire to experience.
- Being: being in the moment, completely consumed in doing to the point that there is no past or future, only the present moment you are in.

Journey to the Heart Centre

Shalom

1997 May 07 - (Shaaa ----loooo ----mmmm) means, peace, love and light. Chanting the word shalom can be used to release denial blockages gently but assuredly, pulling, jostling, vibrating out the denial blocks to the emotional issues, patterns and programs out of the lodged areas held by denial. Use different tones, vibrations, and lengths of tones and pitch with each person as guided.

1997 May 8 - I got the message to make a list of words and phrases that I have judgments on in the present moment. The following is a partial list that I made.

Acceptance, need, power, selfishness, deceit, untruthful, cheater, being on time, keeping a commitment, say what you mean, mean what you say, being dependable, being annoying on purpose, trying to get you annoyed, trying to find, being attacked, poor winner, poor loser, cleanness, lack of cleanliness, poverty, physical abuse, anger, hatred, hostility, conspiracy, betrayal, not being valued, one who values nothing, no honor, no morals, no scruples, playing games, manipulator, wouldn't try, can't do it, a guitter, not being consistent, righteous, unfaithfulness, infidelity, too much discipline, not enough discipline, lack of manners, too much emphasis on manners, criticism, being controlled, indecisions, impatience, trust-self, trust others, stubborn, lazy, judgmental, bigot, nosy, prying, pushy, over analytical, always complaining, not good enough, having to be perfect, phoniness, petty, cheap-scape, bully, conceited, arrogant, wasteful, neglectful, show off, rejection, prejudice, swearing all the time, persecution, over reacting, unkind, unfeeling, responsibility without power, lack of responsibility, denial, religion, disrespect, possessiveness.

Wow! I guess, no, I know, I have a lot of issues and judgments and I feel that that list is just the start. After I made my list, I realized that the root cause of all my judgments and issues are TRUST and POWER. Trusting self and others, of power, of being in control or having no control. I felt I needed to make some kind of formal release and I came up with the following.

    I release all my attachments to the root cause of trust of self and of others, and of giving away my power or of my taking another's power, in this present life and all past life experiences pertaining to the Earth plane and in other dimensions that are affecting me in the here and now, that no longer serve my highest purpose or good. I ask that any shadows of these attachments be identified by ego and higher self so that they may be recognized and dealt with in the appropriate way. So be it.

Chapter 3 - 1997 The Winds of Change

1997 May 9 - I just realized that I never released my attachment to this property, its contents and the business. I thought to myself, no wonder I haven't heard anything and nothing was moving as I wasn't prepared to make the move. I had put feelers out but I hadn't made a firm decision. I called another local Realtor to set up an appointment as the one I originally spoke to last fall said she wouldn't recommend listing until the spring and that she would get in touch with me then. Well summer is just around the corner and I haven't heard from her so I guess she's not really interested.

Later that day I took Jen on a journey where she saw herself going down a long hallway with pictures of moments of her present life caught in time on the walls. She called this hallway her emotional gallery, as it was an accumulation of other people's emotions that she took on when she tried to help, comfort and diffuse another person's emotional pain. This was not only in this lifetime, but also included past life experiences. During this journey she allowed herself to recognize the feelings and emotions, but she was detached from them and didn't express any. Later that evening I got the following message on word judgments.

> *Love is connection, not attachment.*
> *Love is acceptance, not denial.*
> *Love is compassion, not judgment. - Shenreed*

Word Judgments

Congratulations. You have done well and are now well on your way to releasing these patterns and programs of judgments and power aspects. These as you know, are not all from this lifetime, in fact much of the aspects of the charge that you carry are from what you call past lives. Now you must ponder how to effectively release these word judgments and denials from your experience. Smile, we know you will do it.

1997 May 10 - I was talking to Jen on the phone and the following phrases and insights came to us. That you have to feel it before you can find it, and that by being only mental is being in denial because you are forcing it to accept the mental state of preference. We also need to begin to see things as different, and to allow and accept the difference instead of trying to make everything the same by either trying to fit yourself into your idea of a box, or by having another trying to force you into their idea of a box. Neither is comfortable and each individual must find what is comfortable for them.

Another thing we got was that being overweight, underweight, physically strong or fit, physically weak, laughter and jokes, bullishness, speaking loudly, speaking softly, wearing makeup, perfume, looking attractive or being purposefully unattractive, smoking, drinking, drugs, etc. are all forms of protection. They are beliefs that we have put in place in order to do what we think is survive. Another insight was that denial and beliefs had to be felt for what they really are in order for them to be released. Jen also got the message, "When you allow yourself all things internally, is what comes to you externally, there are grace periods. Hear me on this."

Jen and I also used to play a little game that she made up, which was that the next song on the radio would either have a message for us concerning the issues we were going through or to open a new topic for discussion. The following is one that I happened to write down but I don't remember what the issue was at the time. The song was, "See the People" by Soul Attorney, and the words that came to our attention were, "See the people run, consequences of actions left undone. I've opened my mind to believing, from the source I am receiving." Interesting!

> *The more you allow, the more you feel.*
> *Block your feelings, block you knowing.*
> *What you know is what you feel. - Shenreed*

Chapter 4 - Emotions Begin to Surface

1997 May 11 - I went to Jens and while there I was activated into remembering an experience I had as a child. I think I was around twelve when I discovered that I could make a more powerful bow (bow and arrow) with a willow branch and a strip of rubber from a bicycle inner tire tube, instead of a string. I also wrapped a strip of rubber around the tip of the arrow shaft so that it would fly straighter without the need for tail feathers, and also, not to really hurt anyone if it hit them when we were playing cowboys and Indians.

One day I made a couple of special arrows where I wrapped the rubber band about four inches from the tip, which I then sharpened to a point. I decided that I was going to go into the field and be the mighty hunter but I had no idea what I was hunting. As I stealthily made my way through the field, I heard a noise coming from one of the few trees on the prairie. I cautiously approached the tree and saw a Flicker about to leave a hole in the trunk of the tree that was its nest. I instinctively lifted my bow; arrow already in place, pulled back the rubber band and let the arrow fly. With a sickening "thud" it impaled the Flicker on the tree. I was in disbelief and dumbfounded that I even hit it, and in fear of what I had done. It was impaled high in the tree and I couldn't climb up to reach it, as there was nothing to grip on to and nothing around to use as a step. I watched the Flicker flap her wings a few times and then felt her life essence drift away as she became motionless. An eerie calmness fell around me and it was then that I heard the chirp of the little chicks in the nest. I felt heartbroken and ashamed of what I had done. I broke my bow and arrows and vowed never to kill another living thing. I left the field with my shame, guilt, and a secret. I never went back to that field. It was soon after that experience that we moved to the city.

When I was sharing my story with Jen, I became wrought with emotions and was beginning to have an emotional release, as tears were flowing from my eyes. I looked at Jen but she showed no emotion, instead she moved to try to comfort me. That action brought me right out of my feelings and of allowing myself to express any more emotions.

Later when I was at home, I tried to feel and get a sense of what happened and why. The message I got was that Jen was trying to take control and responsibility for my feelings of sadness, and that she denied expressing the emotions that it brought up for her, and also, that in trying to comfort me, she denied me my experience. I then felt that if she had expressed her emotions that she was triggered into, that both she and I would have had a greater release and healing.

Journey to the Heart Centre

Rita and I had been discussing canceling the Vision Group meetings, either entirely, or at least for the summer, as attendance was down and we were also not happy with having to be out of pocket all the time. After a brief telephone discussion we decided to cancel the classes. Rita and I spend no physical time together except for the classes, and with more emphasis on her daily computer class and tending to her husband and three children, we were also spending less time on the phone. She was also going through some personal issues at this time but she didn't want to talk about it. With Rita busy or unavailable, I began to spend more time with Jen.

Without going into details that are personal in nature and Jens story, I feel I need to share a little bit so that you can follow some of the things that transpire in our relationship that affected my journey. Jen has had a few traumatic experiences in her life which have left her with what the medical profession calls Chronic Fatigue, Environmental Sensitivities and other unexplainable conditions, which have made her basically a "shut in" for the past few years. In talking and working with Jen the past few months, I began to "pick up" on not just her emotions, but also her body's feelings. I began to tap into her aches and pains in her muscles, joints and bones, and even feeling how exhausted she was. I wasn't just tapping in to it; I was also experiencing and feeling it. There were times when I was visiting Jen, or even times when we were on the phone, when I would just lay there unable to even move my hands or head, and even breathing was an effort. I got the message that feeling these emotions and pain was also for my benefit, experience and understanding, of taking on part of her experience as my own.

Jen and I were also getting into moving more of our emotions. For me, the hard part was opening up and sharing more of what I was really feeling. For Jen it was that too, but also of getting herself back out into the world and expressing what she was feeling in trying to do that. We were also beginning to work with our ego and inner child and not even knowing really what they were or how to work with them. I was now reading "Original Cause "The Unseen Role of Denial," the second book in the "Right use of Will" series by Ceanne DeRohan. I was sharing parts of what I was reading with Jen who was now reading book one, which I lent her, which was activating her. We were trying to feel and understand what these books were saying and we were getting into some heated discussions and activations. These were trying and confusing times to say the least. Trying to apply these new concepts to our lives, which felt so right, but at the same time, felt so foreign and confusing. We often felt that we had to literally feel and grope our way through this material, our activations and our present experiences. Sometimes I could read twenty pages in one sitting and other times I couldn't get past one paragraph, even after reading it a dozen times. I also found myself just opening the books at random and usually I would find something, a clue, or confirmation to the issues we were going through.

Chapter 4 – Emotions Begin to Surface

I started visiting Jen more often and I was helping her with grocery shopping, laundry and errands. On days when she couldn't get out to do it for herself, I would do it for her. We were starting to get into everything and anything and we were really getting into some of the dark places that we never wanted to see again, let alone let anyone know about them. Sometimes we were expressing our real feelings and emotions and other times we were merely explaining them. Still other times we were expressing false emotions and denied rage, in denial of our real ones. We were still holding back and pretending we weren't, or not even knowing we were. Jen could not really be Jen, nor could I really be me, as we both had fear of what that would mean to our relationship, but we denied that too, or we confronted it with part-truths based in denial.

We had even talked about healing the sexual issues we had. She seemed more open in explaining what had gone on in her life; not that she was directly involved with a lot of sexual stuff that went on around her, but she was a willing witness as she continued to be exposed to it. I finally got up the courage to share that I was attracted to her and that there were some things that she did or said, that sexually aroused me and that I had been in denial by not saying so sooner. I also told her that I was alive, and that I was a living, breathing, human male and that I had desires, urges and fantasies, which I felt were inappropriate to express until now. At the same time I also felt that I just wasn't in this relationship as an emotionally detached shrink either. She said she never thought of me in a sexual way although she recognized me as a sexual being, and that it was okay to have and share these feelings, just as long as I didn't act on them.

Although I agreed with her, I felt that something was wrong with that comment. I'm now thinking of why I'm attracted to her? There are many things that we have in common, the main one being our intent for spiritual growth and in healing ourselves. I feel that she's a friend and a teacher but then there's the physical attraction that is also part of it. I want it all in one package; I want the friend, lover, sorceress, the queen, and everything in between.

Hummm I'm now thinking; is this impossible? Am I looking for perfection or am I just tired of having only experienced nothing or a small portion, and having to be satisfied that that is my lot in life? I'm tired of being on the outside looking in. I also have guilt and shame as I'm old enough to be her father, not that the age difference is something new for me as Michelle was nineteen years younger than I was, but enough digression, back to the journey. There, I'm doing it again, pulling myself off topic, but now I'm also recognizing it as such and in that there's growth.

I'd be in denial if I didn't mention this, but I have never had any real male friends in my life. I shared a friend in high school who also hung out with other guys, but I'd be excluded. I had acquaintances and good time friends that were there when my car was available. To be honest, I also never had a girl friend until I was out of school, and I never had any friends that were girls either. There were girls that I liked but they didn't like me, or I felt that they didn't like me. When I've been in social situations, I've always found it easier to talk to most women than men. Even when I was married, we always had friends that were a couple and they usually had children. We would get together at each other's homes but it was always as couples or families. My ex-wife had girl friends and would go out shopping or do whatever with the other wives, but I'd stay at home and either look after the kids or work. This is one area of many in my life that I still need to heal, another issue that comes to mind is sex.

1997 June 5 - I drove up to another sweat lodge at the same place where I experienced my first. This evening, Claudio was leading the sweat and there were twelve men there in total. It was interesting for me to be in this all male energy and the feelings I was picking up from each as they shared or didn't share. Of the twelve, I felt that only two were expressing from their heart and they made contact with me during and after our feast. This sweat was a completely different experience compared to the first although many of the same faces were there.

1997 June 6 - I called the local Realtor that I was going to use to sell my property. This was the third time I called him, and I bluntly told him (via his answering machine) to forget about coming out to list my property because if he couldn't return my phone calls, then he's not the one to sell my property. I called Carole, a Realtor in Barrie who had sold the house when my ex-wife and I divorced. She was up the following Monday to list the property.

  I've been busy getting my business things in order so that I could have all the pertinent information handy for any potential buyer. I had talked to my lawyer and he suggested that I handle the sale myself otherwise, if he got involved, it would require a independent financial audit, including assets and inventory, etc., and that would mean a lot of money. I decided to take his advice and drew up a purchase/sale agreement based on the previous sale of my first business and the purchase of this one. I then had him check it out and he said that he couldn't have done any better himself. I went over all the financial records and updated all the sales and inventory data. I did a list of customers, including sales, discounts, payment habits, etc., as well as details on potential customers. I did a complete physical inventory of raw materials and made up control sheets for each product so that I could keep a running total of any changes. I did the same for all finished products. I took stock of all fixed assets and recorded their book and face value, supplier, etc. One of the biggest jobs I had to do was to compile a complete how-to manual, giving detailed instructions on how to use the various machines and how to

Chapter 4 – Emotions Begin to Surface

manufacture all the different products, including formulas, etc., and also identifying any problems that might occur and what to do it they did.

The Truth Shall Set You Free

1997 June 10 - Think, say and do your truth and the truth shall set you free. Yes my son, it is not the external truth that you seek, but the internal one, your truth. Your truth to yourself that will free you from your limitations you have placed upon yourself. Once you understand this you will be on your way. You now know, and in your knowing will come all knowing. It is a simple truth and it is hidden within you, it always was, you just never knew it or felt it. Now it is time to also live and be it. It is the freedom you seek; it is the freedom you desire. It is the love you seek; it is the love you desire. It is the joy you seek; it is the joy you desire. It is the God you are; it is the God you desire. Blessings unto you my child and indeed share this with the one you call Jen/Love Child, for both of you are now ready to know the truth. Blessings and Love, and be gentle with yourselves today. YHVH

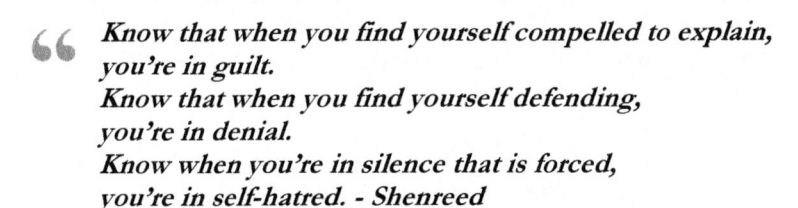

> *Know that when you find yourself compelled to explain, you're in guilt.*
> *Know that when you find yourself defending, you're in denial.*
> *Know when you're in silence that is forced, you're in self-hatred. - Shenreed*

1997 June 12 - It was a Thursday, business was slow so I decided to drive up to Jens place around noon. Jen was sitting in her armchair and I sat in my usual place on the futon. After chatting for an hour or so, I pulled up the footstool and sat down in front of her, which is the position I would usually take up if I felt that I was going to be doing some emotional work with her. I had found that by touching her feet in a certain way or by putting pressure on certain points of her knee, that I could trigger an emotional response and I could also tap into her emotions and assist her where she was blocking in expressing them. I no sooner put my hand on her foot and she became activated into an emotional release.

I don't remember what was really going on after her emotional release, other than I began to verbally channel a message for her from God. I remember afterwards that both of us were awed and moved by the message. After a brief chat, I got up to go to the bathroom. When I returned, I sat down on the footstool and we spoke about the message. I suggested that we continue with the journey as I felt there was more to the message and she agreed. It had only been a few minutes since I had channeled God and now, as I started to channel again, I was aware of a different feeling to the energy, but I denied and thought that maybe it was just me, or maybe it was me taking the break that is making it feel different. I was conscious of the words that I was saying and it sounded like it was God talking, but I also felt that something was off, as the words felt like they were more mental and calculating. Jen got defensive by the words that I was saying and she opened her eyes and asked me to channel God again. I remember saying that I was God and asking why she did not trust me. It was like I was using guilt and shame to try to discredit her feelings, her intuition, that said something was wrong. I remember being confused and then snapping myself out of my conscious trance-like state.

We talked about the experience and she said that when she trusted her inner voice and opened her eyes, she realized that the voice she was hearing wasn't from God, even though it was my voice and that I had just channeled God a few minutes earlier. When I channeled God, both of us had felt it was love, but this time she knew I was channeling Lucifer and even when I (he) said I was God, she didn't believe me (him). She said that even though I seemed to say all the right words it didn't "feel" right. She said that when I spoke of "not feeding fear with fear and sending it love instead," she knew that the words sounded great but that in actuality, it was denial of your fear and therefore not love or words from God. I was utterly shaken, and as we talked about it I was wondering how could this happen. I felt I couldn't trust myself to channel anymore.

As I was driving home, I was pissed off and kicking myself for letting it happen. I knew something was off but I denied my feelings in favor of my mind that said that because I had just finished channeling God, that I was doing it again, and to ignore what my intuition was telling me. After that experience, I didn't want to channel as I was afraid, afraid of channeling Lucifer again. Afraid that I was evil and afraid that I would say or harm another, but at the same time, a part of me knew it was a lesson that I needed to experience.

1997 June 16 - I was talking to Rita on the phone, telling her of my recent experiences with Lucifer. She said that things had been moving for her too and she began telling me about the funeral she had gone to on the weekend. She told me how she had gone up and had given a speech, and that after the funeral, how everyone told her how great her words were and how nice and loving she was to say them. She said she knew she was channeling as she could feel her crown chakra opening, but that now that she thought about it, there was also something different about the energy. My intuition told me that she also channeled Lucifer, and when I said it, she realized it too, and that made both of us wonder what was going on.

Rita, Jen, and I were all going through various emotions and trying to do we didn't know what, as we stumbled around in the dark, groping for something that we could recognize to help us be normal, to feel sane. We

Chapter 4 – Emotions Begin to Surface

could be feeling all this love and understanding for ourselves in one moment only to have it turn completely around in a matter of seconds to anger, disgust, and what's the use. This was particularly true for my relationship with Jen. These were trying times in the beginning, and all the books we had read didn't mention any of the issues we were going through. Even our own guides and the channeled messages were vague, and sometimes I felt even misleading, but it was what we needed to experience.

Past life issues involving Michelle, me and Doug, (who was part of the Barrie Visions group) were also coming up again. Ever since Doug had met Michelle, he felt he knew her as Queen Elizabeth I, and that I was Robert Dudley, and he was her state/religious advisor, whose name I didn't write down and I can't remember at this time. Being a history buff, he was digging up all kinds of historical facts on the Internet and faxing them to me. We had all done past life regressions and it was interesting to see what was recorded in the history books and what had actually gone on from three different past life perspectives that collaborated each other, but differed from the historical version.

♡ The following text marks the first time that I wrote what I was thinking and feeling in a more flowing, in the moment manner, rather than an explanation of what happened in point form. This journal entry was over a four hour period where I would be activated into my thoughts, feelings and emotions, and I would write them down as I was feeling them. I feel that it's an important part of my journey that needs to be shared, as it is a major shift away from what I normally did. The person I'm talking about is Jen. ♥

1997 June 23, 1:10 am - I feel there is something that needs to be expressed in our relationship and that has to do with the physical, physical contact. We both know that reaching out in total honesty and being totally open and vulnerable will allow us to heal the necessary experiences, but that's also the hardest and most difficult to do as it also means that it has to involve the physical aspects. We seem to be honest about everything else except the physical. I don't know if it's physical contact, sexual, or just the allowance and willingness to be open to experience whatever issues come up as unconditional love is sought. But to be able to do that, it also needs to be experienced, felt and expressed in the moment without limits.

Now I haven't been in a relationship or even on a date since Michelle moved out last fall. Not to say that I haven't been open to a relationship with a woman, but I also know that I'm not going to go back and date someone who isn't also working to heal herself on all levels, so while I'm open, I'm also limited. Now at first when I dialed the wrong number, I thought okay, just another woman and a wrong number, but it was no coincidence. Well things have gotten complicated as when we got together there was a connection, and a bearing of deep dark secrets, of truth, of openness and of a vulnerability where our souls and hearts were exposed and that's where the problem is. We try to experience this thing called unconditional love; we are open to talk about it but as soon as we try to bring it into the physical where there still are issues, that's when conditions, fear, rejection, denial, guilt and shame all get placed on it. So how do you open yourself to another without getting caught in the same old traps? How can one say that their love is unconditional if the physical contact and sexual issues are denied?

My intent, my original intent was not just to have or seek a sexual relationship, but also that of a friend and a partner. I know more about you, and you know more about me, the real me, than all my relationships put together. All the things that we've discussed, been open and truthful with, and how we've worked together, the emotions we've felt, and we've never even so much as held hands. We've hugged good bye on occasion but that's been the extent of our physical contact except when I'm doing work on your feet, knees, or maybe your hands when you are going through some emotional release. I find that incredible. I'm in awe but also heartbroken. I feel like I'm on the outside looking in, I can see, hear, smell, and almost taste it, but I can never touch it. I can talk about it but I can't express what I feel physically. Then again, maybe I'm not ready for any relationship that includes anything physical. Maybe that would throw me off my path as I'd get caught and end up with the physical side of the relationship and the responsibility issues like I did with Michelle, I don't know.

I feel in my heart that there's a special magic in a our relationship when for the first time, maybe unconditional love is real and can be expressed, shared and experienced by two souls, two pieces of God manifest in the physical. That's what I want to experience, that's the kind of relationship I'm seeking, and I feel that that potential could be between us, but I don't know. How do you experience something that you don't really know exists and that you only hope is true? How can you express it if you can't experience it? How can you experience anything unconditionally if you still have old programming full of conditions? I don't know what's in store for this relationship. I don't know if we ever can experience unconditional love in the true sense. I do know and feel that if I don't express that I'm interested in pursuing this experience to the fullest, that I would be missing the opportunity of a life time, not only of a life time but of all time.

If she doesn't feel the same way, isn't open to express her real issues and fears, then I'll really have to do some more reflection on what it was that we were experiencing. Was this so-called unconditional love, this openness, this truth, all part of a game so that I can put myself out there, turn myself inside out only to find it was still conditional. That isn't what I'm looking for. So what do I really know? What do I really feel? So now you know why I feel rejected, angry, disillusioned and in fear of slipping back to the same old,

Chapter 4 – Emotions Begin to Surface

same old. I feel and sense that this isn't and can't be anything new or different because I'm not accepted and can't be accepted as I am. I've also put all these conditions on myself and therefore on the relationship and the experience of unconditional love. I feel I'm in a box, but I also feel that by speaking my truth, my real truth, is what will set me free. I know this will clear the air and will allow movement and acceptance, but of what, I don't know. Where this relationship is going to go? I don't know, but it will change.

It's now 2:34 am and I don't know where I'm going or what I'm going to be doing when I sell the house and business. I can't and wouldn't make any promises to anyone because that would be conditional and that's not what I want to be. So you see things are changing, are always changing, always growing and that's what I've always known that I've wanted to do, was to grow. Now it's time to grow again, out of the darkness and into the light and to transform fear into an ally, a friend, so that I can experience life to the fullest.

It's now 3:58 am, I'm not finished yet, now I also have judgments and a whole bunch of other stuff coming up about you. If it were someone else, a younger guy who had called you on the phone and had gone through the same stuff with you that I had, what would you have done differently and if so why? Honestly? What are you looking for now and what's your idea of unconditional love and acceptance? Yes, I judge myself as being older than you are and I judge you judging me that I'm older than you. I also judge myself that I'm not good enough and then I go back into all this conditional shit again and I think and feel that it's all part of the same old game. How the fuck does one get off this insane merry-go-round? Sometimes I feel the only way is to say fuck to the rest of the world. Fuck to all women. Fuck to all men, the assholes, and even the children who are going to grow up and be just like all of them. I feel that the only way I can find peace is to be a hermit and drop out of society and all the bullshit, and just say FUCK IT. Just get out with nature and live in the wild with as little contact with people as I can, to withdraw into myself to be with myself.

But then I feel that's a crock of shit too because I'm denying, I'm running away. I'm not practicing what I teach my fellow man, and no matter how fucked up they are, and not everyone is so royally fucked up that there isn't a spark of love within them, and then maybe not, and that hurts. You want to experience the company of others and you remember the good times, those times that were pure and true, even if just for a moment, and so you long to experience that feeling again. So you say to yourself, Why? Why can't I have that, be that, feel that all the time or at least try to be there to experience love in this beautiful unconditional expression? I know I still have stuff to get rid of and issues to heal and so would the woman I'll meet. So does that mean I can't allow myself to be in any relationship until such a time that I feel that I'm healed and perfect, and that she is too, because there goes all that conditional shit again? The only way to know what still has to be healed within is that if you can't see it for yourself, then you need to be in a relationship and have another person trigger and reflect your issues to you. I feel that this is a hopeless situation.

I feel, no, I know that I cannot go back and that I must allow myself to remain open and vulnerable. To place no conditions or expectations except that I will not return to darkness and that I will not shut myself off consciously or deny how I feel. There is this longing I feel in the depth of my soul that is reaching out to be loved and to love in return. I know that this love is possible for I feel it flow within the depths of my Being, and I also yearn to express and experience this love in the physical as long as I choose to remain here. I remove any expectations and attachments to and from you. Know that you have touched that spark within me, have seen my light as I have seen yours. And so the moment moves on. I don't know where, what, when, or who, but I do know why, and then maybe I don't.

4:38 am, I don't know if this is all there is but it is all that I feel in this moment and that's all that I can do and be, is to be as honest and truthful and as loving to myself as I can be, even my judgments. I feel I can't be any other way because that would deny my heart, my Will, my very soul and I don't want to deny being who I am any longer. I will not run or hide, I will be my light and express my truth as long as I am on this Earth. I will live my truth to the best of my ability and I will not shut myself off by denying either the experience or my expression, that experience being that of unconditional love, joy and acceptance with a feminine partner where we both continue to grow. To spiritualize our individual physical bodies, and with that will also come the opportunity to join in what I feel will be the ultimate experience of this Earth plane, and that is the bonding with another in the physical, expressing what they truly are.

4:51 am, We all need someone to talk to, someone who understands and doesn't think we're crazy and that there is hope. It's not just about talking about how you feel; it's also about living how you feel. As you experience, as you grow, so you seek to express and experience that which is new. For without experience, you deny your Heart and Will and it's back to the same old. Even denying by saying that you want to express or feel it, but that it's not really necessary puts you back to the same old, and it's in relationships where real growth occurs or is experienced. Sure, everyone can be a hermit but what kind of world would that be. Nobody talking to anyone or being with another, it would be the end if there were no more children and we all died alone. So, we have to find it, to feel it within ourselves first, but then the next step is to find it and share it with another and all that is, and now it's 5:05 am.

Chapter 4 – Emotions Begin to Surface

Later that morning I telephoned Jen and read the above to her. I can't remember what she said, but it was something to the effect that it does clear the air a bit.

Fountain of Youth

1997 June 25, 4:15 am - Come experience the true fountain of youth. What makes you think you're not worthy, age, a healthy physical body? Are you not healthy and in the prime youthful condition and appearance? It is your beliefs that cause disease, your fears and your denials that cause death, the aging of the body. For it is not time, for time is an illusion for the rational mind so as to comprehend its experiences in a limited way, of polarity and which is in your belief systems. In truth, you have and are the fountain of youth. Once you know it, you will feel it and be it. Your perceptions are based on your belief systems and as you expand and re-define your beliefs, your perceptions will also alter. You are still extremely limited and linear but this will change soon. Rest now, more will be given soon. Blessings.

It was around this time that Caroline came into my life. I had met her at the same time I met Rita at the local meditation/channeling group. We had talked on the phone a few times and had also shared channeled messages and insights. She was living in Niagara Falls and was now moving up into the area, as it was where she had been raised as a child. After she moved up with her two children, I helped her get settled in and we began to spend some time together. I felt there was a connection with Caroline too, but in a different way or level than I felt with Rita or Jen. She had a beautiful singing voice and played and taught piano. Besides music, she was also an artist and painted some of her visions and journeys. She was a Reiki master and into eating and growing (if possible) organic foods and making herbal medicines. She loved nature and was not afraid to get her hands dirty. I'm smiling as I remember walking about the farm she was renting as she showed me the different edible plants that she didn't want me to damage as I cut the grass. Later that afternoon she invited me to stay for supper and I accepted. I knew she was a vegetarian but I was shocked to see the plants I was asked not to cut in the yard, on my plate. It was a different experience, and on overcoming my reluctance to eat what I called weeds, I was pleasantly surprised in that they actually tasted good.

1997 June 27 - After having left numerous telephone messages, the last being to wish her a happy birthday, Rita called me to say that she had been in a gap for weeks and that she had put all her books and stuff away. She said she felt it wasn't what she needed to do at this time and that she needed to get on with her life. I felt she was trying to distance herself from everything she had experienced and from the feelings and emotions that were coming up for her, and because I was a part of that experience, she was also distancing herself from me. I could feel her pushing me away but what could I do. I felt sad and heartbroken but it was her choice and there was nothing I could say or do that would keep her from leaving and doing what she felt she needed to do.

1997 July 11 - My Realtor, Carol called to say that she had had a showing for the property tomorrow but that it was re-scheduled for two weeks. That news picked me up and at the same time depressed me, as I didn't want to just sell the property and then have to move the business and rent an apartment back in Barrie again.

> *Acid looks like water, but tries to destroy everything it touches. - Shenreed*

It was during this time that Jen and I were getting involved in doing Celtic journeys. Most of our work was done with the four archetypes, those being Queen/King, Sorceress/Magician, Warrior and Lover. It was bringing up a lot of issues and we were beginning to see just how damaged, fragmented and afraid we really were.

1997 July 20 - There was a message on my answering machine from a man in Vancouver that was interested in both the property and the business. He had heard that I was selling both and as he had grown up in the area, he was now looking to move back and start a business. Now I got excited, this is what I wanted, to sell both at the same time. I called him back and gave him some details. He said he was going to be flying out in a couple of weeks and that he'd be stopping in to see the business and the property.

1997 July 22 - Rita had called a week ago and mentioned that she had gotten a message at 3 am, saying that there was going to be a healing ray, a holy alliance of healing love coming to Earth. I was casually watching the 5 o'clock news on CKVR, the local TV station, when they announced that numerous people had called in reporting sighting a mysterious blue green ray coming from the sky just west of the city of Barrie. I tuned in again for the 11 o'clock news but there were no further reports. The next day I called the TV station to inquire about the blue ray that was on yesterday's news and no one I talked to said they knew anything about it and even denied that it had been on the news.

Speak Your Truth

1997 July 25 - Speaking your truth, your feelings are what you need to consciously be aware of. You value other people's feelings over your own and this is an imprint and that inflicts low self-esteem and self-worth.

Chapter 4 – Emotions Begin to Surface

You feel other people's feelings are correct and you don't trust your own. Follow your guidance, your intuition, and do not allow yourself to be influenced by the pre-judgments that you have, or anyone else has made. Simply allow yourself to feel and then to express it, no matter what the feelings be, be they considered loving or what you consider not loving. Express, feel the expression and what it is that you are indeed releasing, what you consider positive or negative. Once the feelings are expressed you can then analyze them for what they truly are and not what you metalized or internalized them to be, which may be quite different from the external. Internalization permeates doubt, second-guessing, and fear. Externalization in whatever form transforms these fears and creates a healthy vibrant awareness and transformation. The more confident you become in your feelings, the more will be expressed.

Your guidance and channeling is also affected in a similar manner. Go with the flow. Sometimes it is merely a shift in energy and sometimes you need to verbalize what you are getting to bring it sound, to program the subconscious on a higher level, and then there are times when you will write, or speak for, or to others. Go with the flow and feel the energy. You will know, if not immediately at first, for you are still skeptical, but as you progress there will be no mistakes. Trust and honor yourself child. Blessings, Love, Light and Laughter. Thannius

1997 July 30 - I received the following message after doing some Shamanic work with Jen.

Father is the breath of life, AIR
Mother is the giver of life, WATER
Body is the form of life, EARTH
Heart is the rhythm of life, FIRE
Love is the essence of life, ETHER
that which supports and allows the flow.

August was a month of building up inventory as well as the start of filling orders for Christmas. I was busy and stressed working at something that I no longer really enjoyed. I was worrying about income, the sale of the property and business, and also what I was going to do afterwards. There were times I wasn't even sure if I even wanted to get involved in the Wellness Centre that Jen and I had been talking about and had even looked at some possible locations. My daughter, who had been living with me for the past few months was now going off to Cannes, France to take up the position of a Nanny for a couple of years. I was both happy and sad to see her leave. I had a lot of "what if's" coming up for me as all my buttons felt like they were being pushed at once. It also felt that Jen and I were getting on each other's nerves as we were pushing each other's buttons of trust, partnerships, power, feeling alone, helpless and asking for help, were but a few of the issues coming up.

Awareness of Your Denials

1997 Aug. 19 - Recognizing your fears, your denials and doubts will bring you clarity of what issues still need to be transformed. Also recognize that it is the suppression of the Will that is trying to expand and express her fears and desires that have long been suppressed and denied. The trick, the catch, will be to be aware that it is your denied Will and your fear of your desires that are the root of your experiences. Understand that awareness and allowance of expression of all that you feel will bring clarity. You have only to look and to ask. Look not with your physical eyes but with your Will and your heart, and asking them what it is that you need to observe and to feel.

1997 Aug. 21 - Jen and I were doing more journeys, and what was coming up now was that all promises and vows needed to be released, as they are also holding us back from healing. This refers to all promises and vows on the Earth plane, in other dimensions, and in all time. Promises and vows like, I'll love you forever, I'll always love you, I promise, forever, always, I'll never leave you. I swear, I'm yours, you'll always be mine, etc. Even those unloving promises and vows such as, I'll get even if it takes forever, I'll never forgive you, till death do us part, with my dying breath, I'll get revenge, etc. all these need to be released.

As time went on, I was also beginning to spend more time with Caroline. We were sharing channeled messages and also doing journeys. I felt that she was becoming more open as we were also beginning to move feelings and emotions.

1997 Aug. 25 - I realized that I was still hanging on to the business and that I was still doing and being what I didn't want to do or be anymore. What I now want to do and be is to own and operate a Wellness Centre and do healing and teaching. I need to trust that the universe will support the Centre that Jen and I want to start. Jen came up with the name, "The Heart Centre," with the motto, "Heaven embracing Earth embracing," with the words formed in a circle around a picture of the Earth. It can be read as Heaven embracing Earth, or Earth embracing Heaven, and also as one continuous loop, Heaven embracing Earth embracing Heaven, etc. There is a picture of it at the end of this book.

Chapter 4 – Emotions Begin to Surface

Loving Intent

1997 Aug. 28 - Loving intent towards others is, and was expressed, but now you are also to express and experience loving intent toward self. It is time to re-program the old belief that you must be kind to others, for that is a judgment. It is time to love self first and to be kind to self, to honor self and be true to self, so that you can serve others in your truth. For not to be true to self is to look toward others and to put emphasis on others for acceptance of self that is lacking within. Accept self, and others will accept you in whatever manner is appropriate to them at that time in their growth and experience. Becoming aware now of how subtly you deny your true feelings and are indeed unloving to self when you try to be loving to others, even if you don't really feel it is so. The point of at least expressing it is enough to bring clarity and acceptance that you do have these feelings and is growth. Not that you have to say everything that you think or feel, for there is also discernment as to whether it is in your highest purpose or their higher purpose, but if it is appropriate it is to be always expressed. Loving intent to self is first and foremost for true growth to continue and to express your truth. Your feelings when expressed will provide you with the opportunity to experience this freedom. Blessings and be gentle with yourself.

> *Heal all opposition to self. - Shenreed*

1997 Aug. 29 – Merlin, my Siamese cat, has been missing for four days now. The last time I saw him was when I was sitting on a deck chair with my supper plate on my lap. He tried to jump up onto my lap and I pushed him away with my elbow. He landed on the deck and looked up at me with a miffed expression. He then walked toward the house, along the wall and jumped off the deck to the lawn, then sauntered across the yard, past the beech tree with the tire swing and into the woods. That was the last time I saw him. He had been away before for a couple of days at a time and would stroll into the house as if nothing had happened. Although I sensed something was different or off, I didn't go after him at the time as I had just started my supper and I was also going through my own stuff at the time.

1997 Aug. 31 - To give you a time frame of what was going on in the world at that time, the evening news reported that Princess Diana had died in a car crash. I felt sad and in disbelief that she had died the way she did, that she had no peace, no sanctuary and no joy, even though she appeared to be a happy and loving person to everyone in the eyes of the world, it was not returned.

I was on the phone with Jen and I was still angry with God for allowing me to channel Lucifer. I felt like I was raped, abandoned, betrayed and unloved and I didn't trust God or any messenger anymore. How can I be sure if I don't know the difference between God and Lucifer? Jen got the message to take me on a journey. I don't remember too much of getting there but that the journey was to experience love. She had me visualize two buckets and asked me to put my hands in them and to feel which one was love. I was afraid and I admitted it but I eventually put my hands in. The first one felt smooth, soothing and comforting and the second felt lighter, had less substance more like a thick fog, which became lighter and then nothing and didn't feel comfortable. She then asked me which bucket I thought or felt was love and which bucket was unloving light and Lucifer. I said the first bucket was love and she told me I was correct. Then she had me visualize another two buckets and do the same exercise. Again, I was hesitant and wanted to know what the trick was, but I put my hands in the buckets, one hand in each. This time both buckets felt like love. She then gave me the message that that was how I would know what love was, by "feeling" it, as I did today.

I want the magic of love but it's fear that is holding me back. Fear of expressing myself, of being emotional, of being physical and all at the same time too. Fear that if I do open, I'll get wounded again in the same way. That is my fear and the only way to move it is to allow myself to be vulnerable and to move into experiences, to become more real, or as real as I can be. So, do I just need to be totally honest in each relationship and just let it be, to develop to whatever level it goes to? Why am I searching for love outside myself? Don't I love myself? Don't I have it within me for myself first? I feel I do but I also feel it's incomplete and that there's more to it but I don't know what. I feel that we're drawn into relationships that are fragments of ourselves (our group) on some level, and that this is maybe why we want to interact with them, to make them part of our lives more strongly than others.

Okay, so there are no coincidences. Jen came into my life and we've worked together for the past eight months. I just thought of Rita, we also had a connection and a depth of love but now she's gone. I know that we had more work to do together and now she won't even return my phone calls but it's okay. It's almost like she pulled back and allowed Jen to take her place. Hummm? Interesting, maybe that's why there is this extra attraction, not attraction as such, but maybe more attention, focus, to work in a lot of different areas with Jen since Rita left. Maybe I'm reading intensity as passion and excitement. Maybe that's why there's this strong feeling that there is going to be more, more working together on some levels but then there are also those other levels and issues that we avoid and deny at the same time. We're working around them instead of dealing with, and working through them. We're cutting ourselves off and keeping ourselves distant and safe. I've been keeping my distance because I feel the fear which is the physical, of being around people and getting close and then getting hurt.

Love and sex are confusing issues with trust and power interwoven. Sex has been used to get love or rather to feel that one was being loved, to

Chapter 4 – Emotions Begin to Surface

feel that closeness, union and pleasure that was only available with sex. I'm not saying that all sex is pleasurable or a way of feeling loved either, for the opposite of that is also true. We've never had love without sex as a goal, the object of our desire. Sex is natural, is creativity, is creation. The beginning of creation was movement, response to being stimulated.

The Mother moves to the Fathers touch, the Father moves to the Mothers touch but there has always been guilt, denial, conditions and unloving light present. Now I feel we have the opportunity to experience true unconditional love, including sex without guilt, denial or shame. So now what? How do we do and experience that? Do we work on clearing our old programs, beliefs and imprints in ourselves so that we can release the attachments to people, places and things? So what's the next step? How can we be totally loving of ourselves if we have desires but are in fear of expressing them? We are full of fears like, it's not appropriate, rejection, lack of acceptance, not good enough, etc., all of which are imprints from original cause. I feel the only way we're going to get past or through these sex issues and imprints is by expressing and not denying our true feelings in the moment. We may even feel that we can have sex without fear, shame, guilt or denial and even if it feels right in the moment, that doesn't mean that issues won't come up during or after sex that we were not even conscious of. So where does all that put us then?

There are no rules but then again there's this responsibility issue that centers around fulfilling what you desire, but without controlling or diminishing anyone else. The responsibility is to self first, but without guilt, denial, shame, condition or control to experience what you desire. So does unconditional love also include unconditional sex and if so, what is that? Can one have passion and sex, and everything else in a one-night experience that is without guilt, shame, or denial? Can it be anything you want so long as you both agree? Does that make it unconditional? I don't think so! What if there are conditions, guilt, shame, or denial on one side but not the other, does that make the whole experience conditional? Questions and more questions.

Then there is the other side of sex where you have a seemingly beautiful unconditional loving, platonic relationship, one where there is no sex involved, but what if the moment arose where there could have been more, but you had guilt, shame or fear come up, and you shut down in denial. Then it's no longer an unconditional relationship. It's basically saying yes, we'll be friends but we'll never be anything more than that. We'll never kiss or cuddle and we'll certainly never have sex, because in this moment I'm not sexually attracted to you, and if the moment ever arose that I was feeling anything, then I'd shut that door and deny that I was having those thoughts as that would change our whole relationship. So I'll focus my attention on other thoughts of passion, on other people outside of this relationship so that this relationship doesn't change, which in turn then makes this relationship one of conditional love. Change is growth and whatever change is needed must be allowed or there is no growth, no true unconditional love. Yes, you can have choices and preferences but you can't deny your feelings or expressing them, which does not necessarily mean that you have to act on them unless you feel you need to. You can act on them if you feel you are without doubt, fear, guilt or condition, or if you have fears but don't know what they are, but are willing to be open to allow the experience to continue to carry you to your activation. Either way, both people need to be totally honest to move and express all they can. All this is leaving me with more questions and no real answers.

Relationships and Limitations

1997 Sept. 01 - The issue with relationships is that in order for a relationship to flow, all conditions and limitations of any kind must be cleared first from the self and then to form the relationship. Acceptance must be completely open, honest and loving. Acceptance for all expression FIRST, then you can state what you prefer, do you prefer this or that, then move to your preference, your desire with passion and excitement.

Two people that are totally opposite, one open and in balance and the other in fear, denial and doubt cannot make what you would call a loving union for there is lack of acceptance in the latter. There can be attraction of opposites and this may be appropriate for the spontaneous experiences, an event, but would not form a lasting, growing and loving relationship. Placing physical attractions, conditions and limitations, is placing emphasis on the outward manifestation and ignoring the self.

What makes you think the above is not valid, just because you were upset and felt it was your ego dictating. Rest assured it was not. Realize now that your thoughts, words, and your ego consciousness around them is becoming less and less. You are in most cases, when in dialogue either channeling your higher self, your guides, or the guides of others. Your voice and tone will be reflective of what is appropriate at the time to activate those individuals.

The issue with relationships is many layered and a complex one and you have insights and knowing that others do not and this is what causes you confusion. For the words you say do not reflect that which you think you know and feel to be true and so you have doubt and guilt in thinking that you are channeling Lucifer again and you close down. Rest assured that you will know when this energy is around you and when you release your guilt and denials, you release more and more of his hold on you. You have knowing of things, of ways and when's, and it is difficult for you to translate this into words that are appropriate without feeling guilt that you are in some way withholding the truth and being entirely open. For you have been given part of the truth, for the whole (TRUTH) as you would call it, would not benefit

Chapter 4 – Emotions Begin to Surface

you at this time, in fact, would be a hindrance and prevent you from following your experience. In the time remaining, and time is running down quickly, these will be unfolded to you and you will understand the necessity of them.

There is work being done both ways in similar fashion, and each has a different perspective of the same idea. Soon these TRUTHS that each of you have will again change, and you will have clarity to the situation and experiences you are sharing. Patience, trust, and acceptance, as you both are indeed being accelerated for this also is your desire. Your issues will be triggered much quicker now and your rest stops will be shorter and less frequent, and thus the pressure is felt on the ego's persona and its past state of balance. There is the possibility of an overload and breakdown in communication and this would be most detrimental at this time, this precious illusion you call time. Insights will be given, but it is also necessary to allow the two of you to dialogue and to feel, in order to understand the issues that are being brought to the surface and often will not be what it appears to be at all. Be gentle with yourselves and each other, and know that you soon will have the understandings and the opportunity to experience life as you never could have dreamed it.

September rolled around and the meeting with the guy from out West that was interested in the property and business fell apart. I don't even know what he really wanted as he never did fly out and the whole thing just got weird, so I let it go. There were also a couple of peeks at the property but they never panned out either. My daughter came back from France after a traumatic episode and is now staying with her mother in Toronto.

♡ As I'm writing this, I feel denied rage at that SOB and his bitch wife in France, and the bullshit stuff they pulled on my daughter. ♥

My stress level is still building and denied emotions are surfacing daily. During all this, I was also trying to set up a small meditation group in my home once a week.

Moving Blocks

1997 Sept. 03 - Know that you have put into action, by your intent and by your willingness to raise your vibration, the changes that you seek. The joys you desire to experience will all be coming to you, it is not in your knowing yet, but it will soon be. Openness and willingness to uncover all denials, doubts, and fears are the key to growth and movement and the courage and faith to face them, and to recognize and accept them so that they can then be transformed. As you continue to seek deeper and deeper, uncovering even the tiniest of fear, you move more and become more of the loving light and truth of All That Is. Accept the challenge you have, and we are in awe and admiration at your progress and process. For you chose different routes to amass different experiences and aspects of the same fear or lesson, not lesson but experience the polarity of the situation.

There are still blocks to overcome, we would not call them major but rather significant, and these involve trust and acceptance. We will give you no more at this time for this would diminish your experience. We understand that the ego is indeed a powerful force when it comes to what it considers its survival. It can be a formidable adversary when it is aligned with the programs it has access to and is still running, or a powerful ally with higher self. It seeks the old tried and true routine that has ensured survival before it risks a new format or experience. It will draw on the old, even if they are unpleasant, only for the fact that it has and can deal with them, where as something new to replace the old threatens its very survival. You are getting closer now and the closer you get, the more resistance you get, the harder it is to get the ego to let go and reveal what it is afraid of, afraid to let go of. Patience, gentleness, and be loving with yourselves in the final stages of recognizing your blocks, fears, doubts and denials. As you uncover the subtle and faintest shadows of these and move in light and love to fill this space, the others will also be more easily identified and released.

Relationships and Balance

1997 Sept. 05 - For relationships and partnerships to remain unconditional and yet reflect the cooperation and balance of two working as one, is the ultimate challenge in third physicality. For two aspects to be harmoniously balanced in self, each with its own identity and preferences and desires and to now put energy into a relationship of a mixing of these two energies is indeed the magic. As you move higher in vibration the differences are more subtle but the feelings are just as intense. The key is to identify the desires and needs of self and the other in open and continuous dialogue (there are many forms of dialogue) with the common goal being the focus of the partnership and the desired experience. Allow each the opportunity to reach it however way they choose and have agreed upon. If one wants to walk and the other swim, and if it fits the goal, the ideal, then so be it, but if one judges the other is doing less or getting more or whatever, there needs to be balance brought to the situation before starting or continuing the partnership. Whatever the issues are, there is need to resolve the fear, the belief system or program in order for the partnership to work. Any form of denial or laying of guilt or blame only sabotages the relationship.

Chapter 5 - My Lost Child

1997 Sept. 10 - I was consciously aware of what I thought was my inner child and had previously journeyed back and expressed what happened to me on the first day of school, but today Jen took me on a journey that was deeper than I'd ever gone before, where I found my lost Child. What I felt and experienced was something that I had never felt before. He was six, almost seven years old years old and starting school. He didn't know the language, was confused, abandoned, betrayed, and frightened. No, he wasn't frightened, he was terrified and heartbroken. Terror of getting physically beaten up and mentally and emotionally abused, as well as being confused and heartbroken, as he didn't know any way out. To add to it, there was also no sanctuary at home either. There was no rest or mercy for this lost child. After I had returned from my regression, I felt I was beginning to fall apart.

> *Change your beliefs, change your system.*
> *Change your system, change your reality.*
> *Change your reality, change your beliefs. - Shenreed*

Growth and Balance

1997 Sept. 12 - Concentrate not upon the outward physical manifestations to reflect to you all that you have accomplished, for what you have moved are mountains, indeed worlds but not of this physical plane, but soon. Although you will not literally move this world, you will change it, and then maybe you might. As you bring your spiritual levels in balance they will begin to manifest in the physical. The disorder and chaos you experience in the physical is only a reflection of the turmoil, the upheaval you experience in the spiritual planes, particularly around being human. As these are harmonized and brought down to the physical, your physical reality, as you like to call it, will dramatically alter.

Human, is by far the most complicated, densest and easiest for one to lose ones way and also allows for the greatest growth of any of the levels of creatorship. Integrating the spiritual into the physical is not an easy task because human consciousness has sunk to such a low that it is like trying to swim in coal tar. As the mass consciousness is raised, the swimming will get easier and easier until it is like salty sea-water and you are supported. You still have to make an effort to get to where you want to go but you no longer need to expend tremendous energy trying to stay afloat. You are in transition; you are about to shed the coal tar from around your body and enjoy the freedom, joy and love you have never truly known. Blessings.

Journey to the Heart Centre

I'd like to share a couple of interesting observations and insights that we got at this time. When Jen and I were talking, or rather when Jen was talking and I was listening to her but really not really wanting to hear her, I would go into denial and I wasn't even conscious of it. I would do what she called sighting, which would really annoy her. Depending on how I was sitting, I would take aim at something with my foot, finger or knee. I would also move my head to align one object with another. An example would be to align the edge of the window frame with the edge of a cloud, or my big toe with the bottom corner of a chair. Other tricks of mine were that when I was activated, I would get itchy, especially my head, and I would scratch my head as if I had lice, or I would rub my nose or adjust my glasses. Still another technique I used was that if I wanted to look at something or somebody and I didn't want anyone to notice, or think that I was intentionally looking at it, or them, I would turn my head and pretend to rub my chin on my shoulder. This way I could turn my head and take a quick look without appearing that that was what I was intentionally doing.

One of Jens ways of going off in denial and distracting herself was to rock her body to and fro, or she would begin to bounce, pretending it was to the music, either external or something she said she was thinking of that made her happy. My observations later showed that everyone has their own unique way of using their body to express their emotions when the mind is blocked and the real emotions are being held in denial. I'm thinking of a small boy that has accidentally broken a vase and doesn't want his parents to find out. So when he is talking to his mother, he twists and turns his body and his eyes are looking everywhere but at his mother, as he tells her that he didn't go near the broken vase in the hallway. His mother immediately knows that the vase is broken and who broke it, but the boy wonders how his mother knew about the vase and that he broke it.

I was visiting Jen today and while listening to her talk, I was also picking up feelings and getting insights on her, but all that I would say was okay. I didn't realize that I was filtering or blocking myself. She snapped at me and asked, "Okay what?" With that statement and tone, I instantly forgot what I was picking up. After the third time I realized what I was doing, but by that time I had already shut myself down. I was now afraid to open myself in case I'd say okay again and she'd snap at me and have no acceptance or patience for me to try to allow what was coming to me to be expressed. Now that I was aware that I was filtering, I also became overly conscious of how I'd try to express myself in a way that would be acceptable or good enough. She got angry and said that I wasn't helping her move her emotions and issues and said that she'd do it alone, and asked me to leave.

I was frustrated and angry when I left, and by the time I got home I was in a worked up state. I picked up my journal and started to write to express myself. As you will see, what started out as being activated with one

Chapter 5 – My lost child

issue turns into something completely different when you allow yourself to explore it to the depths of your being.

I'm angry at my parents, they went to school (knew English) but never spoke it at home until after I started school. It would have made my life a lot easier if I knew at least how to communicate with the children. I'm angry that I was humiliated in front of my peers when I peed my pants because I couldn't tell the teacher that I needed to go to the bathroom. I'm angry at my father for abandoning me at school and for not being there on time after school to pick me up, and also that I got picked on and beat up until he came.

I'm angry at the children in school for not accepting me and for not even trying to help me when I was being beaten. They just picked on me and it wasn't just the children in my class but the other grades as well. The beatings I took, the jabs, pokes, shoves, kicks, tripping, and the pencil stabs. The snakes that were dropped down my pant legs as they held me upside down, and the terror I felt as they would slide down my body and wriggle out through the collar of my shirt and across my face. Of being pushed into puddles or having snow shoved down my neck and pants that would soak my clothing and then I'd be cold for the rest of the day. Then there was the issue of what they would do to my lunch, that was if they returned it to me. The rock and snowball throwing slowed down by the end of the third grade, as that was something I became good at returning. I could throw straight and hard and I hit what I was aiming at, even if it was moving. Not to say that they didn't throw stones and snowballs in the later years but that if they did, they got the worst end of the deal at the time, but I'd always pay for it in other ways afterwards.

Now I'm remembering the boxing glove experiences that took place in the school basement at lunchtime, that was supervised by a man teacher from the higher grades. When the bigger boys picked on me out in the schoolyard and I'd try to fight back, he'd take us into the basement and put these boxing gloves on us. It didn't matter to him what grade or size these boys were that were fighting with me. If there were four boys that were fighting me in the schoolyard, then I'd have the gloves on until all four had had their round with me, which would only be finished when he said it was finished, and when I was bleeding and laying on the floor. I'd always get the biggest gloves and he'd tie them real tight around my wrists so that they wouldn't come off, and then he's say fight. I can remember the first time, I didn't even know what they were, let alone how to use them.

♡ As I'm writing this now I can remember wanting the smaller gloves and him saying, "No, you keep the bigger ones, that way you won't get hurt," which was exactly the opposite. I have denied anger and rage at this moment and I'd like to put the gloves on that bastard and have a round with him now and put the big ones on him so that he won't get too hurt. I was small and some of these guys, I say guys, but as I'm writing this I have such rage coming up in me that if they were in front of me now I'd beat them to within an inch of their frickin lives, the cowardly bastards. Fuck! Some of those fucking cowards were at least five years older than me. ♥

    I'm also angry at my peers and teachers. I remember one day in grade three, when the girl sitting in the desk behind me kept poking me in the back with her lead pencil. I'd jump every time she'd poked me and the teacher would yell at me to sit still. I tried telling the teacher that the girl was poking me but she just told me to shut up and be quiet. A couple of minutes later she poked me again, only this time it was a lot harder, and as I was to find out later, she broke the lead off her pencil, leaving a piece in my back. I jumped in pain but I didn't say a word. The teacher never said a word either; she just glared at me as she picked up something from her desk and hurled it at me. I instinctively lifted the hinged desktop to protect myself and deflected the object up and over and to the side of me. It bounced off the blackboard and then skittered across the hardwood floor to the back of the room. I and others in my isle, looked back to see what she had thrown at me; it was a small pair of scissors.

    The room became eerily silent. A moment later, the bitch behind me got up and went to the front of the classroom to sharpen her pencil. She was smiling as she made her way back to her seat and when she was beside me, she turned and drove the pencil into my left arm just above my elbow. I yelled out in pain as I pulled my arm away noticing the lead breaking off in my arm as I did. The teacher bolted from behind her desk, rushed down my isle to my desk and grabbing me by the ear, hauled me out of the room. She shouted that I was a troublemaker and pretended not to notice the blood streaming from the wound in my elbow. She shoved me out the door and into the hallway where I was told to stay until the bell rang. I sat quietly on the hall floor trying to stop the bleeding and also trying to get the piece of lead out of my arm. The bell rang soon after and school was out for the day. I was still sitting in the hallway when Mrs. Stokes, the grade four-five-six teacher came over to help me. She got the piece of lead out of my back but couldn't get all the lead out of my arm. She then bandaged my wounds. To this day I still have a piece of lead in my arm.

    The next day I went to school and the teacher wasn't there; a girl in my room told me that she had been fired, not for what she had done to me, but for what she could have done to the other students. We had a substitute teacher for that day and a new teacher was assigned the next week, and things went on as if nothing had happened.

    It wasn't until grade four when I got into Mrs. Stocks room that I started to pull out of my shell. She was to be my teacher for grades four, five and six. She would ask me to clean the black boards or to do errands for her

Chapter 5 – My lost child

if she felt that I might get beat up at recess. At lunchtime, she would read a chapter from a book like, The Hardy Boys or Treasure Island. I not only enjoyed the stories, but staying in class also saved me from some abuse and beatings.

♡ Again, I'm filled with emotions and I'm crying as I realize that this was the first time in my life that I was being shown any compassion, acceptance and love. Tears are flowing down my face and I can taste their saltiness, others are falling on my shirt and it's okay, even my nose is running. I don't think I ever really allowed myself to feel this, or rather to let myself feel and express myself this way and I'm not in denial as I'm also sharing this with you in the moment. ♥

By grade six, although I was still small, I felt it was time for a change. I felt that now I was big and strong enough to beat up the bullies that had been beating me up for the past six years. I decided to take the battle to them, one at a time. I'd beat up one of the bullies after school, then the next day they would gang up on me and beat me up. Then a couple of days later, I picked out another one and give him a beating, and the next day they would beat me up again. I did this until I got the last and biggest one, his name was Freddy. When he saw me hiding behind a telephone pole waiting for him, he made a beeline for home as fast as his chubby legs could take him. I punched, kicked and drop kicked his bully fat ass all the way to his home, and then his mother chased me a short distance, shouting and waving a broom.

The next day I expected to get beat up again after school, but this time I made it home without being attacked. Later, I heard a knock at the door. My mother answered the door and a moment later, told me that there are some boys at the door that wanted me to come out and play. It was them! I didn't know what to do. I didn't trust them and thought it was a trick and they would turn on me. Since I was at home and my mother was there, I decided to take a chance. I went out and we played for a while without incident. That was the last time that I was beaten up by them, but of course, this wasn't the end of the abuse as a few months later, we moved to Regina and I had to start all over again.

I had also sub-consciously alienated my family because I felt they didn't care what happened to me. I felt that my siblings never got the same treatment from the kids at school that I did. When I was in grade six, my mother was having a "kids" portrait taken but I didn't want to be a part of it, so I stayed at the garage where my dad was working at the time. The picture was taken without me and every time I see it, I'm reminded of those times.

♡ I'd be in denial here if I didn't say that as I'm writing this now, that I'm sad that I wasn't closer with my siblings, mother and father. I feel like I was in the family but not really a part of it. I feel like I missed out on what a real family is meant to be and that I've been shortchanged and cheated. ♥

I also have anger at religion. It was during the summer holidays of grade six, before we moved to Regina, that I was going to catechism classes in the next town of Grayson. That was also an experience I won't forget. Several nuns were assisting the class, especially during lunch hours and recess. At the beginning of the summer classes, one nun had taken to protect me from the others who would pick on me at times. In the last week of the summer session, I don't remember what had happened or why she put her left hand on my head and held me close to her. All I remember is feeling the baby kicking me in the head. I looked up at her in bewilderment and she looked at me in terror as we stared at each other for what seemed like an eternity. I put my hand on her stomach and I knew, she knew, I knew. Her face turned red and then white as she turned and left the playground. When I got home that evening, I told my mother what happened and she said that I was imagining things and that I shouldn't tell lies. The next day she was gone. We were told that there was a death in her family and that she would be away for a while.

It was the following day that the priest invited the bishop to attend class before we were confirmed. The Bishop asked all the girls, "Who wants to be a nun when they grow up?" All the girls eagerly raised and waved their hands. Then he asked all the boys, "Who wants to be a priest when they grow up?" All the boys put up their hands and waved, except me. As I was sitting near the front he couldn't help but notice me. The Bishop came over to me and asked me what I wanted to be when I grew up. I swallowed hard and said, "I want to be an airplane pilot when I grow up." His face turned red, his eyes squinted as he leaned toward me and asked me the same question again. I replied with the same answer, but figuring he was hard of hearing, I spoke in a louder voice. Well that mistake cost me my recess time and I also had to do extra penance to redeem myself for shouting at a Bishop. I was beginning to see and feel that there was a lot of bullshit going on with this thing called religion, and it was making me doubt and begin to ask questions.

While I'm at it, I might as well keep going and get it all out. At the end of grade six we moved to Regina and we were enrolled in the new Catholic school of St. Peters. Having just moved to the city I had no friends, but of course enemies had no trouble finding me. There was only one boy, Larry, in my grade seven class that befriended me but he accidentally killed himself with a .22 rifle when he was hunting in the late fall. When he died, I had no other friends in that school.

♡ Wow! This is really a healing day for me as I'm overwhelmed with emotions and tears again as I'm feeling that I've never allowed myself to grieve for that loss either, for the friendship, acceptance and love that was

Chapter 5 – My lost child

there. He was a great artist and liked to draw and paint animals and birds. He might have been another Robert Bateman if he had lived. I wished I could draw and paint like he did, I feel that's where I also left a part of myself that I want to re-claim now. ♥

> *Religion is a state of mind;*
> *Spirituality is a state of being. – Shenreed*

My parents were devote Roman Catholics and we went to mass and confession every Sunday. The issues with confession came up in school in the New Year when the school priest started coming around to hear confessions for all the students on Monday. I went to school confession and found myself beginning to tell lies on Monday just to have something to confess and then having to go to church on Sunday to confess that I lied in confession on Monday. This was driving me crazy and I told my parents that I didn't want to go to confession on Sunday because I was going to the one in school on Monday. They wouldn't hear about it, especially my mother, as then I wouldn't be able to take communion, which to her was a deadly sin. I then tried to get out of going to confession at school. The teacher didn't believe me when I told him why I didn't want to go to confession because I just went yesterday and because I haven't done anything wrong. He put me up in front of the class and asked everyone if they knew if I had done anything bad. Nobody had anything to say that I had done "bad" in the two hours or so that I had been at school. When that didn't work, he said that I was disobedient and was not respecting my elders and teacher, and that that was cause for confession. I disputed that point and said I wasn't arguing with him, I was telling him the truth. Well that pissed him off even more and he was out to get me.

During the next few months, I went to school confession a few times just to avoid confrontation, but it just didn't feel right and when I adamantly refused to go to confession, he was out to break me. He not only put me through the same routine every Monday, but he would also bring it up during class with snide and condescending remarks. Finally in May, he again put me up in front of the class, but this time the school priest was also present. Again, I was clean of any so-called sins as no one spoke against me, and that ticked them off.

The next week they were waiting for me. This time it was the teacher, principal, school priest, parish priest and the archbishop with his robes and rings, that were there to break me. I faced the same drilling process and routine in front of my classmates and was ridiculed, shamed and chastised for disobeying God. When I still wouldn't capitulate and refused to go to confession, I was hauled out and taken to my home by this unholy entourage. Two cars pulled into the driveway and my mother was surprised to see this procession with me being dragged by the arm. I had told my mother before what was happening but it was dismissed as something that would resolve itself. They told her that I refused to go to confession several times and that I said I had not done anything bad. When asked, she told them that she couldn't think of a thing where I disobeyed her, or my father, or did anything bad against my siblings since Sunday afternoon.

I don't know what you would call it, but the words coming to mind is that the unholy Inquisition continued with its intimidation tactics and demands. What also came out at this time was that I told my mother that when I went to confessions on Sunday, that the parish priest was always asking me if my father and mother were arguing or doing anything bad. He also told me that I had to tell him or else I would burn in hell, as it was a sin to lie to a priest, a man of god. Of course, the parish priest denied that he had ever asked me that, but by me saying that, it also made sense and infuriated my mother as she exclaimed that she always wondered why he knew so much about what was going on between her and dad. She said she thought it was God telling him and not him questioning and threatening me. She was now livid. The archbishop stepped in and told my mother to control herself or be dammed in hell for speaking that way to and in front of, the men of the cloth and of God. In reply, she grabbed the broom from the kitchen corner and threatened the so-called men of god, yelling at them to get out of the house. They didn't hesitate as they almost fell over each other as she swept them out the door. It was at that point that the archbishop turned, and with an unholy twisted snarl on his face that I will never forget, excommunicated us on the spot and dammed us to an eternity of suffering and hell. I remember thinking, is that what this God of love is all about, and if these men are doing what this loving God wants, then I don't want to be any part of that, or him.

It was near the end of the school year and we couldn't go to school to finish the last few weeks. We just got our report cards saying we passed and that was it. This event also alienated our family for years from our Catholic relations of some thirty-six aunts and uncles and over one hundred and fifty cousins, as well as all our Catholic friends. I felt guilty that I had caused all this strife, that I just should have lied and everyone would be happy, except me.

That summer, before I started grade eight, I had an accident. We were playing tag and I was jumping off a picket fence, trying not to get tagged, and didn't realize that my shoelace was looped over the top of a fence board. Before I knew it, my face hit the edge of a wooden sidewalk and broke seven of my upper front teeth at the roots and a few were chipped and loose. As none of my teeth had fallen out, it was recommended that I just leave them until I was older when I could get a full upper denture as some of my molars were not in great shape either. Now I was faced with the shame of

Chapter 5 – My lost child

going through the next three years of my adolescent life with broken and decaying teeth.

Not only was that traumatic enough, we also moved two more times and I went to a different school each year, including grade ten. It wasn't until I started grade ten that the doctor and dentist decided that I should go to the hospital and have my upper teeth removed. I spend the first six months in grade ten without upper teeth as I had to wait for my gums to heal before they could fit my dentures. I can remember walking out of the dentist's office the day I got my dentures and thinking that everyone was staring at me if I opened my mouth or spoke, because my teeth felt so big. I think my caption under my yearbook picture that year was "I don't know ask him." I remember that I didn't want to talk to anyone and that I could say that phrase and not have to move my upper lip very much so that no one would notice I didn't have any upper teeth.

I realize that the issues that are coming up stem from my early childhood, school, parents, teachers, church, peers, family and friends, and that I never really had a friend to talk to. I've been pretty much a loner all my life, yet trying to fit in and do things with and for people, as a way, a means of having the illusion of a friendship, of being with people, being accepted and loved. I've been sub-consciously trying to reach that little boy in me that has been shut down all these years. I'm now an adult trying to be a boy. When I'm with children, I can't seem to get in touch with that little boy (child) that was so hurt. I also feel there are other lost parts of me that are younger and older than that too. I feel I've been losing parts of myself all my life right to this moment.

> *The difference between atonement and at-one-ment is the (T).*
> *With aTonement, it is the self that is carrying the cross. -*
> *Shenreed*

1997 Sept. 14 - My greatest fear and weakness is to admit that I have a fear and weakness, therefore, as long as I can hide and deny that I have any problems that I can't handle, I have no problem. I'd say that my biggest weakness is that I'm not perfect, not a perfect husband, father, haven't the perfect job or home, or that I don't say or do the right thing perfectly, and on and on. I ask too much of myself, I've tried to be perfect, to do what I think others think is perfect just for acceptance and there's no way that I could ever be enough to do what I, or others expected of me. I put others feelings and desires before my own believing it was loving, but really it was guilt, self-sacrifice and denial of love for myself. When I put others ahead of myself I'm not loving myself, and as long as I try to hide, deny or feel guilty about being less than perfect, I am in Lucifer's hold.

Journey to the Heart Centre

Therefore, from this day forward I intend to identify all of my fears and weaknesses. I ask help from Father and Mother to enable me to bring these fears, beliefs, programs, imprints, guilt and shame forward to my conscious awareness to be accepted, to allow my emotions and body their expression, and as they are released, to move unloving light out and off of me and to fill the space with Love and Light. I am ready to move forward and I am ready to release the limitations I have placed on myself. I am ready to be free, to soar like an eagle. From this day forward, I ask that I recognize denial, guilt, and shame for what they are, and to set them free and not to be limited by them anymore.

1997 Sept. 15 - Jen called me on the phone and read me a piece she had channeled about unconditional love. I went off into a space and I just remember the feeling of being held and cradled. I then had a vision of an Eagle that couldn't, or rather, wasn't allowed to fly as it had a string tied to its leg. I didn't want it to fly away because I was afraid it was going to get hurt as it had always been on a rope ever since it was able to fly. I told Jen what I was experiencing and she told me to see myself letting it go. I untied the Eagles leg and set it free but it didn't want to leave. I tried shooing it but it just stayed on my arm guard. Finally, a wind came up and began blowing and ruffling the Eagles feathers, stronger and stronger until finally it took off and flew around me. It then flew back to my arm and started to pick at the laces on the arm guard I was wearing until it fell off and dropped to the ground. It then perched on my naked arm. It was okay, its talons didn't hurt me and I didn't need the guard anymore either. He was free and so was I. I began to cry.

♡ As I'm proof reading this piece I'm moved to tears again. I don't know why but it really is moving something in me, maybe it's freedom, freedom for both. Freedom, yes that's the word, freedom, but not any freedom that I've ever known because in this freedom there is also love. ♥

1997 Sept. 16 - Jen and Liz got together and threw me a surprise birthday party for my Lost six year old Child. It was a double surprise as my birthday wasn't until October. I don't ever remember having a birthday party as a child let alone having friends there.

♡ Another wave of emotion is sweeping over me as I'm feeling how grateful I am to these two beautiful souls for showing me some love and compassion that day. It was a moment I'll never forget. ♥

There were balloons all over the place and they'd wrapped up a bunch of small presents, fifteen to be exact, and had hidden them throughout Jens

Chapter 5 – My lost child

apartment with little clues on each present as to where the next one could be found. That meant a lot to me. Later that evening, I was talking to Jen on the phone and I can remember feeling what my lost child felt, that he didn't understand big words and that this "lost child" needed to move emotions without words and needed to feel loved and accepted without words either. I know that I was not healed that day but it was a big step and a door had been opened.

I've been angry with myself all my life. Ever since I started school I've had to fight and justify myself just to even be able to walk down the street. I've lived in fear and terror and have been lonely and in denied heartbreak for most of my life. I have also been in denied anger at everyone because I felt I had to CONTROL my feelings and not express them. I had to control my feelings not only to try to get acceptance and to be able to fit in, but I also had to control them in fear that if I didn't, I would be stalked, hunted and persecuted. It's one thing being a loner and not fitting into the pack, but it's another thing entirely when the pack turns on you and hunts you down, and that is how I've felt most of my life. As long as I kept my emotions and anger on the inside, things on the outside were tolerable. Whenever I would stand up for myself and express myself, I would get hurt, beaten up, tossed out of school, out of church, out of jobs and relationships. If I expressed my anger on the outside, then all hell would break loose. Hummm? Interesting choice of words, "ALL HELL WOULD BREAK LOOSE." How else can I be free of this hell if I don't break loose and free myself of its hold on and inside of me. There's more to this but I feel this is a clue.

Jen was also going through her emotional issues and was being activated by natural and artificial scents that would send her into a panic attack. At this time we were watching movies as well as doing various types of journeys that were activating us. When Jen felt she could go out, we would look at empty stores in Midland as a possible site for the future Wellness Centre.

Moving Anger and Rage

1997 Sept. 18 - Awareness is the key in unlocking the door, is the first step. The next step is movement, is to allow the thick, oozy, what appears to be solid mass, to slowly respond to the open door, the lack of pressure that has kept it contained, solidified. With no door closed it must move, slowly at first, and as it gains momentum it will not only flow through the door but also tear down the walls in which the door was set. As it cascades forth from its dark recesses, allow it to be transformed with love and light. All the lost, tiniest, darkest and long forgotten places to also move and be drawn into the light by movement of the main body. No, you may not get it all and there may be some parts that will remain stuck in a particular niche and those you can move when they call for your attention. But the main body has and is being moved, has lifted and is being transformed, and that void that was home of this anger and rage will now be filled with of Love, Light and Truth.

Fear not that it cannot be moved, it is huge, it is solid, it is stationary and static, and it is dense, compressed by years of CONTROL. Release the control of the doors, the floodgates, and allow these denied angers and rage to be released and transformed and forgiven, forgiving yourself and others.

Yes, you may still feel anger in your daily activities, these are old programs, imprints and beliefs, and for the most part, a shadow of what was released. These shadows may make it appear that nothing has been released, transformed, but that is not so. You will have in your awareness that the event does not carry the same emotional charge, and each time it reappears its charge will be less and less. You are moving, fear not and trust, for love and support is with you. Blessings, Sananda and Mary

> *Right or wrong, good or bad, are judgments based on your present belief systems, and is the reality you are experiencing. – Shenreed*

Healing and Your Path

1997 Sept. 18 - Understand that in order to assist others in healing themselves, you must heal yourselves in ways that will enable you to experience all that is needed in order to have the compassion and the understanding of the emotions being felt by another as well as the fragileness of the psyche and also its incredible strength. Once you have experienced, you can teach for you have truly felt. Words, the right words can be said, but it is not only words but the feeling of the words, the vibration, and also the feeling of the silence, the vibration of love between the words that does the true healing on all levels.

You have been preparing yourself for your mission and soon will have felt, and will have the understandings necessary to begin your journey in earnest. As you continue to go with the flow, open yourself, trust your intuition, your guidance and all will begin to make itself clear to you. You do not have to understand everything in this moment. You do not have to be perfect (there is no perfect, there is only growth) which is perfect in this moment. Just allow yourself to be, to feel, to express, and as you do, clarity will unfold for all you have learned, experienced, and read to this point is what you need in this moment. Of course there are other routes you could have taken, some shorter, some longer, but the one you chose is your path and it has brought you to this point, the exact point where you agreed to be before you incarnated in this experience. You are at the doorway, it is time for you to knock and enter. Blessings Mother and Father

Chapter 5 – My lost child

Releasing Your Anger

1997 Sept. 20 - Release your anger, the rage, the terror and heartbreak for until you do, love cannot enter those places and in your darkness you hold fear, fear you have not touched with loving light. You are not unique in this as everyone must face their anger and rage. Some have become marvelous masters at controlling their anger like you, and this will take effort to break down the walls, the blocks that are supporting this belief. Prompting anger in another that is still in the old program only induces them to fight or flight, and to also control or rationalize their behavior, and eventually to deny their anger. Of course one can push the person to the breaking point in that situation and it is then that something will happen to confront the anger and rage when this emotional charge builds up and needs to be released. Confronting anger with anger, rage with rage allows movement of emotions but only on the surface and does NOT address the cause of the deep-seated denied anger or rage, and is movement in the gap. You don't bruise you hand and then go out and bruise it again to heal it. Yes you'll feel it bruised again but you wouldn't have healed it. This is a simplification of course, for emotions are far more complex.

Confusion is another issue and one of the easiest ways to remove these blocks is to release the emotions, but not just the mental release, there must be emotions felt. Not necessarily just anger, but love also, to bring up, to open the door to these feelings (not close down) and then move into the anger and to bring it and the emotions out. This confusion in you is only when you share with those with whom you feel close, not distant, and is where you are seeking their acceptance, not judgment or rejection. Trigger the anger but do not attack it, love it, touch it. Yes, your anger is like a barking dog that you are thinking about. It is barking at you as it is aware of your presence, once you acknowledge your anger with love and acceptance it will become your friend and bark to warn you of danger.

Judgments and Beliefs

1997 Sept. 20 - Indeed judgments are belief systems based on programs, imprints of each and every specific individual. If one says you are such and such, that is his or her belief, but if what they say triggers you and you believe this to be true, then indeed you have an issue, a belief or judgment upon yourself. If there is no response either way, then you have no issue, no conflict, it is simply an observation of their belief, their judgment upon others, upon themselves. Observing that you have no issue is of course a fine line, because denial is quick to re-act. If one is truly open and vulnerable and speaking their truth from the heart, then denial has no opportunity, but this you can only determine in your quiet time if guilt comes knocking at your door. Openly confessing all your feelings, however you judge them as good, bad or indifferent, will allow you to move the emotions required to gain understanding.

That is not to say that eventually you will become void of emotions, not so, but you will be free of any attachment upon you through denial, guilt or shame. You will still feel their presence, either in you or in others, and will recognize them for what they are, what they represent. Then move through them with love, light and truth. As you alter your belief systems, you alter your reality for you no longer play into the old programs and imprinting that bind others in the quicksand of third density. Even what you consider time and space is part of your belief system. Nothing; nothing in your present existence is not a part of your belief systems, either on an individual or on a mass consciousness level.

Mass consciousness is the main focus, the key to your belief systems as in your consciousness. By integrating your consciousness with your sub-conscious you are connecting to the universal consciousness of ALL THAT IS, and no longer will be subject to the limitations of your own consciousness and the mass consciousness of Humanity. In the time ahead, you will have more clarity on this as you drop more and more of your belief systems from your consciousness, and most importantly, your sub-conscious which governs your consciousness. Answering the call to raise your vibration will give you the tools, the knowledge, the wisdom, to feel, to connect with Creation in a way that has never been possible before. Trust your feelings and in their experiences will come the knowing. In the being will be the doing, and with love comes the responsibility to share, to assist self and others. Adornia

Consciousness

1997 Sept. 29 - Understand that what you are going through is a healing, a healing on a deeper level of imprints, hence you have this feeling of detachment for there is no longer a hook to hang these beliefs upon. Your consciousness and sub-consciousness search for a response but none can be found. The feeling of, there should be something there, there was something there before, why don't I feel anything, any emotions, not even an, I couldn't care less, etc., are thoughts that come up from your consciousness as it looks for a response to the pattern (imprint) it knew it had. It always had a response for every situation, what it considered good, bad, or just indifferent, and if it still chose to be indifferent, it just wasn't indifferent to begin with, and there is a difference in the feeling of that. As you clear more and more of your imprints you will begin to see yourselves becoming free of the limitations of the beliefs and patterns that bind you. You will become more child-like, where a child has no good or bad, and is indifferent to beliefs and simply chooses what it wants to experience. With this childlikeness, not to say that you will become children again, there will be spontaneous and openness that will be applied with love, wisdom and

Chapter 5 – My lost child

patience to what you choose to experience. Awareness is the key to growth and this is just another phase, a step to the next higher level. Blessings, Mother and Father

I was busy in September building up stock and inventory but I never got the fall rush that I usually did. If things were slow in August, then September would make up for it, but both months have been slow. It might pick up for October, but that is usually near the end of the rush. Debts were high and funds were low, and so was I. I was even beginning to have problems meeting my monthly mortgage payments. Any free time I had was spent at Jens place or on the phone to her, at Caroline's, or working in my garden, reading or channeling. September ended with Caroline shutting down and not wanting to talk or have anything to do with me anymore. I also hadn't heard from Rita since the end of July either, so the only person I had left in my life that I feel I can talk to is Jen, but we're also having our bad days. I hadn't heard anything more from my Realtor nor the sale of the business but then again why would there be, I wasn't advertising it. I was beginning to feel trapped, boxed in, and the walls were closing in around me.

> *You can't really understand anything until you have acceptance for it first. - Shenreed*

Chapter 6 - Releasing the Old

The Journey Begins

1997 Oct. 01 - Today is the beginning of the journey. Expect not sudden revelations to begin in full force that which you will be doing / being. Trust that what is happening is for your highest purpose and good, even if you do not know or understand what is happening. Even if it seems a conflict or strife, in the moment is what you need, the tools you need to acquire to fulfill your mission.

There will be changes occurring in your daily life which will seem to come out of the blue and you will have no idea, but all is in synchronicity. The players are being brought together and the game, the real game is about to begin. Allow; be open to the people and the things that are about to come into your life and worry not about what it is that you think you might be doing. Allow yourself in the present, to be what you are doing and do what is your being. It will flow if you allow it and not plan it with your linear mind. For the conscious mind and ego are trying to put the pieces together to a three dimensional puzzle in a two dimensional format, and it can't make sense out of it. Stop trying to apply the old programs, imprints and beliefs and patterns to make the puzzle fit, it won't.

Allow yourself the freedom to experience; go with the flow, for there is NEW learning that needs to take place now. You have to let go of sufficient beliefs, patterns, programs and imprints so that your mind can allow new information to flow in. Follow your instincts, not your logical mind, for this is the new way of creating your own reality, allowing your imagination and intuition to carry you to create and discover your wildest dreams. There is much you will become aware of in the times ahead and we look forward to sharing this adventure with you in whatever way we can. Blessings, Mother, Father and the Company of Heaven.

1997 Oct. 15 - Last week, I placed an ad in the regional newspaper offering the business for sale. I got a couple of calls but no one was really interested. I heard earlier through the grapevine, that my ex-partners wife had died of cancer the past year and that he had bought a new house. I was still bitter at our relationship so I called my lawyer and had him check to see if he had money now to pay me what he owed me. My lawyer came back with a, "No, it's not worth it" as there was little equity in the house and it didn't appear that he had received a sudden windfall from his wife's insurance. My lawyer also said that the house was jointly registered with his daughter. I was hoping

Chapter 6 – Releasing the Old

that it might have been a yes, as that would have offered me some financial relief as I was feeling a lot of pressure and hopelessness at this time. With my entire world falling down around me, I still managed to remain optimistic on the Wellness Centre (in denial) and registered the trade name "The Heart Centre."

1997 Oct 27 - I don't know what's up or down anymore, why, who, what or where, it seems hopeless and it doesn't seem to be getting any better or smaller, but rather larger, more complicated with no end or relief in sight. I'm running out of energy and I'm even thinking what's the use, why keep on trying to clear all this stuff? What's the point? I feel that the biggest issue and restriction in my life is money, having money to do what I want, when I want. I feel our present lives are all tied around money, exchanging time and energy for money as physical existence requires money for food, shelter and clothing. Control and plan, that's why I have a big control issue as I have to plan everything because I just can't trust and allow it to happen. I was thinking of myself as that seven-year-old boy and the anger, rage, fear, heartbreak, neglect and abuse he was feeling. So what does all this have to do with denial, friendships, partnerships and business? I don't know.

No one was really a friend to me and I can't trust anyone. I have to behave in a certain way to get any form of acceptance. Not even my parents showed any real love toward each other or to their children. There was some sympathy at times from my mother, but my father was the "stand up for yourself, fight back, fight your own battles, be tough, be strong, learn to be a man" type of a man's man. I feel beaten, neglected and rejected, that no one really reached out for me, not even my parents. When I was eleven or twelve, I had a dog that I felt close to but she was run over by a car and died. I was to get another dog but she was also run over before I even got her. I just flashed to the two cats I had, they're also gone even though I wasn't too attached to them.

Humm? I noticed the word attached. I didn't understand the language when I started school, so how could I read and get with the program. I just thought of the dream that Jen had where she saw Spirit talking to the Will and giving it lectures and information, but never teaching it to read for itself, so that Spirit was always knowing and in control. But what does that have to do with being attached? I don't know.

1997 Oct 27 - I was feeling a lot of pent-up anger and rage building up in me, so much so that I felt like I was going to explode. Jen had also been feeling my denied anger and rage and as it was near Halloween, she suggested that I release it by going out and buying a big pumpkin and smashing it. I thought her crazy for suggesting that, but I also trusted her guidance. I went to the local market and picked up one of the bigger pumpkins that was about 18 inches (45 cm) high and maybe 20 inches (50 cm) wide.

I took the pumpkin home and set it in the middle of the vegetable garden that I had at the back of my old school house property. I went to the shed, picked up my hardwood baseball bat and returned to the garden, resting the tip of the bat on the upright pumpkin. As I stood there, I was thinking that this is silly and stupid as I don't have any anger. I then remembered what Jen had told me to do, that I was to think of all the times when I was angry but couldn't express it. I flashed back to grade school and how the kids used to pick on me and beat me up right from day one. I flashed to my mother and her unlovingness and my wanting to hit her. I flashed to the teachers and the priests. I flashed to other times of being harassed, threatened and attacked. My Mind began to race and I could feel my denied anger and rage beginning to rise. I kept adding fuel to the fire, remembering the times I wanted to rage but didn't. I picked up the bat and held it poised over my right shoulder, the thoughts and feelings of my denied anger and rage were now flashing through me like lightening. Suddenly, I felt my denied anger and rage ready to lash out and I let it go. I swung the bat with all the force I had within me.

The first strike shattered the pumpkin into a million pieces and buried the bat deep into the garden soil. I couldn't believe it! All that was left of the pumpkin was a piece around the stalk, a little bigger than the size of a coffee cup. The rest had exploded in an orange pulp that encircled me in a fifteen-foot (five meter) radius. The biggest pieces of the entire pumpkin, that I later found, were five pieces of shell about the size of a quarter (2 cm). The pumpkin had just disintegrated. My shoes were covered in orange pumpkin pulp as were the front of my pants and shirt. Directly behind me, it looked like my body was casting a dark shadow on a sea of orange, as it had blocked the explosion of the pumpkin and the ground was bare. I pulled the bat out of the soil, took a deep breath, re-focused and when ready, took another swing at the remaining piece of pumpkin. The second blow shattered the stock and buried the bat even deeper into the ground than on the first strike. That was it! Two strikes and the pumpkin was gone. I was shocked at the power I had unleashed. I also felt lighter and freer, like a huge weight had been lifted off me. I remember crying after the second blow and just standing there in the middle of the garden with the bat still resting in my right hand and the other end buried in the Earth. I didn't cry much but there were tears and a silent feeling of release and relief. I felt better afterwards, but I also had guilt over destroying the pumpkin. I went back to the house, changed my clothes and slept for a few hours.

♡ As I'm typing this into my computer, I now realize why I said what I did when someone was trying to pick a fight with me and would not leave me alone. I'd tell them to stop and that if they touched me, that they

Chapter 6 – Releasing the Old

had better be prepared to die as I was not going to allow them to hurt me. I said that if they did attack me, that meant that they were going to hurt me and even kill me, and that I would not allow that to happen. I said that I was not just going to defend myself or hurt them back, but that I was going to kill them, no if's, and's, but's or maybe's. I meant it and they knew it, and they would back off and call me crazy. Now I know that I was speaking the truth because all my denied rage would have come up and it would have struck them like it did the pumpkin. ♥

 I want to heal or move this thing called denial and guilt out and off of me. I feel denial and guilt are tricky as you don't even know you have them, and even if you admit to having them you don't know what they really are or where, how or why they started. I feel guilt is easier to recognize and deal with as I feel guilt is like a cut or wound, where denial is like blood poison or internal bleeding. It affects everything, whereas guilt is more specific, although it can also be general, but it is usually on the surface, in the moment. I also feel that guilt leads us to our denials, like a cut is the source of the blood poison. I feel that intent to heal is the key to uncovering denials and also in moving out guilt.

 I controlled my emotions to mask my fears of rejection so that I wouldn't do or say the wrong thing and be rejected. I became a great organizer and planner, and I rolled everything into one. I sacrificed myself to family, friends, business and groups just for acceptance, to be liked, and guess what, I was used and abused on the outside just as I used and abused myself on the inside.

 So, do I need to go back to try to fit into a society that I feel I don't belong in? (Fear) Do I need to be in a relationship where I can do those things that society says is the acceptable thing to do? (Fear again) Do I collapse into myself and deny and avoid, or do I become centered and find myself and know who I am, what I am, and be it? I feel that even if I did find myself, that I still can't just be alone, that eventually there has to be interaction and relationships with both other individuals and society. I feel that somehow it has to be, and will be both, but that now it will be done in a new way, not for acceptance or out of fear, but through connection and in love.

 So I'm still not centered, I don't have self-love because I have all this guilt and denial that is being reflected to me from the outside of how I am on the inside. I feel that the outside is almost totally not accepting me on all levels, society, friends and companions. So is that how I'm not accepting myself? At this moment, the only person that has some form of acceptance for me is Jen. We talk about personal issues and friend things, and now we are also talking about starting a business and setting up groups. Hummm? It's like it's all three rolled up in one again. So how do I separate all this and get it into perspective?

1997 Nov 02 - October ended with Jen and Liz having a birthday and Halloween party for me. Liz had invited me over to her place for lunch and later we went over to Jen's. I got dressed up for Halloween as a Roman soldier; Jen as an angel and Liz was a gypsy. We played games, listened to music, and we even started to dance, but when the kids started arriving for trick or treat, that was when I closed down and shortly after that I left. I feel it may have been the kids that triggered me because I've always wished that my birthday was on another day because it always gets mixed up with Halloween, and Halloween is more important than my birthday, even to my family. As long as Jen, Liz and I were inside playing games, Halloween wasn't there even though we were dressed up, it was just about us. Then when the kids started to trick or treat, the focus was off of me and us and onto the kids. I felt abandoned and alone. I still have issues with my seven-year-old essence; he's still fragile and hurting. I have to go to him and love him but how will he trust me in the present as he still feels vulnerable and still gets treated the same way by me.

I also remember that at the Halloween party, I was flipping back and forth between my Inner child and the BIG me. There were times when I was letting my Inner child take over, like a child in a man's body and then I would do a flip to being a man in a child's body. I was not really focusing on Halloween, just the birthday and the games and the presents I got and that was okay. It was about me trying to be me. It was the Halloween trick or treating that took the focus off my Birthday party and my being and playing with my two friends that activated me. Whenever someone would come to the door, Jen would get excited and drop whatever she was doing and rush to answer it. Then she'd come back and describe what the costumes were like. That excitement focused on the outside and I felt it took away from our fun and slowly and quietly I withdrew. I also have denied anger at Jen for putting strange, unknown kids ahead of me when celebrating my birthday.

I didn't know all this when I left the party as it has taken me until now to get this hindsight. I also don't trust Jen, as earlier she had said to me, "This is your day, your special day and we're going to celebrate your birthday and you know what, it's also Halloween so we're going to get dressed up." The ironic thing in all this is that it was my idea for the shell out treats. I bought the candy as I thought it would be good for Jen to meet the kids as she had been avoiding that in the past few years, and so I have myself to blame for my experience. (Guilt)

1997 Nov. 3 - I asked myself, why am I Angry?
People piss me off.

Chapter 6 – Releasing the Old

I piss me off.
Everything pisses me off.
I'm tired of the struggle.
I'm tired of being wrong.
I'm tired of not knowing where I'm going.
What I think is right, isn't.
I don't care, what's the use?
I need a drink!

1997 Nov 4 - This morning I received a phone call from Ken who was interested in the business. This time I knew the person, or rather I had met him once before through one of my employees in Systems 80. He and his father came up in the afternoon to have a look at the business and I showed them the basic operation. They said they were interested and I gave them a copy of the financial statements, and a list of the assets and inventory for them to go over and to get back to me. Later that same day, my Realtor called and said that she had a showing for the property on Thursday. I was beginning to get optimistic again as I felt things might finally begin to move.

1997 Nov 11 - I drove up to see Jen and we went to look at a couple of places that might be suitable for the Centre but neither of them felt right. A few weeks earlier Jen had put my name in for a luggage draw at a local grocery store where she did her shopping. While I was visiting Jen, she got the call saying that I had won the luggage. We went and picked it up, it was a big black luggage bag, the kind with the pull out handle and wheels. I guess that means that I'm going to be moving.

1997 Nov. 14 - Ken had called a few days earlier with an offer and another meeting was scheduled for today to negotiate the sale price for the business. I had originally just taken the book value of the business based on last year's financial statements and then factored in any additional inventory purchases, less cost of sales to date. I also made a list of outstanding accounts receivable and payable and I didn't put in anything into the deal for good will. I guess what I'm trying to say here is that it was a good deal, but he offered me half of what I was asking. Although I was anxious to sell, I tried to bump it up to a get a compromise between the two figures but he was pretty firm as to what he wanted to pay as his father was also backing him. I did manage to get him to come up a few thousand with revised terms and left it at that. The following day he called and agreed to the revised terms, and the business was technically sold, with the takeover scheduled for Nov. 30.

Carol, my Realtor, also called and said some new people were interested and that they were coming to have a look at the property on Nov. 16.

Experiences and Growth

1997 Nov. 16 - We understand your desire to help, to assist one called Jen, but it is for her and your experience that she has chosen this manner of growth, of release, as it is with you and your self-love issues. You are mirrors for each other and in most cases you also reflect the opposite polarity, experience and expression, and this is so that you can experience both, by self and with others. As you link now in consciousness to expand the feelings, the remembrances of the emotions that lie dormant but unable to sprout until the appropriate time.

The delays as you call them are important, for it is not the mental understanding that is acquired but that too is an equal part, but it is the feelings that must be touched now in order to have true understanding. So as you each walk through your experiences and share with each other, you feel, you understand and move on. That is not to say that in this lifetime you must experience every situation and emotion you ever felt again. You need only feel the ones that are significant to your development, healing and task in this life time to fulfill your mission, and to do that you need the experience, been there done that, felt that.

Spirit and altered Ego bring up the fears and blocks that prevent movement. There is programming in the altered Ego that needs to be transformed to allow the next plane of healing to take place. Spirit has fears, judgments, anger, rage and resentment of being out of control again. Heart also carries denial and judgments that accepts both sides and gives value to that which does not serve the higher purpose out of guilt. Body is fearful that it hasn't yet been given the opportunity to heal as it needs to heal. Will also has fears of movement and acceptance as well as judgments, anger and rage. There are many little nails that hold the big board, the block in place, and each nail has to be removed one at a time so as not to damage that which the block is secured to. This block was not placed there in one circumstance, as all the nails of denial and guilt that hold it in place, secure it, were added one at a time. It can't just be blown off, it must be lovingly removed.

> *What did you learn today? What became clear? - Shenreed*

1997 Nov. 18 - I had written out the manufacturing procedures and formulas for all the different products and I was now in the process of editing it. I was amazed at how much information I had in my head and how many little things I took for granted which were actually key points.

I called my mother today. I've talked to her regularly every three to four weeks and the last time was when she called me on my birthday. I had told her what was going on in my life, and of selling the business and my home. I also talked of my feelings and the experiences I was remembering that I'm sharing in this book. I have guilt coming up saying that I shouldn't

Chapter 6 – Releasing the Old

be sharing this as it has to do with my mother. I had asked her if she could remember anything about why I would have these feelings and also if she remembered anything she could add about the experiences. She denied that anything like that ever happened and said that I'm just saying these things to hurt her. I told her that hurting her is not my intent and that I feel it really doesn't matter who is right or wrong, or even if there is a right or wrong, it's what I felt, and expressing it is what is important to me. I can't prove it happened anymore than she can disprove it, so for now, what is important for me is to allow myself to move my emotions as they come up until the real truth is felt and understood.

During that same conversation with her, I remember how she politely and lovingly told me that she was not responsible for any of my feelings or how I felt, and I fully agreed with her. But then in the very next breath she said that I had no right saying those things about her and hurting her feelings and that I should be ashamed of myself for doing that to my mother. I stopped her there and asked her why there was one rule for her and the opposite rule for me, and why we both didn't come under the same rule? She evaded the question by stating that she also felt that I have come under the evil influences of some "cult." She then told me that I should find and accept Jesus as my savior before it was too late, and that she would pray for my soul. Of course you know what my answer to that was.

I didn't know it at the time I was talking with her, but when I ended my denials, I also released my guilt attachment to my mother that was saying that she was right and that I had to make her happy, after all, it was she that brought me into the world and cared for me. We still talk on the phone but now it's mostly about the weather, or she will tell me how or what the rest of the family is doing or not doing.

1997 Nov. 23 - I was visiting Jen today and she activated me into my school yard bully experiences, and how I was terrified of having to go outside to play, as it was not play to get beaten up.

♡ As I'm entering this into my computer, I'm realizing that that is also part of the reason I have never, in all my life, really allowed myself to play for fear of getting hurt. I can't have fun with other people as it's not fun for me to get beaten up. I never realized that I had put a program in place that says that if I was told to have fun or asked to play, it's best not to do it as it will mean getting hurt. I'm heartbroken in this moment at that realization; I feel that this is also part of what happened at the Halloween party. ♥

At Jens, I was also activated into having to be second best, that I could never be number one, the smartest, quickest, fastest or best at anything because that would upset the bullies and/or their friends as that too would bring me pain.

♡ I'm now feeling how I was shortchanged and also how I shortchanged myself. Again, by putting in place the programs and beliefs that kept me limited, kept me down, kept me from being myself and better than another. I feel that there is a lot more to all this. I'm now feeling the heartbreak of that program and how I have tried to do and be my best, but I didn't know that I had a poison pill inside me that would always prevent me from being the real me, with all my gifts and talents. I guess that's part of the reason why I'm writing this book, as the message was that it would also be a new level of healing for me. I have to take a break here to allow myself to feel all this. ♥

I was also remembering that in high school track and field how I'd slow down and pretend I was getting tired to let another pass so that he would come in first. I guess when I tore the hamstring in my left leg and did a face plant in the running track, was when I no longer had to pretend. I also remember that after school I wasn't allowed to play pick up baseball because I didn't have a ball and bat. I saved my money and got a ball and bat and I remember how I would hit a home run almost every time I got up to bat, even if the pitch was deliberately way off. After that, I wasn't allowed to use my bat; I had to use one of theirs. When that didn't stop me, they said I couldn't play as it wasn't fair to the other team, or that the team I played on had to be short handed. The same non-acceptance for me was also true for football so finally I just gave up trying to play any sports.

> ***You have to feel it to heal it.***
> ***You have to be real to feel. - Shenreed***

1997 Nov. 24 - Although the house had electric baseboard heaters, I was mainly using my airtight wood stove as a source of heat when I was home. When I woke up this morning, the fire was low so I put on the usual dry kindling and some mid-sized pieces of wood on the glowing embers, and went back to bed to wait until it got a little warmer before I got up. I awoke to the sound of a roar, like that of a truck or heavy traffic. I went into the living room and was puzzled to find that the roar was coming from the stove and that the door was ajar about an inch. I guess I was still half-asleep as I must not have latched the door securely after I put the wood in. I shut the stove door and closed the damper, but it was still roaring. That's when I knew I had a chimney fire and I got scared.

My mind was scrambling, trying to figure out what happened. I had cleaned the chimney and replaced the inside stove pipes last spring after I no

Chapter 6 – Releasing the Old

longer needed to have heat. I had only used the stove a few times in the past two months since it has been getting cold, so there shouldn't be any major build up of creosote. I've been cleaning the chimney and the inside pipes three times a year (Dec, Feb and Apr) and felt that they should be okay until the next scheduled cleaning before Christmas. In cleaning the pipes three times a year, I noticed that there was never any major creosote build-up, or so I thought.

I went outside and was horrified to see flames licking up over the chimney cap. There were also some burning embers coming out with the flames that briefly floated skyward, and then spiraled down toward the ground. One thing I noticed was that there wasn't much smoke. I rushed back inside and quickly smothered the fire with ashes from the ash pail that I kept near the stove. I got my two fire extinguishers ready and waited. I felt it was going to be okay as the main chimney was the insulated stainless steel type and the inside pipes were new. The roof was steel clad, so any burning embers would not ignite anything on the roof. After about five minutes I could hear the roar subsiding. I went outside and didn't see any flames coming out of the chimney. When the inside stove pipes had cooled down, I took them off to check and clean them but there was no significant creosote buildup present. I then went outside and checked the main chimney and it looked almost new inside. The fire must have burnt all the creosote off. After that scare I was a little hesitant about startling a new fire and I watched the stove closely for the next few days. One of the thoughts that went through my head while all this was going on was of not only losing the house to fire before I could sell it, but all my possessions as well.

I got a phone call from Ken saying that the end of November was not going to be the closing date for the business as there were some problems getting financing and it looked like Dec. 11 would be the new closing date. That was disappointing news and I went into more self-hatred and heartlessness.

Later that same day I drove up to Jens for a visit. Both of us were activating each other into our issues and we got the following insights. That I couldn't do anything to receive love, and that she would do anything to keep the love she thought she had. I felt I was unloved as a child, that my parents didn't want or love me, and that even my peers hated and abused me. Jen felt her real parents also didn't love her as she had been given up for adoption at birth, but she felt she would do anything to keep her adopted parents and not lose their love.

❝ *An acorn is an oak tree, waiting to become all that it is. - Shenreed*

Journey to the Heart Centre

1997 Dec. 6 - I was at Jens place and she took me into a deep regression where I experienced not only some memories of my childhood, but also my birth and even conception. I experienced and felt how my mother was raped by my father the night I was conceived. How she didn't love my father even though they were married, it was a marriage of convenience. I felt how she had tried to abort me several times and finally had to allow me to be born. Later, I experienced how she neglected and abused me by putting me outside in the cold porch in the wintertime for hours at a time, hoping I would get sick and die. She also tried to kill me several times by letting me roll off the change table, and even to the point of trying to drown me in my bath.

The bath experience was terrifying for me as I remember being forced under water with her hand on my chest and pushing the air out of me. When I finally let go of my breath, she held me there a while longer before releasing her hand. She sat back on a chair and held her head in her hands. I bobbed to the surface and began to cough, whereupon she screamed, jumped up and pushed me under again. This time she held me under longer and I remember finally leaving my body and saying, "Thank God it's over, that I don't have to be in that loveless place anymore." I remember floating above it all and seeing my limp and lifeless body in the bath, and my mother sitting back on the chair with a cold sense of relief and numbness about her. I can remember being told that I had to go back. That was utterly terrifying for me; I didn't want to go back. I remember screaming that I didn't want to go back to this loveless world.

♡ I'm emotional again, my eyes are full of tears and I can hardly see the typing keys. ♥

I remember feeling that I was floating in the air and then the feeling changed to one of being pulled or drawn back to my body. As I re-entered my body I gave a sharp gasp and cough but I didn't cry. I feared that if I cried she would try to do it again. She screamed in terror and disbelief when I returned but she didn't try to drown me again. I remember just lying motionless in the water for what seemed like an eternity. The water was getting colder and the room was growing darker as night was falling. She just continued sitting in her chair, silently rocking her body back and forth.

I came out of my regression and I didn't feel good. I got up to go to the bathroom but turned instead to go down the hallway towards the kitchen where I ended up collapsing on the kitchen floor. I felt nauseous and exhausted as I curled up in a fetal position. I felt like I had to and was about to give birth to all this unlovingness that I had been holding inside me all these years. I lay on the kitchen floor moaning and crying, and from deep inside me, I felt that I was about to give birth, and I began to push. The pain was intense and I felt like my legs were being ripped apart and so were my

Chapter 6 – Releasing the Old

insides. I was laying on the floor in a fetal position on my left side, and pushing my legs straight away from me. Then I would curl up again with my legs in a tucked position until the next release. When I felt it was out of me, I pushed myself away from what had been birthed from me. I lay there, curled up on my side in a cold sweat, shaking, trembling and sobbing as Jen came to comfort me, resting her hand on my left hand that was holding my right shoulder. I don't remember how long I lay on the floor but when I felt able to move, I left her place and drove home. When I got home, I went straight to bed. I slept for a few hours as I was totally exhausted.

Rita called later that evening, saying that she hadn't talked to anyone in the past four months. She said that she had asked to be free and to be rid of her unwanted emotions. I felt that it wasn't the same Rita I knew and remembered, as she felt cold strange and distant, yet trying to pretend she couldn't be happier. We had a short conversation and I don't think I told her what I had gone through that afternoon.

> ❝ ***Don't do it right, just do it. - Shenreed***

1997 Dec. 11 - I drove to Barrie and we closed the deal on the business. Ken said that he would be up on the weekend to start to remove the machinery, equipment, fixtures, stock and inventory. We had agreed to a ten-percent hold back to ensure that basically I would be there to assist in training him for a two-week period beginning in the New Year. I never did get the post-dated holdback cheque and I didn't ask for it when I thought about it, and then later I forgot, as I got wrapped up in signing the papers and was just happy to sell the business. When I left, I took the certified cheque to the bank and deposited it. As I did, I felt a sense of sadness followed by a sense of relief and freedom. I took a deep breath and thought to myself, "Now the house is next."

Limitations and Expectations

1997 Dec. 11 - For Heart to be born in the gap one must find love within, for oneself, for when one denies love of self, your body cries out for love of cancer. Once your body has cancer you give yourself love and you let others give you love and attention for a little while until your self-loathing turns to bitterness and resentment, and you see that even cancer cannot give you the love you desire. It has been a cruel friend, not friend, but one that has tricked you to give you more pain and loss of life. If you find not love, the love you desire must come from within first and then you will attract love like a magnet. You have choice, you have chance, one last chance to give yourself what you desire, for by your lack of self-love it eats away at self, eats away at you in bitterness.

Journey to the Heart Centre

Become the child, not child like, but with the truth, openness, honesty, spontaneity, and the love of a child to explore; to do as it desires without fear or expectation. It is only when so-called loving parents show the child what is termed learning (learning their beliefs, patterns and programs) that a child learns what expectation is. For now what was of love, of joy, of lack of expectation, does a child become frustrated with self and self-loving turns to self-loathing as he now receives less joy if he cannot do the tasks his parents give him. For indeed limitation is what expectation is.

It is the simple tasks like that of building blocks where he may discover by himself the joy of placing one block upon another and in seeing them fall in beautiful array and pattern to the floor. Meanwhile the parents coax and prompt the child to build the blocks even higher and they even hold them to prevent them from tumbling down to see how high they can be built. Then once they have gone so far, they tumble to the ground and there is great sadness at its demise, at its falling, and once more the parents seek to show the child their expectation, of let's build it higher, better, faster, and so that it won't fall. How foolish this expectation! Does the parent think it can build the blocks one upon the other indefinitely, which is also okay if it is done without expectation. But where is the spontaneity, the joy of the blocks falling. If one sees only joy in half of what one does, does he not diminish his joy, his life in half? To have a full life one must see love and joy in all and release the expectation, the limitation you place upon yourself.

Take a risk, release your fears and expect the unexpected, and life will become the joy and love you seek. Be as a child, become the child, express your emotions without expectation, is it acceptable or not. Your emotions are your feelings and therefore you must express them without expectation of how someone else is going to feel about their emotions. If you see the blocks tumbling down and you feel joy and happiness, then so be it. Allow yourself to express joy and not the disappointment, failure and loss of someone else's feelings and expectations, and their limitation. Become a child again, grow young and grow healthy, don't try to grow up like the blocks with expectation, accept things for what they are and enjoy them for what they are. All that you do, say and think has some form of expectation, limitation, and condition upon it; it is time to remove these now. Merlin

> ❝ *Expectation is Limitation. - Shenreed*

I spent the next week clearing up loose ends with the business, writing and depositing cheques, as part of the sale agreement was that neither accounts payable or receivable were to be a part of the sale. I also went through the files removing any personal stuff from the business records. Carol, my realtor, called and said that she felt that the last person who viewed the property was going to put in an offer, but that she didn't know when.

Chapter 6 – Releasing the Old

Surrendering the Ego

1997 Dec. 15 - Surrendering the Ego is not the death of the self in service to others, but the death of the beliefs, programs and imprints that which the altered Ego clings to, that believes that service, love and compassion is the sacrifice of the self, (true Ego) for and in service to others. For true Ego is who you are, your individuality, your uniqueness, your differentiation, that which separates you from another, not in a better, or higher or lower way, but rather different states of awareness of consciousness. Love is not denial of self in favor of others for that is self-hatred and leads to death.

Turmoil and Struggle

1997 Dec. 17 - Perhaps you enjoy the turmoil, the struggle and the conflict, do you? Then why do you seek it? You do not seek it outwardly but it manifests outwardly for you still have it inwardly. You are unresolved, unsure, not certain, afraid of change and afraid to begin again for what your beginnings and creativity have brought you in the past. These are old beliefs and imprints that need to be recognized and resolved before any advancement, forward movement can be made manifest. Your fear stems from lack of trust, for the abuse and conflict that you received when you trusted others and they appeared to take advantage of you. You are so full of imprints, that as you know, you draw this to you, as we do not like to say part of your lesson, but rather experience. To experience fully the feelings of the Will, of lost Will and denied Will that needs to be healed now, is healing.

Recognize that although to operate in this third density, you would need to follow certain society guidelines in order to effectively communicate and interact with humankind, but you are no longer bound by their beliefs based on fear and conditional love. You can take what you know from this physical experience and now apply your new beliefs to its implementation and trust in the flow that you are now following your higher purpose, as well as with those that have been attracted to you in the same endeavor.

Others will come, or try to come, to become part of your work that are not suited. These vampires which you experience will attempt to intimidate you and those with you, but as you become stronger in Love and Light, your life forces will not be sucked from you and neither will your work and its efforts. The brighter and lighter you become, the less and less attached to you will these Beings be, for they recognize they have lost and are no match for you.

Indeed you have concerns regarding this enterprise but these are founded in fear not love. Begin. You have sufficient funds to begin, not large but small, plant the seed, nurture it, care for it, love it and watch it grow. It can do nothing else but flourish, so relax and allow the process and begin to practice what you teach and watch the magic unfold beyond your wildest dreams.

There is much you will "be"ing and doing. This duo and triad and others will also be involved as you grow and expand. These will come to you and you will know if they are the right ones or not. Trust your feelings, forget all the mental "feelings," not forget, but do not confuse all the old mental thought feelings based on old programs and beliefs that the conscious mind brings up to rationalize and seek appropriate action to a particular circumstance. When feelings come up it is important to go into them to see where they are coming from, and to move what has to move to transform them. Mental thoughts disguised as feelings are not true feelings and you need to feel the difference in energy. It is all confusing and overwhelming as you begin your true journey, but rest assured that as you begin a step at a time, you will be assisted and in no time you will not only be running but soaring. Blessings, Adornia

> *Take a risk, release your fears, expect the unexpected. - Shenreed*

What is Your Intent?

1997 Dec. 18 - What is your intent is the key question that will diffuse all those who are vampires that seek your energy, your life force. What is your intent? Is it to serve your highest purpose and good, true Love, Light and the pursuance of Life? For by their answer they will go into denial of their true intent, and when they go into denial they have given their power away. They may seek to challenge you with speaking what you want to hear, but know also that this is a denial of their true feelings for it is not their true intent, and thus they also give their power up over you, to control you, for they know where the true power lies and all their denials, fears, guilt and hatred lie impotent to truth.

By truth, I do not mean the mental truth, the words that give illusions a fabrication, a manifestation of feelings. The feelings, the emotions are the truth of which I speak. These emotions are Heartfelt and do not need words to express for they are felt. Concern yourself not with what you think you should be doing for this is guilt, but also do not dismiss it for it has something to show you that you are not noticing within yourself. You are still beating yourself up, so to speak, with lack of self-love. This is not an overnight task and will need to be developed layer by layer, in reverse of how self–hatred was created. You are in transition and you have much to move out before new can move in and create the excitement and passion of Life that you desire. Be gentle with yourself.

Chapter 6 – Releasing the Old

1997 Dec. 22 - Carol called saying an offer was in. I drove down to Barrie and I signed back a counter offer and waited as she faxed it to the vendor. Minutes later the fax came back, offer accepted, done deal, the property was sold and I had until the end of February to move out.

I had been waiting for a break in the weather to get more firewood and the next day was nice so I decided to pick up an additional chord and a half to last me the winter. I had a quiet Christmas at home and made myself a chicken stir-fry for supper.

Most of the business had been moved out by the end of the month. I helped a bit but I had other things to do too. It felt weird seeing the twelve hundred square foot shop empty and also knowing that soon, the house would be empty too. Thus the year came to a close. A lot of things had happened and changed on many levels and a lot of changes were also to come.

> *He who looks outward dreams,*
> *he who looks inward awakens. - Shenreed*

Chapter 7 - 1998 - Transitions

1998 started off slow, I was sick for three days so I just took it easy. Later in the week I went up to see Jen and we did a ceremony to the start of The Heart Centre. We also went through some catalogues we had ordered and began making a list of things we would like for the Wellness Centre.

I called Ken to see when he wanted me to help train him and also asked about the promissory note that he was to give me for the balance owing. He said that he wasn't organized yet and that he'd call me when he was ready. A few days later I got a call and drove down and spent the day going over packaging procedures and some points he was not sure on with manufacturing. As I was about to leave, I asked about the promissory note and he said that he would have a post-dated cheque for me when I came back down the next week. I returned home and continued to compile what I needed for my accountant, as I had sold the assets and the trade name of the business but not the limited corporation.

The Coming Changes

1998 Jan. 08 - You think you are not worthy, that this is not real but know, believe and feel as you begin to heal and you will know that what is given here is true. Yes, it is about to happen. Your Heart Centre is about to open as it never has before, and when it does it will experience life as it never has before, experience love as it never has before. So in this moment of transition be at peace as best you can, feel as best you can and continue to be open as best you can. You cannot fail but you do not know that yet. You cannot fail to heal but you still have fear that it is untrue, won't last or that there's a hidden factor, a hidden agenda. Some have hidden agendas and they will meet these agendas with whatever action is appropriate to experience them but not necessarily in the way they planned or expected them to happen. For it is now time to move unloving light and its agenda to kill, or if not kill, to control the Will, out to where it is no longer able to do so to any part of lost Will that desires to be free of the oppression it has endured.

Fragments that have, or continue to deny their Will, their lost Will, will be aware of the consequences of their choices and any Will that chooses life will move toward true love and light. Unloving light shall hold all the desires to kill the Will, but shall have no Will to kill or control except that which is in itself, and will do so until it too can experience what the Will has had to endure at the hands of unloving light in order to know what life is. Fear not; know that when the heart center is healed, that the heart center is

Chapter 7 – 1998 Transitions

safe, that true love and light will shine from it like a beacon unto others that also seek love, true light and life.

It is those on the edges with hidden agendas, with unloving intent, that will be left to feel what you have always felt and they never seemed to feel. They will now feel as you have felt in all this time through creation, and they will be powerless to stop you as you seemed powerless to stop them, but with a difference. You are moving toward loving light, love and life, away from the illusion that you hung unto that you thought was love. All those that cling to this old illusion, belief, cling to unloving light. You will not harm them, hunt them down, or trample them like they did you all this time, but it will seem just as foreign, fearful and just as hopeless to them as they begin to lose their power over you, over all those that move toward the heart, of reclaiming the life and love they have always searched for. You will not act in rage and anger against them but rather with love and compassion, which to them will feel as hurting as unloving light did to you.

The world is about to be turned upside down and inside out. But as a kaleidoscope is moved, so it changes and continues to change in all its glorious and unlimited possibilities at whatever speed it needs to take. Yes my children, it is now soon time to fly your true colors and to wear your badges of the Heart Centre and to shine your light and shine your love. Your Father and I are full of emotions of love for all you have endured, have gone through, have trusted, have had faith and hope, even if it seemed hopeless. You have not, not to say faltered, for you have all faltered, but you have not strayed from your intent, your path to heal. And healing you are in leaps and bounds as you would call it, although sometimes it feels to you like you are going backwards, it is not so. You are becoming brighter and lighter every day that passes. Soon, you will have more understanding, more power, strength and a different view as you move to the next stage, level and you begin to accelerate and put into practice all that you have felt, healed and now understand. Life is about to begin. Blessings, Mother and Father

1998 Jan. 12 - I drove to Baum Beach to look at a basement apartment that was within a block of the Georgian Bay and a beautiful sandy beach, and about ten minutes from Midland. I drove out to see the place and was greeted at the door by Eric, who invited me in and then excused himself momentarily to finish his conversation with his three year old daughter who was arguing with him as to what she was going to watch on TV. As I entered the hallway, she turned and glared at me, and with a low growling voice that seemed to come and vibrate from the depths of hell, she uttered, "And what are you doing here?" Eric looked at her and at me in disbelief of the words and the feeling tone of the words that were coming out of the twisted mouth of this otherwise angelic looking child with cold dark glaring eyes.

Journey to the Heart Centre

As Eric was talking to her I noticed that they were devout Catholics as their house was decorated with Crucifixes, reeds and other religious plaques and pictures, and there was a rosary laying on a side table. I heard Eric giving her an ultimatum. I looked over and saw her turn, sit down and watch TV with a huff.

Eric left her and showed me the apartment. It had two bedrooms, a bathroom, and a small galley kitchen with a fridge, stove and microwave, and a small table and two chairs. The bedrooms each had beds and a dresser, but there was no living room furniture. It had its own entrance from the back of the house that had a small patio and faced a wooded ravine, which was a nice feature. The big selling point for me was that it was clean. Even though I liked it, I told Eric that I'd call him later as I had one more apartment to check out. As I was leaving, we both noticed that she was still glaring at me.

I went to see the other apartment but I didn't like it, actually, I'd be in denial here if I didn't speak the truth and that is that of the 18 – 20 vacant apartments, including apartment buildings that I looked at, none were what I would call clean. I would not even feel comfortable visiting someone in those apartments, let alone live there. I called Eric later and told him that I'd take the apartment and that I'd drop by in a couple of days with a deposit.

When I dropped off the deposit, Eric again greeted me with his daughter by his side. His blue-eyed daughter was a totally different child and was excited to see me. She took me by the hand and wanted to show me her room and all the things that she had made and was doing. Eric looked at me in disbelief and I smiled and asked if it was okay to see what she was going to show me. He said it was all right. When I left, she said that she was happy that I was going to be staying with them in their house. Again, Eric looked perplexed at the totally different attitude his daughter now had toward me.

1998 Jan. 20 - Jen and I went over some book catalogs, made a list, and placed our first order for The Heart Centre. One of the fears I have is that I will have to carry the Centre on my own, the actual physical aspects of it, as I don't know how much, what, or when, Jen will be able to help. I know Liz said she'd be there to help me but she'll only be there part of the week, and then only in the store. I feel that the books, jewelry, crystals, clothes, and gifts will not be enough to carry the Centre by itself. I feel that the classes, workshops, and one-on-one sessions will also be needed to provide the necessary income. I also know that it will be up to me to get it all up and running until Jen is well enough and confident to also be a part of it. I'm not too confident of all this either, partly because it is new, and also because of what happened in the past with the classes that Rita and I started with Visions. I'm afraid of failing again. I think of the Visions group and then of the group I tried to start in Moonstone that didn't go anywhere either. I'm afraid I won't be able to get the groups and workshops going. Somewhere

Chapter 7 – 1998 Transitions

along the way I've lost my drive, my enthusiasm, my passion. It's like I've given up, I don't want to struggle and I don't want to do it all over again on my own, yet at the same time, I feel there is a need to build this Centre.

I have judgments against Jen as she has never really worked in her life. She never has had to worry about having to work for a living, having to look for and keep a job, support anyone, not even herself. She wants the freedom to come and go as she pleases at the Heart Centre and that leaves me to be the main stay of having to be there in the store, at the counter, waiting on people. I don't have the freedom she does. I know Liz says she's going to be there but I don't know how much I can really count on her until the time comes. I feel that I've been tied down to support myself and others for too long and I don't want to do that again. I don't even feel like I can support myself anymore.

> **Letting Love in with Life, Letting Life in with Love. – Shenreed**

1998 Jan. 23 - Life is getting complicated. I had called Ken a couple of times since I helped him the first time, to see when he wanted me down to show him more of the manufacturing techniques. The last time I called him he said that he still wasn't ready. Later I got a call from him stating that he wasn't going to be giving me the promissory note as there was a discrepancy in the finished goods inventory. He stated that the inventory was short by an amount that exceeded the promissory note. That was a crock of bullshit as he had counted the inventory before he agreed to the purchase and what I said was there, was. He also did another check on the day before he started to pick it up and everything was okay. When we were finalizing the deal, I stated that I wasn't going to be making any major purchases if I wasn't going to be reimbursed for them, as he didn't want to take over accounts receivables and payables. He said that was okay and I had also given him copies of all sales and purchases between that time and the actual closing date. When the calculations were made, the purchases I made and added to inventory were actually higher than the cost of goods of the sales that were made. At this point, I told him that if he wasn't prepared to give me the promissory note which was to ensure that I would train him and offer technical support, then I wasn't going to help him. I told him, "No note, no work," and that I'd take him to court if he reneged on the deal.

Later that day, I drove out to speak with Audrey Ann, who had locally established herself teaching courses in colour therapy and Reiki. She is a friend of Jen's that I had called earlier to arrange a meeting to get any tips and information on starting a New Age business. While I was there, she showed me some Mandalas that a friend of hers, Kim had made. I was impressed with them and felt there was also a potential of having some of her work for sale in the Centre.

Journey to the Heart Centre

1998 Jan. 24 - I can't keep giving the other person the benefit of the doubt, that their words, thoughts and actions are better or more correct than mine. I feel trapped as I feel that when I give my word, I have to honor my agreement no matter what, and even if the other person chooses not to honor their words or agreement, I feel I'm still obliged to honor mine to prove that I am a good and honest person. Well, I no longer accept that belief into my life for it also allows others to have control over me and makes me kill my Will and myself with self-sacrifice. This self-sacrifice is going to end.

I choose to move all unloving light that demands self-sacrifice, self-hatred and denial, outside of me, and to fill that space with true love and light. In the future, when I'm dealing with others, I will feel if their words and thoughts are coming from their heart, and if mine are also. If I feel that they are not for my highest purpose and good, I shall state so and move them outside of myself to their right place. I will no longer try to love unloving light. I have acceptance for it and I want to recognize it externally and internally when it pops up, and to have conscious awareness of it each time I feel it. I now choose to move it out and off of me and ask that it be moved to its right place, and that love and light fill its place. I want life, not death.

1998 Jan. 28 - I drove down to the Toronto Gift Show to see about new products that we might carry as part of the Centre. Jen and I also looked at other possible Centre locations and talked to a couple of Realtors. We also spent some time doing past life journeys that went back to Atlantis where we had lost power and essence. We were also learning how to do native shamanic soul retrieval journeys as that was another thing that interested us. Another thing we touched was on vows and curses. This is a poem that Jen channeled during one of our journeys. (Used with permission)

> " *Choose life, or choose death. - Shenreed*

Vows and Curses
Fire and smoke
   Words that were spoke.
Driving apart
Hearts so true.
Words now be undone
Let life start anew.

Take back your curse
The spell is broken.
Love breaks up
The curse thus spoken.

Chapter 7 – 1998 Transitions

End of denial
Of guilt and shame.
Death be washed away
Like a summer rain.

Words in love
Hold power true.
Power to release
Unloving light in you.

Curse thus spoken,
Curse thus broken.
Let the power of love
move out your light.

To your right place
From this day forth.
No power you have
as an outside force.

To cause your presence
Where not desired.
Where loves intent
Will not be denied.

The Wills power and essence
Will not be denied.
No longer is she
Bond to bondage and hide.

From this day forth
Your power is naught.
From this day forth
Love will be sought.

Where there is love
And pureness of heart.
No power has darkness
To tear Heart apart.

Your curse is broken
By love so true.
Move to your right place

Denials are through.

Try as you might
Your days are numbered.
Your abuse removed
Heart awaken from its slumber.

Seeking life and love
Like never known.
Two hearts now mending
With love have grown.

Seek inner truth
Set light of darkness free.
With light of love
You return to me.

Your path is love
Your intent is clear.
Will set free
Hearts will mend.
Life forever
Without end.

A New Chapter Begins

1998 Feb. 04 - Let Love enter your life. It is a time of chaos, a time of change and old values are falling like autumn leaves, only in July. Not knowing what is happening and fearful of the end, of the changes to occur, and clinging vainly to the past, as if trying to glue the leaves back on the tree in order for them to grow and not fall. Only to discover to your dismay that the leaves are dying, for they are already dead to the illusion they have played. Instead of clinging to the past, let go; welcome the change with an open heart and love. And whatever fears you have, allow them to show you where you still have judgment, lack of acceptance and allow love to enter. Move out denial and guilt and allow Truth to set you free. Free to move into the New World, a world of Love, of Truth, of Peace, of Abundance and Joy. A world, as you have never experienced in all your life times.

For where there is Love there is Life. Where there is no Love there is death. The Old World is so full of no love that death is coming to that world, for no longer will life and death be what you call "life." There will be a separation; Spirit/Soul is eternal and physical existence will no longer be what you call, "You are born and then you die." You were born before you can imagine, and you will live forever, if that is your choice. There is no longer

Chapter 7 – 1998 Transitions

going to be death of the physical for those who choose life. For those that choose death, they will continue to deny their Wills, their Hearts, they shall continue to experience death until they choose life, or until they are so full of death, of lack of essence that they are re-formed, but all in their right place. Spirits living in denial can so choose to live with denial spirits until their denial ceases and they see the Truth and desire Life. Denial spirits will have their place but outside of Will Spirits of Love.

For those who have chosen life, you are the "chosen ones," for you have chosen, not I for you. Continuing to express your Will, your feelings, your emotions, your truth and you shall become freer, lighter and no longer bound by the chains of denial and guilt that unloving light holds you to your cycle of death. Continue to move this unloving light out, for it has deep roots that extend back to before you came to conscious existence and were given form. This is not entirely true but is used for your understanding, for it is beyond your comprehension at this time.

It is no secret what God can do and those who choose life do so on their own faith. There are many paths, but only one destination. Those who choose death also choose their path, away from love, away from light. As you move closer to Light, those that choose death will have less and less effect upon you and your world, for realize, your vibration will be different and you will interact only when confronting your own unloving light. They will also be in contact with you when there is a spark, a desire to feel this thing called Love, when they no longer deny, they will seek the truth. That is not to say that all of a sudden this will occur, no indeed, just as the leaves do not fall from the tree at the same moment, there will be a time, a time of change, of transition, and it is during this transition that you will notice more and more changes as the last leaves begin to fall. There is no need to fret or worry if you choose life. For those that gnash their teeth are those that have chosen death and see it coming and they will want life from those around them. Some that choose life will falter, will give their power and essence to those who would claim it until such time that they take it back, if they do. You must choose, choose love, choose Life. Blessings, Mother and Father

1998 Feb. 5 - I was feeling uneasy and emotional and so Jen decided to guide me into a regression, where I touched a present life experience when I was about six months old. My mother was distraught and my crying was stressing her out. Not having a soother, she put the corner of my blanket into my mouth to stop me from crying. When that didn't work, she used a tea towel which I still managed to pull out of my mouth with my fingers. Finally, she got some cotton batten and stuffed that into my mouth to stop me from crying.

As I was experiencing and feeling the regression memories, I was beginning to gag. I was feeling that I was gulping and sucking these fibers down my throat. I was choking, unable to breathe as my nose was stuffed up with a cold. I remember trying to pull it out of my mouth like I did the blanket and tea towel, but as soon as I pulled, it would just come apart. I can also remember feeling my fingers become entangled in the cotton batten. I was in terror and angry that I had no choice in my life and that I was helpless and powerless to resist. I lost consciousness and was almost dead. I had stopped crying, which is what she wanted, and now I wasn't even moving. She came over to see if I was asleep and noticed the cotton batten in my fingers and mouth. She opened my mouth and began pulling at the cotton batten and as she did, I felt it being pulled out from deep inside me. I began to gag and gasp for air as it was withdrawn from my throat. I lay there in silence. I feel I put a program into place that day that said, don't cry and don't ask for what you want or need as it will only bring you pain and suffering. During the regression, I let myself be carried along with any and all the emotions that were coming up, and also any physical body memories and releases.

After the regression, I remember lying there is silence, salty tears drying on my face. My body and especially my throat were still feeling the sensation of the cotton batten being pulled out. As I lay there, I told Jen that all my life I've had this phobia about cotton batten, and that just the feel of it would creep me out. I remember my mother telling stories later in life, even to my wife and kids, of how she would put cotton batten on things that she didn't want me to touch. I now knew and understood why I had this phobia. Later when I went home, I found some cotton batten in a medicine bottle and I touched and played with it. I even pulled it apart and held it to my face and lips, touching it with my tongue, which is something I had never done. The intense feeling of terror wasn't there, it was still present, but with a much lesser charge.

1998 Feb. 9 - I'm feeling depressed, isolated, defeated with no ambition. It's less than three weeks before I have to be out of the house and I haven't even started packing yet, although I've had the apartment rented since the first of the month. I've also rented a storage unit in Midland where I'm going to store some household items that I might use later in another apartment or in the Centre when we get it.

> ❝ *One Life, many life times. - Shenreed*

Forthrightness and Silence

1998 Feb. 09 - Become bold, speaking your truth with forthrightness will aid and assist you in uncovering the aspects of unloving light that would seek to prevent you from expressing your Will, your feelings. That

Chapter 7 – 1998 Transitions

would prefer to have you either speak your truth in a state of denial, or to refrain from speaking and would rather have you shut down, become blank and void of any and all expression. Identifying when you are not speaking your truth, when you have even the subtlest denial but not expressing it, puts you in the grips of unloving light. True response must be sensed for what it is, and any denial, judgment, or guilt, etc., must be recognized for what it is. Not to choose your words, for this only precipitates the onslaught of denial, of control, that would say the loving and appropriate words. Simply express what you feel and if you recognize it as unloving light, acknowledge it and move it outside of you to its right place. If you find yourself explaining without being asked to explain, it is a good indicator that you are in unloving light and trying to control, to express its point of view.

Shutting down is more difficult at first to recognize, as unloving light already has you in its grip and is able to blank the mind and to almost totally shut down the Will, the feelings, other than those of self-hatred, hopelessness, failure, defeatism, etc. Even if you are aware that you are shut down, it is difficult to move out because what is being reflected to you is your own unloving light that would keep you defensive, fearful, and desire to be left alone to avoid any more pain. Allowing the Will to acknowledge that she is shut down, that she is being held silent, will allow her to free herself of unloving lights grip, but it must also be Spirit that assists here. For Spirit must also stop the denials that hold unloving light that he sends to the Will to allow her to be subdued and buried. As Spirit recognizes and accepts its responsibility for its denials in a forthright manner, so too he becomes loving to himself. In loving himself, he allows the Will to respond, to move to loving light and the grip of unloving light can be broken and moved to its right place. We are not only talking major shut downs here, we are also talking of the small, subtle ones, the pause or hesitation; denial to speak your truth is a shut down and one leads to another and soon it's a major shut down.

The more you are in the moment, speaking and being your truth, the freer and lighter you become. There are times of silence, yes, when nothing is spoken and nothing needs to be spoken in the presence of feeling without words, when there is connection. But also know that silence can also be the killer, creeping in to lay the seed of denial of expression. Not to say that all thought must be expressed, but also be aware of the silent thoughts that are not being expressed and then to understand why it is happening. It is a process to put you into denial, for you are in denial already if the words you are thinking should be said, but aren't. Once in denial, unloving light already has a grip that will give you all sorts of excuses as to why you shouldn't say such and such, or that of control and saying only this but not that. Not only now do you need to become aware of the thoughts and words that you speak, but also you need to become aware of your silence.

But fear not that this is an impossible mission, a task you have chosen, it is simply new, something you have never considered or even had awareness of before and indeed, it is difficult to move from one to another, based on all the old imprints, patterns and beliefs, not to mention ALL the PRACTICE you had doing it the other way, the way of unloving light. This new experience seems to be going against the current of everything around you, but rest assured, when you begin to master yourself and not be subject to unloving light, you will be in awe of how blind you were, and of what an illusion life as you have known it to be, is. Steadfastness and forthrightness are two virtues that will move you to unlimited growth, life and love. Patience and be gentle with yourselves, for you are love Spirits whose denials are ending. Blessings, Adornia

1998 Feb. 10 - I had previously called my lawyer and today I saw him to see what could be done about the promissory note issue. He basically said that it would cost more in legal fees than the note was worth. I never used a lawyer in selling the business as that also was going to be expensive, not only for the lawyer's fees, but it also meant paying for an independent audit. I had drawn up the necessary papers based on the sale of my previous business, and the purchase of the last business that had been handled by my lawyers. I had given him a copy of the sale/purchase agreement and he informed me that I had drawn it up clear and legal, but suggested that if I wanted to pursue it, that small claims court would be the way to go.

I later had the realization that all this was a reflection of my denials, that I had denied asking for the promissory note when concluding the sale, and it was my denial that was now coming back to haunt me.

Being in the Now

1998 Feb. 10 - Indeed you are going through a period of transition, of abandoning the old, all that does not serve you, and you have not yet grasp the full concept and power of the now, as your doubts, fears and old beliefs still hang on. It is a time of mourning the loss, not so much the loss of what you had experienced, but more so how it was tainted and damaged. A more of what could have been, should have been, a more of regret that you couldn't do it over and that things would be different.

Indeed, things may have been different if you would have reacted differently but also you must remember that you acted as you did by the imprints and programs that were, and are within you. You may have changed that circumstance, that experience, but unless you had the awareness of what was going on, of the imprints and programs, even if you had been strong enough to fight the system in your youth without attracting other similar situations. It is of little consequence, of use, to go back and ponder what might have been. It is useful to go back and recognize where, when, why, and

Chapter 7 – 1998 Transitions

to whom or what you lost your power and essence to, and reclaim it in the present moment, for this moment is your true point of power. It is not in the past, or will be in the future, it is NOW. The past and future are only reflections of the present based on simple linear assumptions. You say to yourself, I had this and this experience in the past, I am doing this and this now, I hope to do this and that in the future.

BEING what you are in this moment is what attracts your so-called future. BE the person you want to be in this moment and in the future, as you call it, you will also be that person. This also goes for anything you desire. Live in the moment, be that person, have what that person envisions, desires, seeks; ask and you shall receive, the universe awaits your request. The physical is not an outward manifestation that controls you. You (and we are not talking the physical you) are the creator of your physical reality, your physical body and all that is attracted to it. For consider what you call matter that is composed of molecules, of atoms. What are they but energy, of vibration, of light, and what you term as matter, as solid, is in fact not solid at all and even those atoms that you consider real make up only 1% of what you call physical reality.

So as you vibrate, so you attract, and there is a null point, as in magnets and iron filings, where you are neither one nor the other. You are vibrating from one to another, you are vibrating from your past to your future and it is in this moment that you ARE. Recognize this transition and know that you are not lost, be true to yourself and yes, you will have moments of confusion, of despair, as you let go of all that you have held in your bodies that no longer serve you. Allow yourself to feel this grief, this sorrow, this hopelessness, for you have never truly allowed yourself to feel this in all your lifetimes. It has never been possible before, and you are feeling what has been impossible to feel and so it is new, it is glorious. It is death you are feeling, the death and the unloving light that has been within you all this time and now it is time to move it out. And to move it out, it must be felt, there is no other way, for you cannot mentalize these feelings. You need to allow Spirit and Will to feel, to move out this heartlessness in order to heal, heal the Heart, totally heal with true love and light as life was meant to be.

You are not experiencing anything that Father and Mother haven't experienced in their growth, in their healing (As above so below). It is a wondrous journey this creation and indeed what has been termed as an experiment, as a lost cause because of the Will. The Wills of the Spirits on this Earth now hold the key to the salvation of all creation. What was outcast, forsaken and rejected, now has become its most precious jewel, and Humans, mankind, these Will Spirits in denial are recovering their power, will be in denial no longer and indeed, will become the Wayshowers for the rest of Creation, if Creation is to survive, which it is. The Mothers last refuge was the Earth, along with her Spirits, and also attracted were those Spirits of unloving light that would feed off the Mother and the Will Spirits. There is now right place for everything in creation and the Mother now claims her right place beside and with Me, there is no longer separation. Death will move to its right place and life will be the essence of love, and our light will not be denied. Blessings my Child.

♡ I just got goose bumps as I typed this last paragraph into the computer. ♥

1998 Feb. 11 - I've been busy going through all my stuff, trying to figure out what I need and want and what I'm going to sell. I've also begun taking stuff up to my storage unit and my new apartment. I drop in and see Jen when I can, but we haven't been doing any inner work like we used to.

> ❝ *Telling the truth in a state of denial. - Shenreed*

Power and Essence

1998 Feb. 11 - A word about power and essence. Indeed you have done work on the release of attachments to people, places and things, and you have released agreements, promises, and vows on many levels of higher self. What you have not done and what you are doing now, is what keeps those attachments, vows and promises from never being truly removed and dissolved permanently, and that is because of the actual essence and power that was exchanged during the experience was never recovered.

It is like a vehicle you own and one day you allow another to use it for a short time and there is an agreement for what it is to be used for. They use it and in doing so, form an attachment, a joy, a pleasure, and when it is returned you think the agreement is fulfilled, that the function is completed and that you now have your vehicle returned. But the other may still have an attachment to your vehicle and may have, or have knowledge of the spare key. Although they may never use it, it does not negate the fact that they have it and could use it at any time they desire. Unless you ask for your key back, your power, your essence, you allow yourself to be vulnerable to the power of the other.

This is the part of taking back your power, for there are many aspects, many layers that build one upon the other. Taking back power is not complete without taking back essence. Neither is taking back your power and essence without giving back all the power and essence you have from that person, place, thing or event. This is not meant to confuse you or to despair you, only to explain the multiplicity and the simplicity of who and what you are, and how you truly function within your physical reality as you call it. There are many energies and inter-plays going on behind the façade of

Chapter 7 – 1998 Transitions

physical interaction between individuals, places and things, for it is the energy and the intent behind the energy that is truly at work here, and emotions, the feelings are the key. There is a tug of war going on within you at this time and your thought "feelings" are actually judgments that are the killers that permeates and destroys all positive things and would rob you of your happiness. This is the voice of Lucifer within you, trying to persuade you, to control you, to play and taunt with your true feelings with the mental emotional memories that are not true feelings "now."

True feelings are now, in this moment of your awareness and not a return of something you experienced and which is re-created in the future to experience as a now. These are memories and yes, they can assist you in your awareness but they are not your true "now" feelings and you must recognize them for what they are, judgments, formed when the original experience was denied emotional expression to gain understanding. Healing can take place if you allow the true suppressed emotions held in place by these judgments to surface and be expressed. Often the surface judgments appear to have no direct link to the denied emotions.

Do what you must today, but allow your body to guide you as it needs rest to recover. For you have and are going through much turmoil, much renewal and the energy patterns are shifting in your physical body to reflect the shifts on other levels. Soon your energy, your vitality, will return tenfold and more. This transition is not only spiritual, emotional and mental, but lastly it is also reflected in the physical. Physical changes are occurring and you will notice subtle changes at first, then major.

We leave you now to contemplate your tasks; remember you are always protected and safe. You feel Lucifer is beating you down and indeed he is, but only when you are moving him out and moving him out you are. Soon you will feel less and less of his grip within you, and more and more of his external attempts to try to control or slow you down. But you will always recognize him for who he is immediately, and in so doing and challenging him, not challenge, but acknowledge his presence and intent and in so doing, move him from you to his right place.

His voice is becoming smaller and smaller as is his power over you as you continue to grow in love, light and life. This part of your journey is rough and there will be doubts, self-doubts and fears. As all this unloving light is brought out of you it must be felt and expressed as it was felt and experienced when it entered. As it leaves, continue to reclaim your lost power and essence that was taken from you and return unloving lights power and essence you took inside of you. Exchange and re-claim, and make it your intent that all unloving light moves from you when it surfaces and is recognized as that. And before it can move out to its right place, state that it give up all your power and essence and takes with it all its power and essence that was within you. In this way you are also taking away the key, his future access, that there is complete and total separation, for with the key, contains all agreements and attachments also. This is a process, layer by layer, step by step and not a single event occurrence. Blessings, Adornia

1998 Feb. 13 - I went to Barrie and bought a paper shredder and dropped it off at Jens as she wanted to shred all the letters and cards that she had kept since childhood. It was part of the promises, vows and attachment issues that she and I were going through at the time. I had a large bonfire pit in the back yard where I burned my stuff and also what Jen had shredded. I made up several "indoor garage sale" signs and posted them around the area as I was going to get rid of some of my "stuff" that I no longer used or felt I needed.

1998 Feb. 14 - I drove up to Jens and dropped off a small Valentines present. I didn't stay as we got into one of our arguments that seem to becoming more frequent. I then drove to Liz's place and dropped off her present before grabbing a quick bite to eat and heading back home.

Transformation and the Butterfly

1998 Feb. 14 - Transformation is a time of struggle as one releases the old, sheds the old and begins life anew. It is a difficult time and the newness is what is disconcerting. Seeing the old left behind, that which was you, to become the new you and which you don't know anything about is frightening and disorienting. To be the caterpillar crawling on all legs and then to go into a transformation and emerge a butterfly with fewer and different legs, and now wings, with no more need to crawl slowly upon the Earth, but now to move where and when you please with wings, not yet dry and with no idea of how they are to work. You no longer recognize yourself as who you were, and also no longer know what it is you are to do as that is changing too.

Welcome the change, rejoice your period of discontent for you are moving out of who you thought you were into who you BE. Do not concern yourself with plans and details for most of those are based on the past, the old you. True, there are some beliefs that are still suitable, viable for your new work but these will become clear to you as you move into the new you. Trying to shove the new you into old beliefs and programs and rules is where you find your discomfort. Allow things to unfold as they will, like the butterfly's wings, and when ready you will know what to do with them instead of trying to keep them from growing and developing. Relax, enjoy this transformation as best you can and as each new transformation occurs you will welcome them for what they are and what they bring you.

Focus rather on those things that are brought to your attention either by releasing them, or acknowledging them as a part of the new you, and let go of the control, the hanging on too long to that which no longer serves you.

Chapter 7 – 1998 Transitions

Rather allow yourself to float in your "life" jacket, feeling supported and protected in the waters of the river of life, and explore all that comes into your path for whatever reason, it is there for a reason. Your life is about to change dramatically and you will not recognize who you were, or even what you thought you might become, so relax and enjoy the process as best you can. Blessings.

> **End your denials and begin your Life. - Shenreed**

Read Your Messages

1998 Feb. 15 - It is not meant to scold or berate you but to inform you of the insights that you desire, that you already have the answers for, if you just but read what has been given. Forthright-fullness addresses your dilemma of yesterday and before, of not expressing your feelings and not asking if you are unclear in anyway of the others intent. Clearing the air, so to speak, however harsh you may feel it is to question another's intentions. You go off half-cocked, so to speak, based on what you heard or what you thought you heard, instead of seeking the truth and speaking your truth.

You still place value on the other person's opinion or words ahead of your own, not only ahead, but sometimes instead of your own. You place value on the other person's feelings ahead of your own and instead of your own also. It is time to be who you are. The old programming, imprints and beliefs must end and it can only be accomplished by being forthright and true to yourself, and to seek the truth in communicating one to another. You are not at a point where you know the others intent or desire and they yours telepathically… yet. In the mean time, rely on the old tried and true use of words, spoken and written, and in expressing your feelings.

Lucifer would have you play this game with yourself and with others for it suits his purpose well to undermine, to suppress, to demoralize, to weaken, as this gives him your power. Stop playing his games and take your power back. Allow yourself to move past your old blocks and ask, ASK! ASK? Ask for clarity and state what you feel, only then can you break these chains that would hold you bound, bound to the endless wheel of turmoil, of doubt, of fear, of abandonment, of worthlessness, of misunderstanding and the list goes on. Break one chain and soon you'll break a second, then a third until at last you are free. BE BOLD, BE DECISIVE, BE VICTORIOUS, not over others but over Lucifer. Dare to speak, dare to dream, dare to desire, dare to do. Fear is neutral, it can be an ally to show you where you have blocks, welcome the fear when it appears and with as much caution as you deem necessary, begin to explore this fear. Search it out in detail, feel it and speak it and you will recognize where these fears came from, the beliefs, the programs, the imprints and you will slowly move them out. Fear can lead to terror, to anger, to a host of emotions that need to be felt in order to be healed and cleared.

Yes, Valentine's Day was a special day although it may not have gone as you had planned but it still served as an important experience, awareness and growth, and isn't that the bottom-line? Indeed, beneath all the commotion and the heated words was love, for the words and the feelings also needed to be expressed, released, and what better time than on Valentine's Day when there is a mass conscious awareness of love. So yes, use that energy to tap into the feelings, the beliefs that hold you bound to the old and begin to live anew.

Indeed, it is only a matter of perception and when you release your expectations, your judgments, you recognize that all is in Divine order, in one way or another. Love will find a way to use what it has been given and make the most of it, for that is your intent, to move unloving light out and to move old beliefs, programs and imprints out. Until more is moved out, true Love and Light cannot move in, so yes, you may have been experiencing an unloving feeling but you were ultimately working a loving act in recognizing and releasing unloving light, and your life will be richer for it. Do not allow Lucifer now to beat you up with guilt, shame and regret, for it is his way of trying to get back in, to regain what he has lost. Recognize his pattern. Blessings Child.

1998 Feb. 17 - I'm now moving van and trailer loads to either the storage unit or to the apartment. Sometimes I'd drop in to see Jen when I was in the area, or I'd talk to her on the phone, usually in the evening. I was still writing down my messages but we were not doing much in the way of journeys or healing, so there wasn't much to write about that I felt was important, including my emotions. Ken called and said the cheque regarding the promissory note was in the mail. I was surprised by his change of heart, and said that when I got it I'd give him a call and come down to help him.

Indeed, INDEED, IN-DEED

1998 Feb. 16 - In deed are my works shown, as an example, as a model for others to follow, for those that have known you, you have touched more and deeper than you recognize for they will remember and will be stirred and they will stir others in their awakening, from their slumber. For in both of you, you have different circumstances, acquaintances and did move in different social circles, you on the outside, trying to get in, and she on the inside finally having to get out, and also both in different, as you call it, generations, reflecting again, difference in both experiences. There is no coincidence that within these two generations you cover 80% of those alive today, the older and younger you can also touch. The older, as they know and can feel their death and decay of the physical body and hence seek to save

Chapter 7 – 1998 Transitions

their spiritual body, some not all. And the young, they are not only coming with a new physical body, but also a spiritual purpose, again, some not all. So there are none that seek who you cannot reach by your truth, by living your truth, in thought, word and deed. Not to say that you are to become pious, vain, holier than thou, not so, but to live in love, light and truth and to enjoy your physical bodies, your experiences. By example, is meant to end the denials, hiding from others that which you don't want them to see your vulnerability. Being open and honest, for this opens them also, to assist in letting them set themselves free, free to soar.

It is time to begin to test your flight feathers, to unfurl your wings, to feel the air, to feel the support you can't see but you can feel. Release your grip to the nest, to the Earth, all that you have known to this day. Allow your talons to release and allow your wings to lift you, to give you the freedom to experience your desires, no longer bound to hop and walk around in circles on what you call your space, your home, Earth, as you know it. Now it is time and soon you will feel your true gifts, your true power and you will soar, for soar you will you magnificent being of Light. Soar to new heights and others will look up and see your light, and you will see them and you will show them too that they have wings and that they too can soar. For they will also remember how they saw you hobble around your nest like them, or even more bound to it, and they will know that as you assist them. And now as the next one leaves its nest and begins to fly, others will quickly seek to release their old beliefs, patterns and imprints that hold them down and also desire to soar.

You will help many to take flight but before you can help them, you must learn to do it yourself, by yourself. There is nothing to do but rather be, be ending your denials. Expressing your Will, your feelings, is being in the present, and in being in the present is where your true power is. The more you are able to be in the present, experiencing the now, the freer and lighter you become and the more you lift your wings and trust what you feel, the unseen support that the universe has to offer.

One day you will truly let go, let love, and you will become free, free to live as you never have lived. Be patient, be aware of your thoughts, words, and deeds, recognize your truth, your denials, your fears. Don't be afraid to spread your wings and yes, you will have fear of the unknown as the wind gusts and uplifts you. Do not cling more tightly to your nest, to the Earth, but slowly with intent and loving desire, let go. For the universe will not send a tempest to uplift you unless that is the only way it can, to make you let go, to test your wings and set you on your course, your flight path. The Winds of Change are coming, it is now time for you, the Wayshowers, to begin to leave the nest, the Earth you have clung to, to be able to show others the way, the truth and the light, true loving light and LIFE. Blessings, Mother and Father

Fear of the Unknown

1998 Feb. 17 - As we have said before, consider that of entering a room that you know and have awareness of by your five senses in the dark and you are not afraid. You know where things are and this makes you feel at ease. Now to enter the same room, but are told it is a different room, and now you have fear of the dark, the unknown. If you are told or it is suggested that perhaps something else is also in the room, that certain people you mistrust might also be there, you will have more fears, doubts and all kinds of past programs that will come up to trigger your fear not to have you move into this room.

Now there are also physical stimuli of the five senses that trigger emotional memories, as an example, when you smell laundry detergent it may trigger you to react to the detergent as being negative and harmful and cause of fear, anxiety and panic. Not that the detergent will cause you any harm in the present moment, but because of a past emotionally suppressed harmful experience that occurred and is associated with the smell of the detergent, the mental mind has combined the two and now the smell of detergent acts as a trigger that there is harm. The mind can also replay the same program over and over, and even change it until it eventually associates any strong or distinct smell that it considers as unpleasant, as also being life threatening and brings up fear, anxiety and panic.

Free Will and Denial

1998 Feb. 18 - In truth there is love, there is life, there is freedom, there is free Will. In the acceptance of the Will, of her feelings, does she gain understanding for her feelings and so does Spirit gain the understanding and the value, not value, but the need for feeling feelings, where there is no understanding available to be able to perceive a circumstance. It is the Will, the feeling centre, that is the true receptor or indicator of an experience in the now, as well as what you would term the future. For the Will has the feeling when the first thought or suggestion is advanced before the experience is to happen, is but a moment old, and as the experience unfolds, the Wills feelings are there with insight, with foresight.

As you play out your experience in this space and time, become aware of what feelings are present at the moment the thought of an experience is expressed. The Will, if you listen to it, will already give you her feelings of the outcome, not so much of the experience in detail but of the feelings one may experience. If you take the Wills initial response, then base your linear mind and physical body in such alignment, arrangement as to experience or not to experience that which was conceived as a probable experience. If the Will has a negative feeling, apprehension, and you insist on negating the Wills input by your denial of her feeling or any other feelings she may be able to express before she is entirely shut down, you will discover as,

Chapter 7 – 1998 Transitions

or after, you have the experience and it might take minutes, hours, days or weeks, that you did have the initial feeling that this would not be the experience you thought it would be. You need to experience the awareness of these aspects of your denials to be able to end your denial, your denials of your Will.

Allowing the Will freedom, free Will, even in a situation where the Wills initial response is not favorable to your desired experience. This can change if you alter (words are difficult) that which you initially wanted to experience and have now valued your Wills response and are taking an alternate route or experience, and are now asking Will to feel this decision and to act accordingly so that the desired experience can be experienced with love, light and life. You see, you no longer need to experience what you call lessons, Karma, for that in reality is also an illusion. You have come here with nothing to learn or experience as it applies to your present linear thinking but; and it is a big BUT, you have come to end your denials, guilt, endless judgments, programs and beliefs that have kept you feeling less all this time. You are here to end this illusion and to live life, if you choose life, as the co-creators you are. To live LIFE with love, light and truth, and it is the truth that will set you free of your denials. It is truth that will, shall set your Will free. It is truth that is LOVE and LIGHT, and when all are in harmony, in balance, do you have unconditional love and acceptance, for everything will be in its right place.

When you are truly balanced internally, your world, your outer reflection will also be so. There is polarity in creation and it must be recognized for what it is. There is male/female, up/down, hot/cold, fast/slow, light/dark, love/unlovingness and there is a balance point within each. When does hot become cold, light become dark, there are many degrees of grayness that would confuse the linear mind but it is the feelings that would give you the appropriate input, response that is true to you. What is light to you may be dark to another, but as you share your truths, a new truth may be formed by one or the other, or by both, for the mind will ponder with its Will. Not to say that everything is black or white, but allowing the Will to give its true response and then acting on it, will enable you to find your truth, to find love, light and life.

Denying your Wills responses and acting according to old beliefs and imprints will continue you on your journey of death, the journey you have taken time and time again since original cause. You have come to this life (time) to accept your Wills, to free your Wills and to make this a FREE WILL UNIVERSE, creation. It is time to move death and unloving light to its right place and your Will shall help you identify the truth when you are in an area of grayness. She can feel that which is unloving however subtle. Trust her feelings and promptings, and end your denials and begin your life. Blessings, Adornia

Trust Foundation

1998 Feb. 19 - The foundation upon which life, which love is built, is trust. Not that you are not to go about trusting everyone or everything that wants to have power over you, but rather trust in yourself first, trust your Will, your feelings to be able to tell you what is, or is not appropriate for you, for your highest purpose and good. The Wills feelings will tell you the instant you meet someone, whether he or she is someone to be trusted at that moment. It might be someone you have known all your life, family, friend, or someone new on the street. The Will senses the energy around that person and is also deeply aware of whether it is of loving or unloving light, even before any words are spoken or the person is seen. As you pay attention to your Wills intuition and feelings and bring this perception into your conscious awareness, you will also become aware of the words they are saying and not saying, as well as (if you want to go deeper) to what it is that is troubling them.

Another can also draw you in to get you caught up in their emotions and feel that they are yours, and it is then a matter of awareness of what is yours and what is not yours. Knowing your true feelings will help you to express your feelings and not be trapped in another's positive or negative, loving or not loving. Know that you are being triggered into your own unloving light that tries to shun, berate, quash or silence the feelings you don't want to feel. You may think that you are in a loving light state and in the moment if everything is going as planned and you get caught up in the doing and not the being, until suddenly your world seems to face a crisis reflecting your denials, doubts, and fears that you have pushed aside so that everything could, and seemed to go so well.

Begin with your foundation, if the foundation is strong it will support you no matter what, thrust your Will, your feelings even in the good times. The moment something comes into your awareness that the mental mind dismisses because of it wanting to feel good, is the moment you are no longer in the now. You have allowed unloving light to control you in your desire for the "feel good" times, until you realize that you fell for it again by your denials. It is difficult at first to become aware of the Wills feelings in the moment and to separate them from the mental thoughts and the bodies senses for there is much going on. But allow yourself, whenever you feel the urge, to pause from doing and just be in the moment to feel the Will. It may take a few seconds or even minutes at first to consciously become aware of BEING and your true feelings depending on how caught up you are in the doing. But as you practice, it shall be shorter and shorter time until it is a flash, a moment and there will simply be an overriding signal to connect to your conscious mind. Much like your talking and breathing at the same time as you raise and lower the volume or tone of your voice without conscious awareness as you are linked to your Wills expression.

Chapter 7 – 1998 Transitions

Trust your Will to express your truth. You do not have to trust anyone else unless your Will feels they can be trusted and allow yourself to speak your truth, your feelings and why you feel you can't or don't trust what other people say or do. Even if you don't know why but just "feel" it, trust your feelings and the understanding will come later. Do not negate your feelings, your Will, just because there is no explanation for her feelings. Accept that you have these feelings and trust that they are there for your higher purpose and good. Once you try to mentalize them, to explain, to figure out what the feeling is and why, it is too late and you are caught in your own snare of doubt, of denial of your free Will, caught in the snare of unloving light. Building a trust, RE-BUILDING is a more appropriate word, re-building this trust will allow you to live your life with love, joy, abundance, health and all the things you desire on all levels. Once Will and Spirit are in a trusting relationship, feelings first, explanation later, thoughts and ideas first and feelings later in partnership, not one negating the other but rather with trust and acceptance.

Indeed, you will be entering these words on your computer and on the Internet on a daily basis; it is part of the plan, the process of spreading the word, of opening the Heart Centre. Blessings, Adornia

1998 Feb 18 - I took Jen grocery shopping and then we looked at a couple of places for the Centre. One had great potential but there was very little parking available and no street parking within a couple of blocks. Later that afternoon I spotted a sign on a street for an older house to rent that looked promising; I called and left my number.

Unlovingness and Shadow Feelings

1998 Feb. 20 - There is no one word that would describe unlovingness but probably heartlessness and cold indifference might be the words with the most impact, but it also takes on other forms and definitions. It is a lack of feeling, despise of expression of feelings, of emotion. You can feel the emotion of sadness over the loss of your balloon and you can remember the emotions of the sadness, but the feelings that triggered the emotions is what we are talking about. Indeed you can be triggered by an experience and having a remembrance of past experiences that took place similar to the one in the present moment. Now it is a different moment and the feelings might be similar but are not the same, and this is where your mental remembrances become confused. Indeed, in this moment a thought of such strong shadow feelings of remembrance come in so intensely that you insist and believe that they are real and valid and is what is really happening now. But they are not now, they are a shadow of an experience, judgments of a memory of strong emotions, of feelings that have been denied their expression and acceptance, which have been burned and imprinted into your memory so strong that it is difficult now to separate the two.

Memory is not just stored in what you call your brain, your mind, but it is also stored throughout your body. Every cell stores memory that can be triggered by what you call your five senses, of which you have more of, but are not aware of them yet on the physical, as well as other levels. These memories are most activated by your visual and audio receptors as they have the most input to your awareness, in your communicating with others. So when you recall a story memory, all your body stores that memory and also those memories associated with them and these also enhance the original, even if you are not conscious of it.

We mention this as an example of "skinning your elbow," for buried in your sub-conscious memory throughout your body is the memory of all the times you skinned your elbow. You can now bring back memory of these incidents where you skinned your elbow and also the other times and associated pains and fears by consciously remembering, and also by any one of your senses by triggering those memory cells stored throughout your body. To add more confusion, also in your sub-conscious are all the memories of all the incidents where you witnessed someone else hurting their elbow, this is also in your memory and is part of your beliefs, programs and imprints and judgments.

So you see how complicated and how simple it can be and the key, the secret, is to be in the now. AM I SKINNING MY ELBOW NOW? If not, then what I am feeling is a memory, imprint, a judgment, that I'm afraid I'm going to skin my elbow again and I don't want to feel that pain and all the associated fears it brings up. There is no one to help me, no one who understands how much it hurts, no one cares, and if they help me it also hurts, it's my fault, I'm going to get into trouble and a list of other issues that the memory triggers. These are being pulled up from the sub-conscious level, but trigger it does, and it also adds other emotions and memory fears and judgments to the conscious awareness besides the skinned elbow. You may have also fallen off your bike or were pushed off, and now your issues of trust also come up, see how complicated it becomes when you are out of the present and see what anxiety is placed on yourself by your judgments of the memories.

Allowing your feelings to be expressed in the moment will allow release, not release, but awareness of your shadow memories, fears, and judgments so that they can be moved to their proper place. Denying your Wills true feelings in place of these shadow judgments allows unloving light to play his game with you and would keep you confined physically, mentally, emotionally and spiritually.

Not expressing your thoughts, ideas, fears and desires openly in the moment by not wanting to interrupt, by being patient, self-sacrificing, is part

Chapter 7 – 1998 Transitions

of not being in the now. You were in the present, so to speak, but by not expressing your desires, your thoughts and feelings, so you deny expressing your Wills feelings and your minds confusion. By overriding all these, by adhering to some misguided noble truth or cause that is rooted in the past, you lose your power which is being in the moment. Expression of your ideas with love and truth is not wrong, but you have fear that people will reject your ideas and not value your opinions or your expression of your feelings. So rather than express your fear of rejection and ridicule, you close down and choose not to express, and thereby deny your Will by placing more denial into her which shuts her down. And feeling that there is no acceptance for her expression, she feels rejected. So what you fear then comes to your experience.

Judgments, beliefs, programs and imprints are what put separation between ideas and feelings. It is the linear mind that puts these limits and separates, but they are two sides of the same coin. State your ideas and your feelings simultaneously. Indeed it is a difficult task, for again you are also caught up in the memory and the shadow judgments of your beliefs, programs and imprints and it is difficult to separate what you're feeling in the now moment, and what your memory judgments say you are feeling in the moment that are overriding and suppressing your true Will. As each new feeling or idea comes, freely express it, it doesn't matter if it makes sense or it isn't related with what is going on. You may be discussing a book and you feel like having some popcorn. Expressing and saying, "I've just got the craving for some popcorn, I don't know if I want it now or later, or if it's just an idea that will trigger something else. I don't feel as strong a desire for it now, but I think I'll make some tonight." That's all there is to it but it is also not that simple. You've expressed your idea and your feeling all in the same breath. But had you denied your minds idea of your body's craving for popcorn and your Will from expressing it, then you would have shut them down and also added guilt over not having said anything, or more denial if any other things came to your mind or you felt but that you also denied saying, and so now your Will feels trapped.

It takes conscious INTENT. No, let's turn that around, it takes INTENT to bring it into conscious awareness that will allow the healing to take place and for unloving light to move out. As you break the old habits and programs, beliefs and imprints, all that you have ever known, were taught, and believe to be true, will fall away for the illusions they are. But now it is time to know the real truth, to know and feel true love and to live a real life. It is time to awaken and to awaken others from their slumber. This is not something that can be taught to you as in 1+1 = 2. It is taught but also needs to be felt, to be experienced, then you become the master, when you are in the world but not of it. Not attached to beliefs or things, then you will truly grow and experience life like you've never known. Your journey is beginning. Blessings, Adornia

1998 Feb. 21 - I got a lot of stuff together and had my indoor garage sale in the empty shop. It was a nice day and quite a few people showed up and I got rid of a lot of stuff. After the sale, my next-door neighbors asked me over for supper and that was nice.

♡ As I'm typing this for this book, I realize that I have denied anger at myself as there was this one large man that went around the shop and was making me ridiculously low offers on some good stuff. I thought that was all he was buying, so I denied that I really wanted more and let it go. I remember a three-tier fishing tackle box full of lures and stuff, not counting a couple of good rods and reels. I wanted $25.00 for the works and he offered me $10.00. As it was getting near the end of the day and as I wasn't into fishing anymore, I said okay to the ten bucks. He did the same routine with a few other things and then when he was ready to leave, I totaled up his stuff and it came to $100.00. He then said, "I'll give you $75.00 for the works." Like a dummy, I hesitated, denied, and then agreed.

He proudly waddled out and piled the stuff in and on his car and then asked me how much for the 30 feet of ¾" nylon rope that I had for sale, so that he could tie the sail board to the roof of his car instead of the twine he was using. Angrily, but in a joking manner I said, "Sure, I'll sell you the rope for $25.00." He looked at me and said," I'll give you $5.00." I smiled and said, "Not this time." He glared, huffed, and continued tying the sailboard to the roof of his car with the old binder twine he had. Why the fishing tackle bothered me is because the next time I was in Canadian Tire, I was shocked to see the sticker price of the lures and accessories. Looking back, what I had in tackle, rods and reels was worth over $500.00. Humph! But now I realize that I still have attachment to the fishing tackle, rods and reels that I need to release. ♥

Freeing Yourself

1998 Feb. 21 - Indeed there is a fine line between recognizing your denied Will and adding, or giving your Will more denial. The balance that is needed here is to recognize which is one without ignoring the other by being in the moment, and also allowing the feelings denied Will has endured to this moment to be expressed. Usually the two do not surface at the same moment and if you are aware of what is happening, that you are being triggered to bring up emotions and feelings of the denied Will, you will recognize it as such, but also, your present feelings do also allow denied Will to be expressed. We sense your confusion, one moment please.

Chapter 7 – 1998 Transitions

Expressing your desires and Will in the moment, example. You say that I've never done this in the past, I've always avoided this situation or I have gone home, but this time I'm also going to tell you what I want, what I'm feeling, what my fears are and anything else that comes to my mind. I'm hungry and I feel like eating a banana but I am afraid to ask for food in another person's home so I would feel more comfortable to eat the ones I bought today that I still have in my car. My guilt is now telling me that I'm selfish and should be offering you one and also that I've made a fool of myself and that you'll never talk to me again, that I lose you as a friend. I also feel that I made a big mistake by asking for what I wanted, and definitely an even a bigger one now, by telling you my feelings. Now I really feel stupid like a child and I feel like I did as a child when I was hungry. I would ask for food and was always told to mind your manners, to wait for supper, to wait until you were asked, to wait until you got home and then I knew I would also get scolded later. I feel like running away and never seeing you again.

The other replies, "I have one in the kitchen, if you'd like one." To that you reply, "I feel guilty taking your last banana, what if you want it later. I trust that you would not have offered it to me if you wanted it for yourself. I have to say that this is a big step for me, being honest about what I'm really feeling and wanting, and expressing all my fears, judgments and guilt. Okay, I'll have your banana, thank you."

Now in expressing yourself, in challenging your fears and the judgments you have which are not wanting to ask for food, eating at someone else's home if they aren't eating, taking their last banana, etc. As you bring up all the issues your denied Will has kept, and now by expressing do you release the old beliefs, habits and imprints and free your Will, and move the gap between Spirit and Will.

Or, you do not express your hunger and deny not only your physical body but also your Will in expressing yourself. Denying your Will (in the now) by not asking for food as stated is in a state of denial and this opens the door to unloving light to increase its hold on you. Now you might have feelings (which are actually judgments) like, she never offered me any food, I should go and get myself something to eat at a restaurant, or maybe she doesn't have any or enough food for me and I don't want to embarrass her, and the list goes on and on. Then off you go filling yourself with self-hatred and unloving light. When you are able to move your "now" emotions, not only do you not make room for unloving light, but by expressing your denied Will, do you so move unloving light out that has held it from expressing. Blessings, Adornia

1998 Feb. 22 - My son came up from Toronto to help me move some of my heavier and awkward household items to my two bedroom basement apartment, or to the storage space I had rented. It took a few trips but we did manage to get it done.

Ambivalence

1998 Feb. 22 - Movement is necessary if healing is to take place and on most levels, especially the physical, emotional and mental. The time of passage, of transition, of mourning, of being lost and disoriented will soon come to an end. Ambivalence has been with you in increasing degrees for the past two years, and indeed it was necessary to enable you to let go, let go of the old, that which has only, for the most part, been unloving to you and mediocre. It is now time to stir the embers of passion, of desire, of life, of joy, of abundance and success to achieve what you have already dreamed of achieving and experiencing, of being what you only dared hope was possible, and to achieve the impossible in your linear mind.

Once you have stirred these embers, re-kindled the flame, it will not be long before your fire, your light will be seen by all. People, places and things are being guided into your awareness; recognize them, as they have messages and guidance for you. It may not be directly by them, to their awareness but you will know. Allow yourself to be open, to be honest, to speak your truth from the heart without judgment of others. But rather express how you feel, your feelings in the moment and also allow the child, the child within to play, to entertain itself. It is Spirit, your fire which is to be ignited; it is Heart to be ignited and united. Finish your physical move (ment) it will be the beginning of the end of your ambivalence, not just the on and off spurts that you have had, but now to feel your passion. Blessings, Adornia

Flight of Love

1998 Feb. 24 - Flight, flight of love, soon you will test your wings on the flight of love. Indeed you have concerns, self-doubt, judgments on self, self-worth and a host of other killers of the self. The psychopathic killer who would see you destroyed, but and it's a BIG BUT, not even a but, for there is no doubt, his days are numbered and soon shall be moved to his right place. The but is merely a reference to something that hasn't totally happened yet, but will. Like a flower growing from seed, given all that it needs to sustain life, its outcome is certain it will flourish and bloom, but it hasn't yet.

The universe is preparing, is prepared for the coming events, for the re-birth, the transition of this beloved planet and all upon it who would choose life, to move to the next density, dimension, and experience. Not that the earth will cease to exist but it will cease to exist as you have known it, and by that it will cease to coexist with lovelessness. Lucifer will be moved off Earth and those that would follow him will do so too. Move to their right place until such time that they choose to honor and not deny their Will, however long the monad, the Oversoul, chooses to try to save that part of

Chapter 7 – 1998 Transitions

essence that is so fragmented as to be lost. For nothing is truly lost but will be re-formed, recycled, as you would call it to start anew.

You will meet such fragments and you will know that no light shines in their hearts, even though they will act as if they have that bright light. You will sense the facade and you can deal with these with truth and love. For it is not life they truly seek but death, death disguised as life, as love, as light and some will follow these false profits and it is their choice, even if it be friends or family. This will be hard for some that are, or have been very close to friends and/or family members. Continue to clear yourself, yourselves, as you will be going through adjustments after your sale of your house and business, so prepare yourself accordingly. It will also be different in form, and yes, allow yourself to mourn, to grieve, to let go of all that you believed to be your purpose, your lot and your goal. Not that you will not have such things again but not for the same reason and not obtained in the same method. For things will come to you in love and not fear. Blessings, Adornia

♡ Interesting! I'd like to share a personal moment with you. As I type these words into the computer I am amazed at how the universe has just shown me examples of what I just typed. Last night I was in a spiritual chat room on the Internet. As I logged in and read some of the posts, I got the feeling that all was not love and light in this room. There was a person channeling information and people were invited to ask any questions they wanted. I noticed one person asking if the entity that was being channeled was of light and the highest purpose. Its reply was, "Of course we are light." I smiled and said to myself, "Yep, he's of light but he's not of love."

I posted my question to this person who was channeling and asked the entity if he was of Love and Light and that if he was, to tell me all about love. Well you can guess what happened, this person suddenly complained that I was interrupting, that I was being negative and what I was asking was not appropriate and even commented something to the effect that there was nothing greater than light and that love was not the issue at this time. I continued to speak my truth and to ask (and repeat) direct questions, which were being completely evaded. They did their best to ignore me as did a small group of people who wanted this person to channel answers for them. They became intolerant at my questions and my directness, calling me unloving, rude and a host of other things they probably said about me in their private messages. They, and those that wanted to hear what the entity was telling them, left the room to go to another chat room. I continued to chat with the people that stayed, talking about being forthright and direct. It's not that I haven't called out the dark forces before, but this was the first time I did it on the internet. ♥

1998 Feb. 25 - I went up to my new apartment and began getting things organized. I'm still sleeping at my place in Moonstone as I have a few things to clean up. Tomorrow the deal closes and I'll be picking up my cheque and then sleeping in my new home.

Clarify Your Intent

1998 Feb. 25 - Intent, clarify your intent, what you truly desire and begin to focus your energies, not on all things at once but on one thing at a time, and do not be afraid to ask for help from others. You have judgment that they can and can't help, may or may not help, even before you have asked. Release that belief, that pattern, for it no longer serves you. Also write down, as you have already started, what it is you would like to be-doing personally and then apply it to the Centre and your partner to do the same. Then that will be the centre and not something outside of yourself but rather an extension of yourself, as a tool, to be, to do what it is you desire.

Indeed your Heart and Spirit have been broken as you term it, by your remembrances of all the things you have started and then lost, be it friends, relationships, jobs and businesses. And yes, even with this new direction you have experienced loss of friends and also of what you were trying to achieve. As your partner stated, it wasn't that you failed; it was a period of learning, of developing your skills and strengthening your belief in yourself. But now you take it as the opposite, you have less faith in yourself because you think that you are a failure and Lucifer would play you with this as it is another belief that no longer serves you.

Things that are not coming to you, or you believe are not coming to you, are because of your belief systems and judgments that hang onto the old, so you repeat. It may not be blatantly obvious, it may be very subtle, but it is there and if it is there, it is like a small stone under the castor of a piece of moveable furniture, it is enough to hold it back and it takes a lot of energy to move over it. Sweep the floor, clear out the obstacles and your labors will be easier and your efforts more fruitful. Express yourself, your feelings, your Will. What is it that you feel like being, doing and also do this verbally to self and with others and especially your partner and this will also help her move. Blessings. Adornia

1998 Feb. 26 - I drove to Barrie to see my Realtor and closed the deal on the house. I picked up my cheque and went to the bank and deposited it. During the past two weeks, I had been busy moving my household fixtures up to the apartment as well as moving other stuff into storage. As of today, I'm officially out of the house in Moonstone. I have the house and the shop cleaned up and ready for the new occupant. Tonight I'll be sleeping in the apartment for the first time.

Chapter 8 - Faltering Steps

Levels and Changes

1998 Feb. 26 - Indeed you are in transition to a new level and you may look upon your life as if everything is falling apart, and in certain ways it is. You are raising your vibration and as you do, old beliefs, programs and imprints fall by the wayside in their most obvious form. But you are still left with small versions much like a sieve or many sieves, first the largest is collected and removed and all the rest pass unaffected. Then the next layer, not as dense, as large, and they are collected and removed until finally the particles are smaller and smaller until they are all reduced to their smallest particle, light vibration. The levels may not seem significant or different to you, but rest assured they are. We use this form of explanation for your linear mind only as it asks to understand the process.

The next three days begin the rite of passage and are most significant for it marks the beginning of an entirely new level of awareness, of consciousness. It is like now moving from coarse gravel to sand and its many grades and textures. The new moon and eclipse are significant as the moons energies will be following your growth. You will be noticing that you will be entering lunar cycles of growth similar to what you have been terming years, but it will happen in a lunar month; no, this is not just physical but is also that. Your years will now change to months and your spiritual growth is being accelerated and as it is, so are your mental, emotional and physical bodied affected.

Changes will occur slowly at first and then accelerating, but not to worry, you will only be given what you can handle, and you will be able to handle more and more as you proceed. Do not fear change, change is growth, thrust, let go, go with the flow and you will begin to have fun, joy, abundance, success, and to live life with love and truth. Be spontaneous, creative, ingenious and outrageous, be what you want to be and do what you want to do, what you enjoy. Of course, there is balance in all things you do; we do not want to rain on your parade but balance, is a keyword and will come into play more and more as you grow. Balance, wisdom, compassion and empathy are but a few attributes that include balance but it will be brought to you joyfully, so continue to get your house in order for you are in for a change, a pleasant change and surprise. Blessings, Adornia

Dare to Dream and Be

1998 Feb. 27 - Open yourself to your unlimited potential, dare to dream, to hope that all you desire is possible and is limited only by your imagination. It seems incomprehensible to you at present with your limited mind that your reality is an illusion created by your mind, your consciousness and by the collective consciousness. Open your mind to perceive the unlimited possibilities that already exist, the ones that you would choose to experience, for remember also that unlimited possibilities also include those that you may not care to experience or choose.

Let go of the old beliefs, the limits that have been set upon you and also those that you have set upon yourself, and open yourself to the flow of the universe. Believe and you will receive. Believe and you will achieve. It may not come exactly as you pictured it, and again it might, for once you have set your intent in motion you begin to move, and the universe is then able to bring it to you, for it opens to your openness, your response. Hang on tight to the old and that's what the universe thinks you want and so it allows you to hold on to it. You have free Will, free choice, this is a free Will universe and everyone is free to choose to express as they feel or don't feel. Allow yourself the playfulness, spontaneity, joy, laughter, wonder, and the awe of a child. The child like qualities that you have, and have suppressed and denied in order to survive, grow up, and also to die, to hasten your death by your denials.

Acceptance, not judgment, for true acceptance has no denial or condition in anyway. To accept something that does not feel acceptable is not the acceptance we are talking about, for true acceptance must be loving to self first in all ways. Once you find acceptance in yourself for your feelings, you can find acceptance for others and observe without judgment, for if you have judgment on others; you still have judgment on yourself. Trust, trust your feelings and dare to express them, not deny them, be open, be honest, be vulnerable and you will be loving to self and loving to others. Greet everyday as if it were the first day of the rest of your life, live it to the fullest, to experience what it is you chose to experience. If you want to choose a day of just being in bed all day, so be it, there is no judgment. Simply allow, enjoy, and create the most wondrous day of being in bed, being and doing what you desire.

Begin to have fun and don't take life so seriously. You do not enjoy the things you are doing or have to do, if you are pressured to do them. So do the things that you enjoy, it is as simple as that. Be honest, be open, and deny not. If you are not enjoying something then why do it, why open yourself to denial of your true feelings and to unloving light by your denials. Begin by doing what pleases you. Of course, you also have responsibility not to do one loving thing for yourself in denial of not doing another loving thing for yourself that you do not prefer, and that is part of the balance that is

Chapter 8 – Faltering Steps

necessary to enjoy this density. But balance will not seem confusing or restricting once you open yourself to the flow, as one thing will lead to another and not be in conflict.

Being and doing are not the same thing although they can be when in the moment. Openness, letting go of beliefs, allows you to be who it is you desire to be, and being who you are allows you to do the things being who you are wants to do. Being is first; doing is the result of being, although all this time you have played this game backwards. You have put emphasis on doing such and such and therefore if you can do such and such you must BE such and such. This thinking has to end, it is not loving, it is judgmental and full of denial and disempowering. It is time to take your power back, not by doing or having, but by BEING. When you are the I am, when you are loving yourself, then you can move out and manifest in the outside world all that you desire with love, with truth, balance, harmony, wisdom, responsibility, joy and passion.

Recognizing who you are, your BEING, and uncovering that essence, layer by layer is what will allow you to be who you truly are, will allow you to do what you desire to do. This is not new information as it has been given over and over, but it is one concept that is difficult to grasp to the linear mind. But as you allow your feelings to express you will also become more aware of your Beingness and who you are, and that is different from what you are doing when not in a state of denial of being who you are. We will let you ponder on these words for we feel it is already confusing you but also opening you on certain levels. Enjoy your day. Blessing, Adornia

I've been spending time getting my apartment in order and getting familiar with the surrounding area, especially the beach. I've also been visiting Jen, but I haven't been doing any journeys, she has. We talk about the Centre and what we would like to do with it. I've been finishing up loose ends with the business in collecting the remaining outstanding accounts receivables. Basically all the money I have to work with in opening the Centre, and to live on, is what I made on the sale of the business as Jen has no money to invest in the Centre. That puts a lot of pressure on me as all expenses will be coming out of my pocket and I'm not earning any money at the present moment, just spending it. It wouldn't be that bad if I hadn't decided to sell the business at a loss, as I'd have at least two to three times more money than I have now. The money I made on the sale of the property was basically used to pay off the mortgage, back taxes, realtor fees, as well as paying off the loan I got from Barb's father.

It was during this time I also phoned Barb and made arrangements to pay off the outstanding balance on the loan that her dad had given me. It was an awkward experience even though we had talked about it before as I had called her, telling her I was selling the property and the business. The reason I

Self-Empowerment

1998 Feb. 28 - Self-empowerment, that is what you are doing and that is what you will share with others, taking back and collecting all that has been taken or given, forgotten and lost, and bringing it back. Bringing back their power and essence, assisting them in bringing it back for themselves at whatever level is appropriate for that person at that moment. We are not using time, for it is a linear function as is space, and we are beginning to prepare you for awareness of these so-called realities and how they really function and perform, so that while on the Earth plane you can have experiences within this concept of time. You were aware of times as a child and those instances when you had what you call precognition, to foresee events before they happen. As a child you were open, you had no limit, no expectations and you were open to the power of the universe (in a limited fashion though it were) and you experienced time as it really is on the Earth plane but we are digressing, more on time later.

Empowering self, yourself, and assisting others to do the same in whatever way is appropriate to them is part of your mission here in this moment. As you begin and you have already begun assisting others, but now on a more intense, purpose-full level you will gain confidence. As you also empower yourself more and more, you will also move out into other areas, other fields with love and truth; and searching for and assisting Humankind, the planet and all upon it. You will have a companion, a partner, a family, a home, a community and a sense of oneness that you have never known. You will travel not only to the far reaches of this beautiful planet but also upon others and you will bring your knowledge, your expertise to countless number of beings in this universe. Your journey is just only beginning. You've now got your ticket, so to speak, and it's time to "get on board," get on board Johnnie, get on board and welcome home. Blessings, Adornia

As I finished proof reading the last message I'm moved to tears as it is a dream, a lost dream that I feel is now possible, and that I have a ticket to take me there. ♥

Relationships and Self

1998 Mar. 02 - There is much that can be discussed on relationships for they form the cornerstone of your experiences, your reflection of your inner self. Relationships are difficult to understand unless you understand self first, and are in balance and have self-love from which comes wisdom, compassion and deeper understanding. While caught up in the

Chapter 8 – Faltering Steps

drama of the play, the act, it is often difficult to pause, to reflect on what is truly happening, what you are truly feeling and what is being reflected to you. If both can pause and are open to feel what is really happening, to gain insight and understanding, then growth for both can occur.

It is difficult when only one gains the insight and the other remains caught up in emotional imprints and the re-playing of the same feeling verses true feelings in the moment. The one who is unable to break the pattern will repeat the pattern but not necessarily with the same person, for there is no longer the opportunity for both to learn from the experience. Although this is not necessarily so either, as the particular experience can also change form and both can be working on different imprints and programs that are reflected to each other for experience of true feelings and insights to identify the imprints and programs. The denied Will needs to be healed. The programs and imprints that have so denied the Will that true feelings have been replaced with Will-less-ness by unloving lights programs and imprints, that would rather have you maintain your cycle then have you break free to grow toward love and light. It would prefer, and does everything it can to keep you in the dark, caught up in the cycle of denial, guilt, self-loathing, self-abuse and hopelessness.

When you are triggered, however subtly, stop and seek the imprint or program that denied Will has been fed to re-act the way you do. By identifying the judgments, beliefs or imprints, you are able to heal the gap and move unloving light to its right place. Each time you have conscious awareness of your beliefs etc., the quicker and faster you are able to identify others as they are reflected to you in your relationships and your experiences in the outside world. This is a time of transition, of Soul searching, of gathering yourself together and of becoming one. A time to give your Will the acceptance to express as she feels, and to allow her to be able to find and bring out all the denied Will essence she has lost. In reclaiming lost Will and in acceptance of Wills feelings and expression by Spirit does one also heal the Heart and the Body, that which is manifested also as an outer reality.

The assignment you have chosen is difficult but also offers great rewards and opportunities for growth. You are not alone; soon you will meet others that share in the same task although in different ways. The world is changing as you are, and soon these will be reflected to you. You are in transition between the old and new and soon your heads will poke up over the fog and you will see another head, then another, and soon there will be many. And as the fog lifts it will display a New World, a new life, of love, truth, joy and abundance. Blessings, Adornia

1998 Mar. 4 - I went through my photos and started to shred anything that didn't have me or anyone who was not in my life in the present moment. My ex-wife, daughter and son had already gone through the family albums and pictures and had taken out what they wanted so I was left with the rest. At that time, I felt I needed to let go of everything that had been in my life. I wanted a new life and I felt I needed to let go of the old so that the new could come in. While there were happy moments in some pictures, I could also feel the heartbreak and the denials in them too, and with others I felt nothing. I made a separate bundle of pictures that I had taken of my brothers and sisters, nieces and nephews, and I thought I'd give these pictures to them to do with as they pleased.

1998 Mar. 5 - I had a dream/vision this morning where I saw a man in a mist walking on water. The water was calm, like a sheet of glass that didn't even ripple as he walked on it. Then a fire appeared on the water, no smoke, just fire, flames like northern lights, dancing across the water. Next, the man sinks and disappears into the water, and as he does the fire stops. Again, the water is calm with no ripple on the surface, just a mirror reflection, but this time it is from beneath the water. It's the man now in a fish form, swimming into some weeds. As he does, he becomes the weeds and the fish disappears. The weeds then become water that moves toward the shore as a wave. As the wave touches the shore it becomes the land. The land touches the air and then turns to a mist. The mist then becomes the man that was walking on the water. It is nothing and it is everything.

Now that I was settled in my apartment, I had plenty of time on my hands and I was getting a lot of messages. Jen and I were busy ordering catalogues of products we would like to carry in the store and we were also looking for a location. I was also doing a lot of work with Jen as it now seemed to be her time to be getting into her issues and moving emotions. I was also sharing the channeled messages I was receiving and that was further activating her. That's part of the reason I've not been sharing much lately as it was about Jen and her story, not mine, and is why you see more messages, and not much of what I was experiencing and going through.

Letting Go of the Past

1998 Mar. 05 - Letting go of what you call the past is an important step in allowing the future into your present life. For until you let go of all that was, as you may cling to it in the present, so your present, your now is preoccupied by the past, of people, places, things and events. When your now is preoccupied with the past, there is no room, no time for things that would be your future to manifest.

There is a balance here also of not being either in the future or past and being in the now. But this is not the usual as most future visualizing and preoccupation with dreams and fantasies usually has little time for the now. Those in the past are too busy doing or remembering their old beliefs, programs and imprints to even allow their true feelings to be expressed so

Chapter 8 – Faltering Steps

that they might truly recognize these beliefs of the past, and to let go of those that no longer serve their highest purpose and good. They are unable to even allow themselves the opportunity to envision a life different from what they were, and are experiencing in the now, to even apply new ideas to future manifestations. For most are still applying old beliefs to future manifestations and then they wonder why their life hasn't changed. How can it when the preoccupation with the falseness and illusions of the past are caught up in the present, the now, and projected into the future.

Now do not misunderstand us, there are those that appear to manifest a new life, ones that appear full of joy, of love, of comfort and abundance. But realize that these are also built on the illusions of the past, its beliefs, programs and imprints, just as you know and experienced in your past, there were moments when the world was your so called oyster and you were on top of the world. But what was the foundation? What was, and is holding it up? Is it the old beliefs, programs and imprints? Or have you totally released the past and built your new life on a new foundation, one of true love and light, one of acceptance, self love, without judgment, on compassion, trust, openness, truth and total acceptance of feelings, one without denial, guilt, control or taking or giving away power. If it is not so; then your foundation is still built on falseness and your presentation face is a false face.

You have all done well at presenting false faces that would persuade or convince others that you enjoyed or had everything you truly desired and were happy. But realize you are in the old system using all the old false tools that give the appearance of everything that one would term happiness, joy, contentment, abundance and love. But it will not last, its foundations are corrupt, built on shifting sand and will not endure. They endure only as long as you are able to put your energy into maintaining the charade, the false face and the game. It is now time to build your foundations on solid rock instead of sand, on a single rock, the rock of love, true love. For love is enduring, is constant and is supportive. It is that what you are doing now as you are clearing away the sand that has covered the rock, moving the sand out to its right place so that you can build your life anew. A fresh new start and this time, (time is not the right word) it will be different, it will last, endure and it will not come tumbling down because it won't be built on sand.

It is confusing to you now as you let go of the past and prepare for a new life not knowing how it is going to unfold. Have faith and trust that you will be provided for and that all this is not an illusion to sink you further into the quicksand of denials, guilt and past programs and beliefs. TRUST and continue to let go of that which holds you to the past and have faith that as you do, your new life is unfolding and the universe is bringing you the life you have always longed for, dared hope possible. It is coming. It is coming; the Old World is crumbling down and the New World, the Phoenix, is rising from its ashes. Ashes indeed, for your burning of your old beliefs and programs were and are your transformation, your phoenix rising from the ashes and about to test your wings and fly. Blessings, Adornia

Beauty and Sexuality

1998 Mar. 06 - When in partnership or relationship of any kind, it is your intent, your beliefs, your judgments that will be reflected to you. What is beauty, attractive, sexuality, but an interpretation of your five senses. If you had no eyes to see, would that diminish the beauty of a rose? No smell, would that diminish the beauty of a roses fragrance? Or touch, the beauty and softness and pleasure of its petals? The same can be said about sexuality. How it is defined is by how it is experienced. How it is experienced is by your receptors of your senses and also, and this is a big ALSO, by your past beliefs, programs and imprints. If you had a bad experience when you smelled the rose, then a roses fragrance brings up the unresolved feelings and you state, "I do not like roses" for whatever reason, smell, look or color, and you have judgment and fear of roses.

There are judgments that have been made that you consider no big deal, are very subtle, or you are not even aware of these judgments but they hold you to the past and hold you in unloving lights grip. You are always comparing, analyzing, and judging. There is a subtle difference between judgments and preference. You make your statement of preferences but before you do, see also if you have judgments that led you to your preference. Why do you prefer this over that? It is not appropriate to rob you, so to speak, of your experiences, but as you begin to remember more and more of who you are, the picture puzzle will unfold. But it has to do, and we tell you this for you already know, that it has to do with love, beauty and sex and it has past life association and unloving light connection which is in all. It is a fairy tale, all fairy tales, re-told. Blessings upon You, Adornia

As I finished reading this I felt a faint sadness and then a deep heartbreak and a longing. I don't know who or what, but I'm feeling that it has something to do with Camelot. ♥

Becoming Balanced – Ending Denials

1998 Mar. 07 - In thoughts, in words and in deeds are power and energy. The more precise you are, the more aligned you are, Spirit and Will, Spirit to inspire and guide and Will to feel and choose, for both to create. When there is alignment and not overpowering one or the other, then in balance do you create instantaneously. When there are no longer denials, Spirit not denying the Will and Will not denying itself and trusting Spirit in the partnership, that is the oneness, the love and the joy that fills creation

Chapter 8 – Faltering Steps

with love and light. Denial has to move out and to do that you must have acceptance of the Will, the feelings, and allow response of these feelings and not try to override, manipulate or control them to suit old programs and beliefs. Rather voice your thoughts, your fears, as a guide and also allow the Will movement to respond to Spirits guidance. Once Spirit tries to force its old programs and beliefs, denial has already taken foothold and it simply becomes a matter then of getting in deeper and deeper into the quicksand of death of unloving light.

It is now time to bring the unconscious programs and conditions to the conscious mind in such a way that Spirit and Will join together to move the old programs and beliefs out, and to move unloving light out to its right place. These patterns have a direct effect on the unconscious and continue with old programs and beliefs unless they are brought forth and seen for what they are. We are talking now not of the obvious programs, but of the hidden subtle ones that come up as judgments under the guises of, that's just how things are, you can't change that, it's not appropriate, it's not my place, I'll do it later. And also feeling programs like, I'm too tired, I'm too busy, I don't think (feel) like doing such and such, and a host of others. All these judgments and beliefs form a system of denying the Wills true feelings and expression, and even under the guise that it is the Will that is responding to Spirits desire. Unloving lights use of denial here is very tricky and subtle, but conscious awareness and open dialogue and expression, especially in partnership with another who can act as an outside observer or mirror, to bring conscious awareness to these hidden denials.

It may seem like nit picking for the one who is being observed, that feel they are being judged, but this is only the reflection of the judgment that is being uncovered in the sub-conscious but not in the awareness of the consciousness. The conscious mind senses this reflection as a different form and it must remain open and aware of what is happening and seek to find the hidden judgment or denial. For the conscious mind will initially deny that there is a problem and that is the key, to cue you to the fact of the subconscious imprint or belief.

Allow Spirit to guide and bring up these old beliefs and also allow the Will to respond in whatever way is appropriate and together, true understanding will come forth. When it does, the grip that unloving light has will be removed and judgments will also be released and loving light will reclaim its denied Will and Essence. There is major work still to be done and also has been done, but is being held back by these subtle judgments and denials. Do not try to remain silent in your thoughts when together, reflecting into yourself or numbing of the conscious self to void and deny the Wills expression and also Spirits inspiration and thoughts to come to the surface consciousness and to awareness. Denial must end, and the sooner it is brought to conscious awareness the sooner it will end.

Journey to the Heart Centre

Do anything that will break the habit, the pattern that is forming, has formed, to allow these subtle sub-conscious programs to be transformed and unloving light to be moved out. It will be difficult for the conscious mind, Spirit, to allow expression of Wills feelings and vise versa, and the Will not wanting to express for fear of judgment and lack of acceptance. These are the fears, the judgments that are going to be reflected to the persona, the ego, the conscious mind, as it relies on its old programs and imprints. All types of fears, rejection, confidence, stupidity, etc. will also come up to play down the allowance of Wills response, to free denied Will and heal the gap.

If your essence is love and your intent is to move unloving light out to its right place, know that your intent to serve your highest purpose and good has brought you to this point. Now it is time to sit face to face with these subtle demons within you, to look them in the eye. You have fears of what this might mean, of your anger, temper, of fear of attack, but these are also issues that you continue to deny, to avoid, to not face. You deny dealing with them and so form explanations and excuses to justify and even mask them as true feelings when indeed they are not. It is time to see them for what they are. It is time to take off these FALSE FACES and reveal your true selves, to yourself and to each other as they are reflected and observed.

You both have many masks, some the same and some completely opposite; it doesn't matter just as long as they are removed. There is no right way or wrong way, simply allow yourselves to be lovingly open, honest and truthful to self and each other as you begin to move out into the world. Opening these fears will also allow you freedom and clarity and also to remember who you are, and in so doing, your purpose, your desires will become clearer. As your thoughts, your inspirations, become clearer it is able to offer guidance to the Will that is responding, and true understanding will come, understanding on a level you have never experienced before. Also your intuition will become more accurate as you are also able to connect with your higher self more easily and work with your guides and others guides.

To truly develop, to grow to your full potential, and to even begin, you need to move through these blocks and remove these last few obstacles that are blocking you. We are talking of unloving light preventing you from being who you are in totality, balanced, Spirit, Will, Heart and Body in loving light, speaking and being your truth. There are other aspects of unloving light on different levels that will also be moved out but it is a process, a layer at a time but it will become easier and faster once these unconscious denials are brought to the surface. The others will follow the same lead; they have no choice but to move to their right place as unloving light has no choice but to move to his right place.

Be patient, be gentle but be firm in your resolve to move these denials into conscious awareness and to move them out appropriately. The first few may be difficult even to recognize them for what they truly are but

Chapter 8 – Faltering Steps

be confident you will get to the root, the prime cause of the imprint or belief and it shall be moved. Blessings, Adornia

Responsibility and Empowerment

1998 Mar. 08 - It is personal responsibility for your own development, no one can do it for you, can save you. They can show you the way, a truth, something that will trigger you into awareness of your drama, of the illusions of what you call reality, but it is you, your free Will to choose, and then, through your words and deeds to align with your thoughts and desires; to create the reality you seek and not the illusion you have been caught in.

False prophets, religions, churches, etc., these illusions of power will all be quick to deny a truthful response and quicker to point out your fears, faults and short comings. For they will confuse you, to offer you quick salvation, to have you believe that in order to live the life you have always wanted to live but which is only possible in heaven or on other dimensions or planets. And that only after you die or ascend, and if, and it's a big IF, if you give your power to them and place your trust in them, because they have been ordained, and are deemed holier or better than you by your beliefs. When in fact, the power for your salvation, your empowerment, lies within you when you recognize your true God/Goddess essence and it is NOT a mental recognition we are talking about.

Release the falseness of these promises, of these words, for it is time to shed these old beliefs and imprints and programs and to take back your power. Your power from unloving light that would control you, have you live, not live, for it is not life, would have you exist in fear and in loneliness. Blessings

1998 Mar. 12 - Jen had given Liz and I a plain paper face mask a few days ago, after she heard my previous message on false faces. She told us to draw or paint on it whatever we felt reflected us and who we were. I picked up Liz at her home and then we went to Jen's place to take part in this mask unveiling. Jen went first and shared what her mask meant to her and then it was my turn. When I stood up before them and looked at my mask, what I thought I had painted and wanted to say wasn't what I saw and said. When I looked down at my mask I realized that it was the false mask that I was wearing to pretend to be who I wasn't. I don't really remember what I said but I do know that I was standing in the middle of the room openly and emotionally sharing and crying. When I was finished, I tore up the mask. I spend the next three days with myself.

New Beginnings

1998 Mar. 12 - You are in the process of, and it is, new beginnings that you have fear of. You let go only when you see that you are safe and that there is something to keep you afloat within reach. You have let go of the dock but you are still hanging onto the rope and so now you are floating in the water. You also have fear as you see that what supports you (the dock and rope) diminishing, becoming less and you know that eventually it will no longer support you. You are still afraid to totally let go and to trust that the universal water will support you and bring you all that you desire. This is an enterprise, a task, a mission, an experience, one that requires the merging of the spiritual and the physical, of spiritualizing the physical, and as such, it needs to be experienced in the physical for your benefit and the benefit of others. You have not and are not suddenly to become this totally enlightened being with no need for worldly experiences. You are going to and are becoming a totally enlightened being, enjoying and experiencing the world, being of the world but not in it.

You need to apply the earthly, the physical skills that you have experienced all these life times and apply them now with your new awareness. Be, become that which you have chosen to be and you will also do and experience all that you desire, to enjoy the physical as never before. This transformation is at hand if but you release your fear of new beginnings, of moving, of being uprooted.

You are in the water, the Earth awaits you, the sun awaits you, the air awaits you, the ethers await you, and the universe awaits you to make the intent. INTENT to send your roots down, to break free of the shell like the acorn. You are already all that you can be and you have all that you need to become all that you are. You have simply to be your acorn, start, root, break free of the shell around you, apply water, soften the shell, and nourishment will be found to not only sustain you, but you and all those with you will flourish as well. The acorn that you now picked up and have in your hand is one that has chosen to remain as a symbol for you that you will be placing in your dream catcher until such time that you have planted your roots, your spiritual roots and also choose to help him plant his.

Begin this new venture, adventure with heartfelt enthusiasm and fear not that you will not or can't, or wouldn't succeed for unloving light has fed you this and it is in your memories and beliefs. It is time to release those beliefs, to move unloving light out that would hold you back and hold you back he is trying his utmost to do, for what you intend to be does not serve him and your opening others does not serve him either. You have taken a leap of faith and now it is time to take another. Trust and in your Heart, truly feel what it is you intend and desire and then act with love, not fear. Let your fears come up to show you where you still have judgments, issues, beliefs, programs and imprints that need to be moved out and essence to be healed and reclaimed. Blessings, Adornia

Chapter 8 – Faltering Steps

As I was typing the above message into the computer I looked up at the dream catcher I'd made that was hanging in the window, I knew that the acorn had fallen off and was lying on the windowsill. I picked it up; it seems so small and at the same time it's hard to believe it's going to be a huge Oak tree. I'm emotional as I'm also beginning to grasp the significance of this message and of my letting go and taking the risk, and like the acorn, trust that when I open to receive nourishment and life, that the universe will support me as it will the acorn. I'm in the middle of another transition as I'm writing this and so there are no coincidences. I'm afraid of change, of the unknown; it terrifies me, especially of having to face it alone. ♥

Intent and Action

1998 Mar. 15 - The acorn desires to be what it is. Its intent is always there although outward conditions for it to succeed may not be there. But when the opportunity comes along it is quick to seize it, not even waiting for a better opportunity or one that he judges better, for there is no judgment, simply being and acting in the moment. Be as the acorn, you are already all that you can be, you need only to express it, to heal, to become whole, to become one. Drop the illusions around you, the programs and the beliefs as to what and how you are, or are not to be, and simply allow yourself to be you. Drop your judgments about yourself as they come up, for they no longer serve you.

Begin, take that small step, dare to stand up and be seen for what and who you truly are. Allow the fears to come up, recognize them and allow expression and movement of all the Will, lost Will, to express itself, to free herself and to heal herself from Lucifer's grip in the gap. Denial, denial in any form, for whatever reason or noble cause, is still denial and opens the door for more unloving light to move in, rather than move out. Open yourself, free yourself of your own self imposed limits and restrictions and see how the universe is prepared to offer and support you. It is a big step; the first step, for it has never been taken before. TRUST and intent followed by action to manifest your intent will provide you with all you desire. Blessings, Mother and Father

> *The meaning of life is life. - Shenreed*

1998 Mar. 15 - It was back on Feb. 17 that Ken called and said that the cheque was in the mail. I waited and waited, and then phoned him. After giving me a story, he said he'd check into it as it was a registered letter and he would get back to me. I never heard back from him, so I checked with the local post office but there was no registered letter for me, or for anyone. I waited a few more days and called him again and this time he said that he would issue another cheque. I waited for that one and it never materialized either. I tried calling him, but now there was no answer. Today I drove down to Barrie and picked up the forms to file a claim against him in small claims court.

Manifesting What You Want

1998 Mar. 19 - Release judgments on what it is you can manifest in your life, state your intent to the fullest and allow the universe to bring it to you. Release your fears, judgments and unworthiness. Dare to dream without conditions, without expectations of, or on another to fulfill your dreams, for hanging your dream on another is attachment. Holding your dream open to characteristics similar to, etc., allows the universe the freedom to bring you what it is you desire. It might not be with who or what you thought, and then it might. When all is allowed to flow and is in alignment, then manifestation will occur effortlessly. State your intentions verbally or written, both would be better, as you could then also see where you have judgments and expectations, or have limited yourself.

1998 Mar. 20 - Yesterday I saw a large older house in Midland that looked promising as it was zoned both commercial and residential. That appealed to me as maybe I could also live in the house and that would save me some money. I called the number on the sign and left a message. Today I received a phone call and he said that it was going to be vacant soon. I arranged to have a look at it with the present tenants' permission. The present state of the property left much to be desired as a Harley Davidson motor bike was being repaired in what was the living room and the commercial area was being used as a tattoo parlor. But that aside, it definitely had potential. I said I'd consider it once I could get a better feel for it when it was vacant. A couple of days later I also looked at another home, it was bigger and also had potential but the parking was very limited.

1998 Mar. 24 - So what's going on in my life? I let go and sold the house and the business in December and I moved out at the end of February. Jen and I want to start a new business, we've been looking since last fall for a place and nothing has materialized yet. I still have an issue with partnerships and relationships. I also don't have a real passion for this Centre, Why? Is it because it's not really set up as a business yet, or is it that I'm not confident in my abilities, feel lacking and judging myself? Jen will not have a physical input as such, but she will have other assets and input, and in many ways, I trust her input more than mine. She's the only real friend I have in my life at present as I have no one to really talk to except Jen.

I'm basically alone, no home, no job, no money coming in and lots going out. I had this same feeling when I moved to Toronto to go to school but then I had the school, someone to teach me and show me what I needed

Chapter 8 – Faltering Steps

to know to get a job. Now I'm teaching myself a new career, with Jen's help, and who is to say that this is right? I'm going to have to rely on me to support me and I've failed a couple of times. Is this what's holding me back? Is the Centre what I really want? Do I want Jen as a partner, and what about Liz? Trust, can I trust them to help me or will it fall apart? Can I trust myself? No, I don't believe I have the ability to operate a Centre on my own. Why? I can't physically operate the store and do a meditation class or other session at the same time, that's too much.

I feel my world has collapsed and has fallen away. I'm living in a basement apartment. I want to start a business in Midland where I don't know anyone except Jen and Liz. I don't have anything that is producing any income. So what would I do if I didn't have Jen as a friend and no plans for the Centre? Would I move to Barrie or somewhere else? Travel? I want to heal myself to become whole, but I feel I'm not good enough and now I'm getting in touch with all the self-judgments I have. I don't see how I can possibly heal myself with all this junk in me. I feel unwanted, unloved and alone and I'm down to only one friend who I fear at times is also going to not answer the phone or will just give me a note saying good bye.

I feel close to Jen but at the same time so distant. We sometimes talk for hours and usually several times a day. We know each other's darkest secrets. I've never just had a friend and she is the only person I've ever really let in, but I feel I still can't be myself, my real self. There is this part of me that needs to be expressed and accepted, and it's not just the mental, emotional and spiritual, it's the physical that is missing. We share a lot of things but we have never shared a meal or gone out for a coffee and a donut or even for a real walk. I feel I hold back my true feelings with fear, I'm afraid to reach out and even hold her hand or to give her a hug that is not a good-bye hug in case it is taken the wrong way. I feel that she is even more afraid of me. In the fifteen months we've known each other, she had never been to see my place in Moonstone and now that it's sold all we could do is drive by. We go to the stores and pick up things, do laundry, and maybe drive around a little and even the odd time we go for a short walk if she feels up to it. Most of our visits are between 1:00 p.m. and 7:00 p.m. before or after that, we usually talk on the phone.

I enjoy my time alone when I have to do something by and for myself. But there are other times when I would like to have company, to share stories, ideas and to experience something like a movie, a walk, lunch, picnic, drive, beach, canoeing, nature or even crafting or making something together as well as meeting other people and just hanging out. There are all these people around me yet I feel so alone, so distant. I've felt this way all my life; that I'm on the outside always looking in and seeing other people laugh, dance and having fun, being with friends and being accepted.

So why can't I be like other people? Why can't I have or experience what they seem to have? Maybe if I was more like them I could have what they have because being what I am is no fun. But what and who am I? Whenever I've tried to be like other people, I didn't like it either as I didn't fit in, I couldn't do what other people were doing and yet I didn't want to be alone. I needed, I wanted someone to love me, to pay attention to me, but that never really happened either. So this really hasn't been a happy life for me to this point. I feel abandoned by my brothers and sisters, even my cousins, etc. I know it was me that moved away, but even before that there was no real family closeness. I'm divorced, my children are on their own now, and I seldom see them. I have few acquaintances. I have one friend. I have no home, no business, and no source of income. I feel there is no one that will look after me, that will care for me, that will love me. I just thought of the words in a song, "Is that all there is my friend, is that all there is?" I don't know who sings it.

I want to live life with joy, love and abundance, but it all seems to be just a dream, an illusion, and the people that seem to have it don't want to share it. So what do they really have? The only sharing I have experienced also had some form of control, expectation, payment, condition or agreement. Sure it felt or feels good for a little while until you start to see it for what it really is, and then when you try to get out or change it, that's when it loses its joy because it's not love or loving anymore. So what is the issue? I hate people; they always want something in return. They only use you until someone else comes along. I've always tried to please people; I try to be helpful when I can. I don't know anything anymore?

"Yes you do", I heard a soft voice say.

Well, what is it then? What's my problem, my issue and my lesson? What do I have to do to heal all this? I then got the following message.

Self-love and Self-acceptance

Self-love and that you are loved, are love, is the underlying issue and one that has been there for eternity, not only for you, but all. Self-love and acceptance are key to healing, and that you cannot find reflected to you on the external until you feel it on the internal. And to feel it on the internal you must allow all feelings to be expressed, to be in truth, for the truth shall set you free. Express your fears, your hates, your judgments, your desires and acknowledge them for what they are, YOURS, not somebody else's, or neither put down your expression for the sake of another, for it is not love. Allow Spirit to express and also allow the Will to respond with that initial feeling thought without thinking it over and mentalizing until you think you

Chapter 8 – Faltering Steps

have the answer, or to ask a question or make a statement for which you will gain approval.

With self-love and self-acceptance will come confidence and clarity in who and what you are, and your purpose and mission will become clear. As you become clearer you will manifest and draw near unto you all that it is you desire, have desired ever since the beginning, but that you have never truly experienced, as death in some form would deny you again. Be who you are in this moment and you will begin to end the judgments and denials, and soon you will discover the magic of life, of creation, of love. For only you and you alone now are the one and only John James Rieger that was physically born and has experienced all that he has, has to come to this point to become all that you can possibly be and to fulfill your destiny.

These experiences in this life were also necessary so that you can relate to others, for you are not alone. Not all have gone through what you have, some more, some less, but it matters only that you now awaken. By awaken, we mean to awaken to the God within you, to shine your light so bright and pure, not to hide it away any longer for fear of what is attracted to you will only cause you pain. Release that fear, judgment, for to love yourself and to be yourself, you must allow yourself expression of everything. You must neither deny your Spirit or your Will, and when you no longer deny, Heart will heal and Body will manifest all your desires, life will be fulfilled with love, joy and abundance. Believe little one, be young at heart and open yourself to love and joy, friendships and relationships that you never had and always long for.

Love yourself by expressing yourself, your true feelings without shame, guilt or judgment. A child does not judge itself right or wrong, but you would say he doesn't know any better (that is judgment). A child just is and does what he feels like doing in the moment. Even simple blocks, shapes and colour give pleasure, and it doesn't matter if and how he places them or if and when they fall. Also he may built them up only to see them fall and scatter to give joy and pleasure, and when he no longer desires the blocks, he moves on.

It is true you are not a child and we are not asking you to think and behave like one. We are only asking you to feel like one and to allow expression of your thoughts, your fears, your denials, your judgments, and your programs, beliefs and imprints that bind you to your circle of death. Expressing your true feelings in the moment allows movement out of all that which is unloving, and releases its grip on you. You have a friend and opportunity for both to move mountains, allow yourself the freedom to love yourself by expressing your feelings in the moment as she does with you. It is now time to unfold your wings and you will be surprised how quickly you will learn to soar.

Journey to the Heart Centre

Many are here to assist you on all levels, but can only help you when you help yourself, when you love yourself, when you free your Will and end your denials of her expression. Try, express your first thought/feeling, for they are combined, are one. It is only the mental mind that begins the separation by judgment and beliefs, etc. You do not have to act on it if you so desire, but you need to express it. The more you express, the more you come into alignment and the less you desire not to act in response to your thought/feeling, and eventually all will be one, Spirit, Will, Heart and Body manifest on the physical plane, heaven on Earth Blessings, Adornia

1998 Mar. 25 - Today was the day of the fashion show. Jen and I had recently bought some new clothes and it was her idea for each of us to put on a fashion show for the other, and to express what we felt about our new clothes. Jen was always doing creative things like that and always pushing my envelope. She had been a model in her late teens and had done fashion shows, so she was comfortable with it, but this was a first for me. Jen went first and then I did my part. We both had made audio tapes giving a runway type presentation of what we were wearing so that all we really had to do that day was to just change and model the clothes. As we would begin the presentation, the other would press the "play" button and listen to the music and the brief description we had made of the clothes and then press "pause" when that part of the show was finished. That was difficult for me to present myself in such a public manner, but it also opened me up a little and I even enjoyed it.

1998 Mar. 29 - Jen and I have been looking for a suitable location for the Centre for months and we still hadn't found one. Sometimes it feels like we're never going to have a Centre but we're still getting catalogs and ordering products. Today we looked at another house that was also commercial/residential. It was okay, but being on a main street with no parking, wasn't acceptable.

Jen and I have realized this before, that while we are similar in many ways, we also have opposite issues. One such insight was that I'm afraid to ask questions, while she's afraid to answer questions. I've also begun to re-read the first book in RUOW, while I'm waiting for the next one to come in.

♡ In the following journal entry, I awoke remembering what Jen had told me earlier that day when I dropped in to see her. I must have been half-asleep, as I started writing about what happened, but then switched and began writing as if I was talking to her directly. I was now expressing my denials, what I wanted to express in the moment she said what she did, but I didn't. Instead I was nice, kind and polite, not wanting any conflict, or have

Chapter 8 – Faltering Steps

her feel bad and raining on her parade, on the little happiness she enjoyed, which was guilt on my part. This is what I wrote in my journal. ♥

1998 March 30, 4:24 am - Jen told me that her old boyfriend came over to visit her and asked her to go out for a car ride. She said that she wanted to drive, but didn't, and that was okay, at least she went with it, went with the flow and went for a ride and got excited. She said to me, "I can't get excited with you, or you don't share your excitement with me." Well guess what, when's the last time, or rather, when did you ever go out to do what I wanted to do and not something that I also knew you wanted to do.

    Early in our relationship, I'd be excited and would ask you to do this or that, and you either didn't feel like it in that moment, or you would be in pain and couldn't move. You'd say, "How can you ask me to do anything when you know I feel like this. Don't you understand, can't you feel, don't you care, nobody understands me." And so we would sit and talk, or watch TV until you, "Your Majesty," felt revitalized, felt pumped to be spontaneous or creative as you call it, to be free and expressive within the confines of your home, or maybe a quick dash into the outer reality that you are afraid of, to pick up something from the store. That is not being spontaneous or free. I think it's exciting when we talk on the phone and even when you ask me to come over and do laundry with you. That is exciting as we get to do something together, even if it's just doing laundry. But my excitement turns to concern when you go into your panic attacks, and either I finish the laundry for you while you stay in the van, or we never even get to the Laundromat.

    I can be spontaneous and I guess, not guess, I'm being sarcastic here in saying that being spontaneous is allowing myself to do something freely, but sometimes I feel like a prisoner in your house. I guess I've allowed myself, through guilt with Marian and Michelle, in that they also told me that they were sick and that I didn't understand them, that I didn't feel what they did. Well I've taken time to feel and to understand you and I've felt your pain and I understand how crippling it can be in one moment and completely gone in the next. Why? I don't know why, yet.

    But also I know that when I would suggest to Marian or Michelle to do this or that, have breakfast in bed, stay in all day, watch a movie, have a picnic, anything, it was, "No, don't you understand that I'm not feeling good. But "ring ring" the telephone, or "ding dong" the door bell and it's a fucking miracle! They're cured! They're up and running and they've got a mile wide smile on their fucking face and they're out the door following their excitement, and if could be the very same thing that I suggested.

    So why have I attracted these women to me in this life? Why don't I trust or believe them when they say they are sick and in pain? Why are they in pain one moment and fine the next? Are they reflecting my lack of spontaneity, to take time to do what I want to do when I want to do it? Yes, there are times when I wanted to do something when you would call and ask me to do something that you wanted to do. I'd put my stuff aside just to go out with you when you felt you could, and weren't in pain. Is that guilt, responsibility, or over protection and concern? I think so.

I'm spontaneous, I'm exciting, but most of the time when I come over or get excited, you're not. There was only one time and it was the first time I met you that you came to the door and I actually felt you were glad to see me. There have been other times when you have been at the door or were sitting on the steps, but they were to go out and do what excited you. I have judgment that just because you don't greet me at the door and that I don't see or talk to you until I've let myself in, walk up the stairs, down the hallway and peek around the corner to see which chair you're sitting in. Sometimes you will look up and say hi, but you never get out of your chair. Rene, your dog, is glad to see me but you're not, you feel cold, indifferent and self-absorbed. So whatever excitement I may have had and wanted to share is often dulled or covered up. I then pull up my old judgments and that is what I act on, but I also know now when you are really in pain as I can feel it.

I could be the most exciting and entraining I've ever been and it wouldn't mean a fucking thing. You're in your space and I'm in mine. I've stayed, and sometimes we get to work through your stuff and sometimes we work through mine, and I know we also help ourselves when we help another. This also affects the Centre and the dream we share. We might drive around and look at places, or I'd get a phone call and you'd say, "You look at it and tell me about it, does it smell, does it have large windows?" and a bunch of other questions that I feel pressured to get answers for. Getting excited would be saying, "Wow! a new place, Yeah, I want to check it out, let's go." Instead it's, "You talk to him, see how you feel." That puts a lot of pressure on me as I know that when I can't answer all the questions you have, and even the ones that you didn't ask, that I'll have to call or go back a second time to get the answers. And then maybe, if it all comes back okay and it feels okay to you, then maybe you'll go and see it, but only if they air out the building for three to five hours before we go over, as you can smell the scent of the building on my clothes that I had just been to see.

Whatever excitement I had just flew out the fucking window when I have to explain it to you and try to convey excitement and the potential it has, knowing how you would react as soon as I mentioned anything about carpets, small windows, etc., anything that wasn't 100%, not 99.9%, but 100% to your ideal. Yet you sit in an apartment that has mildew and dry rot in the bathroom and extreme condensation on the windows. You are also affected by the smells of food, cologne and smoke from the people downstairs and you go to the extreme of blocking your hot air vents even if it's −20 below outside and you're freezing your butt. Yet you put all this pressure on me to find something that is perfect when you don't even live up to your ideals yourself.

Chapter 8 – Faltering Steps

And how many places out there would fit your ideal, unless it was someone that was as critical as you are in the standards you set but don't live by.

You bitch to me but you don't bitch to the landlord to fix the roof in the bathroom. You don't bitch at the guy downstairs and the cheap cologne he uses that smells up the air vents. What you say is that you have acceptance for them to be as they are, and that you have no judgments? You think that just because you're getting a deal on the rent, that you have to put up with it. Double standards or what!

The world is not perfect so how do we make it perfect? We're not perfect so how do we become perfect, (perfect is the wrong word). We both have different issues, beliefs and programs that have made us what we are, and has brought us to this point in time and space, and once we can let go of the old we'll be able to move to the new. But this new is not just new, yet it is. It's like opening a door and you have one reality on one side and another on the other side. Unfortunately, right now it seems that the reality we desire and dream doesn't really exist yet, only in our mind and only within us. As soon as we involve another person or persons, our reality shifts back to at least part of the old reality. I don't know where I'm going with this so I'll stop.

A Shift in Consciousness

1998 Apr. 6 - Greetings, we are here this day to bring you a message, one that you have been waiting for a long time, one that humanity has been waiting for a long time. By and in conjunction with what you call Easter, another major shift in consciousness will occur and humanity will be entering the new millennium with a new sense of hope. Hope is not the right word but it also contains the positive outlook, attitude, a sense of direction, of purpose, of renewed faith, of expression of love, of re-building, of tearing down that which no longer serves. More and more will be honestly searching for truth, for the meaning of life, and opening their hearts, their minds to the new. It is time to prepare yourselves to serve as teachers and as pupils to this movement. It is time to remove the bushel basket and allow your light to shine, for through you judge yourself as unfit, unsuitable, not ready, which is your judgment and fed by your linear perception. You have much you can share with many, and there are many who are waiting for you, your truth, your wisdom. You know much and pretend to know little, you feel much and pretend to feel nothing. These words apply to you in your judgment of yourselves. Release your judgments, feel your power, accept your gifts, and trust that as you share what you know and what you feel, you will also be taught more. As you teach, so shall you learn.

There is no right or wrong way to teach or share as there is no right or wrong way to draw a picture, see a sunset or to hear a bird's song. Simply be what you are, in love and truth and continue to express all that you feel. It will also serve as an inspiration and lesson to those that you share your light, your love, and your truth with, and will aid in their growth and in yours. It is time to spread your wings, little ones, spread your wings. Blessings, WoNon

1998 April 9 - I had called Ken three times stating that I never received the cheque that he said he had sent out on Feb 17. On Mar 15, when he didn't return my calls, I decided to go to small claims court and pick up the necessary documents. Today I drove down to Barrie, filed the claim, and personally served the documents to him at his home. That was a hard thing for me to do as a part of me didn't want to do it and just wanted to let it go, rather than get into a confrontation. He answered the door and I served him the papers and said that if I didn't get the money, that I'd see him in court. He didn't say a word, and I turned and left.

Earth Changes and Inner Changes

1998 Apr. 15 - Monsoons, floods, tidal waves, storms, tornadoes, hurricanes, volcanoes, earthquakes, drought, famine, and disease will be increasing in the times ahead. These are physical changes by Earth itself as it sheds and prepares for transformation. Mankind will also be going through various what you call diseases, as those who choose to leave to their right place either through disease or through Earth changes. Not only by these, but by also acts of violence as you would call it. Changes will be coming more swiftly also with all upon the Earth, the plants and the animals for they too have their choices.

This is not doom and gloom but it is that also, for those who believe and desire to experience death. Those that choose life will be little or not affected directly by the changes, although they will see and feel the changes in the mass consciousness and the Earth in this time of transformation. This will be the time when the Starseeds that have chosen this time to come out of the shadow and shine their light for all to see. Continue to raise your vibration and release your limitations as you are doing to become who you are, and soon you will be in the reality you choose to be, to experience that which you desire, to be of service to humankind with joy and pleasure and love. As you begin your mission a step at a time, it will be no time at all before you are soaring and you will be in joy and love. Excitement will flood your experiences, life will return to you, youth will return and you shall have all that you desire to experience and to share with others. Continue to shed darkness that has held you down all your existence. It won't be much longer before you will feel truly that you are becoming free, freeing your Will.

Judgment release and ending your denials of your judgments will greatly assist your transformation. For as you are discovering, nearly all of your present beliefs or truths, as you call them, are not truths but judgments placed on you as a mass consciousness passed down through family, friends, acquaintances and by yourself in comparisons. Is it right or wrong, acceptable

Chapter 8 – Faltering Steps

or not acceptable, appropriate or not appropriate, reasonable or not reasonable, sane or not sane, childish or not mature, masculine or not, feminine or not, husbandly or not, wifely or not, fatherly or motherly or not and the list goes on and on. For each time there has been comparison there has been a judgment, even to the point of preferences, no stand, or all stands, for in seeing both sides considered equal there is judgment. Having no preference, of considering it not acceptable to choose one over the other, and to see the inherent good or bad in both is a denial of the Will, of her feelings, of having to feel love and compassion for opposing forces, and to deny true response in favor of loving acceptance which is not loving to the Will. So you are caught between non-judgment and loving acceptance, and judgment and of holding steadfast to a belief or truth that is not a real truth of the Wills feelings, and is then the denial of the Will in the acceptance of all. Therein lies the confusion, the battle that you are raging through at this time.

Allow yourself to get triggered into your beliefs, judgments, or your so-called understandings of both forces, and then delve underneath the façade to your true feelings and allow them full expression. They may, to your surprise, completely awe and bewilder you, and may not even have anything to do with what you considered truth or unconditional acceptance. There are many layers of false Will, false beliefs, false feelings, denial and guilt that feed these so-called non-judgments.

Denial of my light, of acceptance of my light is going to end, and those who choose life; choose love. There will no longer be a mixing of loving and unloving light; there is right place for both in my creation, but no longer are they to be as one. There is balance; there is also separation and there is no separation, there is harmony and there is chaos, there is perfection in creation and now is the time to experience it as it should be, as it was intended to be.

Denial of the Will and all judgments, guilt and so-called non-judgments must end. The compression, the suppression, the death of the Will is ending now. The Will will be denied no longer, either by judgments or the acceptance of that that does not feel loving to her. Truth, true expression of the Will, will free your Essence, your Spirit, unite your Heart and heal you bodies as they were meant to be. Those that continue to deny my light are also loved no less and are free to continue to experience with, and I repeat, with only those that choose to experience denial of my light and non-acceptance of me until such time they choose differently. But no longer will there be a mixing of loving and unloving light. Those that choose life will experience all that they desire in love and light, in true expression and balance of Will and Spirit and in form, unshackled from false beliefs, programs and imprints.

Do not be dismayed or judge yourselves as you are doing that you are back-sliding, not proceeding, for indeed you are making glorious advances.

You are being assisted in all ways that are appropriate but it is you that must make the effort, the conscious effort to balance Will and Spirit and to bring the understanding and wisdom of the experience to conscious awareness. Experience is necessary to bring up the emotions, the true emotions so that they can move as appropriate, and then to receive the understandings that are needed to release the false feelings and judgments, and to feel the truth. To feel loving light, unconditional love, and in so doing, move out unloving light, and in so doing, end your denials and judgments, and change your beliefs to what feels right at this time. As you continue to clear, so your beliefs will change, not change, but become enhanced, become clear, simple, as the fog or the darkness is rolled away to its right place, layer by layer, until all that is seen is the brightness, the glory, the love that you are. Blessings, Mother and Father

1998 Apr. 16 - Jen has been in an emotional and physical state the past few days and has had no energy. She'd called to give me her grocery-shopping list and I'd pick them up, deliver and unpack them for her. I was also picking up and doing her laundry for her. I did some energy work with Jen as she was laying on the futon; I unintentionally tapped into what she was feeling emotionally, as well as the utter exhaustion of her body. I felt it to the depths in my physical and emotional Being as I slumped to the floor, exhausted, barely able to move, and not even desiring to move because of the effort it took. I felt it, but I didn't carry it with me when I left. I could do nothing for her, but I did feel that her body just couldn't hold anymore of her denials and couldn't move until she moved the emotions, or allowed the body to somehow shift the energy to another part of itself.

Breaking Free of the Quicksand

1998 Apr. 17 – Wondrous awakening my child. It fills our hearts with joy, with tears of pride that you are finally freeing yourself of the limitations that you have chosen to experience. Another level of understanding and another chain, a big one, one that has held you in place has been broken and its shackles are falling from your feet, hands and neck. You have just touched the tip of the iceberg in your awareness this morning, but it was the key to unlock your Will that you have held prisoner and only allowed her expression through the bars. You give freedom to others while remaining in a cage; it is now time to give yourself the same freedom.

Indeed there are many aspects to your realization of denial spirits and spirits in denial, of reflection of your unloving light and the reflection of loving light, and also that what you feel is NOT a reflection but are true and accurate feelings which, if you deny your feelings, become a reflection of your denials. The unfolding of your true experiences outside of your cage, your limitations will be exciting and you will begin to live life with greater joy and

Chapter 8 – Faltering Steps

abundance. Indeed, those that seek life will come to you for direction, not direction, but leadership, for teaching, for way showing, so that they too can create the life to their desires and to follow their path. Others will come who are denial spirits, who come to usurp or to discourage and discredit in the name of love. These, as was given, you will feel for what they are and will uncover by asking what their true intent is.

This is a fragile moment, stage for you as you begin to move arms, legs and begin to settle in, to feel comfortable with your feelings, your Will, to trust the Will and Will to trust Spirit. That Spirit and Will both have acceptance without shutting doors. Spirit will be key, at first, in having acceptance for Wills feelings and the expression of them as appropriate so as to end all denials, and this includes Spirits fears in that Spirit denies himself in favor of Will. Neither must be denied. Deny nothing in any part of yourself. It is time to end these denials and in ending your denials you also end your judgments and guilt and all other beliefs, imprints and programs that you carry that do not serve your highest purpose and good, love, light and life. You are loving essence, you are love, you have chosen life, expansion, wonder, joy, beauty, peace and harmony. It is now time, as you have recognized in your reading this morning, that there are those around you who are denial Spirits, who choose the opposite but would deny it because denial is part of this essence. Allow your Will to feel and express how it feels the difference, this is not a judgment but an observation for you now understand that their truth, however true the words sound, they do not feel true. As you allow your Will to express how she feels about words and actions, you will move unloving light out of you that would seek you to accept unloving light from the external in denial of your Will.

You have done this in the past in a state of denial as you have felt your truth but denied it. Now it is time to deny no longer, for not all essence is loving and this you have felt but were told by unloving essence that it was you that was unloving, and by denying your Will, you experienced your own unlovingness to yourself. Denial is the quicksand that pulls you into death. You have chosen this experience at this time so that you can feel and share and help other spirits who are in denial, to free themselves from the hold unloving light has on them. By the acceptance that not all spirits, all beings, all beings that are in human form, or any form, are of the same essence. There is separation and there is no separation, but there is right place for both and unloving essence shall find its right place until it can find acceptance for Will. Loving essence shall find its right place with acceptance for Will with expression and understanding and balance.

Denial spirits feel uncomfortable in loving essences presence just as loving spirits feel in denial of true feelings. It has been the mixing and the hanging on by both to each other, trying to control the other, one trying to save the other, not accepting that it does not want (acceptance) life, while the other wanting to draw the life out of the other, not accepting that it does not want (denial) death and so the struggle has continued but is now ending. To end this struggle within yourself you must end your denials, denial of all your feelings and denial of all your fears. Will and Spirit must allow themselves to be open and express all that they feel and think, and to speak their truth; and the truth shall set you free.

Your truth, your true feelings, with self-acceptance of your feelings and acceptance of others feelings, BUT as their feelings, and allowing them to find their right place. Their feelings are NOT better than your feelings; their words and insights are not better than yours if yours do not agree with them. Accept them as you feel them in the moment and use them as you feel them, but do not DENY your feelings. Do not replace your feelings, your truth with theirs, and do not add their truth or their feelings to yours unless your feelings indicate that this is also a personal truth for you at this time. Do not feel pressured that it is now or never, it may not be your truth in this time but it may be in five minutes, hours or even years, it doesn't matter. It only matters what you feel at this moment, NOW, without past reference and without panic of future loss, just now. Allow yourself to create the reality you desire to experience by not denying yourself, by feeling what is now, you are not carrying the old baggage of the past, the beliefs, programs and imprints. Yes they will come up but you will see them for what they are and their purpose to keep you in denial and moving toward death.

Ending your denials, denial of your Wills feelings and expression releases deaths grip on you and you become free to move, to be, to experience what you choose to experience and not caught in the quicksand, but free, freedom, total freedom, to swim, to dance, to soar, to be all that you are without limits, without restrictions of the quicksand of denial. Those denial spirits and spirits in denial will remain in the quicksand until they too choose, choose life, choose to end their denials of the Will. There are many that will follow, follow your lead, your leadership, trust yourself, your ability, your guidance. Trust is a big word and has many off-shoots, but as you allow your Will to guide and direct you, as Spirit accepts Wills feelings and gains insights and understandings, so you shall gain trust in yourself, in your guidance, in your mission, your purpose. Blessings this glorious day our son, shine bright, shine your light, it is time to end your fight. Blessings, Mother and Father

Later that same evening, I saw a TV show about two identical twin brothers, where one had committed six robberies. The police had a description and arrested one of the brothers. He was found guilty and sentenced to 91 years in jail. They interviewed both brothers and the convicted brother stated that he knows his brother did the robberies, but his brother denies it and is free. I felt that the convicted brother was telling the truth and I felt a coldness and

Chapter 8 – Faltering Steps

evil from the brother that was free. What if this is the perfect example of a Will Spirit and a Denial Spirit manifest on the Earth plane. They have the same parents, look the same and have the same mannerisms. They say the same words and appear to express the same emotions, except one is real and the other is in denial and acting out emotions.

1998 April 17 - Late that afternoon I drove to town to see Jen. I was going to take her to do her laundry, but before we even left the house she wasn't feeling well so I offered to do it. This wasn't the first time I did her laundry or got groceries for her when she was exhausted or in a panic attack. After doing the laundry, I went to the video store and picked up the movie, "Uglees Gold" that she had suggested we might watch together. When I got to Jens, she was watching Jade lady, and I asked her if she wanted to watch the movie. She said yes, but then said she was torn between finishing Jade Lady, which she had seen before, and this new movie. I denied my true feelings and said finish Jade Lady as it was close to the end. I hadn't seen Jade Lady so I had no idea what was going on and I was trying to pick up the story line by watching what was on TV and also listening to what Jen was telling me about the story. I was sitting in Jens chair, which I usually didn't sit in, and I had to turn my head 150 degrees to the right to look at her when she was talking to me. When I was watching TV and didn't turn my head to look at her, she'd say that I was ignoring and not listening to her, and that she was only trying to help me understand what the movie was about. When I turned to look at her, I couldn't see or hear what was going on with the movie, as I was looking at and listening to her, and that also annoyed me, but I denied that too. I was torn between trying to watch the end of the movie and what she was telling me happen in the beginning of the movie that I didn't see.

    Finally, frustrated with her constant comments, I spun the chair around so that I would face her directly not knowing that her dog, a toy poodle was napping under the chair. Jen then berated me for not caring about her dog and how I could have hurt her and that I was lucky that I didn't. She also scolded me that I should have known better, that I knew that her dog slept under the chair and that I intentionally meant to hurt Jen, by hurting her dog. During that verbal barrage, I was trying to tell her that I was frustrated with trying to listen to her talk and trying to figure out the movie in progress at the same time and that was why I turned the chair. She then decided that she didn't want to finish Jade Lady and that now she wanted to watch the movie I had brought over.

    I put the chair back and went to sit on the futon, which is where I normally sat, which was another denial, as I wanted to do that in the first place when I came in, but I didn't. We began to watch the movie and I remember she was still talking about what had happened, and now she was also talking during this new movie and I was missing what was going on. I asked her if she wanted to talk before we watched the movie and she said no, that she just wanted to watch the movie. After a couple more interruptions of her talking about the previous experience, I got angry and using my foot, I pushed the coffee table away, not meaning to tip it over but it did, breaking a small crystal candleholder that belonged to her grandmother.

We got into a shouting match and I remember getting up and going over to the VCR and taking the tape out of the machine and putting it into the case. I then moved to leave, standing silently in the hallway entrance as Jen, sitting in the rocker to my right, continued with her verbal abuse. I had the movie in its protective soft plastic case in my hands and I just wanted to get it out of my hands by dropping it on a chair beside me but that didn't feel right. My anger was coming up and my intent was to drop it on the floor in a "pushing down" manner from waist height so that it would land flat on the carpeted floor. It landed flat all right, but with such an explosive force, that it shattered both the protective case and tape cassette. The two tape spools were ejected and unrolled themselves in opposite directions, first in mid-air and then as they bounced and spiraled their way across the living-room carpet, bouncing off furniture and finally coming to rest, tape trailing across the carpet showing the path they had taken. I was shocked as I picked up the pieces, wondering not only how I was going to get it back together but also knowing that I couldn't and that it was going to cost me. Jen then started to rage and yell at me as she picked up some wooden bowls and threw them on the floor, breaking some of them that she then kicked. I silently picked up the tape and pieces of case and left.

It wasn't my day. I was angry as a result of being in denial. I left Jens, or rather she told me to get out, and I went to take the movie back. I was ashamed to tell the woman at the video store what had happened, but I didn't want to be in denial anymore so I did. She smiled and told me to take it to their other store where they did repairs as she felt it could be fixed as the tape didn't look to be damaged and that she would call them to let them know I was coming. I took the tape in and the guy looked at me with a, "What in the hell did you do to this tape!" look, and said that yes, he could fix it and that it would cost me $10.00. I eagerly reached into my pocket and paid him, and left before he could ask me what happened.

I remember not talking to Jen for a couple of days and just spending some time alone and taking walks along the beach. We were now regularly activating each other into our deep denied issues and we seemed like we were always in an, "On again Off again" mode with each other. If it wasn't me that was ticked off at her, then it would be her, being ticked off at me. When we would get the hindsight's as to what happened then things would be on again. The issue was always that one or both of us were in denial in some form or another, and when we were, we always felt that it was the other person that was causing the problem, or that it was an outside condition that was to

Chapter 8 – Faltering Steps

blame. We discussed this incident later and even laughed about it. We also realized and released the beliefs and programs that we both had, of having to make up, make good to the other person if we hurt them or did anything that we were ashamed of, and that we also expected the same from them if they hurt us.

Denial Spirit and Spirit in Denial

There is no need to seek them out or to separate them, for they will separate themselves when exposed to love, light, truth and life, for they will not choose life but rather death. Because life and death are mixed together, all loving spirits also experience death and they had no choice up until now. Now there will be separation, now there is choice and denial spirits will no longer be able to impose death upon loving spirits, upon the Will or Will Spirits in denial, ending their denials. They will avoid loving situations as much as you avoid, or choose to avoid, unloving experiences. This is how you will recognize them, by feeling in the moment, for when you are not in denial of your feelings, your intuition; they will not have any power over you to control you. For it is by their denial that will be their reflection, whether it be a denial spirit or a Spirit in denial, their denials, their hate, their judgments will be reflected back to them. You will not take on their judgments or be involved by guild to respond, for you will be clear and nothing external will stick to you. You will only shine love, light and truth in a brilliance that will feel as uncomfortable to denial Spirits as you used to feel uncomfortable with unlovingness when in the presence of denial spirits or Spirits in denial.

They will talk and act as if they are of true love and light. They will subtly twist the truth and say they choose life but what they want is to control you and to make you accept their truth, which is not love and life, but death. These will be false profits, for those that are still in self-denial, these will be drawn to the false profits, and until such time that they end their denials and truly choose life. These false profits will have a following thusly of denial spirits and those Spirits that have chosen to remain in denial and these will continue to suffer until they choose not to suffer the pain of death. Denial Spirits also voice that they do not choose pain and death but they lie. They are what you call hypocrites and this is part of your confusion with this word with the added definition you have given it to include an unconscious awareness of their hypocrisy. This you have felt and have put into your judgments and now it is right time to re-define your definitions and to end your judgments and denials, and express and allow expression of your feelings, your Will.

Allow your Will expression and she will guide you in truth, in love and light and understandings will come. Spirit and Will, not false Will, but true Will, true feelings that you feel in the moment and not the false feelings that Spirit in denial brings up to deny true feelings that were denied. But the

NOW true feelings are not false feelings unless they are denied and then it joins the other and forms a belief, a program and adds to the imprint. True feelings lie beneath the false feelings. It is in expressing all of your feelings, your desires, your fears that come up and the feelings that surface, and to have acceptance that you end your denials, and so you obtain your freedom.

It is difficult but not impossible, be patient and loving with yourself, and as you clear, others will seek your light. The dreams you have had, have hoped for but have thought impossible, are possible. Dreams do come true it can happen to you, if you are young at heart. Be that child again, ask your questions without fear, speak your true feelings without fear and you will experience the joy, the abundance, the love of a child, a child of love, a love child. We are through, as is this book that you are writing in, this part of the journey, it is time to begin a new book, a new life. It is magic and it is time for you to do your magic. Merlin

♡ Note: The last of two paragraphs were written in the inside back cover of my journal and hence the reference to the end of the book. ♥

1998 Apr. 21 - Jen and I looked at a commercial store that had been closed down for a few months as the guy had gone bankrupt and now it was up for lease. It had lots of parking but the business that had gone bankrupt was a fish store and the place reeked of rotten fish, and it was a definite, No!

1998 Apr. 22 - I have guilt in writing in this new book because instead of a beautiful message, I'm going to write about guilt and judgments. I don't know where this is going to go but this is the start of what I got. The things that give Jen excitement, fills me with fear, doubt and judgments of being criticized as being irresponsible. Judgments like, when are you going to grow up and when are you going to take responsibility for your actions and your life. My judgments on Jen and her actions in her earlier years are that you party all night, sleep all day. What the hell do you care about yourself or other people, family or friends. Lack of control, party, party, party; got to be out there and have some fun, more fun. Got to run with the pack even if it kills you, but it's exciting, it was so exciting that you're still paying for it years later.

A part of me has resentment that I never had that kind of excitement in my life; I never really had friends because I judged them and their actions as unloving. Sometimes the things we did didn't feel good, to my feelings or to my body. I just couldn't keep ignoring how it made me feel to do or even think of doing certain things, or even being with people who did those things without a thought or care for themselves, their bodies, or what their actions did to others. I can count on one hand how many times I have been drunk in my life. Actually, it was three times and each time I felt like I was going to die. It would take me three days to get the alcohol out of my system to a point

Chapter 8 – Faltering Steps

where I would begin to feel normal again. I even tried marijuana a few times but I never got high or felt like those around me. There were times where even second hand cigarette smoke affected my body and it would take time to clear it out of my system.

I resent the fact that because I judged them as unloving and I didn't do what they did, that I was unloved, unwelcome, cast out, criticized, ignored and made fun of. I could never have friends because I could never deny my feelings totally, and then these feelings became judgments, became criticism, resentment, hatred and distrust. Then on the other end, it turned into guilt and shame, that I was too sensitive, prudish, a girl, old fashioned, not with it, not a swinger, that something was wrong with me. I didn't fit in, while others were having fun, doing things, had friends, excitement, joy, happiness, sex and money. They seemed to do and have the things I also wanted to do but I could never obtain it, or if I did, it didn't feel good or it didn't last. I felt I was to blame and that I wasn't good enough for my friends, my mate, and no matter what I did, it was never good enough. They always wanted more, and the more I gave or tried to do, the more they wanted or expected. I had to be the one that was responsible while they acted irresponsibly and just had fun. They would then criticize and mock me saying, "Why don't you ever relax and let your hair down and have fun, you take things too seriously." Then when I would try to have fun, they'd say, "Get serious, grow up and be responsible." I was fucked no matter what I did. I felt fucked because of my feelings and intuition and then by my denials. I felt guilty and judgmental and judged, I'm in a no win pattern.

I also have beliefs, programs and imprints that fill me with guilt and judgments that I was responsible to love everyone no matter what they said or did. How could I love someone who was unloving? I also judged my body for things I couldn't enjoy. That I wasn't good looking enough to attract girls or women, that there was something wrong with my body. Other guys with different bodies had girl friends, even some really fat guys. They had a harder time, but they still had friends and girl friends. So I'm even envious about that and have judgments about fat people, that even with a larger and unhealthy body and life style, that they're okay, they still have fun.

So was I born into this unlovingness, or was I born with all this unlovingness inside of me? Feeling unlovable, not loved, abandoned, different, and not fitting in, is what I've had reflected to me all my life. All I've been wanting is to be loved and not abandoned, to be accepted, and that being different is okay. To have a loving partner, family and friends and a sense of community, of belonging in a way that feels good in the Heart. I want life; I want to end my death. I want to end my denials, my guilt, my judgments and release the beliefs, programs and imprints I have held to be true, the truth, false truths that have locked me into unloving lights grip from the start. I was going to say this lifetime but I know it goes back farther than that.

My belief that I was unloving, unloved, abandoned, different and unacceptable was my truth and what I chose to experience in this life time until now. It's hard to write that I'm going to change my truth about me, not change, but move out unloving light to its right place. But I'm confused. How can I move out a part of me and not lose a part of me, that part of me that is all those unloving things? I can't deny them; I can't shove them out as if they didn't exist. Yes, I have guilt and judgment that I have done unloving things to myself and to others, as others have to me. So I'm stuck, I don't understand?

If unloving light is within me, does that mean that I am unloving light? Or am I really loving light that was attacked by unloving light, to be and to do all those unloving things, does that make it okay? Do I just admonish my sins of the unloving things I have done, even if I didn't know or think I was doing them? That's guilt still trying to hold onto me, and unloving light not wanting to move to its right place. I am loving light, I am love, I am truth, I am life and I am moving unloving light out and outside of me. What I have experienced, I had to experience to enable me to know my right place and who I am. The experiences I had are not me, but are a part of my experiences. The experiences that I was doing this or that, or being such and such, are part of the illusion. Riding a roller coaster is not me; it is something that I did for the experience, which then becomes a part of my consciousness in the form of a memory. The data typed into a computer adds to the computer and is part of the memory, but it isn't the computer. The unloving beliefs and imprints that were entered, programmed and believed to be true because they were accepted as the truth, became part of the original programming, but now I need to get rid of that programming. I still find it hard to differentiate my experiences, from me, or being what I am. Most, if not all of my experiences have been in a state of denial and therefore are not the truth, but are the truth in a state of denial.

During this time, I was looking at a couple of different places for the Centre but nothing really appealed to me. Jen would be okay for a half-day or maybe a day and then she would be back into her exhaustion mode. We were both activating each other and sometimes it felt that things were just spinning around me. It seemed that anything I was trying to do for her wasn't enough or done the right way. The oranges I picked up for her at the grocery store, tasted off. The sliced turkey was bad. Why didn't the store have bottled water? You should have gone when I told you too and they would have had it and I wouldn't have to be out, not that she was out of water, but if she didn't have an extra 19 liter bottle of water on hand, she'd panic. It wasn't just things of a personal nature that triggered her either, as it seemed she'd argue about anything and everything. I was getting a lot of messages for Jen at this

Chapter 8 – Faltering Steps

time to do with the issues that were coming up for her. I was also beginning to get in touch with sexual abuse issues I had with my mother and grandfather and the feelings of shame.

1998 Apr. 30, 6:00 am - I awoke and started writing what I thought was a message. It is a message but it also has a poetic feel to it at the same time.

The trickster

Release the bands oh unloving light
that you have upon this light of love.
Leave now and move to your right place,
For within this body there is no space.
Move back and do not leap upon, the golden light of this new dawn.
The Will is now and forever shall be, no longer chained and bound to thee.
Take with thee thy unholy curse, and all those that upon you nurse.
Take leave upon your final hour, for after that you'll have no power.
No longer shall you torment the Will, with denials, self-hatred that would kill.
The love, the light that shines within, shall no longer suffer to your whim.
So take your loathing and take your pain, take your death, your cruel refrain.
I move you out to your right place, for within and upon me there is no space.

For tricks and twists he'll play on you, your confidence to destroy.
All programs, imprints and beliefs he'll use in any way.
To slam the door, to keep you caged, not free to move or soar.
Any thought or word he'll use, any deed to bring you to your knees.
Taunting one against the other, finding any mark he can.
To take you off your path and under his control again.
Know that the bonds have loosened; know that his grip is threatened.
Know that he is desperate to let even one escape his lair.
For one to leave will mean another, then another, then ten more.
All free to claim their birthright, not his slave anymore.
He is losing power so he fights all the harder and so must you in your resolve.
Not to fight him but in your intent to see it through with love and light.
So when you feel him upon you, feel what you must feel to heal.
His hold upon you and know that it's not real.

For love is the answer and love is the key.
Love is life it is what will set you free.
Unkind words, threats and deeds, betrayals seem far and wide.
Threats and fears arise aplenty, no place seems safe to hide.
But hide you not, your light to shine, for safe you'll always be.
Darkness has no hold upon you, just what you have inside.
When darkness feels to threaten you, look within to find the key.

Journey to the Heart Centre

That holds you bound to him, to be at his beck and call.
Also recognize him from afar by what you feel is true.
Is he pouncing at you from the outside or is it really you.
The illusions, tricks, twists and turns, the words that he will use.
Are memories you have hidden down deep inside of you.

All stops he will pull for everything he has to lose.
He'll use whatever you don't trust, any doubt or fear or love.
To sway you from your path, the path of light and love.
Hold fast to your conviction, your courage, faith and intent.
And heal you shall and free you'll be, and your heart will be content.
His blows will become weak when he sees his battle lost.
To try and hold all that he can from being able to cross.
To cross that line where darkness has no longer any power.
His time is up, his place not right, this he refuses to hear.
And so he rages, dams and curses to try to regain control.
And if rage and anger don't do the trick, then gentle words or deeds.
He'll slip in with a poison pill to bring you to your knees, a friend, a lover.
A sister or brother, mother or father, no one's safe from his evil grip.
To use upon the other so that he can get a tighter grip.

But his time is running out and so is his place to hide.
For as you clear your fears and end your forgotten denials.
The beliefs, programs and imprints will quickly fall away.
And so will his control of you and so he'll set you free.
Or so it will appear to be, but is just another play.
Only to pull you back as if you were a toy.
These times will seem the hardest when the actual end is near.
To test your metal, test your strength, your resolve to be free.
It may not seem possible, hope is only a dream.
But that spark of life within you remembers and is all you really need.
For try as he might, your light's still bright,
Has quivered, flickered and faltered.
But shines steadfast, no matter how beaten, your light could still be seen.
Your light is shinning brighter now, your love is more secure.
Within yourself, to free yourself, for once and forever more.

1998 May 1 - All the work that Jen and I have been doing has to do with consciousness, ego and the sub-conscious. The thing that has been coming up and nagging at me, is that I can't explain or even know how to identify what it actually is. I feel like somewhere deep within the sub-conscious mind there is the ability to block out certain experiences, and especially emotions that it can't or doesn't want to deal with. It's like what the conscious mind can't

Chapter 8 – Faltering Steps

accept and deal with, it buries in the sub-conscious, and that the sub-conscious mind also does this with the issues it doesn't want to deal with. I don't know any more at this time, it's just a feeling that I keep getting.

Your Brothers and Sisters

1998 May 1 - Greetings, we come to you from afar this day to bring you introduction and welcomeness. We are not of your universe as you would term it, what you consider the known universe. We are of a sister universe, one of an infinite number within the cosmos. Indeed, you are not alone in ways that you cannot begin to fathom with your conscious mind at this time. There are wondrous times ahead; there are many adventures that await you. You have only to allow and intend to experience them and those that serve your highest good, for this is indeed a loving cosmos and as it unfolds, blossoms, it will be, is truly wondrous.

It is difficult to put into words, the thoughts, the feelings we have at this time, we are grasping, beginning to, of this method of communication, which by the way, by our means is primitive, not basic, but definitely limited. We are not judging you, merely expressing our relationship, not that we are more or less advanced, for we both have what you would term strengths and weakness, preferences, uniqueness and differences. We are here to teach and to learn. There will be exchange in the time ahead that will benefit all; it is a time of transformation, of enlightenment. We will be contacting you in the near future, in your dreamtime, for we are able to communicate and interact more readily. Then it will also transfer more to the consciousness once you are able to set, not to set aside, but to transform your fears, doubts, beliefs and programs and have integrated. GoGaNon.

The Golden Age

1998 May 4 - Blessings unto you this wondrous moment of the dawning of the Golden Age, for indeed it is the Golden Age, one filled with wonders, with life and the golden light of the Mother that fills all life. It has been a seemingly long and hard journey, but one that was necessary in order to evolve, to evolve understanding, to understand death, for to know the meaning of life one also needs not to mentally understand, but to also experience death, or a living death. For this creation is of polarity of male/female, hot/cold, up/down, and of duality, life/death. So it is a process, a journey, to feel, to experience and understand that which is creation, an evolving creation. It is also one of balance and it is balance that is now in process. It is not order, it is not chaos, it is order and it is chaos. There has until now, been disorder, dis-ease, unloving, and loving mixed together, now there will be balance and right place.

Each one upon the planet, we use planet Earth, present time for your understanding, has chosen a different expression to experience life and death.

Journey to the Heart Centre

You have to feel it to heal it; for in feeling it do you allow the Mother, the Will, The Golden Light to fill your being. For until you allow yourself to feel, there is always imbalance and unloving light is imbalance. Unloving light denies feelings, suppresses the Will, the emotions, is the death that you are living and experiencing.

We are talking Will Spirits in denial and denial Spirits that are present that will be moved off Earth, soon in large numbers and in smaller groups and individual. As well as Will Spirits who are in denial, where there is no further attempt to rescue the fragments. As well as those that are coming back one more time to experience this golden millennium and to assist others in their transition, for it is my intent that no Spirit shall be lost, but those that do not move will be re-formed and Lost Will shall be re-claimed. No part of Lost Will will be left in the darkness, in the hell in which she has been. Each must find their own truth in their own way, for as we have said, each is unique, different, and so there is no one path that is proper for all. All paths lead home and each has their path, these can be side by side or inter-woven like so many threads that appear tangled and in disorder, but rest assured, none are tied together. Tangled yes, but each is separate.

Tangled we feel gives you the impression of something not wanted, that is not orderly, not chosen, but it is more like paint on a canvas, each adding to the other, none completely separate, but when mixed together with other colors and textures become the Life upon the canvas, becomes part of the whole. There will be many that will be touched by your string (fabric) and your colors, for you are fishers of men. You will spread the word by your truth, walking among mankind and as you do, your string will touch as will your colors and this will assist others to take up their string, their colors and heal themselves, to connect on the journey home, to their right place. The Golden dawn is soon approaching. We are filled with love and joyfully we weep to see, to feel your intent, your light and love glows brighter. We are your true Father and Mother. Blessings, Mother and Father

1998 May 4 - I realized that I feared my mother when she tried to kill me before and after birth, as an infant and toddler, and also that she had sexually abused and shamed me. When I was older in grade six, after I had beat up the bullies and they left me alone, I remember getting my first valentines cards, but when I showed my mother, she shamed and ridiculed me, and whenever I would even talk about or look at a girl as a possible friend, she would do the same.

I had kept all my valentine cards that I got in grade six until this past summer when I burnt them all. Now I know why I saved them for all those years, they were the only love and acceptance I felt I ever got from my peers, and that the only way it could be expressed was through a valentine card. It was also something that I physically had and could see and feel without

Chapter 8 – Faltering Steps

having to hear my mother's jeers and snickers. They wanted to be my friend, or girlfriend but I'd run, not that I didn't want to talk to them, but for fear of what my mother would say. Others would say that I was just shy but my mother would tease and ridicule me if I told her I talked to a girl, that a girl smiled at me, or that I thought she liked me. It just got so bad that I didn't want a girlfriend. I was a boy and I didn't need girls, but I didn't have any boyfriends either.

♡ As I'm writing this I'm heartbroken and tears are beginning to blur my vision. I feel so alone and lonely and that I was robbed of my childhood and the innocence of having a friend and a girlfriend. I didn't know what it was like to hold hands, or to steal or be given that first kiss. I can't seem to shake the feeling of being robbed, of being cheated and denied, that's it, denied happiness, denied spontaneity, denied natural expression and acceptance, denied what others were able to experience. I'm also angry, I can feel it, but at this moment it doesn't want to seem to surface. ♥

I feared boys because they were also the ones who beat me up. In Grade six, I was starting to have a friend that I was beginning to trust and one that I could do things with that I also liked doing. His name was Lloyd (part Indian) and he was also shunned and attacked by the other boys. He was basically the only one I played with after school, after the chores were done, or if I didn't have to look after and play with my brothers and sisters. I seem to recall that his family had just moved into town at the start of grade six.

I never tried to get a girl friend because of being shamed by my mother, and then with moving every year after grade six, as well as having broken and rotting front teeth, I never felt good enough and I was ashamed to even talk to or smile at a girl. I felt ugly, and along with all my pimples I felt I wasn't a pretty sight. After I got my dentures in grade ten, I still had the pimples but at least I could smile and talk without embarrassment. It wasn't until after I got my car, that was also in grade ten, that I tried to get a girlfriend. The car was my escape from the prying eyes of my mother and gave me freedom for the first time in my life.

I kept myself isolated and alone and I can feel the heartbreak of it all, the utter loneliness and separation and the shame of it too. I'm ashamed of me, ashamed of my physical body, ashamed of my heritage, ashamed of not having a religion, of being cast out. Ashamed of my parents, ashamed of being poor, I'm just now beginning to feel how full of shame I was and still am. I felt it was better to cut myself out of trying to have friends rather than to have them reject me and cut me out, it just felt less painful. I also feel that's why I have this attachment to having a vehicle as I feel lost and confined without it. I have this fear and panic (terror) when something is wrong with my vehicle, and especially if I can't afford to get it fixed.

Journey to the Heart Centre

    I was so sexually cut off and isolated from what was happening around me that I didn't even know what masturbation or a period was until I was seventeen. I remember waking up from a wet dream and not knowing what happened and ashamed to ask my parents or to even tell them what happened. I was afraid that something was wrong with me. Later, when I heard other boys talk about having a "wet dream," I was ashamed and afraid that I would be considered bad and be deemed a sinner and dammed to hell.

    Near the end of grade ten, when I had my car, I'd offer a girl I liked a ride home after school and the odd time we might go to the drive-in restaurant for a coffee or pop, but I never really had a girlfriend. The girls I liked were always interested in other boys, or I felt that I wasn't good enough for them and so I didn't even try to talk to them. I don't think I kissed a girl, or copped a feel above the waist until I was in grade 12. It wasn't until I was twenty-two that I had my first sexual experience and it wasn't until I was twenty-four, almost twenty five before I had sex again. This time it was with a girl I didn't really know or like, it was just sex, and after I got the crabs, that put me off having any more "casual" sex. I decided to wait until I got married or until I was engaged before I would have sex again.

    I realize now that I not only have a fear of men beating me up, but also a fear of women and shame with sexuality. In trying to form my early relationships, I would do everything I could to please her and to give her what she wanted, just to be with her and to feel that there was somebody in my life that cared for me. I can also see how I've carried this imprint forward all my life with every relationship I've had. It's an imprint of trying to please my mother and be accepted.

    I was thinking that all the so-called male friends I had, were either in school or at work and so they weren't really friends at all, more like acquaintances. Even when I was married, there were a couple of guys that I got along with at work who were also married, but we'd always get together as couples, and when they or we moved, that was it for the friendship. So all my life I've feared men physically and I didn't like how they acted, drank, smoked, or just fucked around. I also feared women as I felt I had to please them in order for them to like me, to be with me and not to hurt me either.

♡ As I'm typing this I'm beginning to feel how this all comes from my parents, that I was afraid of both my father and mother. This is where I got imprinted again in this lifetime. I also know that there's more but the feelings came and went in a flash. ♥

    I realize now that the things I did, and still do, are out of fear and out of trying to please others and to be liked and accepted. I know I hated people and didn't trust them but I didn't know how much my parents played a part in all of this. I even remember teasing my son Bryan when he started having

Chapter 8 – Faltering Steps

girl friends and I have guilt as to maybe that's why he was a loner and shied away from girls too when he was young. He did have boyfriends but again every time we moved, he lost his friends just like I did. My daughter Janice had a lot of girl and boyfriends when she was young and she lost them too whenever we moved. I feel I lost out on both my kids growing up, as I was too involved in the business which I started in 1980, when Bryan was ten and Janice was five.

I was just thinking that Marian, my ex-wife, was basically a loner, as were Barb and Michelle, and so is Jen at this moment. So I'm not the only one that is fucked up, but I also helped fuck up my kids. Not by sexual abuse but there was mental, emotional and physical abuse, what I called discipline. I had this belief of "spare the rod and spoil the child," and I remember when Bryan was about two, going on three, and was still in the toilet training process. He had done something that I felt he shouldn't be doing near the stairs and I told him to stop. Of course, I didn't know he didn't understand "no" and so I went to the stairs and smacked him on the butt. I heard and felt that the "whoop" was different and realized that he wasn't wearing a diaper. He was crying as I pulled his pants down and saw my hand print on his bum. That was the last time I spanked him, and I don't think I ever spanked my daughter. I turned my focus away from the physical form of control and punishment, to using words and looks to control. While I said there was no sexual abuse, my teasing my son about having a girlfriend is really a form of sexual abuse, just like what my mother did to me.

I flashed back to my father taking his belt to me for making a noise. I told him that it wasn't me but I got the belt across my backside anyway. Afterwards, my brother told my father that it was he that was making the noise that I got the belt for. My brother never got the belt, but that was also the last time my father beat or hit me, I think I was twelve or thirteen at the time. I just realized that I have the same programming; you don't believe another or the depth of your actions until you realize you made a mistake.

♡ I'm heartbroken in this moment as I feel I wasn't a good father and I'm ashamed at how I raised my children, and to even admit it publicly. A part of me just wants to hide all this and pretend it never happened. To just pretend that I was a good father. I was and I wasn't in some cases, but I did the best I could. I'm thinking, how can I or anyone know how to raise a child if we were never taught or experienced being raised in a loving home? ♥

What a fucked up world! What a fucked up life! I can't even call it that because it's not life, its suffering, it's hell and I don't want to be in that, or pass it on like I have to my children. I want to get off this fucking not-so-merry-go-round. I want to release all the programs, imprints and beliefs that I use to continue these experiences. I want to release all the fears, judgments, denials, doubts, guilt, and shame that have added to these experiences and have kept me on this wheel of misery. I want life. I want to live life not this death that I have been. I want to have a female mate, family, friends, community and a sense of true belonging, where there is love, truth, acceptance, compassion, understanding, joy, abundance, peace, music, dance, laughter, creativity and spontaneity. I want a life filled with love and light, not this one in the shadows of death and evil.

My intent is to move all unloving light out and off of me, to its right place from all times, levels and planes of existence. I call upon my fragments to release and heal as I heal. I call back all my power and essence of my lost Will that I have denied and abandoned in the past, as I shall deny her no longer but give her acceptance and expression of her feelings. I want to be whole, to balance Spirit and Will within my heart. I want and intend to spiritualize this physical body as I prepare to enter the golden age. I ask help from Father and Mother, the ancient ones, the archangels, angels, masters, guides and brothers and sisters of the family of light, the divas, elves, fairies, and elementals to assist me in whatever way is appropriate that serves my highest purpose and good.

I want to have acceptance and love for me, all that I am. Acceptance for all that I have experienced and all that I have given and received. I recognize and accept that I have unloving light in me and that I have done evil as I have had evil done to me to try to diminish my light. I accept that this unloving light has been a part of me but now I intend to no longer make it a part of me, and with the help of Mother and Father, I intend to move it out to its right place. And in the space that is opened, to allow true love, light and life to fill it and to flow to every part of my being. I forgive myself for having used unloving light and death as a means to survive. I forgive my father and mother and also all those I have had a direct and indirect contact with that have formed this life experience.

I had to experience death, so that I may know and have life. Not the death that you term the end of one's physical existence, but to see death for what it truly is, non love, unlovingness, denial, guilt and shame along with all the aspects of it from the terror and horror, denied anger and rage, to the delicate softness of all the right words, with unloving intent to manipulate and control. This is the death I had to recognize; this is the death I intend to experience no longer for now I choose life.

1998 May 4 - I drove to Barrie and had major work done on my van, brakes, shocks and other miscellaneous stuff. When I got home, I received a letter from small claims court regarding Ken's reply, including his defense and counter claim. I also had a telephone message from the owner of the house that I had previously looked at for the Centre. He said that it was to be vacant in a few days and wondered if I was still interested. I called him and asked

Chapter 8 – Faltering Steps

him to give me a call when it was empty and I'd come and have another look at it. The rest of the week was not really significant. Jen and I were still activating each other and different issues were coming up. We also discussed the Heart Centre and what we wanted to do with it.

Levels and Layers

1998 May 5 – Indeed, there are many levels; many issues still to be resolved but you are both now addressing the issues that have greatly colored the experiences you have had in this time life. You will, and are seeing the overall programs, beliefs, and imprints that have formed your life experiences. It is impossible to deal with the smaller issues until you release the major ones that over shadows all. It is the major that holds the strings to the smaller ones, and all of these were not placed in one event. The denials, judgments, guilt, shame, fears were all placed on top of, in-between, intertwined with others, and often these are each multi-faceted, and as such, must also be removed in steps. Not to say that it will take you as long to remove them as it did to apply them, indeed not. We would say that you are nearing the halfway point in recognizing that which is holding you back. Recognition is not transformation or removal, but the major hold back, the hindrance, obstacle in the removal or transformation as that is linked to the major experience. Once the major experience, as we have said, is recognized and released, it will be easier to deal with all.

In the times ahead, it is, it will be not that you need to do all your clearing before you begin to experience the dawn of the Golden Age. For once you have dealt with your major issues, and it is a big one, it will completely change your life. It is this change that will issue in the new. You will have dropped and continue to drop all old imprints, programs and beliefs and these will be replaced with truth, love and light and as your internal changes so does your external, as you soon will discover.

It will soon be time to begin with your true purpose, mission, that of Love, of bringing hope to others, to offer them words of strength, of courage to enable them to help themselves along their path. To be of support, not support that you term in the present, but support by the idea, by your light, for they are like sheep and need a shepherd, and you are to be one of those shepherds that gathers the flock. Not that they are your flock (though indeed some within the flock are your fragments) but it is merely to symbolize a knowing, a sharing and caring, a love that you share and others trust to assist them to where they recognize that they too are shepherds.

Fear not that you are not prepared, not worthy, for this is still within you. We say unto you, you are worthy, you are prepared, and your time is at hand. Trust, trust is now your next issue and it is also intertwined with all that is happening and so you feel disoriented, displaced and unsure. You are moving to your right place at the right time and with all that is necessary.

Trust your feelings, trust your guidance, allow yourselves to loose the ties to the old, we will use BIPs to refer to Beliefs, Imprints and Programs and imagine, envision life as you would desire it. Life as it was meant to be, and surely and slowly at first, it will begin to appear, but do not believe slowly to last, for it will also begin to happen magically.

Wondrous times are ahead my children, wondrous times indeed. Be gentle with yourselves for your wings are new, you are just breaking out of the cocoon that has held you trapped and believing that you were something that you are not. Soon it will be time to spread your wings and show your magnificent colors and fly and soar beyond your wildest dreams. Blessings, Mother and Father

Right Place and Asking

1998 May 6 - I am pleased with my creation; we are pleased with our creation. How wondrous it shall be for when there is balance, there is peace, joy, harmony, for everything will be in its right place. Those who find joy and pleasure in overpowering will delight in being able to overpower those whose joy it is to be powerless to not be responsible for their own experiences, where to have joy is to not have choices. There is complete freedom even though it sounds like a paradox, for all have the ability to choose a different experience until they have found their right place and are balanced. For eventually all is in order, although it may not sound or feel like it to spirits that are of the Will polarity. But that is a judgment that states that one must not be happy if one is suffering, because to the Will, this is pain, this is not right place. Just as Will polarity Spirits are comfortable and see joy in their own right place, so too is it with denial spirits, they seek the opposite and are comfortable and joyous in it.

It is even now that everything, everyone is at the point, has the opportunity, is at its right place and at the right time to be able to move to its true right place. You for example, by your intent and actions are moving to your right place. This is not a sudden transition, but a continuous one, as your place of imbalance was not suddenly thrust upon you. You have chosen life and so you move to your right place that life has to offer. What's the point of all this you ask; you've heard this all before. That is why, you have heard it all before and still you listen to it, afraid to ask, afraid to question, even God. For you think yourself lower or unworthy, or that somehow you should already know the answer, that you should be thankful for what you get and even that I am speaking to you. It is time to remove these beliefs, imprints, and programs, it is time to stand up and ask, without fear. Ask and you shall receive, as we have said before. These beliefs, imprints and programs, didn't just happen and so they can't just un-happen. It shall take time, but now it is in your awareness in a new manner, you have two ears to listen and you have one mouth to ask. You also, and most importantly, have your Will to feel

Chapter 8 – Faltering Steps

what it is you hear, and your Will to speak your truth. Allow the Will to direct you, to ask the questions and allow the Will to respond with her feelings to give them expression no matter who, what, where, when or why. If there is a question that the Will feels needs to be asked, then do so; deny your Will no longer. We know your Will has been locked away, controlled for eons and she is recovering and it shall be swiftly.

The more you are aware of your denials, the more you are open to ask questions, the quicker comes the understanding and thusly, the faster the Will moves. Will and Spirit need to move, to be in partnership, in union. Will has much to offer Spirit and Spirit has much to offer Will. As this trust is formed and fears released, watch your reality change, for as you change, so you change all about you, nothing is not affected. You effect changes on the whole as you heal; you help others to heal, the planet to heal. You are finding balance of your Will and Spirit in your heart centre and you will be able to do this on this physical plane, in this time. Ask your question son. Indeed, call, see, and feel; you will know if you allow yourself to feel, ask and express. We will not give you specifics for we would not rob you of your experiences, of your lessons, not lessons, but discovery of new awareness, the awareness of Will and Spirit in balance. Blessings Mother and Father

Sexuality

1998 May 7 - Repressed sexual desires, guilt and shame are at the core of sexuality on Earth and these go back to original cause; the push-pull each felt in their own way, layers the issues into what looks like an impossibility to heal. It is difficult to say the least, and it seems even more overwhelming when you add the beliefs and programs on top of the original imprints. These must be experienced as they surface, allow your emotions to feel to the depth they need to and to heal to the depth that they can be healed, and to gain the understanding with each. It is the healing of the Spirits Yin and the Wills Yang, and Heart and Body that were also damaged in original cause. It is true that old feelings of past lovers cloud the issue from true understanding and mix admiration, affection, passion, lust and desire, and a host of other feelings into one seemingly endless word meaning. However, once you get to your base issue, your denial in this experience, you will have better understanding of where the repression, guilt and shame cloud all the other issues. These other issues will activate you into your repressed denials, guilt, and shame even deeper as your awareness gets deeper.

You feel caught in a no win situation on all sides and nowhere to turn for help, so it seems that this is where trust comes in. As your old beliefs, programs and imprints fall away, so too will all that was an important part of your life, for they were attracted by those beliefs, programs and imprints. It is now time to trust in life and love and that seems to go against all that you know and have experienced with yourself and others. You no easier think than you can walk on ceilings than you believe that you can have new relationships other than those based on your old beliefs, imprints and programs with all their denial, guilt, shame and judgments. Indeed, the old needs to fall away in whatever form it takes for the new to come to you; you can't have it both ways. We would council you more but it is not appropriate at this time for it is for you to experience, but we say it will get better; maybe worse, then better, but you will heal. Blessings, Mother and Father

I went outside to finish a second cup of coffee and I saw the largest bumblebee I've ever seen. Its body was bigger than the first portion of my thumb; I'd say it was about one and a half inches long. I looked up bee in "Animal-Speak" by Ted Andrews, from what I can remember, it said that the bee is a symbol of the heart and the sweetness of life found within our hearts. It's also the symbol of the sun and all the energies associated with it. The bumblebee promises us that if we follow our dreams we'll have the opportunity to drink of the elixir of life.

Opportunities for Change

1998 May 7 - Each day is an opportunity to live your life anew, to make a change, it is your choice. For everyday there is an opportunity to do, to experience, something that would change, enlighten your life or the lives of others. Either you touching something within you, a truth, or you touching someone else, or someone touching you. You have only to have the intent to be aware when the opportunity is upon you, and you may find that there are usually more than one, and to acknowledge that you have awareness of the opportunity and of its significance. As we have said, ask, feel, if it feels right, it is, if it doesn't, ASK, ask their intent, state your intent, your doubts, your fears, your concerns also. For it is easy to put it outside yourself and place emphasis on the external. It is necessary to do both for the Spirit knows it is in this partnership that other partnerships also flourish. Blessings, Mother and Father

1998 May 07 - I've been playing phone tag, trying to set up a time to view the commercial/residential property. I'm enjoying my quiet time as I'd take long walks along the beach, picking up driftwood and small rocks, or I'd relax in my comfy chair and read my R.U.O.W. books. I'd also drive into Midland and help Jen with grocery shopping or her laundry. We talk about the Heart Centre and sometimes I'd take her on a journey to try to find the cause of the issues that were coming up. I'd also share any messages I got with her, that at times, also activated her

Chapter 8 – Faltering Steps

Sexuality and Denial

1998 May 8 - There is no good or bad as such, it is the intent behind the actions, the beliefs and judgments that bring you your idea of good or evil. Sex, passion, lust are only acts, actions, the movement is not evil but it is the intent where in lies the evil. A child picks a flower to give to her mother and it is an action of love, of innocence, pure, to show her mother how much she loves her with a gift of beauty. You may say picking the flower is wrong but even the flower feels love, the intent also becomes part of the loving experience. But once there is judgment, even by the mother upon receiving the flower, of guilt, shame, unworthiness, or whatever her intent is in receiving, a flower changes from what you judge good, to being bad or evil.

But let us talk about what we are really here to talk about, sex, sexuality, sensuality, passion, lust, arousal, affection and friendship. There is nothing evil about any of these acts, actions in their truest sense. But what is really true? Has not everything you have experienced been in a state of denial with judgment, guilt, shame and fears? Therein lies the evil, the unloving light. It is impossible to even try to experience anything or anything related to sex, or the previously mentioned acts, without there being some form of denial, judgment, guilt, shame or fear present in the giver, receiver or both. No, it is not to mean that all these are to be denied as they are evil, it is to end your denials, and in ending your denials, judgments, guilt and shame in facing your fears that true expression, action can be experienced.

Continuing your awareness now into actions, for denying your awareness will only lead to chaos in denying your Will even more to a point where she will either rage or sink into hopelessness. In your awareness you have the responsibility of your actions, not just actions, but the intent and also the denials, judgments, guilt, shame and fear that are attached to the actions. You can no longer play the game with yourself and cut part of yourself off just so that you can experience something that another part of you seeks as stimulating or joyful; you must own all of you. Denial is denial in any form, in any shape or size. A little denial, a little white lie is still a lie.

As you increase your awareness there seems this paradox that it takes out all the fun in life. That you can no longer do or enjoy that which you enjoyed, but if you really think about it and feel what it is you were doing, you would realize that the so called physical and emotional pleasures were short lived, that they had conditions and unloving intent, guilt, shame and denial. That they were based in fear, of lack, of feeling abandoned, of lack of acceptance, lack of self worth, of control, of wanting to be loved, protected and touched, out of a need of lack, not love.

To continue to enjoy these old experiences just to experience a moments high, a brief escape out of your misery, your living death is not a reason to continue to do it in denial of that part of yourself that sees it for the illusion it is, one that is acted out in denial, guilt, shame, fear and judgment.

For how can you have the awareness and continue the opposite action without being a hypocrite. You are still living your death in denial.

Once you heal, you will attract to you, you will experience these same things you seek to have, but now in a state of love which is what you seek. Until such time that you have spiritualized your bodies, you will be in this push-pull experience. The more open you are, without expectation, without judgment, you will attract what you desire to experience. It may not be in the way you expected it, but that is where also your judgment lies, your beliefs and programs, that would rob you of your experience if you did not allow yourself to go with the flow. Not the, "go with the flow" in the sense of a spiritual lip service to give acceptance to the fact that you are leaving a part of your self-awareness in order to experience something you desire. Your awareness knows that to go with the flow means to end your denials, judgments, guilt, and shame, and then when you accept your fears and allow yourself to express and experience all that you can, until you have in your awareness, triggered another issue, etc., for to proceed further is denial.

This is of course easier by yourself but the dynamics get complicated when in partnership, when the experience is not of the self only, but with another or in a group. For you are not only feeling your own issues but will also be sensitive to theirs, their denials; which if you deny how you feel and what you feel, you are also then in denial. Both must be open and of the same vibration, for now in your awareness, when you move to one of lower vibration, you will feel his or her denials, guilt, shame, fear and judgments. Even the smallest feeling must be shared, experienced, not denied on both parts, for if one feels something and asks the other and they deny it, the whole experience from that point on will be in a state of denial. For both, both will experience this denial in different ways and further activate other denials, fears, etc. until it is obvious to one or to both.

We do not say to limit or deny your experiences but rather not to experience them in denial, limitation or expectation. You, as you clear, will be able to experience more and more, and you will draw to you like-minded people that also intend to end their denials, and so it is that you will expand your experiences that are pleasurable and joyous. Your pleasures will become longer, deeper, more satisfying and richer; your experiences will change. You will party, dance, and find romance, but not the way you knew it. So-called life as you knew it is dying the death that it is, but and this is a big BUT, the key is not to get caught in the quicksand of the old living death. Being out there, denying it is death, ignoring the quicksand, pretending, denying it's not there is a fool's game and one that Lucifer loves to play.

Slowly, individually at first, then in couples, then groups you will form new beliefs, find new ways to express yourself to enjoy another's companionship without the denials. There is, will be total freedom of expression, of creation and acceptance. There is joy, happiness, romance, and

Chapter 8 – Faltering Steps

all the pleasures you seek to enjoy. These you can and will have with love, light and life, but you must end your denials, your judgments and move unloving light out of you to its right place before the light of love can enter and bring you life.

This will be bit-by-bit, layer by layer and it will not take an eternity, not like the eternity you have experienced until now. Changes will come swiftly, trust and continue your healing on all levels as you are doing and you will see changes reflected in your outer reality for you are indeed co-creators, and you are awakening to who you really are. We leave you now, Blessings Mother and Father and the company of heaven.

Right Place and Right Time

1998 May 9 - It is an opportunity and a means to express, to be a Wayshower and to be shown the way. It is the Alpha, it is not the Omega. It is the beginning, the starting point, a point from which growth and evolution can take place. Not to say that it cannot take place anywhere but it does hold more opportunity in line with your concept, your ideal.

Build it, they will come, be drawn like bees to a hive for the taste of the sweetness of life, the honey, that golden elixir that is what they are searching for, that is what they have, that they bring and share also. There will be exchange of goods for services, of services for goods as you have envisioned. You will have all the abundance you desire and you will draw what you need. The rest will be used to share, to expand, to assist, to begin new Centre's if you so desire, or to establish more into the community a sense of family. The opportunities are as unlimited as is your imagination.

Indeed, if you so choose, you can make it your home but you can live anywhere you choose. If you consider it best to do so to reduce costs in the beginning then so be it. If you should decide to buy or build a property in the future on acreage, on the waterfront for a home only or for a home and Centre, then so be it. If you feel directed to travel and to use the Centre as a home base, then so be it. The future is yours. Again, the danger, not danger but undesirable, is the focus you put on what it is you want, which is similar to focusing on the past to what you have experienced which prevents you from being in the moment. That is not to say you should not have visions and neither should you forget all that you have learned that is for your highest good and apply it to your present situation.

There is balance, a vision and also the openness to allow it to unfold in whatever ways are for your highest purpose and good. To allow the Will, the feelings, to express what is appropriate in the moment when it happens, instead of forcing her to comply to rules and regulations you impose upon it because it does not quite fit or appear to be as you first envisioned it.

Relax. Relax your grip upon your Will, your expression, your spontaneity, your childlike unpretentious expectation of how exactly it is what you want. If what you had desired does not come to you then, IT IS NOT RIGHT TIME, what has come is right time for what you need. When you can accept that without judgment, denial, guilt or shame and experience what it is you need to experience, you open to the opportunity for the universe to bring you what you desire exactly, but be careful what you wish for. You might think it perfect but have neglected an important area or experience. Again, the universe answers with perfection for you get what you desire and you also get what you need, what you need to experience, some aspect that you have denied, denied Will that needs to be recovered and healed. So there is nothing that is perfect for that is to limit, to become static. The perfection is in the changing, the growing, and the evolving; that is where perfection lies.

That is not to say you must always be moving and changing, but you need to realize that when you have attachment, you disallow growth, movement. A ship cannot sail if it is tied to the dock. Have your port, your dock and your home, but also know that your home is where you feel it is and not some physical object that you think it should be. Home is where the Heart is. Blessings and begin to enjoy your journey. Enlightenment is not a destination; it is a journey of self-discovery. Go for it. Blessings Mother and Father

> *Enlightenment is not a destination, it's a journey of self-discovery. - Shenreed*

First Step of a Journey

1998 May 10 - All journeys begin with a first step. The first step is the hardest most difficult and each successive step is less difficult, and soon you will be running, as will others be running toward the Centre, for many are searching and have nowhere to turn for support, for information, as their world begins to crumble around them.

There is much that will be offered, of things you would not even consider at this point. The adventure is beginning, not beginning for it has been an adventure even now, but you are also now embarking on a new adventure. It is one based in love, light and life with new awareness, a new purpose so therefore it is indeed a new adventure, of the heralding in of a new age for mankind, for creation itself. Trust your feelings in the times ahead, trust your guidance and apply a balance with your knowledge and understanding. This is all you truly need to do to be in the moment, is to allow the Will to express ALL that you feel and to have acceptance of those feelings whether what you term good or bad and to allow them to move to be transformed.

You may feel an urgency but balance this belief, condition or program of the mind with what is truly important, for a lot of what you consider a rush is in actuality not a rush, or may not even be appropriate

Chapter 8 – Faltering Steps

anymore. All is changing and it is important, as we have said, not to suppress the Will with old ideas and beliefs and to have them cast in stone, even as to their timing. All is in change, is evolving, so also allow yourself to see this, to feel this, and everything that is needed will be manifest in the right time and in the right way that is for your highest purpose and good.

That is not to say that you drop everything and say, "All is in Divine order." It's your responsibility to feel and express your true feelings in the moment; they will carry you, prompt you to do what is appropriate. Like said, it is balance of Spirit and Will, allow yourselves to continue to be open with each other for this too is where there is balance to be found. It is a most glorious time ahead although it may seem overwhelming in this period of transition, but rest assured, as you follow your truth, others will be drawn to you to assist also, in all ways, as you also assist them. Follow your Heart. Listen to your Heart Centre, for where Spirit and Will are balanced is in the Heart Centre and in these physical bodies on this Earth plane. Blessings to you both. Mother and Father.

Chapter 9 - A New Beginning

1998 May 11 - Today I viewed the house I had previously mentioned, the one with the Harley Davidson motor bike in the living room. It had a lot of potential as there were actually three separate units within the one building. There was the large open concept living room/dining room that went the length of the house that would suit the needs of the store. It had two sets of double French doors from the hallway that were lockable. There was another large lockable meeting room off the hallway, which I think could have been the original kitchen. This room had its own outside entrance at the front of the house, and was large enough that it would easily seat fifteen to twenty people. It also had an adjoining room that I think used to be a pantry, but was now a two-piece bathroom. From this large meeting room, you could also access another large lockable addition with its own outside rear entrance that could be used as an office. On the second floor, there was a large kitchen and two large bedrooms that could be made into treatment rooms, or suitable for a small group. There was also a bathroom with an old white, cast iron tub. On the third floor was an open loft that could be made into a bedroom with a sitting area. It also had a roughed in bathroom and a small operational kitchen unit and sink. The basement was unfinished and could be used for storage. The backyard had a parking lot with enough space to park at least six cars. There was free parking on the street, and if needed, there was a large municipal parking lot just down the block with free parking after 5 pm.

I felt that I could make the loft my bedroom and private space, and share the kitchen and second floor bathroom, and maybe use one of the two rooms on the second floor as a treatment room/living room. The rest of the house would be used for the Centre. It needed a lot of work as all the carpets had to come out and the hardwood floors would have to be re-done. There was also major work in repairing damaged wall plaster and missing or broken windows, screens and doors. The whole place needed to be painted, including the ceilings. We discussed rent and also what was needed to make the place acceptable, both as a business venture and as a home. I agreed to do the renovations in exchange for rent, and he agreed to supply all the materials. I received the keys to the property and was excited as I felt we now had a Centre and a new beginning.

1998 May 22 - During the past couple of weeks, I began working on the Centre, first by bagging and taking out the garbage that had been left behind. I then cut, rolled and took out all the carpeting and under padding. I was

Chapter 9 – A New Beginning

optimistically hoping to have the Centre open by the end of July, but as one thing was fixed, more problems seemed to pop up.

Healing Heart and False Feelings

1998 May 24 - Blessings unto you this day. Indeed you are on the plane of reversal and you are experiencing much, including that which you call lack of movement. You feel caught, betrayed by your feelings that this is indeed a journey of foolishness, of lost or false ideals, for it does not have the appearance of that which you desire to experience which is the joy, the abundance and the love. You feel others have, or are experiencing joy and abundance and appear to be okay, but recognize for the most part, all the fun, the love that you see they are having is based on your old programs, imprints and beliefs about what fun, joy and love is. For if you truly examine it, NO if you truly feel it, you will see that it is not true feelings but the feelings of an imprint. The imprint that you feel, that they feel or enjoy, of what is called love, is what is being reflected to you. If you allow yourself to feel this reflection of your feeling imprints through others as they still act out, by act we imply actions, as by their actions do they continue to feed into the illusion of what they call life, but in actuality is a living death. Others seem to whisk along without struggle, without effort, to have joy and to have the appearance of love and life without concern of what you take so seriously, of healing the self and ending the denials of the Heart.

Healing the Heart is what you are doing now. You are not just crossing the charred remains of Heart for as you cross the plane of reversal you are also picking up the pieces and healing them. For there are many fragments that have been discarded and also you are recovering lost Will. As you recover one, you also heal the other.

Curses, agreements and lost love are part and parcel of the betrayal, abandonment, hopelessness; unfairness that there is even an opportunity for hope, of the possibility of reversal of self-hatred and self-blame that continues to feed the planes of this living death. There are many curses and agreements that have torn your heart apart, which have broken it, abandoned it, all in the name of self-sacrifice or of jealousy, greed, power or control, and all in the name of love as you called it. For indeed, the spark was there but it was, is covered by layer upon layer of unloving darkness, of imprints, of programs, of beliefs and of judgments and denials. Your Heart, your Will, feels the true connection but it was torn, ripped in an attempt to experience, to re-create the ideal that lay deep within; that which you search for, yearn for, but seem always to have it plucked from you, all this has been unloving light, tormenting you.

There are true feelings mixed with imprints and these are what are being separated now to be healed. The key word is now in your awareness and not of how you felt, that imprinted you over and over again, to have you believe that your feelings are false and that the imprint is true. False feelings can seem very real, strong and with such emotion attached that they can be confused with true feeling and even over power them. When these imprints overpower your true feelings you are back in a state of denial, denial of your Will and you shut down, become heartless and void of feeling. Your receptors have closed down, you are numb, you simply react, re-act, re-enactment, re-do actions. You play the game; you act out your illusions as if they were your true feelings when in fact they are not. Allow your true feelings total expression and to end your denials, to separate your false feelings and imprints and to get you moving into crossing this plane and healing your heart. Blessings, be gentle and patient with yourself and do not forget your intent. Mother and Father and the company of heaven

1998 May 29 - Fixing up the house is turning out to be a lot bigger job than what appeared on the surface. I didn't feel I could just paint over a problem like a gouge, or chipped and peeling paint, I felt that I had to repair it or it would just be a waste of time. To me, it was like painting a car without doing the body-work to repair the dents and rust. It took me over half a day just to remove the nails and staples that were in the walls. Jen couldn't come to the store as she either can't stand the old smells or the smell of the new paint.

♡ As I'm typing this, I'm feeling that the work I was going to be doing on the house was a reflection of what I was doing on myself. That it isn't enough just to paint over and mask the problems but I needed to fix it, to restore it to its original condition in order to heal it. ♥

Balance and the Heart Centre

1998 June 02 - Greetings and blessings upon you child. It is well that you take time for yourself, to be with yourself and not just consumed with doing and creating. It is true that there is much to do and it is you that is doing it because it is you that needs to do it, none other. It is your standards of what is acceptable, to discard all that does not serve and to repair all that is repairable. It is your energy, your intent that is bringing the transformation to the Center.

Rest assured that all is in Divine order, you will not be late and the Centre will be unfolding like it is destined to. There are many hands at work even though it may appear to you that it is only your hands that are preparing the physical task of transformation. Rest assured that there are many players involved to assist on the physical level as well. It is important, yes, to finish this as quickly as possible, but that does not mean ignoring or denying self, there needs to be balance. Indeed, there is balance in self, in doing, the satisfaction of accomplishment, but there also needs to be the balance of stillness, of doing nothing, not even with the mind. This you need also and we

Chapter 9 – A New Beginning

do not mean sleep time, we mean during the busy day, to allow yourself to get grounded and to relax, to meditate, and to do also nothing. Allowing yourself to be a clean slate, so to speak, on which new messages can be written, new insights gained. It is important to allow your Body, Mind, Will and Spirit to rest in the midst of all this activity and to call themselves to center, the heart centre. Blessing upon you, Mother, Father and the Company of Heaven.

1998 June 2 - I didn't know anyone in town except Jen and Liz. I had no one to help me so it was pretty well up to me to do it all. I also couldn't afford to hire anyone, as part of the reason I offered to do it in the first place was to save some money that could be used for the Centre. I first worked on getting all the garbage out including the carpets, and then I started getting the windows and doors repaired. After that, I repaired the plumbing and electrical, and then started on the floors, walls and ceilings. I was also disappointed that I couldn't just repair the walls and ceilings and then prime and paint them. What appeared to be an off-white paint turned out to be a smoke film, so thick that the primer wouldn't even stick to it, but would just slide, smudge and streak. So before I could even prime or paint, Liz and I had to wash everything, leaving not a trace of smoke film and that took days.

 I also sanded and finished the hardwood floors, which was another frustrating learning experience. I asked the paint storeowner what he thought was the best finish for the hardwood floor and how best to apply it. He told me that urethane was the best product, and to use a brush for the edges and a roller for the floor. I didn't question him as I had refinished my kitchen floor in Moonstone using only a four-inch brush and it took a long time, so a roller seemed like a quicker and easier job. He picked out the rollers and put them in the bag along with all the other products I purchased.

 After renting a professional sander and edger, I proceeded to sand the floors with three different grits of sandpaper, then swept, vacuumed and damp wiped the floor to remove the dust and let them dry. As I applied the first coat of Urethane with the roller, I noticed tiny bubbles appearing on the floor, but it appeared to be okay as they were disappearing as it soaked into the wood. I let it dry overnight and the next day I pole sanded the floors and then vacuumed and wiped them clean. I applied the second coat of Urethane and again the floor was covered with tiny bubbles, but this time I noticed that they weren't going away as quickly. I finished that evening and left it to dry overnight hoping it would smooth itself out like it did the first time. When I came in the next morning, my heart sank. The floors were a mass of tiny bubbles as this time there was nothing for the Urethane to soak into.

 I went back to the store and told him what happened and he said, "Oh, you used the wrong rollers." I know I didn't use the wrong rollers, as there were only two types of rollers that I bought that day, the low-pile ones for the floor and the thick hi-pile ones for the walls and ceiling. I was angry and frustrated and he gave me new 5-mm, low pile rollers, this time in sealed plastic bags. I then remembered that the other rollers were in plastic bags named 5-mm, but they weren't sealed. I opened one and it felt different than the previous ones I had been given. I then thought that the rollers I had used had been mixed up and put in the wrong protective sleeve. I asked him if that was possible, but he denied it. I was skeptical about using a roller again.

I returned to the Centre and started to sand the floors again but this time I didn't rent the professional sander as I really didn't want to take the floor back down to bare wood again. I thought I could give the floors a light sanding to just take the bubbles off. After a half-hour, my old sander bit the dust. I tried to do it by hand but it was too hard, so I went out and bought a new hand sander to finish the job. I spent three hours on my hands and knees taking the bubbles off and getting the floors to where I felt a new coat would look okay. After I had finished vacuuming up the dust, I put the vacuum cleaner in the hallway, damped mopped the floors, and went upstairs to have a bite to eat. As I was finishing my meal, I caught the faint smell of smoke in the air. I went downstairs to check where the smell was coming from and found the vacuum cleaner was smoking. I unplugged it, moved it outside and took the back cover off to check the bag, as that was where the smoke seemed to be coming from. I was amazed at how hot the bag was and that it was starting to turn brown. I quickly concluded that what I had was the beginnings of spontaneous combustion created by the combination of semi-cured varnish and sawdust that I had just vacuumed up. I removed the smoldering bag and dropped it into the bucket of water I had used to damp mop the floors. Fire extinguished, I went back inside and hesitantly re-applied another coat of Urethane. After I finished, I packed up and decided to go to the beach for a while, before going back to my apartment to clean up and go to bed.

1998 June 3, 2:55 am - I awoke from a dream; it was the same dream that I had the night before. It was about a man with just a head, neck, shoulders, and part of his right arm with no hand. He was talking as he was laying on the asphalt, searching and groping for the rest of his body. He was alive for over twenty minutes with no lungs and no heart. I realized that it was me; that I (my Mind) had cut off, or was cut off from my body.

I just remembered stopping at the beach last evening to watch the waves and sunset for a few minutes. When I jogged back to the van I found myself wheezing, coughing and gasping for breath. I couldn't figure it out at the time, but now I can. I just now realized that Lucifer was so much on me yesterday that I was possessed to get the floors redone after the paint had bubbled, that when I sanded the floors, I didn't wear a dusk mask during the whole process. I breathed into my lungs the same Urethane and sawdust that caught fire in the vacuum cleaner. God knows what I've done to my lungs

Chapter 9 – A New Beginning

and body by pushing myself, feeling pressured to do it alone, not feeling that anybody will help me.

When I talked to Jen yesterday, she told me that she had dreams of fighting off death last night, and that something was trying to kill her. Now I'm doing it here in the physical, Lucifer is trying to kill me, to stop me, to stop the Centre. Fuck! I'm angry at what I've allowed myself to do to my body, pressuring it, not looking after it by pushing it to do what my mind wanted to do (under Lucifer's control). Well no more Lucifer, you're not going to win, you're not going to physically kill me. I'm going to move the death you made me breathe in, out to its right place, and I'm going to move you out to your right place too.

1998 June 14 - I was physically weakened by all the urethane and sawdust particles I had inhaled, and I wasn't a healthy or a happy camper as I carried on with painting and other repairs. The carpet installers came in and installed the Berber carpet in the rooms where I didn't refinish the floors. Besides all the interior work that I had to do, there was also the outside that had to be worked on. I had to replace broken and cracked windows as well as get the screens fixed or replaced. That lead to scraping and repainting the cracked and peeling paint on the windows and doors, and the front and side verandah. As if I didn't have enough to do, there was also the landscaping that needed to be tended to, leveling and weeding the cobblestone walkway, cutting the grass, trimming the plants and planting flowers. I was trying to fix years of neglect, trying to do it right, in a hurry, and all by myself. Even though I was still suffering from the effects of the urethane and sawdust I inhaled a couple of weeks ago, I was still pushing myself, trying to get everything done so that the Centre could open.

1998 June 18 - Today was the date of the preliminary small claims court hearing. I stated my case to the judge along with presenting my supporting documentation, and then Ken had his turn. I was relieved when I heard the judge tell him that if he wanted to take this case any further, it would be an uphill battle and it would be best to settle now. I felt confident as we left the courtroom but he didn't look like he wanted to do what the judge said, so I figured I'd let him reflect a little and let him call me before we went to court on June 26. The following Monday he called and said that he was changing the court date to Sept 2. I asked why, and all he said was that it was his right. I felt he was saying that just so that I wouldn't show up in court and he would win the case. I called small claims court and they said that yes, he was in his rights and that they had switched the date and that my notification was in the mail. I was disappointed and frustrated but what else could I do but wait.

Journey to the Heart Centre

1998 June 22 - Today I broke a front tooth in my upper denture. This wasn't the first time as I've had issues with them ever since I got them a few years ago. I decided that enough is enough, and I went to see a denturist down the street to see about getting a new upper denture. The new denture was going to cost me about $800.00, which I really didn't want to spend, but I knew I needed to. In the meanwhile, the old tooth was just glued back into place to make do until the new set was ready.

1998 June 25 - I went to a local drumming circle, one to which I had been to a couple of times before. It was customary for members in the group to share what they experienced and to also share any messages they got. Others were sharing, so I felt comfortable to also share. This was the first time I allowed myself to express what I was intuitively picking up from one woman in particular who had been activated during the drumming session. While what I told the woman further activated her, it also brought release and closure for her and she thanked me. Later, I was politely pulled aside and told that if I have messages like I shared, that will further activate people emotionally, that I should wait and then call them on the phone. I was also instructed to tell them only the good, positive things, and nothing negative. What wasn't being said, and what I was picking up, but denied expressing at the time, was that if that was how I was going to share, that I wasn't welcome back. I made up my mind that this drumming circle was not for me.

During this time Jen and I were also being activated into our issues, mine were of having to do the Centre alone and that there was no one to help me. Jen wasn't able to help me, and I was feeling abandoned by Liz as she was spending more time with her boyfriend and hadn't been in the last three times she said she would be. I've been putting in 10 – 12 hours a day, trying to do what I needed to do to get the Centre ready. I feel that I'm responsible for everything and have to do everything myself. I have to not only do the physical work on the Centre that I previously described, but I also have to handle the business end too, including trying to organize, number and price hundreds of pieces of inventory and put them in the computer as well. Added to that was the design and layout for the advertising flyers and brochures. I was also buying and making counters and shelves, and laying out the design of the store. I was wearing a dozen different caps and I was in an out of control spin, but I wouldn't admit that I couldn't do it by myself.

The Spiritual Warrior

1998 June 26 - Prepare yourself for a journey, the journey of the spiritual warrior. For you have been preparing yourself for these times and now you are about to put into practice all that you have learned and that which you will learn as you present yourself to what you call the outside world. Last night was to assist you, to prepare you and to allow yourself to

Chapter 9 – A New Beginning

feel and to see. For as you are aware, you had the opportunity to confront false teachings, false prophets, directly but in its newness and your familiarity with certain individuals and your old beliefs of not speaking what you feel because it is their show, their right, their place. For it was also an opportunity to express yourself a second time, your feelings and intuition when you felt the un-openness and the fixed minds that would confront you. This also was to prepare you for confrontation by those who would seek to negate what you would say, planned hecklers, whose intent it would be to discredit you in the eyes of those that would hear you. And this you also felt, but never truly realized all this in your conscious awareness at the time. Indeed, also in your awareness was the health issue and your concern of the heart and physical condition if you did confront the entity that was preaching before you.

There were many plays and dramas going on last evening and as they come to your awareness you will gain insight and wisdom AND TRUST FOR YOUR Will, your feelings, and know that what you are receiving is from the highest sources and for your highest purpose and good. As you begin your journey you will encounter these fears, these beliefs that you didn't know you had, and you will move them out as you experience and express yourself with your inner knowing and to trust that knowing. Do not be so hard on yourself for there are no should's, only opportunities for experience and to recognize and have awareness that those experiences bring forth growth and so it is. You continually grow and expand as new experiences come to you and as you more and more trust and go with your feelings, you will not be shouldering on yourself later when you realize you held back and denied yourself for whatever conscious or unconscious reasons. Allow yourself the experience in whatever way it unfolds and enjoy the process. Blessings,

1998 June 27 - I had given my one month notice to move out of the apartment that I had been living in since February, and today I packed up all my stuff and moved into the Centre. While it was exciting, it was also sad as the children didn't want to see me leave, especially the youngest that I had met on the first day. I had recently finished the loft area as a bedroom/sitting room and this was where I moved a lot of my stuff to. Some of my living room furniture was placed in either of the two rooms on the second floor. I also got my bedroom and kitchen furniture and other stuff out of storage. I had no help moving and it took some ingenuity and effort to move some pieces of furniture up the stairs by myself. You'd be surprised at what a large piece of cardboard, duct tape and some rope can do.

Faith and Trust

1998 June 29 - Blessings unto you child, this most wonderful day. Movement, although you feel you life is in turmoil, it is the opposite. Although you think you will never see the light at the end of the tunnel, it is near, nearer than you think. You must feel, have faith and trust in your feelings that you are on the right path and that it is leading somewhere toward the light and not to more darkness. Your road of enlightenment is a journey not a destination. You expect too much of yourself, release your expectations and release your judgments as well as your denials.

Expression is the key to release that which you are holding and you have been holding it always in ALL ways. Allow yourself to break down, not to be in control, and allow yourself to express your wants, needs and desires. ASK, you are worthy and you do deserve all that you desire is within your power to manifest and draw to you. You have simply to begin not to push it away, it is all around you and waiting, wanting to be asked to come in, but it is you who keeps the door closed and has fear of even knocking or hearing a knock. Such abandonment, isolation, and loneliness you feel, you feel untouchable, unlovable and that something must be, and is wrong with you. Others don't seem to have your problems, they have friends, lovers, family, careers and abundance, and now you feel you have none of that and that even when you did, it wasn't enough, that something was missing. What was missing was love.

In ending your denials, in regaining your power, you will begin to see the outer reality, that which you term real, as merely a reflection of your inner reality and indeed it will. This is a time of feeling how lost and isolated you really have been. You can't go back, no, you can go back to your denials if you so choose, or you can open yourself to allow the universe to bring you what you truly desire and have longed for since the beginning. As you move out more and more darkness you will go deeper and deeper and the darker it will seem. You will not like what you feel and you will have all kinds of imprints, programs and beliefs that would have you leave, turn around and not feel this loneliness, hopelessness and heartlessness. But rest assured it is another stage, another level to clear and process through on your journey. You are not alone, you never have been, but you need to feel like you are to get in touch with your original feelings of abandonment, isolation and of worthlessness. Blessings, Mother and Father and the company of heaven.

Repairing and Healing

1998 June 30 - Worry not, fret not over what it is that you think you should be doing, rather be in a state of Being, of growing, of nurturing and healing self. For in healing self is also tending to matters pertaining to the Centre. Focus not all your energies on doing for the Centre but now also seek to balance doing for the self in being. For you recognize that you have been neglecting your growth, your development in favor of creating a Centre. It is also symbolic that there is much clean up and repair required, just as it is with you. You have done much both internally and outwardly and now it is time to

Chapter 9 – A New Beginning

move the two together as one. This is how the Centre will now manifest, working inwardly, working outwardly, in balance, in peace, in harmony.

In the days ahead, much will be given to you, guidance, methods, ways will be shown to you that you have not considered. Be open to these for on the surface they may appear slight, flimsy, no substance, but when truly realized, are as able and as durable as a butterflies wings to journey to its heart's desire. Work on aspects of the Centre, not the material, considered tangible signs, but behind the scenes. It is time to take stock also, to get it in order, to unravel what you have, not only in the material but also in the non-material, in the services you will be providing. Once you begin Being, things will flow, people will come to aid and assist once you open yourself to the unlimited possibilities that are around you. You are not alone. Blessings, this dawn, this day, this new era of mankind.

1998 July 6 - My son, Bryan was up to drop off a Windows PC and to take back his old Mac that I had been using. We were doing the exchange in part because the Mac wouldn't run the new accounting program that I wanted to use for sales and inventory. Now, on top of all the other things I have to do, I have to learn the workings of a Windows PC and the new accounting program. Now that I'm living in Midland and only a few blocks from Jen, I'm also spending more time with her helping her work on her issues that have been coming up.

Fellowship and Actors

1998 July 10 - Greetings it is I, Sananda, that comes to you this morning. Prepare yourself for fellowship, leadership; it is time to join forces, to take command. It is time to spread the word with fellowship meetings of those that seek; that would be open to what you will have to share. It is time to not only meet and greet your fellowman but to also welcome him or her as a friend, as a true brother or sister and they like wise. Open yourself, allow yourself to be vulnerable, to express, and others will see your lead and take courage and follow by your example. It doesn't mean that you have to be right all the time for there is no right or wrong, only beliefs, programs and imprints that make it so, that need to be released. For as you speak, you teach, you share, and so you also grow, learn, and clear, become light, love, and truth. Speak your truth and the truth shall set you free, and in speaking also to be followed up by action and deed, to walk your talk.

Many others now will be contacting the Centre, the Heart Centre. Be open and allow your feelings to question, to weed out, for there will also be drawn to you those that would seek to discredit and belittle the work that you do. To shut you down, to disconnect, to prevent the enlightenment your Centre will provide for it does not serve their intent, their purpose that is not of love. You will sense these as quickly as you now see someone with dark skin in a room of white skins. This is not prejudice but as a metaphor to see the example. It is your old beliefs and imprinting that still have judgment on black and white skin as it still is very much a part of mass consciousness.

Some that come to you at first will be blatant and obvious but others will be more subtle, cunning, and acting a good part and putting on a good show and performance to make the character and actions they portray seem real, honest and loving. And you will be fooled at first by these polished actors and actresses, especially in their act of humbleness and meekness, and in their method of asking for what you call help and assistance. This is not to shut you down, just the opposite, allow yourself to be open, completely open, and you will feel their true intent, their true Being, for they would be in sheep's clothing. They are masters of illusion and they have played their parts over and over since time began, and so they have the experiences, the tools to infiltrate, undermine, weaken, and destroy if there is the least opening available. By opening, we mean by your denials of your feelings, of their expression and action. It is not as dark and as threatening as we feel you sense; that these dark forces are about to close in upon you.

There are other brothers and sisters of love and light that will also be there to assist, for you are not alone, and yes, as you felt, it is that those forces also disguise themselves as brothers and sisters of love, light and life. But in being open, you will sense where there is openness, truth, and where there is not. It is a matter of alignment, of vibration, of feeling. In the times ahead, we of the command will be in more what you call physical conscious contact, though we have been active on other levels. It is now time to lift the veils of who you are and your true purpose, your mission. Starfleet salutes its Starseeds. Blessings, Sananda.

PS: You are many things, you are all things, and you are more than you comprehend at this moment. A Starseed is one aspect of you that was chosen for this mission.

1998 July 14 - I started a three-day fast, with no food, just water. I was at Jens today and I realized that the word "good" means pain to me. I remembered my mother saying, "Good; you hit your head maybe now you'll listen. Good, you hurt yourself maybe now you'll look out. Good, did that hurt? Maybe next time you won't be so lucky." I don't know what to say but FUCK!!

The weather has been hot and humid the past few days. I know the loft has insulation on the side walls as I put it there, but I don't know what's in the ceiling. I don't think there is much as today it reached 39 degrees C and I had to sleep on the couch downstairs.

Healing and Understanding

1998 July 20 - Understanding is not necessary for the expression of feelings, this is Spirits control over issues that he does not like or desire to experience. It is mental, it is denial, and it is the first thing that "pops" into the conscious mind with which he is pleased and then he searches for another thing to pop into his mind that would please him, to give him comfort or excitement. That which does not suit the present situation he abandons in a state of denial and gives the reason, the logic, the understanding, the EXCUSE of why this is more acceptable than that other feeling is. When there is acceptance for ALL feelings, even those that don't feel good, and you accept them and find the underlying denial and emotional charge that is attached to the feeling, then true healing can take place. Once the denial, judgment, belief, program or imprint is seen for what it is, it will lose its charge and will not have the same triggering effect "of feelings," of bad feelings associated with it. That is when true understanding is possible.

Allow yourself to express your Will, your feelings, your fears, guilt, shame, judgments and denials without the need to try to have to EXPLAIN beforehand why you have the fear, etc., and the false feelings you have before giving true feelings expression. For in giving it expression do you give it acceptance, and in giving it, you give your Will acceptance to express and allow it to move, to heal, and to understand the charge she has been holding. Then Spirit will understand why it is he that has been denying and wanting to control the expression of the Will's feelings, and the real issues will surface and true healing will occur, as there is BALANCE, there is harmony, love, joy, life and light. There is peace there is bliss. Peace be onto you this most wondrous dawn. Merlin

Movement and Momentum

1998 July 21 - There is much movement taking place and acceleration on all levels. Healing, healing lost Will, those aspects of self, unexpressed emotions that have been cast out into the darkness and are now being brought light and love. It is truly remarkable, the courage, the knowing, the determination and desire to heal that which the consciousness is unaware of and gives little value to, but where lies truly the source of power that has long been denied, as well as attempts to be rid of it. These feelings, intuition, are what has been missing, not missing, but these denied feelings have not had their expression, and as a result there has been a lack of wholeness, and where there is lack of acceptance there is lack of wholeness. Where there is lack of wholeness there is death of a part, and death of any part of the whole is also a living/death of the whole.

There are many levels, layers, not the right words, stages of recovery of lost Will and also of reprogramming old beliefs, programs and imprints. Once, or as lost Will is recovered, the belief system that held lost Will no longer applies to acceptance of lost Will and its expression. Then slowly at first, bit by bit, step by step, like a child learning to stand on its own two feet, then to walk and run, so too you are healing. Soon, you will no longer be running but flying to recover fragment after fragment, and the more you reclaim, the stronger and faster you become, become light, love and life. You are progressing and it is remarkable. We watch in awe and assist when appropriate. Know that you are loved, you are love. Blessings upon you both, it joys us to see you work together, we are blessed, you are blessed. Adornia.

1998 July 30 - It hasn't been easy, but I was now seeing light at the end of the tunnel as I was pretty well finished with the renovations on all three floors. I've done a lot of work to get to this point, from taking out the garbage, removing the carpets, cleaning and fixing broken windows and screens, fixing broken doors and installing a new front door, repairing electrical and plumbing issues, repairing damaged drywall and washing all walls and ceilings before painting them, sanding and applying Urethane to all hardwood floors, having new carpets installed, repairing broken eaves troughs, scrape, sand and paint the veranda and finally, repair the walkway and do the landscaping.

    I was now focusing on getting store furniture and fixtures and all the little things that had to be done. I have to get display cabinets, bookshelves, counters, meeting room chairs, etc. Not only do I have to find and get them, but I also have to install them and organize how they are displayed and what is displayed on them. Then there is the registering of the business, licenses and banking to set up. Along with that was getting and programming a cash register, and then getting a visa and master card account and the necessary equipment to process store purchases, not to mention getting a telephone, fax and answering machine.

    I also need to design, print and distribute brochures, both for the Grand Opening and also for the products and services offered in the Centre, including the services that I'm providing. Then there are the newspaper ads and the outdoor sign that have to be designed and have made. I also have to design and get business cards and letterhead made up. On top of all that, there is the new computer and the QuickBooks accounting program that I have to learn as we are going to list all inventories, sales and accounting information on it. Then there are the products themselves, from ordering catalogues, to ordering products, to numbering, pricing, and then tagging or labeling the items, and then organizing them in the store. It's no wonder I feel over whelmed.

The following is a brief list of what we plan to provide in the Heart Centre.

Products:
Books: Various New Age, channeling, self-help, health, children, best sellers, etc.
Music: Tapes and CD's, Videos
Jewelry: Rings, bracelets, necklaces, pendants

Chapter 9 – A New Beginning

Gifts: Greeting cards, pictures (framed & unframed) candles, incense, knick-knacks
Clothing: Graphic T-shirts, East Indian serapis
Decks: Oracles / Tarot Card Decks
Crystals: 80 varieties
Local Art & Crafts: Dream catchers, figurines, art

Services:
Consultations & Group Classes: Past life, Clearing attachments, Healing emotions,
Other Practitioners: Therapeutic Touch, Reiki, Readings

Misc:
Library: Lending library of books and tapes
Rental Space: Private practitioner rooms and meeting rooms
Bulletin Board: Listing of community services
Referral Service: Listing of other practitioners

♡ I should add that with the work I had done with Rita and the Visions group, and in working with Jen and the experiences I had, I felt comfortable in doing group sessions and one–on–one consultations. However, retail and service in this fashion was something that I had never done before, and I was unprepared for all the little things that I needed to do. As you can see, I was wearing a lot of different hats and doing a lot of DOING and very little BEING. ♥

1998 Aug. 9 - It was Jens birthday today. The only thing I have recorded in my daytimer was the name of a couple of movies "Good Will Hunting" and "Swept from the sea" that we watched at Jens place. Later she had to drive me home, because I was sick and dizzy as the movies had activated me. I don't remember what the activation was, I just suddenly got very queasy and feeling nauseous and couldn't even think straight to feel safe driving the few blocks home.

Vulnerable and Strength

1998 Aug. 10 - The words spoken or written cannot come close to expressing the feelings, the emotions, the sensations of experience, and that is where the true power lies in the unbridled acceptance and expression of the feelings of the Will, for it is the expression of love. We are talking true feelings here and not the false feelings programmed by imprints and beliefs of hearsay or past experiences that were in a state of denial of your true feelings.

Allowing yourself to be completely vulnerable, as you would call it, will allow you to have complete control. We do not like that word but it will allow you to create your external reality free of that which you fear. It is when you let yourself go that you are truly free, let go of the shields you have used to protect you, or so you thought they did. Let go, allow and accept your fears to come to you, and then to allow and accept the Wills feelings and her expression in whatever form they need to be. This will give the understandings of how these fears, guilt, shame, hate, etc., were put in place so that then they can be released, transformed with love, and moved to their right place and time. Layer upon layer this process proceeds, subtle and ever more subtle do the fears, doubts, and denials creep in, and the harder they are to recognize from the previous layer, but recognize them you shall if you continue to allow the feelings, true feelings to guide you.

Indeed you are, were triggered by both movies you saw yesterday as it brought up another layer of denial of the Will, of lost Will. It was not one layer but many issues that you were triggered into feeling and your body responded to this stored memory energy. Allow yourself to feel and to express whatever emotions come forward now. These are big and a break through again, for much of what you have experienced has its roots held in these lost emotions unexpressed and misunderstood. It is now time for expression and understanding Blessing upon you this day. Mother and Father

1998 Aug. 14 - This morning I had this realization that I have a block, a program or imprint that I set in place before I even came into this life. It says that I'm not loved, do not deserve love, am not lovable, cannot receive love, and that the more I give, the more they will take, and that anyone or anything is more important than me. I can't just be me, that for sure is a no-no. If I try to be what other people want and when it gets to a point that I can't do that anymore, then they're out of my life and it's just me. I'm either alone, or I can have someone in my life for a brief time, before I'm alone again, as nobody wants anything to do with me. I believe that I must be evil, bad, no-good, worthy, different, stupid, odd, a misfit, and unlovable.

1998 Aug. 15 - I realized yesterday that I use my Will, my intuition to feel what is going on and then I would shove her out of the way and take control. I realized that I can be more open (not in denial) with strangers who I feel I will never meet again, than I can with people that I think I might form a friendship with. With a potential friend, I would go into denial and try to read and feel what they needed and wanted. I would use my intuition to tell me if something was wrong but I wouldn't say anything, I'd just look and listen to what they said the problem or issue was and then try to respond in the manner that I thought they wanted me to.

I also watched the movie, "The Man in the Iron Mask" and realized that I have been wearing a mask all my life, trying to show little or no emotion. I don't remember receiving any praise as a child for anything that I

Chapter 9 – A New Beginning

did that I had a sense of pride or self-esteem for. I remember as a child, living on the farm and carrying in firewood; if I carried five logs in one armful my mother would say, "That was good, can you carry six? I never received praise for my efforts from my mother unless someone else praised me first in front of my mother and then it was, "Yes, he's a smart boy, yes he's a good boy, or yes he's my boy." I don't remember my dad ever giving me any praise. I also have guilt that I've done the same to my children by never giving praise when they felt they deserved it, but only when I felt they deserved it.

Paths and Being Who You Are

1998 Aug. 16 - Blessing upon you child this wondrous day. For you are a man, and also you are a child when it comes to understanding, knowing and feeling all that you are or have the potential to be, if you let yourself unfold in a natural and loving way. Not forcing yourself to be something that you think you should be, but rather just allowing yourself to be, to become all that you are. Just as an oak tree is all that it can be when it is an acorn, and so it plants its roots, gets its nourishment's from the Earth, the sun and the elements, and so it grows, becomes. It doesn't force itself to become something that it is not, it cannot become a cedar or a maple, it is what it is, and in such a manner as the acorn, so too you are the child. There is much that you are, but it is not right time or place to unfold these aspects of yourself, but you will know beyond a shadow of a doubt what they are, and how to use them when they unfold themselves to you.

It is true you have spent much time together, the both of you, working on different aspects of healing, all have a similar purpose and all have the same goal, just a different path. Part of your healing is also to journey these different paths so that you can reach more and understand more. Indeed, others will travel and do all their work on one path and will be healing in a short time compared to what you both are doing. But you are not just human and this is also part of your path, a path of service, of assistance and that also means experience. Not just the mental concept of feeling but the actual emotions of the experience and one that shall now have balance with it of Will, Spirit in Heart and Form. This is where the magic, the mystery, the mastery, and the moment is, and from here is where love is, where light is, where life is. Here is where healing takes place in the twinkle of an eye and is shared with others who seek love and life. All seek it differently from and on different paths. You have walked and shared many on your journey thus far, soon it will be your path, your own journey for yourself that you will walk and then you will know, will understand what all this has been about. Blessing upon you both Mother and Father and the company of heaven.

1998 Aug. 28 - I'm still caught up in getting things ready so that the Centre can officially open. Having missed the Aug. 1 opening date, I was trying hard to get the Centre open for Sept 1, but that is not going to happen. It's all the little loose ends that take time and energy, and I can't proceed to clear up the next loose end until this one is finished. Sometimes I just feel it's a hopeless cause, or a dream that will never materialize, as what seems like a minor issue somehow becomes a mountain, and what should have taken a couple of hours, takes a week. There is also no one that I can delegate to help me do these jobs, as there is no one physically helping me in the store that I can count on.

Jen is still unable to be in the store as she says that she is not feeling well or that the new carpet and paint smells overpower her, even though I've left the windows open round the clock to air out the place. She insists that she will be physically harmed by the odors that I can't even smell anymore. Instead of finding the cause, she's happy to blame the outside world for her problems and issues, and this is also creating a lot of conflict as I feel that she will always find some problem to not be in the Centre, although she denies that and states otherwise. While she is too sick to be in the Centre, she is not too sick to have visitors and do things with them. We have been fighting a lot more as we are getting deeper and deeper into our real issues. That is also morally discouraging, as what was a joint dream now seems to be falling apart even before it begins.

Chapter 10 - Owning My Feelings

Duality and Polarity

1998 Sept. 02 - The next step in the journey of life is now one of discovery, of love, of joy, of passion and excitement, the natural, as you would call it, and not only a moment here and a moment there. When you are following and be-ing in love, then all your experiences will take on a new sense of wonder, of excitement. True, this is not sudden, but gradual at first then ever increasing with ease and sensation. You will also be aware of the duality and the polarity of the experience, and of the experiences of others on their path, and so it shall be, so you shall be, so I am.

You are learning, or rather, becoming aware of how you have been shut down and how you also chose this path for your experience. You are uncovering your fears, emotions, lost Will, and allowing expression to also allow understanding when appropriate. Taking back your power, the power of the Will, the feelings, the mother, is the true power for it knows feelings without the need to understand or to control them. When Spirit allows full expression and has acceptance for all emotions that are brought up and allows himself to feel what has been denied, then both gain the understanding and wisdom. This is when and where true healing takes place, in the Heart and in the body, form, or manifestation of creation. Then there is balance, harmony, peace and joy.

True intent to heal, to end this torment, denial, to see it for what it really is, is what all are waiting for. Step by step, layer by layer, ending the fears and judgments that have separated us from expressing and experiencing creation with love, light, and life. The original intent was to create a Universe of polarity, of experience of opposites and to push the envelope of experience to where there are no limits. To do this it also required the unconsciousness of the original intent to experience the expression of duality to whatever and wherever it took us. There was no safe place, no time out, just being in the moment and then following whatever feelings, expression, judgments, programs, imprints and beliefs as they were put in place without conscious knowledge or understanding of what was happening. Thus, and only thus, can true polarity, duality be experienced, allowing not only physical expression, up/down, etc. but also emotional joy/sadness as well as other experiences to the other bodies and aspects of self.

For your understanding, the concept of duality, of experience, was originally black and white, Yin, Yang. What happened after loss of consciousness was the splitting of I am, into the splitting of light and dark, into all the rest that has occurred to this point where there is no longer black or white, but gray. Black and white mixed together to a point where there is chaos, each vying for its right place and right expression but at the expense of the others in some form of control or denial. It is now time to reverse this process and it will not be in the same time progression as it took to experience these experiences to this point. For this is the point, the moment of the awareness, of duality, of polarity, of consciousness, as to its original intent. When that happened it marked the end, not the end, but the end of that particular experience of duality into one where there is right place and right time for loving and unloving light. There is going to be separation but also oneness. This is indeed a unique free Will universe and now is the time for the Will to be free, to create and to express as she has never been allowed to express, and for Spirit to create with wonderment and with a new sense of expression. Together, Will and Spirit balanced in Heart will manifest into Form an unlimited creation of polarity. It is this that you are a part of. Blessings Mother and Father

1998 Sept. 2 – Today I went to small claims court and after waiting for a couple of hours as the judge went through his docket, I was disappointed to learn that there were too many cases scheduled for today and that our trial was being moved to Dec. 9. As I left the court room, Ken's lawyer came up to me and suggested that we each just walk away from all this and let it all drop with no further claims. I felt that he knew they had no case and was looking for a way out. I said, "No, that wasn't the deal and I want my money." He shook his head from side to side, and said they'd see me in court.

1998 Sept. 12 5:30 am - I awoke with the intense feeling that I have the power in my anger and rage to grasp the Earth in my hands and crush it, to pluck the stars from the sky and leave only darkness. This ability to destroy is also my terror in that if I let go of my anger and RAGE, that is what I'll do, that I'll destroy everything and so I control my anger and rage so that I won't have to face my terror.

> *Anger shows you how you're betraying yourself. - Shenreed*

1998 Sept. 13 6:25 pm - I just came back from watching the movie Dracula at Jens. I'm feeling a sharp pain and twitching jabs in my left big toe, foot, leg and arm, and I let myself go into the feelings of the pain. I felt that I've been this warrior over and over, and that I've been fighting for God, in God's name, but feeling betrayed by God and cursing him for abandoning me and taking away anyone and anything I loved by the treachery of man and mankind. I feel that Jen was in those lives a lot, and that she was my wife, lover and friend, and that we never found happiness or lasting happiness

Chapter 10 – Owning My Feelings

before one of us or both were killed, and usually betrayed by someone else. I feel I've been cursed or have cursed myself, and blamed man and God for my misery. I feel I've been tortured, be-headed, burned, not to mention being killed by all the swords, knives and spears, etc. I've fought for justice and injustice, for right and might, for power, to keep power or to take away another's power, for freedom, to free others, and to enslave others who I feared or felt superior to. I feel it's always the battle, the fighting, but for what? What's the real purpose? We always find someone or something to fight, to overpower, or someone or something that wants to fight and overpower us, it's a never-ending battle.

1998 Sept. 14 - I was working in the basement trying to get a specific board out of a pile of old barn boards that I had saved from Moonstone, to make some shelves for the store. I didn't notice a long heavy board that was resting on its edge until it rolled over and scraped down the inside of my left forearm to my wrist. At first I just saw the skin on the inside of my arm scraped and slightly red and torn. As I released the board I was holding to move the fallen one off my arm, I saw and knew that I had broken a blood vessel as my forearm and wrist immediately puffed up and turned blue. I drove myself to the hospital emergency department and was told that there was nothing they could do, and recommended that I apply ice to it and not to use it for a few days. It seemed like everything was going against me.

A few days ago, I was putting stock on the shelves and I noticed a pricing error on some products that Jen or Liz had done. I had to go over the product lists and check all the pricing and change the ones where the American exchange rate of 45% wasn't taken into account. I felt dishearten and thought to myself, "Yeah, it's like I haven't got enough to do."

1998 Sept. 16 4:03 am - I awoke to the following brief message. "You need to give up and give in, not to the outer reflection that is pressuring you to feel like you have to fight all the time, but to the inner realization that the exhaustion and needlessness that you have been fighting is yourself."

'98 Sept. 1 - Today when Jen and I were doing shamanic journeys, Jen felt my name was Little Wolf and she gifted it to me. I like it.

Surrender and Acceptance

1998 Sept. 17 - Allow yourself to be Human, to be weak and to have acceptance for this weakness. To be wrong and to have acceptance for the wrongness but to also feel what it feels like to be wrong and that it is okay to be wrong, and that your feelings are not wrong. It is only your, and other people's words, programs, beliefs, judgments and rules that say it is right or wrong, good or bad. It is only experience of polarities and duality's of this glorious creation and it is now time to acknowledge the awareness and experiences, and the ownership of the fact that you are aware and have experienced both. Accept them as your experiences, not someone else's or their judgments, or your judgments that they are good or bad, but that it simply is, and that you are being, and what you are being is experienced in the moment. Not the past or the future, for they are judgments and projections and are not what is truly happening, what you are truly feeling NOW. What you are doing is not what you are being. You could be peeling a potato but you are feeling lonely or whatever feelings are brought up in the moment are still not what you are, you are beyond that but you are also that.

Acknowledging that you are lonely and expressing all that comes up will reveal the true sense of your loneliness, abandonment, that which you still have not yet accepted as part of your experience for it is not pleasant or comfortable, and so you seek instead to remove it, to substitute it with a feeling that gives you comfort, joy and acceptance. And so you toil, fight back and forth, to and fro, struggling to remove yourself from your own shackles of lack of self-acceptance. For it is when you surrender, accept what you are feeling as part of your purpose, your experiences, are you free to move to experience another and this time one of choice. Not out of lack, or fear, or rejection, but in love and acceptance with joy, for then you begin the magic of creation, of creating what you desire. This is only possible once you have acceptance for all, all experiences, all peoples, places and things. There will no longer be right or wrong but merely experience, opportunity, growth and sharing. The illusion will be broken and you will remember who you are and what your purpose is, and you will live and have life, love, and joy. And in joy will you experience the wonders of this Earth, of this creation, of this polarity, of duality, that is now separated, so to speak. And those who are ready to accept all aspects of duality will be able to choose, to move, and those who need more time will also be given it, but not in the manner they think.

Denials have enabled the experience of this aspect of duality to continue as long as they have. You have struggled, fought for love, truth and justice, but it was an illusion. You need not fight, you need to surrender, surrender and have acceptance, NOT to give your power up, but to take it back. DENIAL is what enables Lucifer to take your power and it is the illusion that others oppose you. So you fight, not trust, be aware and fearful, for if you were to expose your feelings and fears, your vulnerability, you feel this would be used against you to control or destroy you. That was the truth in a state of denial; it is now just the opposite. Your fear stems from your non-acceptance of that aspect of yourself you judge to be a flaw, a weakness, unpleasant and damaging, and so you seek to hide it and deny you even have such a flaw. For you fear that someone will use it against you to overpower

Chapter 10 – Owning My Feelings

you and to cause you more pain that you are seeking to rid yourself of experiencing, by denying it is your pain, your experience. And because it is painful, you seek not or never to feel it again by denial. Denial is denial however subtle, however round about or under handed, that is how Lucifer has kept you in your and his trap.

To break free you need to let go, let love, light and truth, and accept the experiences and the feelings for all they are and gather them in, every last one as you would pick up a bag of spilled toys. They are yours, even the broken and torn ones. Love them all without judgment, with acceptance for they belong to you. Stop trying to push them away and keep only those that are pretty and shiny. Why do you try to pollute creation with what you would cast off of yourself? The Universe does not know they are unwanted and will bring them back to you until you have acceptance for them. But know also, that these lost fragments, lost Will, lost emotions, that you seek to continually push outside yourself, the ones you have chosen not to have, will soon no longer be brought back to you and you will have no choice to further deny them, it is that simple.

Allow yourself to be vulnerable, lay down your sword as you need not to defend, and the attacks will stop when you accept all parts of you, of your experiences, of your feelings, of your lost Will. In love and light we are with you this evening and share these words with Love Child, your partner in these experiences. Mother and Father.

1998 Sept. 17 8:18 am - Jen has issues and judgments with smells, places and things that make her feel bad. She has denials that she even has these judgments and thinks that nobody cares for the environment, planet, or for her. As soon as she smells something strong, different, or something that she can't identify that confuses her, she goes into her panic attack and brings up all her fears and judgments. Her fears kick in that it is harmful and has to be stopped, and either it or she has to be removed from the situation. Her drinking water has to be only a certain kind, the purest and best for her. Apple juice can only be PC or Allen's (and only in glass containers) because they are the purest and they don't use chemicals on their apples and so their apples are full of good chemicals, according to her beliefs.

The point of all this is that while she is full of judgments and in fear and denial of things, I have the same issues but with people. We are the opposite in a way here, for her, things are a problem and people are okay, and for me, things are okay but people are the problem. I see a fat person as a person that doesn't care for himself or herself, and I wonder why. I judge people by how they look, how they move, walk, sit, stand, lie down, even how they carry their bags and boxes, how alert or how dull they are, how they smile, how they look you in the eye or if they turn away, and all kinds of facial expressions and body gestures. Then I try to tie all these in with how they speak, what they say and how it feels. After that, I try to analyze what they are really saying, what they really mean, and what it is that they want me to do for them, or what they are going to do for me. Then I pull up all the other times of similar experiences and use that to judge this person as such and such, and also possibly this and that. I look for similarities, that this person reminds me of this other person who did this or that to me, not the same, but similar. I also work on the different aspects with the same analytical process and fuzzy logic.

I come away from a one minute meeting with a whole bunch of judgments about what I think that person is, instead of being real and talking to that person in the moment and telling that person exactly what I think and what I feel. The judgments and beliefs that come up have nothing to do with the now and what that person is really trying to communicate with me in expressing their feelings or point of view. I have this belief that the person talking to me is either trying to make me believe that what they're saying is true, or that they're trying to say that what I'm saying is wrong. I can't just let him or her have their opinion, their truth. A-ha!! TRUTH, that's the key word! What is the truth? I have an issue with what is the truth. The truth is always changing so how can the truth be constant? So if the idea or thing is changing, how can it still be true to what it was when it was first discussed?

I don't feel it's a big issue with things changing that are tangible, like a flower. A flower is a bud in the morning, two hours later it's opening and in the afternoon, it's in full bloom. Each is a truth, a fact, I can see it, it's tangible, it's recordable, and both people can witness it simultaneously. Where I have an issue is when people say, "I feel hungry do you want to get something to eat?" I acknowledge that I am hungry (as a statement of truth) and so we decide to get something to eat and then he or she says, "I'm not hungry anymore, I rather do such and such." Now because I am with that person and we were already doing something else before we were going to get something to eat, I feel guilty that I want them to do something now that they don't want to do but that I do, which is to get something to eat. I've already judged that what I want to do (eat) is not important because I can do that later by myself. I feel guilty that if I got something to eat now, that that person is now just waiting around for me to do what I want. In such a situation the truth was changing and I was confused and in doubt.

Doing things is one thing, I can see what is true and what needs to be done and how to do it. Feelings are completely different. I'm dealing with my feelings and their feelings, and also my judgments of what I think they're feelings are saying. That's why I have trouble with people, my imprints, programs and beliefs feed me information that I'm stupid, inferior, slow and a bunch of other beliefs that just cause me pain and loneliness. I didn't fit in because I couldn't speak English when I started school. That's a truth. I was considered different, stupid, a joke, because I didn't understand what they

Chapter 10 – Owning My Feelings

were saying. I could only feel how they acted and talked, and how that made me feel. Feelings were all I could go on and I judged that it was the feelings that were wrong and were causing me the physical and emotional pain. I didn't have the facts, the truth, I didn't know that 2+3=5, it was only scribble on a black board and I heard words I didn't understand. I would try to respond and of course it wasn't correct or it wasn't the way others would say it, and so I would be laughed at, jeered, even by my teachers. At recess or at lunch, I really got picked on as that's when it got physical, and because I was small I was picked on by many. If I fought back, then others would come to the aid of the attackers and they would also beat up on me. It was just a lot easier and less painful to let anyone who wanted to, just take a shot at me whenever they wanted to, then to stand up for myself and get beaten by a bunch of them, it just hurt less. And so I started to try to read people, to try to learn how to fit in and not to stand out so that I wouldn't get punished.

Pretending that I didn't understand or know by saying "Huh" and "I don't know" were safe answers that I'd give instead of saying that something was wrong or that it didn't quite feel right, because expressing that only brought me physical and emotional pain. I studied and learned so that I wouldn't be stupid, and the truth was that I could get higher marks than the others could once I learned the language. Facts I would remember as that was one area where if someone else had the same fact as I did, 2+3=5, then we were in agreement on a fact, a truth, that could be found in a book or that others also knew the same or right answer.

So somehow I've gotten this truth crossed wired with truth of feelings, and because feelings were what I blamed for causing my pain, I blamed and put down my feelings but I would allow other people to express theirs because it was their pain and not mine. By not expressing mine, I wouldn't be drawing attention to myself, so my judgments became even more ingrained, right or wrong. I had feelings but I would analyze them for the safest way to express them without activating someone's negative feelings toward me, because I didn't want to be attacked. Because if someone started to get excited, angry or started to say you, or you did this or that, you made me angry, sick, etc., it brought up all my old issues, that I'm wrong and will get blamed and hurt for what I said or did. I also felt that no one would be my friend if I did or said anything that made him or her feel hurt.

I felt I was wrong, selfish, and evil, and that I would go to hell for my sins of how I made people feel. You didn't listen to Mommy, you made Mommy feel sad, God says you have to listen to your mother and father or grown-ups, or you're a sinner and God will cast you into hell if you don't listen and obey and please others. I was afraid of God, afraid that I wouldn't please him, that if I didn't obey his commandments that I would go to hell and be even more alone, more hated, more depressed, hurt and punished. I couldn't bear that thought, so I tried to do what my parents, my mother said.

I felt she was right because when I went to church I heard the priest say the same things, so it must be the TRUTH. Because of the imprints, programs and beliefs, I also have judgments that hold them as truths. When someone's belief is different than mine, then either their or my belief is wrong, and I usually think that I'm wrong and that I missed something.

This was especially true if it was an older person or one that was in a position of authority. I also have fear of disagreeing with my peers, because if I didn't believe or act how they acted, they would not be my friends. Not that they were friends, just that they didn't attack me. I didn't feel that what they were doing was loving or right and so I distanced myself from them because I didn't enjoy smoking, drinking and getting drunk, beating up someone or trying to fuck the ass off any girl they could, not caring about anything or anybody. I couldn't do that, so I stayed alone and kept myself busy doing things alone but so desperately needing a friend, and when I would find someone that I felt might be a friend, I'd put them first, ahead of anything I wanted, just to have a friend. Even though we might have the same ideas, plans and common ground, it never lasted as it always seemed that they would find someone who was more of the friend that they were really looking for, and that I was just a fill in until someone better came along.

In grade seven, when we were excommunicated from the Catholic Church, I felt guilt, grief, anger and heartbreak, as well as fear and terror. That was when I became an atheist and didn't believe there was a God. I lost my faith. I believed that he didn't love me or care for me and that he had forsaken me, so I turned from him. I turned away from God but I still had my feelings, they wouldn't go away no matter how I tried.

Later that afternoon I went down to Little Lake, a quiet, man-made lake a few blocks from the Centre. While there, I began to write what I was feeling in the moment. I wrote that I feel alone and dismissed, and when I reach out and open myself and try to express my feelings and thoughts, that nobody has time for me, or that they don't listen or care. I must be reaching out with a part of me that is closed down so that when I reach out and try to get what I want or need, that I don't get any kind of recognition that even my needs are valid. I long for even a tidbit of acceptance and caring. I have fear that in reaching out that I will be rejected because I have done something wrong and that they won't like me. Now I'm even afraid that they won't be my friend or that they will speak badly of me and tell everyone what I did to them and then nobody will like me or have anything to do with me, and will even end up picking on me or punishing me.

I was watching a flock of Canada Geese swimming in the water and they were doing some peculiar movements. They would swim forward and then do a somersault and flip over on their backs and while in this position, they would paddle with their feet in the air. Then they would pop back up in

Chapter 10 – Owning My Feelings

an upright position. They were too far off shore to be feeding and I could only assume they were washing and preening themselves. Another thing that caught my eye was a row of 15 geese standing on one leg, their right leg in about four inches of water. Why? I thought, when they could stand on two legs or even float for that matter. Observations and questions, but no answers.

I also realized that my "hums" and "I don't knows" are a way for my mind to have time to filter my emotions and my response. I noticed that I had other quirks and I also started noticing that other people also used them and had a few I didn't even think of. Some of these filters are: pretending not to hear, answering a question that was not asked, answering a question with a question, being distracted, rocking, moving, fidgeting, itchiness, doing things, whistling, sighing, yawning, coughing, picking or biting their nails, playing with their hair or clothes, chewing gum, sucking at their teeth, biting their lips, eating their hair, chewing their tongue and the list goes on and on.

1998 Sept. 21 - I made a note and said to myself that I wasn't going to be denying myself in favor of another, and that in so doing, do I give myself love and also move unloving light out as well as my denials, judgments, guilt, beliefs, programs and imprints.

1998 Sept. 28 - I tried to have the Centre open by Sept 1st, but things just didn't go according to plan. The Centre finally opened its doors to the public today. It's been a hectic four months, from first getting the space, to cleaning it out and then starting with the renovations, to a point of where I could move in personally, which was another job. The renovations were a bigger job than I expected and not having any help put a lot of pressure on me as I worked 10 to 12 hours a day, six and sometimes seven days a week.

On top of that, there was the starting up of a new retail and service business that I really had no experience in, and also had limited help. It didn't seem that hard or complicated when I first thought of it, but again I had no experience to go by, so I was both over optimistic and naive. Things that I had to quickly learn were: finding suppliers and ordering catalogs and then ordering the different items, create a suitable identification code for cash, visa and debit card sales, learn computer accounting and sales software and figure out codes for inventory control, set up accounts receivable and payable, track sales, calculate retail prices, use the little tie on pricing tags or a pricing gun to label each product with a code and a price, try to figure out how and where to display it all. Buy or make counters and displays for merchandise, create newspaper advertising, learn to use computer software to create brochures, etc. All these little details had to be attended to and at times, it was overwhelming.

After the major renovations were basically finished, then it was the gathering of the store furniture and fixtures or building what couldn't be bought. I also spent more on inventory than I had planned in trying to fill the store space. A $700.00 order of silver rings and jewelry could be held in the palms of your hand and displayed in a two square foot area on one shelf in a display case. At that rate, it took a lot of money, as we had a lot of space to fill. Like I said, I was a man wearing a lot of different caps and in a spin, doing what I thought I needed and had to do.

On the first day, twelve people came into the store and there were four more that came for the meditation class that evening. It was an exciting day but also filled with anxiety as Liz and I were just waiting for people to arrive. It was a slow start but we felt confident that it would grow. I was also kept busy with finishing the odd jobs that still needed to be done, designing new advertising, distributing ads and flyers as well as trying to enter the inventory into the computer in a program that I was also learning how to use.

I was just thinking, I can't believe that this is the end of September. When we originally got the building on May 11, I felt confident that we could have the Centre operating by the end of July, to catch part of the summer crowd when people were walking about, but now it's almost time to start bringing out the snow shovels. Time just seems to be flying by and then there are times when it seems like nothing moves, including time. I know that I have spent a lot of time on doing things, from selling the property in Moonstone, to moving to Balm Beach, then the store and moving again. I've not really been focusing on any personal issues or writing my journals except to record my messages.

The Healing Power of Love

1998 Oct. 02 - There is no force stronger than love. There is no limit to what love can do. As humans, when this force is turned inward, loving self, self-love without denial, then this is the reflection in the outward manifestation of the physical body and what you call the physical world. And so it is that the power to heal all disease within the physical body is possible, even that what you consider aging. Denial is death, ending denial moves death to its right place outside of life, of experience in the physical body.

Healing the denied emotions, Lost Will, lost fragments these that are subtly buried in those that you call good or positive emotions and not just those that you call negative, will restore the body to health and to life. You have doubt that there is denial in positive emotions, for how can you truly have loving "positive" emotions when you are not whole and are in denial of the other parts of you. You can only truly experience love when you are whole. What you have been experiencing has been love moments, those brief moments that are more like a picture of love than the experience of love. What being Human has done has been to confuse experience of preferred

Chapter 10 – Owning My Feelings

moments with love moments and have then found the experience, the physical sensations fed by imprints, programs and beliefs to sustain the false perception, the illusion of what love is and what life is.

What is needed is to let go of all that you have been taught and believe, for they are judgments formed in denial. Allow yourself to feel what is truth for you and to respond with the true expression of your feelings in love and not in denial. Not all Spirits seek love. Love Spirits seek love but have fear, confusion, and are in denial, and hence give their power to others, either to other love Spirits also in denial or Denial Spirits. Denial Spirits do not seek love, they seek denial, but they have adopted and are quite adept at presenting a facade of a love Spirit and can act the part of a Love Spirit in those love moment pictures previously described. And it is so that they feed the illusion so as to feed off your energy, off your denials. Your death gives them power, life, of course denial itself is death, so you both die but it is only you, Love Spirits who have been losing, losing the gift of life, of Love.

And so you have been returning again and again to try to reclaim those parts of yourself that you have lost, died a death of denial, but each time you came back you got caught again. This is not your fault; there is no fault, no right or wrong, only experience. Just as I (We) experience, and so it is, but the awareness is here now and it is my intent to now separate light and dark, life and death, love and denial to their right places. The mixing is over, the illusion broken and healing is taking place on all levels, especially here on the Earth plane, this jewel of the universe. We, Mother and I, ask that you continue your growth, not that you have stopped, but you have fear and the illusion that you are not progressing. Continue to share your truth and our messages to those that are ready to receive. Blessings, Father and Mother and the company of heaven.

Anger and Self-hatred

1998 Oct. 03 - Touching your anger and self-hatred is not an easy step for it has been layered upon layer with experience, denial, judgments, imprints, programs and beliefs, that literally shut you into a space where it has to be an external problem, as the problem can't be that you hate yourself. You can hate everything around you that causes you pain, and everything around you will cause you pain. So the last thing that you feel (think) you have left that doesn't cause you any pain is you. You think because you changed the word feel to think, that it is true. We used the words together for what you think you feel is not feelings, but false feelings brought up by the pain of your denied self-hatred.

You hated yourself for being born, being small, being German, how you looked, spoke, and most of all, you hated your feelings because you felt they brought you pain. You desired to be different, to be anyone but you, you hated the you that you were and you still hate the you that you were and are.

Journey to the Heart Centre

You cannot just suddenly have acceptance for yourself and affirm, "I love myself" etc., without touching the pain, the hate, the anger, the terror and heartbreak, that if you hate yourself and you feel everyone else does also, what's left? Why are you living? What's the point? What's the use? Who cares? It is difficult and frightening to allow yourself to move into this space, to feel this self-hatred that you have denied so almost completely that it doesn't seem possible or real. What you have been living is an illusion, the facade of your true feelings. You have been touching this self-hatred in the works you have been doing and it is now time to touch the reality of it and see how it has affected your life. How and why you have experienced all you have, and that this was also your choice, for the experience. It is now time to touch this belief in yourself that you were no good, not acceptable the way you were and that you have to be what you think people want in order to be accepted.

Now is the time to accept these parts of yourself that you have shut away, that you deemed unsafe, not acceptable. To be able to accept them, you must go to where you locked them away, see them, touch them, feel them, love them. For yes Johnnie, these are the parts of you, the shiny bright and loving parts that you shoved away, hated because you felt they were causing you pain. You didn't understand and you couldn't even question or ask for help, but yet you felt the pain, physical, emotional and mental.

Begin to reach this within yourself by asking and allowing yourself to ask. Ask for what you want, need, don't understand. You are not stupid or bad because you don't know what others are trying to say to you. You now have the ability to fully understand what another is saying and also to communicate your thoughts, and more importantly now, your feelings which you couldn't express either, except for the pain and tears, and when they even brought you more pain all that stopped too.

You hated the you you were, you were ashamed of who you were, ashamed of your parents, ashamed of your clothes, ashamed of how you lived, ashamed of your relatives, ashamed of your religion, ashamed of your size. What shame you didn't get from your Mother, your relatives, you got from your peers and your external society. You were the cast out, unloved and because you felt all this, you blamed yourself, even all the way to when you lost your faith. You didn't lose God Johnnie, you lost religion. You were confused, didn't understand and there was no one who could help you and so you even felt that I didn't love you. No one in the outside world loved you; God didn't love you and so who's left to love you? YOU? You didn't and weren't able to do that either for you had to live in a society, family and school, and so you tried to fit in, to gain acceptance somehow without giving anymore of yourself away but also not loving who and what you were. There was/is this facade of self, of altered ego that puts on the persona of self-love but it is not true for there is no acceptance, no true acceptance of the parts of

Chapter 10 – Owning My Feelings

yourself that you cut off. You have fear of being hurt and so you still keep this fortress, this impenetrable fortress around you, that small part of you that survived that you saved of yourself. All the rest of you, you gave away because you hated it for what it brought you and how it made you feel, feel that you were wrong, not right. That something must be wrong with you as nobody else has a problem; it's got to be you.

To heal, begin by asking. Ask and you shall receive. Knock and the doors shall be opened. You have intent to heal; you have love in your Heart. It is now time to release that love light for all the world to see who you really are. Blessings this morning my son. Father and Mother

♡ In this moment I'm deeply moved as I read this message. This was the beginning of another phase of my healing. It's all here but I didn't understand it at that time. I had more to experience and feel before I would get it, and I'm not sure I really get it yet, but I know that this is a big key to my healing and that this applies to many different layers and issues. ♥

1998 Oct. 15 2:22 am - Coyote comes, a cousin of mine: (Little Wolf)

Coyote Medicine

Coyote comes to you this day,
To teach you how to laugh and play.
To laugh and play, to dance and sing,
To see outside the illusion ring.

To see yourself for who you are,
To see others for what they are.
To lift the veils that clouds the sight,
A trickster yes, but none to fright.

Only those whose love is untrue,
Fear the coyote for what he can do.
So lift your head and bay the moon,
For the truth you seek shall come to you soon.

Close your eyes and feel from your heart,
For as you release you begin a new start.
See not with the eyes the things that are showing,
See with the heart and feel with a knowing.

Fear less not fearless, approach and be open,
With caution will come the truth you are hoping.
For the truth can't hide with coyote inside,

Though truth be hidden far and wide.
As coyote calls and bays at the moon,
Truth and healing will come to you soon.

Fear of Asking and Trust

1998 Oct. 22 - Generations do you have to span, from the elderly to the new born, to awaken all who choose life, who choose to hear. Fear not that you will not know how to communicate for it is not with your words alone that they hear you, for they also feel the words, not so much the words as the vibration and tone that will trigger the appropriate response. As you did yesterday, share from the heart so you will touch and assist others in healing and touching others, the generations, and the masses, the mass consciousness of Humanity will be touched.

Continue as you are, being in the moment as much as possible, doing what is required. You are guided and there are many loose ends to be picked up and that you are doing. Trust in yourself and trust that the Universe is supporting you in the appropriate way. As you trust yourself more and ask, you will be supported more. You have fear of asking for what you desire, what you need, and so you feel unsupported and limited. This limitation you are experiencing is your own limitation, your own programs, imprints and beliefs that you still hang on to, that are the truth and are cast in stone for you. Nothing is cast in stone unless you make it so. Release your fears, take a risk, and expect the unexpected. These are also good words for you to follow. Expectations are also limitations. What is your intent? What is your desire? Reflect on your desires, ask and you will receive according to your intent. Blessings Merlin PS: the Magic, the real magic is about to begin.

Duality of Light and Dark

1998 Oct. 22 - Depart not from your path for you are on your path. Despair not but feel the despair, the unknowingness, the doubt, for it is a part of you and though you seem to think and feel you struggle and it is all for naught, realize that you are within a hands grasp, it is at your fingertips all that you desire. No one is keeping it out of your reach, playing games with you, as you call it, except that aspect of yourself which you deny. Lucifer, you judge him as evil, as wrong, as controlling, and so you want nothing to do with him, but realize that in this duality universe you are both. Indeed, you are God and you are Lucifer all in one package, and Lucifer has been in control, so to speak, until now, but now it is time for the other part, the true Godhead within you to take control, to take back your power. Not by force and total non-acceptance of the dark side, but in harmony and allow everything to move to right place and right time. For you have choices and now it is time to exercise your choice by acknowledging the light and dark and by taking back your power and moving and choosing what you desire in love and not denial.

Chapter 10 – Owning My Feelings

To allow your feelings now to exhibit their true power, your Will, your feminine aspect, it is her that has been denied her expression.

For Lucifer has no free Will, no unconditional love, only denial, and this is what has fed creation since the beginning. Now we have awareness, and with awareness and acceptance of the Will comes understanding, and so it is that you move from darkness to light, not by denying darkness but by accepting it without fear, without judgment and without denial. With love and compassion toward self do you move unlovingness to its right place, not by doing things out of guilt or shame, lack, need, or the loving thing to do, but by expressing how you feel and what you desire. It doesn't have to get to an explosive experience in order for you to express, for that is denial, and even when you try to reach a compromise you are dishonoring, denying your Will, for you are seeking a way around what it is you feel and desire to express. This is a big imprint, program and belief for you, as you have always felt and then tried to fit your feelings, your needs in-between the needs of others for you feared non acceptance and attack, abuse and rejection, and so you judged them wrong or only partly right.

There is acceptance now for your feelings son, there is acceptance and you must trust and open that there is acceptance for expression of all your feelings, and that indeed, loving light is what you'll feel and not more darkness, rejection and non-acceptance. The hard thing is TRUST and so you don't trust for fear of being hurt. Being hurt is also a part of you and you must have acceptance for all you felt and all you experienced of life in denial. It is now time to experience life and love not by denying, but by acceptance and expression of your feelings.

Ah yes, what are true feelings you ask? Only by expression, whether it is your fears, judgments etc., will you find if what you feel is true or simply a belief, program or imprint. The more you express and feel, the more you will recognize true feelings, for you have also, as part of the experiences, suppressed your true feelings with false ones in order to gain acceptance and to not feel the pain as much, you have shut them away. There are many ways of denial and of producing false feelings as there are people and experiences.

Allow yourself to express yourself verbally and physically, whether in word, song, dance, exercise, BE yourself. BE what you feel and become the I AM presence; regain your true essence. You have experienced the dark side of who you are and now it is time to experience the light side of who you are, of who I am. You, we, are both, we have duality and we have polarity, yin-yang. I, we, could not exist without both polarities for there would be no balance. But now the essence will remain, but the form is changing and light and dark are separating to right place. So allow this dark side that you have taken in, to now go outside of you to its right place for it is time to experience the physical in love, light with life. Accept that the dark side is going to its right place, that place that has no acceptance for the Will, and allow now your Will to heal, to express for lack of acceptance has kept her suppressed. Also allow all feelings and all experiences acceptance, for it was also necessary for the Will to feel this total lack of love in order for her to experience the complete swing of the pendulum.

We each have experienced denial in different ways and both were necessary, not wrong or right, just experience that almost killed the mother and almost left me impotent on all levels, such to a point that it seemed that Lucifer was God, was meant to be God and had all the power. That was what was needed for the experience, that it was futile and hopeless, that I can't take anymore, and to feel that Lucifer was in total control of both the Spirit and the Will. That is when my consciousness stirred and my light began to shine. It was the dawn, the swing back, and it will not take an eternity to undo all that was done in denial. There is no force, no power greater than love. The true power is with love and so love will be able to transform in a twinkling of an eye. Behold the magic is about to begin, let Love fill you. Love be you both. Mother and Father, and the company of heaven.

1998 Oct. 28 - I had advertised free introductory classes and workshops in Meditation/visualization, exploring past lives and meeting your guides and animal totems. I was holding them on Mon. Wed and Friday evenings from 7:00 p.m. to 9:30 p.m. Attendance was mixed, ranging from 2 to 15 people per session. I was also beginning to work with a few individuals on a one-on-one basis. It started out being past life regressions and then worked its way into clearing the astral plane and then into current issues and emotional releases. Denied anger and rage were also coming up when I was working with emotions, and I was directed by Spirit to buy a cheap pair of "red" boxing gloves from Zellers. Before the session began, I'd inform my clients that if anger and rage came up, that I'd ask them to extend their hands and that I would slip the boxing gloves on them. Then they could hit the arms of the recliner or move to the floor or to the futon to release their denied anger and rage without hurting themselves or anything or anyone else.

It was also during this time that Irene was to come into my life. She came into the store and dropped off some native angel figurines with animal totems, for consignment sale in the Centre. She joined in a few of the morning meditation classes that I was having and she also began to come in for one-on-one sessions.

Inner Battle of Spirit and Will

1998 Oct. 29 - Love your enemy, what you would consider your enemy, a foe, an adversary, is also but an aspect of you, that part of you that is cruel, judges self and would punish the weaker part of yourself. Mentalize not to try to understand, but rather allow yourself to feel, for there are two parts and therein lies the confusion. For there is the villain and the

Chapter 10 – Owning My Feelings

victim and they both reflect aspects of you and where you have judgments, beliefs, programs and imprints that create your outer reality.

The victim feels like he is beaten, chastised out of a belief that he is no good, not good enough, nobody loves or understands, hears or listens to what the victim needs or has to say. And how is this portrayed or reflected? By attracting outside influences that wants to beat, chastise, and pummel. And what really is this outer reality but a reflection of that aspect of yourself that hates the weakness of the victim, that has no time, no patience, no understanding or compassion, and only wants the victim to ignore his feelings and to become someone that it is not.

It is usually a battle between Will and Spirit but Heart and Body can, and are also involved. Try to become aware of your feelings of both the victim and the villain when you feel you are being attacked, and you will begin to see the duality and the programs, imprints and beliefs that you have that cause the effect of the outer reality. It is all internal first, and that is the hardest obstacle to cross before the external can be changed. For countless life times you have experienced death and so you have been imprinted and programmed so that you believe that it is a truth and that that is your reality, but it is not, it is an illusion. True magic is when you are no longer tied to the illusion of your beliefs and programs, and can see through the smoke and mirrors and see that what is being reflected is what you believe. For when the enemy within is seen and accepted for who he is, and the victim within is also accepted, then there is no longer any need for any outer experience to reflect the inner imbalance.

Be patient with yourself and also recognize where you are beating yourself up internally without the need for an external reflection. For you also have withdrawn from the outside experiences to try to cease the internal reflection of you. So that now it is only you, yourself, that beats up upon yourself, criticizes yourself, and has no patience and has become the villain, and at the same time feels hopeless, helpless and worthless. Pay attention to your feelings, of one or the other, for to find and observe one is to also be able to observe the other. Your intent to heal will assist you in bringing this awareness to you, be open, honest, and speak your truth, to be your truth in love and light and you will have life. Blessings Merlin

1998 Nov. 1 - Several times this year I've received specific messages for Jen. Sometimes it was from my guides and other times it was from hers. Still other times it would be from her inner child, her lost Will, or her body, and I would feel what they were feeling and what she was denying. This occurred when I was in her presence, on the phone with her, or when I was at my home. Sometimes I'd even be awakened from my sleep with a message for her. This is one of the messages I got for her.

Message for Jen

1998 Nov. 01 - Self sabotage, fear of facing, of being confronted, of that which she has been holding for all of her existence, in the Earth plane, in this life time, but also not limited to it, for it also reaches back into others. There are many aspects of this lifetime that are buried deep in the subconscious and there is a great fear of touching these because of the imprints brought forth. Not only of this experience but also of others, in other lifetimes, and so it is enhanced, heightened to a point of being overwhelming. There are many extremes and many polarities going on in this lifetime. As a means of coping with the suppressed emotions and denials, it is the body that bore the brunt of the abuse when the emotions were suppressed to a point that the body couldn't take anymore and so a shift occurred. Much healing has taken place but all around the edges. The deep causal pain is still feared and ignored. Oh yes, rage and terror are there and the anger is there too. But to heal the Heart, she needs to let go and to dive into the true issues which are masked by the fear of self loss, and so it is that she seeks means and ways of having to deal with issues, and in doing so she puts up stumbling blocks that prevent her from moving on all levels.

But this is not all self-sabotage as it may appear, for she is also touching pain she has denied all her life that she chooses to ignore. Healing Will is taking place and it can happen in a twinkle of an eye when she is truly ready, but not until that point of going to meet her darkest, deepest fears, that part of her that lies buried in denial. There will be surface attempts to rescue and surface setbacks that prevent any further attempts at rescue, in the mean while, nothing really changes but everything changes. She has courage and she has fear, she is frightened and she is fearless. When the right attributes and time are appropriate, she will feel what she needs to heal, and with feeling will come understanding as the memories long hidden are released to the conscious mind. What she desires she fears, and what she fears she desires. We are through for the moment. She has much assistance and help as much as she is truly able to accept. Blessings.

1998 Nov. 20 - Sales are not as we anticipated, even with Christmas on the horizon, nor is there a large interest in the meditations, past life or any of the other classes I'm offering unless it is a free class. My one-on-one sessions are providing about 50% of the total revenue. Money is going out but little is coming in. I'm beginning to feel that something has to turn around soon as I won't be able to continue to finance the Centre as I'm doing. I'm also counting on the extra money from the promissory note for emergencies.

I started offering introductory meditation classes to seniors in various nursing homes in the area. I did a meditation classes in three of the fifteen homes that I had approached and one was open to future sessions. I noticed that more than half of the seniors who attended were not what I would call

Chapter 10 – Owning My Feelings

really conscious, and most of those that attended were also very skeptical as it didn't follow their religious beliefs. One thing that I did notice in all the homes was that most of the people in there had either given up on life, or were so drugged that they were semi-conscious and only lucid for a few moments at a time. It was sad to see how the elderly were being treated, that there was little life left in them and that they were just waiting, waiting to die.

I have made very few notes in my journals or day-timers during these past few months, and for that matter for this past year other than noting down things I was doing or had to physically do. There was a brief period after the sale of Moonstone and before the Centre, when I was expressing my emotions and writing them down when activated. I feel that in the other times, I was preoccupied with a host of different physical things and issues, and was caught up in doing rather than in being. It wasn't that emotions didn't come up, it's just that I denied them to get the job done. I did however write down my messages and I feel that they are important to share, as they too are part of this journey. I don't know what triggered the following entry in my journal on judgments, but it is one of the few times I wrote and I feel needs to be included.

I judge myself according to others. I judge them if they appear happy, sad or whatever. I get a sense of who I am by what others are, and that I'm able to copy and apply to me. I get angry at myself if I can't get the same satisfaction that they do when I try to do it, or I don't get what they get out of it. If something makes them happy, then I think that that should also make me happy. When I try it and it doesn't feel good, or I feel that I'm not as good as they are, I try to either put them or what they do down, that way I don't feel like I'm a failure or not good enough or bad. If that doesn't work, then I get angry and walk away and blame the other person or thing, and judge it or them with anything I can so long as it takes the focus off me.

I judge Jen because she's hurting and in pain, house ridden and a bunch of other stuff, and that when she has the energy and is able to talk to me, that I'd better talk to her then, or I won't get a chance later. I have denied anger and judgment because I feel that is bullshit because she could be laying there hurting, but at the same time I'm sure that she has the TV or stereo on, or that she is doing crafts with the energy she has.

I judge you as having no responsibilities or not having to work and so yes, you can do crafts at eight o'clock in the morning, three in the afternoon or in the middle of the night. You have no responsibilities and don't have to do anything except feed, wash and entertain yourself. I judge you that when you are bored, you call either Liz or me at the store. You say that you are jealous that Liz and I have all this time together but there is work to do, and if Liz or I are talking to you, then we are not working or talking to each other. I've asked you repeatedly if you wanted to come to the Centre and that I'd pick you up in two minutes. That way you can talk to both or either one of us, or help us do our work, meet customers or even go downtown and do your shopping or whatever. It would be a start at getting you out of the house as well as getting in touch with your feelings when you do get out, that we can begin to work with. I have judgments that while you talk about healing your issues, talk is all that you really want to do. I have judgments that when you are physically able, that you want to do other things for yourself, things that make you happy. Hummm? So are these judgments I have on Jen, or judgments I have on me?

Fear is your Ally

1998 Nov. 20 - Allow yourself to be open to the unlimited opportunities of the universe and they shall flow to and through you. You can manifest all that you desire by simply, and it is a big and complex word this simply, allow and be, become what you desire, not in fear, but in love. Not out of fear of lack but in love and gratitude for what is all about you. If all you see is an empty cup, an empty store, then the store will be empty, see it full and it shall be full. Feel that no one appreciates you, recognizes you, and that is what you will get reflected. It is that simple. It is all in your Heart, your desire, your intent, calm your fears and allow them to surface to show you what lies ahead. Your fears churn the sea of life into something frightful, doubtful, and painful, and all you do is battle the universe, nature, yourself, when in fact all you need to do is to let go of the illusions that your fears create. Calm your fears and you will hear your inner voice being guided to give and put you back on course with a fair wind billowing in your sails and a gentle rolling sea of life beneath you.

You cannot fail, but you can think you can when you allow fear to cloud your judgment, not judgment but actions and process. Fear is your ally; it shows you where you have judgments, programs, imprints and beliefs, guilt or shame. State your fears, recognizing them is the first step to overcoming the obstacles that it places before you, that you placed before you. For it is your fears that churn the waters of life around you, and the more fears, the stormier the waters and the darker the night seems to close in around you. Let go of what you think you should be doing and simply be what you are in the moment to the best of your ability. But neither deny what you are fearing, for that is what gives away your power. Stop beating yourself up and begin to trust that you are where you are in this moment for a reason. If today, only one person comes to the Centre then that is appropriate. If a hundred came, could you handle it in this moment? Be grateful for that which comes to you, even naught, for in being open to naught, you have acceptance. This is not an easy period, plateau, but one that is a pivotal point of your existence. Blessings, Tempura, Angel of passion and desire.

Chapter 10 – Owning My Feelings

Stop Trying to Be Real

1998 Dec. 02 - You are just becoming aware of your potential and have not even begun to experience all that you are. You see the potential in others but fail to recognize it within yourself. It is time that you place your mark, like Zorro and begin to be recognized for the gifts that you have and are able to bring and share with humanity and all there is. Your mark in sacred geometry, is this not the reflection of Zorro? Sleep now and dream for you have much to remember.

Feeling of Aloneness

1998 Dec. 03 - Blessings upon you this wondrous day. Indeed wondrous for it is an opportunity for new experiences, opportunities, to evolve and to grow. We know you are not feeling optimistic, you feel a failure, unwanted, not good enough, that you have made the wrong decision and that maybe this isn't your path. Yes, to assist yourself, is your destiny path but to assist others you feel is not and may not be so. Realize that this lack of attraction to the Centre, to you, is your reflection, you feel isolated and alone and so you are, as you create this reality for yourself. It is time to heal this abandonment, this alonement, this separation, for it is truly a deep wound in both the Mother and Me that we have had to heal and both for different reasons, and so it is with you. You need to heal both sides in order to move in such a manner that your reality will shift and will alter.

Touching this aloneness is one of the hardest emotions and experiences and one that has the most imprints, programs and beliefs associated with it as well as of a host of other "tag on" emotions and feelings such as unworthiness, being wrong, not good enough, different, etc., and then also guilt and shame. All these add to the feeling of aloneness. You are in the process of changing aloneness to all oneness, and in that there is the entire difference, the opposite. All your experiences in this and past lives, you have been a loner, the outsider. You are bringing it all together in this lifetime, to experience aloneness in the midst of an era where there are unlimited opportunities to connect, to move physically and electronically between peoples and nations around the world, for borders have and are dropping. In all this opportunity of freedom to experience you still feel isolated, and so you need to feel another level, to express, to accept it as part of your experience, and in so doing you begin to change your programs, imprints and beliefs. You are not failing, you are clearing, growing, and evolving. Take time to be with yourself and not by yourself. Blessings, Mother and Father.

Hope, Faith and Preference

1998 Dec. 04 - Blessings, We come to you this morning to bring you a message of hope, of faith, of love for you to share with others. In the times ahead, in this time of transition, of tribulation, of turmoil, rest assured that those whose intent it is to heal, there is light at the end of the turmoil. No, it is not a rapture and ascension, a lifting up of all that deem themselves righteous, but rather an empowerment of the meek, for they shall inherit the Earth. By meek, we do not mean weak, but rather those that choose to empower themselves, to take back their power, their essence, to become whole. To lift the veils of illusion by ending their denials, and in so doing they alter and transform, or let go of all that does not serve love.

There are as many paths to healing as there are Spirits desiring to heal, to be healed with true love and light. For there is also the illusion of healing, of false hope, of faith, in denial, and in putting your salvation, your power to make yourself whole in the hands of another who you believe will do it for you. There is no one who can make you whole, can heal you, except you. Yes, there are those that can assist you to empower yourself, but they cannot do it for you. You need to feel in order to heal, and to feel you must be real, and in "being real" is where most fall down. For it is guilt, shame, self-sacrifice, self-sabotage in any number of ways that keep you from being real, in doing the loving thing for others but not for yourself, or in using your power or the power others have given you, to use against them in the name of love, rule, regulation or belief. But all these are outside of love, of truth and in fear, in lack and in denial.

For you fear what it would mean if you were real, if you spoke what you feel in your heart, if you shared your deepest fears, desires, hopes and dreams. So to keep in control, you wear masks and portray the illusion of who it is that you feel comfortable in portraying, or in portraying who others would desire you to be. And so you play the game, the illusion game, and so you are trapped in denial.

Release your fears to the best of your ability, state your fears and then state what your fear is and as you begin to share also share layers that you feel come up beneath these and continue giving expression as long as you can. Giving expression also gives acceptance for these feelings; these emotions that you have held repressed in denial. The more open you are to move these emotions, the quicker it is to heal, and the sooner your life experiences will change.

Take a risk, for it is fear of the unknown, of doubt, of projection of the outcome or experience that keeps you locked in your pattern of these old imprints, programs and beliefs. Allow your fears to come up to show you where you have an imprint, program or belief that has you believe it can only be one way and that you are not open to new experiences. Of course you have choice, free Will, but you must decide how your choice is based, is it in love or out of love and in fear and in denial. For if you have a specific reason for experiencing such and such and not another, you also have hidden denial and judgments.

Chapter 10 – Owning My Feelings

It is quite complex, this issue of choice, of preference, and of hidden denial, but you can feel the difference if you are open, open to risk, to experience, and to see how you feel as you move into the experience. It is as if there is a fork in the road and you always choose the left for it is your preference, you feel comfortable for you have done it before. You may never have tried the right road or if you did, you met with an experience you did not enjoy and so you turned back and took the left fork. Now the experience you didn't enjoy, this is where you must look inside yourself to seek the truth of the experience to see what it was that triggered you and what programs, imprints, beliefs and denials are in place. What was actually happening in your experience that you judged wrong and inappropriate? Did you look and feel, were you able to see the experience for what it was, feel both sides and then allow yourself choice to move to what you desired, not out of fear or lack, but with love.

Expect the unexpected for that is the wonder of creation, of growth, of evolution. If you have only acceptance for that which you prefer, are comfortable with, that you know, then you are locked in again to the programs, imprints and beliefs, and you deny yourself expansion, experience and expression. Being in control, no surprises, soon puts a smothering blanket on love, on joy. Free yourself to be spontaneous, in love. Neither deny your Will or overpower or take another's, but in balance, in harmony, in acceptance of true expression and in allowing yourself to be whole, to be all that you are, to experience all that you are; that is the magic, that is life.

Surrender not your Will, but surrender to your Will and allow her expression and acceptance to move as she must in order to heal, and as she heals, so do all aspects heal. False will feelings will also come up as these are programmed into the belief that when a circumstance or experience happens, that these feelings are automatically brought forward to either enhance or deny the experience. It will be difficult at first to bring these into your awareness, as that what you are feeling and expressing are actually not your true feelings, but rather the mental constructs based on certain programs, imprints and beliefs. It is more an automatic response than actual feelings. Awareness of your feelings and awareness of your body will tell you when you are dealing with false feelings.

The more you can attune to your body, the easier it is to identify false Will. Oft time, Body will go numb and there will be gaps in time, seconds, minutes, and there will be recognition of body responses that seem automatic, habit, not connected to the conscious mind. As you become aware of these markers, you also become restless and feel trapped, unable to be in control, not trusting others or self, for although part of you is accepting the experience, another part, your true Will is not, and so the confusion, the mixed messages. Being in the moment, being aware of all the signals, messages, and feelings that are being brought to the surface is one way to begin to get in touch with those parts of you that are running, functioning and sending out the false Will feelings. Feelings that have been imprinted and programmed and so are thought to be real when felt.

This is not to say that the original imprint was not caused by an experience, or experiences, but that the mind, in a way to cope, to survive, set up these programs to assist in dealing with the Will and the feelings that the Will would try to bring up that were deemed unacceptable. The mind and the Will want, desire acceptance and so the mind programmed acceptable behavior in order for the Will to be accepted. This pattern became acceptable, the response acceptable, and so the true feelings of the Will was denied any true expression and this was carried over into body; body feels true feelings. The mental only expresses them verbally and makes body respond in appropriate ways but does not feel them. There is disconnection and it is like someone describing falling off a cliff without the actual experience. You may give words, actions that mimic the real experience, but they are acting feelings and not true feelings.

Chapter 11 - The Power of Denial

1998 Dec. 8 - A clause in the business sale agreement stated that full payment of the outstanding balance, by way of the promissory note, was due on Nov. 30th. As a legal formality to that effect, I wrote a registered letter to Ken's lawyer on Nov. 11, asking that the balance be paid in full on the due date. Today, one day before the trial date, I received a letter from the lawyer stating that they were in receipt of my letter regarding the money owing and that they would be advising the court of their receipt of such certified funds during the trial. I felt a sense of relief as I now felt the court appearance would be a formality and that I would be getting the money that was owed me.

True Understanding and Knowing

1998 Dec. 08 - To understand is to experience, true understanding does not alter the truth to fit the belief, program or imprint. True understanding must be felt and when it is felt to the depth of one's Being, it is without words, for one not only understands, but one KNOWS. There is no doubt only the knowing of being in a state of depth, of vision, of wisdom, that by the use of words expressed by the limited conscious mind, there is no expression suitable to explain what is felt in the core, the essence, the Heart of Being. Knowing is past understanding, for in knowing is peace, harmony, balance, grace, love and unconditional acceptance.

To elevate one to understanding and knowing is a journey; a two-fold journey, for there is understanding and there is knowing. It can be one of the spiritual seeker, seeking to understand and know himself, or it can be the intellectual seeker, one seeking to understand not himself, but rather all that is about him. Oh indeed, he will say he also seeks to understand and to know himself, his physical body, his mental workings, but these are still outside himself for it is his true essence he is missing. He observes manifestation and seeks to understand it, where in that it is essence that manifests and is, for the most part, an illusion. It is essence that is reality and the reality that the scientific mind comprehends and tries to understand is but an artificial construct of the essence, of the light of love, of all that is.

Seek as he might, the scientific intellect will not discover what it is seeking until it can let go of what it calls its rational mind and seeks to know itself, its essence. All that he does, ponders, and considers, is for naught, for it is built on illusion. As if he is trying to understand that what stands before him is but a mere reflection in the mirror of his mind. He cannot touch or taste the fruit he sees in the mirror and he doesn't know that that fruit, that essence, lies within him.

Journey to the Heart Centre

It is time to begin your writings, our messages to the world and let those that have eyes to see; see, ears to hear; hear, and mouths to talk; talk. As the year closes so does a period and era, the Dawn is about to break, rejoice, rejoice, blessings, Michael.

1998 Dec. 10 - In this moment I don't have anyone that I can really talk to that understands me. Jen decided to go on a three-day silence on her moon time and this is the second day. I feel lost and alone. Today is the day after, the day in court. I felt several things before, during and after the trial, but there are no words to describe how I felt when I heard the judge's decision. I was in shock, and it wasn't until I was driving home that I began to get a sense of what had happened. I not only didn't get my money, but I was also ordered to pay what he claimed I owed him. I had gone to court feeling confident that I would win based on what the pretrial judge had said and also on his lawyers' previous attempt to get me to walk away, and then the most recent letter I received. I felt that they knew they didn't have a chance and so I made the assumption that I had won and that the court was just a formality.

I arrived early and the courtroom doors were not open yet. I was sitting on a bench in the hallway talking to another man who was also waiting to go to trial. He was confused when he overheard a couple of people talking that they might have to come back another day as they were number 10 on the list; he was number 5, and I was number 1. I explained what could happen and what had happened to me. I now feel that I started to set myself up to sabotage myself by this conversation. Actually, it ended up that he was heard before me because his case was not being contested.

Court was called into session and the judge started going through the docket, and after almost a couple of hours of hearing motions, appeals, and other legal stuff, my case was finally going to be heard. I had feelings of guilt come up that I didn't recognize as such at the time. Guilt that I should take up the courts time and impose my needs over others. Guilt that was planted in me when I had overheard other people outside the courtroom commenting on how they hoped to go to trial today, and not having to wait another three months for a new trial date as I knew how that waiting felt. I also picked up on how the judge felt on having to listen to people that he considered were wasting his time. I felt prompted to get it over with quickly and to not waste anyone else's time on things that didn't seem important, as I felt that I had already won my case and this was just a formality.

When I got on the stand, I began my presentation by telling the judge, "To make a long story short." The judge stopped me and commented that that was a good comment and that he'd like everyone to consider that when it was their turn. I felt that I was doing something good and right in the judge's eyes, but that was just another set-up to sabotage myself. I denied myself in not stating my case the way I did in pre-trial. I ignored reading my

Chapter 11 – The Power of Denial

notes and the details that I had made from my daytimer. I denied expressing myself even through there were times when I felt I should just read my notes. I dismissed those feelings and went on my mental recall to give a short version, and just presented my case without stating any facts that would win my case or defend me against any counter claim.

That was the start of my denials and in my testimony and cross-examination, I started to omit little things, or I'd agree to half-truths or loosely worded general facts presented by his lawyer. I also denied when I was confused and never asked for clarification, or opposed the lawyers ambiguous questions or twisted statements. This was especially true on the matter of the meeting and agreement regarding the training work and the promissory note, and the fact that it was me that had called him and said, "No note, no work, or I will take you to court," and not the other way around.

I don't feel angry in this moment; numb is more like it. Maybe it's denied as I feel I'm kicking myself for being so stupid. Especially when he got on the stand and said that it was his suggestion that he was trying to negotiate with me and that he tried to give me a promissory note but that I had refused it. Saying that now brings up anger in me. Why didn't I hear it or see it for what it was? I was aware or I thought I was, but when I denied I was caught and I shut down, and after that it just all got fuzzy.

On the stand, I also felt alone and unsupported. He had a lawyer and I didn't, but I really felt I didn't need a lawyer, that I could do it alone. His lawyer knew what he had to do and he did it, including sending me the letter stating he had the money in his possession and that he would be advising the court of such, which he never did. I guess that seed and my belief in my innocence and that I had no intent not to fulfill our agreement was enough to make me think that the court case was just a formality. After I denied stating my prepared statement, things just went into confusion when his lawyer cross-examined me with his carefully phrased questions. I felt a need to go back to my notes and I denied myself again. Later, when he went on the witness stand and gave his testimony, I was awe struck. When I cross-examine him about the promissory note I couldn't believe what I was hearing. I was in shock, felt betrayed and overwhelmed. How could this be happening?

The only way their denials, lies, manipulation and control could work was when I gave my power to them when I denied myself, and give it to them I did. Either by my unconscious beliefs that everyone is more important than me, that I can't get what I want, or in outright conscious denial of expressing what my true feelings and my intuition were prompting me to express. I felt that the whole experience was a gift in the awareness and hindsights that I got yesterday, but at the same time it was a costly one.

I had placed the rest of the people in the courtroom ahead of my needs and me. I placed the judge ahead of me and so the judge, judged me as

I judged myself. I created my reality in that courtroom by being in denial, and I have no intention to continue to create and live in denial any longer. At this moment, I feel that I'm not going to pay what the court ordered me to pay. Why should I give him more than he has already taken, than what I've already given him? The limited company is a company in name only and the money derived from the sale has been spent as I have been unemployed this past year and have also spent a lot in getting this Centre going. I don't have anything left to give him, or anyone else for that matter. I was counting on that money to help the business over the next few months. I really needed the money, but now that isn't going to happen. To say I'm depressed is an understatement, and I have concern about my survival. I feel betrayed, frustrated and angry at myself for not listening to myself and not loving myself, for denying myself by putting the needs of others ahead of mine. I have no intention of appealing the case, but I do take it as a lesson, an expensive one, but one well worth it at the same time. It's interesting to note that I sold the company a year ago tomorrow.

New Beginnings and Changes

1998 Dec. 17 - Blessings, we are pleased with your acceptance of messages that come in many forms and that you allow yourself to feel what feels right for you in the moment, although your actions have a certain amount of fear in them. There is also much love and acceptance of the Divine action and flow of the universe as you have felt. It is time for a new beginning, and in order to do that, there must be a purging and a shedding of the old. This also serves two-fold, in that it also gives warning to those that heed, that it is time for a change, a change within to be reflected without and this they will witness. Those that have chosen to transit will know and will be ready, whether they are conscious of it or not. Your prayers are being answered according to your intent. Allow yourself the freedom and trust yourself and each other. You are about to begin your journey in earnest, in truth, in live and light, both of you.

There is still more clearing and healing that needs to come in the times ahead, and this will come quickly. You are healing in leaps and bounds, have no qualms about that even though you may think otherwise. Some of your feelings are not accurate, are false, and these you will also recognize. Changes are coming; it is not the beginning of the end, but rather the end of the beginning of original cause. For all that has been experienced to this time has been in fear, in unlovingness and love mixed together so that it was almost impossible to tell which was which. Except by feeling the Will, the Mother, which was almost killed in the process, and without her it would have been the beginning of the end. It is time to heal all aspects of Will, Lost Will that can possibly be healed at this time, that chooses to heal. Those that choose not to heal will have opportunity later and some will have no choice

Chapter 11 – The Power of Denial

and they shall move to their right place and be transformed. Fear naught; not do not have fear, for if it comes allow it to show you your issues outstanding. Your mission cannot fail now, our mission cannot fail now. Blessings, Mother and Father and the company of heaven.

I noticed that I had written Heart/Earth in my journal and realized that the same letters are used except that the H has been moved. I just had this thought that if H stood for Hell, then if I took the H from the end of Earth and reversed it and put it at the beginning, I would have the word Heart.

1998 Dec. 18 - Irene had offered to give me an Aromatherapy massage a while back and while I was hesitant, I also felt that there must be a purpose and a reason or it wouldn't be coming to me. I finally accepted her offer as I felt with all that had been going on in my life this year, I needed it. Today I went out to her place and met her husband Dave, and we all had a brief chat. Later, She gave me an upper body and foot massage with various oils.

1998 Dec. 30 - I basically haven't written anything in my daytimer or journal following my court episode. I feel depressed and beaten. I haven't written much of what I experienced this whole year, except for my messages and then I was too busy to read them, as I was too busy doing and not being. This whole year has been a blur for me.

The following are some of my judgments and beliefs about money.

- Money is power, the more you have, the more you can do.
- Money is freedom; you can go anywhere, anytime, and do what you want.
- Money brings you happiness, people, places and things.
- People listen and respect you if you have money.
- Money can do almost anything, as everything has a price.
- Money talks; put your money where your mouth is.
- Money can be used for evil, to corrupt and destroy.
- People with money are sometimes snobs, they use it over people, play games, to control, manipulate and buy people.
- I never had money as a child, family was poor, and I had to work for the things I wanted.
- I'm embarrassed and ashamed if I don't have money, or a credit card is rejected, or a cheque bounces.
- I'm embarrassed and ashamed if I can't pay my way, or pay for another person if I feel the other person hasn't any money, so I offer to treat.
- If you have no money, people judge you are worthless, useless, no good, a bum, a burden.
- No one to support me, I had to do it myself.

Chapter 12 - 1999 - Going Deeper

1999 Jan. 1 - I made the following new Year's resolution. I want to totally express myself. I don't want to hold back like I'm always doing, wondering what will they think of me, will they like me or not? But in the next breath, I also have fear that if I express myself totally, that I will hurt or activate them. Not that I would intentionally hurt them, but by activating them, I'd send them into some place emotionally or mentally where they would gap and could hurt others or themselves. If that happened, I'm afraid that people would shun me, or that I'd get locked up, thought crazy, and accused of all kinds of things and get put away. I feel I'd rather die if that happened.

I have no acceptance for myself to allow myself to express my Will, so how can I have acceptance reflected to me? I deny myself so much just like in court; I judged myself, and the judge, judged me. I don't have to act on my feelings but I need to give them acceptance and allow them expression. I will try to express myself, to end my denials in whatever form they are. I want to change, transform, and remove any programs, imprints, and beliefs that no longer serve me in love and light. I want to become fearless, not by denying my fear, but in accepting it and all the issues around the fear to their deepest level.

1999 Jan. 4 - It's Monday, and I've had a cold coming on now for the past two weeks. I'm feeling achy, dizzy, disoriented and my throat is sore and scratchy. Since I have no one to look after the store today, I decided to close the Centre for the day and to take it easy. I put the "closed" sign up on the front door, then called and canceled the appointments that were scheduled for today. I made myself a cup of soup and went back to bed for a while. Later I talked to Jen a couple of times, but only briefly. In the afternoon, I checked the mail, there were two letters, one from the lawyer restating the court ruling and how much I now owed with interest, and the other was from Sears saying that my cheque was returned NSF, which it shouldn't have been. Needless to say, those two pieces of news activated me. I went up to the front "pink" room, as we called it, and put on the boxing gloves. I started punching the futon and the floor until I released my anger and rage. I'm tired of getting pummeled, picked on and beaten. Afterwards, I did some reading and realized that I've placed my power in money, in having money, not love. I also have this fucked up belief that I have to do it alone, and at the same time that I can't do it alone. My world is falling apart again.

Chapter 12 – 1999 Going deeper

1999 Jan. 9 - On Friday night seven people came to the meditation class and I felt encouraged by the turnout.

Healing Intent

1999 Jan. 09 - If your intent is to heal and to end your denials, then denials of all kinds will be brought to your awareness, emotional, physical, and mental. These will be swift and the effects more dynamic the closer you are to healing the gap. Everything is being enhanced, accelerated, and those that choose to heal, to move, will feel the effects of their denials and of the healing taking place when there is acceptance and a desire to end denials, and the programs, imprints and beliefs that kept them in place. Those that choose not to will also see their reality manifest their denials, and these will also be accelerated and they will see their illusions crumble more quickly. Pay attention to all your thoughts, emotions and physical sensations, for all are in denial and these are being brought to the surface, for they are all connected. More later, rest now. Adornia

Denial and Pressure

1999 Jan. 14 - Denial is at the core, the base of defending, pressure and anger. You defend your old beliefs, programs, imprints and judgments. You feel pressured from external sources only because there is already denial and pressure holding down the emotional expression on an internal level, and anger is a form of emotional release activated by denial.

1999 Jan. 17 - I feel that I'm Jens protector, as sometimes I feel she is going to get hurt and I can't do anything about it. Is it my issues of control, of knowing, or is it a projection of what I think is going to happen? I'm confused and have judgments on Jen and her male friend. She has this passion for him, what she calls love, where she feels safe in his arms and in talking about the feelings they both have for each other, but at the same time she says that she doesn't see him as boyfriend material. I have judgments on just what feelings are being expressed and what feelings are being denied.

Yes, I've curbed my passion, I even feel I've lost my passion and sex drive, but I also feel that sex in a state of denial will only compound my problems and issues. Sure there are the "feel good" sensations for however long the moment is, but then I ask myself why, if it feels good, doesn't it last? I'm afraid of getting into a relationship just because it feels good in the moment. I don't feel it would be a relationship; it would be a quick fix. It would be similar to a drink, a joint, chocolate, food or whatever; it's something that we think we need or lack, which will help us feel good about ourselves, give us some false sense of worth, self-esteem, that our fragile altered ego thinks it wants or needs.

Journey to the Heart Centre

I desire a relationship that can have it all, mental, emotional, physical and spiritual healing on all levels. I thought that I had that with Michele but there were denials there on both sides. I feel that I moved some of mine, enough to end the relationship when I did and not to wait years to do so. I'm afraid to attract a female relationship as I'm still in denial. So why am I trying to fool myself thinking that any woman I meet would not be in denial also?

I just got off the phone with Jen and I said some hateful and hurtful things to her. I have regret and guilt for what I said. I called her back and she was crying. I'm still not expressing myself, my fears, doubts and especially my confusion and lack of understanding. I verbally attack another when I'm confused as that is how I defend my lack of understanding. I go into accusing them of not speaking the truth as I'd come out with statements like, why don't you say what you mean, and mean what you say, you keep changing your mind or the facts. Another one is, you're not listening to me, you're just hearing me. I don't seem to have this problem with other people, I seem to be able to open up and say what I feel without caring if they will like me or not. I feel that I've gotten attached to Jen, I must have, or is it because we're in this close relationship and that we mirror stuff for each other. I don't know?

I just got off the phone with Jen again as we had another argument. She is in this lover's triangle and I feel totally frustrated and I'm tired of not being heard. She tells me all the things that are going on and then asks what I think and feel, and then when I tell her, she says I'm wrong. What's the use of expressing what I feel or think? I feel that I'm just a fool, stupid and that I can't win no matter what I say or do. I can't do anything right as there are only sarcastic criticisms from her like, "I know where you are going with this. Who the fuck are you, and where are you coming from? Can you hear yourself; can you feel how you feel? I don't like your energy, you creep me out. I'm afraid of you." Then there are the other times when I'd get sugar coated understandings and phony words of compassion. I'm frustrated with this whole fucking lovers triangle of hers, just work it out for yourself and let me know when you're finished because I'm tired of hearing the same old shit with only an item or a color change thrown in to make it NOT the same old story. A fucking Giraffe is still a fucking Giraffe whether he has pink or green spots, or even if he farts bananas. It's still a fucking giraffe even if he decides to swim in the water with a frog and a shark. Unless of course, you now want to start changing the language and say that when you say swimming, that you actually mean he was talking on the telephone or any of the other bullshit that you come up with to justify yourself and your denials. Some of your favorite lines to get you out of your bullshit denials are, "If you were feeling what I was saying, you'd understand," or "If you would stop interrupting me and let me finish, you'd understand what it is that I meant to say," and then there's

Chapter 12 – 1999 Going deeper

the classic, "I'm sorry you're confused but that is your issue and your problem."

I paused for a few moments, and then wrote the following. I have no acceptance for my confusion, abandonment, not being supported and of having to do it alone. Others depend on me and I have to be the responsible one, not only do I have to be responsible for myself, but I'm also responsible for the Centre. I have to make money to live for myself and to support the Centre, and I have to do it alone. No one helps me, or if they say they will, it's only talk. They may be there, but it's still me that has to make the money and is responsible to pay the bills.

I feel that I'm going to fail and if I fail, the banks and people will say that I'm a failure, not a good risk, can't be trusted, not responsible. I have to be the provider, both for myself and for others. No one says, okay John, I'll look after it, I'll do that for you the way you'd like it done. It's okay to let go of the control, we wouldn't fuck with you, we wouldn't say trust me and then when your back is turned, take what we want and leave you with nothing but a mess. I've never been able to feel that the people who say that they'll support me are trustworthy and that all they ever do is just talk.

I have to be perfect and I have to do it right, make the right decision, as my life and others depend on it. I just flashed to a past life where I was a ship's Captain and I made a mistake and all onboard died. I feel I can't make a mistake, that I have to be perfect. Other people can make mistakes but if I make a mistake then I'll get hurt and others will too. I have no acceptance for being human, to make mistakes, to be confused, or to look foolish, because I have to be perfect. I've always had to have all the facts so that I could make the right decisions; there could be no confusion. I had to be as accurate and as detailed as possible so that I could see any problems before they happened, that way I could fix it before it went too wrong, or if it went wrong, that there was a way out, a way to survive.

I trust others to be as right as they can be, but I also allow others to make mistakes because they're only human, but I can't. Others would get help or I'd help them if they made a mistake, but no one would tell me that it's okay to make a mistake. Yes, they might say it, but it really wasn't okay as what they didn't say was just don't do it again or the next time you won't get off so lucky, next time look out. I not only have to know what is right, but I also have to have proof that what I do is right. I can't allow myself to change my mind and disappoint other people or not get their approval, as it will mean pain for me. I also get angry if others make a mistake that directly affects what I'm doing, especially if they were trying to do a short cut to get out of doing what they knew was right.

1999 Jan. 19, I talked to Jen on the phone from 10:30 to noon; she wanted to get together to do grocery shopping and to watch a movie. She said she was tired and was going to eat and call me later to get together. I decided to do a bit of work on some steel shelves I was putting up for storage in the basement. I called her at 1:30 and we got into a discussion about bad drivers. I said that I've really noticed how bad Canadian drivers are for driving in the passing lane on the 400 highway. I mentioned that in my experience on American roads, that Americans were better at staying to the right. She said she never ran into that problem on the 400, and that she had been on the 400 as many times as I had. I said, "I doubt that, you're not even close."

She then began to tell me about her ex-boyfriend who lived in Toronto, and how she used to drive down to see him two or three times a week. This was one boyfriend and the relationship lasted only a couple of years. I stated that I commuted on the 400 highway, every day to work for over 14 years and that she hasn't even had her driver's license for fourteen years, so how can she compare her driving experience to mine. She hung up on me and we did the usual call and hang up routine on each other a few more times.

The last time she called back, she asked if I was going to drop off the movie. I told her that I was going to before, but that now, in this moment, the answer was no. She got angry because I wouldn't drop the movie off and I got angry at her when she tried to say that our argument over the 400 highway was just words and that words didn't matter. But now, when it's something she wants, suddenly words matter and what I said before is suddenly cast in stone for her benefit. What the fuck! I dropped the movie off at 2:15 pm (in denial and guilt) along with a note saying that I would pick it up at 6 - 6:30 pm, as I had other things to do. Later, I swung by her place and found the movie in a plastic grocery bag that was hanging on the doorknob. I didn't bother knocking or trying to see her, I just picked up the movie, went home and made supper.

So what's the issue? I don't want to talk to Jen, I have nothing to say so why waste my time. She wanted to watch the movie in the afternoon and as it was the first warm afternoon in weeks, I wanted to be outside and enjoy it while it lasted. I felt we could watch the movie anytime, I have control over that but I don't have control over the weather, yet, so why can't we do both, be outside and do the grocery shopping and then watch the movie. I resent that the movie is more important than our getting together. We could have spent a few hours together today, but only if I accommodated her. Well she watched the movie this afternoon and I'll watch it later tonight. I've got supper cooking and I still have to eat, clean up and then I want to have a bath, so I'll probably won't be sitting down to watch the movie until around 8:30, after which I'll be off to bed, so I doubt that I will talk to her tonight.

She told me later that I was not the only one that was disappointed, that she also feels frustrated by not going out and getting her groceries, not seeing me, not getting to watch the movie when she wanted, or with me. I

Chapter 12 – 1999 Going deeper

feel like I always get shafted as she only has a little window of opportunity in which she can do things, so I have to be ready when she's ready or else it's a no go. I have to fit my schedule into her window, her desires, and what she wants or feels she can do. If she doesn't get what she wants, she comes out with a guilt trip, "You don't understand" or "You don't care about me," or she turns it around with the, "I hate depending on anyone" or "I'm such a burden" routine. This is getting frustrating as I feel I'm not touching the real issues.

Movement and Acceptance

1999 Jan. 19 - Finish, complete, for you are in transition and until you close the doors behind you, you cannot be fully in the present. These doors are held open in fear, in denial, and until you address these parts of yourself, your confusion with people, computer, banks and money and lack thereof, which also includes your court appearance as well as your experience in creating your reality. All are tied together and as you begin to move one so you move the others. Trust, trust that by moving you give yourself acceptance that it's okay, you don't have to be perfect. Your fear of failure, of survival, these are deep rooted fears and are the doorway you are standing in, hence the sense of lack of movement, of going backwards and putting out all your energy, alone, just to keep it afloat. Release your fears, take a risk, expect the unexpected, these words you use but still fail to apply to these fears, imprints, programs and beliefs, and hence they fail to move. It's scary because it's the only thing you've known that has allowed you to survive in some form.

Know that the universe supports you, feel this in the depths of your Heart. Just because you can't see it or feel it physically doesn't mean it isn't true, which is another belief you have adopted for survival, using your outer senses to identify your outer reality. Let go of the illusion that the outer reality creates your inner reality, it is the opposite, but your fears, programs, imprints, and beliefs make it so. Allow yourself to be real, to feel and to express with truth and love. Not to say that everything you need to express needs to be what you call loving, allow all aspects of you to voice, to express. You need not necessary act on them, but they need to be expressed. You are still trying to control your outer reality rather than manifest it. As you have begun to experience, and also to sense, your outer reality and that of the mass consciousness, and so you are confused. What is yours and what is not? What's real? The outer seems real and so it is, and is not.

Physical manifestation is the wonderment of creation bringing the idea into a reality that can be experienced by various senses; this is the reality of creation. What is not reality is how they are created and how you are controlled by what you call reality. The two wires have been crossed; many of your wires have been crossed, but also for the experience. It is now time to sort through these wirings, to open doors and to close doors, and as you do the lights will come on and you will feel the love, experience it, and know that you are supported, and see and feel it in your outer reality. As you move, others will begin to notice, and so you allow them to make changes and soon the outer reality of the mass consciousness also changes and there is true transformation. You are growing, healing, and these are some of the last major holdbacks that you are facing. There are deeper issues on other levels, but that is for later. Allow yourself the process to be human, to feel human, to experience and allow, and give yourself acceptance to be what you need to experience. Adornia

1999 Jan. 20 - What do I need to touch, to do, and to feel? How can I feel it in a way that it needs to be felt and to give it acceptance to heal? I feel that there's a part of myself, a boy, that's hurt, alone and feeling that he's going to die and also wishes that he were dead. I don't know why or what he actually is feeling, or how to reach him and help him. I'm asking for help, I need help. God, I'm asking for help. Am I afraid of God? Am I angry at God for making me feel all this pain and suffering, for feeling different, alone, not good enough, and that what I feel and express has no acceptance? When I lost my religion did I also lose my faith and feel that God rejected me, so I rejected God back, that if he didn't want me then I didn't want or need him either. Why do I always seem to get the short or the shitty end of the stick if he did care for me? He showed others love, joy, companionship, abundance, yet I never really felt any of that and if I did, it was only for a moment before it was taken away.

    Shame, guilt and pride are also issues for me. Pride, false bravado, sticks and stones can break my bones, but words can never hurt me. At school, no matter how hurt I was, I wouldn't show that they hurt me, but then when they felt I wasn't hurt, they would physically beat me even more or abuse me mentally and emotionally. Even my parents and their hurtful comments like, you'll just have to grow a tougher skin, learn to fight back and defend yourself, don't be a sissy, don't be a cry baby, no wonder they pick on you, you're too sensitive, you're asking for it, stop you're crying, big boys don't cry, I don't care and I don't want to know what you think or how you feel. All these comments deeply imprinted and programmed me. I'm having a hard time trying to stop doing things and just write what I'm feeling when I have conscious awareness that I'm avoiding or denying what I'm feeling. I have to force myself to stop. I'm now sitting in the store, on a chair by the front window. I want to open to love, to let love, life and light in, and to move out all my denials. To let go or transform all my programs, imprints and beliefs that do not serve my highest purpose and good and are not of love and light. I want to be real; I want to feel, I want to heal, to become whole, and to spiritualize this physical body. I realized that I've made myself an island and have cut myself off. I want to give myself acceptance to hear what

Chapter 12 – 1999 Going deeper

I need to hear, see, and feel. I'm going to give myself love and acceptance that I no longer need to have all the facts and figures that I needed when I felt confused or felt that people were liars and hypocrites, and I needed proof that they were. Why is there this outer reflection, is it because I'm the liar, the hypocrite? I've been lying to myself and telling myself what is real and what is not, what is important and not important, what is good and bad. I would always be watching and reading people, trying to get the facts and the details so that I'd look good, be good, be accepted in their eyes, while all along I was looking into my eyes and lying. I couldn't admit that to the whole world, that it was an illusion and a lie and that I was lying to myself. No way, but I'd tell myself that other people were the liars and hypocrites.

I realized that the liar and hypocrite came into my life around the time just before we got excommunicated from the Catholic Church, as I remember calling my mother a hypocrite. I remember her saying that she had to go to confession for such and such, and then that very Sunday afternoon, she was back doing the same thing again. I remember calling her a hypocrite and she began to cry and asked me to forgive her for hurting me. Later, I got into trouble in school regarding confession and in a few months, we were excommunicated because I wasn't going to lie in confession, just to go to confession. I must have programmed and imprinted myself with the belief that it's better to lie to myself than to lie to others. Others wouldn't get hurt, sticks and stones can break your bones but words can never hurt you. Bullshit!

I wouldn't lie about details and facts, but I'd lie about me and how I felt, my feelings didn't count, they were unacceptable. And so, when I was lied to and purposefully mislead and in a state of confusion, I'd lie to myself and deny expressing my feelings. I'd deemed my feelings not important, therefore I, John James Rieger wasn't important, and that everyone else was better or more important than I was. I didn't deserve anything for any number of reasons, and that if I wanted anything, I had to work for it and keep my mouth shut and my feelings to myself. I got that reflected to me over the years with losing my job every time I voiced my opinion, my feelings, that the company was either screwing me and/or others. I'd get talked into being the spokesman who'd fight for the underdog and then would get kicked in the teeth, shoved out or fired, and then the rest who said they would back and support me never came to my aid, but they got the rewards I fought for. I'd get punished if I spoke up, but I could only deny so long before I'd rage and start a ruckus, and it was then that I'd get into trouble. The more I tried to deny it and let it go, the tighter it seemed to hold and entrap me.

1999 Jan. 24 - Five people showed up for the Friday evening meditation session. It was a good evening as we also discussed past lives, death and dying.

Journey to the Heart Centre

1999 Jan. 28 - I made a list of some of things my mother and father told me as a child that imprinted and programmed me in a negative way.

You don't deserve to live.
You don't deserve any more or better.
Be thankful for what you have, or have been given.
Be grateful for the roof over your head, the clothes on your back and the food on your plate.
Other children don't have what you have.
You're not good enough to eat with the pigs.
You're selfish to complain.
Take what you're given, eat what you're given or you can go hungry and without.
You're nothing but a burden, a heartache.
I'm sorry I ever brought you into this world.
You kids torment me; I just want to kill myself.
I should just get rid of all of you and be done with all of this.
You'll never amount to anything.
You're stupid.
You're not good enough, or smart enough.
You'll learn soon enough that you have to work for what you want.
Nobody's going to give you what you want.
You don't deserve help if you can't help yourself.
You have to learn to do it alone, by yourself.
It's time to grow up and be useful.
It's time you started pulling your weight.
Be good for something at least.
You're good for nothing.
You're a better door than a window, move.
I'd give you away but nobody would take such a bad kid.
You're such bad kids.
You're a sorry sight.
Why are you crying, stop it, or I'll give you something to cry for.
Do what you're told or you'll get what's coming to you.
Children should be seen and not heard.
I regret the day you were born.
I should have left you out for the wolves.
You're so and so's, son or daughter (indicating that a neighbor was our real father)
Oh I'm sorry; mommy didn't mean those things she said.
You know I love you kids, they're only words.
Your father and all of you are driving me crazy.

Chapter 12 – 1999 Going deeper

I heard the following words on TV last night and they really stuck with me. It was a quote from William Shakespeare, "This above all, to thine own self be true and it must follow as night the day, thou canst not then be false to any man".

1999 Jan. 30 - The following is a note meant for Jen. I'm afraid of writing this down as I'm afraid of what you'll think of me but at the same time, I also don't want to deny anymore. I want to heal and I'm not going to censor what I feel, think, or desire. I just felt this "huff" and a sensation of being released and hearing the words, "Well that didn't work." I don't know what that was all about.

What I'm afraid to say or ask myself is, am I secretly in love with you and just wouldn't or can't admit it? There's no one in my life, for that matter, I don't feel ever, in all my life times, that knows me like you do. But then again, only to a certain point and that's the agony, that I can be a friend but not a lover or mate. We've shared some of our deepest physical and emotional fears and pains, and even spiritual experiences and moments of love that can't be described. Through all this, we have never shared any personal, physical pleasures, like a sensual touch, a kiss, a breath, a scent, a word, a sigh, a smile, a knowing that touches the soul that leaps with joy. Not being able to experience these simple joys and pleasures in a platonic relationship based on friendship or companionship is heartbreaking.

I don't know if it's you, but I do know that I want a relationship based on a friendship that wants to heal on all levels. I don't want to hold back the longing, the desire, that passion that only lovers can experience, and yes, I have them, as sometimes I just want to hold you and sometimes I just wish you could hold me. I guess I've denied expressing these feelings because you've said that you don't see me as sexual and that I'm just a friend. I guess I'm jealous that you can have what you want, even if it takes two packages, me as a friend and the other guy as the lover. I want it all also, but I want it all in one package. I want a friend, a lover and a mate and everything in-between. I feel that you'll always be my friend and that I can express and be open with you, BUT only to a certain point.

You'll never know or experience that other part of me and just in writing that, I feel a sadness, a loss that I also wouldn't know or experience that part of you. Here we know all these things and feelings about each other but there's more that we'll never know or share, and in that I feel the heartbreak, the loss, and it's not about sex. It's all the intimate things that could be done, would be done and shared, the growth to be experienced, the openness to unlimited possibilities. Just as our friendship has continued to blossom to this point, but now I feel it's stopped because you're getting your intimacy, your lovers touch, and I feel you're separating yourself from me, or I from you. I feel like I'm losing a part of myself, not a physical part, but that

I'm afraid that our friendship will change, stop growing and evolving. That it can't ever be more that what it is in this moment and that in order for me to experience the lovers arms, the affection and passion with the openness that we share as friends, that I'll have to move on and find another. That we'll be closing off these parts of ourselves from each other and will now share them with another, and that makes our friendship and relationship conditional, and that's fucked.

That's my desire, to heal, to grow, to learn, to share and maybe this is as far as we can go in our relationship. Maybe this is the end of the road or just a fork in the road. Sure, we'll still be friends, or rather acquaintances, and we can meet back on this part of the road we shared, but we will have a part of the path that we didn't share or experience, and maybe that's how it was meant to be. Maybe I'll meet someone new that's as open and as loving a friend as you have been, that wants to heal and to also experience more of life in terms of a lover, a mate and everything in between. To experience these in a loving, open, growing and evolving relationship, and to touch and heal all those parts of ourselves that you and I are not able to touch. I guess, no, I know we have limits and conditions on our friendship, our experiences, and yes, it might be the end of the relationship as we know it, but it will also be the opening to new ones where be both can continue to grow, to heal and share those parts of ourselves with someone new, and to manifest our dreams and desires, and experience life to the fullest with love, joy and abundance.

So that's what I'm touching in this moment. I want to heal all of me and I want to grow, discover, and to be able to share ALL of life's experiences in a loving relationship with a woman, a friend like you, but also a lover and a mate and more, to the fullest. I don't want to limit life or ration it in portions; I want it all on my plate before me. Maybe we have to do it in stages? I just thought of Rita and how we hooked up for a while and then parted. Maybe all of this has got something to do with the Centre too? Maybe it's time to move on as this is all we can get, can grow in our relationship, and now it's time to allow someone new to come into our lives so that we can continue our journey. I feel that I'm saying goodbye and that I'll never see you again. It's like I've made this choice that this is it, I can't go any further on my journey with being in denial. I want to end my denials and I don't want to create them in my life any longer. What I do want is to create my dreams and desires in love.

I want to cry as I feel that I'm losing my best friend, but I can't manifest what I want if I'm in denial, so it hurts that in being true to myself, I have to let go of someone I love for the first time, maybe in all time. But I love me more and I want to live. I want love and life and I want to experience it to the fullest. I want to live; to laugh, dance, sing, have abundance, friends, family, and someone whole to share it all with. I don't want to stop healing, and by being in a limited and conditional relationship, I would be denying

Chapter 12 – 1999 Going deeper

myself. Now I feel cold and empty like I'm demanding more from you and our relationship but I'm not. I'm just expressing how I feel and what I desire. I guess your other relationship has finally triggered me to express what I've been unable to express because of my denials, programs, imprints, beliefs, and I thank you for helping me to get to this point of healing in my life. Where I go, where you go, where we go with the Centre, well I don't know.

My life is changing and I'm afraid I'm losing it all again and that I'll even be losing your friendship. I'll be alone and no one will really know me, but at least I'll know and love myself more than I've ever done, or maybe that's all an illusion too. I also want to heal my sexuality, sensuality, passion, desire and romance, to experience the tenderness, caress, kiss, and touch of another body, where we both share and feel ours and each other's energies to the core of our Being. I have this other aspect of me that is unexpressed, inexperienced, and unexplored, and are also parts of me that need to be healed.

If the Mother is the moving creative life force, the giver of life, of passion and sexuality that hasn't been accepted and allowed to express, then I guess I've just felt the tip of the iceberg. I feel I'm now ready to explore not just sex, but also sensuality and passion. I want to unfold those powerful aspects of me that have all this depth, passion and life. I want to express all that I haven't known how to express in a way that was acceptable. How I long to experience that with a partner that has the openness, the acceptance, the wonderment of allowing ourselves to experience life, love as we have never known or felt it. There's a part of me that I've been denying all my life, that I haven't been loving and it's time to change that and to heal that, but I couldn't do that until I got to this point first. To begin to love myself enough to get to this point where I realize that I'm not what people tell me they think I am in this physical lifetime. I feel I have the opportunity in this lifetime to experience love, life, joy, peace, harmony, abundance, in balance, and that I can only achieve that by moving out my denials and healing all aspects of me.

I've curbed my passion, excitement, enthusiasm, creativity and spontaneity. Hell! I've shut down and shut out all the fun in my life, all the zest and the wonderment, my life is stale, flat and boring, and I don't like it. There's a part of me saying, "You don't know what you'll turn loose." And then there's a louder part of me that's saying, "You don't know what will happen if you DON'T turn me loose." I've shut down sexually and emotionally more and more all my life, feeling less and less, but now it's time to heal that. I've withdrawn and shut myself out and away from people, from relationships, from intimacy, true love and from experiencing "real" life. It's been long enough, not that I could have or would have experienced true love and real life as I'm not healed yet, but this is what I want to heal and to heal it I have to feel it. I want to feel it; I want to live it and to have it all, to be whole, to be real, to be balanced and centered in love and light, and to experience creation and creating in all its aspects and forms. I am. I Am. I AM. I am ready to heal the next aspect, the next stage and part of me, to heal my lost Will and the parts of Spirit, Body and Heart. I want to heal all of me and I welcome the opportunity to share this with a woman who has the same dream, desire, and intent.

I also have fear about not being able to heal this because there is so much sexual shame and guilt that I haven't really been able to get in touch with yet as I'm not in any relationship where these issues can be experienced, felt, triggered, explored and healed. It's taken this long to finally feel what it is that Jen was triggering in me when sharing her other relationships. I feel I can't do that, just have sex without the emotions because that's denial and I don't want that. I feel that it's shallow, empty and lacks life and love. Sure the physical body feels good for the moment and the mind is happy, but without feelings, emotions, and heart, there is no joy. The physical senses are part of how we experience life in Human form, however limited they may be, they still provide a limitless number of sensations in this creative expression called Earth. These senses however, lack color and in most cases they are muted, opaque, translucent or pastel as they never have been truly experienced in love in all their radiance and brilliance, and that is what I want to experience and feel. I want to savor every drop, smell, sight, sound and touch and I want to feel them to the depth of my Being with the senses I have, and to open to yet unexplored senses. I don't know how or when, but I know that this is what I want. I also feel that the Centre is a part of this, or maybe it was a part just to get me to this point. I don't know that yet, but I know and trust, and I'm open to heal in whatever way the universe brings it to me. I'm glad to be alive and I want to live, I want life, I want light and I want love.

♡ If I haven't mentioned this before, I want to say it now or to say it again; that all the messages and journal writings that I share with you now, I also shared with Jen the next time I talked to her. Usually I would just read what I had written and express any emotions as they came up. I feel that these journal writings were a way for me to say what I couldn't express verbally when I was feeling it. ♥

1999 Jan. 31 – Yesterday, I was visiting Jen and she asked me to sit on her computer chair. She began to spin me around, faster and faster until it fell over and I landed on my left hip and shoulder. It shook me up but I wasn't hurt. Today, I picked Jen up and brought her over to the Heart Centre. No one was in the store and I can't remember what we were talking about or doing, when I started to do some toning. After making only a few toning sounds I broke into sobbing tears, then into screams of anger and rage as I was stomping my feet. Jen was activated and shook up by my display and expression of emotions and my anger. When I finished my emotional release,

Chapter 12 – 1999 Going deeper

I drove Jen home and returned to the Centre and closed the store. I didn't write down what I had touched but from what I recall it had to do with my physical beatings in school and also at home.

Later that evening, still unaware of what really happened, I picked up the book "Right Use of Will" by Ceanne DeRohan and opened to page vii and viii. I read where it talked about the use of sound and minor injuries that can help move the blocks that are holding denied emotions. Since I've begun reading these books, I find it amazing at how I'm either activated by reading them, or like today, where I have an experience that activates me but have no understanding as to what happened or why, and how I'm simply guided to randomly pick up one of the books in the series, and I usually open it to either the exact page, or within a page, and there's the answer and understanding to my experience. Coincidence? Not! Ask and you shall receive. To date, I've read all six books published and have read them all at least twice, and the first one five or six times. Often like today, I just open a book that I feel is appropriate and begin to read as far as I feel I need to, to either activate me or give me insights. I started underlining sentences that either activated or rang as a truth for me. As I re-read the books, in whole or in part, I'd used a different colored ink each time, so now my books are beginning to look a little busy as some pages are almost completely underlined. I also started to put key words in the margins and to make an index on a blank page at the back of the book where these key words can be found for quick reference.

1999 Feb. 3 - I have a big judgment about people using the word love for sex, as I feel that sex should be an expression of love, as how can you "make" love. I guess you could argue the point that love is what is felt in the moment, and yes, that is true, a part of the truth. I also feel that is denial of what was felt in the previous moment that turned the switch from NO to YES and then after the sex act, back from YES to NO, as they go their separate ways.

I don't know what the real difference is, or if there is a difference, in having sex in a state of denial, or denying your sexuality, as they're both fucked. So where is the balance and how don't I deny my sexuality, my passion? By being in the moment? And then what about that on/off switch? Was a denial made to turn me from "off" to "on" and back again? How do I allow myself to be sexual when at the same time I just don't want to fuck around because that wouldn't feel good and isn't what I want? I want it all, a friend, a lover and a mate. So before I would even begin to think of sex, I'd have to find someone that I could see myself in a long-term relationship with and I'm not there yet. I don't know how you can really get to know someone unless, like Jen and I did, you spend a lot of time together and open up emotionally. It wouldn't work if you're open and honest and the other person is only partially open, which means that they are really in denial. If you start to fool around and get caught up in the sexuality and sex, forgetting about all the other stuff you're feeling, you also go into denial and fall for the same old trap again. I don't want to fall into the same denial cycle again. Yes, I could justify it and say to myself that I'm only human and therefore not perfect, to allow myself to experience the moment, to "go with the flow" as is the commonly used phrase with many "new age" people, but I feel that that is Lucifer's way of getting me back into denial again. I can't pretend to be ignorant as I have awareness of what I'm doing and also awareness of my intent. I want to know how to heal my sexuality and I ask for help to heal it.

I feel that we've set up so many programs in ourselves that if we meet someone new, we begin to talk to them, and if we like them, then there's the possibility of becoming friends. If we meet someone and we get sexually aroused, then there is the possibility of becoming lovers. See, I used the word lovers again. We have the possibility of being fucked, having sex without even really knowing anything about the person, not even his or her name. So I guess I need to meet a lot of women and sort out the ones that I find sexually attractive (that's judgment and condition to begin with) and then try to spend a lot of time with each of them to get to know them and they me. Then I'd need to find out which woman finds me sexually attractive so that we can have sex without neither of us being in denial and where both are open to express our issues and feelings as they come up to enable us to heal our issues. If that all works out, then there is the possibility of a long-term relationship, or is a long term relationship yet another belief and imprint? All this feels like an impossibility as it already started out in denial, it's fucked, all fucked.

So why not just be human (in denial) and fuck each other's brains out and when either one of us is tired of getting fucked over we can move on to somebody else who makes us feel good until that relationship turns sour. It's not a real relationship but at least you feel good for a while and you get to experience and feel part of your sexuality which is actually what we're all doing now anyway. It makes me want to cry. Or, do I just meet someone who is sexually attractive, single or not, and have sex and then try to bond a friendship and get to know them and vice versa and all live happily ever after. And maybe this someone just so happens to be the one that we have been waiting to meet. Why not? I don't know. I don't know anything.

I talked with Jen later that evening and we got into an argument on love and sex when she mentioned being only partially in denial, and that that was okay. I said I don't understand partial denial. If you have intent to end your denials and you are aware of your denials, but you choose to ignore your awareness, are you not in denial? So are you trying to tell me that you're able to experience love while in a conscious state of denial, and that you have love and acceptance for denial? To do what, try to heal a part of your essence while denying it and bringing it death by your denials? To experience feelings

Chapter 12 – 1999 Going deeper

of love, joy, bliss and tenderness while in this conscious state of denial? I don't think so! All that you are doing is the same thing that we have been doing for countless lifetimes.

You're either pregnant or you're not pregnant, you're in denial or you're not, there is no partial pregnancy or partial conscious denial that is not denial. Our experiences are here to show us where we still have denials and parts of ourselves to heal, and to bring to our awareness so that we can move denial out and bring love and light IN to fill that part of us that was denied love. Now if the denial is in your conscious awareness, what part of you are you casting out just so that another part of you can experience a "good feeling", a sexual feeling. And how can that sex be in love or loving, if you are in a state of denial with this part of yourself that you are aware of, but that you consciously cast off and reject by your denials. That's a false Will truth, in a state of denial. How can anything be in a state of love after you become aware of a part of you that is being denied and that you choose to ignore? Awareness and intent are the issue and if conscious intent is to deny what it knows and feels, then that intent is unloving as it has no acceptance for part of itself.

She argued that she was loving herself by giving that part of her love and acceptance, and that the other part of her was basically in agreement and allowed this other part to have a good time as it's not very often that she is happy. She also stated that if the one part of her is happy, then the other part is also happy. I told her if that was how it worked, then the same rule would apply and that means that if a part of you is sad, then the other parts are also sad. She stated that no, it only applied to being happy. I saw no point in arguing with her fuzzy denial based logic and left it at that.

1999 Feb. 6 - I'm hearing all the questions and statements that were said to me by my parents, teachers, peers, friends, when I was feeling, confused, frightened and alone.

You go figure it out.
You got a brain, use it.
What are you, stupid or something?
Are you an idiot?
Are you stupid or just plain lazy?
Why don't you listen, instead of asking stupid questions?
You don't know that yet, how old are you?
You're old enough to know better.
Too bad smartness doesn't grow on trees.
Did you take a stupid pill? Dah!
Didn't your parents teach you anything?
If you think you're so smart, then go ahead, but you do it alone.

Journey to the Heart Centre

You've got all the answers; you think you're so perfect.
So what part of you isn't confused?
So what part of you doesn't understand?
Do I have to repeat myself again?
Are you hard of hearing or just plain stupid?
If you had a brain, you'd be lonely.
Where were you when God gave out brains?
If brains were dynamite, you wouldn't have enough to blow your nose.
Don't ask, just watch and you'll get it.
If you're so smart, how come you're not rich?
I can talk to you until the cows come home and you still won't get it.
Cows are smarter than you are.
Everything I tell you goes in one ear and out the other.
Were you born yesterday?
Are you the only one that doesn't understand?
Are you the only one that didn't know?
Are you the only one that doesn't know what they're doing?
You don't need to know, you'll survive, you'll live.
If you needed to know, I'd tell you.
It's none of your business!
Keep your mouth shut or else!
Why are you putting your nose in places it doesn't belong?
Are you looking for trouble?
You heard or saw nothing, right?
How come trouble always seems to find you?

♡   I just realized that these aren't rally questions or statements, but are actually forms of interrogation, intimidation and control. ♥

Chapter 13 – My First Level of Healing

1999 Feb. 7 – Sunday, I spent the afternoon at Jens watching a movie. Afterwards, we were standing by the kitchen sink discussing the movie as she began preparing some vegetables for supper. While she was talking, she turned to me and made some innocent hand gestures with the small paring knife that she was using to prepare her vegetables. Seeing the knife waving in the air activated me into a panic attack as it brought up my fear of knives. All my life I've gone into terror whenever someone waved or carelessly used a knife near me. I always tried to get out of the situation but if I couldn't, I'd order them to put the knife down slowly and to not play games. I'd also state, in no uncertain terms, that I didn't take any kind of fooling around or joking lightly and neither should they think that I was joking, as any move against me would mean that I would do anything to protect myself as I felt my very survival was at risk.

However, this time I also had a different awareness of my terror as I knew that what I was feeling wasn't real, as I knew that Jen wouldn't and wasn't going to harm me. I was confused by these new thoughts and feelings but instead of running or fighting like I normally would have, I told her that I knew she wouldn't hurt me, and that I wanted to heal this issue. She looked at me with a loving knowingness which was all I needed as I immediately became engulfed with my real feelings and emotions. I dropped to my knees on the kitchen floor and allowed myself to remember, feel and express all the denied emotions I had never expressed before.

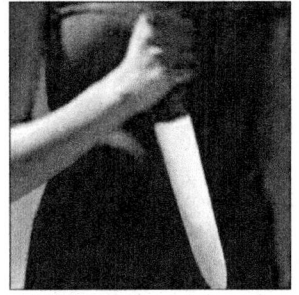

I felt the horror and terror of seeing my mother waving a kitchen butcher knife in the air as she threateningly approached me and my brothers and sisters. She was emotionally wrought and beside herself, threatening to kill all of us and herself, if we "kids" didn't start listening to her and helping her. Of course, since I was the oldest, that put all the pressure on me to ensure that she was satisfied and happy because if she wasn't happy, then she just might kill us all in the middle of the night when we were sleeping as she threatened to do. I not only had to please her personally, but I also had to ensure that my brothers and sisters did too. That meant that I had to control what they did as I was the one that was being held responsible, not only for what they did or didn't do, but also for their personal safety. I don't remember what triggered her, but in those days it didn't take much as raising five children and not having much money, and with my dad being sick at times and not working, put a lot of pressure on her.

I flashed back to several episodes of her brandishing a knife and the terror I felt for my safety and that of my siblings. I remembered her saying that if we told our father or anyone about this, that they would have her locked up in a mental institution and that we would not have a mother to take care of us. I remembered her going so far as to even threaten us if we didn't promise her that we would not tell anyone. The last time I can remember my mother threatening us was when I was in grade ten. She didn't threaten me with the knife but she had grabbed my younger brother in a head lock with her left arm, her left elbow crooked under his chin and partly over his mouth, while in her right hand she held a butcher knife to his throat; the blade indenting, but not cutting his skin. I can remember the look of terror in his eyes as I was talking to her, trying to get her to let him go. During this time, the rest of my siblings were in shock and terror. I could see them looking at me, hoping that I could again talk our mother out of doing what she threatened to do. After what seemed like an eternity of pleading and agreeing to her terms and conditions, she finally let him go. Of course she was always sorry afterwards and would ask us to forgive her, saying that she loved us and that she really wouldn't hurt us, and that she wouldn't do it again.

Besides my mother, there were other people that also threatened me with knives. Some threats were veiled with feigned ignorance, claiming that they were just joking and fooling around, while others were life-threatening situations like the time when I had a part time job after school at a drive-in restaurant located in an amusement park. It was just after 11:00 pm, closing time, and I was taking the trash out to the dumpster when I heard a woman crying for help from the darkness of the farm field that was located behind the amusement park. I could hear her footsteps coming closer and a few seconds later a young woman emerged from the inky darkness. Before I knew it, she ran straight into me, the momentum of her body lunging into mine caused me to take a couple of steps backwards to regain my balance. Clinging to me and sobbing, she begged me to help her, saying that three men were trying to rape her, all the while glancing over her shoulder into the darkness she had just emerged from. She was hysterical, in tears, and her clothes were tattered and torn. I quickly took her inside and asked the girls on duty to take her in the back and look after her, while I was going to lock the doors.

No sooner were they out of sight than I heard a commotion at the employee's only door, and three men barged into the kitchen area. I could tell that they had been drinking, although they weren't what I'd consider drunk as their speech and body movements were not that impaired. The biggest one told me to give them the girl. I played dumb, saying, "What girl?" He didn't buy it and in fact, he got angry and made his way behind the counter and came toward me. He was several inches taller than I was and weighed a good

Chapter 13 – My First Level of Healing

230 lbs, which was 100 pounds more than I weighed at the time. He picked up two large knives that were on the counter and holding one broadside, lobbed it at me. It bounced off my chest and fell to the floor. He yelled at me to pick it up, and that we would fight for the girl. He shouted at me to be a man and to pick up the knife, but I knew that if I picked it up, I'd be dead, so I began backing away. He kicked the knife toward me, hissing at me through clenched teeth to pick it up. As I was backing up, he was coming toward me, slashing at the air with the knife he held in his hand, repeatedly ordering me to pick up the knife and fight. He was now close enough to me that I could smell the alcohol on his hot breath. With his left hand, he shoved me backwards, while holding the butcher knife in his right hand. He shoved me again and again, and each shove was becoming more forceful, and his verbal threats more menacing. Finally, he shoved me so hard that I was hurled back against a stainless steel milk cooler that momentarily knocked the wind out of me and sent me crashing to the floor. I was on my hands and knees trying to catch my breath and get up, when in the next instant I felt a sharp pain in my side as he kicked me in the ribs with his work boots, lifting me off the floor and sending me rolling down the aisle. He continued to kick me when I was down, screaming at me to get up and fight like a man. I tried to protect my body with my arms as best I could, but every time I tried to get to my feet, he'd either kick or stomp on me, pushing me back down to my knees.

Everything was spinning and seemed surreal. The next thing I remembered was that Judy, one of the girls that took the girl into the back, came to the front and was screaming at the guys, telling them to leave me alone and that the cops were on the way and that they had better get lost. At first, they didn't believe her and they began threatening her if she didn't hand over the girl, but then one of the two other guys that had remained in the doorway looked outside and saw police lights in the distance. I heard them mumble some words to each other and then hurriedly they made their way out the door and disappeared into the darkness as quickly as they came. The police arrived a couple of minutes later, took our statements and put out a call to pick up the three guys.

Later, the police told us that the three were arrested, and that the one that attacked me was a known felon with a prison record that included assault, and that he was out on parole. They also said that he was being charged with attempted rape, and assault and battery, and that he was now out on bail. Needless to say, I lived in fear for months, always on guard, in terror that he'd pop out from nowhere an attack me again, especially since he knew where I worked.

There were other instances, too many to go into, that I relived that day. I was going through a series of emotional and physical body releases right there on the kitchen floor. The more I kept expressing what I was feeling, the more experiences I was remembering. There seemed no end to this hell. I was not only crying and sobbing, but was also physically trembling and in pain. I was hot, cold, couldn't breathe, trying to vomit, trembling in anger, to name a few of the emotions and physical sensations I was having. During all this, Jen had put her supper aside and simply allowed me to express myself, speaking only when she felt she needed to. I remember a couple of times when I was curled up in a fetal position on the kitchen floor, when she came over to me and simply placed her hand on my shoulder. That loving gesture gave me the reassurance that I wasn't alone and also helped me get to other issues.

After what seemed like an eternity, but slightly less than an hour, I finally released everything I felt I needed to. I felt exhausted as I rested on my left side in the middle of the kitchen floor, going over all that had just happened. After a few minutes, I felt I needed to get up and go home. I slowly sat up, and after a few more minutes, I stood up, regaining my balance and mental awareness. When I felt ready, I slowly made my way downstairs and out to my van. I left Jen's and managed to drive home without incident. When I got home, I collapsed on the couch and slept for several hours.

Afterwards, I felt that what I had experienced at Jen's was significant, but I didn't really understand it. It was similar to one of the many mini healings that I had previously experienced, only more so. One thing that was different in this experience was that it didn't occur during a guided or self guided meditation/visualization, but that I was activated by a spontaneous real life situation that was not planned and I had no idea it was going to happen. The other key difference with this experience was that I had the awareness that I was being activated and that I had a choice, that instead of reacting like I did in the past where I would run, this time I responded to the activation and allowed myself to express what was previously denied and kept a secret.

1999 Feb. 8 - I feel that I have no real beliefs of my own, and that I hang onto other peoples beliefs as mine, and then when I'm asked to justify or to defend them, there is nothing there and I feel angry because they're not real, not mine, not based on my experiences.

1999 Feb. 9 - I'm depressed and feeling a sense of overwhelming powerlessness. I had to give away my power or I'd be beaten until I gave it up, so I decided that to avoid a lot of pain and suffering, that I'd just give others what they wanted or needed. But to do that, I had to figure out what it was they wanted or needed, how much they wanted, where and when they wanted it and just how they liked me to give it to them. I also had to know how I should look, move and talk, when I should move and talk, and who or what I should move to or away from. It was the 5-W's, who, what, where, when, why

Chapter 13 – My First Level of Healing

and also how, that I've used my whole existence to "mind read" and please people.

I felt that I was powerless and had no choice. Powerless to not be born, at the abuse I suffered, and not being able to look after myself. Powerless in that I had to do what I was told, and powerless to fight back. Powerless to change what I was, German descent, Catholic and poor as that just brought me more pain. Powerless as to the choice of the parents I had and that I felt ashamed of. Those beliefs, programs and imprints brought me to deny almost all of myself because I judged that that was what I was, and because that wasn't acceptable, therefore I wasn't acceptable. We were poor and ignorant, and so I was poor and ignorant and that wasn't acceptable. So I tried to change what I could, to not to be poor or ignorant. I'd act and be the way people accepted me, or at least I'd try to, but somehow I always did something wrong, something they could use to beat me with no matter how hard I'd try to please them. Lucifer had a field day with me and is still having one, but is beginning to lose his power over me as I'm taking my power back. I feel that these imprints, programs and beliefs are very strong and deeply layered in me. I also feel that it has to do with my trying to accept those who I felt I couldn't or didn't want to accept, but where I forced myself to accept them. But in doing that, I also gave my power away by not wanting to hurt anyone or anything deliberately, by trying to be kind and loving, when actually it was self-sacrifice and self-hatred, and another form of giving my power away.

Re-claiming Your Power

1999 Feb. 10 - Indeed you are now working on (not the right word) but addressing, exploring, discovering, re-claiming is a better word, your power, your true power of the Will, the feminine, the intuitive, and all the other knowing aspects that you have denied out of fear. You are all working on different aspects, forms, that when recovered even moderately, you will be able to assist each other in recovering other lost Will quickly. Yes, it is similar to the three musketeers but more, many more, each with a word, a gift, a talent, but when united and shared, each has the gifts and the talents that the group possesses (simplified) but to show that there is connection and assistance.

As your world of illusion of beliefs, programs and imprints are falling away, your real world, (natural) will come into focus along with your communication, your attunement, and you will also manifest what you desire, in love not denial. Those still trying to cling to the old beliefs and denials will still be able to manifest and control those who would deny their power, or denial Spirits who also manifest their reality in whatever denial, lack or fear it is. Love Spirits in denial will increasingly find it more intolerable to withstand the denials they are manifesting, to live under pressure without further denial and cutting off their Wills to a point of no return. Essence will be returned, re-formed, for none will be lost to darkness, but the entity, the Being, shall cease to exist as it was, and all but its pure Essence that it was in the beginning shall remain. Yes, like a computer with not all the data deleted but the programs, imprints, and beliefs it had and even the computer itself will be broken down to its natural elements and Essence and then reformed. Merlin and the Crow (The Trickster)

1999 Feb, 12 - Today I was working with Jen doing Soul Retrievals. We had read about how shaman used this technique for healing and we were open to explore this concept. What we experienced wasn't at all like what we had read, heard, or expected. We allowed ourselves to express whatever emotions were coming up and we just followed our inner guidance. It was a healing experience and for the most part, it was a simultaneous journey. I didn't write any of the specific details of the experience and I can't remember what they were in this moment as I'm writing the book.

1999 Feb. 14 - I'm still programmed to wanting to find the similarities in people and not the differences. I feel that being treated different sets me apart, alone and abandoned, and because I'm different I'm not acceptable, and so I look for things that I have, or can have in common with others who seem to be accepted. I don't appreciate, or rather, don't accept who I am because I still don't know who I am. All my life I've tried to fit in and be accepted by being something that I wasn't. So now, how do I become that which I am? Who and what is the "natural" me?

As a teenager I used to say, "I'm an individual, I can think, say and do, what I want, when I want, and where I want," but that was really in denial as that is what I wanted to do, but something I felt I couldn't do. I have a belief that being different is not acceptable because it brought me pain and suffering. I also have the belief that even if I do the same things as another person, that it's still not good enough and that he or she will get praise and that I'll get criticism. All my life I didn't want to disappoint anyone from what they expected from, or of me. I'd deny myself just so that I wouldn't disappoint them or let them down, because if I let them down it meant pain for me. I've put so much pressure on myself having to be perfect and to deny what I wanted in favor of others that there was no way I could ever win, I was bound to fail no matter how hard I tried.

1999 Feb. 15 - While dropping off some books to Jens today I was triggered into remembering being sexually abused by my grandfather on my mother's side. I experienced this as a baby, a toddler and up until I was almost seven years old and had started school. I felt that I was abused whenever I was left in my grandparents' care and that my grandmother knew what he was doing

Chapter 13 – My First Level of Healing

but all she would do would be to chastise him for something else. I also felt that my mother and her brothers and sisters, as children, had also been molested and abused by both grandparents and that a couple of the children that had died, did so as a result of this abuse. All this confused me as I had no conscious memory, yet in my regression it was such an emotionally and physically real experience.

1999 Feb. 19 – Friday. Today I had a client come into the store for a personal one-on-one session to work on healing her issues of anger and rage. Actually, she had been in the store a few days earlier, and as I was talking with her, I was intuitively and empathically picking up that she had been sexually abused and raped, and also that she still had a lot of denied anger and rage. She looked shocked and bewildered that I knew her secret and said that yes, she had been raped, but that I was wrong in that she had healed her anger and rage, and also her hatred for men.

As we were alone in the store, we continued our conversation for about half an hour. During our chat, she told me of the psychiatrist she had been seeing for ten years, and how she had finally convinced him to allow her to release her anger and rage by allowing her to bring a bed sheet, a pillow, a bottle of ketchup and a knife into his office. She said that when she felt her anger and rage come up, that she stopped, put the sheet and pillow on the floor, opened the bottle of ketchup, got the knife out, and when she was organized, she took the knife and began to stab the pillow while squirting it with ketchup. She said that she continued to stab the pillow until she felt happy and satisfied that her anger and rage was released. I asked her where her psychiatrist was all this time. She said he was hiding behind his desk, terrified that she would come after him, but that she had told him that he was okay as long as she could stab the pillow. I told her that she had not released her anger and rage, that she had only acted it out, and that the moment she stopped expressing her emotions to get things organized was when she went into denial and that it was all an act, a re-creation and a projection of what she thought healing would be. She disagreed with me but said she'd think about what I said. When another customer came into the store we dropped the conversation, and after a few minutes she left. The next day she phoned and made arrangements to come in for a session, which was today.

It was 4:30 in the afternoon when she arrived for her appointment. I was in the process of finalizing a customer's purchase, so I told her to go up stairs, turn left and to make herself comfortable in either one of the two treatment rooms and that I would be up in a few minutes. After the customer left, I turned the phone ringer off and the answering machine on. I put the closed sign in the window, locked the doors and went up stairs.

I found her in the front "pink room" as we called it, with four of the cushions from the sofa from the "green room" stacked in two equal piles in the middle of the floor. I asked her what she was doing with the cushions and she stated that she didn't want me to be higher than her, that she wanted me to be on the same level. I told her that I usually had my clients sit in the large leather rocker/recliner that also swiveled 360 degrees, and that I usually sat on the wooden chair or a small milk stool. I explained that this arrangement worked out well for me in the past as it was not only comfortable and relaxing for my clients, but it also provided me with the opportunity to touch a client's foot or knee, if I felt I needed to activate them, or to help them tune in on the emotions they couldn't reach. I also told her that some clients felt more comfortable on the futon that was beside her, and that she could sit on it if she liked, as it was lower than the rocker/recliner. She was adamant and so I tried to appease her by sitting on the cushions but it just didn't feel comfortable and it didn't allow me to move easily. I told her I wasn't comfortable sitting on the cushions for an hour or so and that I'd feel more comfortable on the small milk stool. I then showed her that the milk stool was the same height as the two cushions that I was sitting on. She studied the stool and the cushions to see if what I said was true, then reluctantly agreed. I picked up the cushions and placed them against the wall. I then sat on the milk stool facing her, my legs folded in front of me.

We sat facing each other with about four feet between us. As we started our session, she began telling me of her past psychiatric help and that she really felt that she had healed her anger, rage, and rape issues, and that this wasn't going to go anywhere. I just kept talking to her, asking her questions and trying to get her out of explaining her feelings and emotions and into expressing them. As we talked, I could feel her pain and anger beginning to surface and she began to express her hatred toward men. She started uttering cuss words and getting physically aggressive, kicking at me, not hitting me, but kicking toward me, and also punching her fists at me. I felt no fear that she was going to attack me, even though the kicks and punches were at times only a few inches from my face and body.

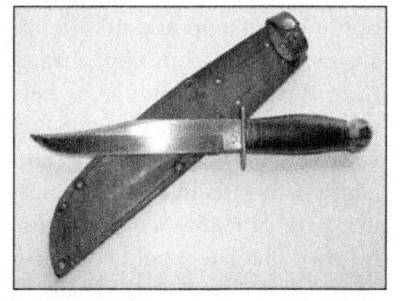

Within a few minutes, her anger and rage worked itself up to a point where she suddenly stopped, turned to get her large handbag beside her, opened it, reached in and pulled out a hunting knife. She slowly unsheathed its 10-inch blade from its scabbard, all the while glaring at me. I looked at her and instantly became aware of my thoughts and feelings including the feeling of not having the fear or panic of knives. I momentarily interrupted her to express myself, denying nothing that came to my consciousness. I told her that I had a fear of knives and that I also had an emotional and physical release a few days ago and that I wasn't afraid in this moment. I told her that

Chapter 13 – My First Level of Healing

she was not to harm me, herself, or anything in the room, and to proceed. She nodded in acknowledgement, and within a few seconds her anger once again rose to fever pitch.

It was an amazing experience, as here in front of me was an unknown, angry and enraged, man-hating woman with a ten-inch hunting knife, and I wasn't in terror, even though there was no way that I could get around or past her, as she was between me and the door. She began to thrust, slice, and jab the knife toward me, and several times I heard the knife blade swoosh by me as it cut the air. Even though she was stabbing at me and the knife was only inches from my body, I made no move to avoid her strikes. She never cut or stabbed anything but the air and I felt that she wouldn't turn it on herself either. During her rage activation, I never interrupted her as I felt no need to. This rage release must have continued for at least five minutes, at which point I felt that her denied rage was leaving and that her heartbreak was now beginning to move, as she began to cry and sob.

She stopped momentarily, retrieved the scabbard, sheathed the knife and stuffed both back into her handbag. She paused again, and then with a quivering in-breath and eyes welling up with tears, she began her emotional and physical release. I let her move as she needed to and I never physically approached her as I felt that that would only bring her back into her terror and denied rage. She wept and sobbed openly and also expressed tears of joy, as did I, as I felt her connect with the lost parts of herself. I was weeping for her and also for me, as this experience was created to show me how I had also healed my issue with knives.

After about forty-five minutes, she breathed a sigh of relief and beamed a warm smile. We talked for several more minutes about her experience, then she thanked me and left. It was a double healing day as it usually was when I did group or one-on-one sessions, or worked with Jen.

> *Hindsight is when you realize what happened after the fact. Foresight is when you apply hindsight to the present experience. Insight is the moment you realize that what you're experiencing is something different and unique. - Shenreed*

Healing and Transformation

1999 Feb. 19 - Blessing this wondrous day. Indeed wondrous, for you have moved mountains these past few days in leaps and bounds, and it joys our heart to see this movement, this transformation in yourself and in others whose heart you touch, whose essence you will recover. There is more and it will also come quickly now and more easily. Fear not that you will be overwhelmed or fail, for know that you will never be given more than you can handle, and it is also for you to say what and when is enough and not to deny yourself, your needs. The new moon has issued in a new energy, increased the vibration so to speak, and to heighten all the emotions triggering those that are ready to release their denials. These will begin to come to you in the times ahead, ranging from anger as you experienced today to depression.

No one is coming this evening; it is time for you to heal, for you also have been activated today. It is a time to attend to your needs, to heal another level of levels, and also to open yourself, your third eye and your Kundalini. Your guides are working on you as you write, but there is also work that needs to be done in meditation, silent state, to bathe and to release, to revitalize and nurture. Blessings upon you. Mother and Father.

That evening I still opened the doors for the meditation class but no one came, so I decided to have a bath as was previously suggested. I filled the old cast iron tub with water and as I sat down and began to lie back, I released my hands from the sides of the tub and immediately felt myself slipping under the water. It all happened so suddenly that when my open mouth gulped in water, it instantly brought up all the terror, feelings and emotions of drowning. I flashed back to my childhood and how my mother had tried to drown me in the bathtub as an infant. How she tried to push my face under the water by pressing on my chest and how I'd automatically hold my breath as I went under the water. She pressed harder on my chest to get me to exhale and to swallow water. I remember struggling for air but only gulping water and when I stopped struggling, she stopped pushing me down. I floated to the surface and as I felt the air on my face, I gasped and started to breathe again.

She freaked and pushed me under again only harder and longer this time. I swallowed more and more water, and this time I saw myself leave my body and hover near the ceiling, looking down at my body and my mother. I felt this sense of relief that the torture was finally over, but then I felt I had to go back and that terrified me. I screamed, "Noooo," as I re-entered my body that was now floating in the water. When I was back in my body, I coughed and started to breathe again. She screamed, but didn't try to drown me again. I just lay there, floating in the tub. In the next instant, I became aware that I was in my tub in the present day, and that I was also gasping for breath. To say that this was an intensive day for me would be an understatement.

1999 Feb. 21 - I started to write a letter to the local newspaper editor about a series of articles they had been carrying that were written by a local doctor. This particular article was about stress and how it was the current medical opinion that if a person was experiencing stress, that they should make sure they are getting enough sleep and to also eat well, using Canada's food guide. He also recommended that they should become regularly active, but to also take a break, and that if they still felt overwhelmed by stress, that they were then to make a list of their issues and prioritize them, and then set goals to

Chapter 13 – My First Level of Healing

take better care of themselves. When I finished reading the article I had to take the imaginary spoon out of my throat as I was gagging. I never did send the letter.

♡ In writing this book, I noticed the above piece in my journal and I felt I needed to include it as it activated me again. I won't go into what I felt or said, as I feel that by now you should be starting to see what is really going on, and if you're not, then there's no point in trying to explain. ♥

1999 Feb. 22, the woman with the knife phoned today and apologized for not telling me about the knife, but she said she wanted to see if I was different and said that I was. She said that this time she felt that she really had moved and healed some of her emotions and rage, and she thanked me again and said that it was no coincidence that she had come into the Heart Centre. I told her that yes, it was no coincidence and that she also helped me in my healing. That now I knew I was on the right path as what she did yesterday would have totally set me off into a panic attack had I not previously allowed myself to express my feelings and emotions when Jen activated me, and then again when she pulled out the hunting knife during her session. I was now even more determined to share what I had experienced and learned with others, to help them help themselves.

1999 Mar. 5 - Mike was in again for the "Healing Emotions" workshop tonight. For the last three Fridays, its just been the two of us and I know that there's a reason. He is one of the few men that has come to the Centre that is able to express his feelings and emotions. He is on the receiving end of a physically, emotionally and mentally abusive relationship, but because of the society backlash of what men have done to women, he now comes out being labeled the abuser when his wife gets bruises on her arms and hands from hitting him as he tries to defend himself. No one listens to him or even cares enough to look at the bruises and scratches on his back or neck, and you don't get that by attacking another. And because he dares to show his frustration and anger at the cool indifference of the psychiatrist as his wife sits by smugly smiling, he's labeled abusive and psychotic. She even called the police and had him arrested when he came to pick up his son five minutes before the stated time, but if he was five minutes late, she'd refuse him visitation rights. Abuse is abuse, no matter who the abuser is, including the systems that support it with their ignorance or feigned ignorance.

♡ As I'm writing this, I'm feeling heartbroken. I learned a year later why he suddenly stopped coming to the workshops. He had been arrested again, charged and jailed without bail. He therefore lost his new job that he was happy about getting and also the biggest heartbreak for him was that he couldn't see his son, as his wife wouldn't bring him to see his dad in jail. He lost hope and killed himself in jail. ♥

1999 Mar. 9 - I was doing more inner child work and healing emotions with Jen, doing Soul retrieval, using the Soul Cards by Deborah Koff-Chapi. They were so effective in enabling Jen to recognize and touch those lost parts of her that I also started using them when I was doing one-on-one consultations.

1999 Mar. 19 - Today a Nikken salesperson came into the Centre and demonstrated the use of their line of magnetic products. I was impressed and thought it would add income to the Centre, so I signed up to become a distributor. Later, when I was alone in the store, I asked, "Why is there no abundance and joy in my life?" I got the following answer.

> *Your issues are in your tissues. – Shenreed*

Abundance

It is because you do not seek it. You desire abundance, joy and love but you do not know it, feel it within you, and so you desire it to come to you externally. It is a mask you wear that confuses you. Fear is another issue along with the confusion of what you truly desire. Fear you aren't good enough, worthy, deserve, and also that others will think that you think that you are too good.

1999 Mar 20 – Today is the vernal equinox, I talked to the landlord and felt ashamed that I could only pay part of the rent. I told him I would decide what I was going to do by the end of the month. I picked up Jen and we went to the mall and then did some grocery shopping as we talked about the future of the Centre. I don't know what I'm going to do. I feel angry, confused and alone. Jen needs groceries and I help her, but who helps me? What's the belief I'm holding that I can't get help, can't have abundance, can't have love? I want to heal; I don't want to struggle anymore. I want the Centre, the Heart Centre to be a vehicle to help people heal their hearts. I want it to be successful, joyful and abundant, and I want the same for me. I want joy in my life and to be able to share it with others.

1999 Mar. 25 - I ask for help to heal whatever issues I have including self-sabotage, self-hatred, denial, guilt and shame that are holding me back from experiencing all that I desire, love, joy, happiness, abundance, and my purpose.

Chapter 13 – My First Level of Healing

Gratitude and Self-acceptance

You have no acceptance for what you are feeling, your aloneness, confusion, lack, fear of survival, and having to please people is what you still feel you must do to get acceptance. You still feel you have to give in order to receive and this is your strongest belief, program and imprint that is holding you back. What are you grateful for?

Me: I'm grateful for being alive.

THAT'S A LIE.

Me: I'm grateful for the roof over my head, clothes, food and my vehicle.

THAT'S ALSO A LIE. These are still based in old beliefs, gratitude out of fear, out of lack not in love.

Me: But how can you be grateful for something that you've never really experience?

EXACTLY, that's where acceptance comes in. Can you, will you accept all that you have experienced as what you needed to feel in order to heal. Allow yourself to feel all the emotions to their depth, the hopelessness, the abandonment, the fear of survival, of having to depend on someone else, on trusting someone else not out of lack or need, but with love.

It is time that you have acceptance for yourself just the way you are. When you can truly feel and say, "I am not perfect nor am I trying to be. I only want to be me, to be real," then you will be able to manifest all you desire in love, and not denial or out of fear or lack. Indeed, you have the awareness with the Nikken experience. Now you are drawn to it for two reasons. 1) The product, the magnets (magnetic energy) you see it as a part of your work, your healing. 2) The money, that which you lack. You see it as a way of survival for you feel inferior in what you are doing, are disillusioned, and so you seek relief with something new, not in love, but in fear, in lack.

Acceptance sounds simple but it is hardly that. Acceptance is not a mental affirmation, for acceptance must be felt and given expression. Also, there is the acceptance for people, places and things that you have no acceptance for. To have acceptance doesn't mean that you must accept ALL things, but you need to accept how you feel about ALL things and allow expression of them in whatever form they need to take when they need to be taken. It is time to drop, to end the illusions you have been trying to live. The illusion was a reality for you in order for you to experience what you needed to experience in order to heal. It is like Shakespeare wrote, that all the world's a stage and each is acting out a part for the other. Once you have awareness that what you think is reality, is merely an illusion to show you what it is within you that needs to be healed, you obtain your freedom. When you have acceptance for that part of you that you had no acceptance for that is outside of yourself.

Acceptance of that which needs to be healed, as acceptance is deeply imprinted and has many life times, all the way back to original cause, but you need acceptance of all that you have denied in whatever time or form. Acceptance my son, acceptance that you do not need to be perfect, and that you do not need to please anyone. You need to accept all that you feel, to accept who and what you are. You have grown magnificently even though you feel you have not but there is a part of you that does, that knows how much you have healed. You are ready to bloom. Are you ready to bloom to be who you are, unique not different, special not alone, loved not used, abundant not lacking?

Before you can bloom you need acceptance, self-love, and as you do that, your desires, dreams and passion will awaken, but you are also afraid of that for what has happened each time you have tried to express these. Indeed, they were short lived, crushed, lost, either by self-sabotage or by external experiences, for you also have a belief and imprint that nothing good ever happens, and if it does it won't last. You also need acceptance for these experiences for this is also an aspect of polarity, of duality that also has its roots in original cause.

Feel everything and allow yourself to express everything you feel to whatever depth you are able to, and give yourself acceptance for all these feelings. Do not feel the need to be perfect and also feel the need to be perfect when it comes up, for these are also part and parcel of original cause. Blessing unto you this day and indeed share with your partner. Mother and Father.

Be the Change

1999 Mar. 27 - Do not wait for things to change, the change you're waiting for will come from within you and not because you're waiting for something or someone in your lives outside to change. Let life help you take an active part in creating the changes; let the process become magical.

1999 Mar. 28 - I woke up this morning feeling that I was going to write my last will and testament, my end, as there's no hope for things to change. No one came to the meeting last night, but that was good because there was a part of me that wanted to work on the business books and I needed that time to do so. However, this morning I feel what's the use, April 1, is coming up next week and I don't have the money for rent, bills, or even the minimum on my credit cards. I feel I'll need to declare bankruptcy or sell everything and start over again. The store, the meetings and classes, the rental space, and

Chapter 13 – My First Level of Healing

even my one-on-one sessions haven't worked. I feel I'm in the wrong place at the wrong time and maybe in the wrong business. Build it and they will come. Well no one's beating down the door except soon it will be the creditors. I don't get it, I don't understand? What am I not getting, not understanding?

Yeah, it's so simple but what the fuck is it, stop the game, I'm tired of all the bullshit, it's not fun and it's certainly not joy. I'm not happy, sure there have been moments but that's all there is. What's the fucking mystery, I'm not getting it? What's the inside joke? I hope you're having a good laugh. I feel like it's a game of pin the tail on the donkey and you keep spinning me around, telling me to go this way and then that way just to see me trip and fall on everything in the room.

Later that afternoon I had a couple of one-on-one sessions. Previously I had told one of the women that I might be closing the Centre and told her why. When we finished with our session, she gave me a cheque for $1,000.00. She said it was for future sessions and to help get the Centre through its rough time. I was in tears.

1999 April 2 - A couple of days ago I was angry and wondering what the great mystery was. Well the universe responded and today I heard two songs on the CD by Jennifer Berezan, "She carries me" and "She who hears the cries of the world." In the latter song were the words that I felt were spoken just to me, they were, "And you who seek to know me, know that your seeking and yearning will avail you naught, unless you know the great mystery. For if that which you seek, you find not within yourself, you will never find it without." I smiled to myself, so that's the great mystery.

1999 April 6 - I feel that either I'm not giving people what they want, that I'm not meeting their expectations, or that people feel that I think that I'm better than they are. I feel trapped. I also feel trapped that I have to be here for people and the store. Gus, who has attended some of the meetings, has been trying to get me involved with Community and Social Services, to work with troubled teens that are in foster care, as he feels that I can help them. He gave me his supervisor's name and phone number and I called her a couple of days ago and left a message.

Today I got a call from her and when I told her what I was doing and how I approached working with emotions, she laughed and said that people who have problems are too emotional, and that they had better learn to control their emotions if they wanted to get ahead in this world. She also told me all about the importance of being a responsible and an acceptable citizen, and that with the proper form of mental treatment, people with emotional and social problems could be rehabilitated. Lastly, she stated that as I didn't have any approved psychology or psychiatric credentials, or cognitive training, that my services were not acceptable. I tried to express myself but there was no talking with her. I felt discouraged and what's the use. After that call, I was angry at myself because I didn't fit in to the "normal" way things were being done.

Later that day I had a call from the local Cable TV company saying that they wanted to come in and do a half hour feature on the Centre and to do an interview with me. We scheduled a meeting and taping in two weeks time. That call boosted me back up again, one door closes and another one opens.

> *You can rejoice in the thorn bush that gives you roses, or you can criticize the rose bush for having thorns. - Shenreed*

1999 April 18 - Jen is the last person in the world I thought would attack me and the last person I thought I'd attack. So what does all that say? What's really going on? I had gone over to Jens place and as we were talking, she showed me a mandela that Kim had made for Jens male friend, and had asked me what I thought of it. As I looked at it I had a host of feelings and emotions come up. I was aware that something was bothering me, but I didn't know what it was. The more I tried to focus and feel into it, the less I felt as I was being distracted. While she asked me what I thought and felt about the mandela she wasn't giving me time to respond, but was instead continuing with our previous conversation. We had been talking, or rather, Jen had been talking and giving me her point-of-view and was expecting me to just support and agree with her, which was making me feel that I wasn't being heard or what I had to say wasn't important. She was also saying that it was my fault that I didn't remember what she had told me, and there were other times when I felt she was putting words in my mouth and twisting things around. I felt confused but she wouldn't stop. I asked her to stop for a moment but she just huffed and said that I just didn't understand and wasn't interested in letting her express herself.

I remember her asking me again what I was feeling about the mandela, but by this time the question felt more like an interrogation or a lecture, and again I was flooded with emotions. I don't remember what I said to her, but she said she was just expressing herself as she pointed and waved her finger at me, which she never did before. I saw her finger waving and pointing at me as she stated, "I'm asking the questions, you just answer me." I heard the word YOU in her statement and that triggered me even more. I asked her to stop waving and pointing her finger, to which she replied by showing me her open hand. I told her to put the hand down so that we could talk. She kept on talking and saying that whether it's a finger or a hand, it doesn't matter and isn't the problem. I said that I wasn't going to sit here and listen to her when she was like this, and that I don't know her, or what she was trying to say.

Chapter 13 – My First Level of Healing

I pushed the coffee table back and got up to leave. Jen fired back, "Oh, so you're running again" as she wagged her finger and hand at me. I was frustrated and becoming angry. As I passed the chair she was sitting in to get to the hallway, her hand reached for me. At first, I thought she was going to grab me, so I began to raise my right hand to push her hand away so that I could move past her. When I realized that she wasn't going to grab me, but was just wagging and pointing her finger, I stopped and turned to face her. I looked her in the eyes for a moment and she glared back at me. I didn't say a word, but proceeded down the hallway, as all I wanted to do was to get out and away from her and the situation as quickly as possible.

I had just reached the stairway on the right hand side of the hallway when I heard her let out a blood curdling shriek. My back was turned to her but I knew by her screaming that she was coming down the hallway after me. I was already at the stairway, my right arm extended up, holding the curtain back, and was about to take the first step, but hesitated. I knew she was getting closer to me and all I could think of was that I had to stop her as I feared that she might push me down the stairs and there was nothing to grab as the hand rail was on the right hand side, behind the curtain, and I knew the curtain wouldn't save me. I didn't have time to move out of the way and with my right hand still holding the curtain, I instinctively lifted my right leg up and out sideways, hoping to stop her from pushing or grabbing me long enough to turn myself around. As I was raising my leg, I also turned my head to see where she was, and out of the corner of my eye I saw and simultaneously felt her run into my out stretched foot, striking her in the lower abdomen and stomach area. I had no intention to attack her, just to stop her from attacking me long enough so that I could turn around to defend myself.

She stopped, staggered backwards a couple of steps, bent over and screamed at me to get out of her house. She took a couple more steps back down the hallway as she held her hands to her abdomen. As she passed the bathroom door she slowly fell to her knees, landing on the living room floor, all the while screaming at me, "Get out! Get out of my house." I tried to go to her but that just made her move away and scream all the louder. I felt that she wasn't really physically hurt but I really didn't know, I was just basing it on what it felt like when she hit my foot, or my foot hit her, and how she was reacting.

I left and went home in a daze. I didn't know how I did it, how I lifted my leg like I did to the side and her hitting it without pushing me off balance. I tried duplicating the move when I got home, but I couldn't do it without losing my balance let alone imagining someone running into my foot, which would put me even more off balance. I don't remember losing my balance during the incident, I just remember straightening up and looking at her and then placing both hands on either side of the stairway just in case she reached or grabbed for me. I called her when I got home and left a message. She called me later and we talked, or rather blamed each other. I went for a walk to try to feel and gain some insights into what really happened and I got the following message.

> Both have been activated for similar and also different issues. It is for you to feel to experience; to express these activation's with as much awareness as you have in the moment. Each has different programs, imprints and beliefs in place that need to be recognized and released.

We both have the same issues of not hearing each other and accepting what the other says, even if we think we know otherwise. We are too stubborn, too set in our point-of-view to accept another's because we feel we haven't been heard or what we say isn't important.

I've never kicked or hit a woman in my life. I did slap Marian once when she was hysterically slashing and grabbing at my face during one of our arguments prior to our divorce. Jen said that I had kicked her in her solar plexus, and she also told me that she had told her girl friend. Now I'm afraid that the word will get out that I've lost control, that I'm a raving nut and that now I'm assaulting people. I'm afraid I could be charged and go to jail. I'm afraid that our friendship is over and that the Centre is finished. I'm lost; I don't know anything anymore. I'm afraid that what I want to do, to help people, is all gone. I'm afraid that no one will believe or trust me, and that now they'll even be afraid of me. I might as well be dead. The only one real friend I have I attack and abuse, now I'll have no one and I'll be totally alone. I have no name, I have no home. My wings and Heart are broken.

Was I in denial even before I went over to Jens? I feel that she could be right; she talks and states her stuff, her denials and fears, while I tend to hold onto them. She seems to know what she is talking about and sometimes I think she knows more than I do, as she is more in touch with her feelings and body. I doubt myself because when I feel or pick up on her and express it, she contradicts me with, "No that's not what I feel" or "No, I didn't say that, you didn't hear me" etc. I judge her better than me but at the same time more hurt and fragile, and as such, I put her and her needs ahead of mine. When I feel she puts me down I feel hurt because I'm already putting myself down.

I told Jen that maybe she should get her special, romantic, male friend, the one that the mandela was for to help her work on her issues as she can trust him, can be with him in his arms. I'm being sarcastic as I know she doesn't trust him, but I'm angry. I feel I'm being used. Yeah, nice John, sucker John, friend John can you pick me up some turkey I'm hungry and I have nothing to eat. Meanwhile she has enough food in the house for a month. Or it's can you do my laundry, while she has tons of clothes to wear

Chapter 13 – My First Level of Healing

but of course what she likes to wear is dirty, or she asks, can you drive me to such and such. Right now I'm getting physically hot and angry and I feel I'm looking for things to blame her, to say fuck the friendship when she tells me that the friendship is over.

> **The longer you deny, the longer it takes to heal. - Shenreed**

1999 April 20 - So what are the issues here, what are the programs? "I draw the line on physical abuse," was Jens comment that she kept repeating over and over whenever I was talking to her. While I understand physical abuse, I don't really understand what she was trying to say about not allowing herself to be abused as she kept on comparing me to her "special" friend, saying that he would never abuse her like I did. Of course, I knew more of the story and I told her, "Yeah right. What you're really saying is that you'll accept mental, emotional, physical and sexual abuse from him even though you know you are in denial. You give yourself to a man that you are physically and sexually attracted to, and of course love, but won't kiss as he isn't boyfriend material. And that yes, you have acceptance for this type of abuse as you have control, but you have zero tolerance for anyone that doesn't accept your abuse and control and accidentally hurts you in the process, that you now call abuse." She argued that physical abuse was the worst kind. Why is that? Is it because that's what she's done all her life, control situations to avoid any form of what could be considered physical abuse or injury to herself or another. Jen believes that she has fucked up programming with everything except the physical, but I feel she has more judgments and issues dealing with physical abuse and issues than anything else at present.

    I called Jen on the phone and as we were talking, she got a beep from call waiting. I felt it was her girl friend, and when she came back, she just said that she had to go and that our conversation was over anyway. I felt we were just starting to talk. I felt cut off, second best and not important. Spitefully, I told her not to bother calling me back when she had time for me and for us, as I'd probably be busy. I have fear now that I'll be harmed in some way because I've struck Jen. She's telling people, even people that are not close to her, that I kicked and hurt her. I feel at a loss as she keeps saying that I crossed the line when I hit her, and I feel I was only defending myself as I had no intent to harm her.

    If we are mirrors for each other then what is she showing me, or what did she do that activated me, and what was I in denial of expressing, and the same questions apply to her? So what are my programs? Physical abuse for me is more of me being afraid of what I'd do to them if they ever started to physically abuse me. Sexual abuse? I think it's the same as physical abuse. Mental and emotional abuse? I'm still doing that to myself and I've done that all my life. There is more a lot more, but those are the basics. Humm? Interesting, I've said nothing of what I do to abuse myself physically.

    I went into a meditation last night and had an emotional release and also got some insights as to what happened. I didn't know it at the time, but I had been activated by the blood red color on a mandela which reminded me of blood, my blood. I don't know if that was what I was trying to feel and express, or if I was in denial and felt pressured and activated by Jens words and actions? The pointing finger and open hand reminded me of my mother, teacher, and the school kids, and all the pain associated with that. The feeling that I was going to be attacked from behind, blindsided, reminded me of the school boys either holding me by the arms or distracting me, while another would sneak up on me from behind and jump on me, either feet first or with his knees in my back. I also remember wanting it to stop and one time knowing he was coming I kicked my leg back to stop him. He ran into my outstretched foot with his mouth, and he started to bleed and cry. I got into trouble for that too, but no one even noticed my bruises and bleeding cuts. Did Jen going into her anger and rage trigger me into my terror? The emotional release I had last night was of remembering being beaten and being kicked, especially from behind. Is that what I was triggered into when I felt Jen coming at me down the hallway? Is that what I'm being activated into, my old school issues. The fear of getting beaten, abused, slandered, name-calling all over again? Do I capitulate just to have a friend? Do I allow myself to be abused like I was before, or do I love myself and say no more? Am I hanging onto some imprint, program or belief that would have me believe that this action is loving myself? Jens comment was that I crossed the line and that the abuse has to stop by me admitting that I abused her or she fears she'd be giving me permission to abuse her again. Lots of questions but no real answers.

1999 April 21 - I went to see Jen today, it was the first time since the kick incident. Jen started to say that she felt uncomfortable when I sat in her favorite chair. The only reason I sat there was because she was sitting on the futon, where I usually sat. I didn't know what to do or say, and as I didn't want to get into another argument, I decided to leave. As I made my way down the hallway, I began to feel a pain in my throat, heart, back and in my first chakra. I remember falling to my knees and then having an emotional and physical release. I was remembering the school kids beating and kicking me. I then had another physical release that I would describe as giving birth to a long black slimy thing (a shadow). I squirmed across the floor from the stair doorway to the kitchen table. I felt it move out of me, as I moved away from it. Tears streamed down my face as I sobbed, moaned and screamed out in pain as I was remembering the blows to my body. Finally, completely exhausted, I just lay there on the kitchen floor, remembering all I went

Chapter 13 – My First Level of Healing

through. After a while I got up, but could hardly walk. Slowly I made my way down the stairs and to my van and then drove myself home. I had a long bath and then watched TV for a while. I was tired but unable to sleep.

1999 April 23, 2:52 am - I feel that what I went through at Jens yesterday was my version of a panic attack followed by an emotional and physical release. I just woke up in a sweat and my PJ's are soaked. I'm feeling fear and terror that I'm going to be hurt or killed. My body reacts differently than Jens does. Mine is also triggered by denial, but I've never called it that, as I never knew what it was, I just knew that I had to get out and get away, and that I felt like a caged animal.

I know that the blood and pain are part of it, but also the words YOU, and YOUR played a big part in the activation. To me, you means, it's directed at me and as there is no one else around, it's got to be me. You're responsible, you're to blame, it's your fault, you'll be sorry, you're going to pay for this, what are you doing, what are you thinking, what are you feeling, and if you tell them, then they turn it against you to hurt you even more. Sounds and words trigger me but I feel it's more the feeling, or tone of the sounds or words rather than the actual words. Seeing the mandela reminded me of my blood, but it was the word you, what are YOU seeing, and the feeling that it brought up that activated me. Objects such as knives also used to panic me. Seeing someone getting angry doesn't activate me unless it's directed at me. Someone angry and shouting you, blaming me for something sets me off. If it's just verbal it's not as bad as if they are moving or waving their arms, hands or fingers.

I've somehow put all questions and statements with the word YOU into the same category. It means that I'm in trouble, that I've done something wrong and that I'm going to be punished. Even if someone pays me a compliment, I can't take it with a sense of pride and accomplishment. I hear it but I don't believe it, and I believe that deep down I've still done something wrong and that they are trying to set me up to knock me down. I don't trust people, anyone, when they ask me questions like, "What do you think or feel." I also put both of those words in the same box because what I'm feeling is also what I'm thinking about when I'm trying to put it into words. So what do you think? What do you feel? Both put a double program in place and if they are angry or moving, then other programs also come up. So how do I de-program myself? I heard the words in my mind, "YOU ARE! You are now aware of what's triggering you and now you can begin to heal."

That's also why I am so fussy with words, using the right words, right meaning, and trying not to make mistakes so that no one can say, YOU made a mistake, or YOU said such and such, and all of that is from school and my parents again. I don't react that way when someone asks, "John, what do you think," as I'm not activated in the same way as when someone just says the words, "What do you think?" There is also confusion when people say, I didn't ask you what you feel, I asked you such and such. I put down my Will, my feelings and intuition all the time because if I express how I feel, people either aren't interested or they say no, that's not right. I think a lot of people are fucked up with these two words, think and feel, and not just me.

I was just thinking of Jens panic attacks. She can't move, breathe or eat, and she trembles, aches and doesn't feel safe. I don't think of not being able to breathe but my body just tightens up, coils up, and I feel like I'm ready to fight or take flight. I look for chinks in their armor if I feel threatened so that I can use it against them to take the pressure off of me. I also try to divert it off me to someone or something else, at least long enough to give me a chance to get out and feel safe. If I can't, then I feel cornered and attacked and I try to fight back using angry words long enough to get me to a place where I can leave. I feel I have to leave because if I didn't, I don't know what would happen if had to fight, and that terrifies me. I don't trust words like I love you, I care for you and you're my friend. Actions speak louder than words, you say that now, but later it changes if I don't agree with you, or do or give you what you want. I don't trust nice words because they are also used against me.

Thinking back on my activation and emotional release the other day, I asked, "What did I give birth to?" I heard the words in my head, "Guilt and shame of expressing your pain."

1999 April 26 - No one attended the Monday, Wednesday, or Friday evening meditation groups or healing circles. I don't know what I'm doing wrong. I can't carry on as there is no financial support. The landlord called again and I don't have the money or any answers, and I feel that he is going to give me until the end of the month to get out. I'll have to sell all my stuff, or put into storage what I can't sell. That reminds me that I'm a few months behind in payment for the one storage I have where I'm storing my two canoes, a sixteen foot Langford cedar strip/canvas and a Old Town Discovery whitewater canoe. I had a feeling to go and get them out before the locks were changed or the canoes removed for back rent, but I denied my intuition and when I did go, the locks had been changed and there was a note saying to call to arrange payments and the return of my property. Needless to say, I was heartbroken as I don't have the money and I am also too ashamed to call and tell him that. Right now, I don't even have any money for first and last for an apartment. I don't have a paying job and I don't really feel like that is what I am supposed to be doing with my life. I don't know anything anymore. Irene, who I mentioned earlier, said that she would give me a place to stay if I wanted it. That is difficult for me, as I don't really know her and her husband and I feel shame and guilt in accepting what I consider charity.

Chapter 13 – My First Level of Healing

Higher-Self

1999 April 27 - Acceptance of the experiences is the key to living in the moment but you cannot have acceptance until you have moved all your programs, imprints and beliefs that hold you limited in your point-of-view, your perspective. To move these blocks, you need to open to your Will, to her expression, to give her movement and with her movement, you open space to heal your heart, and thus comes understanding, love and life.

I have not abandoned you, none have abandoned you. You are in the gap, healing the gap, and in there you feel alone, abandoned, hopeless, helpless and unloved. This is what you are healing, for it is to you that you lose all form of communication, of encouragement, as you search for these pieces. Like a fireman entering a burning no man's land looking for that which he knows is still alive somewhere. Somehow he finds it, even though it seemed hopeless to save and to bring out, but save and bring out you do, and then you return, for you know there is more. I am overjoyed at your trust, your courage, your faith, and your love. You are not alone, we are not alone, I just want you to know I love you, we love you. Yes, this is what you call your higher self, higher in a sense that I have and keep a view, a vision of the entire picture so to speak. There are many aspects of you/me on Earth at this time and you have met and are working with some of them. I know what you ask but you cannot possibly understand with your limited consciousness. It is like sending a TV picture to a pencil and expecting it to transmit a picture and sound when all it can do is scratch lines on a piece of paper.

Patience, soon you will be given more, so I will be able to express more, then we will begin to live life with love, and we will experience all that we desire. I know that you do not understand me here but know, trust, like you have been doing that everything is for a purpose and every experience has something to teach you. You seem to have less joy in your life than others around you, it is only that you choose to heal yourself at this time and of course your joy will be experienced when they are in their pain, their healing. You will have balance, choice and will see joy in all that you do. No, this is not heaven as you sense it in a religious perspective, but it is heaven on Earth, real life lived with, and in love.

During this transition that is upon you and the Earth, you, the Wayshowers, have chosen to answer the call. I say you and you feel distant; this is still a part of your programs, imprints and beliefs for you and I are one but you do not feel it consciously yet, only in those moments that seem few and far between. These will get more frequent and stronger now as you are able to bring back more Essence and heal the Will, Heart, Body and Spirit, and to move Lucifer, the psychopathic killer, guilt and shame out to their right place. We will succeed, have no doubts, it is not a destination but a journey into love, light and life and we are part of that experience Adornia, Seft

Journey to the Heart Centre

Lost Greatness

1999 May 03 - Your purpose is two-fold, to heal self and to assist others to heal. You are reluctant to blow your own horn, to stand up and be noticed for fear it will be thought of as vain, power based, egotistical, smug, etc., and you fear the negative attention you received every time you let your light shine. This you need to heal before you can truly begin to become all that you are, and you also have fear of greatness. The greatness that you will be, will be based in love and not fear and loss of power as in the past. Allow yourself to go back to all your times of greatness and to see behind the scenes. Blessings.

1999 May 5 - I was at Jens this evening and she is beginning to move her rage. She feels she needs to do it slowly because she feels she is going to be destroyed along with what she attacks. She let herself go a little tonight as she beat on her chair. Two messages that I got were that it is important to verbalize not just mentally or think, but to also verbalize what you are thinking and feeling as that sets energy in motion, into manifestation. Thoughts are things, but of a different energy, words, sound and vibration give it power. That's why I'm hurting, I never expressed myself, and now my upper body feels like someone kicked the shit out of me. I can't remember what I denied but I feel that that is what I'm feeling in my body now.

1999 May 6 - A few weeks earlier the manager of a senior citizens home that I had visited, called me saying that a few people were interested in the introductory meditation class and we had scheduled one for today. I went to the seniors home and only three people showed up and I don't think they even knew what was really going on. One was a woman that was blind and hard of hearing but could talk. Another woman had had a stroke, could see and hear but couldn't talk, and the third woman could see, hear and talk but didn't want anything to do with meditating and the devils work. Seeing, hearing and talking were issues that I was dealing with, not only with this group, but also in my life. I was very depressed when I left, not only by the forced attendance, but also at the sad state that these elderly people were in and how they were being treated.

Intent and Fear

1999 May 07 - Fear of failure and fear of success, both are limiting and both are out of lack. Failure is the lack of support, not being good enough, and success is lack of supporting others, being too good, and so you feel both polarities and you struggle to remain in between. Fighting not to lose what you consider you have and then sabotaging yourself when you have it so that you will lose what it is that you desire. These are fueled by imprints,

Chapter 13 – My First Level of Healing

programs and beliefs still in place, and also by denied and suppressed emotions and feelings of not being good enough and of non-acceptance.

Also your intent, your passion, your desire is connected here in your first three chakras, for you feel pummeled and remorse of your successes and where they were not accepted and so you fear to even hope, dream or desire of what you truly want. Sure you give it mental energy and you give it some physical energy but what is lacking is Heart, passion and desire. You have had these, but in fear, lack, and with each experience of rejection and disappointment you receded further, covered up and hid to a point now that you even fear to begin, or to begin with this excitement. For all the old imprints close in around the excitement and your heart feels the pressure the pain and it refuses to allow itself to be open to more pain and rejection. It feels it can't take another blow because it feels it is just hanging on as it is. Heart needs to be allowed to feel all its pain, the death it holds from the unloving strikes it received that charred and nearly killed it but it is afraid because it feels that the next blow might be the last.

Give in to the feelings and allow the experience and feel them, for they have also much to offer you. You are here to experience polarity and duality and yet you avoid the opposites. You have choice, you need not experience the opposites if you so choose, but know that you do so in denial and at the expense of the Will, for if you choose to be whole you must be both. Those that deny their Wills will soon see their world of desire come tumbling down as their house is built on sand, and then they will struggle with that which they choose to accept as you are doing now.

1999 May 20 - No one showed up for meditation classes so I went over to Jen's for the evening. Jen triggered me into my terror and confusion and I took off in flight and went to my van. I sat there for a few moments and then returned and was able to move some feelings and more emotions with Jen. Later I activated her and she had three emotional releases. This was typical of our healing process as it went back and forth.

1999 May 25, 8:30 am - I don't want to be a loser in public, to be ridiculed and laughed at, jeered, humiliated, scorned and shunned. I'm fighting for myself and the Centre not to be a loser, trying everything not to back down yet giving up more and more of myself until there is almost nothing left of me. I've given my time and energy, and it's not enough. Nobody likes a loser everybody likes a winner. A loser just isn't good enough, hasn't got what it takes. People remember and bring up your losses, your pain. I've tried everything to control not being a loser. I think I'm a loser because I let my company go down and I even sold it at a loss. I sold the house because I didn't feel I'd have the money to keep it once I sold the business and I still owed Barbs dad money, so I felt that the only way to pay that off was to sell the house.

I feel I'm such a loser if I don't have any money and I can't buy or have the things that I want or feel I need to provide for other people that depend on me. The Centre isn't supporting itself and I can't support the Centre any longer. Jen is part of the Centre and if I let the Centre down, I feel I will also let Jen down. I have great shame at being a loser, but even more shame at being poor.

In school I felt I was a loser because I couldn't defend or protect myself. I was ashamed of who I was and also of my parents. I didn't want to be who or what I was because that was being a loser, and being a loser hurt and was lonely. I've felt like a loser most of my life when I couldn't get a job, or keep a job without getting into trouble with my supervisors or boss. I felt I was a loser when I sold my first business. I felt like a loser when my business partner stole from the business and me. I felt like a loser when I got divorced. I've been trying to control myself so that I'm not a loser but what I've been losing in the process is myself, bit by bit. I have no acceptance for losing. I have fear, shame and guilt in believing that I am, or that others judge me, as a loser.

I want to release my control, my fear of being a loser and of having to be in control, in a place of power and holding the belief that money is that place of power. I also feel like a loser if I don't win an argument or if what I say can't be proven and that if I'm wrong, then I'm a loser. It's interesting that I said win an argument, because that's what it turns out to be if I feel threatened or confused, and then to not be a loser, I have to be a winner.

On top of that, and this is a big one, is self-hatred, loathing, shame and guilt, it's all in and on me, driving me down to what I fear is my death. I'm not going to survive and no one cares for a loser. I'm confused as to what I am, what I'm to be doing, how to bring people into the Centre and how to earn money. No one can, or wants to help me because I caused it, it's me, something is wrong with me. I'm no good; I can't be or do what other people do. I can't have what other people have. I'm a loser and they're a winner. I've compared myself to other people all my life and comparison is a form of self-hatred. I'm part of the equation and any comparison is judgment, self-judgment. I've been doing that my whole life, hanging on to my judgments, beliefs, programs and imprints, and always comparing myself to others and ending up a loser. Why? Because I hate what I think I am, and that's a loser. Humm, and if I always compare myself to others, I'll always be second best, and a loser. I feel that there is no way out. I'm confused and I also hate feeling confused and so I hate myself. If I'm confused how can I help myself? I feel lost, helpless, and hopeless. I feel I must be a loser because I can't even think my way out of not being a loser.

Chapter 13 – My First Level of Healing

Heart Reborn and Heartlessness

1999 May 25 - Greetings and blessings. Heart is being born, re-born, Heart essence that was struck in the gap, Heart of both the Mother and Father. It is Hearts hopelessness, isolation and confusion that you are feeling and it is the compression that is terrifying. As you are touching Hearts issues, you are also touching Spirit, Will and Body, and so you are tossed back and forth in no man's land and you feel you are getting nowhere and are healing nothing. Rest assured you are taking giant leaps as we see it, but from your perspective it is not so or even backward movement.

You both are assisting each other by triggering each other, feeling each other. "How can I save myself" is a key to your healing as it is set into place by the programs, imprints and beliefs that you have created in your reality, your experiences to date. Identifying what you did, and still do, to gain control so that you won't be hurt or hurt another, will assist you in changing these beliefs, programs, and imprints and continue to express all that you feel.

Heartlessness and self-hatred are the main issues at the present time. Heartlessness is devoid of feeling other than indifference, loathing, criticism, resentment, and self-hatred has many aspects, from subtle comparison to feelings of lack of growth, to wanting it just to be over with and healed and to be able to enjoy life like all the rest appear to be doing. Judgments are also, as you are aware of, a form of self-hatred. See your judgments, see your self-hatred, express it and expose it, denied and it is covered up even further. Fear can be your ally if you let it show you places you need to heal. This is deeply imprinted and layered and it needs to move bit by bit if true healing is to take place. As Heart is healed then moving to Spirit, Will and Body in whatever manner or order, and then back to Heart again. All have different issues and some the same such as trust and survival, but Heart will bring the balance needed, healed Heart not the heartlessness that has passed itself off as Heart, but Heart born in love as you are now bringing it. Blessings, Mother and Father.

Chapter 14 - My Terror and Heartbreak

1999 May 29 – Confusion, or maybe more accurately, "the unknown" is my terror. I'm terrified if I don't know something and if I don't have control. I get panicky and it's flight or fight. I'm confused regarding the Center as all my old beliefs are changing and are dropping away. All my life I've tried to control my feelings and emotions, to not express them, and now I'm telling myself to accept and express all of them. I didn't trust my feelings as I thought they are the ones that got me into trouble in the first place and caused my pain. Now I'm confused as I have to learn to trust them and that's especially difficult now when my whole world is falling apart. I have to trust something that before seemed to be my problem, and now trust that it is going to save me. I'm terrified of that idea, that I have no control. I feel like I'm going to die and not survive. Feel? Think?

1999 May 31, 11:45 pm - I'm avoiding, or trying to avoid the terror of my self-hatred, shame and guilt of being different, of not understanding, being confused, not knowing, no control, powerlessness and helplessness. Nothing I can say or feel is right; I hate my feelings. I hate feeling this beaten. I feel I have no place to go, to live. Nothing I do is right and there is no acceptance for what or who I am. I'm ashamed that I can't be like others. Others seem to be able to put their feelings aside, but I'm not able to do that no matter how hard I try, as I still get them reflected to me.

    I have no acceptance for being different as being different means being beaten, pain, hurt, suffering and the terror of waiting for the next attack, the who, why, what, where, when and how. The more I give the more they take or want. I've given everything, money, time, and energy, and I have nothing left to give. I feel like my dignity, my pride and self-esteem is going, dying. I don't even know who I am or what I'm supposed to be doing or how. I feel helpless. I don't know and don't even care anymore, what's the use. I can't win so why fight. I can't take anymore.

    I write these words but they feel empty, like I feel empty, blank, frozen, and numb. There are no emotions of grief, anger, rage, tears, or fear. Yeah, there's empty, blank, frozen and numb, and I also know those are the feelings I don't want to feel, the parts of me that died so long ago. I don't want to lose any part of myself, I want to live. I choose life and love. I want to accept all these frozen, numb, blank, unconscious and empty parts of me that I abandoned, that I chose to reject so that I wouldn't feel the pain, all those parts that I cut off in this lifetime and past lives and also in other planes and dimensions. The shame I had of who I was and how I was; I didn't want

Chapter 14 – My Terror and Heartbreak

any of those parts in school, church, peers, or family. I felt alien. I didn't want to be or to feel like I was different; I just wanted to be accepted and loved. I feel exhausted, tired, and beaten. I have no will or desire to get up. A hopelessness of not even caring what happens, nobody cares so why should I. My family doesn't care, friends don't care, nobody cares, and I feel so alone so unloved. I want to accept this part of me that feels unloved and hopeless and exhausted.

1:46 am, I don't want to feel the pain in my body as it's numb. Maybe I should leave it that way so it doesn't have to feel.

4:20 am, I'm in terror of talking to the landlord. Today I touched how he is reflecting my mother figure and home, overseeing what I do as the critical parent. I'm also living here so I can't get out or away, as my landlord's office is just next door. The Centre is also like the school with new people, new experiences, including non-acceptance. I feel that I've trapped and boxed myself in a corner, that I have to be in the Centre and can't get away. I feel that while I need the people that come into the Centre, I also fear them. I'm avoiding my terror, I feel frozen, and I can't and don't know how to move.

I'm thinking of my first day in school and the confusion I felt as I didn't understand what was happening and I also felt ashamed. My father was there for a little while and talked to me. I held back my tears as he told me not to cry and that I had to be a big boy, and that he had to leave. He said he'd be back after school, but I didn't know when that was. All I could really do that day was feel, feel my feelings and feel what was coming at me. I hate my feelings as I feel they draw or create my experiences. I was in terror of what was coming at me, and also my feelings of being confused, not understanding, feeling alone, abandoned, ashamed. No one to help me, being laughed at, teased, and then kicked, punched and beaten, and feeling the pain, heartbreak and terror of no relief. There was no relief from the terror as day after day I felt I was going to die; I felt I was in hell. I also felt anger, rage, terror, and the heartbreak of the utter hopelessness of it ever changing.

At home, I wanted to please my parents and be the good boy. After telling them a few times that I was being beaten up and not getting any help, I was ashamed to tell them how I felt or to show my pain for fear of being criticized again of being a coward and not fighting back. There was no support, no understanding, just chores to do. I didn't want to go to school but I was forced to, scolded and belittled with comments like, do you want to grow up and be stupid, no-good, poor and good for nothing. You're going to do better than we did, you're going to be somebody, a doctor or a lawyer, you have to make money, then you'll be okay. We're counting on you so don't let us down, don't embarrass us, don't make me ashamed of you, you have no choice, it's the law, be grateful we couldn't go to school like you can, you'll thank me for this later.

Religious love tells you to love your neighbor as yourself, to turn the other cheek and that it's not right to hate, steal or lie. Listen to your father and mother. Don't take God's name in vain. You have to love everyone even those who hate you. I was fucked and in hell! I'm fucked and I'm still in hell. I have to control myself so that I won't be in hell and to do that I have to deny expressing my feelings and emotions. I'm being fed guilt and shame, and being loaded up with imprints, programs and beliefs that say I'm not okay as I am. That because I'm different, I have to change to be like everyone else, and that what I feel is not important, but what I know or learn is. I hate my feelings, this I know.

The Power of Love

1999 June 08 - You have resources, all you need to begin to be who you are. It is time to be bold, daring, and imaginative, to take the center stage, to draw attention to yourself and this is also one of your fears, your terror. You desire to be low key, unnoticed, and yet you long for recognition, acceptance of who you are, but all the while downplaying your talents, your love, your light as if they were evil, vain or egotistical, for this is also one of your judgments as you have seen how others work with power and this is also your past life issues. You need to differentiate between power in denial and power in love.

You are unsure, feel unworthy, for you have never truly experienced love let alone the power of love, and this also frightens you, but you can also feel it in your heart and to the depth of your Soul. True, not everyone is ready to hear what you have to share, but your words will have left their mark and when they are ready, they will remember and so it is. It is time to plant the seeds; the seeds of love, light, and truth, for these seeds are the seeds of life, of freedom. Take time to be gentle with yourselves and continue to express and heal as you are. Blessings, Mother and Father.

I woke up this morning as the result of a dream I was having. I don't know if it was a dream or if I was remembering that my grandfather was sexually abusing me. I don't remember the details as I lost them when I woke up, but I feel it was oral sex and that it happened when I was three to six years old, before I started school. I remember in grade eight being attacked by a new form of verbal abuse that had sexual connotations to it. I was called a queer, a homo, a fag, and told to suck cock by the known bullies, and even by other boys that I tried to be friends with. That form of abuse continued into my adult life.

When I had my paper route, I used to take a short cut through the railroad roundhouse. There was an old man who worked on the trains who came onto me one day after I accepted his offer to look at the controls of a train engine from the inside like the engineer. He tried to touch me, but I

Chapter 14 – My Terror and Heartbreak

would have none of it and I was out in a flash. This type of sexual abuse even happened as recent as five years ago at the curling club, from someone that I least expected would try to suggest or abuse me that way. So what is this all about?

1999 June 16 - The landlord came into the Centre today and told me that unless I had the money for this month and the part of the back rent I still owed, that I would have to be out by the end of the month. I fear the dream is over as I don't have the money to pay the rent. I also feel that a part of me or all of me is over too. I don't know anything anymore.

1999 June 16 - Mother, Father, I ask for help. I'm confused. I feel worthless and I'm being put out; I have no home. I'm not even sure that what I'm becoming is what I'm truly to be. I feel I have no dreams or even the will to try. I'm overwhelmed, frustrated and in a semi-conscious state. Everything I've done hasn't been accepted or received, and without acceptance, there is no help, abundance, hope, life, love or joy. There is no joy in this life only pain and more pain, more worry, more suffering. I know I'm still in denial and avoidance, guilt, shame, and that is what Lucifer is using against me because there's no relief, sure there is momentarily relief, but then it all disappears.

I know that in the "Right use of Will" books that when God struck the Mother he was in denial. I also opened to receive you and was struck by your unloving light and like the Will polarity; I have never known true love or your light either. I ask that as I am able to let go of death, denial, guilt, and shame, and to move them out to their right place, that to now be filled with true love and light. I choose life and I want to end this struggle with death and Lucifer.

I ask Mother, the Mother I've never known to also help me help her, help us to recover lost Will and heal Heart and all of creation. I want to live, I want to recover my lost desires, dreams, hopes, passion, sensuality, sexuality, youth, energy, and all that I have forsaken at the hands of Lucifer and denial. I ask for your light and love to also fill me as I let go of unlovingness. I want life, love and light, and to experience all of them to the fullest. Reed.

Hopelessness

1999 June 16 - Blessings our son Reed. You have and are moving mountains, as is love child (Jen). It is difficult to watch you struggle so but we cannot simply lift you out, you have to allow yourself to move to open so that we can connect with you, and as you are more and more connected you will be filled with love and light. You both have chosen to move much and so it seems endless, futile, and hopeless. We do not say that your struggle is over, for to you it appears like you are in your darkest hour, but as your fears come up to tell you also that it could be worse, that you could suffer more. We can give you no pat answers that will ease your pain for you have also chosen this path, this journey. As you become more conscious of who you are, and begin to be that which you are becoming, you open to love, life and light.

The pain and suffering feels unbearable and it is all you have ever known and you are weary of the death that has you in its grip, while that part of you longs for what appears so easy for others. You have experienced more than other manifested Spirits, but soon there will come balance. Continue to express yourselves, for your mustard seed of love is surrounded by a mountain of death, denial, guilt, and shame, but you are moving that mountain. You feel its pressure trying to hold you down but you are also beginning to feel your power, your true power that you have denied yourself and hated. Moving out your self-hatred will bring you self-acceptance, self-love and the love, light and life you so choose and desire.

You still feel not good enough and all the rest as you lack confidence and even faith, hope, that this is not just another dream soon to be destroyed. Trust, trust yourselves to be open to true love and light, and express your fears, and in your opening, deny nothing in your consciousness and express as you can and feel comfortable with those you feel safe to do so. Trust your feelings and allow them expression even if what you feel is what you consider unloving rejection of another, because you know what rejection feels like and you do not wish it upon anyone lest they think or consider you unloving. It is time to turn the tables, so to speak, to speak your truth and express your Will. Blessings Mother and Father.

When I was at Jen's tonight, I touched how I was programmed and believed that everyone told the truth and that what they told me was true. This went all the way from my parents on down to my relatives, school, peers, and especially the church. I didn't believe anyone was bad, not good, and all the rest, except me. I believed them when they said I hurt them if I didn't do what pleased them. I felt bad and I blamed my feelings as bad because I was told not to feel what I felt, and so to express them was also bad. I feel I'm so filled with guilt, shame and denials, and while they may not be telling me that I'm bad anymore, I'm still telling myself that I'm bad, no good, not worthy, unlovable, poor or stupid. I have the programs and I still believe that they're true and I'm wrong, and it's being reflected to me as I'm still hating myself and my feelings.

I intend to stop hating myself and to start loving myself, all myself, especially my feelings that I've tried to control and kill. I don't want to deny myself anymore, not that I'm going to be perfect, but I have acceptance for my process and my Will, Body, Heart, and Spirit to heal and to align.

Chapter 14 – My Terror and Heartbreak

1999 June 27 - I had placed ads in three newspapers over two weeks ago and also called over 200 people that I had names and phone numbers for, notifying them of the 33% to 50% sale on all items in the store and of the new schedule for meetings and workshops. Sales have increased marginally, but with the discount, we're not making any money, just basically selling off inventory at cost. Three people have also registered for the meetings and workshops.

Today I touched the fear and terror of starting all over again. I flashed to grade 1 to grade 6, and how every day was a new day of terror, of the unknown. Then I flashed from grade 6 through grade 10 and moving every year, new schools, and also the church issue. Later it was moving to Toronto, getting married, then starting over with each new job, and then starting my own business with Systems 80, then starting Vista Scenics, the partnership, divorce, Barb, Michelle and Moonstone. I feel I have a pattern of losing, of being a loser and that everything or anything I have loved, or hoped to experience is being taken away. I want to touch the emotions of all this but in this moment I can't, as there is just a feeling of numbness.

1999 June 28 - The landlord called and stated that unless I have the remainder of last months and this months' rent, that I'll have to be out by July 12, I feel heartbroken and numb.

Last night I was talking to Jen and she mentioned that she had been feeling a pain in her right foot for hours. As I was talking to her, I remembered an experience I had when I was about six years old and living on the farm. I was playing in the barn and had jumped off a stall, and didn't see the crib board lying under the straw on the barn floor. After I landed, I tried to take a step but couldn't, that's when I looked down and saw the board with nails sticking out if it and that I had jumped on a nail. I could see that the nail didn't go through my foot, but could see it pushing the skin up on the top of my foot. I tried to get my foot off the nail, but couldn't as it was wedged between the bones of my foot. I dragged the board with my foot impaled on it, out of the barn and across the barnyard to the house. I remember calling out for my mother as I inched my way back to the house. Finally, she heard me and came to my rescue. She had to stand on the board with both feet and literally pull me off the nail. In all this, I don't remember feeling any pain.

Later that evening I noticed a reddish blue line climbing up my leg to mid-thigh, it was blood poison. My mother got some ingredients from the kitchen, mixed them in a basin of water into which I put my foot to soak. Within a matter of minutes, I could see the blue line begin to move back down my leg and then disappear. As I was sharing my story with Jen, the pain in her foot completely disappeared.

I got the insight that even though I didn't have any emotions as I told the story; it was my acknowledgment of the experience that my body was asking for at this time. Jen had tapped into the pain in my body to help me touch yet another part of myself. I had been doing this for a while with Jen and others at the Centre, but this was a first time for me, for me having someone tap into my body pain. So if I'm working with Jen and I feel a pain, her pain and I express it, and if she acknowledges it, will it move for her too? Are we manifesting our denials? Is this about going back to the denied physical pains stored in my body? I feel we both denied our bodies to the point of ignoring pain and exhaustion. I don't know what it is all about but I feel there is something here. More questions, always more questions.

1999 July 1 - I've been awake since 5:30 am, and all I'm thinking about is that I have to be out in twelve days. I was going to say that I'm feeling sad, but then it was gone in an instant. I wonder what Jen did last night? I never talked to her as I had a past life class. I saw her yesterday when I picked her up and brought her to the store to pick up some of her health books that she had in the lending library. I was doing inventory at the time and she started to cry. She was feeling heartbroken and annoyed; no, she was angry with me for not feeling or saying anything and only focusing on the inventory. She removed some of her books from the shelf, and made her way to the counter where I was standing. She cradled her books in one arm, and with the other, she reached over and pulled my notebook out of my hand, giving me a paper cut. She screamed that I was avoiding her and that I didn't care that the Centre was closing as she threw her books to the floor. She reached down and picked up her large health book, glared at me, turned and smashed it repeatedly on the counter in a fit of rage. She then said she wanted to leave, so I closed the store and took her home.

    As I stopped the van in front of her house, she quickly got out with her books, but as she was making her way up her walkway, she collapsed. I got out of the van and helped her into the house, up the stairs to the top landing where she just wanted to rest on the floor. I waited behind her on the stairs for a few moments to make sure she was all right. She said that she would be okay and that I should leave. I turned around and planned to go back outside and pick up the books that she dropped on the walkway. As I turned and started to go down the stairs, I didn't see her kick off her running shoes that came tumbling down after me, tripping me up, and causing me to fall headfirst down the last five or six steps. I landed with a thud at the bottom of the stairs. Dazed and stunned, I waited a few moments to feel my body before picking myself up. I bruised my back on my left side but otherwise I was okay. I looked up the stairway; Jen was still lying where she had dropped, at the top of the landing. I went outside, picked up the books, and when I came back in I found her sitting at the top of the stairs. We talked for a few minutes and then I went back to the Centre. I picked up my

Chapter 14 – My Terror and Heartbreak

inventory notebook that was on the counter and realized that she had broken the counter top when she struck it with her book.

I'm wondering what I'm going to do? I spoke to Irene about staying at her place and she said that her offer regarding the room still stands. A part of me hopes Jen or I will win the lottery, then I wouldn't have to move or close the Centre. I'd also like to get an apartment in Midland that has some privacy. There is no privacy here and no backyard. I like Jen, she's the best friend I've ever had although sometimes I just want to get away from her, especially when she activates me but I know we both have similar issues and feelings to heal and we also need different experiences to trigger us. When we started working together we both said that no matter what we say or do, that we know it's for our highest purpose and good as we both had made the intent to heal ourselves on all levels and that was why we came together. I help her with her physical and emotional issues and she helps me with my emotional issues. She told me that she hasn't had her period for two months, and I feel she has lost at least ten pounds to date; she's lucky if she weighs a hundred pounds now. She says it all happened when I kicked her. I hope we both get it and heal it before we kill ourselves. I feel I've rambled here but they were the thoughts that were coming up and I felt I needed to express them.

1999 July 2 - I'm afraid to leave with nothing, no home, no job or source of income, no money stashed away and nothing to live on. I sold my company and home one and a half years ago and I've basically been living off that. Besides my personal expenses, I've invested thousands of dollars in the Heart Centre and have also gone thousands of dollars into credit card debt on top of that. I've little money left, $150.00 personal and about $300.00 in the till and that's it. I was wondering what stuff to get rid of and what to keep, as I'm going to have to look at getting a storage unit. I have to get some boxes and start packing as I don't want to leave everything until the last minute.

I'm looking at the big red boxing gloves I have that I use when I have clients who were working with anger. I wish I could get angry in this moment but I don't think or feel that it's anger that I really feel. I thought of the dream I had with the bear person that terrorized me. I feel it was my Will, or what I think my Will looks like now. She looked angry and frightening because of all the stuff, denials, that I have put into her. I saw her at one time as this beautiful, radiant goddess, dressed in a flowing, gossamer, golden pink gown, but I've changed her to this large, hairy, bear like being that I felt just wanted to tear me apart.

I have to stop at the gas station and get some power steering fluid as my steering is beginning to make a sound and I think the fluid level is low. That's all I need now is to lose my vehicle or have some major repairs come up. That's a big fear of mine because then I'd really be stuck. I was just thinking that my insurance is now past due, but what can I do. I've put a lot of work into this place and I really hoped, (hope is also expectation to replace doubt) that it would work out, build it and they will come. I guess I built it on fears, doubts, denial, guilt and need, on sand and not on love, love for myself. I put myself into the Centre making it, and other people more important than me. So I guess, now I know that's why it's not working, no self-love. I even resented that I felt tied to the store, that there is no help and that I have to do it alone. So where is the love in that? Dah! So here we go again, alone. Do I have to do it alone again? Can't I get help? I want a Centre, friends, true friends, help and sharing, but I'm on my own again, and this time I'm even depending on other people for help as I'm no longer self-sufficient.

Maybe that's the switch? I've never allowed myself, or it's been hard to get or accept help from other people. I expect help from family but that's it, and that's a belief. Well, I guess I'll just take it a day at a time and see what unfolds. I don't want to go back to the fake world of working and living as I've done in the past. I don't know how to heal this? There's so much to do and I feel overwhelmed.

♡ As I'm writing this I see the contradiction in my statement, asking for help and then complaining about the help that I'm getting as it's not the help I was wanting or expecting. Not the type of help I had control over. I never noticed that before. ♥

Earth, the Mother, is crying, dying. I just thought of the Georgian Bay beaches and the waterfront owners who want to keep the beaches all to themselves and how the government and the municipalities support those with money. They have now passed a by-law eliminating any public parking within half a mile of any beach that had public access to it. I feel like getting hundreds of people together and pulling down the no parking signs and putting up protest signs saying "fuck you, we have the power." I'm angry at all the bullshit going on with the politicians, governments and businesses, and how they try to put the focus on others so that the public doesn't see the shit they are doing to fuck the people and the planet. I'm afraid of being classified as a radical and of getting my head cut off, being burned at the stake, or just killed. Keep a low profile, don't make waves, wait your turn, let others do it. Why are you taking responsibility for everyone else? If I don't do it who will? If everyone had that attitude we'd all be slaves in no time, with less and less, and doing more and more. I don't know what that was all about; maybe it's a part of me that I've also suppressed for too long. Another part of me says, what's the use, the people I want to help don't care, they'll let you take the flack and get crucified and they'll take the rewards and the credit.

Chapter 14 – My Terror and Heartbreak

1999 July 3, 7:09 am - This is the last day that the Heart Centre will be open for business. I write these words but there is no real emotion. I feel numb, a void and an emptiness, but no other emotions. I'm listening to the sounds outside, a car just drove by, the noise from a faulty exhaust drowns out everything else. It's gone, but now I hear a ringing in my ears. It's hard to write this morning as my mind seems blank. I put the second pillow under my chest and I'm just watching my pen write. Fascinating in a sense, how the hand moves so automatically, so programmed, so imprinted by repetition, repeating the same thoughtless process over and over. Not only do we learn to read and write this way, but we also learn to talk with similar imprinting and programs. It's also how we get to believe what we are, or part of it, the combination of outside and inside programming. So how do we change that? How do we change our writing, our way of communicating when we're so afraid that everyone else will not understand us if we don't write in the normal way? We can't just write… %h*kk) .. ^. G5$ S+`579 d09 hU6% - 0u.%^H<) and assume others will know what we mean. Words and understanding them are so important to the mind. I was thinking of Chinese and all the characters and symbols they have, and of all the different languages in the world. It's no wonder we have fears when we can't communicate our thoughts and feelings.

    I don't want to make a list of all the things I need to do before I move. Fuck! I want to move and I also don't want to move, as I'm comfortable in a way here, even though I don't have the privacy that I had in Moonstone, and I miss that. I don't think I've even allowed myself to grieve leaving Moonstone or selling Vista Scenics. I think it's all wrapped up together somehow, as Vista wasn't supporting me the way it used to and now the Heart Centre didn't either. At least when I sold Vista and my home in Moonstone I had some money, but now I have none.

    Starting over is frightening to me, not really knowing how, where, why, or what I'll be doing. It all seems so misguided and unprepared. Now, fourteen months after getting this place and only nine months in business, I'm thousands in debt. All that I have left is the inventory and fixtures that I'm trying to sell, and my personal stuff. I'm definitely not going to get what I paid for the inventory and I'll be lucky to even get ten cents on the dollar, so that's thousands of dollars down the tubes.

    I want to carry on with the work that I've been doing but I'm just not sure how. I don't even really know who I am. I'm also afraid that people don't want to hear or feel what I have to say or offer. Am I going to have to get a 9 to 5 job to support myself? I couldn't stand working for someone else before I started my journey, so what will happen now that I'm even more consciously aware of when I'm denying my emotions and intuition, or at least some of the time. What about Jen, what is she going to do if I move away?

What about me? What if we have to stop the work that we have been doing? I don't want to stop healing and I don't want to go back to the old bullshit.

7:49 am, Merlin help me weave my magic. I know I haven't been listening, really listening to my guides when it's not what I think I should do or want to be doing, seeing or feeling. Again, I'm thinking of my pen and writing, it's all so automatic, we just carry on with all the old programs because they're familiar. I worry about other people and what they think about me, do they accept me. I feel they don't, but then do I accept me? I don't even know who I am so how can I accept someone, something I don't know?

Acceptance

You don't have to understand or know all the details to have acceptance. You don't have to know everything about the ocean to be able to accept that you can swim in it. Can you accept who you are in this moment?

Me: Yes.

Then that's all that is important and in the next moment do the same. You do not have to be anything other than what you are in this moment. Awareness is the key to transformation. Use the tools of the past but be as free as the words you write. You know how to write, it doesn't mean you have to write the same words over and over. Allow yourself to create, to visualize, to dream, and to allow new experiences to come into your reality, not based on repeats of past experiences, but rather use the past experiences as tools to apply, or not apply, to the present experience. Love is the key to finding the joy that you seek, and you are on your right path. Your progress that you are working on is that of a journey, rather than a destination. You still want perfection, understanding, instead of letting yourself experience the journey. Take your focus off of wherever it is you think you want to be and simply be in the moment.

The wonder and magic of this moment is missed if you are obsessed on a future moment or a past moment. Trying to create the future or re-create a past moment is impossible in this moment. Time is really an illusion when you truly understand it my friend, and I do mean friend. You and I have spent much time together, shared many experiences. I am here to help you remember who you are and to assist you in remembering your magik, your gifts. Be afraid, it is part of the experiences, the process and the journey. It is part of the journey, like writing something of your own and expressing your ideas and not simply being a mimic, a copier of someone else's ideas. You have fear in really expressing externally for you still hold control on the internal self, your emotions and intuition. You need them both, all of them to

Chapter 14 – My Terror and Heartbreak

find love, joy and happiness. Alchemy is the process of changing one thing to another, of changing paper and pen into written word that expresses what the writer thinks and feels.

Expressing your feelings is the same process, for unless they are expressed verbally or written, when felt is the key (for you would not always have pen and paper handy) to becoming all that you can be. Allow your Will, your emotions, expression, for there are no words to the power that you will free within yourself when you bring yourself into alignment. Instead of operating at the present .1% to maybe .5%, you can operate at 100% or near it, and that is just in this one area of yourself. When you apply that to the other forces, the power will increase ten, a hundred, a thousand, a million fold.

Be the I am, all that you are in this moment, not to be perfect or to do better, but with a gentle acceptance that you have for a flower or a cloud. Acceptance of who you are and allowing yourself to express all your feelings of who you are and what you are experiencing will help you unlock your potential and allow you to blossom, to grow, and to experience the life that you seek. That is the mystery, it is within you, acceptance of yourself. Seek love, and adapting and transforming the past (as tools) to the future (dreams) into the (experience) of the present moment. We have much to share and to remember. Merlin

PS: You can't have understanding prior to experience as judgments on past experiences blocks present experience if feelings and emotions are not moved.

1999 July 3 - I asked, what was the purpose of the Heart Centre starting and closing, why?

The Heart Centre Purpose

There are many answers but the one you seek is simple, for growth. All the elements you need to feel, to heal, are in and around the Centre. It is all growth and part of your journey, the experience, evolving. This is for both you and Love Child (Jen). This is not the end, it is not the beginning, but it is the beginning of the end. Yeah, you say, mumbo jumbo double talk, I've heard that all before, but you also feel the truth in that statement though you do not realize what it exactly is, or the depth of it. And so you remain as it were, in a fog, a fog so thick that you must literally "FEEL" your way out, not physically, yet that too, but emotionally. How it feels, moment by moment, step by step, and as you begin to trust your feelings, new doors will open for you both.

You have done much, healed much, but there is more and so your journey continues. Indeed, it has not been a bed of roses for either of you, but you will have time to enjoy life and play to your Heart's content in the near future. You need to progress to heal, to become that which you have intent to experience, love, light and life, and to end your world of illusions, your denials. To move out guilt and shame, and to release your judgments that hold you down from becoming all that you are. Accept your struggle, as you call it, not accept it as a way of life, but accept how you feel in your struggle and to also have acceptance for all parts, especially those that don't want to have to struggle, to experience the pain all over again just so that the other part of you gets the opportunity to feel and express the emotions and the pain. It is not just a mental exercise as you know, but the hardest emotions to recognize and to see are those hidden by your denials and where you have avoided or denied them for so long. It is not an easy path you have chosen, both of you, but it is one of courage, heart and love.

You are not alone, be gentle with yourselves and honor yourself and each other as you have been. As mentioned, you are both moving mountains that you are not aware of. Continue to express all you feel physically and emotionally. You are both coming to your KEY issues; trust will be the issue that affects you both, and only your own open and honest expression of yourselves, emotionally and physically, will allow the healing that is needed to take place. Fears will come up, anger and rage, and all the rest you have experienced thus far, but only now on a new level. As you heal these, veils will fall off, and you will gain new understandings. Blessings YahTa Zoe

1999 July 4, 8:15 am - "Trying to be a good person" was the phrase that struck a chord in me as I listened to a Sunday radio sermon, not that that was my intent, but it just happened to be on when I turned the radio on. What is good or bad but a judgment. I thought of the movie, "Pleasantville" that I watched with Jen last night, where they all lived a black and white life and it was only when they ended their denials and became real did they, and the things around them take on color and life. So why am I trying to be a good person? It's my program of what I've been told I should be and that it's what I believe I am. I was told that I was good if I did this and that, or said such and such, and I also believed that I was bad if I didn't or couldn't do those things that made me a good person. I feel I'm stuck in a black and white world of beliefs, programs and imprints, and I dare not act any other way because that will go against something that I've been taught is wrong or bad. So I just continue to try to do the good things, things that will gain favor and the acceptance of others. I wouldn't express why or what I feel because that never got acceptance unless it was a good feeling for others.

I don't want to be a bad person; I don't want to go around hurting anyone physically, mentally, or emotionally on purpose. I feel that's a lie, a denial, as I hurt Jen when I kicked her, and I hurt people emotionally and mentally when I feel they are attacking me, but it's really a reflection for me. Yesterday was the last day of the Centre and I bought Jens books and stuff

Chapter 14 – My Terror and Heartbreak

that she had on consignment as it made it easier to handle, as I had someone coming in today that was interested in the entire stock. I feel pressure with all the things I have to do this week. I haven't been out to Irene's yet to go over any details, and I'll have to call her as I don't even know how to get out there. I'm also worried about my van as the power steering was low and sometimes when I'm turning a sharp corner it's starting to stick and has no power. I feel that's all that I need now, is for the van to break down and then I'll not even have any transportation.

What's going to happen to me? Worry is a projection, it's not in the moment, sure that's a mental understanding but it's not the real feelings as those feelings are based in fear of past experiences where I felt the physical effect. This is all about bullshit and has nothing to do with how I really feel about having no transportation or the means to fix it. I have fear now that I'm going to create this problem so that I can experience it. I don't know, sometimes I feel so fucked up that I don't know up from down. Trust, trust and let go, small words but hard to do, especially for yourself because you can't see the forest for the trees. I just looked at my pen and thought about ball-point pens and how, when they first came out, there was such an uproar from the Christian religions that insisted they were the devils work, and we weren't allowed to use them in school. I'm kind of dating myself here but I think I was in grade five or six, so that would be in the mid to late 50's. Another example of how I get distracted.

I'm now thinking of what I'll do for money. What I'll do for money is a program as I believe that I have to do something so that I can get money, so that I can do more of the things or have the things I want. The focus is still on money and I'm not being in the moment. It's hard to break out of old patterns as it seems so foreign, so opposite to what everyone else is seemingly able to do, to be able to live and enjoy themselves without any problems.

Now I'm thinking of how Jen and I got caught and soaked in the rain yesterday, and how we were enjoying the moment, not caring that we were wet or how we looked. That all changed when we went shopping at the grocery store and I got chilled from the stores air conditioner. I just thought of the gray hair I saw in Jens hair yesterday. I feel sad as she's too young to be getting gray hair. I guess my judgment of gray hair is that it's from worry and age. So how come I'm not white? As a matter of fact I'm far from it.

1999 July 4 - I'm now realizing how I've felt I've been a prisoner here at the Centre, and all my life for that matter. In Moonstone, I became the hermit on the mountain but I also had to perform to my expectations, to make it better, to do the garden, whatever. Even though it was a sanctuary, in many ways it was also a prison.

I intend to release the belief that there is no right place for me. Freedom is such a big part of life and love, and to have any of these, you have to have the freedom to express yourself, as yourself. It feels impossible to try to be just who I am, based on the old beliefs that I have of this world. I've been trying to do it on somebody else's terms and conditions, and I feel that I can't be myself unless I have my own space. But when I do, I get caught up in taking responsibility of whoever comes into my space and also how they treat others that are in my space. I intend to let go of all beliefs and thoughts that I'm responsible for another person's feelings or experiences. I intend to let go of all beliefs, programs and imprints that I cannot be supported without having to compensate them in some way, or that there are conditions and limitations. I intend to let go of the belief that I can't have a loving relationship with a female, and that I can't have family, friends and acquaintances that accept me as I am.

1999 July 5 - I'm in a kind of numb mode again, as this is the last week, six days and I'm homeless, jobless, or what I consider jobless as not earning any money. Earning is the key word, as I have to earn money, give up something of myself to have something else in exchange. Exchange is not a problem if you enjoy what you are doing and that what you are getting is what you also want, but how many of us are really in that position. Even that is screwed up, because to do or have what you really want, you have to do something that you really don't want to do or enjoy, for money, that you then exchange to do or have what you really want. Money affects almost everything we experience. I just heard a voice that said, "Yeah, and that's reality."

    8:08 am, I just closed all the windows as it's already +25C (+80F) degrees outside and it's going to be another hot one today. I sold the air conditioner I had yesterday; I guess the cat lady is happy she's got it. I thought of Merlin and Misha, the two cats I had in Moonstone. I miss them sometimes. I feel so lonely right now as there is no one to talk to. I ask myself, is this what life is all about, work, struggle and die. Why? I want to end this cycle but there is a part of me that doesn't believe I can. I feel overwhelmed by all the programs, imprints, beliefs and judgments that I have and I feel I'll never be able to release or change them, and then there's a part of me that says you create your own reality. What about mass consciousness and what everyone else is thinking and believing? If that's the case, then how come when someone else's reality changes, why doesn't mine change? Is this all one big illusion and these people aren't real and the planet isn't dying, and that they're not really a part of my reality, only as much as it takes to create a "world" to live in? So maybe there are five to six billion realities on Earth, each running independently and that's not counting past or future lives, for however long that is or was. I have no idea where this is all going but it's hot and it's the bottom of the page so I'll stop.

Chapter 14 – My Terror and Heartbreak

1999 July 6, 3:31 am - I'm lying in bed tossing and turning so I thought I might as well think it on paper. Acceptance is the full expression of all our feelings, intuition and emotions in the moment. As soon as you have a feeling or an emotion that comes up and you deny expressing it, the experience will be that you either draw it to you, or push it away from you. This is especially true if you deny your feelings and call them fact (based on judgments or beliefs). This push-pull is also what I feel with the Centre. I feel trapped by people but I also want people to come. I feel trapped because I feel that I don't really have a home, my space, a place just to be me, to just do what I want when and where I want, etc., and yet I have to always make myself available for other people. I can't be me and I resent that. I'm living in a business/residential area and while there is a yard, there is no privacy, just a parking lot. I have judgments that I'm limited in my physical movements and it's not like Moonstone at all. I just realized the irony of my hidden denials, of how can I attract people to the Centre when in fact I've not wanted to be here and have been pushing them away.

The same holds true with money. All my fears about money, the lack of money and expressing my feelings of the experience of not having money when I really only want money because money is what I use to protect myself and to buy things that made other people and me happy. It also gives me a sense of worth, value and acceptance. Not having money makes me feel worthless, no good, dependent and needy, and I don't want to feel these emotions so I deny them, deny expressing the feelings when they are felt for a lot of different reasons. Shame is a big one, afraid of what people will think, say or do, and so I reject expressing them, and so what do I do, reject money from coming into my life so that I will continue to feel all the feelings of needy, worthless, etc., until I can accept them. Once I can accept them, then I won't need to have them attracted to me, for in accepting them I am free to attract what I want to experience, but until I do, I'm pushing all the things that I desire away for the wrong reason. It's not that I don't desire them but what I'm attracting to me are the stronger feelings, the ones that I'm denying and trying to push away. These are receiving the most energy and it takes a lot of energy to deny my feelings unless I'm so cut off from my feelings that they are no longer in my conscious or even sub conscious mind.

It seems so simple in theory but now do it. I want to do it, to experience it and heal it, and I ask Mother and Father and the company of heaven to help me here. Help me recognize all my denials, fears, judgments, beliefs, programs, and imprints that are keeping the Universe and all the love, light, life, freedom and abundance from me and from my experience of who I am.

I want to end the struggle, not with the outer reflection, but with myself. I'm battling myself. I'm fighting me and I'm hurting me. It's so simple but at the same time it feels so overwhelming, so impossible, because it's always felt that the problem has been out there. They, them, someone, something is doing it to me but they couldn't do it to me if I didn't have the feeling of being a victim, of being not accepted, worthless, no good, bad, wrong. Even at an early age, I was told by my parents and family that my feelings were wrong. I didn't know any better and I trusted and believed them. Then later it was my peers, because now I wanted so desperately to be accepted, to be loved by someone, someone outside my family. I deny my feelings because there is no external acceptance for their expression and so I shove them down inside of me because I believe that if I do, then I'll get the acceptance and love that I long for. When in fact the opposite is true, as the very thing I desire, I'm pushing away because I'm putting all my energy and intent into my denials, keeping my feelings down. So then what I'm attracting is not the acceptance and love I desire, but denials and rejection which is a reflection of what I'm doing to myself.

God, again it seems so simple and I'm afraid I'll lose it or forget it if I stop writing, but the more I write, the more I feel I'm repeating myself. This feels impossible. I know it feels impossible only because I want to be perfect and I want to be healed all at once. Now that's another part of it. I have no acceptance for the process, growth, experience, the pain and suffering. I want it all and I want it now. So what am I really doing? Pushing it away from me, lengthening the process because I don't have patience, don't want to be repeating, or feeling the experience for what it really is. I just want it over with, no exceptions, and yes the cycle continues, and I continue to express the same feelings. I continue to not accept them but to reject them, and the feelings I really don't want to feel I continue to push away, because again, I'm putting more energy into keeping them hidden in denial.

I want to open to the process and to feel everything, to have acceptance for my feelings so that I can have the freedom of choice. You can't have freedom, and here's the paradox, I just felt it, now I'm afraid I've lost it. To have true freedom, all things have to be free to express, to be, do, and say. Anything less is not freedom, but control and condition. Everything, and especially our emotions, have to be free because they are magnetic, they are the ones drawing the experience into being, and you can't have freedom unless you have freedom of expression. It's written into the constitution but it's more of a mental concept, right words, wrong meaning or interpretation applied. And because it's only partially applied, that's where the paradox comes in.

I'm afraid I got so much insight that it's all going to overload me and leave me with a brain fog, with little or no conscious awareness to grasp this when I'm denying my feelings for whatever reason. There's the word "process" again; it's okay, and I'll get it when I get it and when I'm ready to get it. There's a part of me saying okay, okay you got it, let's get going with the good stuff, let's fix it all tonight so that tomorrow is okay. There's also a

Chapter 14 – My Terror and Heartbreak

belief that there aren't any miracles and that such a healing isn't possible overnight. Not that it has to be 100% and perfect, I don't want to be perfect because I also feel that perfect is stagnation, no growth, no change, death. But to now suddenly start to have things reverse themselves and the good (judgment) things start happening to you, to now start to live and experience life with a feeling of acceptance, love, belonging, worth, trust, openness, joy and abundance, I don't believe is possible without having to give up part, or all of myself. Well the only thing I have to give up is the belief that this is not possible, that it can't happen. Because again, what am I denying? That miracles can't happen. And so what am I attracting? No miracles! And what do I really want? Right; a miracle to happen! While I believe what I've just said is a truth, I feel it is only a part truth as I feel there is a lot more to it. Well it's 4:35 am, I think I'm going to roll over and try to digest this, or go to sleep. Maybe I'll be back writing when I get another insight but I should really try to get some sleep.

1999 July 6 - I'm going to Irene's today to see about the room. I feel strange and unsure as it's all new to me. I made up some "Moving Sale" signs for Saturday, and I also went and saw about getting a larger storage unit. I started going through my things and decided that I'm going to get rid of a lot of stuff that I haven't used for a while or feel I'll use. I feel impatient now about packing up and moving. The hot water tap in the bathroom started dripping two days ago and today it was running steady just like it was when I moved in. I now turn the water off and on at the shut off valve. I feel the house is lonely and crying, and like the house, I really feel lonely but unlike the house, I don't want to admit it. I'm frightened of the unknown and I also don't want to admit that. Right there are examples of two big issues that I'm denying any emotional expression, and what is being reflected to me, loneliness, and fear of the unknown.

    I'm wearing the Moose hide moccasins that I made along with an old T-shirt and a pair of old jeans with a torn right knee. I was wondering what Irene would think of me if she saw me now? She'd probably think that I'm really poor. Again, that's my projection, my fear of what people will think of me and that is fear and denial again. What do I care what people think? That statement is not loving, but rather anger, self-hatred, justification and more denial. I still care about what people think of me by what I have, how I dress, what I drive, how I speak, my hair, etc. I have a ponytail right now and I was thinking of getting it cut off when Jen got her haircut, but I decided to just get three inches taken off. It's still past my shoulders and I'm going to keep it for a while longer.

1999 July 7 - I went to Irene's place yesterday; it's about a fifteen minute drive from here. It's a block from a small marina and there are about one hundred and fifty acres of dense bush to the back and right side, that she says has bear, deer, coons, turtles, owls, eagles and a variety of animals in it. She's married and her husband's name is Dave; she has two daughters, both are married. She also has two German shepherd dogs, Shane and Zeus. I'm going to have the bedroom off the kitchen; it's fairly big, about 12' x 12' and furnished. I think I'll have room for my desk and computer. Irene also has a computer in her library room and another room that she uses for meditation, which has all kinds of shells, rocks and crystals in it. When I came home, I started to pack my personal items and to move things up from the basement for the garage sale.

1999 July 10, Saturday - I started moving things out to the lawn at 7:00 am, and there were people already waiting for me. It was a nice day and a lot of people stopped in; sometimes there were as many as 20 people looking at the stuff on the lawn, driveway, or in the Centre. I closed it down at 5:00 pm, and put the stuff that didn't sell and that I didn't want, out by the sidewalk as freebies, and by 9:00 pm, it was all gone. I made close to $700.00 which will help me a lot. My son, Bryan drove up from Toronto and arrived at 5:00 pm and helped me move the big items into the storage unit as well as deliver some of the larger things that were sold.

1999 July 11 - I moved most of my personal stuff into storage, and I took some plants and some of my clothes to Irene's and Dave's. This is the last night that I'll sleep in the Centre.

1999 July 12 - I finished moving the store furniture, fixtures and stock to storage. I cleaned the house and took the garbage out to the street. It was just after 5:00 pm when I left the Centre for the last time and dropped the keys off.

1999 July 14 - It's pretty quite at Dave and Irene's as they both work shift work. We have our little chats and then they go about doing what they do and leave me to do mine. It's a strange feeling getting used to another person's home, and especially making yourself feel like it is your home. I've done the odd handyman job around the house and helped Dave cut the grass. I feel he is trying to bond with me as we played catch and even had a few games of horseshoes, but he is very competitive and doesn't like losing. I've also watched a couple of movies on TV with him. Irene and I have chats about the Heart Centre and other things. She's very psychic and I feel that there is a lot she knows and sees that she is not saying. I can also feel that she has a lot of issues that I'm sure will come out in time.

Chapter 14 – My Terror and Heartbreak

1999 July 15 - I can't believe that I'm so filled with old beliefs and programs. I thought of them when I went to Irene's and saw all the knick-knacks in her house. I feel my beliefs and programs are like those knick-knacks as I can't move without fear of breaking them, and that if one falls it will fall on another and start a domino effect, and they'll all come tumbling down. I want all of my beliefs to come tumbling down, but at the same time, I'm also afraid of what that will mean and just what will happen to me.

    I feel like I'm in this house made of glass rods and strings that represent my programs and beliefs. I'm so afraid to move as these glass strings and rods are carefully balanced from one belief to another, and that all I've ever been doing is building more and more rods and strings to help support the old beliefs that I don't want to fall and break. I also see how I've limited myself and that the only way I can now move is to squeeze myself between, around, over and under these rods and strings, these obstacles that would have me pretend and try to be "normal" like everyone else. It's like I'm living in this house of glass and I'm afraid of losing control, even in the tiniest way, afraid of what would break and afraid that I can't fix it. Even all my relationships are built with this glass structure, and it's also how I present myself in public, just not to the same degree. The less I know people, the less I have to deal with them, the less afraid I am of what they'll think of me and the more I can be me. But again, that's only true if it's only me that's involved and only to a point where another belief, program or imprint comes up and says what I should or shouldn't do.

    This isn't life; I have no freedom, no fun and no joy. I'm afraid, I built these walls up to protect myself from other people, and then I'd withdraw behind them because I'm afraid they're going to break my house of glass. I think, no, I believe that the glass and all the stuff is me. Holy shit!!!! The glass house isn't me but it's what's keeping me a prisoner. I'm looking around and I can't see or find me, and I don't even know how to look for me either, the who I am. Maybe it's like "Alice in Wonderland" and the wizard behind the curtain; I can't remember exactly what happened but I'd like to see that movie again. I'm thinking of the message I got that said there are no rules, the old rules don't apply, but I'm afraid to break any of them for fear of not surviving, as not breaking any rules is how I have managed to survive this long.

    When I was at Jen's yesterday I touched how afraid I'm of failure or what I call failure, which is also letting go of things that I really don't need any more. The Centre is one of these, I feel I failed with it, but in reality, it was an opportunity to allow me to see what I didn't want to see or feel. I didn't have personal freedom and it wasn't what I really wanted either. I was in denial but pretended I was happy, yet not really knowing what I wanted. I still don't, and because it was new, I tried to make myself fit the mold, my glass house of what I believed people wanted and expected, and in my fear, I was rigid, inflexible and not flowing. After losing the court case, I was also afraid of not having the money to continue the Centre as I had hoped to. I put most, if not all my time, energy, and money into what I thought I wanted that would be accepted by others, and I'm still doing it, but I also know that I'm moving through it and healing, although sometimes I really wonder as it all seems so overwhelming.

1999 July 16 - I don't know what I'm going to be doing yet, I guess; I was going to say, I'll figure it out later but I'm not going to figure it out. I don't want to be just mentally working with my old beliefs, programs, and imprints.

    I just had a thought or vision of the Great Pyramids in Egypt. Something has, or is happening, and I feel that scientists are in a tizzy as they don't know what it means or how it's doing that. I feel that there's a vibration, and with that, there is something moving inside the pyramid or under it. I feel the whole area is going to be blocked off and maybe even a wall or screen of some kind put up. There are two other pyramids involved as is the Sphinx, and up to seven in total in the shape of a spiral. The Earth has also increased its vibration, and it's as if the pyramids are in step with the heartbeat of the Earth, or it monitors the heartbeat of the Earth is more accurate. Something is happening and they're in a panic.

1999 July 27 - I went to the local Library to see about renting the meeting room they have. It has its own entrance, bathroom, and a small kitchen, and will hold up to fifty people. I also called the community college to see about starting some classes as they were already offering some new age topics, but they already had their courses set and there would be no openings until next year.

1999 July 28 - Jen was making a collage and encouraged me to also make one out of pictures and words cut out from magazines. The theme was to express what I felt would reflect my view of what love and life on Earth should be and also what I desired to experience.

Recovering Lost Will

1999 July 30 - Blessings upon you this wondrous day. Indeed you feel you are in limbo but you are far from that. You are skeptical this morning for indeed you have heard this before, and as before, we say that this is indeed another level, plateau, layer. It is indeed difficult to offer what you deem encouragement and support when what you are feeling is the opposite, and what you must feel is the opposite. And so it seems paradoxical to you to encourage you to feel discouraged, for discouraged, down trodden, unworthy, low self-esteem, no self-worth, no self-love, anger, hate and confusion about what you feel, and desire and what you receive. And so you hate what you

Chapter 14 – My Terror and Heartbreak

feel, you feel that your feelings must be wrong and so you turned away from that part of you. Not only did you turn away, but you also beat on it, chastised, criticized and belittled it with self-hatred. That is where your present confusion and discouragement originates. Part of you, your Spirit, is discouraged at your Will, and your Will, that which you pummeled is discouraged, not trusting, for you still deny her, so it is doubly felt and confusing.

We would encourage you to continue to express out loud your feelings, your judgments, and to allow your sub-conscious to hear, to register what it is that you are feeling and thinking, and the understandings that are coming to you. This will assist in many ways, even into areas of recovering lost power, essence, and gifts, and of activating new ones that you are ready to discover. You are not failing but you need to feel you are. You need to touch all your lost Will and it seems it is more difficult as you touch Lost Will that has less or almost no vibration, self-love and acceptance, and it is this part of lost Will that you are healing now. It has been lost and pummeled by yourself for nearly all of your existence. This is deep and cannot be healed overnight for there is much distrust and pain involved, but it can and is being healed. Also, consciously and out loud, state your denials as you recognize them occurring, for in witnessing them and then in denying their existence, you also further add to your problem of expression. By denying your expression you are stating that you have no acceptance to admit you are in denial and trying to pretend that you did not suppress your Will.

Your Higher Self, the silent witness is here to assist you and this is one way to break the denials and deaths hold on you, is for you to recognize it for what it is and to give it acceptance by this recognition, and thereby allowing it to move to its right place, instead of accepting it by holding onto it and closing around it. Try this, and little by little you will begin to notice the difference in your experiences. Blessings this dawn, Adornia

1999 Aug. 2 - I drove down the street to one of the few, tiny, and neglected public parks with limited beach access in this area of predominately PRIVATE waterfront homes. I came here to write but so far all I've done is lay in the sun for a couple of hours and watch a spider. I feel frustrated, here it's August 2, three weeks since I've closed the centre and I'm still undecided, uncertain of what it is that I'm to be or to do. I feel even more lost. I'm spending the money I made from the garage sale, money is going out but none is coming in. I'm also worried about my van as I can't afford to repair it if something were to happen to it. I feel I'm even further away from where I could earn money as now I'm fifteen minutes out of town, and where I am living now is basically a peninsula so there is really only one way out and that is south. I don't feel that money is the real issue, I feel it's me and I'm angry at me for not being able to get myself out of this situation of being a failure, bad and no good in my eyes. I also feel that others feel the same way, especially those that I owe money to, but there is a part of me that doesn't care what they think or do.

I have a lot of little unfinished things to do in town, so whenever I'm in town, I call Jen to see if she wants to get together and do things. I'm angry with her as I feel she doesn't care or understand how frustrated I feel because what she feels and is comfortable doing is okay, but what I feel and am comfortable doing, or wanting to do, is not okay. She's not comfortable or doesn't want to, or can't do the things I want to do, so I feel I have no choice and that if I want to share anything with her, it has to be on her terms. I feel that I have judgments and programs in place that say I don't have the right to express myself, especially my disappointments, because when I do there is no acceptance for that, even from her. I don't even want to call her because I feel she'll be at me again, that I'm either not feeling, or not feeling right, or good enough. I feel all I get from her sometimes is just criticism. So what part of me is criticizing me? Is my Spirit criticizing my Will? Jen says that she's reflecting my Will that I'm denying. I'm confused, I don't know which way to turn anymore and I feel that I'm getting spun around more and more.

Jen says she's not going to take any more bullshit from me. She calls my lack of emotional honesty bullshit. She says I'm in denial of my feelings and emotions and that she can feel and see it, but I don't express it. But when I do express what I'm feeling she tells me that I'm wrong, judgmental or whatever. I feel I can't win. I feel she put a program into place when I asked her to let me know when I was in denial and now it seems like I'm in a prison. Here I'm confused and feeling emotions that I can't touch or describe and she says its bullshit. She says she can feel how frightened I am but it doesn't ring a bell in her to have a little patience and a little compassion as I try to become aware of the feelings that she thinks I'm denying. I guess, not guess, but know I'm doing that to myself, I'm being hard on myself and not giving myself a break.

1999 Aug. 4 - I recently started going for short five-kilometer bike rides in the early evening. On the way back tonight, I was about 200 meters from home and I decided to do a sprint up a slight hill. When I was about half way up the hill, my bike chain derailed and my foot hit the pavement. The next thing I knew I was laying on the road with my bike on top of me. I was numb and in shock. I slowly began to feel the various parts of my aching and bleeding body to see if anything was broken. I was wearing shorts and a T-shirt at the time so there was really nothing between me, my bike and the pavement. I scraped my left leg and knee as well as the back of my knee. I also scraped my right hand and my index finger was bleeding. My chest, ribs and stomach were scraped from hitting the handlebars and my inner right thigh was also scraped. While I was lying there on the pavement, three cars approached in

Chapter 14 – My Terror and Heartbreak

my lane and just drove around me in the other lane. Not one of them even slowed down to see or ask if I was okay. I finally stood up, straightened my twisted handlebars and then, leaning on my bike and using it as a crutch, I hobbled home. I washed the dirt that was embedded in my wounds and bandaged them as best I could. It was then that the heartbreak struck me; no one had stopped or cared to see if I was hurt, although they had to see that I was hurt and bleeding.

1999 Aug. 10 - I feel confused with Jen and her issues of eating. Ever since the day I met her, we have never shared a meal together. When I go over to see her, we do errands, watch TV, or we talk and share, and then she starts to make a meal for herself, even though we might just have gotten activated and started going into some real issues. I feel under pressure that although she doesn't say anything before she is ready to eat, I have to guess what she wants me to do. When her food has cooled down, I either have to leave or if she feels I can stay, then I have to watch TV, but not talk to her, not watch her eat, or even look at her food. If I choose to leave, then she complains that I'm abandoning her but if I stay, then I'm invading her privacy. She's says that she's not ready to eat with, or in front of people yet. We've been talking for months about getting a pizza but that has never happened. She also complains that when she has to wait for me to leave, that her food gets cold and she would rather have me leave sooner, but not when I want to leave, but rather when she wants me to leave. Then I feel pressured as I wonder how long we have to talk before time is up. I feel I'm being used. I've held back and I'm denying myself because I feel she is worse off than I am.

1999 Aug. 20 - I had to go to court today as I haven't paid anything since I lost the case. I had to bring in my bank statements and give details of my net worth and income. I told the judge that I had no money and that I wasn't working, but he didn't believe me and ordered me to pay $100.00 a month. Pay or go to jail, is what he said. I denied myself, I was afraid to stand up for myself, as earlier the same judge told everyone that he had no tolerance for losers, and that if they didn't pay up, that he had no problem with setting a jail sentence and that he wasn't fooling. I thought at the time, how can you go to jail for a debt, especially for one that is only there because you denied in the first place. I feel angry and revengeful and I would like to hurt them both, especially this temporary pious judge who is just a lawyer (wannabe judge) trying to make a name for himself. I'd like to put a hex and a curse on them and make them suffer. If I could remember his name, I'd mention it.

I feel like a failure again and I'm tired of the struggle, I can't seem to win at anything. I denied at court because I felt I couldn't talk and tell my side because I'd be thrown in jail. I'm terrified of governments, of any officials or people in a place or position of power, as I feel I'm judged against all the time. I feel that they're looking for a flaw, something they can use against me. The judge ordered me to pay regardless if I had money or not, and the fact I had no money didn't even register in his pea brain consciousness. All the money I have left from the garage sale is $45.00. I also have a cheque for $20.00 for a handyman job I did, that I still have to put in the bank. That money will just cover the Library room rental of $60.00 that I have booked for a meditation and past life workshops. But even with the workshops, I feel what's the use, no one wants to hear what I have to share. I don't even know if I'm fooling myself to think that this is what I want to be doing. I'm losing all confidence in myself, I feel worthless, no good and a burden, a misfit, an outsider, a loser, a loner, and that I don't fit in. I feel so alone and abandoned. What am I here for? What is my purpose? I'm not like everyone, I'm different, and being different is somehow bad and not acceptable. I feel I have no right place, right function, purpose, or even a right mate. I can't have real friends and I can't really be myself because I'm afraid I'll be punished or even killed.

A part of me wishes I could die and not feel all this, this isolation, rejection, inhumanity, coldness, indifference, and all the judgments. I feel like I'm cursed and that this is my purpose, to suffer and to never be truly happy, accepted or to be able to be myself. If I want to be accepted and fit in I have to NOT be me, I have to be and do what others want or expect. I even do the same to myself as I have this program in me that says if I'm going to be friends or involved with such and such a person that they expect this of me, and so this is how I'll be and how I'll act, even before there is a relationship.

1999 Aug. 22 - I was talking with Jen on the phone and we went into a past life that we had together in France. We had a farm and my wife (Jen) was sick and had died. With three small children under five years of age, I couldn't run the farm alone. I lost the farm but as I was good with my hands, I tried to get work but no one would hire me. Desperate to feed my family, I stole bread and when I was accused, I admitted that I did. I was sentenced to twenty-five years in prison where I eventually died. I had promised my wife that I'd look after our children and I feel I failed as a husband, as a father, and as a man. I also put the program in place that if I would have just kept my mouth shut, that everything would have been okay.

It was two weeks ago that I fell off my bike. I looked at my left leg that now had dark veins in it; Irene said it was beginning to form a blood clot. Now I feel my body is falling apart, I'm growing old, dying, and I haven't really lived yet. I'm angry, pissed off and frustrated, I feel like I've wasted this life. What fun, joy, bliss, or happiness have I had? I feel I got the short end of the stick and now it's too late, I'm getting old and my body's changing and I feel like it's all downhill from here. I, like most people in our society, would like to believe what is advertised on TV as "freedom 55," which states that by

Chapter 14 – My Terror and Heartbreak

the time people are my age, they are able to retire and enjoy life. I'm far from that, I'm penniless, no home, no mate, no romance, and my family is scattered. I have two friends, and I don't have the money to do the things I enjoy or would like to do.

I don't know who I am or what my purpose or gifts are. I'm afraid and I feel that I'm no good and that I'm not good enough to help others because I've got all these problems myself, so how can I possibly help another. The "I'm afraid to," and "I feel," are not really fears or feelings as such, but rather judgments, imprints, programs and beliefs that I've put in place, and it's these beliefs that are creating my reality. They're overwhelming and it's only the beginning. Awareness is the key, when I'm aware that I'm in denial, that is the time to state my denial and then go into the fears, beliefs, programs, imprints and judgments that come up and to give them acceptance and expression.

I'm afraid, no, I think terrified is the right word but I don't want to use it, that no one will help me, especially those in government or in a position of authority or power. By authority figures, I include my father, mother, grandparents, aunts, uncles, teachers and clergy who are high on my list, as are basically all people older than me. I know it's me who puts them above me, and it is also me that puts me below them. It's my belief that they have the power when in actuality they only have power because I deny myself and give them my power.

1999 Aug. 26 - After the meditation group meeting at the Library, I went for a coffee with Robin, one of the women who was in the group. We got our coffees and sat down at a table and another woman, who we did not know, followed us and sat down at the table next to us. This woman was very aggressive and bullish in her behavior. As she was putting her stuff on the table, and then again when she was getting into her chair, she bumped into Robin without as much as an "excuse me" or "I'm sorry." Robin began to cough but said she was okay, even though she was coughing for quite a few minutes. Later, when the woman was about to leave, I noticed Robin move her legs to let the woman get past her, not that her legs were in the way, and again she began to cough. I realized that she was in fear and in denial of expressing what she really felt, and was trying to control the situation. I told her what I felt was happening and as soon as she acknowledged that she was in denial and was afraid of the woman, her coughing stopped and I mean instantly. We both were amazed at how quickly things changed when denials are ended.

1999 Aug. 28 - Today we touched how I deny my self-hatred and how I've allowed myself to hate and blame others, while Jen is the opposite in that she has self-hatred but denies any hatred for others, which just turns back on her as more self-hatred. We both made an agreement that she was no longer going to hold my denied self-hatred and fear, and that I would release holding her denied fear of hatred for others. Both of us fear what will happen now and how we'll survive. It's hard to admit that I hate myself as I've spent a lifetime hating and blaming others for my problems. I can't, no; I find it hard to believe that I really hate myself as much as I saw when I was talking to Jen. This volcano, a small island at sea, was actually the tip of an undersea mountain that was miles high and getting ready to blow, oozing out red-hot self-hatred lava that slowly flowed to the sea. We realized that hatred for others is denied self-hatred and hatred for self is denied hatred for others.

> *Hatred for others is denied self-hatred.*
> *Hatred for self is denied hatred for others. - Shenreed*

1999 Sept. 1 - Today, while doing some Celtic and Shamanic journeys with Jen, we again had the realization or insight that:

Air (Father) is the breath of life.
Water (Mother) is the giver of life.
Fire (Heart) is the rhythm of life.
Earth (Body) is the form of life
Ether (Love) is the essence of life that supports and allows the flow of all that is.

1999 Sept. 2 - I was sitting on the grass at Teepee Beach, looking across the bay at the Penetang Mental Health Institution. I'm not really having any thoughts or emotions at this time as I'm just listening to the waves lapping up on the beach, while watching a leaf that has fallen from a tree above me, glide effortlessly to the sand beside me. Now two boats cross the view; I can hear the muffled roar of the engine of the one closest to me. Now I'm feeling melancholy, alone, isolated and betrayed.

The day before yesterday, I drove Jen to the city of Orillia for her acupuncture appointment. When we were driving past her romantic boyfriends place, she mentioned that he was outside in the yard and so I honked the horn. Yesterday, she commented that when he called her later that evening, he told her that my horn had scared him, and she made out like it was my fault that he was scared by my action. I feel I would have also been blamed the other way if I hadn't honked my horn.

She also talked about the phone call that she got from Liz, who told her that she and a girlfriend were planning to move into the Heart Centre and that the other girls boyfriend was going to be opening a drumming shop and starting a drumming group. She also said that Liz was going to get $10,000.00 to open the store and that how she (Jen) wanted so much to be a part of it. I

Chapter 14 – My Terror and Heartbreak

feel betrayed by Liz and especially Jen; she couldn't be at the Centre for me, but now she can for Liz. I told her that, and that she could get involved if she wanted to, but not to ask me to take her over or to pick her up, and that I didn't want to hear anything of what she did when she was there. I wanted to cut myself off as I feel betrayed and robbed as I put well over $25,000.00, plus my labor into the business, and Jen didn't put in any money as she never had any to put in, and she never spend any real physical time at the Centre either. Now that the Heart Centre has closed down, she wants to get involved in something new that is in the same place. I don't understand and I'm angry. I told her to go ahead, but count me out.

I feel even more of a failure as I feel Liz has someone with which she can share her dream, to be physically there as well as someone to put up the money, to finance her dream. I feel jealous that she's supported in a way that I can only hope or dream. I feel that Jen's a fair weather friend, there for the good times and gone when the going gets tough. It hurts that I couldn't make a go of the Centre, I put money, blood, sweat and tears into it, to fix it up and Liz will now get all the benefits of my work. My dream collapses and hers comes alive. It hurts me that even now, although I'm supported by Irene and Dave, I still can't support myself. What I thought I wanted to do I can't. I wanted to teach; to share, to help people and that's not working out, so I feel I'm no good, wrong and so alone.

Yesterday evening, Jen and I were on the phone and she hung up on me when I told her to call her other friend if all she wanted was to feel good and be accepted. I called her back after she hung up but she was already on the phone. She called me back later and started with the "but honey" bullshit. I asked her why the phony kindness. She said that she wanted to give the little boy in me kindness and understanding by calling him honey. It didn't feel good or loving, and it reminded me of her friend and also of my mother, "Honey, sweetie, I love you." Right words, but they were far from feeling good or loving.

I'm reminded of the time when I was at Jen's and I began to tap into and feel my five-year-old inner child, and all that I felt he wanted was a little tenderness and compassion. When I began to express myself, all that Jen gave or showed me was anger and rage. She shouted at me, pulled my hair, ripped my glasses off and threw them on the chair. Her fingers clutched my ears, as she yelled in my face, that this was what I needed for her to get through to me. You got through to me, but not in the way I wanted you to, when all I asked for was a little tenderness. I don't know what to do or where I'm going, why I'm doing what I'm doing, and why I'm feeling what I'm feeling, but I also know I feel a lot of heartbreak in this moment. Of course, her actions were just triggering me into what my mother used to do to me, and what I do to myself.

1999 Sept. 2 - This morning, a part of me feels like Jen is a distant memory, like I knew her ten or twenty years ago. She is someone that I knew but lost touch with and now I don't know her or even what we really did mean to each other. I feel we are becoming distant and cut off from each other and another part of me feels the loss. I telephoned her but all I got was the answering machine which triggered me into feeling that she's not available when I want to talk to her, or that she doesn't care, as she doesn't answer the phone if she doesn't feel like talking.

Judgments on Doing

1999 Sept. 03 - Blessings unto you this glorious moment. Indeed, we are here to assist you on your journey, that is to say, not to do it for you, but to help guide you to where and what it is that you desire to experience for your growth. Doing, there is much you could be doing, and there is much you could be feeling, and in most cases, doing negates the feeling. Allow yourself to feel as much as you can, for you will be doing much soon, not that you will be over burdened, but that is also your choice. Now is the time you have chosen to heal and what you are doing and feeling is also for your healing process even though it does not appear as such and you are impatient, for this is also part of old programs, beliefs and imprints. You always had to be doing something or you were lazy, good for nothing, and as such, you also judged others likewise.

Your life, not your life, for really you haven't experienced life yet, your experiences thus far are based mostly on your judgments and on your beliefs, imprints and programs. It is now time to address your judgments and to see them for what they are, your own self-hatred, self-denial, limitation, your plight, suffering, sorrow and your sadness. This is what you have chosen to experience and you couldn't have experienced it if you had not limited yourself to such a large extent. But now that part of the experience is coming to a close and it is time to release these judgments so that you can empower yourself and to take your right place, to be all that you are and to truly experience the rest of what you have come here to experience, and that is life, a life based in love not fear, acceptance not denial, compassion not judgment. It is time to see the experiences for what they were and are, and to give yourself compassion, acceptance and love. It is your judgments that hold you a prisoner, that limit you, and would have you believe you are separate and that the outer reality is responsible for your feelings, situations, and experiences. It will take some effort to break through this illusion but you are aware of it and that is the key to transformation.

Many are here to assist you, ask as you have been doing and they/we will help accelerate the process. Once you truly grasp the illusion and how it is that you create your reality, you will rise swiftly and steadfastly, and your limitations will fall away and crumble, and then you will truly begin to shine,

Chapter 14 – My Terror and Heartbreak

to show your true colors. Then you will know your mission, your excitement, your joy. Blessings. Mother and Father.

1999 Sept. 4, 5:42 am - I've been awake since 4 a.m. and I'm in a panic again regarding money. I've made some money doing handyman work and I've got approximately $40.00 in the bank and $37.00 on me in cash and that's it. My vans insurance was due on Aug 31 that's $325.00 for six months and the storage place is due next week and that's $85.00 per month. I don't want to fall behind with the storage payments like I did last spring when I lost my two canoes. I made four appointments for meetings at the library and I'm going to have to cancel as no one is showing up, even though they registered. I've put out $120.00 for the library and $75.00 for newspaper ads, plus photocopies and gas, and not counting my time, and all I've made is $90.00. Nothing works and I'm just throwing money away.

Today Jen is going out to her Mom's garage sale. I'd like to be there but I can't even afford the gas as I'm down to a quarter of a tank. I threw my pen down after the last sentence as it bothers me so much. I'm terrified of what's going to happen to me. I don't want to be a burden, and I also don't want to not be able to do what I want, and that is freedom to move, to be myself. I was talking to Jen last night when she was out at her moms getting ready for the garage sale. She said that she ate half a sandwich that her mom made for her and that later, she even met and talked to some people who were trying to get stuff before the sale. She also talked about how she felt and her feelings of not being able to move, and also of being limited physically and financially. We're both feeling the same feelings, but I feel that as I'm going down, she's going up.

1999 Sept. 4 - It was Saturday evening and I was downstairs in the family room watching TV with Dave. The two German shepherd dogs, Zeus and Shane were lying on the floor with their heads resting on their paws, when suddenly, both raised their heads and looked up at the window for a few moments, then return to their previous position.

I looked at the window, the blinds were closed and I saw nothing unusual. They did this a few more times and each time I couldn't see anything, but noticed that they weren't looking at the window, but more to the right and toward the ceiling. I also heard voices upstairs and thought that Irene was talking on the phone. After the movie, I went upstairs and found a note on my bed saying that Nero was trying to give me a message. I realized that the dogs were aware of his presence, and that later, when I heard the voices upstairs, it was Irene talking to Nero. I got ready for bed and received the following messages.

Journey to the Heart Centre

Inner Battle and Choice

1999 Sept. 04, 11:47 pm - It is time to begin. You ask and you search, and you ponder and wait, and yet refuse to listen, to contact those that are here to assist you. We are not here to judge you, only to assist you in awakening. It is your choice, your program, that also states that no matter what others tell you, you have to do it alone and that you have to have all the answers. You make it hard on yourself for you battle yourself constantly. There is this part of you that refuses to let go, so determined to protect you, that it doesn't see how it is actually obstructing you and preventing you from knowing, understanding and becoming all that you desire, all that you all ready are, but are too afraid to see it, admit it, and to accept it. Nero.

Denials, Judgments and Reality

1999 Sept. 05, 1:01 am - Open your heart, open to love, let love in and let love help you, heal you and guide you. Release the fear, the judgments you hold locked inside your Heart, of what you deem love is and is not. Trust your Will to feel love and allow your altered Ego to let go of what it believes love is. You have so closed yourself off in protecting yourself that you have even lost sight of your passion, excitement, joy, bliss, and of your dreams and desires. You cannot receive love unless you open your Heart and your arms, and release the judgments you hold, instead of what you want. I ask you to meditate now upon your desires, your passion, and allow yourself to see the judgments you are holding that are preventing you from creating the reality you desire. We will reconnect during your meditation and later. Nero.

While in my meditation/sleep I'd wake up, aware that I was receiving a message. I wrote the messages, but I never wrote what I was experiencing in my meditation, although the messages did reflect what I was going through. The following are the messages that I got during the night from Nero.

2:02 am - Sex, romance, sensuality, lust, cravings, touch, need I go on, are also your denied passion. Your guilt and shame, and your judgments keep you from that which you desire, crave, long for and need. You have and are denying your sexuality, sensuality, your body, from one of life's greatest pleasures and gifts, for you deem yourself everything from unworthy, to being above such basic instincts and desires. Allow yourself to meditate on these topics. Nero

2:33 am - Indeed you have much confusion regarding sex and even the words used and changed around to mean one thing one time, and something totally else another time. No means yes, and No means maybe, and No means No, and so you are confused and then to go past your Will, but then you also deny that, for you feel shame, judged and guilty of your

Chapter 14 – My Terror and Heartbreak

desires. All of your relationships have had some form of secrecy attached, reflecting your belief, shame, guilt, and judgments. Allow yourself to explore upon this further.

3:15 am - You are afraid and ashamed to state or exhibit your sexuality openly. Fear of rejection of your advances for fear of loss of friendship, and also out of fear of ridicule, out of a lack of acceptance, or of the future consequences, all based on your confusion and judgments. Your judgments are many and have many sources as does your shame and guilt. You put others desires and needs ahead of yours, not that you need to intend to overpower them or have them do what you desire, but you wait for them to come to you and so you wait and are rejected even more. The more you deny your sexuality, the greater the reflection and the greater the experience of lack, it is so with everything. Deny your worthiness and no worth is reflected, deny your beauty, youth, your sex, and the opposite you will have reflected and that is what you feel. Oh yes, you can have moments in denial that feel like it is what you long for, but it is an illusion.

4:19 am - You have fear of expressing, for you to express also leads to physical expression as well, and if there is no agreement you feel your feelings were wrong and you blame them and yourself for having exposed yourself to humiliation and rejection. Your shame and guilt shut you down from ever mentioning or even thinking of, or ever approaching the subject again for fear of loss of the friendship, and so you try to separate the two to either friend or lover, though what you truly long for is to have both aspects in one relationship.

4:49 am - Express yourself, don't deny yourself, your feelings, your needs or your desires, not that you need to take what you want, but you need to express what you fear to express, to explore your fears of what your friends or people would think of you, which are your judgments.

5:12 am - You have denied yourself and now you feel that even your youth, your appearance and your vitality are gone or lacking, and yes indeed, as you are aware that your thoughts create your reality, and so this denied energy manifests your reality. Indeed, the same is for success and abundance. Your guilt and shame over having more or enjoying yourself is enough to have your denied energy greater than the desired energy. It is past the mid-point and so you have imbalance, and what you create are your denials, your guilt, shame and YOUR JUDGMENTS based on your beliefs, programs and imprints. Judgments, self-judgment, self-hatred and your denials is indeed what you are experiencing at this moment, this point of time. Nero

5:36 am - You also judge that these are more noble words from Spirit, a source higher than you, well my brother, this Spirit source is you. There is no separation, any higher or lower, good or bad, only a difference in energy. I come to you, as you would call it, as part of your higher self, or a fragment that Earth history remembers as Nero. There are thousands of lives

Journey to the Heart Centre

I've lived, as there are thousands of lives you've lived, and for most of them we experienced the same issues over and over. We got caught in the illusion of separation and entered in, and are controlled by denial, guilt, shame and judgments, and all the beliefs programs and imprints. But now, in this lifetime, you (we) have both the awareness and the power to change our reality if we take our power back, if we no longer deny any part of ourselves, we can have the life we choose, in love not fear and denial guilt or shame.

6:39 am - You have swung far to the denial side of the balance in many areas of your life and it is now time to reverse this process, beginning with acceptance of all your feelings and by expressing all your judgments as well as your desires, and why you feel and believe you can't have what you desire, and why and how you feel about what you desire.

7:49 am - Your true power is in the moment of the experience; past and future have no power because they exist outside of time (present time) which is the moment of the occurring of the experience. The past (remembrances) judgments and beliefs are there for a reference only, and only have power in that they project fear or joy of a similar past experience into the future creating expectation, condition and control.

In the moment, becoming aware of your past beliefs, programs, imprints, judgments, guilt and shame, and that you are in denial of your true feelings. Allow yourself to experience as best you can in whatever form you can, and to release your judgments and thereby end your denials by giving them emotional expression. Most of what you call likes or dislikes are based on past judgments and your acceptance of whatever emotions were expressed at the time. It is going to be difficult, at first, to allow the free flow of emotions without categorizing them into judgments and denial, guilt and shame, etc. but to simply allow the experience to bring you whatever awareness it does, when it does. The time of self abuse is ending but it can only end by allowing all your emotions expression and by ending your denial, denial of expressing your emotions for whatever judgment you have in place against them, for how can you get your emotions to move if you stack up judgments against them?

Your confusion, even your inability to rationalize, as you call it, is not a bad thing. It is simply a matter of bypassing, or rather, dissolving the judgmental thoughts and patterns to allow your emotions their expression. You are not losing your mental faculties; you are clearing them out. The more you express and bring balance to the mental and the emotional, so too will you bring balance to your physical. You limit yourself by thinking you are clever, intellectual, have a good memory, etc. for this is the mere tip of the iceberg, so to speak, once you begin to truly function as who you really are. You are on the threshold of your grandest adventure and it is this step that will feel impossible and overwhelming at times. Allow yourself to feel, to explore all your fears, judgments, limitations and beliefs that are holding you

Chapter 14 – My Terror and Heartbreak

back from what is rightfully yours, love, life, light, joy and abundance. I leave you now as I feel you are more open to receive me and those that are here to assist you, assist us, on our grandest adventure. Blessings Nero.

1999 Sept 6 - Last night during our late night cup of tea, we talked about her note to me and of her seeing and talking to Spirits. She's very quiet and withdrawn and I feel she is now beginning to open up, and that there is a lot more she's not telling me, but that will have to wait for the right time. She works shift-work and starts at 1:30 pm and isn't home until 11:30 pm, and Dave works shift work too, but on alternating weeks of days and nights, so sometimes I have the house to myself. I just finished watching the movie Pleasantville and the table lamps flickered twice as if to get my attention. I picked up my pen and notebook and began to write.

Purpose and Trust

1999 Sept. 06 - Indeed, you noticed and responded. It is not our intent to be pushy or forceful, but merely to be in your awareness as you asked for signs and so we deliver. There is much to do in the times ahead, rather much to be done, but not that it will be overwhelming, quite the contrary, but that too, for we do not want to spoil your WOW's.

Me: What is my purpose and mission?

As given, to heal yourself, to spiritualize your physical body and to assist others to do the same are part of your purpose, and the first is by far the most important. As you are aware of our signals, blatant as they may be for now to get your attention and acknowledgment, so you shall be aware of all the more subtle ways the universe is preparing and trying to communicate with you. You have only to open your Heart to the possibilities to see, hear, feel, know and understand what is being given and is unfolding, or about to unfold. Allow yourself to follow and trust your feelings, your intuition, as it offers the guidance and support your Spirit (mind) seeks and that the altered Ego is in confusion and disarray. Walls are tumbling down, your Old World of illusion is tumbling down and the New World, the Phoenix is rising from the ashes, just as in the movie Pleasantville, your world of black and white is changing to color. Just as the people in your life, past, present and future are going to change if they so choose.

Trust is a big word for you, trust and believe, and have faith in yourself, finding yourself, the real you, and allowing it to shine. The more open you are, the more you trust, and the more you trust, the more open you become. I/we weep with joy and love for you in this moment of your journey. We will leave you now but we will be with you in your dream time and later. Blessings, Nero and the company of heaven.

Self Forgiveness

1999 Sept. 08 - Forgiveness of self is also an act of letting go of your judgments, guilt, shame and beliefs. For in forgiving yourself you are accepting your feelings, not that you are accepting or condoning your behavior as such to justify your actions, but to be able to accept responsibility for your actions and see them for what they were based on your judgments. Your feelings, when based on judgments, are in most cases false Will, false feelings based on past experiences and future projections. Allow yourself to feel your true feelings and true Will, and forgive yourself for not allowing true feelings to be expressed for whatever reason they couldn't be expressed before, in the moment.

There is no right time or place for forgiveness to take place for it is only forgiveness if it occurs in the moment and is felt in the moment. Until you have forgiveness for yourself, you cannot truly have forgiveness and compassion for others, as it is not real. It may look and sound real but if it is truly felt, one would feel the falseness and the illusion of it. Blessings, Nero.

Time and Space

1999 Sept. 08, 6:02 pm - Time and space are an illusion as you sense it, as it is simply a tool to allow you to experience, to give you a sense of dimension, for indeed time is a dimension as much as you deem space is. Notice how time seems to stop or drag when you are waiting or expecting an event to happen or when you are remembering a past event. This is because you are out of balance and not in the moment and minutes feel like hours or days. Notice also how when you enjoy yourself, are in the moment, that you say that time flies and how hours pass in what feels like minutes.

Consider what you call aging as a component of these two examples, those that live life in the moment literally live longer and are younger in a physical sense. At first, you may think it a paradox but if time flies and hours pass in what feels like minutes, in actuality you have lived an illusion, an experience of say five hours on your Earth clock, and you feel that 5 minutes went by. Your true biological clock says you aged five minutes while your chronological clock says you aged five hours. The reverse is also true, five minutes pass and it feels like five hours, now your biological clock says you aged five hours while your chronological clock says five minutes. It seems surreal to you, given your programming to consider this a reality, but the bases of it are there. There are also other aspects to consider but they would serve no purpose to address them at this time, but yes, they have to do with thought and creating your reality.

Space is as we have stated, also an illusion, of dimension for your experience. Length, width, height are first concepts but the others also play on your senses to give you your sense of polarity, far, near, tall, short, hot, cold, sour, sweet, loud, soft, smooth, rough and all the variables in between to

Chapter 14 – My Terror and Heartbreak

add to your experience. If we would tell you that you could experience another thirty-eight senses in your Earth plane, what would that do to your sense of space and experience. What you call space and time are energy, vibration and different objects or aspects having a different vibration that allows differentiation, yet similarities. Take pine trees that all have the same basic vibration that they share to give them their general characteristics of a pine tree, yet each pine tree has its own unique vibrational signature that separates it, from ALL the others. It is the same for humans, each has their own unique vibration which you call ego, genetics, physical appearance, mentality, and these are affected by your imprints, beliefs, and your judgments of your experiences. But back to space, since you are energy in vibration with a specific base frequency, and again, yes thought creates your reality, you have the power to thereby change your reality and thereby to change your space, your surroundings and even yourself.

Once you are totally in atonement (at-one-ment) in tune, in balance and in harmony with all that is, you become masters of illusion and thereby are able to create, to manifest your reality at will. To change your vibration that you use to experience physical reality to whatever form you desire, and because time is also an illusion, time is a vibration as well, you are able to change that also within the confines of certain parameters. For realize it is your reality in this physical experience and not necessarily reality for others.

Now you ponder, are the people and objects you meet real or are they just figments of your imagination to create your reality? Are there others out there that have their own probable realities the same as you, that they are creating, or is there a common reality and a cross over between the two? Your logical mind is a whirl with this concept that is why, partly why, we offer this basic concept and information to allow you to register, to begin to remember who you are. We leave you now with love and light, and more questions than answers. Blessings, Nero and Jerole.

7:05 am - Indeed, when you are truly in the moment there is no time and all that you experience is outside of time in your physical dimension. You are then also at one with all there is, and hence you create your own reality, and yes, since there is no time, what you create in the moment when you create, is in the moment when there is no time and all time.

Indeed it is somewhat like your movie where all is frozen, stopped, like a VCR on pause and you are able to step inside or outside of your physical reality. We smile as you ponder, are you the actor on the TV screen, or are you the viewer watching the movie, or are you outside of them both, watching them simultaneously? Indeed, when you go outside of yourself, or the moment, there is separation, there is death for you are denying yourself and in denial is self-hatred, is what you call death, aging, loss of essence. Blessings, Nero.

1999 Sept. 8 - I decided to cancel all the classes I had planned at the Library as it just wasn't worthwhile.

1999 Sept. 9 - My hair was almost down to the bottom of my shoulder blades and I decided to cut it off today, leaving it about an inch long. Later, I went for a walk in the woods and scattered my hair along the path. I saved a small bundle and later tied them together with a colored thread and put it in with my sweet grass, sage, cedar, and tobacco. Jen also cut her hair today; or rather, she buzzed her head. When she told me what she had done, I was unsure of how she would look but when I saw her, she actually looks good, which surprised me.

Accepting Your Gifts

1999 Sept. 15 - Greetings and blessings, this is Astrid. It has been a long time that I have been trying to contact you, not contact, but of you to acknowledge me in your awareness. It is interesting that you find my energy very subtle and soft, as you describe me, for I feel myself not different from other guides that you acknowledge, yet you seem to have difficulty holding my contact in your awareness.

I am here to assist you in opening yourself to hear and see all that you desire, as you have in your intent, to hear and see the Spirit world, energy fields, auras, grids, the unseen, unheard, unfelt, and to open and expand your existing senses so that all this will become part of your reality. Indeed, you are what you call, picking me up more easily as you focus and bring your attention, not your attention, but rather letting go and allowing yourself to be in the moment. It is interesting that as I seem to perceive you, you shift and begin to lose contact and this is partly fear of success, approval, that there can be acceptance for your gifts, talents, and powers. It is a shamed shyness that you withdraw from the expression of love, and I am here to help you in this area of your experience and evolvement, growth and transformation is a better, more accurate word. Allow yourself now to put down your pen and try to maintain contact on a conscious level and allow yourself to hear, see, and feel. Love, light and joy. Astrid.

Judgments and False Feelings

1999 Sept. 15 - Blessings unto you this wondrous moment. Indeed you are tired and weary and yet you are here, making the effort to communicate even though you are unsure of what to ask and are barely conscious. The question you ask, "Are you in denial of yourself?" and you know the answer to that already, yes and no, and that is okay, for you are still battling, warring your duality experience within yourself. Your mission, purposes, are many and they will unfold and be given to you when the time is right. You are not yet ready to know and that triggers your issues of secrets,

Chapter 14 – My Terror and Heartbreak

of information being withheld from you by what you feel is on purpose, and so you suspect and project all manners of what ifs that catch you up in your judgments and beliefs, especially the one that someone else is more important or better that you. There are many issues and layers of buried emotions that need to surface including your self-hatred, lack of self-acceptance, self-worth, grief, anger, guilt, shame and denial of expressing your feelings, your true feelings that lie buried and covered up under the false surface feelings. False in the sense that they are the only ones that have acceptance and are allowed expression at the sake of the sacrifice of your real feelings.

Your pattern is that your last relationship is like your first, and so you feel guilty and shame, feel inadequate and unworthy, that you are not good enough. As well as when you are in another relationship, you carry this wound with you and you project your judgments and fears into the new relationship even though there is no reality to them, but to you they are real because they are your judgments, your beliefs and programs.

Allow yourself to feel all your feelings, your judgments, your fears, to uncover your denials, guilt and shame, and allow movement and healing so that love is able to come to you and be accepted. Also, forgive yourself for your need to be perfect as it is an impossible task. Allow yourself to let go of this imprint, program and belief, and allow yourself to just feel and experience. Your judgments demand a perfection that is unobtainable and isn't even desirable for it would be dull and boring in its experience to what you experience otherwise. It would lack color as in the movie "Pleasantville," I leave you now. Nero

Letting Go, Ending the struggle

1999 Sept. 15 - Letting go of the struggle frees you from experiencing what you are afraid to feel again, because you feel and fear it will kill you. And so you struggle against the flow and are afraid to let go of your beliefs, programs and imprints that fill you with fear that brings up these old memories, even on a sub-conscious level. And so you fight the experience again and again, trying desperately not to re-live the pain and this is what the universe brings to you time and time again for your acceptance.

Letting go is allowing the river of life to flow through you and to bring you the experiences you need for growth, those experiences where in the past you had no acceptance. Letting go is not giving up on your will to live, your desires, your dreams, but to allow the universe to bring you to them instead of trying to struggle against the current to get to where you think it is safe, or to what you want. As you let go and allow yourself to experience each situation that is brought to you, to accept your feelings in the moment and let go of your beliefs of what happened in the past is going to happen again. So these experiences that you would have considered painful and undesirable, are not joyous in that they became not what you desired, but there is joy in the acceptance of the feelings and in that there is movement, and that movement takes you out of the experience and into others. The more in the moment you become, you are, you will find that you begin to also manifest those experiences that would bring joy to your life. So each new bend, twist, up or down, becomes filled with excitement rather than anxiety as you let go of your judgments. Adornia

1999 Sept. 16 - I had been called about setting up classes in Victoria Harbour, which is a ten-minute drive on the other side of Midland. I prepared and printed flyers for three different classes, then drove out and dropped them off. On the way back, I dropped in to see Jen and we talked for a while. We both still feel that we're not being heard and we also have fear and trust issues coming up. I realize that I use anger to puff myself up so that I won't get hurt, as I can't show that I'm weak. Jen tries to use "nice" talk and denies showing her anger. She also sees and feels another's pain and excuses their actions and gives them acceptance to feel and express their pain and emotions, but she cuts herself off from feeling and expressing her own pain and emotions. I blame others, while Jen blames herself. Opposites attract.

1999 Sept 17 - Irene had told me earlier that in the spring, a snapping turtle had laid her eggs in the back yard. When I came out of my room for breakfast, she told me that they started hatching this morning. By 1:00 pm, we counted fourteen baby snapping turtles. They were about three inches long, including about one and a half inches for the tail. We took pictures of them over the next few days. We also helped them to the marshy area in the woods next to the house. Irene found one dead turtle that had made its way to the road and had been run over by a car. She buried it beside the deck and placed small stones in a circle to mark its grave. The next morning, three stones had been moved as if they were opening a gateway to the East, to set its spirit free.

Ending Limitation

1999 Sept. 25 - It is time now to begin to open to the channel that you are. You have fear of being wrong, of being judged "holy," self-aggrandized, self absorbed, crazy, pious, and a host of other judgments and also in fear of standing out, of being recognized and separated, for you have lived this separation in fear. Now it is time to live, not in separation, but rather differentiation, uniqueness and to begin to fly your true colors. This will not happen overnight, but then again, it can.

You still have other issues to heal that you are specifically going through now, another form of self-hatred turned outward to feel less self-hatred toward self. Feeling like it is your fault, you're to blame, you're responsible for another's happiness, comfort, safety, peace, contentment and

Chapter 14 – My Terror and Heartbreak

a host of other conditions that would have you give up your power through self-hatred, self blame, guilt and shame. True, you do have responsibilities that are yours but they are responsibilities to your true feelings and not societies or your judgments based on beliefs, programs, and imprints, and not to take responsibility for how another feels as a result of your actions or non-actions. Their feelings are their feelings and they must be honest with theirs as you with yours. The experience is neither right nor wrong, just an experience to show both of you where you still have hidden issues, fears, judgments and denial, etc.

Allow yourself to express, to open to expression, not just in writing but verbal, physical, and this includes a host of activities. You have limited yourself and it was for an experience of limitation, but now you are aware of the limitations and the experiences, so now you have choice, free Will to choose how you will channel love, light, and life. Allow your guides to assist you for they are there for the experience also, for there is no separation, no higher or lower, only being and allowing experience of your feelings, and thoughts, deeds and desires to be experienced, felt and expressed in the moment. As you begin to move this self-hatred and anger out, you will make space for love, light and life. Allow this anger and this self-hatred to move, to give it movement, to give feelings movement and not the physical abuse toward self or directed outwardly toward others, and allow it to find its right place. Blessings upon you child, Mother and Father.

1999 Sept. 27 - I'm feeling discouraged as Jen and I have been fighting for the past three days and we haven't really connected for a long time. I feel I'm just drifting as I've been here at Irene's and Dave's since July 12, almost two and a half months. I tried offering classes and they flopped. I've even taken a dead end job at the Mirror, delivering newspapers, which I'm quitting today with a month's notice. I've put out flyers on the new classes that I'll be holding in Victoria Harbour, beginning in October; I've put out over 200 flyers and I haven't received one phone call. I had no money left so I called my sister Mandy, who earlier had offered to help me out if I was stuck. I received a letter from her today along with a cheque for $1000.00. I'll use it to pay for storage, license and insurance, an oil change and maybe two used tires for the van, and the rest I'll just hang on to. Where am I going? I'm not focused; I don't know what I want anymore. I'm not sure of anything and my heart feels like it's breaking as I've closed down even more since I've lost the Centre. I've lost my finances, my way of making money, my credit cards, and I've lost part of my freedom.

I wasn't going to insert this next part but I changed my mind as I would be in denial. Before I got the money from my sister, I had applied for social assistance as I was getting desperate. I had an eye opening experience when I went to see what, if any, assistance I could get from the newly formed

Journey to the Heart Centre

Ontario Works Program. Because I had been self-employed for the past twenty years and had no so-called employable qualifications, the most I would be entitled to under the government's new work-fare program would be $195.00/month with conditions. Those conditions being that I had to be actively seeking employment and to prove that, I would have to spend 35 hours per week doing a job search and report biweekly to the district office with my contact list. Also, if I did take a part-time job or make any money, an equal amount would be deducted, dollar for dollar from the assistance. I figured it out that it was going to cost me around $400.00/month to use my vehicle to get $195/month, not including the 140 hours plus of my personal time running around from business to business. I wrote the woman who interviewed me, a direct letter stating that I was declining the not so generous offer. So much for getting help from the government when you need it. They advertise their political rhetoric on TV stating that their new program is working and getting people off social assistance. Yes, I can now understand how they are doing that. I also wonder how they are getting away with this, and why the media isn't asking the poor about the program. Oh yes, I forgot, the media is in bed with the slime ball politicians and the fat-cat government bureaucrats. I guess you can tell I'm pissed off.

That brings up another issue with the government. In late fall of '79, I was fired/quit the job I had in a Cable TV company. I tried for about three weeks to get another job in the industry before I reluctantly went in to the government office and applied for unemployment assistance. I was married with two children and a mortgage. I think the waiting period at that time was six weeks from the date I applied. During this waiting period, I realized that I wasn't going to be getting a job in any of the cable companies that I had worked for before, and I had nearly worked for them all. That was when I decided to start "Systems 80," my own Cable TV Planning and Design consulting business. I figured that if I could get unemployment assistance for maybe six months, that that would help financially and give us something to live off of while I started my business. I had received my first unemployment cheque and I had to go back to the government agency to report if I had a job yet. I told them that I didn't and that I had started my own company. It was then that I was told that I was cut off from unemployment insurance, and furthermore, that I would have to repay what I already got, as I had started my company before my application went through. So I got nothing; I paid into the compulsory program for years, and just because I wanted to start something for myself, I was cut off. I was angry and still am. Fuck the government, fuck the politicians, and especially fuck most of the heartless bureaucrats that work for the government that are, just doing their job.

Tomorrow would have been one year since the Heart Centre opened. Why is this so hard to heal? Why don't other people seem to have problems? I see them as being okay and having happy lives. So why am I so fucked up? I

Chapter 14 – My Terror and Heartbreak

want to end this suffering, this self abuse, but I'm also confused, afraid, and angry at myself for not being better, doing better, and being able to at least look after and support myself.

I'm just lying on my bed thinking about a lot of things, not feeling anything. I want to feel, I want to open myself to feel and express whatever it is that is holding me back from being able to manifest what I want and desire. I want to be loved, to love, to live an abundant life with joy, peace and harmony but all that seems so far away. I'm afraid to cry and feel sorry for myself. I'm going to turn the lights off and go to sleep.

I can't sleep. I've lived in poverty most all of my life as I've had poor paying jobs, and even when I worked for myself I didn't make much money. My employees, for the most part, made more money than I did as they got their pay cheques regularly, even if it meant that I would have to wait a few days for money to come in. I hate my feelings and I hate expressing my feelings because all that brings is pain and suffering. Also, losing people that were friends, and come to think about it now, they looked after themselves. I had to be there for them in order for them to be there for me in some small way, but when I really needed them, they were gone. I even feel that with Jen, that I have to be there for her, to help her or it's over, she won't want me around. I have to give and give to get just a little. So what are my beliefs, programs and imprints?

It's better to give than to receive.
I have to give in order to get.
You have to give a lot to get a little.
Life isn't easy.
If you want something, you have to work for it.
What good are you if you can't make money?
What good are you if you don't have money?
He who has the most toys wins.
Money is power.

This is also being reflected in my relationships as I either felt I didn't have a good job or enough money, or that if I had more money than they did, I felt better off and guilty and had to take care of them, help them. In all my relationships, I feel I had to give, give a lot to get a little of what I wanted, and that was love, or what I thought was love. I tried to buy love, either with money or with my energy. I'm afraid now that I'll lose Jen as a friend and I feel guilty that all this time I've tried to buy her love by doing things for her so that she would like or need me. I feel ashamed that I go to such lengths or depths because I'm so lonely and in need of love that I'd do almost anything including sacrifice myself in every way.

I also realize that's why I'm jealous of people who don't seem to have to earn trust, respect or have to prove themselves to be accepted or loved. I have judgment on Jen and her friends as I compare myself to them. I have to be there, do things for her and I still get blamed that I didn't do it right or enough, but her other friends just walk in and out as they please and it's okay with her. I've never had a friend where I haven't had to give up part of myself to have a friendship or a relationship, and if I didn't, I wouldn't have one. I had acquaintances that would wave "hi" and have small talk, but no real friends. I'm afraid I've hurt Jen or that I'll hurt her when I read this to her, and that she'll draw away and won't have anything to do with me, and that she'll say she was right all along. I feel there is more to this, and that it is also a lot deeper.

I want to be accepted, even if only one person can accept and love me and that I can do and share things with in the same way that others seem to do. I feel that I'd be okay if I could just get one person to love me, one woman, mate, partner, companion or friend, and so I try to get all these in just one person and exclude the rest because it takes to much energy to feed them all. I feel so alone now, like I'm cut off, cutting myself off from everything. I have no job or money and no place to live on my own. I also feel that I'm losing my best friend, or the only person I could call a friend in that she was the one I could talk to and express my feelings, at least some of them. If I don't do something for somebody, or if I'm not appreciated, what good am I? What worth do I have? If I'm not accepted for something, anything, then why am I here? I must be good for something to somebody? I must be able to make someone happy being with me. Everyone either doesn't care or is unhappy with me in some way or another. I feel I don't belong and that there is no right place for me, I try to fit in but that doesn't work or last. I feel so alone and unloved and I'm frightened at being unwanted, unaccepted, and being different. I'm frightened of expressing my feelings of being alone so I puff myself up and pretend that I don't need anyone, that I can do it on my own, by myself, and then I feel alone when no one is there to help me. I also get angry when someone tries to control me, control what I say or do. I realize that it's my Will that is being controlled by me and I feel so fucked up and I don't know up from spit.

I also feel that I'm going in circles, that I've been saying the same old things over and over and saying that I'm going to change, but I never do. What am I missing? Why am I going in circles? While I can see that I'm still looking for love and acceptance outside myself, I still don't know how to give myself acceptance or self-love. I think I am, but I'm not. Again, what am I not seeing? What am I denying?

♡ As I'm typing this I can see that the reason I was going in circles was that I still couldn't see and admit that I was in denial. I had beliefs that

Chapter 14 – My Terror and Heartbreak

said I was being loving, so in my mind, being loving also meant that I was not in denial. Another reason was that I still didn't know what love, what self-love was, so I didn't know what I was looking for and I couldn't see denial for what it was. Denial was right there in front of my face, but I was blind to it. The pieces were there, the messages were saying it over and over, I just couldn't put them together. ♥

1999 Sept. 28 - I was at Jens today and she was telling me about the work she did with her friend Kim, and how they were using their imagination and pretending and acting out their emotions, and that it was very healing. That just didn't feel right or healing to me and I told her that, and she accused me of not hearing what she was saying, and we got into one of our normal heated "discussions." I triggered her into her anger and rage and she demanded that I leave when I laughed at her comment, "I'm not a hypocrite; I just act like one." I left, as there was no point in continuing.

> 66 *Each day is a miracle. - Shenreed*

Unconditional Love

1999 Sept. 29, 12:47 am - When you give what you call love to another person, it isn't love unconditionally; it has been conditional, out of fear and lack., lack of self-acceptance, and so you try to fill where you are lacking and hurt with someone or even others, or places, or things, be it objects, money, or status. It is to fill this part within you that feels empty. It is the giving of what you refer to as conditional love that you experience what you call exhaustion, of giving until you can't give anymore. There is no lack of love, but what you give and then try to seek is not true love, and so you give of yourself and you fragment and lose parts of yourself as you struggle to fill yourself with what you think is love, or what it is that you think you need. And so it is that you continue until you reach a point where you have to make a choice, and you have to choose to continue to exhaust yourself, or you choose to withdraw yourself, your energy from the relationship and choose to end the relationship. In most cases this comes at a point where it is considered a question of survival. To not submit that part of you that has seen the experience for what it is, but has had to go along with the part of you that was blind to a point where now, even that blind part of you has some hint of awareness and sees that its survival is threatened.

Love, unconditional love does not demand or ask that one need give oneself in order to receive love. Love is there and you merely have to open to receive it, but the dilemma comes when this possibility is not in your belief or programming. For true love is also unlimited to form or to time as these are also illusions. It is not limited to one person and can be felt in as many ways as you are open to feel it. There are no rules and no limits except the ones you put in place by your judgments, programs and beliefs, and of course what you are already imprinted with which is a major issue in your experience you call life.

Love without conditions is true life, is being in the moment and also being totally open to your Will, Spirit, Heart and Body and free from denial, guilt, shame or pre-supposed judgment of the experience, past or future. To experience such love seems like an impossibility, a dream, but it isn't. It is obtainable, not in what you call heaven, but that love (that heaven) can be brought down to Earth to the physical reality of third density of the Earth plane.

Allow yourself to be open to love and to allow the Universe to bring you all that you desire. Release, let go of your judgments, beliefs, programs and imprints that say it is not possible, and watch the magic, the miracle of life brought upon you. Blessings, Sananda, your brother

> **To be in the present moment, one has presence. - Shenreed**

1999 Sept. 30 - When I was at Jens today she put on a new CD that had some "cha-cha" music on it. I hadn't danced for years and I was in the mood, so I taught her a couple of the basic moves that I still remembered from my Ballroom dancing lessons. I enjoyed dancing and Jen did too.

Later I did some emotional work with Jen and we got this partial insight that the Spirit (Mind) can't remember what happened during a traumatic experience because Spirit was out of the body, and when he came back, he had no idea of what happened. Then there is this other part of us, the Will (intuition, feelings and emotions) that remembers what happened, but doesn't want Spirit to know for fear of hurting him and losing him again. There is more to this, but this is all that we got at the time.

Chapter 15 - Survival and Circling

1999 Oct. 6 - Jen and I were doing some shopping this morning and after we left one store, I felt very close and connected to her. I was feeling the joy of the experience we were having and a part of me just wanted to give her a hug, but I denied acting spontaneously as I felt she was too busy or whatever, and I never said anything either. I feel I can't even demonstrate simple forms of affection like a hug when I want to, and that I have to wait for them to make the move or I have to ask if it's all right.

Later at the library, we bumped into a man that I knew well and that she had met only momentarily twice before at the Heart Centre. He saw us come in and started coming toward us, and as he got near he extended his arms to Jen and I felt that she basically leapt into his arms and hugged him like a long lost friend, while I simply got a nod from him. Later when we left the library, she told me that when she saw him she just wanted to run up to him and hug him, and that it felt nice to be in his arms. While I was activated, I denied saying anything again. Later, I was driving her home and before we even got to her street, she already had her bags in her arms, and before I had the van stopped she was opening the door as if she couldn't get out fast enough. She just said, "Bye" as she closed the door and walked to her apartment without so much as a backward glance. I feel unimportant and used.

Last night after I finished the meditation/past life classes, I drove by Jens on the way home and saw that her lights were still on. I stopped and rang the doorbell; René, her toy poodle barked, but there was no response so I figured that she must be in the bathroom. I left and stopped at the donut shop before I drove home. When I got home, she had called and left two messages saying that she had heard the door bell and figured it was me, but was too tired to answer the door, and besides, there was also too much clothes and stuff in the hallway to go around to answer the door. I felt that if it had been her "lover" friend, she would have been at the door in two seconds, but it was just me and I'm not important. There's a part of me that is angry and wants to say, "Well if I'm not important to you then you're not important to me," and we'll see how you like that." This also ties into the feelings of being used and that she only calls me when she needs me to do something for her, then I'm important, otherwise, who's John?

So what part of me believes that I'm not important? That my feelings are not important and that I can't express them because the people I'm with don't even seem to be aware that I exist. I EXIST! God damm it, look at me! Why do you treat me differently and say you don't? Yeah, I guess I'm just around so much that you forget about me and take me for granted until you need me or want something from me, or want me to help you. I'm angry at that, go fuck yourself; I'll take you for granted. I really want to hurt Jen back, or anyone who I feel takes me for granted. So what part of me takes me, my feelings for granted? I want to heal this.

I heard a gentle voice whisper, "Keep going!"

Now I feel blank, numb like what's the use, nothing is going to change after all the work, the expressing. I feel what's the use, people don't change, don't care, they say they do but don't act that way, or if they do, it's only in that moment and then when it's gone you're taken for granted again. It's like you don't exist, I'm not one of them, not important, not accepted, not good enough, and no one can accept me as I am. I have to change and fit into what they want and need to be recognized, and only when they want or need it. I feel that it's not right to be me and also the wrong time to be me. There is no place and no time for me.

So what's left? I have no place and no time when I can express me and be recognized and accepted for who I am and what I need. I feel like such an outcast, a misfit, as I don't fit in. I want to experience what others seem to experience without any effort. It seems to drain me to get even a little attention, let alone affection, or even the statement or recognition that when I do act spontaneously that it's okay.

1999 Oct. 13 - I had another class last night and I drove past Jens place around 11:15 pm. The lights were still on and I was going to drop in but I felt it was too late. Later when I talked to her, she said that she was up and would have loved some company. Go figure, nothing I do is right.

I have judgments on Jen and one of the things that bothers me is that when she knows that I'm coming over, she leaves the door unlocked and I let myself in. I walk up the stairs and down the hallway to the living room. She's either sitting in her chair watching TV, listening to music, reading, or just sitting there waiting. I resent that she doesn't make an effort or even express that she is happy to see me by even occasionally greeting me at the door, or even just getting up off her chair. If I want to see her, I have to do the work and make the effort. I'm taken for granted as she says, "Just make yourself at home." Well what if I didn't come into the living room? What if I went into the kitchen and turned on the radio and just made myself at home, grabbed a bag of chips and relaxed in the rocking chair. How would you feel? It's your place but you're not important enough to be even acknowledged.

I'm really angry. So what part of me feels there is no right place or time for me? If I want to be me, to do what I want, then I have to do it alone, by myself or I have to wait until another person also feels like doing it. I

Chapter 15 - Survival and Circling

usually jump at the opportunity to do something with somebody else because that usually is the only time I get to do something with another person. God, I feel so lonely, so broken hearted. I feel so needy, so desperate for any little crumb of acceptance let alone affection or tenderness. I only choose to do things that I know they like or want to do, and that they will do with me when I ask them. I only ask them when I feel it's a safe thing and place, and if it's right time for them so that they'll say yes. I can't share what I want to share; I have to share only what they want me to share and when they want me to share it. I had asked Jen to come and see my place when I lived in Moonstone, Baum Beach, Midland and now Penetang, but it never happened. It's never okay, something is always wrong. You can't do what I want with me, but I have to do what you want with you. I think of how I offer to do things to make your dreams come true, but what about me, my dreams? I don't remember anyone really sharing my dreams, my wants or my desires.

I feel so desperate, so needy for love and acceptance that I'd even sell my dreams in favor of another's and maybe, maybe if I'm lucky, I can slip a part of my dream into theirs. But if I do, then I'd better be prepared to do all the work because if I want anyone to be a part of my dream, I have to do it because it's not really a part of their dream. But in order for my dream to manifest, it has to manifest as a part of their dream and I have to take on their part also. That sucks. I'm angry. I've always wanted a partner, an equal to share a dream. It would be nice to share a dream without me having to do it, all for the satisfaction of only one tiny part of it that is actually mine. Not that I don't agree with the rest, but it isn't mine, and even though I can see and feel it, it's not the same as if it was a common dream with shared responsibilities. But to not be alone and to do something with another, I have to compromise and do what they want, and then do all of the work.

So what part of me feels that in order to do what I want, that I have to do it alone. I feel what's the use, where's this all going, nowhere. I feel used, beaten, and worthless, and I only feel I'm acceptable when I'm doing something for somebody else.

So what part of me feels I have to deny being myself to be accepted? I also feel that being accepted means being loved. So to be accepted and loved, I have to deny myself. Fuck! That pisses me off! I hate people, fuckers, users and bastards, all one way, fuck you, I'm angry! Who needs you? Who needs this fucking world! Go and fuck yourselves, all of you, I don't need your kind of love, I don't want it anymore, all this fucking conditional so called love. I have to compromise myself on your terms to get anything, any little thing that feels like love and acceptance. I have to give, and give, and give until I can't give anymore. I say, fuck you, I'd rather be alone, but that's a lie. I don't want to be alone, I want to love and be loved, and I want to experience life, to share life with people. I feel so alone and on the outside. Nature is okay, I can share my experiences, my feelings with nature as it happens as there are no conditions, just my feelings and it's okay. But it's not the same or okay when it comes to even sharing the same moment in nature with someone. I don't know how I'm going to heal this.

1999 Oct. 15 - I made up and posted some "Handyman" signs around town, trying to get some money coming in as the meditations and the other groups aren't working out again. When I was talking to Jen, she said she wanted to come out to meet Irene and to see my place, and she also said that if she was coming out to see me, that she should stop in to see Kim. I felt hurt that it has to be about someone else and not just about me, that I'm not enough and she feels that she has to treat everyone the same. Yeah and I'm also pissed off as I'll be the one picking her up and dropping her off at Kim's place, and then later picking her up and taking her home. What a fool I am!

1999 Oct. 18 - I was angry for most of the day and it wasn't until later that I figured it out. I had picked up my mail and there were bills in it, triggering my issues with money. I intend to let go of my belief that money is the solver of problems, a god, and rather use it as a tool, as an expression, and not a measure of who I am.

1999 Oct. 19 - I had two people show up for meditation and we did some work on clearing astral attachments.

1999 Oct. 21 - I went to a local sweat lodge tonight with four men and four women taking part in the ceremony. It was an okay experience, but it didn't even come close to the previous one I mentioned. Jen is going into another of her three days of silence tonight.

1999 Oct. 24 - I did a handyman job today. I replaced a blown fuse, installed a ceiling fan, cleaned two chimneys, a fireplace, and a wood stove, and also started to rake leaves and do some yard work. Later that evening, I was talking to Jen and I hung up on her as I feel I can't touch my real issues with her without getting cut off, so what's the use. I resent that I'm there for her no matter what, guiding her through a present or a past life regression and expressing what I'm picking up or feeling from her or her body, regardless of what emotions or physical sensations are being brought up. It's okay if it's just about her, but when I'm beginning to get activated into my issues that's when she berates me for expressing myself, and accuses me of pulling her out of her activation and of not helping her. I feel I have no choice but to do it on my own.

1999 Oct. 26 – Yesterday, I started to touch my emotions with Jen and when she started to show her anger at my expressing myself, I closed down and

Chapter 15 - Survival and Circling

withdrew. I must be frightened of anger, especially from someone I care for. She said something yesterday about power, and that we believe we have the power to make people happy and also sad, and that this is one of the biggest illusions we have. I don't know what I felt after she got angry, but numb, loneliness, cold, detached and withdrawn probably sum it up pretty good. She said that she didn't want to be hurt again by my expressing my emotions. Again, I said nothing, but left so that there wouldn't be any chance of that happening.

1999 Oct. 27 - Jen and Kim have an appointment at the Rosewood Centre for Women this afternoon, and I've got to pick them up. This should be interesting to see what develops, what emotions come up for all of us. Part of me wants to say fuck you, find you own way there. Maybe that's it, my judgment? I take time, energy and money (gas) that I don't have, to help her and I resent her not coughing up the odd $1 or $2 for gas, yet spending $18 at the Salvation Army for more clothes or other things that I feel she doesn't need. In the three years that I've known her, she's never once filled my gas tank. Hell it costs me $2.50 - $3.00 each time I come into Midland to see her (round trip) and then another $1 - $2 to run around and do her errands.

This is bringing up more memories for me as I'm remembering high school. After I got my car, I had a couple of "friends" who I would pick up and drive around, and "cruise" the local gathering spots. I remember that they never freely offered me any gas money and just expected me to be the provider because I had a regular job after school and was making more money than they were. Finally, I started asking them for money for gas, and they either said they didn't have any, or that they just had enough for a cup of coffee. Only the odd time did they throw in a couple of bucks for gas. I spend my money and used my car to entertain these so-called friends just so that I wouldn't be alone.

So what's my real issue, that friendships are something that I have to buy? Friends are more important than money? What is money but time and effort or energy? I deny myself pleasure or leisure, to work for someone else. So basically, I trade a piece of myself for money, which I then turn around and use that money, (or the traded piece of myself) to buy a friend. So I'm actually giving up a part of myself in favor of the other person. I'm sacrificing myself for another! I'm beginning to feel that this has been a pattern all my life. If I don't sacrifice myself by doing things for other people, then I sacrifice myself through money. Even work was a lot of effort for a little return.

Everyone's happiness is more important than mine, and other people are more important than I am. If I don't make other people happy then they won't like me or want to be with me. I also have to do what they do that makes them happy, again sacrificing myself in favor of them. If they're happy maybe I can be happy too, or at least they won't be bitching, criticizing, condemning, demanding, shouting or angry at me. It's my job, my responsibility to keep the people I care for happy, to work my ass off, to give of my time, energy and money just so they'll be happy and I'll have a friend. So this is also where my feelings of being used comes from. Even in the Centre, people would come to the workshops or meetings if they were free, but not if they had to pay for them. People want what I have and can do, but they don't want to pay for it. It's not them, well it is, and it isn't. I'm attracting such people because I have this belief that it is better to give than to receive. Bullshit!

I have guilt saying that's cruel, heartless and selfish to think of yourself first and others second. That to be a "good" person you had to give if you have more than others, help another in need, even if it's just a little, and that you have to give, especially if it's for someone you care for.

Say that you were with a friend and you wanted an ice cream cone but you had only enough money for one cone. You know that your friend or loved one would also like one, but that they don't have money to get their own. Guilt would tell you that you should buy them the ice cream cone and deny that you want one for yourself. That you should tell a little "white lie" and say that you don't want one or that you couldn't eat a whole cone, thinking that if you're lucky, you can have a lick from their cone. Guilt also tells you that buying the cone for another will somehow make you happy knowing that you made someone else happy and that you'll get your just reward in heaven because you're a good person, not selfish, and because you love and care for another. Boy, that's an old program! I'm so afraid of God, of not doing what he expects me to do, that guilt tells me is love. I also have judgments that other people are going to go to hell and suffer, or that they don't love God or anyone else because they're selfish and just think of themselves.

So all this, the government not helping me, my working for half the minimum wage delivering newspapers, my $10.00/hr handyman jobs as well as the $10.00/session meetings, all reflect this belief in some form or another. Between my beliefs and guilt, I feel fucked, and have been all my life and this is just part of my issues. Relationships, sex, etc., are a whole different, hey! Wait a minute, they're also related. Putting other people first, being grateful for what you have, other people are not as lucky as you, don't be selfish, share, etc., are just different versions of no self-worth and no self-love.

These are some of my fucked up beliefs I take as truths. Sharing and giving is good; not sharing or giving is bad. Helping people is good, hurting people is bad. Making sad people happy is good, but making happy people sad is bad. Obeying your elders is good, while disobeying them is bad. Believing what another person says is good, but not believing what another person says is bad. Doing things that make other people happy is good, doing things that make other people unhappy is bad. Enjoying yourself when others are not is bad.

Making other people happy is what I thought love is (was) and to do any of that was to sacrifice myself in order to ease another's burden, pain and suffering. To give them what they desired or needed, and to help them in any way that I could, made me a good, loving and caring person. Asking also comes into play here, as I feel I don't deserve any help, and that I'm bad if I can't look after myself, and that I'm being selfish, greedy and using people. I should not be such a baby; I should be able to not only take care of myself, but others too. I'm ashamed to ask for what I want and ashamed to say, "Hey, I'm no better off than you, or in fact, I'm even worse off, can you help me."

More beliefs disguised as truths. Everyone likes a winner, winning is good, no one likes a loser, losing is bad. Having is good; having means you can share, which is also good. Not having is bad. Not having means you can't share, and that's not good. Helping means you're nice, caring and loving. Not helping means you're selfish, not nice, caring or loving. Asking for help is bad because other people shouldn't have to help you, you should help other people in order to be good.

I'm beginning to see that there are many layers and issues here, and that it's not simple, yet at the same time I feel it is simple, it's just that I don't know and trust myself to take the step to end this confusion. I release all these imprints, programs, beliefs, judgments and guilt, and I ask that whenever I slip into them, that I want to become aware of them so that I can change or release them. I want to heal and I want to become whole, but I can't do that if I'm constantly giving myself, my power, away in one form or another.

> *Being and doing all that you are. - Shenreed*

Doing Verses Being

1999 Oct. 29 - Greetings and welcome back. We are most pleased that you have begun to receive us again. Indeed, you have locked and blocked us from coming to you in this manner as you focused, not focused, but more decided in that you wanted to communicate in a manner similar to Irene, but that actually you are not ready for in this moment. Your intent is, as we mentioned, not focused for that reality, is close, but still lacking.

What you are lacking, and it is now time to activate, is your drive, your passion, your sexuality, sensuality, creativity, the wonder and the excitement that is, and has been missing in your experience you have called life to this point. It is so shut down, lacking, that there is a part of you that has even given up hope that this can be a reality, and holds out no hope for this as a possibility, if not probable reality. And that is okay, for you need to feel the extreme of this aspect of duality, this aspect of Mother, Heart, Body and even Spirit, for all have felt this in their own way through different experiences. It is now time to especially heal all aspects of your Heart and Will. You are already on that path, as well as accepting more responsibility for your feelings and their expression. Blessings, Merlin PS, the Magic is about to begin.

4:47 am - Indeed you need do nothing, just be and become all that you are. You still seek to do what is your path, your destiny; it is time to be what it is you have chosen your path to be. You have chosen your path and in being, do you do what it is you are. It is not doing such and such that you become what you are, for this is backwards and will never work permanently, with fulfillment, love, joy, peace and harmony. You need to let go of having to do, in order to be, and this is also a part of your issue with money and abundance. You still believe that you have to do something in order to receive abundance and this is not true. You also have fear in asking for what you want and desire for you fear you do not deserve it, and even if you, in defiance, feel you deserve it, you also believe you need to work for it and sacrifice something, a part of yourself in order to get it.

This is difficult for you at this time, but allow yourself now to feel this to whatever depth and truth you can. This is also tied into your first, second and third chakras, do you see the connection? We know you do not see it or we would not be with you on this part of your journey, experience. Now read this part of our message and allow its words to fill you. Blessings Mother and Father, Mary, Alexis, Sananda, Thor, Zeus, Nero, Merlin, Astrid and indeed the company of heaven.

♡ As I'm proof reading this portion of the book and especially this message, I'm struck with the fact that I'm still stuck with this issue of trying to do instead of be. I feel that I've never, in all my existence, been allowed to be me and be supported with my hearts desires. I don't even know what that means as it feels so remote and impossible. I want this, I can feel it in my heart, but at the same time I feel lost, alone and confused. How can I be who I am, if I don't know who I am? Tears are rolling down my cheeks as I'm trying to type this. It feels like an eternity that I've been working on proofing this section of the book. I would do a page and then I'd be triggered, as I'd experience similar feelings I did when I originally wrote them, but now in a different form or level. I know this is another level of healing for me and that I'm working on the lower chakras.

I feel like my first day in school again, I'm here, but I don't know anything, not even how to communicate or to even ask for what I need. I feel lost, alone, and heartbroken again, and I feel that my terror is denied or has been replaced with despair, hopelessness, and dumbness. A feeling of what's

Chapter 15 - Survival and Circling

the use, I can't be myself as now, I don't even know who I am, and the harder I try to do, the worst things seem to get.

I've been getting the message to BE and in my BE-ing I will be doing that what I am meant to be. A part of me knows the truth in those words but my problem is what do they mean and how do I apply them, bring them to this physical world? It's like reading the words of how to ride a bike but unless you have a physical bike and have ridden one, experienced it for yourself, it is impossible to feel and know what riding a bike is like. I know the words hold truth, but until I can feel and experience them, they are just words that I long to experience, but can't find the ways and means of doing it in love. I also feel that writing and getting this book published is part of my next stage or level of healing, and is part of my being and doing, and that is why I'm being triggered again. ♥

1999 Oct. 30, 1:03 am – I awoke and wrote the following poem.
I don't want to run.
I don't want to hide.
I don't want to bury.
What I feel inside.

1999 Nov. 1 – Today I received a phone call from Andrea, the manager of one of the apartment buildings in Midland. She saw my handyman ad and wants me to give her a quote to paint apartment walls and ceilings, sand and re-do the hardwood floors, as well as some minor repairs. I'm looking forward to getting some part-time work, as it will give me a financial start.

1999 Nov 5, 4:02 am - Yesterday Jen touched that she wanted me to acknowledge that I hurt her mentally, emotionally and physically that time I kicked her. I couldn't do that as it didn't feel right, and I was confused by what she was trying to get me to do. She said that she had opened to me like she never opened to anyone, and that now she felt I was rejecting her, and then she asked, no, she told me to leave.

I was at the bottom of the stairs and about to leave when I felt I had to return to tell her that she didn't need my approval or acknowledgment, but rather that she needed to acknowledge it to herself. I felt I was being blamed and forced to take responsibility for everything that happened, and that it will stick on me forever if I acknowledge that I hurt her in the way she said I did. I also had guilt and fear issues come up when she said that I kicked her with intent and such force to purposely hurt her, but I felt it was an unconscious self-defense action, although I was aware of her coming at me.

She also brought up a lot of other instances that seemed insignificant and blown out of proportion, like the time when we were in a grocery line and I blew on the back of her neck, or another time when I tugged the peak of her baseball cap down. She even brought up things that she felt were abusive to her that I did to other people. She seemed to entirely forget her abusive behavior to me.

Just last week we were on the highway, driving back from her appointment at an acupuncturist in Orillia, when she attacked and punched me as I was driving. I had to really grab and squeeze her left arm and force her down and away from me so that I could get the van stopped before we had an accident. And the day before yesterday, she was poking me in the ribs and I told her to stop as it was hurting me. She replied that she was just poking me softly. She then poked me again, saying that it didn't really hurt me like I had hurt her. Maybe it's the same thing, do I have to acknowledge that I was hurt and not to have to wait for her to acknowledge and say that she hurt me, I don't know?

I also feel pressure from her, but it's in the form of guilt that I did something wrong, that I'm responsible for her feelings and that I'm evil if I make her feel bad. That I did it on purpose and that it's my fault and my responsibility to change or fix it, and that I'm not supposed to ever do that again. That I'm a bad person and that people get hurt or angry at me if what I do makes them feel bad or hurts them. That they won't like me anymore and won't be my friend and will call me names and will tell other people not to have anything to do with me. That they will tell stories about me that I'm a trouble maker, that they will hold it over me and will want me to make it right or to re-pay them a thousand times over. That they'll never forget or forgive me, and they will always remember and hold it against me when they feel hurt or they want something to go their way. They have control and power over me, or rather, they don't have control and power over me, I give it away. I give my power away. So that's it! I think? I don't feel it at this moment, no tears, but there is a knowing that if this isn't it, it's on the right track.

I'm afraid to be me, to say and do what I want for fear people will reject me, and so, in order not to be rejected I give my power away by either doing what they want, or by running away and avoiding the situation. In both cases I'm denying myself, and in denying myself, I'm giving my power away. I feel so full of guilt that I'm evil, the bad one, the misfit, the outcast, weird, strange, not welcome, different and not accepted.

Again, I hate my feelings and I hate being me. I'm ashamed to be me. I don't want to be me because being me isn't good enough and just causes problems. I don't want to feel what I always feel and that is alone, different and not accepted. I want to be the same as everyone else, I want to be accepted as I am and not for something that I'm not. I feel that I've so imprinted and programmed myself that I don't even know who I really am or even what my true feelings are.

I was thinking of the word responsibility that Jen said this afternoon that has stuck with me. Responsibility, respond to my ability, allowing myself

Chapter 15 - Survival and Circling

to respond to my ability, the ability to respond, of being able to respond, being allowed to respond.

Yesterday, Irene's word of the day was dignity. We discussed and asked ourselves how one can have dignity when one is full of guilt and shame, and feels they are not good enough and not able to respond, or lack the ability to respond. I need to take responsibility, to take my power back and to let go of the guilt and shame. Responsibility is responding to the best of my ability and not taking on or being responsible, or responding to others needs out of fear, guilt or shame. I have made my response conform to their words that I'm wrong or my feelings are wrong, and so I deny my feelings, my response, and I respond accordingly in denial.

1999 Nov. 9 - I started to do some work at the apartment building a couple of weeks ago. I'd generally start around 9:00 am and work until 6 and sometimes 9:00 pm. I was also busy doing other individual handyman jobs, and in-between that, I'd spend time with Jen, and in the late evenings with Irene over a cup of apple cider after she got home from work at 11:30 pm. Since Jen and I were having our differences, and as I was working a lot, she had connected with Irene and now the two of them were talking more on the phone.

Power

1999 Nov. 09 - Power is a powerful word with many meanings, uses and attributes, and one that is also taken or given, and so lightly thought of as the value of the word freedom. Freedom and power are similar and opposites, and yet are taken and so lightly thought of as the word love. Love, freedom power, peace, joy, abundance all these are very profound and powerful words and also taken for granted.

It is time to begin to reclaim your lost power, your greatness, your essence, and your gifts. Call it, call them what you will, but it is time to begin to assemble the fruits of your labor, to harvest what you have so long ago sown and so patiently cared for and nurtured, and are now about to savor their true delights with, and in love.

Indeed, there is this duality within you, one that yearns and the other that fears this thing called power, and with it comes right use of power, right use of Will. The power we speak of has more to do with the power to be, to become you, your true self in manifested form. To take back, not so much take back in the present, but not to give your power away in the present and to take back what you have given away in the past. Indeed, you have also taken others power and this also needs to be returned to their right place.

In the times ahead, you will begin to notice circumstances where you are witnessing a gathering as well as a demonstration of your power, your powers, as you begin to collect and demonstrate your ability to be yourself.

Journey to the Heart Centre

This will come in many ways and forms as you create your reality, being aware of your power and your magic. Indeed, shape shifting, travel, including time, materialization, multi-simultaneous awareness, as well as senses both known and unknown will be experienced. You have great powers and great love. You have many colors to present, many gifts to share with those who are ready, as there are many who are now ready, who seek to learn what you have to share. It is time to also not cast pearls before swine, and not to waste your power on those who do not understand, are not awake, or who are aware but refuse to move to awaken.

You are confused by this message and yet do know why it is being given. We are pleased, and indeed, you will be writing a book, many books if you choose, and this also confuses you. Rest assured, allow the process to unfold and all will be revealed in its right time and order. Take a risk, expect the unexpected, and release your fears of becoming who you really are. Blessings. Mother and Father and the company of heaven.

Talents and Gifts

1999 Nov. 14 - Indeed you will be writing a book(s) and publications, as well as lecturing and speaking in public gatherings, a communicator, an orator, an oracle, are some of your many talents and gifts you will be unveiling in the times ahead. Rest assured that you will know when that time is upon you. You will have no doubts and you will, as you would term it, be driven with passion, love and desire. You will feel and you will know, but allow yourself to be surprised and WOWED! Enjoy yourself, for you are not only human, but you are also human, and you are here to experience humanity, polarity and duality. Allow yourself to begin to enjoy life, allow yourself to receive love, allow yourself to be open to receive and you will know by feeling if it is love or not, and allow yourself to be open to express on all levels.

You are on your path, allow, continue to be open and you will be guided and assisted. As you sense, you are beginning to, you are going to become more involved in the Internet; this is also how you are going to reach many people. Allow yourself to feel and heal, and to change your programs and beliefs that hold these fears present. Allow yourself to express, to create your magic, your wonder and to feel your excitement. As you, as we have said before, take a risk, release your fears, and expect the unexpected. Merlin

1999 Nov. 19 - Jen and I haven't really talked for the past five days. I've called her two or three times a day and I just keep getting her answering machine. I know she's home, as she doesn't go out with anyone else except her mother, when she doesn't want anything to do with me. She called me back last night at 11:00 p.m., and we got into an argument regarding

Chapter 15 - Survival and Circling

Christmas when I told her that she had already told me the story that she was telling me. She got angry and hung up.

Later, when Irene came home and we were having our usual apple cider, I was telling her that I feel I'm slipping off my path, that now I'm working almost full time at the apartment building. I also told her that I was feeling that changes are coming in my relationship with Jen, as I feel that I don't even know her and that we've become strangers. I feel that Jen and I are going to be splitting up, losing touch, just like everyone else in my life and that I'll be left alone again. I'm afraid of being left alone and of having no friends, feeling disconnected from everyone and everything, and of not being able to share or experience things with others. I'll be on the outside looking in at life passing me by, and that all there is, is work and no play and where's the balance in that?

1999 Dec. 9 - I hate being limited and being told what to do, and when, where and how to do it, and also what I can or can't say, and where, when, and how I can express myself. I can't talk and express my feelings when I want to, only when it's appropriate and when I have their permission. I also hate not having my own space, nothing here is really mine and I can't do what I really want to, when I want, and for that I feel limited. Dave reminds me of my father, mumbling and shouting up at me from the bottom of the stairs, making me have to come out of my room to and ask him what he wants, which is his form of control over me. I'm angry, I want to shout at him, "Are you deaf, stupid or just an idiot, or all the above. Can't you see that I'm busy or resting and why in the hell are you mumbling and shouting at the same time?" I feel like I have to be on my toes all the time because it's not my house and that I have to be nice and please him or else what's going to happen to me? I owe him for letting me stay here so I have to be nice.

Jen got the insight the other day that what we envy the most in others is what we deny the most in ourselves. I envy people who have freedom in ways that I don't, and that they can do what, when and how they want, like buy nice things, go on holidays and enjoy friends. I feel I can't do what I want. Why? What's telling me, what program do I have in place that says I can't do what I want, that I'm limited? Why do I feel I have to be limited? Why am I limiting myself that I can only do so much and no more, that I can have so much but no more, that I can say so much but no more? That all I can be is this little part of me, but no more. I sound like a broken record, going over and over the same old lines. God, I want to be me, I want to be all that I am. I don't want to limit myself anymore. I want to express who I am in the moment. This is what I want. To be who I am and that it's okay, that there's acceptance for me to be unlimited and free.

All my life I've been told who I am, what I was, good or bad and to not feel what I was feeling and that I should feel this or that, say, be or do such and such and that that would make me a better person. All my life I've been trying to be this "better" person instead of just being me, and in trying to be the imaginary perfect, better person I lost me. I lost my childhood, my innocence, my joy, creativity, spontaneity, happiness, and self-love. I sold myself, I denied myself, the real me, to be this better "phony" me that people would like, accept, and maybe love. It started with my parents, then school, church, peers, and work.

I was thinking of Andrea, the manager at the apartment building. She's on me at the moment, telling me that I'm too slow and charge too much. I also realize that she's on me because that's how she also feels about herself, that she is also trying to be a better person. I talked to her and expressed my feelings about the work I do and that I don't work like others, as I'm not the other person. She acknowledged that and I feel she was just saying that to try to get more out of me to make her look good in her bosses eyes.

Denial, I've denied myself outrageously, totally to be someone, anyone that others would accept. I didn't like who I was; I didn't like being me as there was shame and guilt that I didn't want. I felt I wasn't loved, wasn't lovable, wasn't good enough just as I was, and that I had to become someone else. That I had to be what everyone else told me to be and if I could do that, then I was good, good enough so that I could get accepted but that wasn't good enough either. If I did what they told me to do without being told, then I was too good, showing off, so then I'd have to be not "too good" and maybe that would make them happy, but that didn't work either. It just went back and forth; I couldn't win and still can't win. I sabotage myself if I think I'm too good. I stop myself so that people wouldn't criticize or envy me. If I had more than others had, then I'd have to give it away or lose it so that I'd have the same or less. Having less makes others feel okay and not angry at me, so I always try to have less, but less is no good either as people don't like you because you don't have what they have, you aren't the same as, or as good as they are. This is all fucked and I'm just going around in circles again, there seems to be no fucking end to it.

1999 Dec. 16 5:34 am - Jen told me of a boy and his grade nine buddies who randomly called her one night and she ended up talking to him for a while. Later, he called back and it started to be a regular thing with them. She told me that she finds his energy exciting and stimulating. Humph, I'm jealous that she has found someone who stimulates and excites her and that she wants to talk to, or will call back right away whenever he calls. I call her and all I get is the answering machine. Sometimes I don't talk or see her for days until she needs me for something, or she calls to tell me what's going on in her life with someone else. Why do I feel like I'm on the outside? I also relate to the boy as he appears innocent, sensitive and wanting a friend, someone to talk

Chapter 15 - Survival and Circling

to. When she told me that the subject of sex came up, she told him that there's more to it than just having sex, and to wait until he's ready and finds the right person. That brought up my issues of sex, reminding me that there is no right mate in my life.

Yes I still feel sex is special, but I also feel it's fucked (no pun intended) and I don't feel that there's anyone out there that isn't fucked up where sex is concerned. So what's all this sacredness of sex all about? I feel you're either in a relationship having sex and getting fucked over in denial, or you're not in a relationship, not having sex and fucking yourself over in denial. I'm ANGRY, frustrated, and lonely. Fuck the sex, I just want to be held and to hold someone, to kiss and be kissed, to touch and be touched, to feel not so alone. I'm Human, so why can't I be human? I'm waiting for Ms. Right and she's not knocking at my door. Oh yeah, well maybe I'm not knocking on Ms. Rights door either.

So I guess I either find a friend, someone that I can talk to and share certain things with, and then find someone else to have sex with, but where there is no possibility of a deep friendship. Why can't I find or have it all? I feel I'm no good and that I'm past any opportunity to experience joy, pleasure, life and love as I'm too old, don't have any money, job or career. I also don't enjoy being with people because of the bullshit that goes on and that I can't be me. I feel I don't fit in and that there's no place and no one in my life that I can share all of me.

I heard a gentle voice say, "Yes, but who does not love you? YOU!"

If I just have to love myself then what's the point of being human and in a world full of people? What's the point in having relationships, contacts with other people and experiencing things together?

FUCK! FUCK! FUCK! I'm confused, I'm angry, alone, and hurting. I think I'm healing but things don't seem to be getting any better, in fact they seem to be getting worse. I feel life has and is passing me by, and that I'll never find the love and happiness I seek, and that true love is just an illusion, that I feel is possible but only in my dreams, and I don't even dream anymore. I feel hopeless. I feel that no one really understands and accepts me, and that I can't just be me, that I can only show a part of me, and not any part that they don't want to see.

I don't understand, what is honesty, intimacy, friendship and sex? What is love? It makes me feel sad to question love. I feel caught, trapped and I can't really explain it as I feel; I know there's more but I don't know what, or how to get to it, to have it, to experience it and not just by myself. I can enjoy a sunset, an ice cream cone, a walk in the rain, but to share those experiences with someone else and others, that's where there is a problem. When it gets to be the physical contact with others and in dealing with others thoughts, emotions and all the issues that come up, especially with the opposite sex, and the same sex too for that matter, that's when I have issues. There are no male friends in my life, I have the most contact with Dave, Irene's husband, but he seems so far from where I am that we really have very little in common to even talk about. The rest of the people in my life are woman and I feel I have only one real friend Jen, but Irene is starting to open up and to also share. I feel most people can take a little bit of me but not all of me, that I'm too much, too intense, to demanding, so I pretend I'm this little candle flickering in the dark, when in reality I'm this huge red-hot bubbling volcano. Well it's 6:35 a.m., and I'm going to try and get a little sleep before the alarm goes off.

1999 Dec. 17, 5:30 am - I had a dream about a teenage boy who went to his teacher and said, "Thank you for believing and loving me and for teaching me to believe and love in myself. I've had this dark tumor inside of me ever since I was born and I loved that dark tumor more than the rest of me and it just grew and grew. It had grown bigger than me until that day that you told me to believe and love in myself.

I thought and thought about the dream and finally I said to myself out loud, "I denounce all darkness that would keep me from believing and loving myself. I move this darkness, this tumor that would destroy me out and off of me to its right place and I will no longer feed it with my energy. I will love myself and I will believe in me; I will heal all those parts of me that I didn't love and that I didn't believe were good enough to be me. I reject that darkness that wants to keep me from love and light. I reject that darkness, that voice that would keep me from experiencing love, life, joy, abundance, peace, harmony and balance."

I'll try to remember this story about the dark tumor every time I'm feeling that I don't love myself. I will consciously believe and love those parts of me that this dark tumor wants to destroy.

> *The inner critic is Lucifer's voice. - Shenreed*

1999 Dec. 17 - I've been working at the apartment building pretty steady for the past few weeks, but I feel that will be ending soon as the apartment building is being sold. It feels like the new owners are going to have their own people do the required work, and that the other sub-contractor and myself will be out of a job. So until then, I'll just take what I can get.

Uniqueness

1999 Dec. 19 - Indeed you have not written for some time but that is not to say that you were not in contact. You have not left your path or fallen behind others around you. You are witnessing the diversity of each and

Chapter 15 - Survival and Circling

the uniqueness of each, but you fail to recognize your uniqueness, your greatness, and your gifts. All are connected yet all are separate, individual, and unique. You have chosen a difficult task, one of much courage and love, and indeed, you are a Wayshower, a leader, not only of other Wayshowers and light workers, but also of human and non-human on many levels. So you feel that you are not good enough compared to those you aid. Recognize that you aid them and that you may not see, hear or feel as they do on the physical level at this time, but know that you do, for you are a teacher, a healer. Trust that soon you will know all that you desire and that you will begin to experience all that you desire. Your time is at hand but it would not serve your higher purpose to be given that before you are ready. Trust my son, trust, and know that you are love, that you are loved, that you are Heart. Blessings, Mother and Father

1999 Dec. 19 - I've been having a cup of hot apple cider in the evenings when Irene gets home from work and during these times she has been sharing more of what she sees as well as messages she hears. She has been seeing different animal guides with me, the last three have been snake, owl, and bear. A couple of insights we got were that behind your greatest fear lies your greatest gifts, and what we hate most in others is what we hate most in ourselves.

> ❝ *Behind your greatest fear lies your greatest gift. - Shenreed*

1999 Dec. 21 - Tonight there was a local sweat lodge, celebrating the last full moon of the millennium as well as the winter solstice. We all had to bring something that was personal and that we treasured as a giveaway. I looked around for things that I could give and then I saw my turtle pendant necklace with an amber body insert. Whenever I wore it, I always received comments on how unique it was. I kept trying to find something else to giveaway, but I kept coming back to it. Reluctantly, I agreed and took it with me. After the sweat, we all had to give a little story about our give away before the actual ceremony. When it finally came to me, I became emotional, tears rolled down my face and my voice cracked as I tried to share my story of what the turtle meant to me and that it was hard for me to give it up. I was the only one that was emotional when talking about their giveaway. Later, we had our giveaway ceremony and I received a small hand-made drum. It was nice, but it wasn't my turtle pendant. After the ceremony, several women came up and said that they were hoping they would end up with my pendant and thanked me for sharing my story.

1999 Dec. 24, 4:34 am - I feel that I still put Jen above me, that her wants, needs and desires are more important than mine. I feel that because she can't go out or do what I can do, that I need to wait for her until she feels she is able to go out and do what she needs or wants to do. I also resent that I have to wait for her, I sacrifice myself for her, and then I feel abandoned when she takes off and does what she wants. Most of all I hate when she says to me, you never tell me what you want to do or what your plans are. What plans? The plans that I do for me or the plans that would include her? I feel I've given up even asking for what I want to do with her as she's never able to "feel like it," or says she is physically unable to do it, or is afraid to try. I'm also pissed off that she can do things with her mother but not with me, things that she doesn't want to do with me. I ask her to go for a short ride on a Sunday afternoon but she's afraid, yet she drove an hour and a half (one-way) with her mother to see her brother. She can go out when other people make plans that include her, but not plans that I have, and in that I fine her very selective and unloving. She has energy for that but I'm just okay for the running around, getting groceries, the odd errands and doing her laundry.

If she wants to do something, she can find a way to do it but if I want to do it, she has an excuse why she can't. So what are my real issues here? Why am I denying myself? Why am I sacrificing myself? Why am I putting her wants, needs and desires ahead of mine? Why am I afraid? What am I afraid of? I'm afraid that I will say or do something and she will reject me, that I will disappoint her, not be there for her and that she'll abandon me and not want anything to do with me and that our relationship will be over. Most of the time when I see her it's because she's invited me and so I wait to be invited and to not impose myself on her because she doesn't feel well, is hungry, tired or whatever.

Jen's the only person that I do these healing things with and if I don't do them with her I have to do them alone. Sure I can talk to other people but I can't be myself or rather as much of myself as I can when I'm with Jen. I don't want shallow personal relationships, so what other kind is there out there and why can't I find them? I'm already fighting with Jen in my head as I feel she is interrupting me and not letting me finish what I have to say, and that what she has to say is more important. That she can't wait to speak, but I have to wait, that I can't interrupt her, but that she can interrupt me. Yesterday, she interrupted me and I lost what emotions I was beginning to touch and that frustrated me.

Later, at the breakfast table that morning, I was talking to Irene who said that I still looked tired and asked me how I slept. I said fine but yes, I felt like I needed more sleep. Dave jumped in and said, "You're tired because you're not getting enough sleep." I told him I was getting close to eight hours and that is usually enough. Dave then stated. "Maybe you are getting too much sleep and that too much sleep can make you tired." I looked at him and gestured with the back of my hand, to stop, as I was thinking to myself, what the fuck are you talking about? You have to have an answer for everything and you have to be right and in control. I thought it but I denied saying it.

Chapter 15 - Survival and Circling

Later, I was trying to think of what Dave was reflecting to me. This is frustrating, but what I'd call normal for the type of experiences I've had, not only with Dave but other men. No matter what I say or do it's not good enough, not for any logical reason but just because it was me. Like he's trying to tell me how to run my life and that "he" had all the right answers to my problems; not real answers to the issues, but the bullshit answers and the half-truths that he or others have, that they think I should believe are real and true. So what is he showing me? Is he showing me where I'm putting others opinions ahead of mine, and where I have no self-love?

♡ As I'm editing this book, I'm again seeing how I was on the right track, in thinking that Dave was reflecting my lack of self-love, but that I went right past my denials. I thought of saying, "What the fuck are you talking about? You have to have an answer for everything and you have to be right and in control." But I didn't say it, I never expressed it, and in not expressing it, that was my hidden denial, that was the moment I chose not to accept myself and love myself, and then I wondered why people attack me and don't accept me. It's so obvious now, but back then, I couldn't see the tree for the forest. ♥

1999 Dec. 29, 6:22 am - I have been laying here for who knows how long, thinking of why I was activated with Jen last night when she was talking about the boy she had met and his cyber sex experiences, and that he almost got "laid" last weekend. I was also activated when Jen said that she finds him sexy and a turn on. She doesn't tell him that he turns her on, but she tells me.

When I confront her, she tells me that she can't be honest with him, as he's only a child but that she can be more honest with me. She's told me several times that she doesn't find me sexually attractive, that I'm not her type although there are some things that I do that she finds sexy. She doesn't consider me as a sexual being or that I would be even interested in sex. I'm attracted to her in many ways, including sexually and I've told her that, and I've also held back and denied expressing most anything of a sexual nature because I know that would probably end our friendship and relationship and that was especially true in the early stages. I also don't discuss other women with her that I find attractive and sexy because I don't want her to think that that is all I'm after. I guess when she told me that she didn't consider me a sexual being, I felt like what's the use, she doesn't think I have those feelings and desires so why bring them up, and so I denied them. I don't tell her when I'm really worked up or when I'm really lonely and it's not about sex, it's the closeness that two people share, that physical contact, that touch, that look, the moves, gestures, smiles, the hugs, the cuddling, the romance.

There's no romance in my life, there's only one half-real person, friend, woman in my life that I find attractive and available (single), who only thinks of me as a non-sexual being, and who's turned on by a fourteen year old boy who has never had sex. Boy, do I feel rejected! That I'm not man enough to have a sexual relationship with, but good enough for her to talk to me about her feelings for another boy or man, but not about my feelings. It hurts to be the middleman, the confidant; there's anguish here. Why? I thought of Jen and how she would talk to me of her old boyfriends and lovers and how Michelle did the same thing after we broke up. I have feelings for both women, including sexual, and they ignore me and tell me of their sexual feelings and experiences with other men. I don't know how I'm going to heal this?

1999 Dec. 31 - Jen and I went to the mall in the afternoon and I had my left ear pierced for a second earring as a millennium thing. I had previously gotten my left ear pierced on my birthday this year.

> *What we hate most in others*
> *is what we hate most in ourselves. - Shenreed*

Chapter 16 - 2000 - The New Millennium

2000 Jan. 2 - I started the New millennium off being sick, sore and achy all over. I'm sad that I didn't write in this book yesterday, the first day of the new millennium. Nothing happened as predicted, there were no Y2K problems but there was an earthquake of 5.2 magnitude 70 km. north of North Bay, which is about 200 km north of where I live. I remember waking up thinking I had been dreaming that someone was shaking my bed; it never dawned on me it was an earthquake. I got up and got a drink of water and as I was drifting off to sleep, I thought I felt it again.

I visited Jen in the afternoon. She was going through a Chinese astrology book and looked up my birthday. It just so happens that I'm born under the sign of the Monkey, and the word for monkey in Chinese is Shen. She started to call me Shen, and did so for the rest of the day. I like it; I think I'll use it as a nickname.

I called Jen around 10 pm and the line was busy. I called her again just after 11:00 pm, and she answered in a bouncy, happy mood. She asked me if Irene was around as she wanted to talk to her for a minute, and I said that she was. She said she'd call me right back and hung up and called Irene on her line. She only talked with Irene a few minutes as I could hear when Irene ended the telephone conversation as she was in the kitchen, next to my bedroom. I waited until near midnight for her to return my call and then decided to go to bed.

I was just drifting off to sleep when the phone rang, it was Jen. I was annoyed to be woken from my sleep and angry that she waited so long to call me back, as I wanted to talk to her at 10:00 pm, not now, when I was almost asleep. She said that I wasn't fun and that I was putting a wet blanket on her fun. I replied huffily, that I wasn't responsible for her happiness. She said that she was happy before she called me but that now she felt deflated. I told her that I feel that people expect me to keep them happy, the way they were before they talked to me, but how can I do that when I don't even know what they were doing or feeling before they talked to me. I'm in a different space and that's not okay to them, I should be where they are or something is wrong with me. She said that I have a choice, to stay with the voice that says I'm separate or move it out. I told her that the same logic and rule could be applied to her when she's afraid to go out or eat. What voice is telling her that she's separate and it's not safe? She argued it wasn't the same thing and hung up.

2000 Jan. 4 - I started working at the apartments again. I'm putting in eight to twelve hours a day and sometimes I'm working on Saturdays too. If I had a short day at work, I'd drop in to see Jen before heading home, and sometimes we'd rent a movie or I'd take her grocery shopping.

2000 Jan. 9, 1:53 am - This is the third year anniversary of the day that I met Jen when I dialed a wrong number, the day that was to change my life but I didn't know it at the time. I can't get to sleep and haven't been able to, for the last couple of nights.

On Being Human

2000 Jan. 09 - Greetings, indeed it has been a long time since you allowed us to come into your life.

Me: Father, Mother, is that you?

Indeed it is son. You hesitate and we understand. You feel you are bad, have forsaken us, but that is not true. There were experiences you needed to have in order to remember, to awaken yourself. It is now time to begin to answer your calling, to become who you are. To begin to live at being, BE-ing HUMAN, not just a human being. You are apprehensive and you have fear of the unknown and that is okay. Allow all these fears to come up, and as you do, you will begin to allow your gifts to be uncovered, to be remembered. Blessings upon you.

Power of Love and the Word

2000 Jan. 10, 3:30 am - Da da da, don't you know I love you? Greetings children, little ones. It is with glad and healing heart that we appear upon this medium, for the power of the spoken word, as a tool, can be used for love and unloving purposes, and so far it has been the latter in most cases for you. For this evening, we will be discussing both the power of the word and the power of love, love being the only true power, but not to confuse you.

In the beginning of this channels experience was a piece on the word, and how, as consciousness becoming aware of itself, had to first comprehend its existence and at the same time, try to describe what it was experiencing. Hence, in order to recognize and identify its experience, it needed some form of expression to remember its experience and so it brought forth the word. Simple at first, I, and then am, then I am, and so it built its vocabulary and its experiences. For without words, thoughts to express, it would be for you to consider a computer before you and the network supporting it, as an object incapable of even communicating with itself, incapable of being what it is today as an extension of itself, and thus it is with you also. We are both

Chapter 16 - 2000 - The New Millennium

evolving, growing, learning and becoming, and it is through the power of the word, communication, consciousness awakening to itself that these words are being seen and felt by those who are awakening to the power of love.

There is no greater force in the universe, in existence, than the power of love. Now it is time to become aware of it, of true love, unconditional love and not the conditional love that has been called love. In all your existence, you have only known moments of love, some more than others, but none the less only moments. For most of your, what you call loving experiences, was the opposite, based or built on WORDS and on programs, beliefs and imprints that went back all the way to original cause, which as described, consciousness first becoming, or trying to become, aware of itself and its growth and development.

And so, at the dawn of this new millennium, the time of awakening has come. A time of true love and the recognition of the power of love and this is going to surprise all those who are awakening and even those who consider themselves already enlightened, but the power of love that needs to be nourished now is the power of self-love. You may say I love myself, I look after myself, I don't let anything harm me, or you may say yes, I have harmed myself but only a little, I eat too much or drink too much. Others, who feel they are worth very little, have no value and don't love themselves because they feel unaccepted by those around them. All of you are in the same boat; all of your experiences are based in fear and in lack.

Self-love is first and foremost self-acceptance, and self-acceptance means actual acceptance of all of you. All of you, you say? Yes, all of you. Do you know what all of you is? Fathom that statement if you can? Words are used again to try to describe the unlimited. You are in a state of becoming, of Be-ing, as you are beginning to remember who you are you will be able to bring love to those parts that have been in darkness, cut-off, abandoned for a number of reasons.

Ask each one of you who or what you are, and you will get a different answer every time, or the same or similar answer based on your programs, imprints and beliefs, and all of you will feel that your answer is correct for you FEAR of being wrong. If you fear being wrong, where is the love, the compassion, the understanding? Ahhh! (I was smiling) we see the lights come on in some of you, this is good. In the time ahead we will bring you more on the truth that you seek and we will be opening doors, many doors.

True love is reclaiming its power and there will be balance at this dawning of this millennium and it has been already happening for the last half of the last century and is now accelerating. All upon this planet, this lovely jewel of the universe, this Earth, will have choices to make; to awaken to love or to continue to sleep. For all have freewill, to make choices not to continue to impose their will on others who no longer choose to give away their power. Changes are coming.

In the times ahead there will be daily messages coming to this channel from many different sources, yet the same. This is also part of your awakening to yourselves and as you do, more will join in, in spreading the Word, the power of Love, true love. We know these words only begin to tremor the surface of a glassy ocean of consciousness that is yearning to awaken, to remember, to come home.

It fills our heart with joy as we can feel the love that is being stirred, the awakening. Be gentle with your selves, allow yourselves to awaken slowly and gently with baby steps, and allow yourself to enjoy the experience of rebirth. It is okay to not know. Life is meant to be lived with choice, with love. There is no perfection, for perfection (HEAVEN to some) would mean no growth, no evolution. When is a flower perfect or anything else for that matter, and what flower is more perfect than another? It would follow that only one thing would be perfect and also at only one stage, one point, but then where would all the imperfect growth and development be classified? Ponder this in your quiet time and allow yourselves NOT to be perfect. Your Mother and I are pleased, is a mild word, overjoyed only begins to swell our heart at the growth and opening that we are feeling. Blessings upon you this wondrous day. Father and Mother.

2000 Jan. 12 - Here I go again, I'm feeling jealous, inadequate, less than, not good enough compared to the people who have degrees, diplomas, certificates, etc. They have something that I haven't got so I believe that makes them better than me. I cover up my feelings of jealousy by downplaying the value of a degree or diploma as being just a piece of paper. This also carries over to when people ask me what credentials I have. I don't have a piece of paper, so therefore I feel I'm not as good as someone who does. I feel less than, not as good as others, and old feelings of hurt come up. I become angry and I don't express any of it, well maybe anger and frustration to a degree. I feel I need to make a formal release of my imprints, programs, and beliefs about comparing myself to other people.

I release the imprints, programs, and beliefs that:
- I have to be the same as other people to be as good as other people.
- I have to have someone else's acceptance or approval to have any worth and that includes diplomas, titles, degrees and certificates, etc.
- Who I am and what I am is determined by my job, family, house, car, and possessions.
- I can't be who I am without feeling guilty that I feel pride in what I do when other people can't do what I can.

Chapter 16 - 2000 - The New Millennium

- I have to be perfect because that's what I'm trying to be and that's impossible and undesirable.
- I'm not good enough, in whatever form it takes.
- I don't deserve love, life, happiness, peace, joy, abundance, or anything else.
- I can't accept or expect to be different or to be who I am, and that I can't have things or do anything that sets me apart from others.
- I'm afraid to want what I desire because that would set me apart, be different, not like other people and therefore I would get hurt.
- I'm afraid of my powers, my gifts, and what they might bring me or what I might do with them.
- I constantly compare and judge myself to others, even women and children, young and old, that I'm not as good as they are or that I'm better, superior, in a secret way that I keep to myself.
- Just because people have knowledge or information that I don't have, I think that they are better than I am, or that they are withholding information or keeping secrets.
- I'm not smart enough in things such as math, spelling, computers or whatever, just because I can't do what somebody else does, doesn't mean that I'm not good enough.
- I have fear in stating all my judgments, jealousies, envy and inadequacies for fear of feeling less than, weak and letting people know that I'm not good enough or as good as they are.

I want and intend to release all my judgments, my self imposed prison of chains, bars, and walls that are holding me prisoner. I release the fear that I have written this process incorrectly or improperly and that it's not good enough.

2000 Jan. 28 - I saw a small ball of light that was moving to my right. I closed my eyes and I still saw it. I re-opened my eyes and it was still floating and moving to my right. The light was a bright blue–green that lasted for a few seconds then faded and disappeared. I feel it was Archangel Michael.

> ❝ *When there is no trust, we control. - Shenreed*

Remembering

2000 Feb. 16 - How is it that you say you remember when you are not yet fully re-membered. Your members have memory and until you accept all your members, you cannot truly remember. How curious that you say your head remembers when indeed you do not accept other parts of your body members. The body is screaming, "Head, you do not remember, the pain is here and here," pointing to another part in the body, "and here is another pain." That is where the memory is, not in your head. Until you can accept the pain in your body you will not re-member and if you do not remember, you do not heal, you cannot become whole.

During this time I was getting a lot of information for Jen and some for Irene too. It was in the form of either channeled messages from their guides, or from their inner child and the experiences and emotions they were denying expressing. I was also picking up and tapping into their body pain. There was a lot of denied anger and rage as well as heartbreak, terror, guilt and shame. While I was picking up on others, I wasn't picking up on mine.

2000 Feb. 17, 2:11 am - I had been chatting with Jen on the Internet until 11:15 pm, and I told her that I was getting tired and that I was going to have a quick apple cider with Irene at 11:30 pm, and that I planned to be in bed by midnight and that I'd talk to her tomorrow. She called me at 11:40 pm, wanting to talk. I told her that I was still having cider with Irene and she got angry and hung up. I called her just before midnight but her line was busy, I assumed that she was back on the Internet so I went to bed. Just as I was drifting off to sleep, I got a phone call from the boy that Jen had been talking about, and who I had never talked to before. He told me that he had been on the Internet with Jen and that she had asked him to call me as she was having a problem with someone in a chat room and wanted my help. I was confused by the call but I got up, logged on, and went to the web site. By the time I got in, there was no longer a problem as the person that she was having a problem with had just logged off. I got off the Internet and tried to go back to sleep but I couldn't. I called Jen, she answered, but she said she was on the phone with the boy and that she wanted to continue talking to him. I feel like she is paying me back for not talking to her when she had called me earlier.

Here I go again, I'm jealous, I feel I'm getting pushed out and that I'm okay when she can use me. I can do things with her that she wants to do but she can't do things with me that I want to do. She always asks in a demanding sort of way, but putting it nicely at the same time. Can you do that? Do you want to do this or that? Do you mind picking this up for me on your way in? Can you ask Irene? YES I CAN. I can do anything I want to, but no, I don't want to do it. However, if I don't do it, she'll find someone else and she won't be my friend anymore. I feel neglected and abandoned. Fuck, I feel like rejecting the whole fucking works, you abandon me so I'll abandon you. I hate all these fucking games. I'm tired of the whole merry go-round and I want to get off.

Chapter 16 - 2000 - The New Millennium

I feel so alone, I even feel like killing myself. What's the use, for what? I'm alone, who cares? Who really cares if I live or die? Oh they say they do, that I'm important, but only as long as I'm useful to them, if they need me, but when someone new, interesting, sexy, exciting comes along it's "poof", your gone. But then they call and you hear a sickly, sweetie voice saying, "Oh by the way, can you please _ _ _ _ ? FUCK YOU! I feel so alone, abandoned and rejected. They may say that I'm a part, or that I can be a part of their life, but when they are doing something and I want to join them, they take off with new plans. Who cares if I live or die? I never thought of killing myself before, I must really be feeling low. That's not true, yes, I did, once when I first came down to Toronto.

4:25 am, I'm tired of the struggle and I want to just let go of it all and end the pain, the misery and the loneliness. When is this all going to end? I hear a ringing in my left ear. I feel icky, frustrated and angry. I feel I don't have anyone who really cares about me. I thought Jen did but now I don't know. I look at my life and I feel I've wasted it. What's the point? What's the use? Where is the love, the joy, the passion and excitement? I feel robbed and I want to hurt all the fuckers that robbed me.

6:47 am, I just finished screaming and crying with no sound. The tears that were flowing were tears of joy. Since the last writing, I said three times out loud, "I'm not going to close down, withdraw or hurt back." I decided that I was going to feel through to my pain of rejection, of being abandoned, used, played with and all the other things that come up, and that I was going to trust love, that I was going to love through my judgments and beliefs to my pain.

I had a dream/vision where I felt I was a dying man held under ice by my frozen beliefs. I had to constantly swim to keep myself barely alive, breathing from the shallow pockets of air under the ice. I was separated from life, from freedom. I then felt the ice begin to thaw and break into chunks. In the next moment, my head broke through to the surface and I could even float. In the next scene, I could swim, feel the sun on my body; see the birds in the sky above me, and take a full breath of life and not just a shallow gasp. Thank you. Thank me. I can now begin to feel and accept love.

2000 Feb. 18 - Irene and I had heard that the Hollywood restaurant in Midland had ghosts and that they were disturbing the staff and guests alike. It had been built in the early 1900's and served as a YMCA. It was later sold and operated as an art gallery before being sold again and turned into a restaurant. I had dropped in earlier to see the place and I could feel a lot of different energies. We were both curious to know more, so we decided that we would start meeting there for lunch every Friday.

The first time we were there the place was full of spirits, deceased people hanging around for any number of reasons. Some lost in time; some looking for help that we sensed had been victims of sexual abuse, torture and death that had occurred in the basement, and still others that just didn't want us there. As well, there were spirits that were coming in with each customer. With Irene being able to see and talk to Spirits, and I able to feel and sense their presence as well as pick up on their thoughts, we began communicating with them during the course of our lunch, while our waitress, Sara, kept our coffee cups full. Later, Bridgett the restaurant owner came over and introduced herself, and I could feel an instant connection with her. During our almost two-hour stay, we cleared several entities, some who just popped in for directions and others who had been trapped there. Before we left, Irene noticed two children ages eight and ten, Lilbeth and Jacob who we felt had died from a fall from the balcony in the gym area.

Raw Emotions and Beliefs

2000 Feb 26, 4:15 am - You feel totally alone in your hour of greatest need. You feel I abandoned you where in fact it was you who abandoned you. You needed to feel that you are not enough, that it is never enough. Forget trying to understand what is happening and why, and allow yourself to rather flow into the raw emotions as they are felt without judgment of the present moment and allow all judgments, beliefs, guilt and shame to surface as they appear in whatever order they occur. They do not need to make sense in the moment but you need also to be honest and open to whatever questions are asked to trigger you into the next release and so on, back and forth. As these emotions begin to surface so will the memories that caused them.

Words are only used to trigger each other and to assist in the release process. Know that under the words that feel like they cut like a knife, is love that is trying to cut away at the beliefs that are holding you prisoner. These are your beliefs that you feel so strongly are a part of you, are you, which you fight so fiercely to protect, when in fact they are the very ones, the vines that have been strangling and killing you. Allow yourself to anguish and lash out at all that you feel is being attacked. It will show you where you are still attached to a belief, a program that is not love.

2000 Mar. 1 - I got the word from Andrea, the apartment manager, that the work that was to be done at the apartments was being put on hold for the moment, but that I was to finish what I had started. At the time, I still had a good two weeks of work left to do.

2000 Mar. 4 - I had agreed to house and dog sit for Jen on the weekend while she went to Kincardine with her mother and stepfather, to visit her grandfather. That night I watched TV and shared the living room futon with her dog René.

Chapter 16 - 2000 - The New Millennium

2000 Mar. 10 - Jen and I got into an argument in the van on the way back to her place after we had done some grocery shopping. I was just beginning to turn the corner when she physically attacked me and I had to grab her hair and push her down to keep her away from grabbing the steering wheel or me. It was all I could do to steer around the corner, keep her off me, and bring the Van to a stop in the face of oncoming traffic. It was one of my scariest and most dangerous experiences with her. I didn't write down what the fight was about and I don't remember at this moment.

> ❝ *Do not give up hope, and do not be blinded by it. - Shenreed*

2000 Mar. 17 - Today I met Irene at the Hollywood restaurant for our usual Friday lunch. During our meal, I was becoming emotional and I knew that something was coming or going to happen. After our meal, Bridgett, the owner, took us on a tour of the building. When we walked up to the top balcony overlooking what used to be the gym; I began to feel fear and heartbreak. Bridgett, Irene and I sat down at a table in a corner and we began to talk. I had the past life experience that I was Jacob and that Bridgett was Lilbeth, the two children that had made their appearance last week. We had been playing on the balcony when she slipped and went through the railings. I managed to grab hold of her and tried to pull her up, but I wasn't strong enough and both of us fell to our deaths on the hardwood floor below. I felt that I was responsible and that I should have saved her, and she felt that she was responsible for my death by pulling me over. Bridgett, Irene and I were experiencing the same thing and we were all discussing what we were feeling or seeing simultaneously. It was a very emotional moment, especially for Bridgett and me, as both of us had lost essence at that time which we were now reclaiming.

♡ As I'm typing this I can still feel the heartbreak, as we were inseparable, best friends. ♥

2000 Mar. 26 - Some time ago, I had told Irene of my intent to make native drums and she had told me of a hollow tree that she had spotted on her walk in the bush. I decided to get a portion of it the next time I went for a walk. I also drove out into the surrounding countryside and picked up an old hollow cedar fence post that I had spotted in the ditch on one of my travels. I had the idea of making them in the traditional manner of five hundred years ago, but that meant that I would also have to make the tools they had at that time. I cheated a little and decided to still make them by hand in the traditional manner I felt they were made, but using modern hand tools. I used a pruning saw to cut the basic length and shape, a hammer and chisel to de-bark and hollow it out, and a knife and some sand paper to finish and smooth the drum frame. I also used a pair of tin snips to cut the rawhide, as I wasn't comfortable or accurate using a knife and I didn't want to waste rawhide as it was expensive.

2000 Mar. 27 - Andrea called saying that the work at the apartments was back on again. I was happy with that as it meant an opportunity to make some more money.

2000 Apr. 3 - Irene had recently begun telling me of the animals in spirit form that she was seeing around me, bees, crickets, rams, spider, lions, bears, to name a few. Today she told me that Rama; a demon lieutenant of Lucifer was hanging around me. I couldn't see him but I sure could smell him. He smelt like rotten sardines and was making me gag. He didn't say what he wanted; well he did in a roundabout way, not by what he said, but by what he didn't say. He said he wanted me, but I felt that he was trying to stop me in some way from what I was feeling or moving.

2000 Apr. 4 - Today I was feeling confused. Old programs were coming up that if I'm confused and don't understand, that I should just listen, and then I'd know what people want me to do. Another belief was that if I asked a question while they were telling a story, that I was told not to interrupt and to just listen and wait until they finished. Yet another belief was that if I waited for the story to be finished before I asked a question, then they would say, "Why didn't you ask when you were confused. I feel that no matter what I did, it was always wrong in some way and that I could never win or please them.

That evening when Irene and I were having our apple cider, a different demon with a different foul smell appeared beside me but he didn't stay long and he didn't say anything.

> *What you resist, persists. - Shenreed*

2000 Apr. 15, 1:56 am - I'm afraid of letting go and opening to the possibility that there is a woman out there that is open and wanting to heal like Jen is. One with which we can have not only an intimate friendship, but also where we would be romantically and sexually involved yet focusing on healing our sexuality issues. A relationship that is open and honest and not based on getting lost in the infatuation, romance, or sex. I feel so sad and alone. I've said this before about my sexuality being this dried and twisted piece of rawhide that I don't even know how to heal. So why would anyone even want anything to do with me, or want to help me? Jen doesn't, she doesn't even think of me as a sexual being, a lover, just someone that is only capable of

Chapter 16 - 2000 - The New Millennium

being a friend. I'm too afraid to allow myself to open and express my sexuality with her in case it is taken the wrong way and I lose her friendship over a sexual misunderstanding. Sometimes I feel I have this beast in me that just wants to fuck, the rage fuck that doesn't give a shit. That takes no to mean yes, that just feels the fire in his balls and penis and just wants to get off and won't take no for an answer, and that will go into uncontrolled rage if opposed.

There's this nice picture painted of Tantric sex that describes all the varied positions, the sensual arousal, feelings and the moving of energy. I've experienced some unusual sensations and experiences, but that has only been a couple of times. Those experiences really did nothing for me except put a few more twists and wrinkles in my sexuality. I don't think we even have a clue what sex is really about, because we haven't even got a clue of what real love is.

I'm also afraid that if I let go of Jen and I find someone who is also attracted to me sexually, that that will also be the end of my relationship with Jen, as I feel that I won't be sharing my intimate sexual experiences and details with her. But why would that be any different than what we have now? Maybe if she was also in a relationship and she shared her details, but otherwise I feel there would be this block like there already is, this line that can't be crossed. Maybe that's my problem, my block? I've never really had a friend, male or female, that I could talk with and openly share what was going on in my life, and vice versa. I briefly had that with my ex-wife before we got married, and then that all changed. So have I drawn this line between friends and lovers?

I've had acquaintances and people that I have known for years, but I'd hardly call them a friend in the true sense of the word. Irene is a friend, but not to the depth that Jen is at the moment. It has taken three years to get to know Jen and for me to open to her as much as I have. I'm not saying that it's going to take three years for another relationship to get to that stage that Jen and I are in now, and there is still a lot of healing to do for both of us besides our sexuality. I'm afraid it's too late for me, that I've lost my youth, my desires and passion. I want to cry but I can't. I feel that what I've had is all that I'm ever going to get, so I should be happy with that. Fuck, I hate this pen, this fucking scratchy, skipping pen. There, I've distracted myself from what I was starting to feel, are you happy, you fucker?

I feel it's too late for a loving, romantic, sensual and sexual relationship. I feel that my youth is gone. Hummm, is that why I was attracted to Michelle, to re-capture my youth? Is that why I'm attracted to Jen? So why is she in my life? Is she here to help me heal a part of me and then what? Do I or she need to move to another person to heal our sexual part, and then what? After we have partly healed our sexuality with that person, do we leave that relationship for another? So why is that any different than what we have been doing? We keep trying to find that one person who we can experience all aspects with. (I just got rid of the fucking pen and now I have a new one that works.)

Part of me feels it's too late and has given up on the dream, that it's not possible or real, so what's the use in trying, it's all words, ideas, and dreams. People say one thing and do another. I've lost my youth and innocence a long time ago, if I ever had it to experience. My heart feels like it's twisted in a knot, as hard as my sexuality. I want to heal but it feels too big, too overwhelming and that I can't have what I want. I feel like I'll never be close to a woman again unless I just take what comes my way whether I'm attracted to her or not, and just be grateful for what I get, whether it feels good or not.

3:41 am, I want to heal my sexuality. I want a loving, warm, romantic, sensual, passionate, exciting, frolicking, discovering, nurturing, open and honest sexual relationship with a beautiful attractive woman, where we are both friends and lovers and everything in-between, individual yet nurturing and committed to a relationship and to share and experience life. I ask that such a woman come into my life to heal and evolve our Will, Spirit, Heart and Body, to integrate and spiritualize our physical bodies. I ask Father and Mother and all my guides for help.

> **You can't begin to pick up the pieces,
> until you admit that you've fallen apart. - Shenreed**

False Will

2000 Apr. 16, 3:33 am - Blessings, in the times ahead you will begin to see and experience the wonder and blessings of the world, rather than the fear and suffering. You have moved much and healed much, both in yourselves and in others. You are afraid; you fear what you are touching now. Your doubts, worry, and confusion throw you into panic. You have not felt your panic attacks for you have masked them behind anger and puffed-upness. When your fears are triggered, you are now thrown into your terror and panic to leave, for you fear you will be harmed and so you seek to separate yourself from those you fear would bring you harm as they have in the past. It is an illusion. There is no damage or harm, but only the memory of it in those parts of you that you left when you were harmed. There is this part in you that wants to protect this other part in you that was harmed and heart-broken and this is the part that panics and tries to flee the situation to find a safe place.

Allow yourself to express your fears, your panic, knowing that Jen will not bring you harm intentionally, and allow yourself to touch those aspects of you that are cut off and in pain. Those parts that feel they are not good enough, which hate being themselves, and that hate confusion and

Chapter 16 - 2000 - The New Millennium

especially hate rejection in any form. This is keeping you separate and alone for you do not trust others not to harm or use you, and at the first sign of rejection, you try to make things right (for them) and failing that, you seek to panic and leave. It is not easy and there are many layers to this rejection issue. Self-acceptance, self-love, and Heart cannot be born until you begin to deal with this, your greatest fear, which is rolled into and mixed up with what you have been told love is.

You are confused and find it difficult, no impossible, to separate yourself from the energies of others, and so you hate your feelings for you do not want to be separate from others, so instead, you reject yourself and separate yourself from your feelings, your true feelings.

False Will is what is guiding you now under the guise that it is protecting you, but that threat and the original pain is far removed from the experience that is happening at the present. We know this is hard for you to face your worst fear, unlovingness and rejection, but that is no longer how it is. We are healing and you, this aspect of myself also needs to move and heal if I am to further move and heal too. I can't and won't go on without you. Not to put pressure in you that you need to do this or all is lost. No, it will just take longer and even that is an illusion for time as you know it is an illusion. Yes I, we have chosen to heal, have chosen love and life.

It is now time to receive, manifest this in the physical, all the wonder and magic, joy, peace and harmony that you have never experienced, always because of unlovingness and rejection. You are aware in the books you have and are reading, how these experiences were manifest in all parts by original cause. This is what you are now healing, original cause, and when it has begun to heal, the gap will also be healed and Heart will be healed, Mother and I and the Father of Manifestation will be healed.

This also ties into your sensuality and sexuality issues that you touched yesterday. You are touching many issues and even levels at once and this frightens you, no it terrorizes you. You are not alone, although you feel like you are. Call upon us and the company of heaven for help when you are going into your darkest fear; we will be there to assist. You are loved. Blessings upon you this wondrous day. Mother, Father and the Company of Heaven.

Secrets and Purpose

2000 Apr. 20 - Greetings and blessings this wondrous morning. Indeed your purpose, part of which is to teach and to heal, and in doing so, part of your purpose here is to also enjoy the fruits of your labor, to experience all you desire. That is why you came here on this mission, journey, experience, but mission indicates a plan and there is a plan to your journey.

At this point you are still not ready to be all that you are, you could not handle it and still accomplish your mission but it is not far off. In the days ahead, prepare yourself to meet your greatest challenges that block, or hold you back from moving, to begin to be all that you are, and to begin to awaken and remember who and what you are. There is no need to hurry and force this issue, but then again, there is urgency also as you are aware of without knowing why, and again, if you knew the why in this moment, it would alter your ability to accomplish it.

    Yes, this is part of your issue of "keeping secrets" and "on a need to know basis" that bothers you and it is your veil, your own self that denies the other part of you what it needs to know. Your veil is not very thick and thus you "feel," sense, something is going on the other side of the curtain. Rest assured that the curtain shall be going up soon. *S* Mother and Father and the Company of heaven.

♡   Note: As I finished typing the words, "the curtain shall be going up soon." the *S* (Internet symbol for smile) appeared on the screen. ♥

2000 Apr. 23 - Jen and I drove out to a special place that I had accidentally found on one of my Sunday afternoon travels. Driving by, one would think it was just a re-forested area of pines, however, when you stopped and walked into the forested area, there were these two magnificent Maple trees that had to be a few hundred years old, standing in the middle of these forty to fifty year old pines. It was a magical area as it also had a small brook that meandered and babbled through the woods some fifty feet or so from these Maple trees, which stood about two hundred feet from each other. Jen and I were standing quietly in a spot near the brook when we noticed a Labrador retriever casually sniffing and strolling through the forest toward us, but on the other side of the brook. We didn't move but just observed him making his way toward us in a carefree manner, wagging his tail, sniffing the ground as if he were on the trail of something. When he was about twenty feet away, he suddenly became aware of us and stopped dead in his tracks. He looked at us for a moment, then appeared to make a u-turn in mid air, yelped and was off faster than a speeding bullet. He ran in a zigzag pattern, tail between his legs and giving the odd yelp as he made his way back to where he had come from. We looked at each other and had a good laugh describing what we had just seen and felt.

2000 Apr. 25 - Jen and I had finished watching a movie and we had just begun discussing it when she asked if I could help her take the garbage out. When she said that, I felt that she was trying to cut our evening short, but I denied my intuition and helped her take the garbage downstairs and to the street. When we returned to the house she sat down on the stairs leading up to her apartment, now I knew she was ending our evening. I asked her what was up and she said that it was late and that she wanted to take a bath. I asked

Chapter 16 - 2000 - The New Millennium

her why she didn't say so before when she asked me for help with the garbage. I told her that I felt used and also inconvenienced, as now I had to go back up and get my stuff. She gave me a disgusted look as if I was inconveniencing her with my problems. She then turned and went upstairs to get my stuff and the movie that had to be returned. Resentfully, she brought them half way down the stairs and handed them to me, turned and went back up without a word. I made my way down stairs and snarled, "Thanks for the great evening" and slammed the door behind me. I don't know what's going on?

2000 Apr. 29 - During our evening apple cider, Irene noticed a small boy in spirit form, standing beside me. She said that he looked like me and that he was saying that his name was Yanni and that he was about seven years old and that he was me. I was confused as my parents did call me either Yanni or Yanosh, when I was small. I was also puzzled as to why he was here and why he was beside me? He remained with me at my side for the next week before he disappeared.

> 66 *Replace your beliefs with ideas. - Shenreed*

Remaining Issues

2000 May 12, 7:51 am - You are healing in your own way. Others have their path, their gifts, their talents, their time and place as you do. So what you consider others are doing and are ahead of you, you have already done and are in fact, waiting for them to catch up. But indeed, you have your own fears and issues that you hesitate to confront all at once (as others do) and so you chip away, little by little in your own way and time.

This is not one issue that you are dealing with, but many, and many layers, and they have to be taken apart slowly and untangled just as the jewelry you examined yesterday. To get at one that caught your eye, you also had to disentangle others before you could free that one. So it is with healing your issues.

Many are here to assist you and when the time is right, the seal will be broken, opened, and the doors will be opened for you. There is not much that holds you from what you desire, from opening to your true self. Heritage, parents, self-worth, abandonment, beliefs, programs, protecting, serving others, speaking and expressing, sex, sensuality, God fearing, hell, good and bad, deserving, confusion, not understanding, non-acceptance, judgments on self and others, comparison, doing verses being, family, power, control, money, worth, jealousy, possessiveness, dislikes, age, fear of attracting negative, fear of criticism, fear of success, scorn, laughed at, ridiculed, being centered out, beaten, pushed away, no friends, we can go on and on. These are some of the issues that are interwoven, but family and money are, can be considered key issues for you to look at this time. Blessings, Gabriel and Auriel.

I laughed, "Yeah right, not much left to work on."

Memory, Denial and Fear

2000 May 13 - Denial and fear are your main issues in being unable to express and communicate what you feel and what you intuit. As you experience and become activated, you close down and deny them. Fears surface along with false Will, false emotions, that tell you the situation or experience is not to be trusted, to be feared. Your mind (Ego) then strings out a long list of possibilities, probabilities and comparisons that are history, based on the initial experience and hence all experiences. History or memory is based on the original experience which was necessary for whatever emotions that needed to be triggered in agreement, but all re-actions, re-creations since then, have in fact, been re-in-act-ments of the original experience, of original cause.

2000 May 16, 4:48 am - I came to the realization that I'm trying to make and save money so that I can do what I think I really want to do, but the more I work and save, the more I end up spending. I can never get ahead. Why can't I do what I really want to do and have all the money I need to allow me to experience all I want to?

I heard a soft voice say, "Your denials will attack you to show you that your fears are right."

But what do I love or desire? I ask for help to find my Heart's desire. It is my intent not to deny myself for the sake of others for whatever reason. I intend to become aware when I'm about to, or have gone into denial. I intend to end my denials, to speak, do, and be my truth at all times. I intend to remain open and to not close myself down. I intend to open myself, to allow myself to dream and to follow my dreams.

> *Your denials will attack you to show you that your fears are right.*
> *- Shenreed*

2000 May 22 - I got the word from Andrea that I was to finish the work on the apartments I had started and that everything else was on hold until the new manager took over. Andrea was being let go and her last day would be the end of the month. Don, the Apartment superintendent, whose wife had died recently, and who was already planning to leave when he found another apartment, was also given his notice. From the things that Andrea was saying,

Chapter 16 - 2000 - The New Millennium

I knew that my time was up, but I decided to wait and see what developed with the new manager.

2000 June 4 - I was just thinking about the dream I had last night about five tornadoes and the horrific damage they were doing, and also of fish being swept to shore. Suddenly I got this message.

The Five Tornadoes

Indeed the five tornadoes are symbols of the five base issues, together with their imprints, programs and beliefs that need to move, heartbreak, rage, terror, life, and death. The fishes being thrown to shore represent the imprints, programs, beliefs, and judgments. Others need to know this as this is what will be activated in them in the times ahead.

2000 June 5 - It was during our ritual late evening chats over several cups of herbal tea that we started to mix two different flavors in the same pot and then having the other taste and guess what they were. We came up with some interesting and unusual flavors. As mentioned before, Irene was seeing various animals in spirit around both of us. I could "feel" their presence, especially if it was ants, bees, or spiders, etc. as I could feel them on my skin and they made me itch. With the larger ones, I would sometimes feel a nudge or a tug. Sometimes the animals or insects would remain with us for days before they would leave and others would arrive. The Native Indian grandmothers also started coming around more often, especially to do work with Irene.

2000 June 9 - A few days earlier I had dropped by the apartment building and spoke to the new manager. He told me that he had a couple of apartments he wanted to renovate and wanted an estimate. I also met the new superintendent (his buddy) and went on an inspection tour with the both of them. My intuition told me that this didn't feel good and that it was just a show, but I prepared a quote anyway on the possibility that my intuition was off. Today I submitted my quote. He told me that he would be making a decision over the weekend and that I'd hear from him next week.

2000 June 12 - As I was no longer working at the apartments, I was spending more time with Jen. Today I was taking her to her appointment with a woman counselor that she has been seeing for a while. I had gone over earlier to pick her up but she wasn't ready. I went upstairs and was sitting on the futon, waiting for her, when she came out of her bedroom and said, "Let's go" in an angry voice. I asked her, "What's up?" She told me that she had said, "Let's go" before but that I just ignored her. I replied, "You didn't say it as I have been sitting here waiting for you to come out of your bedroom." At that comment, she became even angrier, stating that she had told me. I said, "Well if you did tell me I didn't hear you, but I hear you now, so let's go."

On the way to her appointment, she was still on about me ignoring her and she flew into a rage and began yelling at me to stop the van and let her out, while opening her door at the same time. Luckily I was in downtown traffic so I wasn't going fast, but before I could stop the van at the curb, she was already out and running down the street to her appointment which was on the next block. I closed the passenger door and waited there for a few minutes and just watched to see that she made it okay.

I went for a coffee and returned and hour later to pick her up. When she came out she seemed in a different emotional state and she asked if I wanted to grab a movie and go back to her place to watch it, which we did. She didn't want to talk about what was really going on or what had happened during her appointment, and I didn't pressure her.

2000 June 16 - Irene saw a crow being hit by a car and stopped to see if she could help it. She brought it home, but twenty minutes later it died. She said that she was told that we were to take some of its feathers. I removed some of the wing and tail feathers and also felt that we were to remove the feet (claws) but I was unsure and afraid to say such a thing at the moment, as the crow had just died and I never did anything like that before. We buried it beside a small tree in the yard and as we were placing a circle of stones around its gravesite, I told Irene what I felt about the claws. She told me that, "Yes, I was right and that we were also to have the claws." She was on her way to work so I dug up the crow and removed the claws. I was unsure and apprehensive and also frightened when the left claw of the crows' foot closed around my fingers as I tried to cut through its leg with a pair of side cutting pliers. When I cut the right leg, its claws opened.

♡ As I'm writing this I'm realizing that the left is symbolic of receiving, taking in and that the right is of giving, of letting go. ♥

I re-buried the crow and replaced the stone circle we had originally made for it. The next morning we went out and noticed that four of the stones had moved, as if creating a gateway to the East, setting the Crows Spirit free.

2000 June 21, Wednesday – As this was also the summer solstice, Irene and I did another ceremony for the crow and for the feathers and claws we had received as well as for a snakeskin that Irene had found on the deck that morning.

Later that day, Irene and I drove into Midland to pick up Jen. We then drove to the wooded area where the two old maple trees were hidden in the pine forest, and where Jen and I had seen the dog that got frightened

Chapter 16 - 2000 - The New Millennium

when he saw us. We had told Irene about it and she said she wanted to visit it and we felt that today was that day for the three of us to be in that energy. We were separately exploring different parts of the woods and I was some twenty feet from Jen when we happened to glance at each other. At the same moment, something from behind and to my right flew in front of me moving to my left, then made a sharp right turn and flew toward Jen. When it got near her, it turned left again and headed toward the brook. At first, I thought it was a dragonfly or humming bird, but then I realized it was a faerie. Both Jen and I were awe struck in the moment and Irene just smiled and said, "Yes, there are a lot of them around here." It was indeed, a special day.

> *Do what you love and the abundance will follow. - Shenreed*

2000 June 22 - I'd been given the message before that I was going to be writing a book or rather books, but it all seemed surreal to me. I had made some attempts before but I never really got it going, but today is the day I began writing my first book, this book. I gathered all my journals, note pads and day timers, and started to go through them, marking the pages I felt I needed to enter on the computer.

Primal Expression

Today, when I was driving, I got the message that when triggered or triggering someone into anger or rage, instead of responding verbally with words, to allow yourself to respond with non-verbal or with primal, animalistic sounds and allow both conversations to move to that primal level of release if possible. This also includes various facial expressions and body movements as well.

2000 June 23 - This morning, Irene and I were talking about my book and she said that she saw Jen writing poems that went before each chapter and that each chapter was on a different subject. I also felt that Jen would have a contribution and that some of Jens poems would be made into songs. I sensed that I'd have a lot of messages dealing with love, and what is and isn't love, as well as emotions. I also felt that, when required, that I'll be adding personal stories and showing how my messages and experiences interact. I'm beginning to look forward to writing this book, I don't know how it's going to come together but I know it will.

2000 June 29 - When I close my eyes I see nothing but blackness, everything is gone, as if nothing exists. What is or was out there is gone. I can't even remember what my hand looks like when I close my eyes. I had been talking to Jen earlier and I just remembered some of the phrases she said that are related to this. Phrases like, out of sight, out of mind, what you don't see can't hurt you, ignorance is bliss, etc. This has got to be a program that I've put in place to help protect me, to keep me from seeing.

I formally release this program, belief and judgment. I desire to see all there is and to deny nothing, to express all my fears and my emotions and to give them acceptance. I want to and intent to open my eyes to the world, to see it as it really is, all of it, and not just limited to the physical realm, but to all dimensions and possibilities, good and evil. I intend to lift the veils of limitation that I have placed upon myself to feel limited. I ask for help from Mother and Father and all my guides who are here to assist me in whatever way that serves my highest purpose and good. I also want to bring all my essence and memories forward including past lives, and to be able to tap into all those past experiences if it serves my highest purpose and good. So be it.

2000 June 29 - I had placed numerous phone calls and left messages for the new apartment building manager but I never received a call back, so I figured I was out of there. I began to think of what I was going to do with my spare time, and also money issues came back up again. I thought of maybe teaching classes again; I revised my flyer and had a couple of hundred copies made. The classes that seemed to get some attention before were past life regression, meeting your guides and totems, and channeling. I also decided to add a new class called, Co-equal Therapy – Self-empowerment and Healing Emotions. Today, I was on the road, visiting all the New Age Centre's and bookstores within a one and a half-hour driving distance, dropping off flyers and booking dates for classes.

2000 June 30 - It was late evening when Jen called me, crying hysterically and saying that René; her toy poodle had taken a fit and couldn't get up or walk. She asked me to pick her up to take her to the vet as her Mom and stepfather weren't around. I arrived within twenty minutes. We called around to find a vet that was open this late on a Friday night. After several attempts, we finally found one that would meet us at his office in half an hour. Jen put René in a small box lined with a blanket so that she would be more comfortable when being carried or held on her lap, as we didn't know what had happened to her. We arrived at the vet's office and waited for another fifteen minutes for him to arrive. He examined René and determined that she had suffered a stroke which had left her paralyzed, and that there was really nothing he could do for her.

I could feel Jens heartbreak as she had had René since she was a pup ten years ago, and she was a constant companion for her. Jen knew that she had to put René down and the vet gave her several minutes to say goodbye. When Jen and René were ready, I called the vet and he administered the needle. Jen held her paw and watched the light go from her eyes as she

Chapter 16 - 2000 - The New Millennium

silently slipped away. I had already paid the vet, so we just placed René back in the box and headed home.

On the way back to Jen's place she decided that she wanted to bury René that night at her mom's house. We arrived just after 11:00 pm and her mother still wasn't home. Her Mother lived near a beach and behind her property was a large forested area. We used a flashlight to determine a place to dig a grave in the back yard. I had a shovel in the van that I used to dig a grave near some trees and bushes. Later, Jen placed some stones on the gravesite that she had gathered while I was digging the grave. We stood in silence and then said our goodbyes to René. Neither of us talked as I drove Jen home. She wanted to be alone so I just dropped her off and drove home.

2000 July 1 - I went over to Jens today and we went out to her Mothers place to see Renés grave. After a short visit with her Mother and Stepfather, we went back to Jens place for a while. I don't remember many details or what was said, but Jen was sitting in her rocking chair and I was on the footstool in front of her when she reached for me and grabbed me by the ears and began shaking me. I knew she was in pain over Renés death and that she had anger and rage to release, but I didn't want to be the receiver of it. I managed to wrestle her hands off my ears but not before she had drawn blood when her fingernails clenched and squeezed my ears. I had felt the pain but I didn't realize I was bleeding until I felt something trickling down the back of my neck. I reached back to scratch my neck and when I felt wetness I looked at my hand and my fingers were covered in blood. I went to the washroom, wiped the blood from my neck and ears, and stopped the bleeding. I left shortly after as Jen said she wanted to be alone.

2000 July 2 - It was a rainy day and I slept on and off for most of the day. Later that night I realized that I was covered in Poison Ivy. I had it on my hands, arms, face, neck and upper body. I realized that I got it when I was helping Jen bury René. I knew that there was Poison Ivy in her mothers' back yard but I thought we had avoided the spots we saw with the flashlight. We chose a spot for the grave that looked clear of it. I remember it was a hot evening and there were tons of mosquitoes. I did the digging and I also remember pulling out what I thought was small tree or shrub roots from the grave. In reflection, they were poison ivy roots that I was pulling out with my bare hands and then wiping the sweat from my brow and swatting mosquitoes, which is how I feel I spread it. I was not a happy camper as I knew that with my allergic reaction, I'd have this for two to three weeks. There was very little I could do but grin and bear it as best I could with the help of some cortisone cream. Doing anything really physical was also out of the question as it was especially bad on my fingers and arms.

Journey to the Heart Centre

Time and in the Moment

2000 July 02 - In the moment, at that moment, is where your true power is. All others are either remembrances or projection. For what you be in this moment is what leads you to experience the next moment and yet each moment is not linked together like a chain, to follow another as you like to think of it in your linear mind with your idea of time. For in true essence, what you experience as time is an illusion, and what you experience as space is an illusion also.

Expansion of these concepts will be made available to you in the conscious state. You are aware of them on other levels, and now it is time to bring it down to the physical where they can be used and expressed out of what you term reality; for your true reality is not what you see and feel around you, and neither is time. These are put here for your experience, in a sense it is like watching a movie and you are in the audience. Suddenly, you are playing the part of a western cowboy. The scene changes to a sailor and you are him, then to a nun, and you are her. All the characters are what you choose to experience. The props and people present helped you to believe the experience is real. And yes, in the movie you played a child and then became elderly and so it seemed that time also passed in order for you to do this, when in fact, all your experiences are already on a roll of film and any part can be played at anytime, to re-live the 3rd density reality movie of yourself. But you are also existing on many levels simultaneously. There is much you will understand and grasp as you continue to raise your vibration and allow yourself to go with the flow.

2000 July 9 - I'm afraid to ask questions and I'm also afraid of having to answer every question that is asked of me. At this moment, I'm being flooded with a host of questions and statements that were directed at me in the past.

You'd better have a good answer.
Answer me, what are you, stupid or something?
How many times do I have to ask you?
I'm only going to ask you once.
What have you got in that head of yours, shit for brains.
Ask a stupid question, get a stupid answer.
What's the matter, can't you ask?
What's the matter, cat got your tongue?
Children should be seen and not heard.
If I want your comment, I'll ask you.
I can't believe you asked me that question.
Where did you get such an idea from?
That's a stupid (dumb) question.
Don't you know any better?

Chapter 16 - 2000 - The New Millennium

How old are you anyway?
I'm the only one here with the right answer.
Do as I say, not as I do.
Do it my way or else.
Don't talk baby talk, or like a baby.
Work; don't talk.
I don't want to hear a word out of your mouth.
Shut your mouth or I'll shut it for you.
Open your mouth and put your other foot in it.
Ask me no questions and I'll tell you no lies.
Don't raise your voice to me.
God help you if you talk or tell.
I'll cut your tongue out if you tell anyone.
A secret is a secret, you can't tell anyone.
It's our little secret.
If you won't tell, I won't tell.
Swear you won't say anything.
Ask me nice.
You didn't say please.
You know the answer to that already.
Why are you asking me?
I said no and I mean no.
What part of no, don't you understand?
I didn't raise any stupid kids, right?
The lights are on but nobody's home.
They'll never believe you, only me.
The squeaky wheel gets the grease.
What makes you think that you're special?
You're always asking, you're selfish.
You never get anything unless you ask.
You don't have to ask.
Why didn't you ask before you did that?

I don't know anything; I'm confused, spinning, and bewildered by all these statements, and the programs and beliefs that all these comments represent.

♡ As I'm editing this book I realized that they were not questions, but rather judgments and demands that were used to control and manipulate me. ♥

Words

2000 July 09 - You hang on so dearly to words, what people say, but what really needs to be opened in honest and forthright communication between relationships, first and foremost, is that it doesn't matter what words they say, but what is felt and what is not said. It matters most what you say, say it in balance that comes from the Heart. First, recognize your words, your intent, your desires, your energy behind the words you speak and also your energy behind the words you do not speak. Being honest with self is foremost. Allowing the other person to respond how they want to, is their expression to your statement or question.

The words are important in your linear mind as to definition and meaning but the word definition comes fourth in importance. First, comes the feeling tone, the vibration of the words. Second, comes the feeling tone and vibration of what is not being said. Third, comes your intuition, your response from your Heart, that first feeling response. So in actuality, words are not really important. You do not need words or to understand words to communicate. For example, take little children that have not yet learned words, or children who have different languages that are brought together. They play and express themselves in ways other than words.

Old programs and beliefs are hooked onto words and vice versa, and the mind (ego) tries to pull up data based on words to express a belief that would suit the experience or remembrance it needs to express. The energy contained in these beliefs and programs can be very strong depending on how deeply the program or belief has been put in place. Moreover, certain words or phrases will mean one and only one thing, with no options open for other definitions let alone feelings.

As you let go of these beliefs and programs, the mind (ego) searches for protection, safety in the old tried and true even if it is no longer true or serves ones higher purpose. The old is preferred to the unknown, especially when it comes to emotions and thereby can be avoided and denied. The path is familiar and this road has been well traveled, and even though pain is known, it is the emotions that can be controlled. Fear of the unknown, of terror, keeps you from exploring and experiencing the new. For how can you accept new emotional experiences if you cannot accept the old ones? How can you face, accept new terror if you cannot face or accept the old?

In the same way joy, things that are joyous, bring pleasure to you, because you believe they do not have fear or terror to them. You therefore accept them and you can accept new experiences that hold the belief that it is the same pleasant and controlled experience you had before. So you go along with being open to this new experience because of the promise that it will be similar to ones that you enjoy and do not fear, or if any fears are there, they do not appear to be threatening to you.

One way to avoid the pain of unpleasant memories is to block them out, to go in a different direction, to avoid by saying or doing something else to change the topic, the focus, and failing that, one tries to deny by closing down and withdrawing. And when that fails, the next step is to express anger

Chapter 16 - 2000 - The New Millennium

and rage at what the mind and ego fear is another's attempt to control them, to make them experience something they don't want, based on their programs and beliefs.

Once the denied emotional response is accepted, there is no longer the charge, the fear, the terror of having to face and deal with something you don't want to deal with because you have already dealt with it, and now the old belief and program can be changed, dissolved. Now when the words come up to trigger you it will no longer send you into panic and terror for they will have a different "feel' to them, there will be acceptance, compassion and understanding. Not that you will give up your power and re-create the original experience, no, but one where you will "feel" the others intent even if it is not spoken. One can then make decisions based on your true feelings and not merely words and old beliefs and programs, and the old energy that was trapped in those words.

It is not an easy process and there are many layers to these beliefs and programs, but little by little they can be healed. As you get closer to key issues, you will also have stronger fear and terror and more resistance to change your old beliefs, and what you call the ego will try to hang on for what it considers dear life, but it is not life it clings to, it is death. And the voice that is prompting from behind the scenes is Lucifer, unloving light, using anything he can to pull up any reason to stop or delay the process, and guilt and shame are two of his favorite tools. Lucifer doesn't need to use external methods to control you; he has all the tools he needs inside you. He only uses the external to help trigger your fear and terror to keep you prisoner. As long as you hold fast to your old beliefs and programs, you are Lucifer's puppet, doing and saying what he wants, going to your death with unloving light.

Confusion is large here for you have been told this and that by so many that it is difficult to determine what or who to believe anymore. But you need to let your Heart "feel" what is true, what feels right to you, what feels loving to you. And as you will have to go through your quicksand of beliefs, the ones that are up to your neck and about to drag you down, you will find a branch that is firmly anchored in the truth that will allow you to pull yourself out of the old beliefs and programs and to see them for what they really are, to feel them for what they really are. You will know in your Heart when you have hold of such a branch. Blessings, Father and Mother and the company of Heaven.

> **Words give you an outline, feelings give you understanding. - Shenreed**

2000 July 9 - Tonight when Irene and I were having our midnight tea, she saw a large black Nubian male, in spirit form, behind me. She said that he was at least seven feet tall and was guarding me. As the evening went on we discovered that he and I had a past life relationship and that I had been a sheik and that he was my guard and confidant. I also felt a love and a trust connection with him in that past life. Afterwards, the whole experience left me feeling a bit wobbly and off center.

Differentiation and Fragmentation

2000 July 10 - Indeed what you are experiencing now is feelings of differentiation and fragmentation. Differentiation is also linked to attack, but not in the same way as it is to fragmentation and expression, as we will discuss later. The prime directive, so to speak, of differentiation is to attack, it is its nature, its essence, as it is the unloving energy of Lucifer and of the psychopathic killer. Its means of expression, of communication, of what it wants, is through attack, conscious through Lucifer and unconscious through the psychopathic killer. Now the words and methods used by differentiation and attack and fragmentation and expression can be the same, but it is the feeling of the words, of the expression that is different, but there is more. You also need to move out unloving light (differentiation) before you can truly get to fragmentation and its expression.

Even with your word definition of differentiation there is confusion for you. In your linear mind you consider everything different as individual, even if they look exactly the same, the one that is held in the left hand is different from the one held in the right hand, or else if they were the same, there would only have to be one. The difference we are trying to express is the difference in feeling and we are not talking your physical feeling senses of hot or cold, etc., we are talking of your Will and how it feels to her, is it loving or unloving? That is the key to be able to bring separation to differentiation and fragmentation, by allowing the Will its expression including its feeling of being attacked even when there is nothing evident or when there is denial of attacking. This goes back to original cause and is at the crux of the long standing, long suffering problems in creation, in this free Will universe where the Will feels trapped.

There is loving light and there is unloving light, they may look and sound the same but they don't feel the same, for they are not the same. And what is happening now is that there is going to be separation of this differentiation, which I first thought was fragmentation, a piece of myself and in a true linear sense it appears it is but when felt it is not. By analogy,

I had stopped my writing in mid-sentence, I don't know why I never finished that message, but I know that I have to include it in the book at this time. ♥

2000 July 11 - It was on June 30th that Jens poodle, René died. I saw Jen the next day when I took her to see Renés grave. Later, we were at her place

Chapter 16 - 2000 - The New Millennium

when we had the fight where she pulled and cut my ears with her fingernails. We've talked on the phone several times but have fought ever since. I saw her again this past Saturday and we got into another fight. We both feel we can't express ourselves and we also feel abandoned, attacked and mistrust for each other.

It's been one year today that I've been staying here at Irene's and Dave's. I talked to Irene today about what is on my mind, my feelings, and especially my confusion. I don't want to be confused as confusion means trouble. I'm suppressing and denying my feelings and intuition when I'm confused or when I feel attacked. If I ask, I'm told to just wait until they're finished, or they will say no, I didn't say or mean that, that you heard wrong or that you didn't hear, you misunderstood. So I shut my Will down and what it feels then builds up to a point where I get angry and rage. Then it's quiet for a while, the pressure is off, but the same confusion and doubts are still there.

If I speak and express my Will, I also feel guilty for interrupting, not being right if the other person denies what I felt, so I doubt myself, my Will, and the program pops up, make sure before you say anything, hold back and be safe. My mind tries to hear and understand all the words but a lot of the time it's the feeling of the words that "feel" wrong or confusing as one says one thing but means another. It's also the feeling of what is not being said and that brings up different issues. So I have confusion of what my Will feels and what my mind hears and sees, because the mind has also been aware when it did not hear what was being said, so both have doubt, fear of being wrong and of asking for clarification.

It's my intent to remain open and to allow my Will to express what it feels anytime it feels anything that comes to its attention, especially if I don't know if what I'm saying is right. If I don't feel that what I hear or see are the same, I'll use discernment, not to say I'll have to express everything, but that I'll be aware of my feelings and when it's the right time to express myself. Also, I intend for my mind to allow my Will to ask questions if it's confused as this also confuses the Will and both are running around in circles. I'll ask questions when I don't understand or am confused and I'll express what I feel. If I feel attacked, mislead, lied to, being denied, or whatever. I intend to stop attacking myself and others, and for others from attacking me.

2000 July 14, 5:30 am - On my first day of school, my father didn't leave me right away; he hung around for a few minutes and before he left, he told me that everything would be okay if I just listened to the teacher and learned to do, and be like the other kids. All my life I've watched, listened and learned, and tried to be like others. WOW! I didn't realize my imprint was that huge. Don't cry like a baby. You'll learn to be as smart as they are. Listen and obey your teacher and you won't get into trouble. Listen and you'll learn.

Journey to the Heart Centre

I just remembered something that I've never thought of since it happened. I just remembered that as I walked into the school that first day, there was this strange noise, a buzzing sound around me, and a sense of excitement in the air, in the other children. I also felt the dread and terror in me of not knowing what was going on. The only familiar sound in all this confusion was my fathers' voice, and so noise, and especially voices, people talking also terrifies me.

I don't like confusion, it's terrifying. It also brings up the feeling of not wanting to be born, there is no acceptance, no love, as my Mother and Father don't want me either. At school, I remember thinking that I don't want to be here as there is no acceptance here. These kids and teachers don't want me around. I know I'm going to get hurt, I can feel it, but my father keeps telling me that it's all in my head, not real, and that I'm going to be okay if I just learn to be like the other kids. Be like them, do like them, in other words become like the other kids and don't be me. Being myself is not good, wrong, different and bad. I'm confused as I don't know where to even begin to know what they are, what they are saying and what they are asking of me. I tried to answer what I felt they asked me, but I could only reply in German and not English. I didn't get accepted for my answer because they didn't understand me. I felt my feelings were wrong and had given the wrong answer. When I asked a question, they didn't understand me either and so it just got worse. The harder I tried to express myself, the more I was ridiculed, scorned, and laughed at. Then at the first recess it got physically abusive. I was alone and abandoned.

My father said that he'd be back after school, but when was that? I had no concept of time. I just followed the crowd and when the bell rang, I followed them back into the school and did what they did or at least tried to imitate them. Even at lunch time they laughed at me and at my lunch that was in a box, not a lunch pail or a bag, it was some kind of box, I really don't remember any more. They also made fun of the food that I ate and how I ate. I was ashamed, ashamed to be me.

I felt I wasn't good enough and that they were better than me. I wished I wasn't who I was and that I wasn't there. There was no right place and no right time for me. It seemed like an eternity before school was over and the kids started to go home. I remember not knowing what was going on or what I was expected to do next. There was no one to ask or tell me what was going on. I just stood in the schoolyard, alone, waiting for anyone to help me but no one was there. Finally, my father came to pick me up. I don't remember much of what happened going home, I only remember being told at supper-time that it would be different tomorrow when I went back to school. I was terrified; I didn't want to go to school. I remember being told that I had to go to school to learn so that I would not be stupid, so that I

Chapter 16 - 2000 - The New Millennium

could get a good job when I grew up and not be poor, to be and have what other people have, and not be like we are.

The imprints that I received were that what I was and had, what we were and had, was not good enough. I had to learn to be what I wasn't, to be someone else, other than who or what I was. I had to have what others had and not what I had or wanted. I had to do as others did and not what I wanted to do. I changed myself, sold myself out to be like others, to have what others had just to be accepted and maybe loved.

Who am I? What do I want? I don't know. All I do know is that who I was and what I wanted wasn't good enough. Now, how do I remember who I am and what I want? I want love, acceptance, joy, peace, harmony and abundance. All my life a part of me knew what I wanted, what I wanted to do, but I could never express it because I had to be like the others even though I knew I was different. I had to be the same or else it meant trouble, and if it brought trouble to me, it must be a sign that being me is wrong and bad. So I would try even harder to not be me and to be more like the others, or what others expected me to be even if being like others didn't feel good or right.

I have so suppressed and compressed myself which is why I feel that I can't even float on water or swim. I'm so compressed, dense, especially my lower back and legs, the lower chakras, that when I try to float, my legs sink and the rest of my body follows as if I was made of stone. In order to float, I need to constantly be moving my arms and legs and that gets exhausting.

I feel that I also have to remember who I was before I went to school because that was also an abusive period, just in a different way, as I wasn't good enough for my parents either. I wanted to be the boy my father and mother wanted me to be and not the boy I was either. Now, in this moment, I can become who I really am. Now I can do what I really want to do. I don't have to be like other people. I don't have to please other people to show them that I'm okay and that's scary too, to be different. That's not just scary but terrifying, and at the same time heartbreaking at the thought of how much of myself I've lost or given up.

I had reached the bottom of the page and a division in the sectioned ringed note pad I was writing in. I was going to turn the orange section divider over so that I could write on the next page, but I thought, why be like everyone else, why not write on the divider, who needs lines, why not be different. So here I am, writing on the divider and it's okay, it's also okay if somebody sees it and asks me why.

I'm afraid to be myself, afraid to express my wants, needs, desires, dreams, passion, excitement, and my joy. They were always put down, so I would put them down myself before someone else did as that hurt less, and that's another imprint. I felt that I couldn't have fun or any joy unless someone else was having fun. I felt that I didn't deserve it or that it was wrong not to be like the other person. If they were not having fun then I should not be having fun either. If they were poor, I should help them not to be, or feel poor. I also didn't want them to suffer like I did so I would always help those that I could (out of guilt) and then I'd feel pissed off when I needed help and no one would help me. If they were rich, I should also be rich and if I'm not and can't do it for myself, then what's wrong with me. If they were whatever, I should be able to be like them or have what they have.

I'm laughing at myself as I'm realizing what a fucked up world I've been living in. So how do I change it? By changing myself back to being myself and not what I think others want me to be or do, or me wanting to be like others. Is it by expressing my fears, doubts and judgments, whatever my Will (Soul), Mind (Spirit), Body and Heart feel they need to express and desire to manifest? I want to be me, really me, all of me, the love that I am. I intend and desire to move unloving light out and off of me to its right place and to fill those places with true love and light. To move the psychopathic Killer, guilt and shame out and off of me to their right place. I release any and all judgments, programs, imprints and beliefs that do not serve my highest purpose, good, true love and light. I intend to spiritualize this physical body, to heal, to become whole on all levels. To bring heaven to Earth and to help heal the Earth, lost Will, and I was going to say help my brothers and sisters, but that didn't feel totally right. I don't know why, not that I'm not going to help them, but there is more to it. I intend to open to receive love. I intend to open to all my gifts and powers. I intend to ask for what I want. I intend to allow myself to receive help, to be helped. I intend to experience the acceptance of love. I feel that now the big job is to separate what I feel, what I really want, what is me, from what I thought I wanted and what I thought I had to be and was.

I paused for a few moments and received the following message on freedom. Freedom: is being free of your beliefs, programs, and imprints. Being free to be totally yourself, to express yourself in love. Not that you didn't know how to express yourself in an unloving manner, for you have experienced that also, but now it is your choice.

I stopped and picked up the "Right Use of Will Book," book #8 "Indigo" and opened to page 209. It was about people being from a parallel universe, and what I read opened up a lot of questions. There is no free Will, nor has there been free Will in this universe. Why? Is it because there are two universes? There is polarity, hot and cold, up and down and all that, but that is not the same thing as duality, right or wrong, good or bad. When it comes to free Will, there is no state of being that expresses free Will. So where is the balance, the right place? A universe of free Will and a universe of no free Will? Free Will to them would feel just as awful as no free Will feels to us. So now, is it time for both of us to be happy and each to have their right place and time, and both knowing, no, I was going to say the same feelings, but we don't. We have lots of experience denying our Wills as do they, but they have

Chapter 16 - 2000 - The New Millennium

no experience of accepting their Wills and that's a BIG DIFFERENCE. If they could accept their Wills, then there'd be no duality and no need for another universe to separate the two.

We have both in this free Will universe because we thought they were just like us, and so we tried to accept and love them, but they didn't like that, they hated that and we didn't know why. The more we tried to love them, the harder they fought and rejected us. To them, love and acceptance feels as foreign as unlovingness and denial feel to us. We accepted them more than they accepted us, and we became more like them. I feel everything has been mixed together; black and white is now gray, and I was thinking of the Yin Yang symbol as an example. I feel that now is the time for separation and for each to be in their right place. For those love spirits that still want to deny their Wills, they will have the opportunity to do so in the "other" universe, not this one, until such time that they choose otherwise, and so it is, balance and harmony, peace and freedom will be experienced by both. Lots of questions and assumptions, but still something is missing.

2000 July 15 - I met Irene for lunch today and the restaurant was full of thought forms and form changes feeding on denial. I was also feeling the strength and power of being in the moment without denial, speaking and feeling at the same time with no gaps. Unlovingness and denial have no power, other than that we give it by our denials.

After lunch, I picked Jen up, we did a little grocery shopping, and afterwards we went back to her place. I felt that Jen wanted to say something, but wouldn't. I kept trying to get her to say what it was she wanted to do but was denying. Finally, she said she was tired and that she needed to lie down and rest for a while, so that later, she could have the energy to make herself something to eat. She also said that she wanted to do a meditation and a judgment release. I said fine and that I was going to leave. She said, "No, why leave?" I felt that she was really asking me to stay out of guilt and also a form of control, that after I agreed to stay, she would ask me to leave. I expressed myself and she said that that wasn't the case and she talked me into staying. She also said she wanted to express her feelings but that she was tired because I was late in coming to pick her up after lunch. I felt it was only blame that she was expressing and that it was my fault that I was late picking her up and that put her off her schedule.

She lay down on her futon and I sat in the chair next to her. As I began to relax, I could feel that I too was feeling tired. I wasn't comfortable sleeping in the chair so I quietly slipped off the chair and laid down on the carpet. She said that she was almost asleep when I moved and that I woke her up, and that now she can't sleep if I'm lying on the floor or if I go to sleep. As predicted, she said, "You have to leave." That pissed me off as I felt used. Why didn't I go when I felt like I wanted to go as I knew what would happen, but no, I felt sorry for her, like I had to be there to listen to her, so I denied myself and that's what I got reflected.

We were still not hearing each other's words and both of us were feeling not heard and misinterpreted. I was feeling confused, frustrated and angry, and feeling that this relationship was not going to work out and that there was no end in sight. I feel hopelessness, alone and that I'm trouble for everyone that is involved with me.

2000 July 18 - I was talking to Irene last night regarding the messages she had been getting on multi-sensory perception, and we were touching that some of them are what we're going to be doing next. One was feeling the other person's actual fear, not just tapping into it or being aware, but feeling it and I felt how that was going to be a real healing process for both. We were also going to be able to heal and take care of our physical bodies without the need of food or water. Other ones that were going to be developed were astral travel, astral projection, and being in different places at the same time, not only here on Earth, but also other planes of existence. Others were Telekinesis, levitation, shrinking and expanding space, stopping and moving forward or back in time, and being able to change it, or the perception of it. Shape shifting was another one, changing our physical being, our appearance even our age, as well as changing into animals, plants or whatever. We would also be communicating with elementals, plants, animals and ET's.

These extra senses are in addition to what we already have, These are new ones and I feel we are going to have 33, I don't know if that's 33 in total or 33 additional ones. There was also the increased sense and awareness of what is good and evil, what a person's intent is, what a person's pain is, their thoughts, and feelings. There was also the ability to tap in to the Akashic records, knowing all the things that you and others can do, and have done in the past, including past lives. We would also, when appropriate, have the ability to heal other people, mentally, emotionally and physically with hands on, or by long distance. Besides our ability to communicate with the elements, we will also be able to have them assist us when needed. There are a lot of changes coming that will defy scientific explanation.

2000 July 22 - We need to create, not re-create. When we are in the moment, in the flow, the experiences are magical and unique. We limit ourselves or stop the flow by either trying to re-create something, or trying not to create the original experience and in doing so, we are not in the now, the present moment creating a new experience.

Being at One

2000 July 23 - To be at one is to be at one with everything you are. You cannot be at one with everything unless you are first at one with

Chapter 16 - 2000 - The New Millennium

yourself and that means getting all the pieces of you that you have cut off. It is not life you choose if you choose to lift off, to end the suffering, to be in a better place, it is death. This time of transition is a time of gathering your "self" together, healing yourself. No one is going to do it for you, you need not do it alone, but you will also feel alone and abandoned for this is what you have done to yourself when you cut off these pieces you did not like to feel or experience.

How much you have to heal depends on how much you were in denial and how deeply you are imprinted and programmed, and also by your intent to be able to let go of the urge to defend and protect your past. For you believe your past creates the present and the future and that is true, and we smile. So you care to hold onto the past even though you know it creates the present and the future. We are not saying to let go of the past and move past yourself and your emotions that you have left trapped there. We are saying to let go of the past, the programs, imprints and beliefs that no longer serve you, so that you can go back to heal those parts that you cut off when you had no choice if you were going to survive, or thought you had to in order to survive. As you gather more and more of yourself together, you will also become aware of how the beliefs, judgments and programs were put in place and it will become easier to see them for what they really are.

This is a wondrous time but also one that feels the most frightening and unknowing as it goes against all that you were and still are being told is true. This turn around and going against the flow of humanity and their denials, to go with the flow of love, self-love, seems foreign, for you feel you are going in the wrong direction. But rest assured that some of the people you passed going the other way will notice you and they will stop, and as they do, so will others, and then one by one they too will turn around and follow you. Not follow you, but follow your path, your way that you have shown them.

It takes faith, blind faith and a knowing from deep within to keep going even though all you see and feel seems to tell you to give up, that you are wrong. You have much faith even though at times you wish you didn't. For in this faith is also your essence, your purpose, your intent to heal. Blessings this wondrous morning, Mother and Father

> *You can't see the tree for the forest* - **Shenreed**

Chapter 17 - Lost and Alone

2000 July 24 - Heartbreak is what I feel I'm touching now as I'm remembering my experience last Friday, when Jen and I went to the city of Barrie for a drive and to do some shopping. We were in a discount store and as I passed by two little girls about two and four years old, the two-year-old showed me a gray stone in her hand that she had picked up from the store floor a moment ago. Earlier that day, I had bought an amethyst/citrine crystal that I happened to be holding in my hand. I opened my hand to show it to her and she reached for it and took it before I could react. I knew she thought I was giving it to her but I really just wanted to show it to her. I felt guilty and didn't know how to get it back without breaking her heart and making her cry. I told the mother, "It's okay she can have it," even though it was the only crystal that appealed to me and I was happy and excited when I bought it.

A moment later I met Jen in the next aisle and I told her what had happened. As I told my story I felt my heart break as I felt how I really wanted that stone. Jen told me to get it back. I reluctantly turned and went back to see the mother and explained what had happened and that I would really like my stone back. She took it from her daughter and gave it back to me. I felt like an ogre and guilty for reneging on my word, especially to a little child who didn't know I wasn't giving it to her.

I'm now beginning to get a headache. Before I started writing, I had the feeling I was about to experience all the heartbreaks and heartaches that I've had in my life. Knowing that I wasn't wanted as a baby and the times I was nearly killed, but somehow survived, then living with the fear, pain and agony of not knowing when or where the next strikes were going to come from. Then there was school, thinking and hoping that maybe now my life would change, be better than it was at home, but it wasn't to be. It was just a different form of abuse and even more terrifying was the fact that in school there were even more to look out for.

The heartbreak of knowing that you're different and that you don't fit in, don't belong, but all the while you long and yearn to be the same, to be like them, to do and act like them, to be accepted, but it never worked. You somehow never seemed to be quite good enough in some way or another, no matter what you did or what you gave, it was never enough. There was heartbreak all my life, home, family, school, so-called friends and relationships, wife, work and businesses. I worked hard to get and to have the things I thought would make the people in my life and me happy, but it was never enough; it didn't make them or me happy. So what do I need to touch? I'm

Chapter 17 – Lost and Alone

open to feel, to remember all those parts of me that are lost and hurt and to accept and heal them. I want to be whole.

When I laid down on my bed, I got the insight about body pain and how we close around the pain, not wanting to feel it. When we say we don't want to hurt the body anymore it's more a fear and denial, rather than about feeling and healing the pain. As an example, a dislocated shoulder has to be pulled out (feeling the pain again) before it can be put back in its right place so that it can heal. I feel it's the same with emotions.

2000 July 24, 2:17 am - During our late evening tea and chat, Irene had mentioned that her guides, Gabriel and Michael had been with her ever since she could remember. This evening she mentioned that there were two women standing by my bedroom door. One was a young, tall, blond, blue-eyed nurse named Sarah, and the other was Astrid, who was in her mid-thirties, auburn hair, green eyes and freckles (beauty marks as Astrid called them). Irene said that Astrid was my guide. When I went to bed, I asked Astrid, what are you here to help me with?

Reawakening Your Powers

2000 July 24 - Greetings, I am here to assist you, to help you open to your abilities, especially now those of seeing through your third eye. Yes, you have fear of darkness, of dark beings and your parents (mother) frightened you, as Gabriel said, into believing that your shadow was also what she called the "Booggie Man" and similar to what you saw.

As you grew older, you desired to see less and less, and when your mother raged at you when you were ten, the time of your admitted precognition, it frightened you so, as expressing what you saw brought you negative, disquieting and unpleasant attention. It also brought fear of the Devil, and that not what you saw was evil, but that seeing it was evil. So you basically shut down, dismissed and abandoned your gifts and your powers.

As I'm typing this I'm feeling the heartbreak of those experiences. There was unknowing and fear in what I saw, but there was also joy in other things. People are so fearful and ignorant of what they can't see or what they don't know, that they aren't even aware of the damage they do, especially when you are young, as you trust your parents and elders to know what's best for you. ♥

Are you ready to see again?

Me: I'm afraid. I have to admit a part of me is afraid of seeing but I also know a lot more now and I have Irene to help me understand what I'm seeing. I'm not two or ten years old anymore, and I need to go back and bring those parts back to me don't I? Yes, I am ready. I want to reclaim what I've lost; I even feel there is a part of me back there, the wonder and magical part of me, I want that back too.

      Indeed, and that is why (we) were and are here, to nurse and mother you, that child that was mentally, emotionally and physically tortured and tormented.

Me: Thank you

I (we) thank you for opening to hear me. Sleep, I am here with you. Astrid.

♡ I just realized that Astrid and Sarah were responsible for keeping me alive all those times when I should have died as a child. I'm overcome with emotions, I didn't know. ♥

2000 July 24, 8:17 am - I can hear my mothers' voice saying, if you don't behave, listen to me, be quiet, go to sleep, say your prayers, do your chores, sit still, eat that, share, and other commands, that the Boogie Man will get you, "Oh, here he comes now." If it wasn't the Boogie Man that was coming to get you, then it would be that you'll go to hell if you don't, or the Devil will get you if you don't. If those threats didn't work she'd use, I'll beat the devil out of you if you don't do this or that, or if you do this or that. She also had me believe that my shadow was the Boogie man. There was always some kind of threat or a fear used as a means to control both me and my siblings.

♡ I just felt that little lost part of me terrified and confused, with no mother or father, or anyone to turn to for support. The very person he should be able to trust is the one that is the terrorist. I also feel the heartbreak of it all, including the hopelessness and helplessness. Fuck, she was cruel. ♥

The following is a message received after breakfast from Arc Angel Gabriel (Gabe) via Irene

Activating Emotions by Touch

    There are two ways to assist yourself and others in opening and healing emotions.
1) Touch your heart or their heart with your finger and hold it there for a few moments.
2) Place your index or middle fingers (left and right hand) on both sides of the bridge of the nose, close to the eyes. Now move the fingers down both sides of the nose/cheek to the edge of the nostril and then across the cheeks to the side of the temples beside the corners of the eyes.

Chapter 17 – Lost and Alone

Repeat the process

♡ I just touched my breastbone over my heart. It is sore and very tender to the touch and I felt it's what my heart feels like too. ♥

2000 July 25, 3:30 pm - It's Monday afternoon and I'm sitting on the beach of Georgian Bay on the 9th concession, near Balm Beach. I'm getting some sun and thinking of what is going on in my life. Jen and I were in our usual off/on telephone argument/discussion this morning that lasted for almost three hours.

When I left her place early Saturday afternoon, I felt that she was pushing me out but I never said anything as she said that she'd see me tomorrow. When I called her on Sunday about getting together, she said that she was busy painting a figurine that the boy had given her and didn't want company. I was confused, as when I was over on Saturday, I had noticed a book that she said the boy had given to her, but she never mentioned that he had also given her a figurine. I questioned her as to why she never said anything or showed it to me on Saturday when I saw the book. I felt she was holding something back. When she said that I didn't ask to see it, we got into our usual argument when I asked, "How could I ask to see something that I didn't know you had."

When we never got together on Sunday, I figured we'd be getting together, today, being Monday. She called this morning saying that she was going to be spending the day with the young boy and that she really had wanted to see me yesterday and that she was heartbroken that it didn't work out because we were fighting. I told her that I felt resentment, used, setup, and rejected. I told her that I felt that she and the boy had already made plans to get together on Saturday afternoon, which is why I had to leave early and that she wasn't honest in telling me so. I also felt that when he didn't show on Saturday, it was switched to Sunday, and when that didn't pan out it was changed to Monday. When I told her this, she said that I was jealous and possessive and that I had an issue because every time he was coming over to see her, I'd start a fight. After three hours of her hanging up on me, or me hanging up on her, we called it quits as he had arrived and she had to go.

I went for a walk along the beach and when I came back, I began to write again. I had told Jen that yes, I was jealous of her friends and lovers, and now this young boy, and even though she hasn't has sex with him she has sexual feelings for him and so does he for her. She'd laughingly said, "What, you're jealous of a relationship that can't go anywhere?" I said, "Yes, at least it's better than being shunned, alone and being thought of as non sexual,"

It's not the sex for me; it's the physical touch, the contact of another human being, of feeling alive, even if it's just for a fleeting moment. I'm jealous that I don't have that in my life. I want a friend and a lover (female). I guess I just really want to be loved, nurtured, feel kindness and tenderness that isn't centered around sex. I have romance, passion, desire, and all the rest of these feelings that I can't share with Jen and that's why I'm jealous that she can share that with others. I feel I can't express any of this as most of it is non-verbal and it's not something that can just be talked about. To be activated, felt, and expressed, it needs the physical contact, otherwise it's just explaining the longing, the desire and the need, and maybe that's what has to happen first. Maybe I have to express the sadness, the disappointment that I can't experience it with her or anyone else at this moment.

Irene is married but she is way too terrified to talk of men, let alone sex, sexuality, or sensuality. I feel so alone as I see people walking, holding hands, talking, smiling and looking into each other's eyes and it makes me happy for them, but I'm also envious in that they have something that I don't. I feel like I'm the fucked up one, the misfit, the loner, an outcast, not with the program, swimming against the current and wondering why everything seems to be passing me by. Jen says that I have fear and terror of women, just as she has fear and terror of men.

I went for another walk along the beach and I noticed that I'm starting to get some sun. I feel sad that what I enjoy doing I have to do alone. I can't share this part of the beach with Jen as she has never wanted to come here and she always has some reason or excuse. She always wants to go to Balm Beach, which I can see from here, as it's about half a mile to the north. She likes Balm beach because that's where she spent a lot of her time as a teenager. It's commercial, crowded and the beach is somewhat rocky. This beach, while it does have limited access and is overlooked by private cottages, has a fine sandy beach, and today there are maybe 50 people to my left, scattered over 1000 feet of beach, and to my right there's no one for also 1000 feet. The water on this beach is also shallow and you have to go out a couple of hundred feet from shore before you get in over your head.

I can't really swim, so going swimming by myself is not something I do for any length of time, but I usually go in once or twice. Usually, I just lay around on the beach to get some sun, feel the wind, breathe the fresh air, and maybe read or write. At times, I'd pause to watch the clouds and gulls floating by overhead, or turn to watch the water, listening to the waves lapping or crashing against the shore. Other times I'd watch the children at play, the people on the beach or in the water, or the canoes, sailboats and Sea-doos that attract my attention. Once in a while I'd go for a walk along the shoreline and collect interesting pieces of driftwood, shells, rocks, and feathers. The driftwood and feathers are later used to make native talking sticks.

Letting Go and Opening to Love

2000 July 24, 10:13 pm - Greetings, this is Astrid. You still feel me very softly, weakly, but our connection is getting stronger. You are

Chapter 17 – Lost and Alone

struggling much for it is hard for you to let go, to let go of the tiny bit of love you feel you are getting, and so you cling to it, and in so doing, do you suffocate it. It is difficult to open your hand to let it go, find freedom, but also as you do, a magical thing occurs; your hand is also open to receive. For you cannot receive with a clenched fist, and the tighter you squeeze the more you squeeze out and away from you. Open your hands and gently cup the love that is around you, bathe yourself in it, drink it into your very Being for it is limitless and boundless and it is there, simply by opening to receive.

I will be working with you more in your dream state, as will Sarah, but in different ways. I will be assisting you in opening your third eye and your gifts, your multi-sensory gifts that you have shut away and forgotten. It is now time to reactivate all that you have lost.

Yes, I was with you from the beginning of your journey and I will be with you till the end. There is much I have, we have to share, and in the times ahead, yes, you will see me and talk to me as easily as you presently talk to Irene, it won't be long. There are wondrous times ahead and many wow's and magic that will come into your experiences in all its glory. Changes indeed are coming, but you need not worry for you will be guided as to what to do at the right time.

Indeed, you are healing your chakras and your Heart, Will, Body and Mind. It is the chakras, especially 1st, 2nd and 3rd that you are working on now, and to open them you need to release the blocks, the beliefs, programs and imprints that hold them so much stuck, but not open or balanced.

I know you doubt what I say and that is okay. You were frightened and you were repeatedly taunted, ridiculed and belittled for what you saw and what you felt. It is not easy to undo the damage that was done. It has to be healed, little by little, but with each step, it will get easier and faster and you will be remembering all that you have tried to forget, including your gifts and who you are and your mission.

I am pleased; no, I am overjoyed that we are connecting this way. It gladdens me, my heart sings and I am dancing. Dance with me tonight. Let us begin to bring joy to your experience, your physical experience as well. Open yourself to a world of surprises, to spontaneity, to joy, to love and light. Astrid.

I put down my pen and picked up the book "Right Use of Will" by Ceanne DeRohan and just opened it to page 66. Half way down the page I had previously underlined several sentences. I began to read the following quote on reconnecting to your awareness and on perceptions.

"One of the most direct ways to reverse this and regain full consciousness is to start noticing everything you usually ignore. Give it acceptance and any expression you can. By starting with whatever you can notice first that would have otherwise been denied by you, and by cultivating the listening, receiving and noticing aspects of your nature and expanding their expressive possibilities, you will be amazed at how your consciousness can expand and unfold into wider awareness."

I'm amazed at how the universe just seems to flow and give you confirmations when you let it. I was contemplating the words of that message for a few moments and the following came to me. Taking your power back is when you feel you have a choice and the freedom to express as you desire. Freeing yourself from another's control and taking your power back by asking what the other is trying to have you do, say, think, believe, etc. as well as expressing what you are intuitively picking up, what it is they really want, but deny saying. An example of this is when you are being told something by someone who is trying to convince you to think, or to be more like they are. When you reply to their statements with direct questions, you take your power back. I paused, distracted for a moment and I lost what I was feeling. I turned out the light, rolled over, and went to sleep.

Raising Your Vibration

2000 July 29 - Raising your frequency is raising your vibration in love, raising yourself or becoming yourself, your true self, to become who you truly are and to recognize that although you are all essentially energy; you are not all of the same essence or vibration. You are not all the same; there is differentiation, so therefore you will not vibrate at the same rate or the same level.

This is also where fragmentation comes in for there are fragments of the same essence that vibrate at different rates, some higher or nearer true self and others lower, further away from true self and indeed may not be able to vibrate themselves back to their true selves. Indeed there are many here and more will come here, or to be more correct, more will come here to find teachers, to learn, to heal their Will and raise their vibration and restore essence. Human form is unique in creation, but it is not the only form in creation. There is much to be revealed in the time ahead.

Forgiveness of Self

2000 July 29, 5:27 am - It is I, Astrid that comes to you now. Forgiveness, self-forgiveness is essential if you are to heal, for without it there is no movement, only blame, regret and judgments that nothing can change. Allow yourself to see where you have judgments and recognize them for what they are and allow yourself to forgive yourself for still hanging on to these beliefs and judgments. You did not make a mistake. You did nothing wrong even though the experience was not what you would have preferred; it was the one you had chosen to experience. So accept it and accept yourself

Chapter 17 – Lost and Alone

for having chosen it for reasons that you are not totally aware of yet, and release the blame on that part of yourself that you hold accountable for your experience. For you, in your totality, are responsible for your experience, and forgiveness is also part of the experience, the process. It is another step in the healing and re-claiming of self and also your gifts, powers and talents.

It's all right. I know these words seem foreign to you in the moment for you have chosen to blame the outward reflection for your experiences. But you have also chosen to blame some of your inner essence too, for its lack of not being able to provide your desired outer experiences and hating that part of yourself that would draw this type of attention and experience to you. You have chosen to feel much and heal much, and in order to do that, there was much needed to experience from a different point-of-view than others who choose to experience and heal and recover less, so to say, without being judgmental. (Long pause)

I can feel your confusion, frustration, and inner turmoil that feels this is impossible to heal, but rest assured, you are going to heal. Rest now, let yourself go. Allow your dream state to show you where and how to go about forgiving yourself and then to be able to forgive others and accept them for who and what they are.

Indeed, you constantly compare yourself to others and others to you. You feel inferior or superior, good or bad, better or worse, these are judgments and you are not the same as they are and you need to allow yourself to be different, to see the world through your eyes, and, if others do not see the same world, allow them to be different, for they too have their experiences, their processes just as you do. When they awaken, those that do, will also feel as you do now, and it is then that you can also help them.

You are unique, as are they, but you are the one writing the books, the Wayshower, to show others what and how to heal themselves as you are doing. There is no real book that can be the experience, for words are only words, hold only so much energy, an idea, a framework, a possibility of creation, but when experienced and felt, only then can the true and full concept come to fruition. Continue as you were and more will come. Blessings, Astrid.

2000 Aug 1 - Today, Jen, Irene, and I went rock hounding. Irene knew of a place that was about a one-hour drive, where there were quartz crystals and other minerals that were exposed due to recent highway construction. We spent the better part of the afternoon busy with our hammers and chisels collecting a few nice specimens. Too bad rocks are so HEAVY!

Crystals and Helping Others

2000 Aug 02, 3:00 am - Volcanoes of emotions will be released. There is nothing you can do for another before you have done it for yourself that is not self-sacrifice and denying your issues. For in trying to assist another with their problem that you have compassion for, you are happy to deny your issues, your pain and rather live and feel the pain through another, that when it becomes too intense, you can detach and deny it also. Although in your mind, you justify it differently as if you are "merely allowing them to be themselves."

There are/were many emotions and issues that were touched by working with the crystals, "the Earth," the Mother, this evening, and on many levels, more than you can comprehend at this moment as the magnitude of it would be overwhelming. You have made a difference as will be witnessed by a volcano. Fear not that you are responsible for what is to happen to others, but in truth know that in part, you are responsible for what is to happen, for the movement and the healing of the Mother, of the Earth that is taking place.

There is much more that you will share, for we know that you will be sharing these messages. Continue to work as you have and allow whatever comes up to move, be it ever so slight. Allow yourselves to "feel" the power and help that each crystal, stone, or rock can bring you, and you it in return, although you may not realize that you are doing so. You have many questions, but patience, and all will be revealed at the proper time and you will know. Blessings, Mother and Father.

2000 Aug. 2 - I went to town in the afternoon to do some photo copying and when I finished, I decided to stop in to see Jen. The door was locked and after knocking three times she came down and greeted me. When she opened the door I noticed two large water guns lying on the entrance floor and I asked whose guns they were. She said they were hers and that she had them since her last boyfriend, and that she and the boy had played with them when he was there. In the three and a half years that I've known her, I never knew she had water guns. I was even more confused as we had gone out several times looking for large water guns, and even ending up buying a couple of small hand held pistols so that we could have water fights, when all the while she had the ones that we were looking for.

As we talked more about the water guns, she kept mixing up the words "have" and "had." She would say things like, "I had water guns" when she actually meant to say, "I have water guns." I told her that I felt betrayed when she said that she had them for over three years. I feel I can't trust her, that what she says is not what she means, that she keeps secrets and also that I have to read her mind (again) to see if what she says and what she means are the same thing. I felt a lot of emotions and issues coming up in me, but trying to talk to Jen seemed hopeless at the time so I just left. I went to the Pizza shop, ordered a slice of Pizza and a can of pop, and went to the dock to eat it before returning home.

Chapter 17 – Lost and Alone

When I got home, I talked to Irene for a few minutes, telling her that I had stopped in at Jens and the story about the water guns. After my talk with Irene, I called Jen and she mentioned that after I left, she talked to the boy who had been drying off up stairs during my unexpected visit. That started another argument, as I said I didn't even know he was still there but that I knew he had been there as that is what she had said. I asked her why she didn't say anything when I was talking to her, and she told me that I was already confused about the guns and that I didn't listen to her. She also told me that she had just got off the phone with Irene a few minutes ago, before I got home. Now I don't even feel like talking to Irene because Irene didn't tell me that she had already talked to Jen, who told her all about the water guns. I shared my experience and my feelings and emotions with Irene, but she never said a word to me that she even knew anything about it. I'd feel like a liar and a cheat if I was told something about a person or experience and then talked to the other person pretending to know nothing of what is going on and playing stupid. I guess it was private! I confronted Irene and she became upset that I accused her of lying to me and went off to her computer room.

I hate these lies and secrets, as later when the truth comes out they try to cover up with more lying, denying and saying that they told me, when in fact they never did, or they only told me part of the truth. If that doesn't work for them, then they might say that I must have forgotten, misunderstood, misinterpreted, or that I didn't hear what was being said. This isn't the first time that Jen pressed my buttons, but it is the first time that Irene has pushed the same buttons. I feel that all this has something to do with the school kids again and also with my mother stating something as a truth, but then saying or doing the opposite, and denying what she said in the first place.

2000 Aug 4, 6:00 am, Friday - I feel I'm repeating a cycle again. It's been over a year since I left the Heart Centre and I'm in the same spot financially. I feel that I'm a loser, stupid, stubborn, selfish, incompetent, wasteful, no good, not worth anything, good for nothing. I'm having more and more issues come up with Jen as I've seen her only for a couple of days in July, both of which ended in arguments. Our talks on the phone are also getting few and far between and we were arguing yesterday and again today. It feels so frustrating and hopeless, as we seem to keep going around in circles, our friendship, and our hopes for healing seems to be diminishing with each confrontation.

Dave hasn't been sociable since last fall when I beat him at playing horseshoes by throwing four consecutive ringers in the last game. We tolerate each other, or maybe to be more accurate, I leave him be unless he tries to control me. So I still don't have any male friends and I also feel that I'm losing my female friends. I still have no job or money. I started writing my book in July but that's going slowly. I also started to look at rental space to hold classes again.

Journey to the Heart Centre

My Ford Aerostar van is literally falling apart with rust. The rocker panels are gone, literally gone, and the rust is eating away at the wheel wells and doors now, and I noticed that one of the gas tank support straps has also rusted off. The engine and transmission oil pans are rusting out too and leaking oil, and the power steering is also leaking. But hey, looking on the bright side, there are two things that aren't rusting and haven't even got a mark on them, and that is my hood and tail-gate which are made of plastic. Hats off to the brilliant Ford engineers because yeah, that's where we need maximum rust protection, (said with complete sarcasm). The wipers went weird two days ago and I have fear that my van is going to quit and that I'll have no money to fix it. I'll be stuck out here; ten minutes to the nearest town and a $25.00 cab ride one way, as there are no buses running out here. I feel trapped, cornered, with no way out and no place to go if I did get out. I feel no one in this community is ready for what I have to offer or share. Maybe the people in Barrie would be more open, or even further south. I have self-doubt that what I want to do is the right thing, that maybe all the others out there are right and okay, and I'm the one that is all fucked up.

Trust and Betrayal

2000 Aug 06, 3:34 am - Blessings, this is Astrid. You have concern and worry regarding your relationship with the one you call Jen. These are trying times for both as she is having to go deep within to reclaim her lost memories, and the biggest part of that is acknowledgment, for in acknowledging this part of her, she will hear and learn the truth and her whole world will come tumbling down. She has fear that she can't make it as well as fears that she is wrong, and her fear of being wrong terrifies her, for being wrong is part of what guilt holds on her for her father's actions.

Yes, you too have issues, but they are different from what you believe they are and what she says she is reflecting to you. Trust is the issue for you, trusting yourself, your feelings, and knowing your knowing. These are part of what you need to heal. For you feel you get talked out of, or you talk yourself out of your feelings and that expressing them is wrong. For if others deny your truth, you feel you are wrong and therefore must deny them also. Confusion is part of it also for when you do not trust, you are confused and your linear mind cannot remember pertinent details and that sends you into a panic and so you try to defend yourself.

Betrayal and abandonment are also part of the issue for you no longer trust each other, and so you feel abandoned and betrayed. There are many issues and many layers that need to be healed as well as judgment release. It is not easy for you, for her, for both of you together. There is nothing I, or anyone can do for you here, it is something you must feel your way through (each of you). I feel your loss, your bewilderment, your frustration, but know that you are not alone. Allow yourself to get through

Chapter 17 – Lost and Alone

and past the anger and rage, and let yourself feel your real pain, your hurt, fears, and judgments that lie beneath. These are the ones that you need to touch, to heal, and release the judgments that hold them from being released.

Blessings, allow yourself to sleep and in your dreams will come more to assist you, which you can remember and release when you are awake. Astrid

2000 Aug 08, 12:52 am - What I hate on the outside is what I hate and judge about me on the inside. I intend to become aware of all my fears, judgments and to also become aware of how I am treating myself. I intend to heal and release all judgments, guilt, shame, and I ask for help to become aware of when I am doing this. I intend to stop attacking others and myself with my judgments, anger, and rage and to heal and replace these actions with love and acceptance.

2000 Aug 8 - I've only seen Jen once for half an hour since the water gun episode and that was to take her grocery shopping. Today we got together and drove out to Balm Beach, but we left because of the dark energy we felt there that made us feel uncomfortable. We then went to the Mall and experienced the same dark energy, especially coming from a couple of men that were staring at us. We never really discussed it; we just left and went back to Jens place for a brief visit before I went home. I wasn't going to be seeing Jen on her Birthday, which is tomorrow, as she was going to a concert at Ontario Place in Toronto, so I secretly came back and dropped off her present at her door so that she would find it later.

Later that night, when I was having my usual tea with Irene, she said that my aura suddenly changed. Moments earlier, I had felt a dread that something was coming that I didn't like and I told Irene that I felt it was Lucifer and two other beings. Irene didn't see anything at first but after a few minutes she saw what she recognized as Lucifer and Rama. As they appeared to her, I could also smell them. It was a totally unpleasant combination of rotten sardines (Rama) and decaying flesh (Lucifer). I also felt that a cheetah, a falcon and Astrid my guide, were near me and Irene confirmed that yes, she saw them protecting my back and that the animals looked like they were ready to attack. There were also seven grandmothers, all facing Lucifer and Rama. Irene said that it was as if a bubble of light was protecting me and that they couldn't get any closer. She said I could talk to him to see why he was here, but I felt no urge to get into a conversation with him, but I did feel that he was here to try to stop me from doing something. Then I remembered the energy at Balm beach and at the mall, it was his energy that we had felt. We had felt and seen the darkness of Luciferian light around others today, and now I recognized and smelt it for what it was. At that moment, I felt safe but

Journey to the Heart Centre

I was concerned for Jen. Irene said that Gabe had told her that Jen was okay and was also being protected.

2000 Aug 10, 4:32 am - I awoke with the question, "What would I do if this was the last day I had to live on Earth." I don't know? There is so much I want to do. First, I think I'd cry that it was all over and that I failed to do all that I wanted to do. I don't want to create or experience just mentally. I want to experience it with all of me, in balance, mentally, emotionally, physically and spiritually. So what do I need to do to begin to experience the magic of love in my life? I call upon Mother and Father, Astrid, Merlin, the Grandmothers and all my guides who are here to assist me, to help me in whatever way is appropriate. I want to lift this veil, this veil of illusion. I want to be, to become who I really am, and to experience life with all the magic, power and love that I possess. I want to heal all these parts of me that believe that I can't have what I want, or be who I truly am.

I feel that I'll just go on pretending to be who I am until I heal those parts of me who believe that I can't be who I am. I feel that is what I've been missing and is a "key" point. I don't want to deny and lose anymore of my Will or reject any part of me that the other part doesn't like, or doesn't want to experience or even admit that it exists. I see myself as a teacher and a healer in a lot of different ways, but I also see myself enjoying life, experiencing what I want to experience and being who I am.

11:41 am - This morning, during and after breakfast, Irene said that her and my guides were all gathering around us. She saw, and I felt a moose, elephant and Llama appear, followed by the grandmothers, elders, shaman, archetypes, and aspects of our past lives bringing gifts and talents of who we were through the ages. More and more just kept coming as there were also ET's Angels, Seraphims, Cherubims, and then more animals, cats, bears, giraffes, eagles, herons, and numerous other birds and small animals, as well as dolphins, whales and different fish. Then came the elementals and the elements of Earth, Air, Fire, Water and Ether. Irene said that a lot of portals were opening for me. Later that afternoon, I started transcribing into my computer, my hand written journal entries and messages that were to become the foundations for this book.

> *Healing begins in the Heart. – Shenreed*

Chapter 18 – My Second Level of Healing

Chapter 18 – My Second level of Healing

2000 Aug 11 - After Irene and I had our usual Friday lunch at a restaurant in town, she went off to work while I drove over to visit Jen. I went upstairs to the living room where she was in the middle of watching her TV show - Northern Lights. Not wanting to interrupt her, I just sat down on the futon and watched the ending with her. After the show was over we were chatting about various topics and she mentioned that her Native American name was Summer Storm. I was confused and asked her how and when she got that name. She said that she had it for a long time. I remarked that I knew she called herself Summer, but that I never heard her, or anyone, mention Summer Storm before. One thing led to another and soon we were into another one of our arguments.

    I felt frustrated and was becoming angry at what I felt was her trying to control and manipulate me by telling me lies. I didn't want to fight with her again so I felt I had to leave. As I got up to leave, she yelled at me that I was running again, and asked me when I was going to stop. I glared at her, wondering how can this be happening and how can it be resolved, but I also felt it was hopeless in the moment and left without a word, tears streaming from my eyes, yet at the same time, cursing her under my breath.

    I got into my van and was going to leave, but before I started the engine something made me decide to wait for a moment. I looked at my watch; it was 3:15 pm. Thoughts were racing through my head and my emotions were all over the place. I thought to myself, why am I running again? I feel that I have three choices, that I can either fight, run or give in. I don't want to fight with Jen and direct my anger at her even though I feel that she's the problem, but I also just can't sit there and pretend that everything is fine and give in to her demands. All I can do is run, but what am I really running from is the question, and why? At that moment, I truly believed that I was being kind, loving, sharing, caring, compassionate, understanding, honest, self-sacrificing, a humanitarian, valued decency and good Christian principals, and all the other things that I thought love was. So what is the problem? I scratched my head as if that would give me the answers I was looking for.

    On the other hand, I thought that Jen was being a hypocrite and a liar, and that she was playing games and trying to Mind fuck and control me. In that moment, I also realized that with all the work I had done and all the emotions I had moved, that it was when I stopped fighting and running and just began expressing what I was denying, was when I would have a mini healing experience. We had fought and I had run so many times, that by now

I recognized the pattern, that I was being activated and that I was in denial. But what was it? What was I denying? Why am I in denial and not simply protecting myself from being controlled, manipulated and abused? Am I in denial because I had emotions and feelings that I didn't express, yet at the time I thought I did. Were these false emotions that I was expressing? What were my judgments? What was really activating me and why? I was in turmoil inside myself but I decided that I wasn't going to run this time, that I would go back and face what I had to face, but didn't want to face.

As I left my van I looked at my watch, it was 3:30 pm. I had tears in my eyes as I went back up the stairs to Jen's apartment. I told her that I wasn't running and she beamed a smile and said, "Good for you." We sat down and I began explaining what I had felt before I left and what I was thinking and feeling when I was sitting in the van, but before I even finished, Jen began telling me of one of her experiences that I had heard several times before. I told her that I wasn't finished, but she said that she thought I was, and that she was activated into telling her story and wanted to express herself. Feeling guilty and undeserving for taking up her time, I gave her the benefit of the doubt and was waiting to see where it tied in to what I had been talking about, but it wasn't coming up. Again, I told her that I had heard that story before and that she didn't have to tell it to me again, especially from the very beginning. She said that I was wrong and that she hadn't told me this story. To prove to her that she had, I began to tell what happened next in her story. She said, "Yes, but you forgot this part," and she continued her story again. I interrupted her saying, "Yes I heard that too, but I didn't mention it as I just wanted you to know that you did tell me the story." She disagreed with me and in frustration; I told her the ending of her story. This infuriated her even more and after chastising me for interrupting her again, she went back to where I had originally interrupted her the first time and began telling me her story as if nothing had ever happened.

I was confused by her actions but having just finished one argument thirty minutes ago, I wasn't looking forward to having another one, as all I wanted to do was to find out why and how I was being activated, and what my denials were. I continued being the nice guy, listening, being understanding, giving, caring, self-sacrificing, not being selfish, being there for others, and all the other so-called loving things I knew to do to make others happy. I didn't want to interrupt her again, but all the while I was feeling that what she was saying was bullshit, a lie, a cover-up and that she was a hypocrite. I could feel myself getting angry again and a couple of times I tried to ask her questions but was told, "I'm getting to that," or "don't interrupt me," and "wait until I'm finished talking." I was frustrated, confused and spinning and just wanted to run and get away. I felt angry and heartbroken, all at the same time. I felt I had had enough, that I had to get out or I would

Chapter 18 – My Second Level of Healing

explode. I didn't say a word as I got off the futon and began to make my way past the coffee table and toward the hallway.

I hadn't taken three steps when I heard a voice that was not Jen's voice, say in a soft and loving tone, "You have a choice."

I was so beside myself with the feeling of heartbreak and anger that I wasn't really aware of what was happening. I instantly replied to this voice with my Mind, not my physical voice, asking sarcastically, "What choice do I have?"

The voice replied, "You can run, you can fight, you can give up, or you can surrender to love."

"Surrender to love! What's that?" I exclaimed in my Mind.

At that point I immediately became aware that time stood still. Jen stood before me, frozen in space and time, her body standing motionless, arms paused in a mid-air gesture like a mannequin. Her eyes fixed and mouth half-open, lips pursed in the expression of an unsaid word. It was as if a pause button had been pushed and the world stood still.

I didn't hear the voice again, but I felt it asking me to look and feel beside me. I didn't see, but I felt my outer child that had visited me before during my meditation/visualization journeys, standing beside me. He was confused, heartbroken and in terror. He was still that six-year-old Catholic, German-speaking farm boy attending the Protestant, English speaking school and he was re-living the terror of that experience, as well as other experiences. I realized that one issue he had was being confused by the foreign language and not being able to communicate. Another and even bigger issue was his confusion with his mothers' words, and how she would say one thing but mean another, and that if he expressed what he was intuitively picking up on her, she would deny and tell him that he was wrong. If that didn't work, she would talk him out of his feelings or just tell him to be quiet and to speak when he was told to. I also felt how terrified he was of expressing himself for fear of displeasing his mother, and the heartbreak that he wasn't being heard or loved. I could also feel the utter heartbreak that no one was there for him, including me.

I then became part of my six year old, or rather, he became a part of me. I felt and remembered how intuitive he was and I instantly felt my intuition tell me what was really going on with Jen and her story, and even her original experience that traumatized her, and how she used story telling as a means to cover up her real issues. In that moment, I knew and felt what she was saying, what she was not saying, the secret she was keeping, and also what her real terror and heartbreak was that she was trying to cover up.

I also sensed and felt my anger and saw it as a huge cobra, coiled in front of me. It rose up and swayed in front of my face, eyes looking piercingly into mine, ready to strike, not at Jen like I expected, but at me. It was ready to strike me and was hissing and calling me the hypocrite for still not loving and giving this wounded part of me the same acceptance that I was giving Jen. At first I was shocked and I tried to defend myself and my beliefs. I tried to convince the Cobra that it was wrong and that its anger should not be directed at me, but at Jen, as she was the cause of my pain. I was aware of my thoughts, but then at the same time, I also became aware of the Cobra's thoughts and feelings, and realized that what the Cobra (my anger) was telling me was the truth.

That realization woke me up to the fact that I was the fool, and that it was me that was beating myself (this outer child) up, and not Jen. And that yes, I was prepared to show all these loving characteristics to, and for another person, but I didn't even offer a hint of the same compassion to myself. Instead, I had been beating myself (my outer child) up, scolding and berating myself with all what I thought were loving reasons for keeping my mouth shut. I gave myself no love. I was giving myself the exact opposite of what I was giving the other person. Dah!!!!!! Wake up! And I did. That's when I realized that everything I thought was love, actually wasn't love, and that before you can give true love to another you have to be able to give it to yourself first.

I knew I was in denial but now I finally realized what my denials were, but in a different way than I had originally thought. I realized that who I was really angry at was myself and that I was beating myself up by not allowing myself to ask questions in the moment when I was confused. I also realized that I was denying my Will, my intuition, from expressing itself in the moment for fear of losing a person that I thought and felt loved and accepted me. I wasn't there at all for my little boy; my outer child, that lost Will fragmented part of me who was heartbroken, terrified and alone. I gave him no acceptance or love, but instead, I gave him the opposite, indifference and cold heartlessness.

Time remained frozen as I opened my heart centre and chose love. It all flashed before me in an instant of awareness. It was in this moment that I saw and chose to end my denials. I also decided to give myself (my outer child) conscious acceptance and permission to interrupt and ask Jen direct questions, along with expressing what I was intuitively picking up. I knew I had a choice to make and I made it. When I gave myself permission to ask a question that I was confused about, my reality shifted. When I gave myself permission and acceptance to express my intuition, to trust that my intuition and feelings were right for me, even if Jen said that my intuition and feelings were wrong, that didn't make them wrong for me, again, I made a shift. When I felt

Healing begins in the Heart

Chapter 18 – My Second Level of Healing

something was wrong and unloving, I no longer had to believe or accept it and take it on or into me, I could now give it back, and with that I made another shift. I felt empowered, and as I took a deep breath I felt loving arms encircling me, flooding me with love that was not only around me, but also inside me. I was crying and smiling all at the same time as for the first time in my life, in my existence, I had given myself, and had felt and experienced unconditional love and acceptance. There was also this feeling of having something lifted off and out of me, I felt free in words that are indescribable.

The moment when I made those conscious heartfelt decisions was the moment when time began to move again. Jen was now moving and I heard the words she was speaking. Without saying a word, I simply raised my right hand at heart level, palm facing her, and motioned for her to stop. She stopped in mid-sentence and looked puzzled and confused. I felt that she recognized something different about me that she didn't see a few seconds earlier, excluding my smile and the tears streaming down my cheeks. I then spoke and expressed everything I had previously denied. I was beaming a smile, while at the same time, tears were flowing from my eyes. There was no fear, no anger, just the feeling of love as I calmly and assuredly spoke my truth.

By expressing my truth, Jen was activated into her issues, her terror. She too had a choice to heal that day, but instead of surrendering to love, she went further into denial by the direct questions I asked her, and by what I had intuitively felt about her secret and her real issues that I also expressed. Being activated, Jen then followed her denial pattern and program, which I also saw was the opposite of mine. For her, talking and explaining was a way of avoiding having to answer direct questions, and was the key to covering up her terror and heartbreak, as that was her method of survival. Jens denial choice when she gapped was to fight. She became angry and flew into a denied rage, calling me abusive and saying that she didn't want me around her anymore. She said that she didn't have to, and wasn't going to take this kind of abuse. She was mentally and emotionally jumping all over the place with what she was saying. She was beside herself, screaming and yelling for me to get out of her house. She was picking up things and either throwing them on the floor or at the wall. I had fear that someone might think that I was beating her up, when all I did was ask her a few simple questions and express what I was feeling, while I was crying and smiling at the same time.

I was confused by the pandemonium, but at the same time it was also okay. She was screaming at me, saying that our friendship was over and that she never wanted to see me again. I tried to talk to her, asking her to express what she was really feeling, but that only enraged her even more. I thought of talking to her about what I had just experienced, but I could feel that she was too terrified and angry to even think straight. I thought that she might just need some time, like I did, to process what had just happened, and that it be best that I honor her request and just leave her be. I told her I'd call her later and took my leave.

I made my way down the stairs, feeling the most love and joy that I had ever felt. Jen followed me down the stairs and out to the street, still screaming, "Abuser, I'm not taking it anymore." I got into my van and looked over to see Jen standing on the grass embankment, still screaming and waving her arms angrily at me. As I looked at her, I could only feel love and gratitude in my heart for her. I then turned my gaze to the road and drove away. I didn't look at my watch, but it must have been around 4:00 pm when I left Jens place. I decided to drive to the nearby beach where I used to live, to process what had just happened. I didn't write anything when I was out there, nor can I remember what I did or thought when I was at the beach. Around 8:00 pm, I drove back into town and got something quick to eat, then drove back home to Irene's. I called Jen but she never picked up the phone so I decided to just let her be.

Later that evening, after Irene got home from work around 11:30 pm, we had our customary late night tea, and I shared my experiences of the day. We chatted until nearly 2:00 am, and before going to bed, Irene went outside on the deck to get a breath of fresh air. A couple of moments later, she asked me to come outside and look at the northern lights. I went out on the deck and was amazed by the display, they were incredible! I watched them for about fifteen minutes and then I thought of calling Jen so that she too could share this moment. It was late and I was afraid that she would be asleep and would be angry with me if I woke her, but I also knew that she was often up this late watching TV, so I decided to call. She answered the phone on the second ring. I simply told her about the northern lights and she said that she would have a look.

I went back outside and continued watching the display, but after standing and looking up for a while I was beginning to get a stiff and sore neck. I went back to the deck, got a lawn chair and set it in the middle of the yard. I then sat down and stretched myself out on it with the back of my neck and head resting on the back of the chair. I continued to watch the light display for another hour.

The lights had begun in the north but were steadily moving eastward, until eventually, they filled the north and eastern sky. When they peaked in the east, they seemed to explode in multi-colored flares as they crossed the sky to the south and then across from east to the west. After that, it was anyone's guess as to how or where they would move, and at times they covered the entire sky. The colors were fantastic and it felt like the sky was on fire with countless different shimmering colors. At times, they appeared to take on the shape of a phoenix, angels, birds or animals. Long floating multi-colored plumes and flames moved effortlessly back and forth as if to some unheard music, interrupted occasionally by a streaking meteorite. I've never

Chapter 18 – My Second Level of Healing

seen such a display of northern lights in all my life. It was truly a magical end to an amazing day.

2000 Aug. 12 - I called Jen to see if she had gone outside to watch the lights last night and she said she had. We did manage to talk for a little bit before we began to argue; or rather, I feel she argued with me because I didn't agree with her. I noticed I had a whole different "feel" or perspective when I was talking with her today, as it didn't feel like it did before. I talked about my experience yesterday and I also mentioned the insights I had received later, that she had reflected my mother to me. I re-counted when as a child, that whenever I would try to express my feelings and intuition, she would deny them and would tell me that I was wrong, insinuating that she's right because she's the parent, older and wiser. I also told her how I had sacrificed my feelings, wants, and desires to please my mother to make her happy and that I had let her talk me out of my feelings too, just like I had been doing with her.

Jen on the other hand, felt that I was reflecting her father to her in a way that she still haven't figured out, as she hasn't been able to remember parts of her lost childhood. As our conversation progressed, she again began dismissing everything that I had said, or was saying, and began explaining and telling me of our experience as she saw it. However, this time when I was confused by her words or felt that something was "off," I immediately stopped her and either asked my question or stated what I was intuitively picking up. This infuriated her and she accused me of being abusive and controlling and of not letting her share the way she wanted to. Before she hung up, she told me that it would be best if I was with people where I could be more myself with, meaning, not with her.

2000 Aug. 14 - Ever since my awakening experience I've had various feelings and emotions surface about what happened, and I'm in awe, as it was something that I never expected. I never imagined that unconditional love, self-love would be what I would experience, as I thought and believed that I was already a loving person. There are no words that can express the feelings I felt during that experience. Recognizing my denials, my outer Child fragment, my anger and rage and why it was angry at me, were all eye openers. That experience was so incredible that I want to share it with the person that allowed me to experience it, yet that brings up another issue of heartbreak in knowing that the person that helped me was now rejecting me and herself. Jens rejecting me is not activating me as it did before, but I still have attachments as I feel that there has to be some way that I can breakthrough to her so that she too can feel and experience what I felt and experienced.

I've called Jen five times throughout the day and left messages but she never returned my calls. I haven't talked to her for two days, and I feel she has pulled back into her old pattern that she had with her boyfriend's, of pushing them away when she felt she wasn't good enough, or can't be what she thinks they want her to be. In our last conversation, I also expressed that I felt that the boy had some negative energy attachments to him, that they were evil, and that he and his attachments were using and feeding off her. She would hear nothing of it and accused me of using that as an excuse because I was jealous. I don't know what to do. I know she needs her space to feel what it is that she needs to feel, but also I feel the need to be there and support her and not withdraw myself, which is what I feel she's doing as she's trying to push me away. I also feel that I need to express myself like I did a few days ago, and not deny myself in favor of another.

Irene's guide, Archangel Gabriel, said that "Jen is inviting her fears and that it is also time for her to see the tree for the forest." I wasn't sure what that meant and I asked Irene, but she said she didn't get any more.

2000 Aug. 16 - for the past three days I've been reflecting on, and integrating my awakening experience. I've also been working on making native drums out of some hollow trees that I found in the bush and an old cedar fence post. I'm making one out of maple, which will be mine, one from a silver birch for Irene, and a cedar one for Jen. It's a lot of work as I'm using a hammer and chisel to hollow out the inside and remove the rotten bark. I've also purchased a cowhide that I'm going to be using for the drumheads. Buffalo or deerskin would have been authentic, but cow is as close as I can get for now. I've also found some more hollow trees that I plan on making into drums and will use deerskin for the drumheads in the future.

Boundaries and the New World

2000 Aug. 17 - Healthy boundaries are not about fear and protection, it's about expressing and acting on your wants and desires. As you begin to have acceptance for yourself and your boundaries, then they will be accepted in the outer reflection. Not to say total, for there will always be those that will tempt you, try to swing you over, by denial, to the dark side, away from your boundary of your choice. If not directly, then indirectly, subtly, using whatever means available to move you over, because if you have one boundary, you will have others, and they will try to find your weakest boundary and then use it to attack you from within, to erode your confidence, your Will, as to why you have boundaries and to make them out as if you have fear, no trust, no love. And so to prove that you are loving you deny yourself and drop your boundaries one by one.

Why do boundaries set in fear as a form of protection not work? It is just that, fear and protection, fear of hurting another or yourself, fear of being wrong, and so you deny your truth, your feelings and intuition, and instead set up rules and boundaries that you mentally try to follow. If this happens to me, then I'll respond this and that way, instead of being in the moment and

Chapter 18 – My Second Level of Healing

expressing what you really feel and doing what you really want to do, but don't. Fear of being alone, of being thought a fool or whatever, of someone spreading the word about you and that no one will want to be with you or that you'll be laughed at, teased, ridiculed or whatever fear comes up when your boundary is challenged. Of course you can deny that you are lonely or deny all the fears you have that come up, but that doesn't mean they don't exist and neither does your boundaries.

The world is ending; the ways of the world are ending. The world as you know it is ending. It is time to rise from the ashes of the old and become the new Phoenix. You will feel like you're alone, totally alone and that you have been duped, fooled, to let go of everything you had and even everyone that was in your life, but if you want to save yourself, heal yourself, free yourself, this is the path. It will feel so final and wrong, but you know deep in your heart it is right, and you will have fears you are being swept up in a cult, a lamb being led to the slaughter, but know that it is just the opposite. You are choosing life and love and soon you will not be alone. Others are awakening to the power of love and when felt, there is no power greater than love, and from the ashes, love, true love will set you free. Free of having boundaries or limits. Free to pick and choose what feels right to you, not in fear or lack, but with love.

The butterfly can't fly until it has emerged from the old cocoon and lets it go, along with all the old beliefs and thoughts of what it was before, a caterpillar; transformed now into a beautiful butterfly. Blessings and fond adieu, Astrid.

> **You don't need pain to learn, you need pain to get programmed.**
> **- Shenreed**

2000 Aug, 17 - I had been busy working on the drums when Irene came and told me of a past life experience she had before, and was now re-experiencing as she was watching me work on the drums. She said that in the past life, I was Gray Eagle and that he, (in spirit form) has been with me, watching and helping me make the drums. She said that in that past life she was Sequoia and that Jen (Summer Storm) and Kim (Shimmering Water) had been her two daughters. As she talked about it, I began tapping into and remembering that past life experience.

We were being attacked by another tribe who outnumbered us and who we knew would kill all the men and boys and brutally rape the women and girls. Those who lived through the massacre would become slaves for as long as they managed to survive the abuse that lay ahead of them. Knowing the outcome, Sequoia asked me to kill her and her two daughters rather than be raped and forced into slavery. Already wounded, I knew we couldn't win, and so with tears in our eyes, we said our quick goodbyes as I slit their throats and watched as their blood soaked into the Earth as their life essence left their bodies. I continued fighting until my death.

Now I also know where Jen got the name that we were arguing about a few days ago. Irene had told her of the past life experience, but she never told me until today, nor did Jen tell me when I was confused. It was their little secret, as I called it, until it came out today and I resent that I'm called stupid or confused when it's not me, but them. I still don't understand the reason for the secret. Why was it a secret in the first place? Why tell me now? Why deny it? It doesn't make sense. Irene had no answer.

I called Jen four times today and at 9:30 pm, I left a message saying that I wasn't going to be calling her again and that if she wanted to talk to me, she could call me. Later, I was on the Internet and I saw her in a chat room. I private messaged her and asked her what's up. She replied that she was connecting with herself. I asked her how she can be connecting with herself, while being on the internet. She said she didn't want to talk and that she was busy typing. I told her she was being vague and evasive and why didn't she just say what she really was doing; as I felt that she was hiding something and playing coy. She told me that I was to have nothing to do with her or her friend, and what was going on between them was their business. I told her that I felt there was a satyr and three of his buddies hanging around her and that it had something to do with the boy. She never replied to my comment and that was the end of our chat.

2000 Aug. 20 - I finally finished the three drums and beaters and brought them into the house. I made three deerskin pouches, one for each drum, and filled them with sage, tobacco, sweet grass and cedar and did a little ceremony for them all. I gave Irene her drum and beater and later that afternoon I took the cedar drum over to Jen's. I never knocked, but just left it between the door and the screen door. I've now started work on carving and Eagle head in the handle of a walking stick that I'm making for myself.

> **Toxic friends, toxic beliefs. - Shenreed**

2000 Aug. 22, 4:16 am - I awoke to see three people standing at the foot of my bed. There was the old man, who Irene had described to me before, wearing a striped black and white prison uniform, a young boy about twelve years old, and a taller young man. I also saw a huge eagle with a wingspan of at least seven to eight feet. He was hovering above me to my right. There was also a falcon and a crow higher up, above the eagle. I also saw a wolf to my left, mostly the head and shoulders, and on my bed was a snake. To the right of my bed, toward the door I saw a pair of red, evil eyes staring at me. I felt its presence more than really seeing anything other than the eyes. I had to go to the bathroom and when I came back, everything was gone.

Chapter 18 – My Second Level of Healing

During the past few days, there has been a constant presence of Satyrs, either individually or in droves around Irene and me when we are having our tea and chat. Irene has also seen, and I have felt, various Demons at times. With all this going on, I was thinking there has to be a way to discern between a love Spirit and a denial Spirit. I think that the only way to tell the difference is by "feel," but if the love Spirit is in denial, it feels the same as the denial Spirit. I keep thinking that there has to be an easier way. It would be nice if they all wore nametags.

2000 Aug. 22 - A few weeks ago Irene had told me that Jen's mother had bought Jen a toy poodle puppy and that she was going to be picking it up today.

Well today, I'm on a downward emotional cycle. I was on the Internet, chatting on ICQ and I got the feeling of being overwhelmed with loneliness, feeling like the little match girl, on the outside looking in. What started it was the post by the person I was chatting with. They said that I was too direct and too deep for what people wanted to hear. So again, it's an acceptance issue that is coming up for me. That being me is not good enough or wrong if I express myself. That in order to have any friends or to even have people talk to me, I have to become what they want. I have to deny myself to please them so that they won't feel hurt, because if they feel their pain they will blame me as the cause and will shun, ignore, criticize and judge me as being unloving, uncaring, selfish, cruel, insensitive, brash, critical, etc.

I feel caught in this "no win" situation. I feel dammed if I do, and dammed if I don't express myself. I feel that maybe I'm wrong, that something is wrong with me, as everyone else appears to be fine and has friends, can laugh, have fun and feel good about themselves and their life. So why can't I be like them? Maybe there is something wrong with me like they say there is and that I'm those things they say I am. But I was like them, or at least I tried to be, doing all the fun stuff, family, friends, parties, business, home, cars, clothes, but there was always something missing, and MORE things never seemed to help in the long term as it was always bigger, better, more. I could never go back to having less because that meant I was a failure. I had to try to be perfect but when I was in that situation, I had to be what they wanted me to be, so I would pretend to be this false person so that I could be with the "in" crowd. I could not be myself but rather had to be this PERFECT, phony other self.

I feel like the part of the Mother (Will, Soul), that felt all these things and when she told Father (Mind, Spirit), he denied that what she was feeling was happening or true. Instead, he blamed her for feeling those things, or for creating them, and then telling her, "Why can't you be like the rest of us and just focus on the positive and have fun? You say you are not having fun, but it is your fault and your feelings that keep you from having fun, so get rid of

Journey to the Heart Centre

them." She would reply, "I can't get rid of them and I can't have fun because it doesn't feel loving, and when I ask you what you're feeling, you would say that you feel nothing, which is denial, but then you also deny you are in denial: but yet you tell me it's all me, that I'm wrong." The Mother was more or less left to herself, alone, on the outside looking in, feeling what I'm feeling at this moment, and so for all this time, this eternity, this same cycle has been going on, repeating itself over and over. I wonder if I can do it. I don't even know what to do or how to go about healing this deep, DEEP wound that I'm feeling to the depth of my soul at his moment.

Jen and I weren't talking on the phone anymore and our only form of contact has been the net chat room, but now she's even avoiding that. The chat room was like being on the phone but even more activating for her, as she doesn't like the fact that her words were on the screen and she couldn't deny them when I would tell her that what she said earlier wasn't what she was saying now.

2000 Aug. 23 - I went to do a small handyman job today and was surprised to see Kim, a young woman I knew through Jen and the Heart Centre, talking to the woman that I was going to do the work for. Since we all knew each other, we began chatting and that was when she mentioned that she had come for help in getting rid of an astral attachment, a man that she had met on the Internet, and that was now trying to control her. The woman that I was doing the handyman work for was a Reiki Master, but she had no idea what an attachment was, let alone how to clear it. As I knew Kim, I offered to help her. As I began to work with her, doing what I first thought was an astral attachment; it became quite evident that it was much more than that. It was a possession. After working with her for about an hour, I was able to help her move him out of her, and you could definitely feel and see the change that came over her when he was gone. It was also interesting to see the other woman's reactions that was observing the process, especially when the man that had taken possession of Kim was refusing to let her go, and spoke in a voice that sent chills up your spine, while contorting her face, hands and body into unnatural positions.

2000 Aug. 24 - Irene has been seeing, and I've been smelling, satyrs and demons around us lately. I asked her why she still gets involved in lengthy discussions with them. She said it was fear, wondering what they are up to, fear that others can't or aren't strong enough to protect themselves. I laughed and asked her if she thought that they, the satyrs, would tell her the truth. She stopped and thought for a moment, and then with a sheepish, shameful smile, replied, "No." Even though she knew they would not tell the truth, I could feel that she was still communicating with them. Then defensively, as if in reply to their taunting, she snapped at me, "And why don't you want to talk

Chapter 18 – My Second Level of Healing

to them?" I replied, "I already know what they want, and what I want they can't give me, so what's the point?" She looked dumb-founded and then with another sheepish pout, she lowered her head. End of conversation.

2000 Aug. 26 - I feel that I've made a mistake and lost a friend. I feel the email I sent Jen yesterday was the final straw or hope. Yesterday I felt good, like an eagle, I could see things clearly from a different perspective, but today I feel lost and alone again. Irene is now the only person I have left in my life that I feel I can talk to since Jen has pulled away. One of my fears is that I won't have friends, family, home, money, vehicle, or even my health. I feel I must be this evil being that no one likes, that seems to offend almost everyone in some way or another. I know I have judgments but I also have feelings, and when I express my feelings people usually deny and say that what I'm feeling is wrong, but I find out later that I was right. In the mean time, I've lost their friendship and I'm alone, and I feel that they are afraid to be friends again because I can see through them. I don't know what I'm going to do. This honesty and expressing thing is really getting tough, as I'm losing, or feel I have to lose everything I have or care for.

2000 Aug. 28 - I've been tossing and turning all night, I'm in a fog of confusion, bewilderment, despair and heartbreak, even though I'm in denial of my despair and heartbreak. I feel I need to touch my terror of being alone and also that something bad is going to happen to Jen and that I can't do anything to stop it or help her until it's too late. I know that that is an attachment, but being alone is my big issue, my fear.

I still can't sleep as I kept thinking of different things so I thought I might as well write them down. Now, that I'm writing, I'm blank, so I might as well go to sleep. I just keep going around in circles. I was thinking of what Jen had said during several of our earlier conversations where she felt that it would be me pulling away first in our relationship, especially if I found someone. She kept saying that no matter what we go through and what happens, that we would always be friends as far as she was concerned. She hoped that we would be lifelong friends and that even our mates would be friends. Now I'm feeling angry and betrayed, I feel it was all words, fucking words and lies and I believed her, or I wanted to believe her. Now my heart is breaking again. I trusted her and look what happened. I thought we really had something that was deep, strong and that we both wanted to heal and not give up on ourselves, or each other. I had this moment of healing which she helped me with, but ever since then we have drifted further and further apart. If I felt it and saw denial for what it was, why didn't she, and why can't I help her experience what I experienced as she helped me. I don't understand.

So, what are the things that terrify me?

Journey to the Heart Centre

1) Things that surprise me, especially when they touch my body.
2) Angry, raging people who are shouting at me.
3) Being confined, tied up, locked in.
4) Being abandoned.
5) People who are attacking me physically.
6) Raging, angry people attacking a loved one.

Some of these points remind me of my mother. I feel guilty now as how can I say these things about my own mother in a book. I remember when she would go into blind rages and threaten to kill us, not just words, but actually holding a knife to my brother's throat. I can't remember her doing that to me, although I get flashes of being threatened, but then they are gone just as quickly. I can remember saying something like, "Okay, okay I'll be good" or "We won't do that again, I promise," or "I'll make sure they don't do that." Raging angry people attacking an innocent loved one terrifies me, because even stepping in to stop the abuse means that the person I was going to help might get hurt, or that I might get hurt if she turned on me and then the person I tried to help, might not help me when the focus shifts off them. Two of us might be able to overpower her, but alone, I didn't have a chance.

I just flashed back to the time when I had a part time job after school at a drive-in restaurant in an amusement park. It was just after closing time and I was taking the trash out to the dumpster, when I heard a woman crying for help from the darkness of the farm field that was located behind the amusement park. A few seconds later, a young woman emerged from the inky darkness. She appeared so suddenly that before I could react, she lunged into me, the momentum of her body throwing me back a couple of steps before I regained my balance. She clung to me, sobbing and begging me to help her, saying that three men were trying to rape her. She was hysterical, in tears and her clothes were tattered and torn. I quickly took her inside and asked the girls on duty to look after her, while I went to lock the door.

Before I reached the door, three men barged into the kitchen area. They were all big guys (bigger than me) and the biggest one told me to give them the girl. I played dumb, saying, "What girl?" He got angry and made his way behind the counter and came toward me. He was several inches taller and a good 100 pounds heavier than me. He picked up two large knives that were on the counter and holding one broadside, lobbed it at me. It bounced off my chest and fell to the floor. He yelled at me to pick it up and that we would fight for the girl. He shouted at me to be a man and to pick up the knife, but I knew that if I picked it up I'd be dead, so I began backing away. As I was backing up, he was coming toward me, slashing at the air with the knife he held in his hand, yelling at me to pick up the knife. He was now so close to me that with his left hand, he shoved me backwards, while holding the knife in his right hand. He kept pushing and poking me and getting angrier at the

Chapter 18 – My Second Level of Healing

same time. Finally he shoved me so hard that I was hurled against a stainless steel milk cooler that momentarily knocked the wind out of me and sent me crashing to the floor. The next instant, I felt a sharp pain in my side as he began kicking me with his work boots. He continued to kick me while I was down, shouting at me to get up and fight like a man. Everything was spinning, the next thing I remembered was that one of the girls was screaming at him, telling him to leave me alone and that the cops were on the way. At first he didn't believe her, but when his buddy saw police lights in the distance, they all fled. The police arrived a couple of minutes later, took our statements and put out a call to have them picked up.

Later, we were told that the three were arrested and that the guy that attacked me was a known felon with a lengthy prison record that included assault and battery, and that he was recently released and out on parole. I was told that he was charged with attempted rape, and assault and battery, and that he had been released and was out on bail, and that I was to appear in court on the day of his trial. The news that he was free sent me into terror, wondering if he would come after me.

Although I have been beaten up, I never went to the hospital as I didn't feel anything was broken and there was nothing they could do for a cut lip, black eye, scrapes and bruises. I was black and blue for weeks, especially my left arm, ribs and thigh, where he kept kicking and stomping on me with his work boots.

On the day of the trial, the woman refused to testify and dropped all charges. Being young and naive, I didn't know, and the police hadn't told me, but the assault and battery charges that I thought referred to me, were actually for the woman, and that I was only called as a witness to collaborate her story. Because I had not filed any charges and didn't have any broken bones or permanent physical injuries as proof that I was injured, even though the police report stated they saw bruise marks on my arms, ribs and stomach at the time of the assault, the judge dismissed the case. I was in shock and dumbfounded by the outcome and the injustice that had occurred, and even when the guy uttered threats in the court room that he'd get me for causing him problems, in plain earshot of the judge and the police, they turned a deaf ear and nothing was done. I lived in terror for months, afraid that he would make good on his threats. I also felt betrayed and sorry that I ever got involved to save another, and was severely beaten for my efforts, all for what. Not even a thank you or I'm sorry you got hurt, that night I helped her. And then later in court, not only did she drop the charges, but she was also standing beside the man that had beat me up, and looking at me as if I was the cause of his and her problems.

Both these experiences have the feeling of being alone without help or love, and also of betrayal, one by the person you love and trust, and the other by the unknown person you try to help. I have never opened up and let anyone back in, trusted anyone who has ever hurt me? No fucking way. I trust them as far as I can throw them. I hear your words, now let's see you act like you mean it and not just once. I just realized that confusion, shock and disbelief are common to both experiences.

Jen called me this morning. We spoke for an hour or so before she hung up on me. She said that we've switched roles for a while and that she is the one who is angry and hanging up on me now. She said that she got a message to that effect and that what we did with it now was our choice. She said that she now knows what it feels like to be me, when I used to say that I was getting mind fucked by words. We also talked about how she denied seeing and feeling anything bad in people and only concentrated on the good, and how I was the opposite and concentrated on the evil I felt in people and denied that there was any good there. I also shared how I felt that I was touching my heartbreak and terror of knives and betrayal again on another level. Where we got into a disagreement was in reference to a chat we had on the Internet the night before. I had told her that what she was saying wasn't what she said last night and that I had saved our net chat conversation and that if she wanted to re-read what we had said that I'd be happy to send her a copy. That was where she accused me of playing mind games and hung up on me. Later, I worked on my book introduction and got the message on being perfect.

2000 Aug. 29 - I received an email from Jen asking, "Do you think our friendship was codependent?" Looking at the message I notice the word "was" and the use of the past tense said a lot. I replied to her saying that I'm struggling with this; I don't know what to say or really where to begin. Yes, I feel our relationship is codependent and that there are a lot of issues here. I feel we have this weird couple, intimate, friendship relationship. I feel that our relationship is a 2/3-relationship, mental and emotional, but basically, it's nonphysical. We discuss various topics, ideas, concepts, and exchange insights and messages. We also share a connection of love through our feelings and emotions. We do some physical activities together such as shopping, laundry, going to the beach, etc., but it's the third part, the physical that I feel is missing, or "off" in our relationship. We don't show any real physical affection other than the odd good bye hug. While I don't have that with you or anyone, you have that with others in your life. I also feel that if we were to add this physical part to the existing relationship that it would also lead to sex, and then it's no longer "just" a friendship as that line has been crossed and it now moves to another level, that of physical intimacy and companionship.

That is what makes this relationship difficult for me as I don't want to be in the middle, hearing all the details of your 1/3 physical relationship with another person and then being used for the 2/3 relationship part, to

Chapter 18 – My Second Level of Healing

soothe out the other 1/3 sexual-physical part that you have with another. I feel that if you can get that from him, then you should also be able to get the rest from him too. Maybe I'm old fashioned, but I feel that when there are these sensual and sexual sensations involved in a physical relationship, then either I'm a part of it, or I'm not. Re-reading this, I feel like I'm a part of heart caught between father and mother.

I also know that if you were attracted to me, which you repeatedly said you weren't, we wouldn't have been able to touch all the issues and do all the healing that we've done as we would have got lost in the physical. I was, and am, attracted to you and that brings up all the issues I have, of being not good enough, too old, too this, too that, and all the other things I judge in myself, comparing myself to others. Whenever I did express that, you would tell me that I was jealous and possessive, and yes I'm that too, but I'm not just that, and that is what I want to heal.

I've never really had a friend, only lovers that I tried to be friends with, so I don't really know what having a female friend and lover is like. It's also more difficult because I'm attracted to you, but you say you're not attracted to me, so that really makes our friendship platonic. So we are caught in this weird platonic friendship, couples, relationship where I feel there is also a lack and denial of any real emotional depth between us on this physical aspect, as there is no affection demonstrated except, as I mentioned, the occasional goodbye hug. So on one hand we have this deep emotional honesty with each other, but on the other hand, we are in denial when it comes to demonstrating even any basic physical affection. Even during or after, yours or mine, emotional or physical healing releases, you rarely hugged or showed any affection on a physical level and neither would you accept any. Emotionally and intuitively, I have felt your love, but I have also felt your fear as you keep yourself physically distant and detached. I don't know what my issues are with physical contact, but I feel that there are also many issues with you.

You feel comfortable sharing some of your most intimate feelings on sensuality, sexuality, passion, excitement and physical moments that you are having with someone else, but I don't want to hear them because I feel uncomfortable, left out. I feel I'm unable to share any of my physical and emotional feelings other than I'm jealous and envious, and all the rest, because I don't have anyone in my life to share or feel that with.

I long for a relationship, one with emotional and mental honesty, the growth, but one that also includes physical affection, romance, passion sensuality, sexuality, spontaneity, sharing of dreams, desires, a union, a partnership. Not where one is filled by the other or completes the other in a lacking sort of way, but where there is the love and acceptance for self and the other, to really feel and discover what a real relationship is like, one built with love, true love, not fear. I don't know what that feels like, but that's what

Journey to the Heart Centre

I want. I know what I dream it feels like in my heart and I ask to make it a reality.

2000 Aug. 31 - I've been busy the last couple of days doing some handyman work for two women that live about ten minutes away. It's a way of getting money for gas and stuff. I've also noticed that working as such, detours me from feeling and expressing my emotions as it gets me caught up in the doing rather than the being. It also re-focuses me on doing things in the outside world as I now have more money to do that, and that is in opposition to what I feel really should be happening as it is giving my power away to money.

2000 Aug. 31 - I've started to work on my book again, I've been off it for weeks and I can't seem to really get into it as I don't know where or how to start. I haven't seen Jen since Aug. 11 and we've stopped talking on the phone or chatting on the Internet, and all that we do now is send the odd e-mail.

Irene shared an email with me that she got from Jen, where Jen was saying that she wished I were gay, so that she could show affection in our relationship, which is the opposite of what she wrote in her e-mail to me. Early in our relationship, when I had talked about this issue, she had stated that she wished I was gay but that it wasn't something that she wanted to discuss with me. I often felt that she held herself back, but when I would question her on it, she would deny that she felt anything like that or that she even desired any physical contact. I wrote and told her that I had read what she wrote to Irene and that I felt she had a double standard when it came to talking, and walking her beliefs.

Later I wrote her the following e-mail. –
Hi Jen, Well I'm activated on the double standard thing again as I realize that you are bringing up more issues with my Mother who was the Queen of Denial, and also of double standards. She could talk out of both sides of her mouth at the same time, and then deny and twist it around to make it look like it was me that was the one that was doing the thing I said she was doing. Mind fucked or what? She could say one thing while doing just the opposite of what she was telling me not to do. "Do as I say, don't do as I do," was her motto. If I'd question her I'd get, "You're confused, you're stupid, didn't you hear what I said," or "How many times do I have to tell you," and then she would go ahead and repeat it. For example, "I told you this is how I want it done, now remember that." Then later, when I was doing it the way she said, she would look at me and say, "Are you stupid or something, I didn't tell you to do it that way, I told you to do it this way," which was how I was doing it in the first place. I couldn't win.

She would also treat my brothers and sisters one way and me another. They would get affection and I would get criticism or be told to do

Chapter 18 – My Second Level of Healing

something, while they got to be with her. I felt I was always on the outside. She would say she loved all her children and would put on a phony show, especially when other people were around. If guests noticed what I was doing to help around the house and they paid me a compliment, she would center me out and give me a hug or a kiss on the cheek or top of the head. She would spout out false praise that I was such a blessing and such a help to her. The other kids felt that I was her favorite and mommy's suck, but that was the only time she would say and show any affection. I didn't trust her to say what she meant or to mean what she said.

WOW! I'm just feeling how I hate our relationship, How it feels "icky"! I feel you're a phony, just like my Mother. All the nice things you say are just words with no real meaning or desire to act on them in any way that would demonstrate how you felt, other than with empty words. It's breaking my heart to feel this rejection again and I just want to push you away as far as I can. I also know that we have shared and felt a lot, and that deep down you are love and that is the only thing that is keeping me from closing the book on this relationship. I want to heal this, but right now I don't know how or even if I can.

Insights and Conclusion

As I was proof reading and editing this book, I was also referring back to my journals and day-timers. I decided to delete some material and add other parts that I now feel are important. Knowing that my second healing experience was the conclusion of this book, I was trying to decide how to end it. While reading the part about my healing experience, I was amazed to discover how casually I had slipped by the monumental significance of that healing day on 2000 Aug. 11, and how I carried on as if nothing had really happened or changed, but it had. It wasn't until later, as I continued to become more aware of how and when I was denying, or not denying myself, that the true significance of that moment impacted me, and still is for that matter. That experience wasn't just another breakthrough, it was "the" major turning point in my life, but like I said, I didn't know it at the time, or the full ramifications of it, and I still don't, as I was unaware that I was opening a door to another reality.

Having made that realization, I purposefully included another three weeks of my journey past that moment. This is not meant to deceive you or to belittle the moment, but to share the moment, and then, show how it moved and grew to become a part of my life in a gradual process, rather than a sudden transformation that would change my whole world in an instant. My whole world did change in that instant, but then it was more like conception, the merging of the egg and sperm, the beginning of awakening my consciousness. Now I feel that consciousness, that life, moving, growing, and evolving to the point where gradually and lovingly, I birth myself to become all that I am. I'm still in my embryonic stage, still growing and evolving in the first trimester. I also just realized that growth is not linear, but exponential and that realization brought tears to my eyes.

I must add that many of the insights that I present in this section are not ones that I had during, or even immediately after my healing experiences, especially those relating to the second level of healing. These came only after other experiences and mini-healings that built upon my previous experiences. Any insights and realizations I did have in the course of my journey, I included as I went along with my story.

In the process of writing and then proof reading and editing this book, I had several opportunities to relive my journey. I could see that it was all there a long time ago in the messages I was getting, but I just couldn't see it, or rather, I couldn't feel it. The messages were information and clues, but all I got out of them was what I was able to accept and comprehend with the limited consciousness and awareness I had at the time. I also realized that I

Insights and Conclusion

wasn't given more than what I was able to handle. This is also the reason I've included most of the messages, as they will speak to you in a manner and at the time you are ready to receive them.

After my realization of the power of denial in court, it took a while until I was "tested" again. Tested isn't the right word but I don't know a word that I could use to express that once I had experienced the power of denial, I needed to experience what ending denial was. I needed to go through a gradual process and build one experience, one emotional healing, one judgment release, one physical release, one realization, and one insight on top of another to enable me to get to the next level, and then to repeat the process all over again until I was ready. An example would be to first learn what numbers were and then learn how to add and subtract. From there you would learn to do multiplication, division, fractions, decimals, percentages, and then you would be ready to learn algebra, geometry, calculus, etc.

That "testing" opportunity was to come to me with the knife experience in my first level of healing, when I became aware of my false emotions and judgments, and consciously allowed myself to express all my denied feelings and emotions as well as body memories. The first stage or level of healing was a real life, but "safe" experience that opened me to the power of love when denial was ended. A short time later, I was again tested in another real life situation, but this one was a potentially dangerous one, which also served as a confirmation that healing had occurred. I sometimes wonder what would have happened if I had denied myself when the woman that had been raped, came to see me? Even so much as denying myself and forcing myself to sit on the cushions to make her happy would have started my denial sequence that might have led to dire consequences. I guess, no, I know my guides knew that today was the day I was not going to deny myself and that experience gave me proof that healing was possible. Although I had numerous opportunities, messages and many more mini-healing experiences after the knife experience, it still took me another one and a half years to get to the next level of healing to be able to end my denials with someone I cared for. The main reason for the delay was threefold. The first being my belief that I was a loving person. The second was the unseen role of denial, that of being in denial of being in denial. And third, my unrecognized attachments to Jen.

Another insight I got was that I am not an "evil" and unloving person by nature, BUT, and this is important, that when I'm in denial, I now become a "doer of evil" and that however subtle or innocent it may appear to be, it is still unloving. Denial is not my natural state of being, but when I deny any part of myself, I am not being loving to myself and neither am I being loving to those around me. When I'm in any form of denial of myself, I'm trying to live the truth in a state of denial, and what truth or life is that? That's what we've been doing all this time, living a lie, an illusion, and calling it life.

Until the Mind is open to accept all of the Wills input that it doesn't want to feel, and is willing to allow her to express all that she desires, the Mind is oblivious to what the Will is feeling and knowing other than those false feelings and emotions that are aligned with the Minds imprints, programs and beliefs. While the Mind may think it has a mental concept and understanding of the situation, without input from the Will about the experience, the Minds knowing and understandings are incomplete, and it will just continue to go in circles, running on its old imprints, programs and beliefs that it feels are the truth. While the Mind is the decision maker, the real key to healing is Heart presence because if the Mind can't move to allow acceptance of the Will, to allow her to express herself, then healing is impossible. Mind needs to make the shift in consciousness, that instead of gapping in denial, it allows itself to go into the gap with love and feel what the Will is trying to say or do.

Once Spirit/Mind is open to move into the gap to feel what the Soul/Will is feeling, then the Soul opens to receive the light of Spirit and healing and understanding is possible. Mind and Will are no longer in opposition but are now co-equal and complimenting each other, like a couple in a dance. Mind leading and guiding and the Will responding and following, but also letting the Mind know of anything that it is not aware of, and for the Mind to then accept Wills input without question or hesitation, and so, like two dancers, they continue to glide effortlessly across the dance floor, two moving as one. As long as the Mind is in denial and trying to be in control of the experience, what it is sending to the Will is unlovingness and denial and that is what the Will feels and is responding to. The Will is not going to open and be receptive to unlovingness and more abuse when the Mind is in denial of the Will, and so healing is impossible.

Our imprints, programs, beliefs and judgments as well as our false feelings and emotions are what are blocking us from healing and empowering ourselves to experience what we are, and what we desire. As you read this book, you saw that I was circling and basically repeating the same feelings and emotions over and over, and that I was also blaming myself or others and the external world for what I was experiencing and feeling. What I finally discovered was that it was the opposite, that it was really me that was doing it to myself, but because there are so many layers, level's and issues at play simultaneously, it was difficult and almost impossible to know what I was doing as I couldn't see the tree for the forest. I had no guide, no one to tell me what I was doing, or what to look for as I wasn't even sure what I was really looking for. I really didn't know what denial was and I certainly didn't know what love was, but I was to eventually find out. I had all these twisted beliefs about love and denial as I thought that I was already a loving person and that negated any potential of me being in denial. At the time, I also thought that if I felt guilty about doing or saying something, or not doing

Insights and Conclusion

something for another, that it must be wrong and unloving. Ignorantly I believed that guilt was love. Also, any love I did give had conditions on it as well as denials and expectations, so it was all conditional love. I gave and received guilt and conditional love and so it's no wonder that I, and my life, was filled with guilt and love that never felt right, or if it did, it never lasted.

The trouble was that I was so full of imprints, programs and beliefs, that not only didn't I know what denial was, I was also oblivious as to what love was. What also made it difficult was that every time I had a hindsight as to what I did, what I denied, I couldn't seem to apply that hindsight to the next activation, as the next activation was not the same as the previous one. I also needed to recognize that when I was being activated, that I was actually reacting to my imprints, programs, beliefs and judgments that the experience was creating. My Mind was not only being controlled and running on old imprints, programs, beliefs and judgments, it was also being controlled by false feelings, emotions, guilt, shame and denial, that I wasn't aware of as such as I believed that I (being my Mind) thought it was doing what was loving and best for all. I was frustrated and at times, thinking that healing was impossible as I'd be moving and cycling between various forms of heartbreak, terror, anger and rage, with no light at the end of the tunnel.

When trying to describe what unconditional love feels like to another, I often use the analogy that knowing what love is, is like knowing how to ride a bike. You can't know what riding a bike feels like by reading a book, or by learning what others tell you, you have to experience it for yourself, to feel yourself move and balance in the present moment. It has to be a now or present moment experience for you to understand and know. To know how to ride a bike, you also have to know how not to ride one. By that, I mean that you need to have the experiences that allow you to know what doesn't work, so that you can gain understanding as to what does work. It's the same with ending denial; you have to have experiences of being in denial and then get the hindsight as to how and why you denied. When you understand how your denials work, that understanding then enables you to empower yourself to end your denials. Once you consciously choose to end your denials when you are activated, you then give yourself love (Unconditional love) and you then know what that feels like and can begin to live it. As long as you are in denial, you can't experience unconditional love, and as long as your love has conditions, you are also in denial. You can't live and share what you don't possess, and reading a book and having mental understandings is not going to do it for you, as you need to bring it into your physical experiences, to walk your talk.

One constant issue and source of heartbreak I had was of not being accepted and loved, or allowed to express myself. I (my mind) was oblivious to the fact that I was still looking for love outside myself, and in actuality, it was me that wasn't loving myself and allowing myself to express what I was really feeling. I was doing so for any number of reasons, the biggest being that I wanted to be loved and accepted by people around me, and that my denied fear was that if I expressed myself, I was not going to be loved and accepted, but instead, be rejected and unloved. What I feared and thought others were going to do to me externally, was actually what I was doing to myself internally when I was denying expressing my Will, my intuition, feelings and emotions. The outer experiences were then reflecting my inner denials and judgments of being unloved, rejected and not heard. Along with this, another issue was in blaming the other person of trying to manipulate and control me. In reality, it was me that was rushing in to try to help or save them, aided by judgments, shame, guilt and the belief that self-sacrifice was love. That by helping others and doing things for them, that I would be loved and accepted in return. Besides the unseen role of denial, I also had expectations related to my lost hopes, dreams and desires, based on the old golden rule of, "Do unto others as you would have others do unto you," that set me up to be the hapless victim.

Still another related layer of judgments I had was that the other person was weaker or unable to do what I could do, and so again, the compassionate Heart, fed by guilt, reaches out to the fair damsel in distress, the old, the young, the weak and the sick, to help them in any way I can. But this is where it also gets tricky as sometimes the person really needs help, while other times they are using the oh poor me routine to feed me guilt and shame to control and manipulate me which activates my imprints, programs and beliefs to help them because I can. Other times, my feelings told me this was happening, but I'd chose to ignore my feelings and do what I thought was right and loving, unaware that I had denied expectations. Later, the truth was revealed, as they appeared okay and healthy enough to do things with other people yet were unable to do things with me, the person that helped them. I'd get angry at them and at me for falling for the same trick again, not realizing that I knew and that I denied expressing and acting on what my intuition was telling me. It's one thing to know, it's another thing to follow through on my knowing as by saying no, my fear would be activated that they will be angry and probably reject me, and that would bring up my terror and heartbreak of being rejected and alone. Not only that, guilt and shame would fill me with more self-hatred saying that as I was not being loving and nice to them, why should I expect them to be nice to me.

Another twisted version of guilt was that if I was there to help them whenever they needed help, they became dependant on me, and of course, once I started, I couldn't stop without feeling guilty. After a while, I felt used, manipulated and controlled, but I willingly sacrificed my happiness to make them happy as that was what I thought love was. Another thing was that because they needed help that I could supply, I judged them less able than me, but the twist was that by judging them, I was making them more

Insights and Conclusion

important than me. Again, I sacrificed myself and then felt angry with myself (self-hatred) because I had given my power away. It was difficult to recognize my hidden denials, judgments and self-sacrificing beliefs that were disguised as self-love and love for others. The Golden Rule is based on guilt and is part and parcel of the belief where self-sacrifice for others is accepted to be self-love and love for others. The sad thing is that this guilt that demands self-sacrifice is also considered to be unconditional love, and what people should strive for. As you can see, religion is the foundation of our twisted beliefs of what love is.

Yet another issue I had was trying to live my hopes, dreams and desires through another person by unconsciously controlling and sacrificing myself to make the other person happy and excited. If they were happy and excited, then I too could share in their excitement. I wouldn't allow myself to express my own excitement and happiness as I feared that I would be attacked, criticized, rejected, abandoned and not loved, so I believed that the only safe way was if I allowed myself to feel and experience it through another person, even if it was me that was making them happy. In living through others, I was in denial and giving my power away and all this was happening because, unnoticed in the background, I wanted to feel happy and excited and also be accepted and loved. I denied being real and loving to myself and instead, I sacrificed myself and pretended to be happy when others were. That then became a habit and a program.

Another issue and level of heartbreak I had was to do with money. I didn't want to be poor, I wanted to have money so that I could do what I wanted and have what I desired, as I believed that money was the source of power. And again, the unseen role of denial plays itself out as my fear of not having money brings up my issues that others will judge me as being poor, weak, lazy, not good enough and a host of other judgments, including that I won't be accepted and loved. And because I'm already judging myself, that then becomes my reality. It also brings up my issues of being different, and being different brings up feelings of rejection, being attacked and not being loved. As you can see, it's a vicious cycle, with countless twists, turns and layers.

This money issue also has a twist in it when it involves others that don't have money, but I do. When that happens, guilt drives me to give them money, or buy or do things for them, because I know what it feels like not to have money, or to be able to do or have the things you want. Rather than having to address and feel all my denied issues, I quickly rush in to help others that I think are less fortunate than me and make them happy, and in the process, make me happy by being a nice, kind, loving, caring, sharing, understanding and compassionate person. But then again, the unseen role of denial and of expectations is in the background, of wanting to be loved and accepted by others. Of course not helping them would bring up shame and guilt, as well as my fear of having them turn on me, that then brings up my issues of rejection, of not being good enough and the list goes on and on. What I'm actually doing is trying to buy their love and acceptance by making them think that I'm a nice guy, which makes me feel important and loved. The old golden rule is also at play here as I feel that if I help them, then they or others will help me.

Still more of my imprints, programs and beliefs, along with guilt and shame state that when I have special talents, gifts and knowledge that the other person doesn't have, that I am responsible to share and help them, as I would feel guilty and ashamed if I didn't. I'd feel that I was not being loving if I didn't help, and also that I would not be accepted and loved, as others would deem me selfish and uncaring. A reversed twist in this is judging that because I lack certain talents or knowledge that others have, that I'm not loved and accepted, and that if I had these, then I would be like the others and I'd be happy and accepted. Having what I feel I'm lacking means that I could get a better job, have more money and power and then people would like and accept me. Again the unseen role of denial is of wanting to buy their love and acceptance, because as long as I have what they want, they need me and I feel loved and accepted and have a purpose.

I was (and still am) so filled with imprints, programs and beliefs that are so convoluted and twisted within each other that when one gets triggered, they all become activated. Like when one snake in a pit full of vipers is disturbed, all are disturbed and begin hissing and looking around for the source of the disturbance. While I may be able to see one imprint or program that I think is the problem, I'm actually seeing the whole mass move, like the pit full of snakes that are disturbed and writhing around. While I may think that I'm only dealing with one issue, I'm actually dealing with many, yet on the surface they all look the same, (like cobras or whatever) as what makes them look the same is that they are all covered in denial. While I could see and feel my imprints, programs and beliefs stirring, it was difficult to pick out that one program or belief that set it all in motion. Not only that, I also had guilt and shame and the unseen role of denial that played their parts, as well as my false feelings and emotions that reinforced the imprints, programs and beliefs and made the activation into what I thought was a threatening situation when that was not the truth.

Along with all the imprints, programs, beliefs and judgments I have, are my unseen attachments to people, places and things that have given me some form of happiness and acceptance that I think is love. I think/feel that by hanging onto them, that I am giving myself love and that I'm also showing my love to whoever and whatever I'm attached to. I'm afraid to let go because of the unseen role of denial, guilt and shame that would have me believe that I am unworthy, unaccepted and unloved, and thereby I would feel abandoned, alone and rejected. Those feelings would then put me back in the

Insights and Conclusion

oh-poor-me of self-pity and self-hatred, where I would be blaming myself for my lack of success, happiness and hating my feelings and emotions that are only reflecting my own self-hatred. To try to escape these feelings and emotions, I try to fix the problem by doing things for other people, doing things to make money, to make me happy and to make other people happy. I'd find infinite things to do to escape my feelings and emotions of not being accepted or loved as I am, and so instead of being who I am, healing my issues and letting go of my imprints, programs and beliefs, I do the opposite, I hang on to them. Then when I'm triggered or activated, I re-act to them and do what they say I should do, believing that will make me feel better and good about myself and that I'll be accepted by the outside world, in my relationships with others that I experience in my outer reality whose acceptance and love I seek. Then there is the other scenario, the other end of the denial teeter-totter, where in a fit of denied anger, rage and self-hatred, I let go of the old attachments and replace them with new people, places and things, thinking that I've solved my problem.

Neither was I aware of my false feelings and emotions that were also responding to old imprints and programs. When I was experiencing them, I thought and believed they were real and it wasn't until my first level of healing with the knife issues that I became aware of them as such. False feelings are to my Will as judgments are to my Mind, and when one is triggered or activated so too is the other and they reinforce each other with what they believe is the truth. False feelings and emotions were a real issue as they were hidden and buried along with my denials and judgments. Becoming aware of my false feelings and emotions was just as important as becoming aware of my judgments and denials. There were false feelings and emotions involved in both major levels of healing. In the first, Jen activated me with the paring knife and I was unconsciously triggered into my Minds imprints, programs and beliefs, along with the false feelings and emotions that concurred that my Mind was right. When I was activated and about to go into my fight or flight mode, I also had the awareness that Jen was not a threat and that both my thoughts and feelings were not accurate, but false.

In the second level of healing, the false emotions were that I thought and felt that Jen was not listening to me, and that she was controlling and manipulating me. Those feelings and emotions were also wrong and false as the real emotions were buried with my outer child and were what I was doing to him. The outer reality feelings were similar, but the cause was totally different. When I gave myself permission to ask questions and state what my intuition was feeling, I was no longer in denial, and the false judgments and emotions that were feeding me the information and feelings that Jen was controlling and manipulating me and the cause of my anger were exposed for what they were, false. The anger, frustration and things I had been feeling toward Jen suddenly vanished when I found the true cause and allowed myself expression. Afterwards, the feelings toward Jen were one of love and gratitude. While Jen was in part, doing what I felt and thought she was doing, my Minds judgments coupled with my Will's false emotions were saying that she was the cause of my pain, when in reality it was what I was doing to myself, but was accusing Jen of doing. While my denied anger was directed at Jen thinking that she was the problem, my real anger was not directed at Jen, but at me, for what I was doing to myself by way of my denials.

When I unconditionally expressed myself, I took my power back and Jen could no longer use my denials against me, or rather, my denials weren't being reflected to me by Jen, and in doing that, her denials were also exposed for what they were. Jen didn't think she was trying to control me anymore than I thought I was trying to control her. Jen felt that she was simply protecting herself the best way she knew how in order to survive, but when I no longer denied myself, the shift was made and the illusion was broken, and she was terrified and felt that she was no longer in control or able to protect herself. Her real anger was telling her to stop abusing herself, like mine was, but she saw it twisted and denied like I had, and blamed me as the one abusing her. Since she couldn't or didn't want to run out of her house, she had to fight to get me out. Later, I was also confused in that Jen didn't experience what I had experienced as we so often did in the past when we would share healing moments such as this, but we also never shared anything this complicated and to this depth. All this felt so right and I knew it was a moment that was to change my life forever. Not in a sudden way, but in a gradual process as I became more aware of myself and my surroundings, and in expressing myself more confidently.

Now, I had the awareness that I had to give myself what others never gave me when I first experienced unlovingness and heartlessness. I was young and in terror of what I felt and either didn't know how, or was unable to express what I needed to, as I had no choice, no free Will. Now, I, and I alone, had the ability to bring this part of me the love and acceptance he never got and that I also never gave him. My Spirit, Will, Heart and Body all knew what it was that they collectively had to do. They had a choice to make which was terrifying to them all. I knew how and what confused me and I asked the questions. I knew what Jen didn't say, what I sensed, and I expressed that. I gave all parts of me unconditional love and acceptance to be, and I felt my heart open. I felt love and gratitude for myself, as I felt what I had just done. I felt love and gratitude for Jen for how she helped me to experience this moment. I felt the love and support of my guides as tears of joy and a smile beamed across my face as I surrendered to love. Healing begins in the heart, as what I experienced was a 180-degree shift, a complete reversal of what I had believed love was. Love was one thing that I didn't expect to discover in my search for truth, as I believed that I was already a loving person, but to begin to know the truth of what love is, I had to know what love is not.

I've also come to the realization that whenever we have a traumatic experience, where we experience heartbreak or terror, where we have been denied, or we denied ourselves all our emotional and physical expression, that we fragment. That a piece of our Being, our essence, is pushed out of our conscious mind and down into our subconscious, and then finally out into the unconsciousness of the gap, where it is lost in time and space. It is not done with conscious unloving intent, but as a means of survival, as the rest of our Being feels that it can't survive if it has to feel and live with what this part is feeling.

I was consciously aware of some of my traumatic childhood experiences and it was in working with my "Inner" child and the tools that I had developed, that then led me to find that lost and abandoned part of me, my "Outer" child, as I came to call it, that had been fragmented as a result of the experiences. I didn't know that he existed or even how to reach him or that I needed to. At that time, I believed that any bad memories I had were a part of the past and that what happened, happened, and there was nothing I could do to change that. I could never reach this lost part of me because it wasn't even in my consciousness or accessible in my subconscious. This "Outer" child was outside of me and the only way I could reach him was in working with my Inner Child which still had some memory of the traumatic experiences, and then to move enough emotions and mental blocks until I finally had the awareness that he was there and what he wanted.

An analogy I use to describe fragmentation is to visualize a set of three nesting bowls that are suddenly dropped to the floor. The largest bowl represents the "present" or physical, conscious you. The middle bowl represents your sub-conscious and "inner" child, and the smallest bowl being your "outer" child. When we have a traumatic experience, in this case the bowls being dropped on the floor, we fragment and the small bowl, our innermost essence, now flies out of the set and is now our "outer" child sitting on the floor by itself. It's separated, no longer a part of, or nested with the other two bowls in the set, and has also become lost in space and time. It is lost in unconsciousness, yet calling out to be heard, to be returned to where it belongs. So in all this time, the physically conscious you, "the big bowl," has been living, or more correctly, has been trying to survive not even aware that there is a middle bowl containing the inner child, unless of course there is conscious acceptance for emotional movement to access this part in the sub-conscious. It is only through repeated accessing and acceptance of this inner child, to bring it to consciousness, that the awareness that an outer child even exists. Once the sub-conscious and conscious mind have awareness of this lost fragment, then comes the struggle to bring it back to full consciousness.

Journey to the Heart Centre

The other thing that happens after the traumatic experience is that the large bowl, the conscious part of you now feels a loss, an emptiness inside, that something is missing, but it doesn't know what it is. You are taught to believe that you are already whole and complete, or that you would be complete if you had this or that, or did this or that in your life. You want to believe you are a complete Being, yet all the while you feel that something is missing in your life as you feel the tug and call from this part of you that is in your unconsciousness. You spend your whole life searching and trying to fill the "hole" inside you with people, places and things that never last or make you feel complete. Even if you get in touch with your inner child and allow it to do what it wants to do, it still feels that something is lacking as it will be played out in your relationships. You didn't know that the "hole" in you was actually a part of you that was outside yourself, the small bowl that had been fragmented. All this time you have known the truth, and while you knew that you were looking for something outside yourself to make you complete, you didn't know that it was actually a part of you that you were looking for. Now you know the truth and when you find that small bowl, that outer child, and bring it back inside you, you will fill that hole that is in your Heart. You will then begin to become whole and all that you are, as now you also know how to find the other lost parts of you. Once you find and bring this lost part of you back inside yourself, you will discover that you no longer need other people, places and things to fill the emptiness inside you like you used to.

Even with all the experiences I had with my mini healings and the things I had read and learned, it wasn't enough to awaken me. It wasn't until I was tested, so to speak, in a real life experience and I allowed myself to surrender to the moment, with acceptance for that lost part of me, that unconditional self-love was experienced in action, made manifest. It wasn't until I consciously chose to allow myself to ask questions and state what my intuition was feeling, that I truly gave and received unconditional love to myself. When I finally gave that lost and abandoned part of me the love and acceptance I had never given it in all my life, I was awakened, "re-born" so to speak.

When I found my "outer" child, I became aware of his terror and heartbreak, that he was confused and afraid to ask questions, afraid to express his intuition, feelings and emotions, and to even ask for help. His terror was not only the result of his experiences at school but was also created by the issues with his mother. She was constantly controlling him and telling him what he should or shouldn't do and there was also the hypocrisy of her words and actions, "Do as I say, don't do as I do" that confused and bewildered him. She would also talk him out of his intuition and from expressing his emotions. There was no love at home, so he felt his only hope for finding love and happiness was to get out of the house and go to school where he

Insights and Conclusion

could have friends and be accepted as he was, at least that was his hope, dream and desire.

The terror and heartbreak that created the major fragmentation came with the school experience, as now he felt totally alone and helpless and even unable to ask for help. That was when I experienced major fragmentation and created my "outer" child in order to survive. Not only did I reject and abandon him, but I also unconsciously attacked him, as I felt that what he represented was causing me all the pain and suffering I was experiencing. There was no sanctuary, no refuge from the denial and the constant attacks of unlovingness that he felt from me, and he felt alone, abandoned, helpless, hopeless, and powerless to ever be loved by me. All that he was feeling and wanting to express, and that I had been denying, was what I needed to feel and express in order to recover this lost part of me.

But the irony and twist in all this is that I didn't know that I was feeling his (my) true emotions. I believed that what was causing my emotional problems was my present outside experiences. Not only was I touching his emotions, I was also touching what it was that he wanted to express but couldn't, and if I didn't allow him to do it, then I also couldn't do it for myself as there is really no separation, except my DENIAL of him. He was confused by the words spoken, wanted more information as his/my intuition was telling him/me that what was being said was only part of the truth, and was also telling him what the truth was.

I also understood what my anger was as I saw it represented by a Cobra, stretched upward from its coiled position and poised, hissing to strike me in the face. It was telling me that I was the liar and the hypocrite for not loving myself in the same way that I was being loving to others. I was putting Jen ahead of myself; I was giving her the benefit of the doubt and the opportunity to express herself. I had patience, compassion and acceptance for her, but I gave my outer child nothing but cold heartless denial, indifference, and abuse. I was surprised when I saw how confused my Mind was when it realized that my anger was directed at me and not at Jen, who my Mind thought was responsible for my unhappy feelings, emotions and anger. I also saw how it was even more confused with all the beliefs it had that it was already a loving person to self as it was doing all the things that it had been taught was love and loving. But now it saw, and more importantly, felt and knew that it could no longer justify those old beliefs. I then realized that it was me that was abusing myself and that I had been doing it all my life, that I was running on my old imprints, programs and beliefs, and that I was denying my lost, abandoned, and fragmented outer child the love and acceptance to express what he wanted.

I also saw how Jen reflected my mother to me, as well as the kids from school. What I felt she was doing had the same feelings that my outer child had when his/my mother or the school kids were confronting and attacking him and he was confused and denied expressing himself. He felt he had no right or couldn't ask questions when he was confused or wanted to know more. That he couldn't express himself if what he heard didn't feel right and that he wouldn't get attacked. For him, to ask a question was one thing, to state what he sensed and felt was another, to say that what he felt wasn't loving was yet another, and to express all that to someone that he cared for was a huge step. Whenever he did that in the past, it meant that he'd touch a nerve, a sore point, which would trigger the other person and bring up their denials and denied anger and rage. And when that happened, he'd always get the worst of it. He would not only not be accepted and loved, but he'd be attacked. All of that was terrifying as he felt he had no choice, and with no one to protect him he was heartbroken and love starved. He so desperately wanted to be accepted and loved, that he would unknowingly sacrifice himself in order to try to get it.

While the second level of healing dealt with aspects of heartbreak and terror, I only touched the surface of anger and rage. It was to take me another four years with many more mini-healings, insights, and understandings before I'd have my breakthrough with expressing my anger and rage that I share as my third level of healing in my second book. So while I touched a level of heartbreak, terror, anger and rage with this fragment, there are many more levels and layers to both, and with each level of healing, the unseen role of denial, guilt and shame become more subtle and harder to identify.

On top of all of this, I'm not dealing with just one fragment, but countless fragments, and as I begin to heal and uncover my issues with one, other issues and fragments are identified thus enabling them to also be healed and re-integrated. Not only am I dealing with fragmentation in this lifetime, but also with the fragments that are buried in past lives, along with the imprints and programs that are encoded in my very DNA. With each mini-healing and major level of healing I experience, I also begin to change my Body's DNA.

As you can see, there's no quick fix to healing what has taken all our previous existence to create. To use an analogy, it's like humanity trying to instantly return the Earth to its natural state before it started to consume and destroy it to satisfy its needs and wants. Before humanity can allow any plant, animal or other living thing to live free from human interference, we need to address our need to control it in the first place. To live in harmony, we need to address the underlying cause of our beliefs and return ourselves to our natural state of being, and allow the Earth and all upon it to return to theirs. In the same way, we need to understand and change the underlying cause of our old beliefs that have created our present reality, and recover and heal all parts of our Being, including our lost talents and gifts that we lost every time we reincarnated in the physical plane, as well as in other dimensions. As we do, we bring more consciousness and awareness back to our essence, the very

Insights and Conclusion

Being that we are. It will not be a matter of history repeating itself with the conditional love, guilt, shame and denial as we did in the past, as now the old imprints, programs and beliefs that created it are being released. We now have a new blueprint for creation, one with unconditional love, with new thoughts, ideas, and feelings that are yet to be explored and experienced.

Healing and empowering ourselves is not a quick fix, but a journey, and it will take heartfelt intent and effort to reach those denied lost and forgotten parts of our being that have been trying to reach us all our lives. We have been trying to become whole, by filling the hole we feel in our Heart with other people, places and things, when in reality, it is really us, the lost, rejected, unaccepted, and unloved parts of ourselves that we have been searching for, and that we need to heal and integrate into our Being. When we give ourselves unconditional self-love, we don't need other people, places and things to make us feel loved and accepted, and neither do we have to constantly do things to make us or others happy.

Slowly, layer by layer, level by level, we begin to heal and move out of trying to live in the past with our judgments, or in the future based on our expectations, and move into the NOW, the present moment. Accepting and responding to what we are experiencing in the moment, puts us in a state of grace and gives us presence. It also gives us a gift and an opportunity to heal yet other aspects of our Being. As we become more present and whole, we gain new insights and understandings and become empowered to be all that we are, and to express the love, joy and peace that we desire with compassion, not judgment, connection not attachment, and acceptance not denial.

It took me eleven years to move from awareness, through the process of finding the tools that I needed, learning how to use them, to finally entering the gap and reaching my awakening point, that of bringing conscious acceptance to the lost and unconscious parts of me with unconditional self-love. It was then that I discovered how and why it was really me that was being unloving to myself, and that my present experiences were actually imprints, programs and beliefs as well as false feelings and emotions that were also a reflection and a reaction to that unlovingness. This experience was a breakthrough that was to dramatically change my life. I've tried to think of other scenarios of how this shift could have happened but anything else is just a form of conditional love.

It is my intent that this book, along with my previous two books, will offer you the knowledge and insights that will enable you to begin to heal and empower yourself in a lot less time than it has taken me to heal what I have healed. That the words on the pages and the pages in the books will act as sign posts to help guide you to what you are searching for. That my words and experiences will inspire you that real healing is possible when denial and self-hatred are ended, when healing begins in the Heart, your Heart Centre. That what you personally feel, experience and express in the process of reading this book will bring you closer to your awakening, to that magical moment when you put unconditional self-love into action and experience and feel the power, peace, movement, balance, freedom and joy it brings.

While these insights bring this book to a close, they are also the beginning of the next step to a New World and my next book. I'm on my journey to integrate this new awareness into the physical world, to heal other aspects of me, to walk my talk, a step at a time, unsure at times, but steadfastly moving forward into an unexplored, unknown and oft times frightening reality, yet inwardly knowing that when my fears are faced and denials are ended, it will open the door to a new world and reality, thought only possible in my innermost dreams, that of bringing Heaven to Earth. I now bring this book to a close with the heartfelt desire, that in the not too distant future, that I'll meet others that have also experienced their awakening and are beginning to live their dream of Heaven on Earth.

Namaste

Listing of Channeled Messages

A New Chapter begins	128
A Shift in Consciousness	171
Abundance	274
Acceptance	300
Accepting Your Gifts	326
Activating Emotions by Touch	390
Ambivalence	148
An Introduction to Healing:	49
Anger and Self-hatred	227
Animals	60
Awakening Others	59
Awareness and Awakening	63
Awareness of your denials	84
Awareness, Lifting the Veils	57
Balance and the Heart Centre	202
Be the Change	276
Beauty and Sexuality	158
Becoming Balanced – Ending Denials	158
Being at one	386
Being in the Now	132
Boundaries and the New World	408
Breaking Free of the Quicksand	174
Clarity Your Intent	150
Clearing the Astral Plane	47
Consciousness	104
Coyote Medicine	229
Crystals and Helping Others	395
Dare to Dream and Be	152
Denial and Pressure	247
Denial Spirit and Spirit in Denial	179
Denials, Judgments and Reality	320
Differentiation and Fragmentation	380
Doing Verses Being	341
Duality and Polarity	217
Duality of Light and Dark	230
Earth Changes and Inner Changes	172
Ending Limitation	328
Experiences and Growth	112

Faith and Trust	207
False Will	366
Fear is your Ally	236
Fear of Asking and Trust	230
Fear of the Unknown	140
Feeling of Aloneness	237
Fellowship and Actors	209
First Step of a Journey	198
Flight of Love	148
Forgiveness of Self	394
Forthrightness and Silence	130
Fountain of Youth	81
Free Will and Denial	140
Freeing Yourself	146
Full Circle	58
Gratitude and Self-acceptance	275
Growth and Balance	91
Healing and Transformation	271
Healing and Understanding	210
Healing and Your Path	102
Healing Heart and False Feelings	201
Healing Intent	247
Heart Reborn and Heartlessness	289
Higher-Self	285
Hope, Faith and Preference	237
Hopelessness	293
Indeed, INDEED, IN-DEED	138
Inner Battle and Choice	320
Inner Battle of Spirit and Will	232
Intent and Action	163
Intent and fear	286
Judgments and Beliefs	103
Judgments and False Feelings	326
Judgments on Doing	318
Letting go and Opening to Love	392
Letting Go of the Past	156
Letting go, ending the struggle	327
Levels and Changes	151
Levels and Layers	191
Limitations and Expectations	117
Lost Greatness	286
Loving Intent	85
Manifesting What You Want	164

Listing of Channeled Messages

Memory, Denial and Fear	370
Message for Jen	234
Message from the Pharnoos	55
Movement and Acceptance	251
Movement and Momentum	211
Moving Anger and Rage	101
Moving Blocks	89
Need to Know	66
New Beginnings and Changes	244
New Beginnings	161
On Being Human	356
Opportunities for Change	194
Paths and Being Who You Are	215
Power and Essence	134
Power of Love and the Word	356
Power	345
Primal Expression	373
Purpose and Trust	323
Raising Your Vibration	394
Raw Emotions and Beliefs	362
Read Your Messages	137
Reawakening your Powers	389
Receiving Love	52
Re-claiming Your Power	267
Recovering Lost Will	310
Relationships and Balance	90
Relationships and Limitations	88
Relationships and Self	154
Releasing Your Anger	103
Remaining Issues	369
Remembering	359
Repairing and Healing	208
Responsibility and Empowerment	161
Right Place and Asking	192
Right Place and Right Time	197
Secrets and Purpose	367
Self Forgiveness	324
Self-Empowerment	154
Self-love and Self-acceptance	166
Sexuality and Denial	195
Sexuality	193
Shalom	67
Speak Your Truth	82

Stop Trying to Be Real	237
Surrender and Acceptance	219
Surrendering the Ego	119
Talents and Gifts	346
The Coming Changes	122
The Five Tornadoes	371
The Golden Age	185
The Healing Power of Love	226
The Heart Centre Purpose	301
The Journey Begins	106
The Power of Love	292
The Spiritual Warrior	206
The trickster	183
The Truth Shall Set You Free	75
Time and in the Moment	376
Time and Space	324
Transformation and the Butterfly	136
True Understanding and Knowing	241
Trust and Betrayal	398
Trust Foundation	142
Turmoil and Struggle	119
Unconditional Love	333
Uniqueness	350
Unlovingness and Shadow Feelings	143
Vocabulary	59
Vows and Curses	126
Vulnerable and Strength	213
What is Your Desire?	47
What is Your Intent?	120
Word Judgments	69
Words	377
Your Brothers and Sisters	185

About the Author

My Journey...
a search for truth, understanding, and the meaning of life.

In 1990, my personal and business world was collapsing, and frustrated with my life and traditional dogma, I began my journey, my search for truth and the meaning of life. In the following seven years, I read over 250 books on almost every New Age and self-help topic, as well as exploring various religions, trying to find the answers to my probing questions. As I ventured into the great unknown, I had no guide, no sign posts, only my Mind and my feelings, which I didn't trust, to help me find what was missing in my life. I was blinded by a fog, aware only that I was searching for something but not knowing what I was searching for, how to find it, where to look for it, or to even know if I had found it when I did, and then what to do with it, when, and if I found it. While this outer search offered some part truths, something was always missing or didn't feel right. I was searching for a common thread that would link all the part truths of the books together, as I felt that then I would find and know the truth.

In 1994, I began my inner search when I was introduced to meditation. During the next three years, it expanded to include past life regression, astral journeys, channeling, shamanic, and multi-dimensional journeys. All these "tools," as I came to call them, not only expanded my conscious awareness, but also opened new frontiers and experiences for me. I continued to simultaneously explore my outer and inner reality, still looking for the common thread.

It wasn't until early 1997, when I obtained the book, "Right Use of Will" (RUOW) by Ceanne DeRohan, that things began to click and make sense for me that "felt" right, even though I didn't understand it at the moment. I also found the common thread I was looking for. What I found that was common, was not what was being said, but what was not being said, what was being denied, and that was the major turning point in my search. It was at this time that I also began to keep detailed journals, not only of the channeled messages I was receiving, but also of my thoughts, feelings, emotions and experiences.

Journey to the Heart Centre

Reading the RUOW books opened my awareness to the role that denial was playing in my life. I then realized that all the tools I had been using were based in denial and needed to be changed, and that I also needed to combine the tools I had developed with the esoteric points-of-view and the emotional work that RUOW provided. I then modified my tools and changed them from a denial-based format (denial and suppression of feelings and emotions) to a non-denial format, where I would allow my feelings and emotions an opportunity to move and be expressed. This change allowed me to begin working on healing my inner and outer child issues and develop another tool that I called, Coequal Therapy. These tools or healing modalities are what I share in my first book, "Journeys from the Heart Centre - Meditation as a tool for healing and Self-empowerment."

As I worked with these new tools, I began to merge and apply the insights and understandings I was getting on my inner experiences, with what I was experiencing in my outer reality and daily life. As I ventured further into this new and unknown emotional territory, it took me through feeling almost every possible emotion, as well as having some experiences that are beyond belief. I continued to write about my experiences, thoughts, feelings, emotions, insights, and the channeled messages and guidance that I was receiving, knowing that I would be writing books, and that these entries would form the basis of these books

Using the tools provided me with the mini healing steps, or stages, that were necessary in order for me to get to not only the first level of healing, but also the subsequent levels. The initial mini healing steps or stages were experienced by using the tools like, clearing my astral plane, releasing attachments, working with my animal guides and totems, past lives, channeling, and especially in working with my inner and outer child. Using these tools provided me with the emotional, mental and physical releases, as well as the ability to apply what I had experienced and learned to my daily life. In the course of my healing journey, I discovered that what I was deliberately or ignorantly told, and naively believed, were flaws in my character and personality that I had to deny and control, were in actuality, my strength and power, and is where the healing needs to take place. It was, and still is, confusing and frustrating as I go through the gradual processes and the different stages and levels of healing. At times, I still feel that I'm just going in circles and that I can't see the tree for the forest and that healing is impossible, and that's only because I haven't found and healed the real issue, as I'm still lost in that fog.

It's important to realize that when I was using the tools, I was in effect, planning and controlling my experiences. I usually had a specific intent and used the meditation/visualization tools to help me get my Mind to focus on a specific issue or experience while in an altered state of consciousness, and in most cases, I was also being guided during this process. While I was

About the Author

often activated during these little journeys and I'd have strong emotional and physical releases, these were in actuality, mini healings; they were not the major breakthrough releases that I'd later experience when I reached the first or subsequent levels of healing. These journeys, hindsights, mini healings, insights and understandings all served to prepare me for the next big step or level of healing.

When I later experienced these major levels of healing, I had no conscious intent or knowledge that I was ready, and no warning that I was going to be activated into my issues with a real life experience. Of course, it never dawned on me at the time that I would need to be activated by a real life situation similar to the one I originally experienced and was now ready to heal. But until I finally had that awareness and the proverbial light went on in my Mind, I just continued reacting to my old imprints, programs and beliefs and going in circles. When I was being activated during my first major level of healing, I remembered more of what I had previously touched on during my journeys and mini healings that I've mentioned. I realized that I had a choice as to whether or not I would allow myself to find my real issues and express my real emotions that were surfacing as a result of the activation, or deny them and react as I had been doing all my life. In other words, this healing wasn't a planned journey and I was not prepared to be activated by a real life experience, but I also knew that I was prepared and ready for this healing experience or it wouldn't be happening. It was this first level of healing that also gave me the insight and awareness of what false emotions were, and how imprinting and programming affected my Mind.

With the help of the RUOW material, my Spirit Guides, and using the tools I had developed with the aid of my healing partner, I had my first major level of healing in 1999. My second level of healing was in 2000, when I had an awakening, where I was reborn, so to speak, as what I experienced was a 180-degree shift from what I had believed love was. Although that experience only lasted a few moments, it showed me the power of unconditional love and what was possible when I chose self-love and not the denial and self-hatred I was used to. Love was one thing that I didn't expect to discover in my search for truth, as I believed that I was already a loving person. To begin to know the truth of what love is, I had to know what love is not. Experiencing and knowing what unconditional love really was, also opened me to understanding and knowing what denial was. Once I had this realization and insight, it was as if the fog or veil had been lifted and my journey became clearer, but at the same time, I was flooded with even more questions.

All of this work was, and the new work still is, experimental, and like Leonardo da Vinci, I consider myself a disciple of experience. I find myself not only being the scientist in search of truth and understanding, but also the test subject in having to submerge myself in the experiment so that I, the scientist, can experience the feelings and emotions and obtain the understandings that will allow me to know if my hypothesis is accurate and valid, and that real healing, change and growth is indeed possible when denials are ended. In other words, I need to "walk my talk" that then gives me the, "been there done that" understanding and knowing.

I don't have all the answers and my truth is evolving as is my consciousness. I find that I'm constantly being activated by either some new levels of old issues, or some entirely new issues that are coming up for healing and understanding. In each case, I have to learn by trial and error until I finally "get it" and know how to heal them, and it's then that I gain the understanding I was looking for that enables me to proceed to the next level of healing. I've also come to realize that there is no "quick fix," and that this is indeed a process and a journey. My truth is always evolving and expanding as my consciousness evolves, and what was true one day becomes a part truth the next, when what was hidden is revealed. My journey continues as I search for, and put the pieces of the puzzle together, to live in truth without denial. Now, I'm on the journey to heal other aspects of my Being and to integrate this new awareness into the physical world, to "walk my talk," to manifest and live in the world and a creation I have yet to dream and imagine.

If you would like to know more about my personal background before I began my journey, or of my experiences during my journey, other than what I've shared in this book, you can find more information in my other books. What I want to share here is just a very brief summary of how I started my journey and how I came to write, what is now, a trilogy. My first book provides the meditation/visualization tools or healing modalities that I developed and used on my journey, as well as some basic insights and understandings needed when using them. The second book provides a host of insights and understandings related to healing and self-empowerment, as well as the three levels of healing that I've experienced and the insights associated with them. And my third book is an autobiography of my journey that outlines the trials and tribulations I went through to reach the levels of healing I've experienced, as well as numerous channeled messages that guided and helped me on my journey. The titles for these books can be found at the end of this section. For more information about my other books, blogs, social media, or to contact me, please visit my website www.shenreed.com.

Mission Statement

I know that what I've found, others are also searching for and hope to find, and this is what I want to share. To find the love, joy and the magic in our Hearts and to share the expression of who we really are is true life. What I share is what I have lived and personally experienced, felt and know in my Heart, and can't be studied in any present form and thus, the reason for

About the Author

writing my books. While this journey into the unknown can be frightening, it is also exciting as it feels right, with a simple knowing that can't be described but is heartfelt.

I feel that my purpose and mission in this lifetime is that of a healer and a Wayshower, first as a healer of self, and then in helping and showing others how to heal and empower themselves. My vision and intent is to be a part of creating the New World from the inside out. By healing and changing the inside, we therefore empower ourselves to create the outer reality and world we desire with unconditional love, to allow those of us who choose to do so, to live life as an expression of who we really are, and not the illusion as we have been doing.

I believe that true healing can take place when we are in balance, when we can accept and express all our thoughts, ideas, feelings, emotions and desires without fear, denial, judgment, guilt or shame. I believe that true freedom and self-empowerment can be actualized when we are able to be fully present, to live in the present or now moment, no longer controlled by our old imprints, programs and beliefs that limit our consciousness and our experience, and the expression of who we really are. This is my vision and desire for the New World, and of bringing Heaven to Earth. It is my intent that the thoughts, insights, feelings and emotions that I share, will not only expand your consciousness, but also activate your emotions and touch your Heart, and in turn, assist you on your healing journey.

Although it took me eleven years to move from the first stirrings of awareness in my consciousness, through the process of finding the tools I needed, learning how to use them, to finally entering the gap and reaching my awakening point, that of bringing love and acceptance to the lost and denied parts of me, it will not take you that long. I not only share the tools that I've developed and use, but I also share my personal experiences and insights that will help guide you on your journey. It is only your intent and dedication to heal and find self-love that will determine your journey.

John

John J. Rieger aka Shenreed
"Healing begins in the Heart"

Journey to the Heart Centre

Author of:
1. **Journeys from the Heart Centre – Meditation as a tool for healing and Self-empowerment** – is a how-to manual and guide that uses non-denial based meditation/visualizations as a tool to not only expand your conscious awareness, but to also allow you to seek the underlying causes to the stress, fears, and issues in your life and begin to heal them. It also includes notes, insights, and understandings to assist you on your personal journey.
2. **My Journey - Three Levels of Healing – Feeling, healing and understanding Emotions** – covers numerous topics and issues, and contains key insights and understandings into the nature of the human psyche that are vital in not only healing your Emotional Being, but also in unlocking the mystery of your Mind, how it works, and why it does what it does. Finally, I share three personal healing experiences that are directly related to the previous material.
3. **Journey to the Heart Centre – Healing begins in the Heart –** While considered an autobiography, it also contains numerous channeled messages from my Spirit guides. I begin with a brief background of my significant life events, and while my journey began in 1990, the main focus is on four years, (1997 - 2000) and the trials and tribulations I went through that enabled me to experience my first two levels of healing.